CW01081961

GLENTORAN

A Complete Record

A Summary of Glentoran's history as viewed by a comic in the 1950s. Note the mistaken identities of Roberts and Geary.

GLENTORAN

A Complete Record

Roy France

To John
Merry Christmas 2002
R J France.

Published by Westwick Associates

Designed and printed by J. W. Northend Limited, Sheffield S8 0TZ

ISBN number 0-901100-41-2

Contents

Author's Preface

Many people have asked me how and why I have produced this book. Like the person who climbs a mountain because it is there it just needed to be done. Despite its rich history Irish football in general has been a poor relation over the years when compared to the plethora of books on other British clubs. It was a situation that I strongly felt needed to be changed. The highlights of Glentoran's history and achievements are well known but what about all the bread and butter as well – as a fanatical supporter I wanted to discover the complete record.

So after graduating from University in the summer of 1986 I decided to take up the challenge in the last few free months before starting work full-time in England. It developed into a labour of love as day after day was spent flicking through old newspapers in the Linenhall Library and the Newspaper Section of the Belfast Library in Royal Avenue. Indeed when they extended their opening hours the latter became almost a second home for me on the frequent research trips back home. By the summer of 1990 I had traced every Glentoran game I could since 1882. What could I do with this, it would surely be too cold just to publish a list of results. I had read and made notes on every Glentoran match report – why not write it all up and make it appeal to all supporters? So this book idea was born and three years later completed. Then I hit a double brick wall. Around 1993 Glentoran entered into one of the poorer periods in their history and after writing to every single book publisher in Northern Ireland I was left with a complete set of rejection letters. I could not find a willing publisher on the mainland either so things went into cold storage for a couple of years. Meantime I decided to research some more and from all those games I managed to trace the Glentoran line-ups in around 98% of them in order to produce the appearances tables. (As a result the name of every single player ever to don a green, red and black shirt will appear somewhere in the book.) Then in late 2000 things began to fall into place. Funding was secured, a printer who understood both the production of books and football publications was identified and it was game on. The end product of fifteen elapsed years and over 2,000 hours of work is now delivered.

I realised early on that it was impossible to trace every single detail but I hope that you will agree that 99.something per cent is not bad. If anyone can fill in a gap please let me know and if this book is printed again at say ten yearly intervals then it will be enhanced. I hope you enjoy reading and re-reading this book as much as I have in compiling it and if it falls into the hands of supporters of other Irish League clubs then I would encourage you to take up the challenge and tell your club's complete story.

Foreword

from Billy McCullough, Glentoran's all-time leading appearance maker.

The Shipyard, the Ropeworks, Gallagher's, the Aircraft factory and Glentoran Football Club are all synonymous with the history of East Belfast over the last 120 years. For people who lived and worked in the area their main source of entertainment after a hard week's work was a Saturday afternoon game at the Oval. Over the period society has changed a great deal. People are more mobile, have greater wealth and can make choices about their leisure time. Football is only now beginning to respond to these changes and what the future holds in not always clear. It does however underline the importance of recording the story of Glentoran Football Club.

I feel very honoured to be asked to write a foreword to this book. I was born and brought up at Ballyhackamore, which I have always viewed as the "outskirts" of East Belfast. My family all had close links with areas such as the Newtownards Road, Holywood Arches and Bloomfield so it was almost inevitable that at an early age I would become a Glentoran fanatic. Indeed I have a few vague memories as, when a small boy, I was taken "across town" to watch Glentoran play at Grosvenor Park and clearly remember the first game back at the Oval against Linfield in 1949. My boyhood hero was Sammy Hughes and I can still vividly remember some of his goals, although I was never able to emulate his scoring feats.

I suppose at this stage of my life I never dreamt that in the year 2001, twenty-seven years since I finished playing for Glentoran, that I would still hold the record of having played 555 games. My career began with Boys Brigade football and, as a teenager, I played for Ards for a couple of years. In 1961 I was signed for Glentoran by the late Harry Walker, then their manager, and I continued to play until my retirement during 1974/5 season. Relative to the history of the club from 1882 to the present day it is humbling to think that "my era" can only contribute to a very small part of the Glentoran story.

However I do recognise that I was very fortunate to be involved with Glentoran during a period which brought a lot of success and glory to the club. Opportunities to play in European competitions were just beginning and more importantly Glentoran always seemed to attract high quality players and managers. The gap between continental and local teams was not as great as it is currently. Crowds of 30,000 to 35,000 packed the Oval to watch sides such as Benfica, Glasgow Rangers and Arsenal and we always managed to put up creditable performances. Indeed in 1973/4 we reached the Quarter-final of the European Cup Winners Cup before being defeated by Borussia Moenchengladbach. The trip to the United States in 1967, led by the late John Colrain who was a real charismatic manager, is something that will long stand out in my memory. The welcome on our return to East Belfast is something that will never be forgotten.

Other managers such as Harry Walker, Isaac McDowell, Peter McParland, Alex Young, George Eastham and Bobby McGregor all made important contributions during this period but perhaps the greatest influence at the Oval was the late Billy Neill. For me, he was someone who was s playing colleague, a manager, a coach, a friend and counsellor. Glentoran owe him a great debt.

In my time there were many players who made important contributions to Glentoran – Walter Bruce, Trevor Thompson, Tommy Jackson, Terry Conroy, Jim Weatherup, Albert Finlay, Eamon Byrne, Billy McKeag, Eric Ross, Harry Creighton and Arthur Stewart. In reality the list is almost endless.

More recently, in my role as assistant manager to Tommy Jackson, I have seen players such as Jim Cleary, Billy Caskey, Alan Paterson, Johnny Jameson, John Devine, Gary Macartney and Barney Bowers make worthwhile contribution to the history of the club.

As well as great players one has to be very proud of the "non-sectarian" nature of the club and their supporters, even through very difficult periods in the history of Northern Ireland. Players from all backgrounds have always been made welcome at the Oval.

However it has got to be recognised that history can be very subjective. My recollections of Glentoran are based only on my experiences as a child, player, supporter and more recently as a football coach. I know little of Fred Roberts, the half-back line of Ferritt, Scraggs and Emerson, winning the Vienna Cup in Austria or the infamous riots at Cliftonville in 1920. Although I am familiar with other great names associated with Glentoran such as Blanchflower, Bingham, McIlroy, Doherty and Peacock I am not clear about their detailed contributions to Glentoran. This book by Roy France has taken fifteen years to complete and will give details for all of the 5,000 plus games played since 1882 across 119 seasons. It will solve many arguments and perhaps start others.

Billy McCullough, 1961 to 1974, 555 appearances, 12 goals.

Foreword

from Trevor Thompson, Glentoran's all-time leading scorer.

Most Glentoran supporters of my generation will recall the 1950s and 1960s with mixed feelings. From a very good team in the early fifties through to a bad patch from 1957 to 1962 to what I consider to be the best period of that time from 1963 to 1968. The foundation for that successful era was laid by people like Harry Walker, Isaac McDowell, Billy Neill, Gibby McKenzie and John Colrain.

History I believe, will always point to one particular game as being the turning point for the Glens around then. The date 4th April 1964, the venue Windsor Park, the result Linfield 1 Glentoran 8. The cycle of seventeen years without a win at Windsor Park had been broken. From that day the Glens went onto become the 1963/4 League Champions and win many more trophies in the following seasons up until my retirement.

I was delighted at being asked by Roy France to write a foreword to this book and may it give all Glenmen many happy memories. I certainly look forward to reading it.

Trevor Thompson, 1956 to 1968, 463 appearances, 375 goals.

Acknowledgements

The following people made valuable contributions to the production of this book. My sincere thanks goes out to them and to anyone else whose name I have inadvertently omitted. To past players Billy McCullough and Trevor Thompson for their forewords and Billy McKeague, Roy Borne and Billy Walker for access to their press cuttings and memory banks. To Brian McClelland for his copious scrapbooks from the 1950s and him and his family for their meticulous proof reading on the draft manuscript. To Glentoran Gazette editors David McCune, Philip Stevenson and Sam Robinson for their encouragement and support through the club programme. In particular to David for access to the 1923 Supporters club records over many years. To Marshall Gillespie for his expertise in book publishing on Northern Ireland soccer. To Norman Ternahan for his statistics in recent years. To Ian Lemon for sending me the Ulster over many years and accompanying me to many matches in the early 1980s. To the late Eric Wright for access to his memorabilia museum. To Keith Stubley, Ken Stones and the staff at J. W. Northend for their typesetting and printing expertise. To Mark Johnston for general business advice, encouragement and most importantly assistance with funding. To Bryan Milne and George Glass for their assistance with research in tracing details of games in the early years. To Roger Dixon and staff at Belfast Public Libraries in particular Michael Melchett who despite failing health was a mine of information and had the knack of discovering incredibly obscure Glentoran references in local papers. To Thomas Sewell and John Duffy for some excellent photographs. To Colin Crooks of Flynets for help in publicising the book in Belfast.

On a personal note I would like to thank my father for first taking me to the Oval all those years ago and to my mother and sisters for their general encouragement over the years. Finally to my wife Judith for her patience and understanding and results checking as I spent yet another night working on the book.

Roy France

Sheffield,
May 2001

Format and Abbreviations

For each season you will find a textual review and a table of results, sorted chronologically by competition with friendly games at the end. The book has been written with the intention that the reader will refer to both in the course of reading a season. From 1890/1 onwards, when the Irish League commenced, you will also find a table of appearance makers (including substitutes coming on from the mid 1960s) and goalscorers for each season. Abbreviations are used frequently throughout the book for competitions, venues and rounds as follows:

Competitions. AC=Alhambra Cup, BC=Budweiser Cup, BCC=Belfast City Cup, BDL=Belfast and District League, BxC=Blaxnit Cup, CACC=County Antrim Centenary Chalice, CAS=County Antrim Shield, CbC=Carlsberg Cup, CC=City Cup, CCC=Coca-Cola Cup, CDC=County Down Cup, ChC=Charity Cup, CM=Challenge Match, CS=Charity Shield, EC=European Cup, ECW=European Cup Winners' Cup, F=Friendly (Including Testimonials and Benefit games, Practice and trial games), FBC=Festival of Britain Cup, FC=Fairs Cup, GC=Gold Cup, IC=Irish Cup, ICC=Inter-City Cup, IL=Irish League and Irish Premier League, ILC=Irish League Cup, MC=Mercer Cup, NIC=New Irish Cup, NSC=North-South Cup, RL=Regional League, SGC=Substitute Gold Cup, T4C=Top Four Competition, TC=Tylers Cup, UEFA=UEFA Cup, UC=Ulster Cup, VC=Vienna Cup.

Venues. A=Away, Bal=Balmoral, Bf=Ballynafeigh, BS=Ballymena Showgrounds, Bw=Brandywell, CdP=Clandeboye Park, CP=Celtic Park, CrP=Castlereagh Park, CS=Coleraine Showgrounds, DP=Dalymount Park, GP=Grosvenor Park, H=Home, KP=Klondyke Park, MP=Mourneview Park, N=Neutral, NG=New Grosvenor, OP=Oriel Park, Sol or Solt=Solitude, Sv=Seaview, Uv=Ulsterville, WP=Windsor Park.

Rounds. A number corresponds to that round, i.e. 1=first etc., 1.1=first round first leg etc., R=replay, R2=second replay etc, P=Preliminary Round, QF=Quarter final, SF=Semi final, F=final, TM=Test Match, RU=Runners up, PO=Play-off, Q=Qualifying Round.

Others. (p)=penalty, og=own goal, aet=after extra time. If there are two players of the same surname in a particular era where no first name or initial has been traced then they will be differentiated by their playing position. e.g. CH=centre-half, LW=left-wing etc.

For each season a full playing record is given. The percentage success figure (%) is calculated by awarding 100% for a win, 50% for a draw and 0% for a defeat. The overall average is then calculated. Games decided on penalties are counted as a draw.

1882/83

First matches – A cricketing reference – Heavy Irish Cup defeat

Although no exact date of formation can be traced, it appears that a Glentoran team first took the field for a game of football on Saturday 7th October 1882. The opponents Mountavon from Ravenhill, the venue the Ormeau Park and the result 2-2. The sketchy match report from the following Monday's Northern Whig is reproduced here, but the line-up for that initial game is not available. However a team has been traced for the game against Oldpark later that month. In 1-2-2-6 formation it read:

Kerr; Cunningham, McNab; Montgomery, Megaw; Reid, P.Byrne, J.Byrne, Johnston, Stewart, Brown.

A Glentoran cricket team had been in action though on 22nd July 1882. Playing at Avoneil they made 41 for 7 with E.Reid and J. Cunningham batting well before bowling the home side out for a mere 13 with Reid prominent with the ball.

At this time the Irish Cup was the only organised competitive football in Ireland, and Glentoran received a first round bye. Our first cup game resulted in defeat at the hands of the strong Ulster club, when Glentoran were represented by: Cunningham; Forsythe, Johnston; Holland, S.Byrne; Lemon, Megaw, Leslie, McCormick, Elliman, J.Byrne. Note the change in goalkeeping responsibilities - in the 19th Century it was common practice for "outfield" players to regularly play in goal.

Other players to turn out in 1882/3 were Silo, McMillan, Sloane, McVicker, McManus, Wright, Wilson and Steele. It's amusing to note that for the game against Enfield in January we arrived with nine men, however the Whig remarks that "two good subs were taken from the field!" Presumably the team was short as two fixtures were undertaken simultaneously that day. A Second XI were also active in the first season and the following details have been traced:

21st Oct	Distillery 3rds	(A)		Result Unknown
28th Oct	Glencarr	(H)	W	4-1
4th Nov	Clarence 2nds	(H)	W	6-0
11th Nov	Clearstream	(A)	D	1-1
18th Nov	York Road 2nds	(H)	W	10-1
25th Nov	Distillery 3rds	(A)		Result Unknown
2nd Dec	Avoneil 2nds		Game Postponed Indefinitely.	

Lesley(2), Barry, Allen, Miller and Reid were the scorers against Clarence. Clearstream were the 2nd XI of Ligoneil. The performances of the seconds, who also played their home games in the Ormeau Park, augured well for future success.

In general terms 1882/3 saw further development of organised sport in the North of Ireland. A dilemma facing many of the newly formed football clubs was whether to affiliate to Association or Rugby rules or both. (Glentoran have never had any official connection with Rugby.) The season saw Wellington Park form a football club to go alongside their rugby and hockey brethren. Ulster met Distillery in the first friendly of the season on 2nd September. Avoneil, also from East Belfast, held a practice match at their Beechfield grounds on 30th September, before drawing 2-2 with Down Athletics in their first game of the campaign. Malone, a team with no connection to the current rugby club, lost football games to Distillery (0-7), Ulster (0-6) and Cliftonville (4-6).

On the representative front a Belfast and District XI lost 1-7 to Ayrshire in Kilmarnock. No Glentoran players were involved with the three international trial games in February, when one of the trial teams played in brown shirts. The Irish Cup final saw Cliftonville defeat favourites Ulster 5-0 at Bloomfield in front of 2,000 (paying 6d. each) - the largest crowd at a game in Ireland thus far. Scottish League clubs travelled over to promote the game locally, among them Hamilton Academicals and the now defunct Abercorn and Third Lanark clubs. The season closed on 26th May 1883 with a 12-a-side game between Down Athletics 2nds and Rugby 2nds finishing 2-2.

Despite only scant details of Glentoran's games being printed by the local press, the playing records of the more established Belfast clubs were published:

	Played	Won	Drawn	Lost	For	Against
Cliftonville	18	11	2	5	58	38
2nds (Enfield)	20	11	4	5	64	38
Ulster	22	12	4	6	81	33
2nds (Ulidia)	13	10	0	3	45	16
Distillery	14	11	2	1	61	4
Distillery 2nds	10	9	0	1	44	2

To be fair to contemporary newspapers it was deemed the responsibility of club secretaries to forward details of the weekend games in time for inclusion in the Monday and Tuesday editions.

Results 1882/83

F	07/10/1882		Mountavon	H	D	2	2	Megaw, Montgomery
F	14/10/1882		Down Athletics 2nd XI	H	Unknown			
F	28/10/1882		Oldpark	A	L	0	3	-
F	11/11/1882		Ligoneil	H	L	0	3	-
F	02/12/1882		Avoneil	A	Unknown			
F	09/12/1882		Chichester Park	A	Unknown			
F	06/01/1883		Enfield	A	L	2	8	Unknown
F	06/01/1883		Granville	A	Unknown			
F	03/02/1883		Oldpark	H	Unknown			
F	10/02/1883		Enfield	A	L	0	3	-
F	24/02/1883		Mountavon	A	Unknown			
F	10/03/1883		Avoneil	A	L	1	4	Unknown
F	24/03/1883		York Road	A	Unknown			
IC	27/01/1883	2	Ulster	A	L	0	9	- abandoned after 40 minutes

(Irish Association rules.)

GLENTORAN V. MOUNTAVON.

This match was played on Saturday on the grounds of the former, and resulted in a draw, each side scoring two goals. The Glentoran got their two in the first half and the Mountavon theirs in the second half. By a clever pass from M'Millan, Megaw shot the first goal. The ball was then kicked off, and was brought well up to the Glentoran goal, but Silo, with a splendid kick, sent it back to the forwards, who wrought well on the ball, and Montgomery scored the second goal. In the second half the Mountavon played a better game. Shortly after the kick-off they scored their first goal. The play then for a time was about equal, but shortly before call of time Long made a good shot and secured their second goal.

Match report from Glentoran's first ever game

1883/84

Lemon gets a hat-trick – First cross-channel transfer – Development of football

Unfortunately few of Glentoran's games were recorded in the second season of existence, so a summary of the season would be presumptuous. However, we did record a win in the Irish Cup and a player named Lemon claimed the first ever "hat-trick" for Glentoran. Lemon later moved on to England and eventually died in South America.

Glentoran's stoutest players in 1883/4 were Modesto Silo and Cunningham in defence and the forwards Steele, McManus and Reid. Our trip to Lisburn to take on Hertford in January saw confusion in the home ranks. Only six of their players turned up, the rest under the impression that the game was off due to the bad weather. Hertford managed to scrape together nine men eventually and, with the help of a strong wind, built up a 3-0 interval lead. Despite some fast forward play we were unable to draw level in the second half.

In our Irish Cup defeat we showed up well but Ulster were just too strong. Waring did the damage scoring six goals himself in a match played on a very soft pitch.

Only one 2nd XI game was traced this season, a fixture against Lavinia at Ormeau Park on 22nd March 1884. Glentoran 2nds won 8-1, hat-tricks from J.McVicker and J.Meare being supplemented with goals by J.Long and D.Sanderson. McVicker was to become the first Glentoran player to be transferred to an English club when he moved to Macclesfield in 1889.

During this season the number of Association Football clubs passed the 100 mark, as compared with four in season 1879/80. A second competition, the Belfast Charities Cup, was inaugurated, with the gate money from the games going to local Hospitals. W.C.Mitchell was behind the scheme, which was in line with similar competitions organised on the British mainland by the Glasgow and Lancashire F.A.s. Four teams competed in the first Charity Cup, Cliftonville defeating Wellington Park 7-1, and Distillery overcoming Ulster 5-0 (after a 1-1 draw) in the semi-finals. The Reds defeated the Whites in the final. Distillery had already claimed the major silverware, easily beating Wellington Park 5-0 in the Irish Cup final. Again the attendance was around 2,000. Twenty four clubs had entered, 16 from the Belfast area.

New teams to affiliate to the IFA the season included Glenalina, Spencer, YMCA, Hertford and Victoria (the first team from Londonderry). The 30th November 1883 saw the first soccer game played in Dublin when the Belfast Athletics defeated Dublin University 6-0 at Trinity College. Two days later the Dublin AFC held the Belfast men to a 2-3 scoreline at Wesley College, Donnybrook. The Royal Belfast Academical Institution played its first ever Association game, going down 2-5 to Cliftonville. The Reds also managed a 0-0 draw with Bootle. Scottish clubs continued to accept invitations to "come over" for friendlies. Patrons of the Larne-Stranraer ferry were Hearts, Airdrie, Queen's Park and Hamilton Academicals. Ireland continued to have problems at senior level conceding 19 goals in the three "Home" internationals.

The Avoneil club defeated Ormeau (in their first season) 6-0. Avoneil were to be disbanded later in the season and many of their players joined Glentoran. The final game of 1883/4 was on 17th May when Distillery defeated Queen's Island 2-0. The Ulster secretary reported the following record for the club's 1st XI:

Played 32, Won 16, Drew 4, Lost 12, Goals For 81, Against 64.

On a black note, a letter to the News Letter claimed that players who had won Irish Cup medals were selling them for 30 shillings. This was implied as "professionalism" in an amateur game.

14

Results 1883/84

F	27/10/1883		Albert	H	W	5	1	Lemon 3, Reid, J.Byrne
F	03/11/1883		Hertford	H	W	1	0	Unknown
F	17/11/1883		Distillery	A	D	2	2	Unknown
F	05/01/1884		Hertford	A	L	2	3	og, Steele
F	19/01/1884		Albert	H	W	5	1	Unknown
F	26/04/1884		Albert	H	L	0	3	-
IC	29/12/1883	1	Mountavon	Broadway	W	3	0	Unknown
IC	02/02/1884	2	Ulster	A	L	0	7	-

1884/85

Progress in the Irish Cup – McManus plays for Ulster – An active Second XI

With the addition of players from Avoneil, Glentoran developed into a respected club during their third season, although they were still tagged as "juniors". In the Irish Cup we reached the third round before falling to eventual winners Distillery. The first round game against Ormeau kicked-off late and it was agreed to play two 30-minute halves. In a fast moving game Glentoran mastered the wind and a bumpy pitch to move into a 5-0 half-time lead and kill the tie. Controversy reigned in the second round against Spencer.

We held a 1-0 interval lead but the north Belfast XI soon equalised and then had a goal disallowed by referee Mr. Riddle. Although we finished comfortable winners Spencer lodged an official protest and the IFA ordered a replay. The scoreline was repeated second time around and by all accounts, the referee, Mr. McCully, had his decisions universally accepted. In our defeat against Distillery we had the best of the early play but were unable to come back from a 0-3 half-time deficit. The Whites went on to defeat Limavady 2-0 in the final.

Our best result of the season was the defeat of Distillery in early 1885, while we twice held our own against Ulster at Ballynafeigh. The report of the game in March against YMCA indicated that spectators were now taking a lively interest in the fortunes of local clubs. Also the Northern Whig began a regular weekly football column by "Goal". Glentoran were represented by the following players during the season:

Wilson, Megaw, Leslie, P.Byrne, J.Byrne, V.Byrne, Holland, McManus, Silo, Lemon, Fleming, W.Reid, Johnston, Steele and McVicker. Reports of the games hinted that the team had a pleasant style, with the forwards indulging in a neat passing game. The following 2nd XI fixtures and results were traced:

1st Nov	Ormeau 2nd XI	(A)		
8th Nov	Oldpark 2nd XI	(H)	2-2	
13th Dec	Clarence 2nd XI			
26th Dec	Clarence 2nd XI	(A)	1-3	Mears
10th Jan	Ormeau 2nd XI	(A)		
14th Feb	Ulidia	(H)		
28th Feb	Ormeau 2nd XI			
7th Mar	YMCA 2nd XI	(A)		
21st Mar	YMCA 2nd XI	(A)	2-3	Barry, Gaw

McGrath and Fleming played with distinction for the seconds.

McManus became the first Glentoran player to gain a representative honour when he was selected in the forward line for Ulster against Leinster. Unfortunately the provincial Ulster went down 0-1 on 7th February at Solitude.

The Charity Cup had quickly become a major event in the Irish football season. Oldpark defeated Cliftonville 1-0 in the second final attended by Lords, Ladies and local dignitaries, with the Royal Inniskilling band providing the interval entertainment.

Cliftonville, managing to regularly turn out three or more XIs, played Wellington Park in an exhibition at Comber in October. A North Down team was soon formed after the game. Civil Service played their first game, drawing 2-2 with Spencer on 25th October at Ormeau Park. Although the game was developing rapidly in Ireland, the yardstick of International football was depressing. Defeats v England (0-4), Scotland (2-8) and Wales (2-9, after holding a 2-0 interval lead) would have been on the agenda at the IFA's AGM in April 1885.

Results 1884/85

F	11/10/1884		YMCA	A	W	5	0	Unknown
F	18/10/1884		Distillery	A	L	0	3	-
F	25/10/1884		Spencer	A	W	4	0	Reid 3, McManus
F	01/11/1884		Mossley	A	Unknown			
F	08/11/1884		Oldpark	A	Unknown			
F	15/11/1884		Sydenham	A	W	2	0	Unknown
F	22/11/1884		Wellington Park	A	Unknown			
F	29/11/1884		Clarence	A	W	6	1	Unknown
F	13/12/1884		Ulster	A	L	0	2	-
F	26/12/1884		Kilrea	A	D	0	0	-
F	03/01/1885		Distillery	H	W	2	0	Lemon, Steele
F	14/02/1885		Ulster	A	L	2	5	McManus, Lemon
F	28/02/1885		Ormeau	H	Unknown			
F	07/03/1885		YMCA	H	L	1	3	Lemon
IC	06/12/1884	1	Ormeau	A	W	5	1	McManus 2, Lemon, Leslie, Reid
IC	20/12/1884	2	Spencer	A	W	4	1	Steele, Lemon, McManus, Reid – Protest
IC	10/01/1885	2R	Spencer	Bally'feigh	W	4	1	McManus, Leslie, Reid, Steele
IC	24/01/1885	3	Distillery	A	L	1	5	Unknown

1885/86

*Un-seasonal Autumn weather – A marathon Charity Cup tie –
Married men proven stronger*

At Glentoran's AGM on 8th September the following office bearers were elected: CAPTAIN: T.Wilson, VICE-CAPTAIN: M.Silo, TREASURER: Wm. Reid, COMMITTEE: A.McManus, W.Leslie, J.Lemon, J.Byrne, SECRETARY: F.D.Morton, 213 Lorne Terrace, Mountpottinger, Belfast.

They were to preside over another season of good progress as we qualified for our first ever final, the Charity Cup, and again reached the third round of the Irish Cup. Our general play and results made us one of the leading clubs locally, not far behind the well-established trio of Distillery, Cliftonville and Ulster.

Our Irish Cup campaign began easily enough with wins over Montalto of Ballynahinch, and Ligoneil in a game of two 35-minute halves. Against Ligoneil we lined up: V.Byrne, Silo, Sloane, Connor, Baxter, McManus, Steele, Leslie, Lemon, McIlvenney, McVicker.

For the third round game Reid replaced McIlvenney and we could have been satisfied with the interval score of 1-0 to YMCA as the slope was in our favour in the second half. However YM had other ideas racing into a 3-0 lead and not even two late goals and a formal protest to the IFA could save us. Distillery retained the cup without conceding a goal in the competition. A disappointing crowd of 1,000 saw the Whites defeat Limavady 1-0 in the final.

We had figured in two hard early season games with Distillery. The first game at Broadway was played in torrential rain and a hurricane gale - unusual for mid-September! The return at Ormeau Park saw Crone twice give the visitors the lead but we equalised both times. The Whig reported that our goalkeeper, H. Wilson, played splendidly and on the occasion of each score had been charged into the goal.

Our first win over Ulster preceded the first clash between ourselves and Cliftonville. Although the scoreline (4-1) suggested an easy win for the Reds it was a brilliant game between two evenly matched teams. Cliftonville did play one man short, while we had an early headed goal by McManus disallowed for off-side. We could be excused a heavy defeat at the hands of Wellington Park as we had the handicap of playing three men short!

For the second successive season the Glentoran team expressed delight about the treatment and hospitality received on a Christmas trip to Kilrea. Not much charity on the field as the locals took a 2-0 lead, but positional changes at the interval enabled us to come back and snatch a draw. A remarkable event occurred in the game with Oldpark in March. Leslie, one of our backs, was tackling so hard that on one occasion he actually burst the ball!

The Charity Cup for 1885/6 was extended to eight teams and we enjoyed our entry, defeating Ulster in Round 1 "amidst great applause". The semi-final clash against Oldpark has gone down as one of the games of the 19th Century for good reason. A crowd of 3,000 saw Glentoran line-up as follows: Lawther; Silo, Leslie; Baxter, Connor; Steele, McManus, Lemon, Sloane, McVicker, Reid. Against a physically bigger team Reid gave us the lead with a splendid shot. Oldpark equalised when Lawther was charged through his own goal. So at 90 minutes it stood 1-1, another 30 minutes produced no goals, and it was decided to play a further half-hour. With five minutes to go Oldpark scored a goal, but both umpires (the forerunners to linesmen) gave off-side. However the referee over-ruled and the crowd invaded the pitch en masse. The Charity Committee ordered a replay and we gave a much improved performance culminating in brilliant goals from Sloane and McManus.

Unfortunately in the final we couldn't reproduce that form and succumbed meekly to Cliftonville. At least the Cup matches' gate money provided £140 for local Hospital funds.

Some individuals also brought honour to the club. J.Lemon became our first full Irish International when he played against Wales at Wrexham on 27th February (0-5). Lemon and

Leslie had played for Ulster against Staffordshire three weeks earlier with Leslie also appearing against Lancashire. Ulster lost both games 0-3.

January 1886 marked Glasgow Rangers' first visit to these shores when they defeated Cliftonville 8-2 in a game to inaugurate the Reds' new grandstand. 3,000 turned up including 300 in the stand itself.

Glentoran 2nds produced some good football and results. Indeed a game was arranged in March between the respective reserve teams of Glentoran and Cliftonville to decide who was Ireland's premier 2nd XI. Inconclusively it finished 4-4. Glens team: Wilson; Connory, McCleery; Holland, Reid; Fleming, McIlvenney, Knox, Mears, Radcliffe, Wallace. The Seconds played their last game of the season v. Distillery 2nds in oppressive heat on 5th June. Moreover the last soccer game of the season was as late as 18th June when a team of Married men overcame a Singles XI 3-2 in a benefit match for T.Stewart.

Results 1885/86

F	12/09/1885		Distillery	A	L	1	2	Leslie
F	03/10/1885		Distillery	H	L	2	4	Lemon, Steele
F	17/10/1885		Ulster	A	W	2	1	Lemon, Fleming
F	24/10/1885		Ormeau	H	W	5	4	Unknown
F	24/10/1885		Genoa	H	Unknown			
F	31/10/1885		Mossley	A	Unknown			
F	31/10/1885		YMCA	A	D	0	0	-
F	07/11/1885		Carrickfergus	A	Unknown			
F	14/11/1885		Cliftonville	A	L	1	4	McVicker
F	28/11/1885		Wellington Park	A	L	2	6	Leslie, Baxter
F	26/12/1885		Kilrea	A	D	2	2	Unknown
F	23/01/1886		Mount Collier	H	Unknown			
F	06/02/1886		Wellington Park	A	D	4	4	Unknown
F	13/02/1886		Ulster	A	L	0	2	-
F	06/03/1886		Mossley	H	Unknown			
F	20/03/1886		Oldpark	H	W	3	1	Lemon, Unknown 2
F	27/03/1886		Mossley	A	W	3	0	Unknown
IC	21/11/1885	1	Montalto	A	W	9	2	Unknown
IC	05/12/1885	2	Ligoneil	A	W	7	1	Lemon 3, McVicker 2, McIlvenney, Leslie
IC	19/12/1885	3	YMCA	Bf	L	2	3	McVicker 2
ChC	03/04/1886	1	Ulster	A	W	4	1	Ratcliffe 2, McManus, Steele
ChC	10/04/1886	SF	Oldpark	Solt	L	1	2	aet Reid Protest
ChC	21/04/1886	SFR	Oldpark	Solt	W	2	0	Sloane, McManus
ChC	01/05/1886	F	Cliftonville	Bf	L	1	5	Baxter

1886/87

A new ground – Protests and complaints – IFA Suspension

Despite the fact that players Lemon and Leslie were to leave Glentoran and join YMCA, prospects looked bright for further progress in our fifth season. We had secured a new playing ground, moving from Ormeau Park to the King's Field, Bryson Street in Westbourne, Mountpottinger. The land had been obtained from Mr. Alexander King of Ballymacarrett.

The AGM on 14th September 1886 in the Typographical Institute reported that the club was in a satisfactory state. The following officials were appointed: 1st XI CAPTAIN: M.Silo, VICE-CAPTAIN: R.Lawther, TREASURER: W.Reid, COMMITTEE: F.S.Wilson, A.Knox, J.Byrne, D.Macarthur, SECRETARY: John Lemon, 10 Roundhill Street, Mountpottinger. The committee invited prospective opponents for the season to arrange fixtures directly with the secretary.

With a new pitch all of our early season games were at home and some excellent results were recorded. Our first line-up at King's Field was as follows: R.Lawther, M.Silo, J.Connor, S.Scott, C.Holland, P.Kelly, W.Reid, R.Fleming, J.McVicker, E.Steele, J.McCreery.

Although the ground was almost flooded for the game against Clifton Park, it was remarked that Glentoran had rarely played better. Much satisfaction was taken in the win over YMCA, who included our former stars in their ranks. The November meeting with Cliftonville was described as "70 minutes of mud larking." At one stage we held a 3-1 lead and had the advantage of the slope but still had to bow the knee. We paid our first visit to Banbridge for a game against Millmount on New Year's Day.

Hopes were high of lifting one of the two trophies but fate was to deal us a grim hand. The early rounds of the Irish Cup again produced comfortable victories - indeed it was said that against Beechmount, the Glentoran goalkeeper never touched the ball! The scene was set for a big home third round clash against Distillery in December but frost caused a postponement. The match was switched to Ulster's ground at Ballynafeigh with a noon kick-off on Christmas Day. Glentoran took the lead when a corner from Steele rolled along the bar and dropped into the net! Great cheering accompanied a splendid run and goal by McManus, giving us a 2-0 interval lead. Although the cup holders pulled a goal back with eight minutes remaining they could not prevent us qualifying for our first Irish Cup semi-final.

There had seldom been more interest in an Irish football match than that for the semi. Ulster opened the scoring from a goalmouth scramble, Reid headed in a Steele corner, then Ulster took the lead again before half-time. Near the end a fierce Silo free-kick went into the goal only to be disallowed by the referee who claimed that he had given an indirect kick. After the dust had settled Glentoran formally protested to the IFA about this specific decision, demanding a replay. On the Wednesday after the game the IFA disallowed the protest on the grounds that "the referee's decision is final." This ruling was far from consistent with the outcomes of other contemporary protests. Our secretary then wrote another letter of complaint to the IFA Executive and the Northern Whig. The Whig refused to publish this letter, firmly stating that the matter was strictly between the club and the IFA. Finally, on 7th February the IFA suspended Glentoran for "contempt of the IFA ruling", disallowing any other IFA affiliated clubs from playing against us. The Trustees of the Charity Cup reluctantly withdrew our invitation, Limavady taking our place.

Ulster went on to win the Irish Cup, overcoming Cliftonville 3-1 at Broadway. The Reds retained the Charity Cup, defeating YMCA 3-2, and their secretary's report emphasised

Cliftonville's dominance of Irish football at that time. Of their 17 games against Irish clubs they won 16 and lost only one.

It is worth noting that this was Linfield's first full season. Known as Linfield Athletics they played their first game on 18th September away to Clarence. The football clan initially ran alongside the cricket club which had played during the summer of 1886.

Football was continually spreading throughout Ireland, the Mid-Ulster FA was formed and a Junior Cup was thought about, though the progress was not without humorous moments. When County Armagh defeated County Monaghan 2-0 in April 1887, a third goal was disallowed as the ball had been helped into the net by a spectator!

Ireland gained international success, 4-1 over Wales, but Glentoran were left to reflect on a suspension which severely dented progress.

Results 1886/87								
F	02/10/1886		Distillery	H	W	4	2	Unknown
F	16/10/1886		Ulster	H	Unknown			
F	06/11/1886		Hertford	H	W	13	0	McVicker 3, McManus 6, McCready, Steele, Unknown 2
F	13/11/1886		Clifton Park	H	W	10	0	McVicker 3, McCready 2, McManus 3, Reid, Silo
F	27/11/1886		YMCA	H	W	1	0	Fleming
F	04/12/1886		Ulster	H	W	1	0	Steele
F	11/12/1886		Cliftonville	A	L	3	5	Unknown
F	01/01/1887		Millmount	A	W	2	1	Unknown
F	08/01/1887		Wellington Park	A	Postponed			
IC	30/10/1886	1	Beechmount	H	W	4	0	McCleery 2, Steele, McManus
IC	20/11/1886	2	Mount Collier	H	W	6	1	McCleery 2, Steele, Reid, McManus, Unknown
IC	25/12/1886	3	Distillery	Bf	W	2	1	Steele, McManus
IC	22/01/1887	SF	Ulster	A	L	1	2	Reid

1887/88

Our biggest ever win – First meeting with Linfield – Start of the Junior Cup

A resuscitated Glentoran held their AGM at the Liberal Club Rooms on 17th September 1887. D.Macarthur presided over the meeting where the previous season was described as "satisfactory, despite the difficulties." Modesto Silo retained the captaincy of the 1st XI, with Arty McManus appointed vice-captain. R.McCalmont was elected 2nd XI skipper, A.Knox became secretary with H.Wilson as his assistant.

This season brought our biggest ever win - a score now unlikely to be beaten. In his History of Glentoran in the Ireland's Saturday Night of 15th October 1898 Ralph the Rover penned the following passage on the game, which incidentally was to kick-off on the arrival of Glentoran on the 1.25 train from Belfast.

"One of the largest scores the team has ever made was against Montalto in the Irish Cup competition, in the days when a first class club might be drawn against a third-rate country eleven, with disastrous consequences to the latter. On the occasion to which we refer the Ballynahinch men were numbered with the slain to the tune of 18 goals to nil, and would have doubled this number but for the referee, Mr. M.Wilson of Distillery, who asked the Glentoran forwards to ease up some time."

The same day in the cup Distillery defeated United Steamship, also 18-0, while Ulster and Oldpark recorded 13-0 and 10-1 victories over Evening Telegraph and Whiterock respectively. Unfortunately we lost to Ulster in a rough game in Round 2.

October also saw the first clash between elevens of Glentoran and Linfield. Great interest had been generated for this encounter but Linfield emerged the winners. Sam Torrans gave them a 2-0 lead with goals either side of half-time. McVicker pulled one back but Vance, after a late scramble, completed the scoring. The teams for this historic occasion at Westbourne read:

GLENTORAN: Lawther; Silo, Millar; Sloane, Holland, McConkey; McVicker, McCalmont, McManus, Radcliffe, Steele.

LINFIELD ATHLETICS: Gordon; Christian, Clarke; Close, Corrigan, J.Torrans; Vance, S.Torrans, Peden, R.Torrans, Gaffikin.

Linfield also won the return game at the Linfield Mill on a soft treacherous pitch. YMCA had turned into one of the strongest local sides, defeating us 1-0 at their Shaftesbury grounds when ex-Glenman Lemon set up the goal. Silo also moved to YMCA with Sloane taking over our captaincy for the return game at Westbourne. We put up our best display of the season and came within a whisker of winning the game.

Cliftonville claimed the major honours with wins over Distillery (2-1) in the Irish Cup final and Linfield (3-2) in the deciding game for the Charity Cup. The Blues gained some revenge, defeating the Reds in a 4-a-side competition at Cliftonville for Belfast teams. (Glentoran did not enter.)

R. Lawther gained an International cap against Scotland in March and despite conceding 10 goals retained his place for the England game two weeks later. He was joined by McVicker and they restricted the English to a 1-5 scoreline. A feature of internationals in Belfast in these days was the playing of a friendly game between two club sides straight after the main game on the same pitch.

Glentoran Seconds entered the inaugural Junior Cup. In the first round we overcame Stranmillis 7-2 but were forced to replay by the IFA. Distillery II defeated Milford from Armagh 3-0 in the initial final.

Everton travelled to play Ulster for the third successive season and lost 2-3 to the Ballynafeigh club. This reverse must have stung for two days later they thrashed Cliftonville 10-1. The County Antrim FA was formed but the enthusiastic evolution of soccer did not tingle everyone's palate. One Belfast man wrote to the News Letter in March complaining about impromptu games;

"From the time the lads leave school until dark Avoca Street is almost impassable, and the yells with which the games are carried on are objectionable to residents."

Results 1887/88									
F	24/09/1887		Gordon Highlanders	H	W	5	1	Unknown	
F	01/10/1887		Linfield Athletics	H	L	1	3	McVicker	
F	08/10/1887		Cliftonville	A	Unknown				
F	15/10/1887		Distillery	A	L	1	5	"Rush"	
F	22/10/1887		YMCA	A	L	0	1	-	
F	05/11/1887		Beechmount	H	Unknown				
F	24/12/1887		Linfield Athletics	A	L	0	4	-	
F	26/12/1887		Limavady	H	Unknown				
F	07/01/1888		Limavady	A	L	0	2	-	
F	14/01/1888		YMCA	H	D	1	1	Gray	
F	28/01/1888		Ballyclare	A	Unknown				
F	11/02/1888		Belfast Athletics	H	Unknown				
F	25/02/1888		Beechmount	H	Unknown				
F	03/03/1888		Distillery	H	Unknown				
F	17/03/1888		Kilrea	A	W	4	3	Unknown	
F	14/04/1888		Montalto	H	W	7	0	Unknown	
IC	29/10/1887	1	Montalto	A	W	18	0	Unknown	
IC	12/11/1887	2	Ulster	A	L	1	4	Gray	

1888/89

Merger with East End – A fixture in Dublin –
First hooliganism in Irish football

Glentoran Football Club and East End Cricket Club merged at the start of the season, with Glentoran II to play under the name of "East End." The club President for the season was R.H.Allen with James Stelfox and William C. Allen in the VP roles. Goalkeeper Ralph Lawther took over the 1st XI captaincy, to be assisted by new vice-captain P.J.Malone. William Lovell and J.Morrison held the respective East End roles. Harry J. Newbould of 215 Mountpottinger Road was appointed secretary.

Results for the season were satisfactory but we still never really threatened to become one of the land's strongest teams. Against Oldpark in December a 3-0 lead was thrown away but good battling play was displayed against North End Athletics and Cliftonville.

The Irish Cup presented us with our first trip to Dublin. The team caught the 5 p.m. train on Friday, staying overnight in the Metropolis, before taking on Dublin University at Sandymount. A fast and pleasant game was highlighted by a splendid goal from Miller. In Round 2 we faced Belfast Athletics at Westbourne in strong winds coupled with driving rain. The game kicked-off late, but once underway we did most of the pressing and ran out 2-0 winners. Belfast Athletics did however protest to the IFA regarding the delayed start and a replay was ordered. That game took place the next Saturday at Rushfield on the Oldpark Road. Two first half goals were enough to win a well contested game for us.

So to the semi-final and we lined up thus against YMCA: Lawther; McVicker, Baxter; Coutts, Sloan, Gray; McKennie, Irvine, Miller, Meares, McManus. YM took the lead, and after Meares hit the post, Irvine equalised from a Meares cross. However YM, including our former skipper Silo, went on to a deserved win, continuing our Cup frustration. Distillery, who hammered Hilden 13-0 in the other semi-final, overcame YMCA 5-4 in the final.

The less said about our 1889 Charity Cup exploits the better but the Cliftonville-Distillery final witnessed the first example of hooliganism in Irish football. The Broadwegians (Distillery) were trailing 2-4 when handball was given against one of their players by the two umpires. The Distillery team walked off and their "roughs" invaded the pitch, not only threatening the referee and umpires, but also damaging the tennis and cricket pitches at Cliftonville. Needless to say the Reds were awarded the cup and Distillery's deposit was returned by the Charity Cup Trustees.

East End failed to progress past the first hurdle in the Junior Cup, going down 1-2 a home to Stormount. In the same round Westbourne thrashed Edenderry Reserves 19-0.

J.McVicker gained a second cap against Scotland while players to turn out for the Glens apart from those already mentioned included Williams, Mitchell, Long, Holland, Steele, Allister, Scott, Reid, Thompson, Kirkpatrick and Galbraith.

This season witnessed the inauguration of the County Antrim Shield. The trophy created by Messrs. W.Gibson and Co. featured the Irish Harp and the Earl of Antrim Arms. Distillery took first possession of it courtesy of an 8-4 win over YMCA.

September 1888 saw a Canadian FA touring side begin its European tour in Ireland. The visitors accounted for a County Antrim FA XI (6-2), Distillery (3-2) and Clarence (3-2) before sharing the honours with YMCA in a 1-1 draw.

At this time it was fashionable for Scottish and Irish clubs to enter the FA Cup. Cliftonville, Distillery, Ulster, YMCA and Linfield regularly competed but Glentoran never did. In 1888/9 Linfield reached the second round proper after wins over Ulster, Bolton Wanderers, Cliftonville and Nottingham Forest but eventually scratched to Forest.

Results 1888/89

F	22/09/1888		Ulster	H	Unknown			
F	06/10/1888		Oldpark	H	D	1	1	Irvine
F	13/10/1888		Black Watch	H	D	3	3	Unknown
F	01/12/1888		Oldpark	A	D	3	3	Sloane, Williams, Miller
F	08/12/1888		Limavady	H	W	8	0	Unknown
F	15/12/1888		Ulster	A	L	2	5	Miller, Unknown
F	12/01/1889		North End Athletics	A	W	1	0	Unknown
F	02/02/1889		Clarence	H	Unknown			
F	02/03/1889		Distillery	A	L	0	1	-
F	09/03/1889		North End Athletics	H	W	2	0	Unknown
F	30/03/1889		Cliftonville	H	W	2	1	Unknown
IC	20/10/1888	1	Dublin University	A	W	4	0	Miller, Irvine, McVicker, McManus
IC	10/11/1888	2	Belfast Athletics	H	W	2	0	Miller, Irvine
IC	26/01/1889	SF	YMCA	Bf	L	1	3	Irvine
ChC	05/01/1889	1	Distillery	A	L	1	7	Unknown

1889/90

The County Down Cup is won – Junior Cup success –
Historic league meeting

This, Glentoran's eighth season in existence, was significant in that the first silverware came to the club as both the 1st and 2nd XIs won tournaments. The senior side was triumphant in the inaugural County Down Cup while the Seconds annexed the Irish Junior Cup.

The County Down FA held its first meeting on 16th December 1889 with representatives from Glentoran, Glentoran II, Holywood, Botanic, Ulidia, Connsbrook, Ballynafeigh Athletics, Westbourne, Belfast Caledonians (a team of Scotsmen living in Belfast), Ulster, Comber Athletics, Montalto, Rathkeltair, Hilden, Seapatrick and Willowfield present. The draw for the first round of the cup was made exactly a week later with the initial games taking place on 11th January. Glentoran and Ulster, the two senior teams in the county, were exempt from competition until the semi-final stage. No trophy was ever struck for the tournament.

Glentoran IIs battled through to the semis, overcoming Botanic (4-1) and Stormount (5-1). However the Ulster senior team were just too strong for them, although only a single scrambled goal separated the teams. Our 1st XI made an inauspicious debut when a small crowd saw them narrowly overcome Westbourne. The Glentoran-Ulster final set for 19th April caused a logistics problem as both teams had qualified for the Charity Cup semi-finals due for decision the same afternoon. As the two Down teams wished more to play the County final they scratched against their military opponents, the Gordon Highlanders and the Black Watch respectively. In the final analysis, a large crowd saw Glentoran coast to an easy 3-0 win over Ulster at Linfield's Ulsterville ground, fielding the following side: Sloan; Anderson, Mitchell; Dykes, Taggart, Muir; Gray, Irvine, "McDonnell", Miller, McManus.

In qualifying for the Junior Cup final Glentoran Seconds overcame both the first and second elevens of Botanic, recording 5-2 and 5-0 scorelines. Linfield 2nd XI were the opponents in the final at Ballynafeigh on 1st March 1890. After an even first period, Glentoran II kept their rivals on the defensive and triumphed 4-1. Team: McMaster; Boal, J.Thompson; Wright, McVicker, McQuiston; Steele, Larmour, Elliott, Ward, D. Thompson.

Steele and J.Thompson had represented Ireland in the first ever Junior International two weeks previously. An 11-0 defeat was suffered against Scotland at Rutherglen. At senior level R.Crone appeared England and Scotland, adding to the two caps he had won when with Distillery.

Our Irish Cup aspirations were quashed early at the hands of the Gordon Highlanders. They were just one of the many Scottish and English regiments based in Ireland who organised teams and competed against the Irish clubs. Generally they were popular opponents. Gordon Highlanders went on to win the Irish Cup defeating Cliftonville 3-0 in the final after a 2-2 draw.

The remainder of our games this season produced plenty of goals but many were one-sided. The October affair against the Black Watch was described as a "rattling match" and the bond between the two teams was strengthened when four Black Watch players helped us defeat Distillery in November. When the final whistle sounded in that encounter total darkness set in!

Playing with only 10 men on a "diabolical" pitch could have explained our bad loss at Cliftonville in December. From all the matches played in 1889/90 nineteen team line-ups have been traced, with the individual appearances as on the following page.

More hooliganism flared in a final involving Distillery. This time it was during the County Antrim Shield decider versus Linfield at Ballynafeigh. Five minutes remained and

Individual appearances

Irvine	19	McBride	5	Sherlock	2	McCann	1
Taggart	17	Steele	5	Wright	2	McCreery	1
Miller	15	Crone	3	Armstrong	1	McDonald	1
Anderson	14	Graham	3	Bell	1	McDonnell	1
Dykes	14	Holland	3	Boal	1	McVicker	1
Mitchell	13	Meares	3	Bonnar	1	Nesbitt	1
McManus	11	*Shandley	3	Brown	1	Smiley	1
Muir	11	Gavan	2	Coates**	1	D.Thompson	1
Gray	10	Johnston	2	Craig	1	J.Thompson	1
*Sloan	10	McKinney**	2	Gillespie	1	*Wallace	1
Lawther	9	McMaster	2	Hill**	1	Walsh	1
Larmour	6	Malcolm**	2	James	1		

Key: * = Goalkeeper, ** = Black Watch player.
N.B. Sloan played 6 games as an outfield player.

Linfield led 5-3 when a Distillery player was sent off. Whites' supporters invaded the pitch attacking both the Linfield players and the referee. Linfield fans then came on and a mass brawl ensued. The game was abandoned and the Shield withheld.

In March 1890 an historic meeting took place attended by representatives of the leading Irish clubs. It was decided to establish a league competition for the next season, consisting of eight clubs. Seven teams from the Belfast area plus Milford from Armagh were to take part and so the Irish League was born.

Results 1889/90

F	07/09/1889		YMCA	H	L	0	5	-
F	14/09/1889		Clarence	H	W	7	0	Graham, Meares, Unknown 5
F	21/09/1889		Oldpark	H	W	5	1	Unknown
F	28/09/1889		Ulster	H	W	10	2	Unknown
F	05/10/1889		Black Watch	H	L	2	9	Unknown
F	12/10/1889		East Lancs Lilywhites	H	W	7	1	Unknown
F	02/11/1889		Clones	H	W	11	1	Unknown
F	23/11/1889		Cliftonville Olympic	H	W	3	2	Unknown
F	30/11/1889		Distillery	*	W	5	4	McKinney, Unknown 4
F	07/12/1889		Black Watch	H	L	3	7	Unknown
F	14/12/1889		Belfast Athletics	A	L	0	2	-
F	21/12/1889		Cliftonville	A	L	1	7	Unknown
F	28/12/1889		Milford	A	W	4	1	Unknown
F	04/01/1890		Belfast Caledonians	H	W	4	2	Unknown
F	11/01/1890		Ulster	A	W	4	0	Irvine 2, McKinney, Gray
F	01/02/1890		Distillery	A	L	1	4	McManus
F	22/02/1890		Belfast Athletics	H	W	7	2	Unknown
F	31/03/1890		Whiteabbey	H	W	7	2	Unknown
F	Unknown		Glenavon	A	W	4	1	Unknown
IC	19/10/1889	1	Gordon Highlanders	H	D	2	2	Unknown
IC	26/10/1889	1R	Gordon Highlanders	Bf	L	0	4	-
ChC	01/03/1890	1	Cliftonville	A	D	2	2	Millar, McManus
ChC	05/04/1890	1R	Cliftonville	A	W	4	3	Millar, McManus, Unknown 2
ChC	19/04/1890	SF	Gordon Highlanders	Scratched due to County Down Cup Final				
CDC	08/04/1890	SF	Westbourne	Bf	W	2	1	Unknown 2
CDC	19/04/1890	F	Ulster	Uv	W	3	0	"Scrimmage", Unknown 2

* = venue not known

1890/91

A new league and a new ground – First visitors from England

As well as the start of the Irish League, September 1890 also saw Glentoran move to a new ground in Westbourne. The pitch was known as Musgrave Field and had previously been used by the Caledonians.

Hopes were high of a good placing in the league but we only managed to finish fifth out of the eight clubs. Against Milford we were trailing 1-2 until two long range shots from Sloan won the game. Sloan showed his versatility a week later, going into goals when Lawther was injured just before half-time.

Cliftonville provided the opposition to open the new ground and although we won 4-3 it must be reported that the Reds were missing one of their star performers in Clugston, who was otherwise engaged playing lacrosse! We entered our first league game against Linfield expecting to win but the Blues proved too strong, scoring five goals in the second half. In December we exacted revenge on Clarence for our opening day defeat, but not until after Clarence had taken the lead. The same day Linfield defeated Cliftonville 10-2 and Ulster hammered Milford 10-1.

These results bore out the scepticism of the press regarding the success of the Irish League. Indeed as early as the Monday after the opening games the Northern Whig remarked that, "The recent establishment of a Belfast League is not important", allegedly due to the differing abilities of the teams involved. By mid-October the Whig maintained that the league was a foregone conclusion for Linfield, with the majority of games being of little interest to spectators as the encounters were so one-sided and fell flat after dominance by one side had been obtained. As a result press coverage of Irish football dropped considerably from November onwards.

We fared poorly in cup competition this season. The County Down Cup was relinquished to Ulster and we fell at the first hurdle in the Irish Cup against Oldpark. In the Charity Cup Glentoran were involved in a nasty game with Ulster at Cliftonville. During the second half, when Ulster were ahead 4-1, a fight broke out between players and some supporters of both sides. The police, club officials and the referee had to step in and separate the warring factions. Glentoran thereupon refused to play out the remainder of the game and the referee awarded the tie to Ulster. They went on to reach the Charity final but lost 1-7 to Linfield, and it was a similar story in the Irish Cup final where the Blues overcame Ulster 4-2. The Black Watch lifted the County Antrim Shield after defeating Oldpark 4-2.

We met English opponents for the first time in January 1891. The visitors from Barrow, aided by a strong wind, built up a 4-1 interval lead. However we "won" the second half 4-1 and honours finished even. Against Down Athletics in December we fielded virtually a 2nd XI as seven of our players were involved in the County match between Antrim and Down. Our best comeback of the season was against Clarence on 1st November, when we found ourselves 1-4 down just into the second half. After McManus scored our second goal the rest of the game was played in darkness, so it is not surprising that the names of our last three scorers remain unknown!

Martin Miller played in the final international trial but failed to win a cap. In these early days England often played their games against Ireland and Wales on the same day with two different XIs. For example on 7th March 1891 England defeated Ireland 6-1 at Wolverhampton in front of 6,000, while at Sunderland 10,000 watched England beat Wales by 4-1.

Floodlit football was attempted in Belfast in 1891. On 18th March Cliftonville met Distillery at Solitude under 10 electric lights. The innovative game was well publicised with the Lord Mayor kicking off at eight o'clock. The Whites won the match 4-2 but there were difficulties as the lights frequently went out. A second attempt took place again at Cliftonville on 9th April when the home side met the Black Watch. The lights were thoroughly tested beforehand on this occasion and the Northern Whig praised the improvement but pointed out the shortcomings saying, "A glimpse of the ball could be seen now and then but the spectator missed most of the nice play." A final effort came about on 16th April when Cliftonville met a team named the Texas Minstrels. The latest experiment involved mounting two of the lights so that they were suspended over the middle of the field. This apparently caused shadow problems for the small crowd who witnessed a "burlesque" game. Subsequent floodlight pioneering was put on ice for around 60 years.

Results 1890/91

Played 17. Won 6. Drew 2. Lost 9. Goals For 44. Against 50. % 41.2.

IL	06/09/1890		Clarence	A	L	4	5	Elliott 2, Weir, D.Thompson
IL	13/09/1890		Milford	A	W	4	2	C.Gray, Sloane 2, D.Thompson
IL	20/09/1890		Distillery	A	L	2	5	Miller, D.Thompson
IL	27/09/1890		Cliftonville	H	W	4	3	Elliott, Miller, D.Thompson 2
IL	11/10/1890		Oldpark	A	W	3	2	Steel 2, Unknown
IL	18/10/1890		Linfield	H	L	0	7	-
IL	15/11/1890		Ulster	H	L	3	5	Wright, McManus, C.Gray
IL	06/12/1890		Clarence	H	W	9	1	Unknown
IL	20/12/1890		Milford	A	W	8	0	Unknown
IL	03/01/1891		Distillery	H	D	1	1	Unknown
IL	14/02/1891		Oldpark	H	W	2	0	Unknown
IL	21/03/1891		Linfield	A	L	0	6	-
IL	04/04/1891		Ulster	A	L	0	1	-
IL	28/04/1891		Cliftonville	A	D	0	0	-
IC	04/10/1890	1	Oldpark	H	L	3	6	Elliott, McManus, D.Thompson
CDC	11/04/1891	SF	Ulster	Uv	L	0	2	-
ChC	18/04/1891	1	Ulster	Solt	L	1	4	Morrison – Abandoned
F	25/10/1890		Distillery	H	W	3	2	Wright 2, Miller
F	01/11/1890		Clarence	H	W	5	4	Miller, McManus, Unknown 3
F	08/11/1890		Oldpark	H	D	3	3	Unknown
F	29/11/1890		Black Watch	H	W	3	2	Sloane, Ervine, Unknown
F	13/12/1890		Ulster	A	L	0	4	-
F	27/12/1890		Down Athletics	H	L	2	5	Unknown
F	24/01/1891		Cliftonville	H	W	4	3	Young, Miller, Gray, Sloane
F	31/01/1891		Barrow Athletics	H	D	5	5	Unknown
F	07/03/1891		Distillery	H	L	1	3	D.Thompson

Appearances and Goals

	App. (Sub)	Goals		App. (Sub)	Goals		App. (Sub)	Goals
Sloan	12 (1)	2	Boal	5		Moore	1	
Miller	12	2	Christian	4		Morrison T.	1	1
Ervine	11		Steel	4	2	Larmour	1	
Gray C.	10	2	McManus (CH)	4		Purse	1	
Lawther	9		McWattie	4		Kirkpatrick	1	
Thompson D.	9	6	Purvis	3		Wilson	1	
Thompson J.	7		Wright	3	1	Andrews	1	
McManus (FW)	7	2	Morrison A.	2		Weir	1	1
Elliott	6	4	Coutts	2		Young	1	
McVicker	6		Thom	2		Unkown	44	21
Mitchcll	5		Cray (HB)	1				
Bennett	5		Mayrs	1		TOTAL	18/ (1)	44

1891/92

Biggest league win – Weather problems – First Scottish visitors

The Irish League was extended from eight to 10 clubs with the addition of YMCA, Milltown and Ligoneil as Milford dropped out. Clarence were unable to field eleven players for their first game and were quickly replaced by the Lancashire Fusiliers. The Fusiliers found themselves stationed in Belfast as the Black Watch had been moved to Limerick. Problems still persisted with league membership though as YMCA resigned in December and Distillery were expelled by the IFA in April for fielding ineligible players.

Glentoran's opening five league games bore out the differing standards between clubs. Our 15-1 win against Oldpark remains the highest score in an Irish League game to this day. The "big" fixtures were attracting the crowds - 4,000 at Westbourne for the league game with Linfield and 6,000 three weeks later against Distillery. The Whig remarked that against the Whites, "the scenes after McAuley's winning goal surpassed anything that has been seen locally." The Lancashire Fusiliers proved tough opposition and indeed they finished second only to Linfield in the final league table with Glentoran fourth. (The Blues proved their power in April scoring all eight of their goals against us in the first half.) One of our players, Holby, received a month's suspension when he was sent off along with McCabe of Ulster during the second half of the game on 10th October.

The appalling weather at the end of 1891 turned many games into farces. On two occasions "league" meetings with the Lancashire Fusiliers were declared friendlies due to the abominable nature of the pitch. The November friendly with Ulster was played on a swamp and a local scribe applied the following description - "This match was more of a comic show than those advertised as such!"

We entertained our first Scottish visitors, Third Lanark Rifle Volunteers, on New Year's Day 1892. The good result obtained was due in part to our guesting players Torrans, Peden and Gaffikin of Linfield and Forbes of Distillery.

The bright note of the season arrived with the re-capture of the County Down Cup. Ulster Reserves overcame Glentoran Reserves 7-2 but found our senior XI too strong, despite a protest over the first semi-final. Against Ulster in the final a good crowd saw a generally disappointing game. Our best performers were the brilliant S.Clarke and Martin Miller who was "as quick as a deer."

As well as the league Linfield also claimed the Irish and Charity Cups while Cliftonville defeated the Lancashire Fusiliers 2-1 in the final of the County Antrim Shield.

On the representative front McAuley played in the final Irish trial while Miller and Taggart appeared for a Belfast XI which defeated South Derry 6-1 at Dungannon on 30th January 1892. Westbourne, back in good condition, was selected as the venue for the County Down-County Antrim clash in April.

The controversy of the season was the IFA's expulsion of Distillery. Glentoran were admonished too, as the IFA had ordered us to play Distillery in a league game on 26th March. We refused and instead met Milltown, incurring a £15 fine from the IFA, a figure that would have been more than the gate receipts. Glentoran appealed, but this was dismissed as it came to light that we had re-arranged our outstanding league game with Distillery after the IFA had expelled them. However peace was eventually declared at the end of the season and the two clubs arranged a couple of friendlies - each side gaining a win.

A May report in the News Letter surmised that some of the Irish League teams had little interest in the outcomes of the games. Indeed they went on to call for a six-team league consisting of Linfield, Distillery, Cliftonville, Fusiliers, Ulster and Glentoran with the clubs to be managed by men who had "experience and impartiality."

So Glentoran could look back on her first 10 years with pride as we had established ourselves as one of the top teams in Ireland. However the main ambition was still to capture one of the top trophies, elusive thus far.

Results 1891/92

Played 23. Won 13. Drew 3. Lost 7. Goals For 101. Against 65. % 63.0.
Honours: County Down Cup

IL	05/09/1891		Oldpark	H	W	15	1	Unknown
IL	19/09/1891		Milltown	A	W	9	0	Miller, Morrison, McAuley, Unknown 6
IL	26/09/1891		Ligoneil	A	W	9	0	Morrison 3, Unknown 6
IL	03/10/1891		Linfield	H	L	1	7	Miller
IL	10/10/1891		Ulster	A	L	1	7	Morrison
IL	17/10/1891		Cliftonville	H	D	4	4	Morrison, Miller, McAuley, Stewart
IL	24/10/1891		Distillery	H	W	4	3	Morrison, Miller, Stewart, McAuley
IL	31/10/1891		YMCA	A	W	7	0	Morrison 2, Miller 2, Kearney 2, McAusland Game Expunged
IL	12/12/1891		Oldpark	A	W	7	0	Unknown
IL	02/01/1892		Ligoneil	H	W	3	1	Miller, Unknown 2
IL	23/01/1892		Ulster	H	W	6	5	Unknown
IL	13/02/1892		Lancashire Fusiliers	H	L	2	3	Morrison, Miller
IL	26/03/1892		Milltown	H	W	7	3	Unknown
IL	09/04/1892		Lancashire Fusiliers	H	D	1	1	Morrison
IL	16/04/1892		Linfield	A	L	0	8	-
IL	Unknown		Distillery	A	L	2	3	Unknown
IL	Unknown		Cliftonville	A	D	1	1	Unknown
IC	07/11/1891	3	Ligoneil	A	W	5	3	Unknown
IC	21/11/1891	4	Linfield	A	L	0	6	-
CDC	06/02/1892	SF	Ulster Reserves	H	W	6	3	Unknown – Protest
CDC	27/02/1892	SFR	Ulster Reserves	H	W	6	1	Unknown
CDC	02/04/1892	F	Ulster	A	W	5	1	Unknown
ChC	23/04/1892	1	Linfield	Bf	L	0	4	-
F	29/08/1891		Distillery	A	L	2	5	Unknown
F	14/11/1891		Internal Club Practice					
F	28/11/1891		Ulster	H	L	3	8	Stewart 2, Sloan
F	05/12/1891		Lancashire Fusiliers	H	L	4	5	Unknown
F	19/12/1891		Milltown	H	W	11	0	Unknown
F	24/12/1891		Ulster	H	D	4	4	Unknown
F	26/12/1891		Lancashire Fusiliers	H	W	5	2	Unknown
F	01/01/1892		Third Lanark R.V.	H	W	4	3	Unknown
F	13/05/1892		Distillery	H	W	3	2	Unknown
F	20/05/1892		Distillery	A	L	1	4	Unknown

Appearances and Goals

	App.	Goals		App.	Goals		App.	Goals
Miller	9	8	Ervine	4		Dykes	1	
Morrison T.	9	11	Taggart	3		Thompson J.	1	
Stewart	8	2	Loyal	3		Thompson D.	1	
McAuley	8	3	Bennett	2		Wright	1	
Sloan	7		Williams	2		Lawther	1	
Patterson	7		Hamilton	2		Johnston E.	1	
Holby	5		Clarke	2		Ditchfield	1	
Kearney	5	2	McAusland	2	1	McLaughlin	1	
McManus (CH)	6		Woods	1		Unknown	154	74
Purvis	5		Reynolds	1		TOTAL	253	101

1892/93

A team from Derry – Move to the Oval – County Down mystery

Rationalisation of the league did take place prior to its third season. The five main Belfast teams were joined by a club playing under the name of Derry Olympic. The Derry team were an amalgam of players from the St. Columb's Court, Limavady and Rosemount clubs and played their home games at the Brandywell. Linfield again won the league with Cliftonville runners-up and Glentoran a disappointing fourth.

Our opening league game was the last match we played at Musgrave Field, Westbourne. In November 1892 the original Oval was obtained from Sir Daniel Dixon and Kilmarnock travelled from Scotland to officially open the ground on Christmas Eve. The event was well advertised and a large crowd attended. However by January the ground was in a shocking state due to the melting snow of heavy falls. The friendly win over virtually a reserve Linfield XI was reported as a "scrambling and un-scientific game."

Our league campaign suffered frustration on successive weeks at the end of October. Firstly the match against Distillery was declared a friendly due to the non-appearance of the referee who cried off at the last moment due to a family illness. Then Derry Olympic failed to turn up for their scheduled visit on the 29th!

Aggression between Glentoran and Ulster broke out again in the league meeting of 17th December. After 75 minutes play the Glens were holding a 1-0 lead (courtesy of "Ching" Morrison) when a disgraceful fight broke out between Morrison and an Ulster player. The referee ordered both men off but they began scuffling again on the way to the pavilion, causing a crowd invasion and termination of the match. Morrison subsequently received a six month suspension from the IFA.

The outcome of the County Down Cup final was shrouded in mystery. After defeating Glenavon comfortably in the semis we once more met Ulster. The game was locked at 1-1 when, following a scrimmage, Forbes put through his own goal. The game thus finished at 2-1 to Ulster but Glentoran protested on two counts. Firstly Ulster had fielded some Linfield players (the Blues not coming under Co. Down jurisdiction) and it was also felt that Ulster's linesman was partial to this own club. The protest was upheld and a replay ordered. Ulster were not happy, but it is not clear whether they decided to scratch or if a second game took place.

Glentoran had three players in the International trial (Ezekiel Johnston, McFall and Sherrard) and McFall was selected to play against Scotland. However due to injury he missed the game. Seddington was a part of the first ever Irish League XI which defeated the Scottish League 3-2 in April. Glentoran supplied seven and Ulster the remaining four of the County Down side which drew 6-6 with County Antrim at Grosvenor Park in February. Johnston and Conway played for Ulsterville Rangers (Ulster/Glentoran/Linfield combined) when they defeated Greenock Morton 3-0 on 2nd January at Ulsterville.

A combined Glentoran/Ulster team playing as "East End" lost 1-2 to Linfield in November. The game was to aid our Oval Benefit Fund. With the new ground, Glentoran formed an Athletic Club, and announced the intention of staging many sports at the Oval.

Linfield overcame Distillery in both the Irish (4-2) and Charity (3-2) cups. The Grosvenor Park club did lift the County Antrim Shield after defeating juniors Belfast Celtic 2-1 in the final. Incidentally, Celtic, formed in 1891, lost to Glentoran Seconds in their first ever game.

On 13th May 1893 the Oval was the venue for the first games in the Trades Competition, organised by the United Trades Council. A large crowd and a brass band were in attendance to witness the Boilermakers defeat the Moulders 2-0 and the Engineers triumph 4-1 over the Printers. Ezekiel Johnston, our 1st XI goalkeeper, appeared for the Boilermakers. The competition was to continue over the summer months and the Northern Whig suggested that these matches could do more to popularise soccer that any quantity of senior games.

Away from football the Whig gave some interesting figures on the population of Belfast. In 1659 it was recorded as 595 (372 English, 223 Irish), by 1757 it had risen to 8,549 (7,993 Protestant, 556 Catholic) and in 1893 the total figure stood at 275,000.

Results 1892/93

Played 15. Won 6. Drew 0. Lost 9. Goals For 33. Against 36. % 40.0.

IL	03/09/1892		Linfield	H	L	0	5	-
IL	10/09/1892		Cliftonville	A	L	1	2	Unknown
IL	17/09/1892		Distillery	A	W	4	2	Unknown
IL	24/09/1892		Derry Olympic	A	W	2	1	Miller, Elliott
IL	08/10/1892		Linfield	A	L	1	2	Miller
IL	15/10/1892		Cliftonville	A	L	1	3	Miller
IL	29/10/1892		Derry Olympic	H	Opposition failed to turn up			
IL	03/12/1892		Ulster	A	L	1	2	"Rush"
IL	17/12/1892		Ulster	A	A	1	0	Morrison
								Abandoned after 75 minutes
IL	26/12/1892		Derry Olympic	H	W	8	2	Unknown
IL	04/03/1893		Ulster	H	W	3	0	Stewart, Unknown 2
IL	Unknown		Distillery	A	L	0	4	-
IC	05/11/1892	3	Linfield	A	L	1	6	Morrison
CDC	21/01/1893	SF	Glenavon	H	W	6	1	Unknown
CDC	18/03/1893	F	Ulster	Uv	L	1	2	Conway
ChC	15/04/1893	1	Ulster	H	W	3	2	Unknown
ChC	22/04/1893	SF	Linfield	Bf	L	1	2	Unknown
F	22/10/1892		Distillery	A	D	3	3	Miller 2, Morrison
F	19/11/1892		Distillery	A	W	4	2	Unknown
F	24/12/1892		Kilmarnock	H	D	1	1	Unknown
								Opening of the Original Oval
F	07/01/1893		Linfield	H	W	3	2	Unknown
F	11/02/1893		Cliftonville	H	W	4	0	Sherrard, Seddington,
								Unknown 2
F	01/04/1893		Linfield	A	L	3	5	Unknown

Appearances and Goals

	App.	Goals		App.	Goals		App.	Goals
McFall	7		Patterson (FB)	4		Patterson (CF)	1	
Stewart	7	1	Forbes	4		Gourlay	1	
Purvis	6		Elliott	3	1	Lawther	1	
Johnston E.	6		Sherrard	3		Unknown	88	25
Morrison T.	5	1	Spencer	2		"Rush"		1
Clarke	5		McManus	2				
Miller	5	3	Sloan	2		TOTAL	165	33
Johnston W.	5		Conway	2	1			
Morrison A.	4		Seddington	2				

1893/94

League Champions for the first time – Prestigious friendlies

Glentoran came of age in their 12th season by becoming Irish League champions for the first time, finishing two points ahead of runners-up Linfield. Ligoneil had replaced the Derry Olympic team making the league an all-Belfast affair. Confidence would have begun with a win at Ulsterville in mid-September, with Johnston's many saves earning a clean sheet. "Capital" crowds attended the vital away games against Cliftonville and Distillery and great cheers greeted Johnston's late penalty save from Olphie Stanfield against the Whites.

George Louis Silo, younger brother of Modesto, our leading scorer in 1893/94.

We entered the return game with Linfield in October holding a three point lead with four games to go. A very large attendance saw the Blues gain a 2-1 interval lead. The second half witnessed many efforts at both ends come off the bar and posts while Morrison had a goal disallowed but Linfield closed the gap to just one point.

While we were outplaying Ligoneil a week later Distillery held the Blues to a 4-4 draw. (Note: The same day Linfield Swifts defeated our second XI 12-0!). On 11th November we travelled to Ballynafeigh where a good crowd assembled to see us take on the now not so strong Ulster. The home side went into a 2-0 lead but two Silo strikes made it level at half-time. Ulster became "fagged out" in the second period, Longwell scoring our vital third goal and King netting a late fourth. When news filtered through from Solitude that Cliftonville had beaten Linfield 3-1 the celebrations for our first title began.

Our cup campaigns were less successful. We failed to take advantage of a strong wind against Linfield in the Irish Cup and paid the penalty after the break. The Blues reached the final but were beaten 3-2 by Distillery after a replay.

A misunderstanding within the Belview club led to two of their elevens turning up to play us in the Charity Cup on 14th April at Ulsterville. Neither eleven were prepared to give way and so the tie was awarded to Glentoran. A "practice" match was arranged instead, which we won comfortably anyway. The two semi-finals were played as a "double-header" the following Saturday at Solitude. Linfield hammered Cliftonville 7-0 in the first semi, but ours was much tighter and it took a 35th minute goal from King to see off Distillery. A crowd of 4,000 watched Linfield defeat us in the final, all the goals coming in the first half.

The County Down Cup had been restricted to junior clubs only from this season. The St. Patrick's Day final saw Glentoran Reserves overcome Belview 5-2 with the following team: Stewart; Thompson, Elliott; McManus, Dilworth, Wright; Wilson, Millar, Scott, Irvine, Corbett. Glentoran IIs also won the Intermediate Cup.

Cliftonville picked up the County Antrim Shield beating Belfast Celtic 2-1. February 1894 saw Glentoran's first clash with the strong junior team when our full strength side was held to a 2-2 draw. Belfast Celtic had earlier beaten our Reserves 12-0.

We extended our fixtures by travelling to England to play Darwen and inviting cross-channel clubs to visit the large Oval grounds at Easter. On the Saturday Surrey Wanderers, containing many of the full Surrey county squad, began their short Irish tour with a narrow win. The Wanderers also defeated Linfield (2-1) and Ulsterville Rangers (3-2).

Glasgow Celtic played at the Oval on Easter Monday and Tuesday. They defeated Glentoran 3-1 on Monday and recorded an identical scoreline a day later against an "East End Select" made up mostly of Glens players.

Not surprisingly Glentoran were well represented in the Irish League team of 1894, indeed we had seven men in the team beaten 6-0 by the Scottish League at Celtic Park, Glasgow in January. Ireland's players were chaired off the pitch after their 2-2 draw with England at Solitude on 3rd March. The reason - this was the first time ever that Ireland had avoided defeat against the English in 13 attempts.

Results 1893/94

Played 13. Won 10. Drew 0. Lost 3. Goals For 33. Against 16. % 76.9.
Honours: Irish League

IL	02/09/1893		Distillery	H	W	4	2	Silo 3, Unknown
IL	16/09/1893		Linfield	A	W	1	0	Longwell
IL	23/09/1893		Ulster	H	W	5	1	Longwell, Unknown 4
IL	30/09/1893		Cliftonville	A	W	1	0	King
IL	07/10/1893		Distillery	A	W	1	0	J.Stilges og
IL	14/10/1893		Ligoneil	H	W	2	0	Morrison 2
IL	21/10/1893		Linfield	H	L	1	3	Silo
IL	04/11/1893		Ligoneil	H	W	5	1	McFall, Hall, Unknown 3
IL	11/11/1893		Ulster	A	W	4	2	Silo 2, Longwell, King
IL	16/12/1893		Cliftonville	H	W	8	0	Morrison 2, Silo 2, King 3, Longwell
IC	18/11/1893	3	Linfield	A	L	0	4	-
ChC	14/04/1894	1	Belview	Uv	W	6	2	Unknown – Practice Game
ChC	21/04/1894	SF	Distillery	Solt	W	1	0	King
ChC	28/04/1894	F	Linfield	Solt	L	0	3	-
F	28/10/1893		Cliftonville	A	W	4	3	King 2, Hall, Morrison
F	02/12/1893		Linfield	H	L	1	5	Longwell
F	13/01/1894		Cliftonville	H	L	1	3	Unknown
F	20/01/1894		Linfield	A	L	2	5	Unknown
F	03/02/1894		Belfast Celtic	A	D	2	2	Unknown
F	17/03/1894		Darwen	A	L	0	6	-
F	24/03/1894		Surrey Wanderers	H	L	2	3	Stewart, Longwell
F	26/03/1894		Glasgow Celtic	H	L	1	3	Unknown

Appearances and Goals

	App.	Goals		App.	Goals		App.	Goals
Freeland	13		Patterson, (FB)	10		Thompson	1	
Hall	13	1	King	10	6	Coulson	1	
Spencer	12		McFall	5	1	McPherson	1	
Johnston E.	11		Loyal	2		Forbes	1	
Morrison T.	11	4	Parks	2		Own Goals		1
Longwell	11	4	McLoughlin	2		Unknown		8
Stewart	11		Miller	2				
Purvis	10		Somerset	2		TOTAL	142	33
Silo	10	8	Wright	1				

35

1894/95

A new Saturday night paper – Irish Cup loss in Dublin

An extremely disappointing season for the reigning champions, probably due to the loss of some players to other clubs, and Ching Morrison to injury in 1894. Ulster and Ligoneil dropped out of the senior league leaving only a sparse four clubs to compete. As a result the League inaugurated another competition, the Belfast City Cup, to provide competitive fixtures throughout the season. Dunville and Co. supplied the new trophy.

Linfield regained the league title, winning four and drawing two matches, while we only managed one win, against Distillery. The Whites had actually taken the lead in that game. Our City Cup performances were an improvement though we still finished bottom of that table. We came back from two goals down to draw with Cliftonville but then it took three attempts to play off the away fixture with Distillery. Heavy rain caused a postponement on 27th October and the re-arranged game in January was declared a friendly due to the sate of the pitch. It was third time lucky for us in April when Frank Adams' opening goal followed a length of the field run from Morrison. Poor conditions were not only a burden for players, as the 2,500 who attended the Linfield game in February were described as "waders".

Jack Lyttle, secretary and player.

On 17th November 1894 the Belfast Telegraph launched a new weekly sports paper entitled the "Ulster's Saturday Night". The early editions consisted of four large pages and were printed on pink paper well into the 20th Century. The original issues, although in a slightly tattered condition, are available in Belfast's Linenhall Library while the British National Library in Colindale, North London holds copies on microfilm. An inspection is recommended to gain an insight into sporting issues of the day.

Glentoran's progress in the knockout competitions was also limited. After an easy Irish Cup win at Donacloney we visited Bohemians in Dublin. A mere 100 spectators saw us build up a 4-3 interval lead but after one of our players was sent off in the second half we collapsed. The "Bohs" went on to reach the final but came unstuck, losing 1-10 to Linfield.

Juniors Milltown and Ligoneil swelled the Charity Cup entry to six clubs. Despite our taking a 10th minute lead and an excellent display from Morrison, Distillery put us out in the first round. Linfield retained the trophy with a 3-1 final win over Cliftonville. Earlier, in December in fact, the Blues had some bad luck with the weather when a storm blew down a portion of their grandstand. The debris on the field caused the postponement of our scheduled friendly with them.

Glentoran's 2nd XI fared better than the seniors, reaching two finals. In the County Down Cup they overwhelmed Holywood 14-0 but Milltown pipped them 3-2 in the Intermediate Cup final.

Ching Morrison's excellent club form earned him selection for Ireland in all three internationals versus England, Wales and Scotland. W. Sherrard, who had moved to

Cliftonville in mid-season, also played in all three, scoring against the Welsh and Scots. Jack Burnett played against England and Wales adding to his tally of three caps gained while with Distillery. In addition, Morrison and Tom Shannon gained inter-provincial recognition with Ulster, when they lost 2-4 to Leinster in December.

Results 1894/95

Played 15. Won 4. Drew 3. Lost 8. Goals For 35. Against 43. % 36.7

IL	01/09/1894	Cliftonville	H	L	1	3	Unknown
IL	08/09/1894	Distillery	A	L	1	3	Unknown
IL	15/09/1894	Linfield	H	D	2	2	Unknown
IL	22/09/1894	Cliftonville	A	D	2	2	Sherrard 2
IL	29/09/1894	Distillery	H	W	3	1	Sherrard 2, Unknown
IL	06/10/1894	Linfield	A	L	0	3	-
CC	20/10/1894	Cliftonville	H	D	2	2	Sherrard, Adams
CC	10/11/1894	Linfield	H	W	4	3	Morrison (p), Somerset 2, Adams
CC	15/12/1894	Distillery	H	L	1	2	Unknown
CC	19/01/1895	Cliftonville	A	L	2	5	Hall, Shannon
CC	23/02/1895	Linfield	H	L	2	5	Hall, Adams
CC	06/04/1895	Distillery	A	W	2	1	Adams, Woods
IC	03/11/1894 4	Donacloney	A	W	7	2	Unknown
IC	01/12/1894 5	Bohemians	A	L	4	6	Somerset, Morrison 2, Adams
ChC	20/04/1895 1	Distillery	Solt	L	2	3	Woods, Unknown
F	13/10/1894	Junior League	*	D	3	3	Unknown
F	24/11/1894	West Kent Regiment	H	L	3	4	Unknown
F	26/12/1894	Milltown	H	W	3	1	Morrison, Unknown 2
F	05/01/1895	Distillery	H	D	2	2	Morrison, Shannon
F	13/04/1895	Linfield	H	L	0	2	-

* = venue unknown

Appearances and Goals

	App.	Goals		App.	Goals		App.	Goals
Hattie	12		Parkes	6		Lyttle	1	
Shannon	11	1	Sherrard	6	5	Wattie	1	
Burnett	10		Rodgers	3		Conway	1	
Hall	10	2	Patterson	3		Spencer	1	
Freeland	9		Woods	2	2	King	1	
Stewart	9		McFall	2		Black	1	
Adams	9	5	Lawther	1		Bennett	1	
Bleakley	8		Ivory	1		Unknown	33	14
Somerset	8	3	Dunlop	1		TOTAL	165	35
Campbell	6		Browne	1				
Morrison T.	6	3	Connolly	1				

1895/96

Non-appearance of referees – An untimely death - The Charity Cup is won

Ambitious juniors Belfast Celtic's application to join the league was turned down because it was felt that having five senior clubs would be unworkable. Meanwhile down at the Oval the secretarial posts for the Glentoran club were filled by S.Monroe of 22 Schomberg Terrace for the 1st XI, and for the 2nd XI, now known as Glentoran Rovers, by F.Wilson of Witham Street. Ching Morrison was transferred to Glasgow Celtic while goalkeeper Ezekiel Johnston rejoined Glentoran from Burnley. Although we won the Charity Cup and reached our first Irish Cup final there was little improvement in League or City Cup displays.

There must have been a refereeing curse over Glentoran-Linfield games this season. The appointed official did not appear for the September league clash so our new Scottish forward Wattie Johnston had his hat-trick reduced to "friendly" status. The game was re-scheduled four weeks thence and this time the kick-off was delayed 10 minutes as the referee was late. Finally no referee turned up for our City Cup meeting in April so another friendly had to be played.

SUGGESTIONS FOR THE NEXT MATCH AT THE OVAL.

How a cartoonist envisaged a match versus Linfield in 1895 after trouble in an earlier encounter.

The black note of the season was the untimely death of W.Sherrard the night before our league game with Cliftonville. Sherrard, an International outside-right, who played for both the Glens and the Reds, contracted typhoid fever and failed to recover. The game was postponed for a month.

While Jack Burnett was inspirational at the back the form of our forwards was very indifferent in the City Cup. Larger crowds were attending the games now that Linfield were not so dominant. The big attendance for the December clash with Distillery saw the teams turn straight round, taking no half-time interval in order to finish the game before darkness set in. The Whites won the league title, defeating Cliftonville in a play-off, after they both finished on 8 points.

Our path to the Irish Cup final began at Castledawson in November. The game against Moyola Park proved so easy that Ezekiel Johnston came out and played in the forward line in the second half. McMaster, Duncan and Redpath made their debuts in Round 5, but the Scots Guards took us to a replay. Despite having to catch the 7 am train for the return at Beggar's Bush, Dublin a good team performance put us through. The semi-final saw us overwhelm the Derry juniors (who played in Linfield colours) after they had taken the lead on a miserable day weatherwise. Around 7,000 watched us lose to Distillery in the final after we had held an interval lead. The Whites went on to lift the County Antrim Shield a week later, hammering Linfield by 5-0.

We gained revenge on Distillery in the Charity Cup and then annexed that trophy for the first time, defeating Cliftonville on their own ground. Hall's oblique shot, which bounced in via the bar, was the only goal for the 2,000 crowd to cheer.

Leading Scottish clubs frequented the "East End" Oval at the holiday periods. The cold and bitter Christmas Morning weather kept the attendance down to 1,000 for the Hibernian game. After we had a second goal disallowed Hibs notched their third in the last minute. In spite of Glasgow Celtic sending over virtually a reserve XI at Easter temporary accommodation was erected for their two games. On Easter Monday the Celts defeated Glentoran 2-1, with the winning goal coming from Divers of BELFAST Celtic. A day later 5,000 watched Celtic defeat a Belfast Select XI (containing six Glenmen) 4-1.

Only 2,000 rolled up to see us lose 0-2 to Everton, when Scott (Cliftonville and Ireland goalkeeper) and Milne (Linfield and Ireland centre-half) guested for us. The same day Sunderland defeated Distillery 1-0 and Glentoran invited the two English clubs to stay on and play an exhibition match at the Oval the following Tuesday. This they duly did and Everton defeated Sunderland 2-1 in front of 3,000.

Violence flared after a Robinson and Cleaver Shield game between Belfast Celtic and Glentoran Rovers in October 1895. Celtic won the tie 4-2 but many players were injured from stone throwing in a subsequent mob riot. The Rovers had a happier time on 15th February when they beat Athlone 7-1 in The Irish Cup.

Our forward Jim Kelly gained an International cap against England while Jack Burnett captained the Irish League team to a 2-2 draw against the Football League at Stoke and a 2-3 defeat against the Scottish League in Glasgow. Hattie, Hall, Kelly, Johnston(E), Shannon

---

Results 1895/96

Played 19. Won 8. Drew 2. Lost 9. Goals For 48. Against 42. % 47.3.
Honours: Charity Cup

Comp	Date	Rd	Opponent	Venue	Res			Scorers
IL	07/09/1895		Distillery	A	L	1	6	"Scrimmage"
IL	21/09/1895		Cliftonville	H	L	1	3	Hall
IL	28/09/1895		Distillery	H	W	6	2	Hall 2, Johnston 2, Carmichael, Shannon
IL	05/10/1895		Linfield	H	D	2	2	Hall, Shannon
IL	19/10/1895		Linfield	H	L	2	3	Kelly, Howard og
IL	23/11/1895		Cliftonville	A	L	1	2	Carmichael
CC	26/10/1895		Distillery	A	L	1	4	McClatchey og
CC	02/11/1895		Linfield	H	L	1	2	Johnston
CC	14/12/1895		Cliftonville	A	W	1	0	Hall
CC	21/12/1895		Distillery	H	L	2	4	Hall 2
CC	08/02/1896		Cliftonville	H	W	4	1	Burnett, Hall, Carmichael, Kelly
CC	09/05/1896		Linfield	H	L	0	2	-
IC	16/11/1895	4	Moyola Park	A	W	7	1	Carmichael 3, Johnston, Hall, Unknown 2
IC	30/11/1895	5	2nd Scots Guards	H	D	2	2	"Rush", Duncan
IC	07/12/1895	5R	2nd Scots Guards	A	W	3	0	Johnston 2, Carmichael
IC	25/01/1896	SF	Derry North End	GP	W	8	2	Nelson og, Kelly 4, Somerset 2, Johnston
IC	14/03/1896	F	Distillery	Solt	L	1	3	Carmichael
ChC	18/04/1896	SF	Distillery	Solt	W	4	3	Kelly, Carmichael, Johnston 2
ChC	02/05/1896	F	Cliftonville	A	W	1	0	Hall
F	14/09/1895		Linfield	H	W	5	1	Johnston 3, Carmichael, Kelly
F	25/12/1895		Hibernian	H	L	1	3	Kelly
F	29/02/1896		Belfast Celtic	H	W	2	0	Johnston, Carmichael
F	04/04/1896		Linfield	H	L	0	1	-
F	06/04/1896		Glasgow Celtic	H	L	1	2	Carmichael
F	11/04/1896		Distillery	A	L	0	1	-
F	25/04/1896		Everton	H	L	0	2	-

and Carmichael also gained Inter-League honours, while McFall played for the Belfast XI which defeated Derry 4-0 in January. A week before that inter-city game Larne FC defeated Stranraer 6-1 at Laharna Park.

To reflect its more widespread coverage the Ulster's Saturday Night changed name to the Ireland's Saturday Night on 4th January 1896. A Dublin edition was also printed along with the early and final editions of the Belfast copy.

Appearances and Goals

	App.	Goals		App.	Goals		App.	Goals
Carmichael	14	9	Freeland	6		Adams	1	
Hall	14	8	McKelvey	5		Pelan	1	
Kelly	14	9	Spencer	4		Redpath	1	
Hattie	13		Templeton	4		Campbell	1	
Shannon	13	2	Purvis	3		McKnight	1	
Burnett	12	1	McMaster G.	2		Unknown	55	1
Johnston W.	12	10	Duncan	2	1	Own Goals		3
McFall	11		Lewis	1		Rush/Scrimmage		2
Somerset	9	2	Lyttle	1				
Johnston E.	8		Sloan	1		TOTAL	209	48

1896/97

A two-trophy season – Unplayable grounds – Entry to the shield

There were some notable changes prior to the start of the 1896 Irish League. Belfast Celtic and the North Staffordshire Regiment came into the senior set up but both would play their games away from home as Celtic's Broadway ground was unplayable. Glentoran were invited by the County Antrim FA to compete in the Shield while Linfield moved to new headquarters at Myrtlefield Park, Balmoral.

It was another memorable season for Glentoran as the League was won for the second time and the City Cup captured also. Admission to the Oval to watch was 3d (unreserved), 6d (reserved) and 9d (stand) for men with ladies admitted free of charge. The league campaign began inauspiciously with defeat against Distillery and then hooliganism marred the initial encounter against Belfast Celtic. After the game, attended by 3,000, roughs gathered outside the pavilion threatening the Celtic players. A particular target was the visitors ex-Glentoran goalkeeper, Ezekiel Johnston. Police had to eventually break up the mob. (The ubiquitous Johnston moved to Stoke at the end of December.) The press complained that they were unable to describe the game properly due to the crowd blocking their view whereas Glentoran complained to the IFA regarding the stance the Irish News took on reporting the disturbances.

As the league developed our goalkeeper Jim Lewis and defender Willie Purvis (captain) put in star performances. Despite extremely heavy rain 2,000 turned up for the home game with Distillery, after which the Glens were criticised for a lack of covered accommodation. Six successive victories left us only needing to beat Cliftonville on 24th October to become champions. Against a stiff breeze we held the Reds to 1-1 at half-time and then with the score at 2-2, "the leather was sent through the posts in a rush and greeted with loud cheering", to take the league trophy back to the Oval. As Linfield's Balmoral ground had become unplayable the venue of the last league game was switched meaning we played eight of our ten fixtures at home.

Glentoran also began the City Cup sluggishly. The scheduled game v. Belfast Celtic on 12th December was annulled (i.e. no points to either side) by the IFA. The referee inspected the pitch at 2.15 p.m. (due kick-off time) and passed it fit for playing stating a 30-minute each way match would commence at 2.35 p.m.. Glentoran wanted to play a full 90 minutes but the referee ruled that impossible due to the early nights and the game was postponed. The IFA eventually relented and the two sides met at a neutral venue in sweltering heat at the end of the season. Celtic got their first win over us courtesy of a penalty awarded against Lyttle.

At the turn of 1897 the leadership of the City Cup was shared by four teams but Glentoran reeled off six wins to take the trophy. The second half of the Distillery game was played out in a snowstorm. The Whites twice did us 4-0 in cup competition. In the Irish Cup tie only Lewis and debutant Mick Cochrane played well. The referee was attacked after this game when on driving away from the ground his car was pelted with stones and mud! Glentoran shirked responsibility for this event on the basis that it happened outside the Oval grounds. Cliftonville lifted both the Irish and Charity Cups.

Although we won our first County Antrim Shield tie Linfield halted our progress in the semis in front of 8,000. Glentoran Rovers lost to Wesley in the Steel and Sons Cup final.

Glentoran played three away fixtures against junior teams this season. Limavady were a shadow of their former selves while a good crowd attended the game at Larne. It was remarked that these trips must cost a lot but they did the spread of football good. When Easter visitors Third Lanark beat us 3-0 the Belfast Telegraph commented, "A smarter team has not visited Belfast for a while." However a disappointing crowd of 500 patronised the

Tuesday game when the Glens, assisted by Mercer (Distillery) and Darling (Linfield), forced a 1-1 draw.

Trotting meetings were regularly arranged at the Oval while off the field testimonial events were held for Jack Burnett, who suffered a "serious accident" in 1896. The Oval was the venue for the Inter League game with the English and 12,000 saw the visitors win 2-0. Glentoran were represented by T.Somerset and W.McArthur on that occasion whereas against the Scottish League McMaster and Kelly had the honour. Left-back George

---

Results 1896/97

Played 24. Won 16. Drew 3. Lost 5. Goals For 49. Against 30. % 72.9.
Honours: Irish League, City Cup

IL	05/09/1896		Distillery	A	L	0	2	-
IL	12/09/1896		Belfast Celtic	H	W	2	0	"Rush", Carmichael
IL	19/09/1896		Cliftonville	A	W	3	1	Foreman og, McArthur, Kelly
IL	26/09/1896		North Staffs Regiment	H	W	5	0	McArthur, Duncan 2, Kelly, Johnston
IL	03/10/1896		Linfield	H	W	1	0	S.Torrans og
IL	10/10/1896		Distillery	H	W	2	1	Johnston, "Scrimmage"
IL	17/10/1896		Belfast Celtic	H	W	3	1	Kelly, Duncan, "Rush"
IL	24/10/1896		Cliftonville	H	W	3	2	Somerset, Johnston, "Rush"
IL	31/10/1896		North Staffs Regiment	H	W	2	1	Duncan, Johnston
IL	21/11/1896		Linfield	H	D	2	2	McArthur, Unknown
IC	14/11/1896	4	Distillery	H	L	0	4	-
CC	05/12/1896		Distillery	A	D	2	2	Hall, Johnston
CC	19/12/1896		Cliftonville	A	D	2	2	Johnston, Kelly
CC	25/12/1896		North Staffs Regiment	H	W	4	3	Somerset, Unknown 3
CC	02/01/1897		Linfield	H	W	2	0	Johnston, Unknown
CC	09/01/1897		Distillery	H	W	3	0	"Scrimmage", Duncan, Wattie
CC	17/04/1897		North Staffs Regiment	H	W	3	0	Duncan 2, McArthur
CC	01/05/1897		Belfast Celtic	H	W	3	1	Unknown
CC	08/05/1897		Cliftonville	H	W	2	0	Johnston, Duncan
CC	15/05/1897		Linfield	H	W	3	0	Duncan, McArthur, Unknown
CC	22/05/1897		Belfast Celtic	GP	L	0	1	-
CAS	16/01/1897	1	Cliftonville	A	W	2	1	Johnston, Duncan
CAS	13/02/1897	SF	Linfield	GP	L	0	2	-
ChC	10/04/1897	SF	Distillery	Solt	L	0	4	-
F	28/11/1896		Belfast Celtic	H	D	1	1	Somerset
F	25/12/1896		Ligoneil	A	W	8	0	Unknown
F	26/12/1896		Limavady	A	W	2	0	Unknown
F	19/04/1897		Third Lanark	H	L	0	3	-
F	20/04/1897		Third Lanark	H	D	1	1	Darling

Appearances and Goals

	App.	Goals		App.	Goals		App.	Goals
Duncan	22	10	Lyttle	16		Dougall	1	
Lewis	22		Hattie	10		Smith	1	
Purvis	22		Cochrane	8		McWhirter	1	
McArthur	22	5	Sloan	7		Carmichael	1	1
Johnston W.	22	9	McMaster J.	3		Unknown	22	9
Somerset	21	2	McFall	2		Own Goals		2
Kelly	20	4	McCann	1		Rush/Scrimmage		5
McMaster G.	19		Hall	1	1			
Shannon	19		Wattie	1	1	TOTAL	264	49

McMaster played in all three home internationals for Ireland, and Cochrane, Somerset and Duncan helped Belfast defeat Derry 3-0.

The following comment appeared in the Irish News on 14th December 1896:

"The recent proposal of a local writer that the question of a goalkeeper being dressed in a different colour to that of his club has met with the derision it deserved. To think that the most valuable part of a team is to be dressed in a colour that would distinguish him so that a player could easily see the goal instead of as at present is on the humorous side."

How times have changed!

1897/98

Glens on film – Intermediate Cup success - Easter tour cancelled

Glentoran again followed up a championship winning season with a mediocre one. Football interest in Belfast dropped, reflected in both lower attendances at games and fewer inches in newspaper columns. Indeed there were many calls for a team from Derry or Dublin to be invited to compete in order to inject new blood into the senior league. Glentoran did manage to finish joint second to Linfield, losing a test match to Cliftonville for the runners-up medals.

The Glens and the Reds had earlier met in an historic match at the Oval on 23rd October. This was the first Irish football match to be captured on film! A Frenchman, Monsieur Primo, had come to Belfast with his "Lumiere Triographe" and shot various local scenes, including action from the game. Primo then gave a presentation at the Belfast Empire Theatre on the Monday evening and it was "loudly applauded."

The Belfast Telegraph's write up on our last league fixture included the following table:

Against Linfield

	Touches	Crosses	Hands	Fouls	Off-Sides	Goal-Kicks	Goals
1st Half	22	2	2	6	2	5	1
2nd Half	22	4	2	0	2	4	0

Against Glentoran

	Touches	Crosses	Hands	Fouls	Off-Sides	Goal-Kicks	Goals
1st Half	10	1	1	3	1	9	1
2nd Half	25	3	1	3	3	7	1

On three occasions referees failed to turn up for Glentoran games, and friendlies were played in lieu. The most unfortunate case was our scheduled Irish Cup tie against Cliftonville on 13th November. We won the "friendly" on a heavy, muddy pitch but then lost the cup game a week later despite exerting constant pressure on the home goal. The first XI's nearest chance of gaining honours died in the Charity Cup final on a Solitude swamp against the North Staffordshire Regiment. Throughout the season we found the soldiers' goalkeeper, Jack Benton, a difficult opponent.

Our opening City Cup game produced a controversial incident. Glentoran defenders protested vehemently that the shot which gave Belfast Celtic their goal went over the bar. Goalnets were not in use in Ireland then, and the goal stood. The return meeting with Celtic marked our first appearance at their new enclosure Shaun's (or Klondyke) Park.

Proposed friendlies with British mainland clubs did not materialise. Dundee F.C. were to visit the Oval on St. Patrick's Day but no report on the game has been found. Furthermore the Easter trip to Lancashire for games against Burnley and Blackpool was cancelled.

Glentoran II lifted the Intermediate Cup following a 2-0 success over Linfield Swifts. The seconds' biggest victory of the season was a 10-1 hiding of Distillery II in December.

More representative honours came the way of Glentoran players as J.Lyttle turned out for Ireland against Wales at Llandudno. Lewis, Purvis, G.McMaster, McArthur and Kelly were on the Irish League team which lost 1-8 to the English League in November. Willie Purvis was joined by Cochrane and Johnston for the Scottish League game at Dundee (0-5) at the end of January. The Ulster team which lost 2-3 to Leinster at the Oval in December included McArthur and Johnston.

Results 1897/88

Played 25. Won 11. Drew 4. Lost 10. Goals For 50. Against 41. % 52.0.

IL	11/09/1897		Belfast Celtic	H	W	1	0	Duncan
IL	18/09/1897		Cliftonville	A	D	1	1	McArthur
IL	25/09/1897		North Staffs Regiment	H	L	1	2	Somerset
IL	02/10/1897		Linfield	H	L	2	4	Kelly 2
IL	09/10/1897		Distillery	A	W	6	0	Johnston 2, McArthur, Duncan 3
IL	16/10/1897		Belfast Celtic	H	W	5	1	Smith, Johnston, Kelly, McArthur 2
IL	23/10/1897		Cliftonville	H	W	3	0	Purvis, McArthur 2
IL	30/10/1897		North Staffs Regiment	H	W	5	2	Johnston 2, Somerset, Wattie, McArthur
IL	27/12/1897		Distillery	H	W	6	0	Johnston 2, Wattie, Smith 3
IL	11/04/1898		Linfield	A	L	1	2	McArthur
IL	21/05/1898	RUTM	Cliftonville	A	L	0	2	-
IC	20/11/1897	5	Cliftonville	A	L	0	1	-
CC	11/12/1897		Belfast Celtic	H	D	1	1	McArthur
CC	18/12/1897		Cliftonville	A	L	0	5	-
CC	25/12/1897		North Staffs Regiment	H	D	3	3	Smith, Johnston, Duncan (p)
CC	01/01/1898		Linfield	H	W	2	0	Johnston, Gill
CC	05/02/1898		Distillery	A	W	3	0	Johnston 2, Redpath
CC	02/04/1898		Belfast Celtic	A	L	2	3	Lyttle, Johnston
CC	30/04/1898		North Staffs Regiment	H	W	2	0	Willis, Wallace
CC	04/05/1898		Cliftonville	H	D	0	0	-
CC	07/05/1898		Linfield	A	L	0	3	-
CC	14/05/1898		Distillery	H	W	2	1	Johnston, Willis
CAS	15/01/1898	1	Cliftonville	A	L	2	5	Shannon, McArthur
ChC	16/04/1898	SF	Linfield	Solt	W	2	1	Redpath, Smith
ChC	23/04/1898	F	North Staffs Regiment	Solt	L	0	4	-
F	04/09/1897		Distillery	H	W	3	0	McArthur, Duncan, Purvis
F	13/11/1897		Cliftonville	A	W	2	1	Johnston, Duncan
F	09/04/1898		Cliftonville	H	L	0	1	-

Appearances and Goals

	App.	Goals		App.	Goals		App.	Goals
Lyttle	25	1	Kelly	12	3	McCann	3	
Shannon	24	1	Smith	9	6	McKenna	2	
Johnston W.	24	13	Leeman	5		Nabney	2	
Lewis	23		Gill	5	1	Atkinson	1	
Duncan	23	5	Redpath	5	2	McKnight	1	
Purvis	20	1	Willis	5	2	Dougan	1	
Hattie	20		McMaster J.	4		Robinson	1	
McArthur	18	10	Wallace	4	1	Richie	1	
Somerset	16	2	Wattie	4	2	TOTAL	275	50
McMaster G.	14		Boyd	3				

45

1898/99

A brave Irish Cup run ends in dispute – Lewis ever-present for Ireland

Glentoran made another valiant, but ultimately unsuccessful, bid to capture the Irish Cup. The Oval was in a sad state for our opening game against the Whites and we had Lewis in goals to thank for many fine saves. The next two rounds were fairly straightforward. Derry North End played with two men short for most of their game - in fact the Glentoran supporters actually "cheered on" the opposition in the second half out of sympathy. We were saved a trip to Cork to face King's Royal Rifles in the fifth round as the soldiers were unable to find a ground down there. 2,000 saw us win easily at the Oval, both sides missing a penalty.

The first semi-final with Belfast Celtic was an exciting affair despite being played out on an awful pitch. We appeared to have qualified for the final after winning the replay but the Celts lodged an appeal on the grounds that Duncan was ineligible. This was upheld and Celtic duly won the third game. However the wheel turned full circle as Celtic, who were rumoured to be short of players, fielded the Cliftonville centre-half in their ranks. Glentoran's protest was also upheld so a fourth meeting was necessary - this was where the violence crept in. Fights broke out among spectators before and during the game and once Wattie Johnston had put us 2-0 up in the 71st minute the Celtic supporters invaded the pitch. The "worst rowdyism ever in Belfast" began but eventually the police forced all the spectators off the field of play and the referee ordered the teams out to finish the game. Glentoran appeared but Celtic refused and the tie was awarded to the Glens.

However the controversy was far from finished. In the first minute of the final, in front of 3,500, Linfield took the lead. The score remained as such until eight minutes from time when a Linfield defender appeared to punch the ball off the line. Glentoran appealed for a penalty, but nothing was given and the Glens walked off in protest. The referee had no alternative but to abandon the game and the IFA subsequently awarded the cup to Linfield.

The Blues also defeated us in the County Antrim Shield in a match where Somerset and Wilson were sent off for fighting in the second half. Linfield defeated Linfield Swifts 4-1 in the final after a 1-1 draw. The Charity Cup also went to Balmoral when the Blues overcame Distillery 2-1. The Whites had earlier picked up the league title defeating Linfield 2-0 in a test match after the clubs had finished level on 15 points apiece.

Glentoran's silverware came in the form of the City Cup. We finished top of the table with consistent, not spectacular, performances. Linfield were runners-up, two points behind. The North Staffordshire Regiment, whom we had been due to meet in the City Cup on 29th April 1899, were posted away from Belfast and bade farewell to the Irish League.

Our league campaign began in the tropical heat of September 1898 and concluded in November when only 300 saw us beat North Staffs, leaving them defeated in all their matches. Unfortunately there had been more "ruffianism" associated with a Glentoran-Belfast Celtic encounter. On 15th October Celtic's keeper Ezekiel Johnston was hurt and had to be carried off and after the game Celtic fans attempted to attack the referee. They even went to length of chasing and stoning a tram they thought he was aboard. On the field of play it was remarked that Gill was head and shoulders above the other Glentoran forwards.

Jim Lewis played in all three of Ireland's internationals and was quoted as having a "good game" despite a 2-13 defeat to England at Roker Park. George McMaster appeared in the two inter-league games whilst Kerr, Lyttle, Rea and Somerset were in the Co. Antrim team which defeated Co. Derry 2-0. The Ulster side for the 3-1 win over Leinster (attendance 500) included Lewis, G.McMaster and Lyttle. The latter also had the privilege of being one of the linesmen in the Charity Cup final.

We reserved our most woeful display of the season for the prestigious Preston game, but at least the side which lost to Derry Celtic had the excuse of being without six regulars.

Ralph the Rover's "History of Glentoran" article in the ISN on 15th October 1898 concluded with the following paragraph:

"The Glentoran club has a bright future before it. Situated as it is in the very centre of the most densely populated part of our city, it only requires the denizens of the locality to be induced to patronise the matches taking place each week at their very doors to enable the club to rise to that position which it ought and must occupy as one of the best exponents of the game in the country."

Results 1898/99

Played 29. Won 17. Drew 3. Lost 9. Goals For 53. Against 36. % 63.8.
Honours: City Cup

IL	03/09/1898		Distillery	A	W	2	0	Seaton, Johnston
IL	10/09/1898		Belfast Celtic	H	W	2	1	Maginnes og, Seaton
IL	17/09/1898		Cliftonville	A	L	0	3	-
IL	24/09/1898		North Staffs Regiment	H	W	3	0	Gill 2, Johnston
IL	01/10/1898		Linfield	H	L	1	2	Duncan
IL	08/10/1898		Distillery	H	L	1	2	Johnston
IL	15/10/1898		Belfast Celtic	A	W	3	2	Seaton, Unknown 2
IL	22/10/1898		Cliftonville	H	L	1	2	Scott
IL	19/11/1898		Linfield	A	W	1	0	Somerset
IL	26/11/1898		North Staffs Regiment	H	W	3	0	Duncan, Gill, Seaton
IC	29/10/1898	3	Distillery	H	W	2	0	Duncan, Somerset
IC	12/11/1898	4	Derry North End	H	W	4	0	"Scrimmage", Gill, J.McMaster, Johnston
IC	03/12/1898	5	King's Royal Rifles	H	W	8	0	Somerset, Johnston, Smith, Unknown 5
IC	21/01/1899	SF	Belfast Celtic	GP	D	2	2	Johnston, Scott
IC	04/02/1899	SFR	Belfast Celtic	GP	W	2	1	Nabney, McCann – Protest
IC	01/03/1899	SFR2	Belfast Celtic	GP	L	1	2	Unknown – Protest
IC	11/03/1899	SFR3	Belfast Celtic	GP	W	2	0	Johnston 2 – Abandoned
IC	18/03/1899	F	Linfield	Solt	L	0	1	- Abandoned
CC	10/12/1898		Belfast Celtic	H	W	3	1	Seaton, McKnight, Somerset
CC	17/12/1898		Cliftonville	A	W	1	0	Johnston
CC	24/12/1898		North Staffs Regiment	H	W	2	1	Johnston, Gill
CC	26/12/1898		Linfield	H	L	1	4	"Rush"
CC	31/12/1898		Distillery	H	W	2	1	Smith, Johnston
CC	01/04/1899		Belfast Celtic	A	D	2	2	Smith, og
CC	08/04/1899		Cliftonville	H	D	1	1	Unknown
CC	29/04/1899		North Staffs Regiment					Awarded game as Regiment removed from Belfast
CC	06/05/1899		Linfield	A	W	1	0	Unknown
CC	13/05/1899		Distillery	A	W	2	0	J.McMaster, Unknown
CAS	07/01/1899	1	Linfield	H	L	0	3	-
ChC	15/04/1899	SF	Distillery	Solt	L	0	5	-
F	04/03/1899		Derry Celtic	A	L	1	3	Johnston
F	03/04/1899		Preston North End	H	L	0	5	-

Appearances and Goals

	App.	Goals		App.	Goals		App.	Goals
Lewis	29		Seaton	25	5	Robertson	1	
Kerr	28		McMaster J.	19		McKnight	1	1
Lyttle	28		Duncan	18	3	Willis	1	
McCann	28	1	Somerset	13	4	Cullen	1	
Gill	28	5	McMaster G.	12	2	Own Goals		2
Johnston W.	27	11	Scott	4	3	Rush/Scrimmage		2
Purvis	26		Nabney	3	1	Unknown		11
Smith	26	2	Hattie	1		TOTAL	319	53

1899/1900

Our worst season – A stand collapses – Representative honours

In terms of results this was Glentoran's worst ever season. Only two wins were recorded in all competitions, and we suffered our biggest defeat against Distillery in December. The Royal Scots replaced North Staffs as the Irish League's military outfit while Jack Benton, the latter's ex-goalkeeper, joined the Glens.

Our early league games gave no indication of what was to come as against Belfast Celtic we had most of the play while the goalless encounter with Distillery was very even. Many chances were thrown away versus Linfield and, against Cliftonville, Glentoran failed to capitalise on wind advantage in the first half, turning round 1-3 down. The solitary meeting with the Royal Scots saw our 2-1 lead overturned with the help of two late goals for the soldiers. Shortly after this game the Scots were posted to South Africa to take part in the Boer War and their league record was expunged. The same day Linfield met Distillery at Balmoral. During the game a stand collapsed and, although none of the spectators were seriously injured, the Northern Whig reported that some members of the crowd were upset at having their push-bikes damaged!

In the second half of the league campaign only Cliftonville really outplayed us, however we still finished bottom of the table with a meagre two points.

Our initial City Cup result was pleasing in that we twice came from behind to draw with newly crowned league champions Belfast Celtic. A feeble defensive display against the Whites was followed by a tame game with Linfield when the last twenty minutes were played out in darkness. Eventually we obtained a win on the last Saturday before Christmas despite playing most of the second half against Cliftonville with only ten men. George McMaster had retired injured when we were 2-1 up. Linfield went on to finish top of the pile in the City Cup.

Benton's heroics could not prevent a first round Irish Cup exit but we did progress to the semi-finals of the Shield. After having the Linfield defence at our mercy in the second half it took a late A.Leonard goal to force a replay. We tasted defeat on that occasion, despite having more than 50% of the play. The Blues lost the Shield final to Distillery after a replay while Cliftonville pipped Bohemians 2-1 for the Irish Cup. Glentoran were not involved in the Charity Cup semi-finals and a first round game has not been traced.

Although team results were poor some individuals picked up representative honours. In inter-league football Benton and G.McMaster played against the English League at Bolton (1-3), with Leonard appearing against our Scottish counterparts in Edinburgh (0-6). Purvis and Leonard turned out for Antrim in the 5-2 win over Derry at the Oval, while G. McMaster was part of the Ulster XI which triumphed 4-1 over Leinster at Grosvenor Park.

Glentoran players were involved in two other "charity" games during the season. In November a Cliftonville/Distillery XI defeated a Linfield/Glentoran XI 1-0 at Solitude in a match to raise funds for the West Belfast Orange Hall. Then, the gate money from the New Year's Day fixture between McConville's XI (Glentoran/Belfast Celtic/Distillery) and Torrans' XI (Cliftonville/Linfield) was donated to the Boer War Soldiers' Widows' and Orphans' Funds. That match finished 2-2 and as it was too dark to play extra time the Torrans' XI emerged "winners" by the toss of a coin.

Dublin hosted its first ever international on St. Patrick's Day 1900 when 5,000 ventured to Lansdowne Road to see England defeat Ireland by 2-0.

48

Results 1899/1900

Played 21. Won 2. Drew 7. Lost 12. Goals For 23. Against 44. % 26.2

IL	09/09/1899		Belfast Celtic	H	L	0	1	-
IL	16/09/1899		Distillery	A	D	0	0	-
IL	23/09/1899		Linfield	A	L	0	2	-
IL	30/09/1899		Cliftonville	H	L	1	4	Dunwoody
IL	07/10/1899		Royal Scots	H	L	2	4	Johnston, Flanaghan Expunged
IL	14/10/1899		Belfast Celtic	A	L	1	2	Flanaghan
IL	21/10/1899		Distillery	H	L	0	1	-
IL	04/11/1899		Cliftonville	A	L	1	4	Gill
IL	18/11/1899		Linfield	H	D	4	4	Leonard, "Rush", Scott 2
IC	28/10/1899	1	Belfast Celtic	H	L	0	1	-
CC	02/12/1899		Belfast Celtic	H	D	2	2	Flanaghan, Scott
CC	09/12/1899		Distillery	A	L	1	8	Duncan
CC	16/12/1899		Linfield	A	D	1	1	Leonard
CC	23/12/1899		Cliftonville	H	W	3	1	Scott 2, Nabney
CC	30/12/1899		Belfast Celtic	A	L	2	3	Nabney, Gill
CC	06/01/1900		Distillery	H	L	1	2	Nabney
CC	07/04/1900		Linfield	H	L	0	1	-
CC	14/04/1900		Cliftonville	A	D	1	1	Johnston
CAS	13/01/1900	1	Cliftonville Olympic	H	D	1	1	Leonard
CAS	03/02/1900	1R	Cliftonville Olympic	H	W	3	2	Leonard, Nabney 2
CAS	10/02/1900	SF	Linfield	Solt	D	1	1	Leonard
CAS	10/03/1900	SFR	Linfield	Solt	L	0	2	-
F	20/01/1900		Linfield	H	W	2	0	Leonard, Johnston

Appearances and Goals

	App.	Goals		App.	Goals		App.	Goals
Hattie	21		Somerset	12		Booth	5	
Scott	21	5	McMaster G.	10		Rodgers	3	
Flanaghan	19	2	Johnston W.	10	1	Dunwoody	2	1
Purvis	17		Benton	9		Seaton	2	
Gill	17	2	Duncan	7	1	Crothers J.	1	
McCann	14		Nabney	6	5	Bennett	1	
Leonard	14	5	Lawther	5		"Rush'		1
Kerr	13		Cardwell	5				
McMaster J.	12		McClelland	5		TOTAL	231	23

1900/01

An influx from the Whites – Shield success - A visit to Derby

Bolstered by the signing of five Distillery players, including ex-Glens keeper Jim Lewis, Glentoran put the disastrous previous season behind them. Ironically the league championship turned out to be a battle between ourselves and the Whites. After losing to Distillery on the opening day, due to a slack and careless second-half display, Glentoran produced a tremendous run of seven consecutive wins. The sequence began against Cliftonville when we staged a terrific second-half onslaught after being a goal down.

Derry Celtic, in their first senior season, also took the lead against us but we laid siege to McBride in the visitors' goal after the break and "hearty cheers" greeted fine goals from Scott and Rea. Interest and attendances swelled following wins over champions Celtic and Linfield but the expectations of a record crowd for the return with Distillery were dashed as heavy rain arrived on the morning of the match. A crowd of 5,000 did turn up and they "indulged in hat throwing" when McKelvey magnificently equalised the Whites' early goal. An aggressive second half display saw us open up a two point lead with four games to go. A feature at league grounds were the appearances of a "Pearson's Weekly" man. The first spectator to spot the publication's representative could claim a £10 prize and Mr. O'Hara was the lucky chap on 6th October.

To prevent crushing the gates were opened early a week later at Solitude. An estimated 6,000 watched the Glens rain shots on McAlpine in the Cliftonville goal and after only ten minutes we had stormed into a 3-0 lead. Leonard's breakaway fourth put an end to our "3-1" scorelines, while the cool defending of Kerr and Leeman ensured the win. A crowd of 7,000 witnessed Distillery defeat Linfield 1-0 on the day the Glens won at Derry, meaning we carried a two point lead into the last two games.

An early second XI team.

Our momentum was halted a week later as the glorious uncertainty of sport was demonstrated by Belfast Celtic knocking us out of the cup. The Celts' first goal had come when Hattie, in attempting to clear, struck the ball against Kerr for it to glance into the net! Cliftonville went on to win the cup, defeating the Freebooters of Dublin 1-0 in the April final.

Despite a splendid display by our captain George McMaster and close efforts from Black and Rea we were unable to score past Linfield keeper Drennan in November. Distillery, with wins over Cliftonville (4-3) and Derry Celtic (9-0 on 22nd Dec.) lept-frogged above us in the league but it meant we only needed to beat Belfast Celtic in March to lift the title. Unfortunately it was not to be as Celtic netted the only goal of the game through Flanaghan.

Glentoran did manage to gain its first trophy of the century, the County Antrim Shield. We opened up with a comfortable win over Cliftonville Olympic on the "auriferous slopes of Klondyke Park" in January. This was the club's last match in Victorian times as the great Queen, aged 82, passed away at 6.30 p.m. on the Tuesday after the game. Some revenge was gained on Distillery as our lovely football knocked them out after two very fast semi-finals. A large crowd saw a furious final and it took a goal from an 88th minute scrimmage to see off Cliftonville's 1st XI.

Due to wet and chilly weather only a few dozen die-hards attended our opening City Cup fixture. However the Christmas morning clash with leaders Linfield was eagerly awaited and it was reported that trams and trains would pass the Balmoral ground's gates every few minutes. The game in fact began half an hour late for the reason that Glentoran had forgotten their pants! When fully attired we could have won the game but for missing a first half penalty.

The kick-off against Cliftonville was also delayed but this time it was to let all spectators in to the ground. Lewis kept our outside City Cup hopes alive when he saved Kirkwood's last kick of the game penalty. Linfield finally made sure of the cup in April when 5,000 saw them beat us 2-1 at a soft Oval after we had taken the lead. This match also started 15 minutes behind schedule, due to the late arrival of the referee.

When Linfield beat Distillery 4-1 in the Charity Cup final the News Letter remarked that "a cup for this competition is not currently in existence, but is in the process of manufacturing." The original beautiful trophy was presented from 1883 to 1897 but then handed over to rugby union competition. The Irish League clubs had got together and donated £50 for the striking of a new cup.

Our travels to the Peak District, via the Liverpool boat, enabled us to put up a gallant performance against Derby County. The home crowd (approx. 5,000) repeatedly cheered Lewis' saves, and Leonard's goal was apparently a beauty. Steve Bloomer was among the Derby scorers.

Glentoran had three players (J.Connor, J.Black and B.Rea) in the Ireland team which lost 0-3 to England in Southampton. Connor also played against Scotland while H.McKelvey picked up his solitary cap versus Wales at Solitude.

Results 1900/01

Played 24. Won 13. Drew 4. Lost 7. Goals For 50. Against 33. % 62.5.
Honours: County Antrim Shield

IL	01/09/00		Distillery	A	L	1	3	Black
IL	08/09/00		Cliftonville	H	W	3	1	Leonard, Rea, Hattie
IL	15/09/00		Derry Celtic	H	W	3	1	Scott 2, Rea
IL	22/09/00		Belfast Celtic	H	W	3	1	Wattie 2, McKelvey
IL	29/09/00		Linfield	A	W	3	1	McKelvey 2, Rea
IL	06/10/00		Distillery	H	W	3	1	McKelvey 2, Rea
IL	13/10/00		Cliftonville	A	W	4	2	Wattie 2, Leonard 2
IL	20/10/00		Derry Celtic	A	W	4	2	Rea 2, McKelvey, Wattie
IL	03/11/00		Linfield	H	D	0	0	-
IL	16/03/01		Belfast Celtic	A	L	0	1	-
IC	27/10/00	1	Belfast Celtic	H	L	0	3	-
CC	24/11/00		Distillery	A	L	1	3	Rea
CC	08/12/00		Cliftonville	H	L	0	1	-
CC	22/12/00		Belfast Celtic	H	W	2	1	Rea, Leonard
CC	25/12/00		Linfield	A	D	1	1	Johnston
CC	29/12/00		Distillery	H	W	1	0	Johnston
CC	05/01/01		Cliftonville	A	D	1	1	Connor
CC	23/02/00		Belfast Celtic	A	W	4	2	McKelvey 2, Black, Leonard
CC	08/04/00		Linfield	H	L	1	2	McKelvey
CAS	19/01/01	1	Cliftonville Olympic	KP	W	8	2	Unknown
CAS	02/03/01	SF	Distillery	Solt	D	2	2	Black, McKelvey
CAS	18/03/01	SFR	Distillery	Solt	W	3	0	McKelvey, Johnston, Black
CAS	30/03/01	F	Cliftonville	Bal	W	2	1	Black, "Scrimmage"
ChC	20/04/01	SF	Distillery	Solt	L	0	1	-
F	15/12/00		Derby County	A	L	1	5	Leonard

Jack Wattie, Leonard and McKelvey played for Belfast when they overcame Derry 6-1 in the Inter-City match but the Maiden City men gained revenge at County level overcoming Antrim 2-1. Leonard was joined by Lewis and Waddell in the Co. Antrim line-up. Finally, McKelvey and Leonard appeared for a Belfast Select XI beaten 4-2 by Glasgow Rangers at Balmoral on Easter Tuesday.

Appearances and Goals

	App.	Goals		App.	Goals		App.	Goals
Lewis	23		Rea B.	16	8	English	1	
Wattie	23	5	Hattie	15	1	Abrahams	1	
Kerr R.	21		Leeman	12		Thomas	1	
Connor	21	1	Johnston W.	12	3	Scott	1	2
Black	21	5	Purvis	10		Unknown	11	8
Leonard	21	5	McCann	10		"Scrimmage"		1
McMaster G.	20		Wagner	2		TOTAL	264	50
McKelvey	20	11	Layden	2				

1901/02

Crowd disturbances – Shield retained – Glasgow Rangers at the Oval

The Irish League was extended to eight teams with the inclusion of a second Londonderry club, St. Columb's Court, playing at the Brandywell, and the resuscitated Ulster club. This season's outcomes were very similar to 1900/1. The league race between ourselves and Linfield was not decided until the last game, Glentoran retained the County Antrim Shield, finished second in the City Cup and fell at the first hurdle in the Irish Cup. The "plus" of the season was the winning of the newly made Belfast Charities Cup.

Again there were crowd disturbances at a Glentoran-Belfast Celtic fixture. Celtic players protested strongly over three of Glentoran's goals in the first round Shield tie, claiming they were off-side. After the third of these, which put the Glens 5-1 up, Celtic supporters invaded the pitch. The referee promptly picked up the ball, walked off and abandoned the game. A replay was ordered away from the new Celtic Park and strong Glasgow referee Tom Robertson appointed to officiate. Despite the handicap of having Rea off injured for most of the second half Glentoran triumphed amongst great cheering from their fans.

A team group from the early 1900s.

Distillery's juniors were overwhelmed in the semi-final but the Whites' senior XI were a tougher proposition at the ultimate stage. A Johnston header put us in front but Distillery gained a penalty. Parson's kick apparently cannoned back into play off Lewis' head! Despite off-side claims concerning McKelvey's goal the Glens ran out 2-1 winners.

Our Charity Cup success was also hard earned. After a goalless first half on a slippery Solitude pitch Celtic took the lead in the semi-final. Although Johnston was sent off near the end, in what was otherwise an amicable game, we overturned that setback. The Lord Mayor was present for the final with Linfield and he saw a close, exciting game finish in our favour when McKelvey sealed the Cup with a good run and a long range shot.

Glentoran's league campaign had begun on a baking hot day with an irresistible display against Belfast Celtic. This was the first ever game at Celtic Park. Linfield brought us down to earth though, going 4-0 up with the breeze at their backs before we got going. During the next six matches our pretty and effective passing game enabled us to secure wins and go top of the table. However we lost to the Blues in the return at Balmoral and dropped a point at home to Cliftonville after holding a 3-2 interval lead. Three more one-sided wins left us a point behind Linfield going into the last round of matches. At Celtic Park, Derry we were 1-0 up at the turnaround, but could not cope without the injured Blair in the second half and went down 1-2. Linfield defeated Cliftonville 2-0 and became champions.

Thanks to a second minute goal the Reds knocked us out of the Irish Cup, Linfield winning that trophy with a 5-1 final success over Distillery.

The City Cup, featuring Belfast teams only, probably generated the least public interest of all the Irish competitions. Being played on a "league" basis after the actual championship the games stretched from December to the end of May or sometimes even June. This was because the January to March period was invariably given over to the knockout tournaments and international and representative fixtures.

Tempers were sometimes no less frayed. On the day in January when Glentoran defeated Ulster, a shadow of their former selves, on a dismal swamp of an Oval pitch, Linfield met Celtic on the ground of the latter. The Celts late penalty equaliser prompted a stone-throwing riot while Linfield fans sang "Rule Britannia".

Results 1901/02

Played 30. Won 20. Drew 5. Lost 5. Goals For 72. Against 33. % 75.0.
Honours: County Antrim Shield, Charity Cup

IL	31/08/01		Belfast Celtic	A	W	3	1	Leonard, Waddell, Black
IL	07/09/01		Linfield	H	L	1	5	Leonard
IL	14/09/01		Cliftonville	A	W	2	1	McKelvey, Black
IL	21/09/01		St. Columb's Court	A	W	4	0	Black, Smyth 2, Wattie
IL	28/09/01		Ulster	H	W	5	2	Johnston 3, Leonard, Waddell
IL	05/10/01		Distillery	A	W	2	1	Johnston 2
IL	12/10/01		Derry Celtic	H	W	4	1	Wattie, McKelvey, Leonard, Smyth
IL	19/10/01		Belfast Celtic	H	W	4	0	Johnston, Waddell, McKelvey 2
IL	26/10/01		Linfield	A	L	0	2	-
IL	02/11/01		Cliftonville	H	D	3	3	McKelvey 2, Smyth
IL	23/11/01		St. Columb's Court	H	W	7	1	Waddell 2, McKelvey 2, Ferrett, Millar, Johnston
IL	30/11/01		Ulster	H	W	4	2	Blair, Wattie (p), McKelvey 2
IL	07/12/01		Distillery	H	W	3	1	McKelvey 2, Johnston
IL	14/12/01		Derry Celtic	A	L	1	2	Waddell
IC	16/11/01	4	Cliftonville	A	L	0	1	-
CC	25/12/01		Belfast Celtic	A	L	1	2	McKelvey
CC	28/12/01		Cliftonville	H	W	2	0	Smyth, McKelvey
CC	11/01/02		Ulster	H	W	3	1	Smyth 2, McKelvey
CC	31/03/02		Linfield	H	D	1	1	Johnston
CC	12/04/02		Belfast Celtic	H	D	1	1	McKelvey
CC	03/05/02		Cliftonville	A	W	1	0	Smyth
CC	10/05/02		Ulster	H	W	2	0	McCann, McKelvey
CC	17/05/02		Distillery	H	D	1	1	Lynas
CC	24/05/02		Linfield	A	D	0	0	-
CC	31/05/02		Distillery	A	W	2	1	Smyth, Ewing
CAS	18/01/02	1	Belfast Celtic	A	A	5	1	Wattie, Gill, Johnston, Waddell, McKelvey – abandoned
CAS	03/02/02	1R	Belfast Celtic	Solt	W	2	0	Waddell, Smyth
CAS	08/03/02	SF	Distillery West End	Solt	W	6	1	Johnston, McKelvey 2, Waddell 2, Unknown
CAS	29/03/02	F	Distillery	Solt	W	2	1	Johnston, McKelvey
ChC	19/04/02	SF	Belfast Celtic	Solt	W	3	1	Johnston, McKelvey 2
ChC	26/04/02	F	Linfield	Solt	W	2	0	Booth, McKelvey
F	01/04/02		Glasgow Rangers	H	L	0	3	-
F	02/04/02		Glasgow Rangers	H	W	2	0	Unknown

Despite overlapping with the cricket season, the City Cup did maintain public interest on the last day of May 1902. Celtic had finished their ten matches with 14 points while Linfield (13) and Glentoran (12) had each one fixture to fulfil. The Blues defeated bottom of the table Cliftonville 2-1 to win the Cup but the Glens also won to force a test match with Celtic for the runners-up medals. The Irish News reported that it was generally accepted that our winner against Distillery had been yards off-side and the referee was loudly "hooted" at. In any event the test match was held over to 1902/3.

None of our players were recognised at full level but McAreavey, Hattie, Wattie, Johnston and Leonard played in the Irish League team humbled 9-0 by the English League at Woolwich in November. Wattie, accompanied by McKelvey, captained the League team versus the Scottish League (0-3) in February. Wattie also played for Belfast when they went down 1-6 to Derry while our representatives in the Co. Antrim XI which drew 3-3 with Co. Derry were Hattie and McKelvey.

Glasgow Rangers visited the Oval over Easter. After losing heavily on the Monday a "Glentoran United" team , consisting of seven Glenmen supplemented by four top local players overcame the Rangers 2-0 before a crowd of 3,000.

Appearances and Goals

	App.	Goals		App.	Goals		App.	Goals
Lewis	29		McCann	12	1	Booth	2	1
Millar	29	1	Blair	11	1	Turner	2	
Wattie	28	3	Leonard	9	4	McKeown	1	
McMaster G.	26		Ewing	7	1	Tamer	1	
Smyth	25	10	Black	6	3	McCreevy	1	
Waddell	25	9	McClelland	4		Ferrett	1	1
McKelvey	25	23	Beggs	4		Unknown	11	1
Johnston W.	22	12	Gill	3		TOTAL	330	72
McAreavey	21		Lynas	3	1			
Hattie	19		Kerr R.	3				

1902/03

An average season - Marathon charity tie – New Oval ready

With virtually the same set of players as in 1901/2 Glentoran ended this season trophy-less and returned a playing record of marginally more than 50%. St. Columb's Court bowed out after their one season of senior soccer and Dublin gained its first Irish League representatives in the form of Bohemians. This was to be Glentoran's last season at the original Oval as the current ground was obtained and completed in May 1903, coinciding with the club's "coming of age".

The Charity Cup, usually a short competition, was turned into a marathon as it took five matches to decide the Glentoran-Distillery semi-final. In the first meeting the Whites fought back from a 0-2 interval deficit. The goalless replay saw Smyth and Distillery's Morton sent off and with Kerr having to retire injured we played out most of the game with nine men. The Whites thought they had gone through after they won game three but a protest by Glentoran concerning the ineligibility of their keeper Long, recently signed from Aberdeen, was upheld. It was the Glens turn to come back next time after Distillery had built up a 3-0 half-time lead. Eventually we won the tie despite a missed penalty by Dick Kerr in that fifth game. A crowd of 2,000 were present for the deciding episode. Linfield succeeded in the final but the game was spoilt by the miserable weather.

There was a large police presence, "to prevent rowdyism", at our home league game with Belfast Celtic. After the Celts had taken the lead, Lewis saved a Clay penalty and we fought back to win - the deciding goal coming after an 87th minute scrimmage. Two one-sided wins were followed up by unlucky, narrow defeats versus Cliftonville and Linfield when we hammered away without reward. Distillery emerged as league champions, although they were unable to defeat us in either of our encounters. Glentoran finished third.

By having clubs face each other once only in the City Cup it was planned to complete the competition on Christmas Day, avoiding the games dragging on to the end of the season. McKelvey was on top form in our opening match destroying Belfast Celtic single handedly as he shot us into a 5-0 lead at one stage. An obstinate Distillery defence and many missed opportunities against Linfield saw us drop three points in the next two games. Then a crowd of only 1,000 watched us win easily against Ulster. On Christmas Day Millar's late winner saw off a scratch Cliftonville team and when Celtic beat Linfield 1-0 it meant there was a three-way tie at the top of the table. The frustrated City Cup committee decided to hold a triangular play-off at the end of the season. Glentoran lost both their matches and Linfield defeated Celtic 1-0 after a 0-0 draw to take the trophy. Their goalless meeting had been marred by stone throwing. The fixture congestion was increased as it took Celtic and ourselves a further three games to decide the destiny of the previous season's runners-up medals!

Our Irish Cup hopes nose-dived after incessant rain on Friday and Saturday morning turned the pitch for the Linfield game into a quagmire. Distillery lifted the cup with a 3-1 win over Bohemians at Dalymount Park. The Whites also claimed the County Antrim Shield, needing a replay to beat Linfield, after knocking us out with an 86th minute winner in the semis.

On 18th May 1903 the Belfast Evening Telegraph announced that our new ground, complete with brand new playing surface, was ready. Captain Craig, who had "kicked off" our benefit match for the Ballymacarrett New Orange Hall on 27th April, donated a £50 cheque to help fund the ground purchase.

Representative honours continued to come to the club as the Irish League team had a rare good season. When they lost 2-3 to the English League team in October Lewis, Wattie and McKelvey partook. McKelvey retained his place for the Scottish League game in February when the Irish won 1-0. Wattie appeared for Ulster when they beat Leinster 3-1 but Lynas, McMaster, Millar and McKelvey were part of the Co. Antrim team humbled 6-1 by Co. Derry. In the Inter-City match Belfast, including Connor and McKelvey, overcame Derry 6-1.

Press coverage of Irish football had improved considerably when the Northern Whig introduced "Impartial's" column on 21st October 1902. Every Tuesday onwards events in and around the senior clubs were comprehensively analysed, and not without wit.

Results 1902/03

Played 34. Won 13. Drew 9. Lost 12. Goals For 62. Against 47. % 51.5

IL	30/08/02		Distillery	A	D	1	1	McKelvey
IL	06/09/02		Belfast Celtic	H	W	2	1	Smyth, Maginnes og
IL	13/09/02		Bohemians	A	W	3	1	Ewing 2, Waddell
IL	20/09/02		Derry Celtic	H	W	6	0	Smyth, McKelvey 3, Wattie 2
IL	27/09/02		Ulster	H	W	4	1	Lynas, McKelvey 3
IL	04/10/02		Cliftonville	A	L	0	1	-
IL	18/10/02		Linfield	H	L	0	1	-
IL	22/11/02		Distillery	H	D	2	2	Waddell, Smyth
IL	06/12/02		Belfast Celtic	A	L	1	3	Smyth
IL	27/12/02		Bohemians	H	W	4	0	Millar 2, Waddell, Smyth
IL	10/01/03		Derry Celtic	A	L	1	4	G.McMaster
IL	17/01/03		Ulster	H	W	3	1	Waddell, McKelvey 2
IL	07/02/03		Cliftonville	H	W	2	1	Smyth, Ewing
IL	21/02/03		Linfield	A	D	1	1	Unknown
IC	25/10/02	3	Ulster	H	W	6	0	Johnston, McKelvey, Smyth 2, Waddell 2
IC	08/11/02	4	Linfield	H	L	1	2	Wattie
CC	15/11/02		Belfast Celtic	H	W	5	2	McKelvey 5
CC	29/11/02		Distillery	A	L	1	2	Peabody
CC	13/12/02		Linfield	A	D	1	1	Waddell
CC	20/12/02		Ulster	H	W	4	1	Unknown, Waddell, McKelvey, Johnston
CC	25/12/02		Cliftonville	A	W	2	1	Lynas, Millar
CC	13/04/03	PO	Belfast Celtic	GP	L	1	4	Unknown
CC	09/05/03	PO	Linfield	GP	L	0	2	-
CAS	24/01/03	1	Belfast Celtic	H	W	2	0	McKelvey, Ewing
CAS	07/03/03	SF	Distillery	Solt	L	1	2	McMillan og
ChC	18/04/03	SF	Distillery	Solt	D	2	2	Lynas, "Scrimmage"
ChC	22/04/03	SFR	Distillery	Solt	D	0	0	-
ChC	25/04/03	SFR2	Distillery	Solt	L	0	1	- Protest
ChC	06/05/03	SFR3	Distillery	H	D	3	3	Ewing, Connor, McKelvey
ChC	12/05/03	SFR4	Distillery	Solt	W	1	0	Booth
ChC	16/05/03	F	Linfield	Solt	L	0	2	-
CC*	14/03/03	TM	Belfast Celtic	GP	D	1	1	Wattie
CC*	10/04/03	TMR	Belfast Celtic	GP	D	1	1	Lynas
CC*	25/05/03	TMR2	Belfast Celtic	GP	L	0	2	-
F	23/08/02		Ulster	H	D	2	2	Smyth 2
F	27/04/03		Linfield	H	L	0	2	- Ballymacarrett New Orange Hall

*= for season 1901/2

Appearances and Goals

	App.	Goals		App.	Goals		App.	Goals
Lewis	32		Fitzimmons	11		Rea S.	1	
Connor	32	1	McMaster J.	9		Gill	1	
Waddell	30	8	Blair	7		Crabtree	1	
McKelvey	28	18	Johnston W.	4	2	Pierce	1	
Ewing	25	5	Owen	3		Carroll	1	
Smyth	24	8	Beattie	3		Clair	1	
Kerr R.	23		Woods	3		Queen	1	
Lynas	23	4	McFarlane	3		Unknown	22	3
McMaster G.	22	1	Mitchell	2		Own Goals		2
Millar	22	3	Peabody	2	1	"Scrimmage"		1
Wattie	22	4	Booth	2	1	TOTAL	374	62
McAreavey	11		Kerr (LW)	2				

1903/04

Opening of the new Oval – League runners-up – Rangers return

The switch of headquarters to the new Oval coincided with numerous changes to the playing panel. Of the old school from the turn of the century only Kerr, Connor, George McMaster, Lewis and Wattie remained. New blood included the striking Donoghue brothers and a Scottish goalkeeper, A. Cunningham. On 4th February 1904 R.Bennett was signed from Distillery and B.Donaghy joined the club from Derry Celtic.

Team Group 1903/4.

The first competitive game at the Oval was against the Irish League's latest military outfit, the King's Own Scottish Borderers. KOSB had replaced Ulster. Glentoran's line-up for this encounter comprised five Englishmen, five Irishmen and a Scot. The Lord Mayor of Belfast "kicked-off" the game and despite the soldiers' hard play the Glens won convincingly with backs Kerr and Jolly particularly safe. A comment made by Impartial on the new Oval ground was that both the playing surface and spectator's view were good but covered shelter was required.

Our second league game saw Belfast Celtic hand us our only defeat with a 46th minute goal in a fiercely contested meeting. Against the Blues we tended to shoot too often from long range and had Sam Rea to thank for the 85th minute equaliser. October witnessed performances of sound method and steadiness but little flair or brilliance. Bohemians kicked-off with only ten men as their inside-right (Pratt) arrived at the ground twenty minutes late. The drawn game with Distillery on Boxing Day did neither side any good as the result left Linfield clear champions. Our return match with Cliftonville was played on a pitch covered by partially melted snow. Kirkwood missed a penalty for the visitors.

We finished joint second with the Whites and a test match was arranged for the runners-up medals. During that game Waddington's shot was deflected in by Distillery defender Burnison and McKeown made it 2-0 at half-time. The game developed into a "rough-house" in the second period but the Glens held on to win.

Linfield dashed our Irish Cup hopes, scoring all three goals after the break, and went on to capture the trophy with a 5-0 final success over Derry Celtic. Our friendly with the Blues in October was abandoned five minutes into the second half when one of their players (Smyth) suffered a fractured leg in an accidental collision.

We met Belfast Celtic in the Shield a week after they had lost 2-3 to KOSB, giving the soldiers their first win of the season. After a 0-1 defeat we lodged a protest against the Celt Cochrane alleging he was ineligible. The committee ordered a replay with Celtic making it clear that they would be playing under protest. The goalless draw could have been prevented if Waddington had not missed an open goal. A second replay also ended all square but subsequently the County Antrim FA reversed their original decision and allowed Celtic to progress. They reached the final but succumbed 1-4 to Linfield. The "Stripes" did pick up the Charity Cup, defeating us 1-0 in a close, exciting final.

Results 1903/04

Played 31. Won 13. Drew 8. Lost 10. Goals For 43. Against 40. % 54.8

IL	29/08/03		K.O.S.B	H	W	3	0	Harvey, Waddington, Ewing
IL	05/09/03		Belfast Celtic	A	L	0	1	-
IL	12/09/03		Linfield	H	D	1	1	Rea
IL	19/09/03		Derry Celtic	A	W	3	2	Wattie 2 (2p), Waddington
IL	26/09/03		Distillery	H	D	0	0	-
IL	03/10/03		Cliftonville	A	D	1	1	J.Donoghue
IL	17/10/03		Bohemians	A	D	0	0	-
IL	24/10/03		Belfast Celtic	H	W	2	1	P.Donoghue, Ewing
IL	31/10/03		K.O.S.B.	H	W	2	1	Waddington, Rea
IL	05/12/03		Derry Celtic	H	W	1	0	Smyth
IL	26/12/03		Distillery	A	D	1	1	Jolly (p)
IL	16/01/04		Cliftonville	H	W	4	2	J.Donoghue 2, Smyth, Wattie
IL	20/02/04		Bohemians	H	W	2	0	J.Donoghue, Wattie (p)
IL	05/04/04		Linfield	A	D	0	0	-
IL	25/04/04	RUTM	Distillery	A	W	2	1	Waddington, McKeown
IC	07/11/03	4	Linfield	A	L	0	3	-
CC	14/11/03		Cliftonville	A	L	3	4	McKeown, Waddington, Jolly (p)
CC	21/11/03		Distillery	A	L	0	4	-
CC	12/12/03		Cliftonville	H	W	2	1	Waddington, Smyth
CC	19/12/03		K.O.S.B.	H	W	4	0	Rea, Jolly (p), P.Donoghue, Waddington
CC	25/12/03		Belfast Celtic	A	L	1	2	Smyth
CC	02/01/04		Distillery	H	L	2	4	Rea, Mitchell
CC	09/01/04		Linfield	H	L	0	2	-
CC	13/02/04		K.O.S.B.	H	W	4	2	McKeown, P.Donoghue, McMaster, J.Donoghue
CC	27/02/04		Belfast Celtic	H	W	2	1	Ewing, Waddington
CC	16/04/04		Linfield	A	L	0	2	-
CAS	23/01/04	1	Belfast Celtic	A	L	0	1	- Protest
CAS	30/01/04	1R	Belfast Celtic	H	D	0	0	-
CAS	06/02/04	1R2	Belfast Celtic	A	D	2	2	P.Donoghue, Waddington Protest Overturned
ChC	23/04/04	SF	Linfield	GP	W	1	0	Smyth
ChC	30/04/04	F	Belfast Celtic	Solt	L	0	1	-
F	22/08/03		Glentoran 2nds	H	D	2	2	Rooney, Ewing
F	10/10/03		Linfield	A	L	0	2	- Abandoned after 50 minutes
F	05/03/04		Derry Celtic	A	L	0	1	-
F	26/03/04		Cliftonville	A	D	2	2	P.Donoghue, Smyth
F	09/04/04		Glasgow Rangers	H	L	0	3	-

Indifferent displays forced us to settle for a mid-table City Cup position. In both games versus Distillery Jolly was unable to play in the second half and, as substitutes were a thing of the future, we were doubly handicapped. That second Whites' game marked our first Oval defeat. With the Oval playing surface in bad order in December Jack Wattie became another casualty when he twisted his ankle and retired against Cliftonville. The City Cup also found its way to Balmoral.

Glasgow Rangers' second Easter visit to East Belfast only drew a thin crowd who witnessed a "scrambling game."

J.Connor and J.Waddington travelled and played for the Irish League side which went down 1-2 to the English League team at Bradford in October. Connor also appeared at Paisley when the Scottish League overcame the Irish lads 3-1 in February before 5,000.

On 11th June 1904 the Oval hosted the Ulster Cycling Championships, and Irish records were broken in the half-mile, 3-mile and 10-mile events. In the first heat of the latter J.Hanna knocked almost 25 seconds off the old record of 21 mins 49 secs. However in the final Hanna was beaten by Collins, who established a new record of 20 mins 28.2 secs.

Appearances and Goals

	App.	Goals		App.	Goals		App.	Goals
Rea S.	30	4	Ewing	20	3	Mitchell	5	1
Waddington	30	9	Jolly	18	3	Bennett	4	
Connor	29		Donoghue J.	18	5	Donaghy	2	
McMaster G.	26	1	Cunningham	16		Harvey	2	1
McKeown	24	3	Lewis	15		Walker	2	
Wattie	22	4	McLean	14		Crothers J.	1	
Donoghue P.	22	4	Smyth	13	5	Kearney	1	
Kerr R.	21		Tierney	6		TOTAL	341	43

1904/05

League Champions again – Second XI success

Dublin gained its second Irish League side as Shelbourne replaced the Scottish Borderers Regiment. Meanwhile Glentoran had adopted an "all-Irish" team policy and in one preview of the season were billed as "the team of all the talents."

After the first three league games, culminating in defeat on our first visit to Serpentine Avenue, this description had been revised to read "too many old has beens"! However we turned the corner when Doherty's last minute winner defeated Belfast Celtic after their goalkeeper Glenn had threatened to rob us of a point. Three further convincing wins followed to put us joint top with Distillery at the half-way stage. In the game at Derry Celtic the referee had taken the players off the field for a spell during a particularly heavy thunderstorm. Bohemians had their keeper Reynolds, who was also an Irish cycling champion, to thank for restricting us to a single goal in November.

Little consolation could be taken from the assessment that our 0-2 defeat versus Distillery was "the best game in Belfast this season." However the Whites faded after that win, picking up only three points from their last six games, leaving ourselves and Belfast Celtic to vie for the title. An enthusiastic 4,000 crowd saw the Glens, missing the injured Connor and McConnell, come away from Celtic Park with a point on Boxing Day morning. Both teams won their last three matches and so a play-off was necessary to decide the destination of the Gibson Cup.

This came off at Grosvenor Park on 1st April when Glentoran lined-up: Lewis, McClelland, McCourt, Rea, Connor, McConnell, McKeown, Maxwell, Leonard, Kirkwood, Doherty. After he had an early goal disallowed Kirkwood gave Glentoran the lead and within a minute Doherty had made it 2-0. Celtic's second half onslaught was thwarted by a combination of stout defence and Lewis' fine saves and just before time Ralph Leonard clinched the win. So we became Irish League champions for the third time.

Despite brave attempts no other major trophies were won but the Seconds managed to capture the Steel and Sons Cup. The final against Woodvale developed into something of a saga. After two draws Woodvale defeated Glentoran II 2-1 (Napier on target for the Wee Glens in front of 2,000) but we protested and another replay was ordered. The attempt on 17th January was abandoned after only ten minutes play but eleven days later the Seconds lifted the cup thanks to a 1-0 win. The decisive goal was a free kick by Condy King.

The Seconds had a good season overall and recorded their biggest win against Glenbank (10-0). Arguably their best performance, however, came in the first round of the County Antrim Shield when they defeated Cliftonville 2-0 at Solitude. Team: Gray, King, McMichael, Craig, Crothers, Wilton, Mitchell, Baird, Napier, Foster, Ewing. (Foster and Mitchell were the marksmen.) Both Glentoran XI's fell at the semi-final stage on a miserably wet March afternoon. Two Distillery goals immediately after half-time put paid to the first team's hopes while the Seconds went down 0-2 to Linfield at Grosvenor Park. Distillery beat the Blues 2-0 in the final.

We finished runners-up in both the City and Charity Cups. Sir Daniel Dixon, Belfast's Lord Mayor, presented the Charity Cup to the Linfield skipper. In the home City Cup tie with Distillery McKeown had to retire after receiving a kick in the face.

With only the five senior Belfast teams involved in the City Cup it was suggested that the spare club should go "up country" on their idle Saturday promoting soccer by way of exhibition games. In the away encounter with Belfast Celtic the teams turned straight round without a half-time interval to get the game finished earlier due to the heavy rain. Distillery finished two points above us in the final table, leaving Kirkwood to rue a missed penalty against the Whites during our 0-1 defeat at Grosvenor Park.

62

Glentoran's reward for eliminating a poor Cliftonville side in the Irish Cup was a bye into the semi-final. Despite opening the scoring against the Shels at Dalymount Park we crashed out and it was left to Distillery to beat the Dubliners 3-0 in the final.

Connor and McConnell played for the Irish League against the English League (0-2) while Rea, McCourt, McKeown, Leonard and Kirkwood featured when the Leinster League were defeated 2-0 in April. McConnell was on the Belfast team which beat Derry 4-0 but when Ulster lost 1-2 to Leinster in Dublin they included Glenmen Lewis, McCourt, McClelland, Rea and Maxwell.

At Irish international level J.Maxwell gained caps versus Wales and Scotland, accompanied by English McConnell in the latter. James Connor also played for Ireland this season but this was after his move to Belfast Celtic.

Action photographs of matches, replacing pencil sketches, appeared in the ISN for the first time whilst violence was not only confined to clubs' enclosures. It was reported that at the IFA's AGM in the Londonderry Guildhall on 13th May 1905 there were "bouts of fighting and disorder"!

Results 1904/05

Played 29. Won 17. Drew 5. Lost 7. Goals For 48. Against 27. % 67.2.
Honours: Irish League

IL	03/09/04		Distillery	H	D	1	1	Kirkwood
IL	10/09/04		Linfield	A	D	2	2	Leonard, Maxwell
IL	17/09/04		Shelbourne	A	L	1	3	Kirkwood
IL	24/09/04		Belfast Celtic	H	W	1	0	Doherty
IL	08/10/04		Cliftonville	A	W	2	1	Kirkwood, Maxwell
IL	22/10/04		Derry Celtic	A	W	2	0	McKeown, Doherty
IL	19/11/04		Bohemians	H	W	1	0	Doherty
IL	26/11/04		Distillery	A	L	0	2	-
IL	10/12/04		Linfield	H	W	1	0	Leonard
IL	24/12/04		Shelbourne	H	W	2	0	Leonard, McMaster
IL	26/12/04		Belfast Celtic	A	D	1	1	McCourt
IL	14/01/05		Cliftonville	H	W	3	0	"A Charge", McCourt, Kirkwood (p)
IL	28/01/05		Derry Celtic	H	W	3	1	Leonard, Kirkwood 2(1p)
IL	18/02/05		Bohemians	A	W	2	1	McCourt, Rea
IL	01/04/05	TM	Belfast Celtic	GP	W	3	1	Kirkwood, Doherty, Leonard
CC	01/10/04		Cliftonville	H	W	5	0	Doherty 2, McKeown, Ward, McConnell
CC	29/10/04		Distillery	H	D	1	1	Maxwell (p)
CC	17/12/04		Belfast Celtic	A	W	4	0	McKeown 2, Doherty, Connor
CC	31/12/04		Linfield	A	L	0	2	-
CC	07/01/05		Cliftonville	A	W	1	0	Leonard
CC	11/02/05		Distillery	A	L	0	1	-
CC	17/03/05		Belfast Celtic	H	W	4	0	Crothers, Kirkwood 3
CC	22/04/05		Linfield	H	W	1	0	Kirkwood
IC	05/11/04	4	Cliftonville	H	W	2	0	Ward 2 – Bye in Round 5
IC	04/02/05	6	Shelbourne	DP	L	1	4	Doherty
CAS	25/03/05	SF	Distillery	Solt	L	1	2	Rea
ChC	29/04/05	SF	Distillery	Solt	D	1	1	Kirkwood
ChC	02/05/05	SFR	Distillery	Solt	W	2	1	McCourt (p), Ward
ChC	06/05/05	F	Linfield	Solt	L	0	2	-
F	20/08/04		Distillery	A	D	2	2	Unknown
F	27/08/04		Belfast Celtic	H	L	0	1	-

Appearances and Goals

	App.	Goals		App.	Goals		App.	Goals
McCourt	28	3	Maxwell	25	3	Crothers J.	1	1
Doherty	28	9	Connor	24	1	Mitchell	1	
Kirkwood	27	12	Rea S.	23	2	Ewing	1	
McClelland	26		Leonard	20	6	Torrans	1	
McConnell	26	1	Ward	17	4	King R.	1	
McKeown	26	4	McMaster G.	15	1	"Charge"		1
Lewis	25		Gray	4				
						TOTAL	319	48

1905/06

First visit to Windsor Park – From top to bottom in League

A freak 36 hour period of heavy rain caused the postponement of our August friendly with Belfast Celtic and left us with precious little time for practice prior to our league meeting with Linfield. This game marked the opening of the Windsor Park ground and after Glentoran enjoyed most of the pressure in the first half, Soye's goal gave the Blues a winning start to their occupancy.

The Glens, under a stated policy of relying on home grown talents as opposed to "exotic" imports, had an unlucky season. Frequently we found ourselves down to ten men due to injury, and despite invariably playing the better football many games were lost by narrow margins.

Local newspapers carried complaints regarding the public motor service to the Oval. Apparently of the two suitable trams, one arrived 15 minutes too soon with the second causing the spectator to miss the regular 2.45 p.m. kick-offs! The cry went up for a special service.

We ended up with the wooden spoon in one of the most evenly contested league races in history. Indeed, after Cliftonville and Distillery finished level on 19 points, two play-off games also finished all-square. The Whites and the Reds shared the Gibson Cup. Glentoran had dominated the away fixture with Distillery but after missing many chances fell to a late winner. Against Cliftonville at the Oval only an 87th minute equaliser denied us out of two points. Around 4,000 were at Dalymount Park to see Bohemians go 2-0 up within five minutes and then hang on to win. On our other league trip to Dublin King had the misfortune of putting through his own goal against Shelbourne. The return meeting with Distillery saw Davy McDougall fracture his collar bone just before half-time and he was unable to play again until 10th March.

Our hopes in the three knockout tournaments were short lived despite an excellent Irish Cup win over Distillery. Kirkwood had a third "goal" disallowed while debutant keeper Burch made many fine saves. Two weeks later against Shelbourne we made things difficult for ourselves as firstly Maitland, another keeper, dropped a shot into his net and then McCourt had his penalty saved by Rowe. Glentoran were handicapped with the loss of T.Hamilton in the Shield game, while in the Charity Cup tie yet another of our goalkeepers, Reid, saved a penalty.

In order to even the City Cup up to six teams a club from outside of Belfast, Shelbourne, gained entry. Supporters may well have utilised the new electric tram service to Celtic Park on 2nd December. Later the same month, despite the loss of Kirkwood to injury when 2-1 up, we produced our best result of the season against Linfield. The following week we found ourselves 0-2 down to Shelbourne after ten minutes and without McMichael who had been carried off. However a battling display was rewarded with Munn's last minute equaliser. The return game with the Shels was held over to the following season. Hegarty, our latest goalkeeper, saved a penalty against Linfield at Windsor. Belfast Celtic emerged top of the final City Cup pile.

Our Scottish visitors Aidrieonians looked set to swamp us in April when they built up a 4-0 half-time lead. But, in dismally wet conditions, the Glens held their own after the break.

No...9..........

The Glentoran Football and Athletic Club, Ltd.

Season Ticket, 1905-1906.

Admits owner to all Football Matches on the Grounds, from 1st September, 1905, till 30th April, 1906.

Received from

Mr. *James o'Vickell*

5/-

T. D. REID,

Secretary.

NOT TRANSFERABLE.

A season ticket from 1905/6.

In the inter-league match with the English we were represented by McCourt while King, Kirkwood and Ewing played in the Belfast team defeated 3-1 at Derry in February. Ulster played its first ever inter-provincial match with Munster winning 3-1 in Cork. However it was hardly a local team as the solitary Munsterman was joined by ten Scottish and English soldiers stationed in the garrison there.

George McMaster, first XI trainer in 1906 after eleven years service as a player, had a richly deserved benefit game. Unfortunately a smaller than normal crowd turned out as the date chosen clashed with Irish Cup semi-final day.

Results 1905/06

Played 27. Won 4. Drew 8. Lost 15. Goals For 32. Against 49. % 29.6

IL	02/09/05		Linfield	A	L	0 1	-
IL	09/09/05		Belfast Celtic	H	L	1 2	McCourt (p)
IL	16/09/05		Shelbourne	H	W	3 2	Kirkwood 2, McCourt (p)
IL	23/09/05		Derry Celtic	A	L	1 3	Kirkwood
IL	07/10/05		Distillery	A	L	0 1	-
IL	21/10/05		Cliftonville	H	D	1 1	Kirkwood
IL	28/10/05		Bohemians	A	L	2 3	McCourt (p), Ewing
IL	11/11/05		Linfield	H	l	1 2	Kirkwood
IL	25/11/05		Belfast Celtic	A	L	0 3	-
IL	09/12/05		Shelbourne	A	D	1 1	Munn
IL	25/12/05		Derry Celtic	H	W	1 0	Unknown
IL	13/01/06		Distillery	H	L	1 2	J.Crothers
IL	10/02/06		Cliftonville	A	L	1 5	Ewing
IL	16/04/06		Bohemians	H	D	0 0	-
CC	30/09/05		Distillery	H	L	0 1	-
CC	02/12/05		Belfast Celtic	A	L	2 3	Ewing 2
CC	16/12/05		Linfield	H	W	4 1	Hamilton 2, Kirkwood, Ewing
CC	23/12/05		Shelbourne	A	D	2 2	McDougall, Munn
CC	30/12/05		Cliftonville	A	D	1 1	Ewing
CC	06/01/06		Distillery	A	D	2 2	Mitchell, McCourt (p)
CC	10/03/06		Belfast Celtic	H	D	2 2	Ewing, Mitchell
CC	24/03/06		Linfield	A	D	1 1	Hamilton
CC	14/04/06		Cliftonville	H	L	1 2	Fitzpatrick
IC	04/11/05	1	Distillery	H	W	2 0	Hamilton, Kirkwood
IC	18/11/05	2	Shelbourne	H	L	0 2	-
CAS	20/01/06	1	Cliftonville	H	L	0 2	-
ChC	29/01/06	1	Cliftonville	GP	L	2 4	Ewing, King (p)
F	26/12/05		Larne	A	Unknown		-
F	03/02/06		Distillery	H	D	1 1	Mitchell
							George McMaster Benefit
F	17/03/06		Enniskillen Celtic	A	W	3 1	Unknown
F	17/04/06		Airdrie	H	L	2 6	Unknown

Appearances and Goals

	App.	Goals		App.	Goals		App.	Goals
Crothers J.	23	1	McKeown	15		Fitzpatrick	3	1
King R.	21	1	Mitchell	13	2	Burch	2	
Crothers C.	20		McCourt	11	4	Mulheron	1	
Craig	20		Gray	8		Hamilton S.	1	
Ewing	20	8	Maitland	6		McComb	1	
McDougall	20	1	Reid	4		Unknown	44	1
McMichael	18		McMaster G.	4				
Hamilton T.	18	4	Hegarty	3		TOTAL	297	32
Kirkwood	18	7	Munn	3	2			

1906/07

Playing panel bolstered – Ching Morrison returns – Unsavoury incidents

The first team playing squad was strengthened with the addition of Jack Benton (ex-Glens and Stoke City), Dooley (ex-Leeds City), Fred Rea, Sam Rea, Roly Lyner and William (Billy) Andrews. This prompted one previewer of the Irish soccer scene to remark that Glentoran have risen again and "may yet make Ballymacarrett welkin ring with deeds of derring do."

With the Oval Athletic meetings winding down the football season kicked off at the end of August. 1,200 were in attendance in Dublin as we completed our 1905/6 City Cup business with a rare win.

Despite the new faces our league form showed little improvement but at least we managed to finish above Derry Celtic. The Glens' only two wins came in the games which straddled the early opening City Cup fixtures. Against Derry King had mixed fortune. After missing a penalty he made amends when a retake was awarded but had to retire through injury in the second half. Ewing's second goal against Belfast Celtic was lucky in that the visiting keeper, Haddock, "cleared" the ball against him and watched as the rebound ballooned into the net. The Celts gained revenge in the Irish Cup when we missed a penalty for the third consecutive match, McCourt (v. Cliftonville after King had gone off injured) and Sam Rea (v. Shelbourne) the earlier culprits. Against Bohemians, then nicknamed the Gypsies, at the Oval Glentoran adopted a one-back game after Lynas had been carried off with a leg injury. Such tactics forced the referee to constantly blow his whistle for offside but the visitors gained the last laugh with an 88th minute winner.

Ching Morrison returned for the Glens on 8th December against Distillery after spells with Glasgow Celtic and Burnley. Despite his setting up our lead taking goal and McMillen's penalty save we went down 1-3 in near darkness, handicapped this time with the loss of Stevenson to injury. A week later Glentoran were up in arms when Linfield cancelled our City Cup game at very short notice. The reason - the Blues were trying to see off Distillery in the Irish Cup at the sixth time of asking. (They did 2-1.) Our appeal for the points and financial compensation fell on deaf ears and the game was played off at the end of April in a blizzard!

After Fred Rea's own goal had given Belfast Celtic the City Cup points in the first game of 1907, despite a constant bombardment on the visitors' goal, the Glentoran supporters' frustration finally spilled over at the Oval against Cliftonville a week later. Several dubious decisions by the referee earned him and the Reds' players a torrent of verbal abuse, with the official being struck as he left the pitch at half-time. A numerous police presence provided protection in the second half but the matter did not end there. The Glentoran secretary complained to the Irish League regarding the daily newspapers' reports of the events while supporters threatened to "make it hot" for these journalists on future visits to the Oval. Thankfully the unsavoury incidents seemed to blow over, and normality was quickly resumed. Maybe it was just as well that Stevenson and Dunlop scored their own goals against Shelbourne away from home!

Silverware at last returned to the club as we qualified for the finals of both the remaining two competitions. Cliftonville Olympic must have been sick of the sight of Glentoran jerseys as a week after being hammered by us in the Shield they lost 1-2 to the Seconds. The Shield semi-final with Distillery developed into a mini-saga. Goalkeeper McMillen broke his collar bone in the first meeting and replacement Ching Morrison kept a clean sheet until a last minute scrimmaged equaliser. A big crowd saw us take a 2-0 lead after five minutes of the replay but again the Whites fought back. In the third match goals in the 30th and 43rd minutes from Ewing eventually saw us through but even then Distillery had two second half goals disallowed. A poor final finished in favour of Linfield, and they even afforded the luxury of Jones hitting the bar with his penalty.

Results 1906/07

Played 34. Won 10. Drew 9. Lost 15. Goals For 54. Against 54. % 42.6.
Honours: Charity Cup

CC*	25/08/06		Shelbourne	A	W	3	1	Ewing, Lynas, Crothers
IL	01/09/06		Linfield	H	L	0	2	-
IL	08/09/06		Distillery	A	L	2	3	Ewing, Lynas
IL	15/09/06		Bohemians	A	D	1	1	Fitzpatrick
IL	22/09/06		Derry Celtic	H	W	2	0	King (p), McDougall
IL	06/10/06		Belfast Celtic	H	W	3	0	Ewing 2, McDougall
IL	20/10/06		Cliftonville	A	L	1	2	Lynas
IL	27/10/06		Shelbourne	H	D	2	2	Lynas, Ewing
IL	10/11/06		Linfield	A	D	1	1	Fitzpatrick
IL	17/11/06		Distillery	H	D	1	1	Fitzpatrick
IL	01/12/06		Bohemians	H	L	1	2	S.Rea
IL	22/12/06		Derry Celtic	A	L	1	3	McCourt (p)
IL	25/12/06		Belfast Celtic	A	L	2	4	Watson og, King (p)
IL	12/01/07		Cliftonville	H	D	1	1	S.Rea
IL	09/02/07		Shelbourne	A	L	0	3	-
CC	29/09/06		Cliftonville	A	L	0	2	-
CC	08/12/06		Distillery	A	L	1	3	Andrews
CC	29/12/06		Shelbourne	H	W	2	1	Andrews, Morrison
CC	05/01/07		Belfast Celtic	H	L	0	1	-
CC	09/03/07		Cliftonville	H	L	2	3	Ewing, Andrews
CC	01/04/07		Linfield	H	W	3	1	King, Ewing, Andrews
CC	20/04/07		Belfast Celtic	A	L	1	3	Finlay (p)
CC	22/04/07		Shelbourne	A	L	1	3	Unknown
CC	Unknown		Distillery	H	D	0	0	-
CC	30/04/07		Linfield	A	D	1	1	Stevenson
IC	03/11/06	1	Belfast Celtic	A	L	1	3	Fitzpatrick
CAS	26/01/07	1	Cliftonville Olympic	H	W	10	0	Morrison, Andrews 4, Ewing 3, Reid, Fitzpatrick
CAS	02/03/07	SF	Distillery	Solt	D	1	1	Andrews
CAS	18/03/07	SFR	Distillery	CP	D	3	3	Fitzpatrick, S.Rea, King (p)
CAS	25/03/07	SFR2	Distillery	Solt	W	2	0	Ewing 2
CAS	30/03/07	F	Linfield	Solt	L	0	2	-
ChC	08/04/07	1	Belfast Celtic	GP	W	2	1	Rooney, S.Rea
ChC	13/04/07	SF	Cliftonville	GP	W	1	0	Ewing
ChC	27/04/07	F	Linfield	Solt	W	2	0	Willis og, Andrews

* = held over from 1905/6

Appearances and Goals

	App.	Goals		App.	Goals		App.	Goals
Stevenson	30	1	McCourt	15	1	Kirkwood	2	
Ewing	28	13	Wilton	15		Cochrane	2	
McDougall	28	2	Dunlop	10		Doherty	2	
Andrews	27	10	Rooney	10	1	O'Neill	1	
Reid	23	1	Benton	9		Kerr	1	
King R.	22	4	Finlay	9	1	Neeson	1	
Rea S.	22	4	Dooley	8		Unknown	22	1
Fitzpatrick	20	6	Crothers J.	5	1	Own Goals		2
McMillan	18		Lyner R.	5				
Lynas	18	4	Rea F.	3		TOTAL	374	54
Morrison	16	2	Cardwell	2				

Revenge came our way in the Charity Cup, after King had missed another penalty in the semi-final. The final itself was dictated by a strong gale with a Linfield defender slicing Andrews' shot into his own net. For the deciding goal Mehaffey, the Blues' keeper, half-parried Andrews' effort but the wind blew the ball up and over him and so we notched our third Charity Cup success.

Some minor representative honours were bestowed upon Glentoran players. Sam Rea and Morrison played in Ulster's 1-1 away draw with Leinster while Stevenson, Reid and Andrews featured in Belfast's 3-2 win over Derry in February's inter-city game at Celtic Park.

A traumatic season completed the first 25 years of our history.

1907/08

Promising start not fulfilled - Sam Rea's life ban – Billy Andrews capped

For the pre-season friendly with Belfast Celtic Glentoran lined-up as follows: McMillan, King, F.Rea, Stevenson, S.Rea, Reid, Russell, Mitchell, Andrews, Ewing (Capt), McDougall. In the drawn game the Scot, "Do" Mitchell, was carried off. The match was combined with racing - at half-time there was the four mile flat run to decide the champion of Ulster while at the conclusion a 25 mile motor cycle race went round the Oval pitch.

Our league campaign started well and we found ourselves leaders at the end of September. No-one, with the possible exception of Billy Andrews, stood out as a star and it was remarked that the Glens team were "a real bunch of triers." Our opening City Cup tie gave us revenge over Celtic, this time without the rough play witnessed in the league meeting. Visiting keeper Haddock saved another Condy King penalty. Andrews early season form was rewarded when he played and scored against the English League team in a 3-6 defeat on 12th October.

After overcoming Shelbourne our season fell away dramatically. Distillery were one short for the league game on 26th October as their centre-forward failed to turn up. A frantic search of the crowd for eligible players was hastily and fruitlessly undertaken by embarrassed Whites' officials. Despite losing this game we still held a one point lead but by 25th December Linfield had shot five points clear of Cliftonville while we had slumped to fourth place. Insult was added to injury for the fans when they got drenched on Christmas Day as there was as yet no covered accommodation at the Oval. The Blues duly beat the Reds 3-1 to take the championship before they had even played us. Then two purposeful displays against Linfield and a handsome win over the Gypsies gave us a runners-up play-off versus Cliftonville.

Our Irish Cup exit came during the miserable run. Dick Hooper was Bohemians' hat-trick hero in the replay as Andrews watched Sherry save his penalty. The Bohs defeated Shelbourne in the all-Dublin final.

The club was in disgrace following a rowdy City Cup tie at Grosvenor Park on 7th December. In the 86th minute the referee sent a Glentoran player off and was immediately surrounded, jostled and eventually struck by a Glens player. The matter was referred to both the City Cup and the Protest and Appeals Committees with the latter deciding to suspend Sam Rea sine die for his part in the fracas. This seemed to spur on the team as performances dramatically improved. Many Glenmen had the "game of their lives" when Linfield were hammered in January and with three games to go in the City Cup we held a five point lead over the Blues. Over 8,000 were at Windsor on Easter Monday morning for the vital encounter and when Andrews gave us the lead we threatened to carry all before us. However in a furious contest Linfield fought back to equalise and then claimed a winner when the scorer Mercer looked yards off-side. We had one last chance in the final game of the season needing a win to lift the City Cup. Twice we took the lead but two goals from Belfast Celtic in the last 15 minutes sent the trophy to Windsor Park.

The Glens made no progress in either the Shield or the Charity Cup. Two splendid displays from Davies in the Cliftonville goal killed our aspirations in the former tournament. Mitchell's penalty miss against the Blues in the Charity competition proved crucial especially when they scored the winner in the 85th minute.

Our Easter Tuesday defeat against Preston was disappointing in view of Distillery's 0-0 draw with the Lancashire side 24 hours earlier.

Glentoran IIs missed out on honours when they lost to Glenavon in the Intermediate Cup final after a 2-2 draw at Grosvenor Park.

70

Andrews gained his first full International cap in Ireland's 0-5 defeat by Scotland at Dalymount Park in March. He was to pick up two more caps following his transfer to Grimsby Town in 1912/3.

Results 1907/08

Played 29. Won 13. Drew 5. Lost 11. Goals For 53. Against 45. % 53.4

IL	07/09/07		Bohemians	A	W	3	1	Andrews, Mitchell (p), McDougall
IL	14/09/07		Cliftonville	H	W	2	0	Caton, McDougall
IL	21/09/07		Derry Celtic	H	W	4	3	Ewing, Mitchell, Unknown 2
IL	28/09/07		Belfast Celtic	A	L	1	2	Andrews
IL	19/10/07		Shelbourne	H	W	3	2	McDougall, Reid 2
IL	26/10/07		Distillery	A	L	1	3	Mitchell
IL	23/11/07		Distillery	H	D	1	1	Andrews (p)
IL	30/11/07		Cliftonville	A	D	1	1	Andrews
IL	21/12/07		Derry Celtic	A	L	1	2	Garrett
IL	25/12/07		Belfast Celtic	H	L	0	2	-
IL	28/12/07		Shelbourne	A	W	2	1	Ewing, Waugh
IL	18/01/08		Linfield	A	W	3	2	Mitchell, Reid, Andrews
IL	08/02/08		Linfield	H	D	2	2	McDougall, King
IL	07/03/08		Bohemians	H	W	3	1	Mitchell 2, McDougall
CC	05/10/07		Belfast Celtic	H	W	1	0	Morrison
CC	07/12/07		Distillery	A	L	0	1	-
CC	14/12/07		Cliftonville	H	W	2	1	Reid, Mitchell
CC	04/01/08		Linfield	H	W	5	0	Ewing, Waugh, Andrews 2, Mitchell
CC	22/02/08		Shelbourne	A	W	3	1	Garrett, Andrews 2
CC	14/03/08		Shelbourne	H	W	3	0	McDougall 2, Ewing
CC	04/04/08		Distillery	H	W	2	1	Ewing, Waugh
CC	18/04/08		Cliftonville	A	L	1	2	Garrett
CC	20/04/08		Linfield	A	L	1	2	Andrews
CC	09/05/08		Belfast Celtic	A	L	2	3	Waugh, Andrews
IC	02/11/07	2	Bohemians	H	D	2	2	Morrison, Andrews (p)
IC	09/11/07	2R	Bohemians	A	L	1	4	Andrews
CAS	25/01/08	1	Cliftonville	H	D	1	1	Mitchell
CAS	01/02/08	SF	Cliftonville	A	L	1	2	Mitchell
ChC	11/04/08	SF	Linfield	Solt	L	1	2	Waugh
F	30/08/08		Belfast Celtic	H	D	1	1	Reid
F	21/04/08		Preston North End	H	L	1	4	Unknown

Appearances and Goals

	App.	Goals		App.	Goals		App.	Goals
Stevenson	27		Whitten	15		Lyner R.	3	
McDougall	27	7	Waugh	15	5	Caton	2	1
Mitchell	27	10	McMillan	13		Gardiner	1	
King R.	26	1	Garrett	11	3	McKnight	1	
Reid	26	4	Morrison	10	2	Ritchie	1	
Andrews	26	13	Rea S.	5		King M.	1	
Rea F.	25		Bennett	4		Unknown	11	2
Ewing	19	5	McMaster G.	4				
Waddell	16		Brown	3		TOTAL	319	53

1908/09

The Seconds win the County Antrim Shield and the Steel and Sons Cup

This was the season when the Seconds won more senior trophies than the 1st XI! The Seconds had begun their campaign inauspiciously by losing 2-6 to Ards in an August friendly. However they battled through to the Christmas afternoon Steel and Sons Cup final against Larne. A "massive" crowd, paying receipts of £400, saw our reserves win 3-2. Now it was time to tackle senior opposition in the County Antrim Shield. The Seconds travelled to meet Belfast Celtic and trailed 1-2 at the interval, the goal coming from Ritchie. James McKnight twice equalised to leave it 3-3, then further goals from John McKnight and Roly Lyner secured a remarkable win. The draw for the semi-final read: "Glentoran versus Glentoran II at Grosvenor Park." This match came off on the 10th March 1909 when the teams lined out: 1st XI - Kane, Brown, Macartney, F.Rea, Lawrie, Davidson, McDougall, Mitchell, Munro, Black, Carrick. 2nd XI: Harrison, R.Bennett, S.Bennett, Waddell, Ritchie, Lewis, R.Lyner, Lillie, James McKnight, Gillespie, John McKnight.

James McKnight scored the only goal and the Seconds' backs denied the seniors' frantic attempts to get level. Moreover, in the dying minutes, it took many fine saves from Kane to

Glentoran Seconds and their mascot Trixie display the Intermediate Cup, County Antrim Shield and Steel and Sons Cup. Back Row: Kelly, S.Bennett, J.Harrison, R.Bennett, J.Totten Middle Row: J.Magowan (Secretary), G.Kearney (Trainer), D.Foster, A.Waddell, P.Jamison, T.Lewis, J.Gillespie, F.Dawson Front Row: R.Lyner, G.Lillie, James McKnight, S.Ritchie, John McKnight.

keep it to 0-1. Before the Shield final the Seconds had the distraction of the Intermediate Cup final to play off! The first game with Cliftonville Olympic on St. Patrick's Day finished 1-1, but five days later the Seconds triumphed 1-0 in the replay. This set them up for the following week's Shield final against Cliftonville's senior side. About 6,000 were at Celtic Park on 27th March when the Seconds' only change from their semi-final line-up was Jamison for Waddell. The Reds were stunned by the fast play of the Seconds and fell 0-3, with James McKnight claiming a hat-trick to give the Seconds their only ever senior trophy. One Glentoran official brought his Pomeranian dog along to the final. He claimed that the Seconds had never lost while his pet mascot was watching them!

Unfortunately the 1st XI could not match these successes. Despite losing Andrews and Reid, there were six experienced Scots in the squad plus Alec Macartney at left-back and international winger Andy Hunter from Distillery. The league campaign kicked-off at a Solitude ground improved by additional terraced banking. The Sirocco band further entertained spectators but generally the drawn game was "colourless". Two late goals gave us a win in another poor game versus Distillery but the following week we staged a grand comeback against Bohemians after their international army player, Corporal Webb, had given the Dubliners a 2-0 lead. One of Mitchell's goals was direct from a corner but otherwise the visiting keeper Hehir had an excellent game.

The second half at Windsor Park was a debacle after we had held an interval lead. Darling scored a penalty for the Blues in the 46th minute and our defence subsequently caved in while Davidson struck his penalty over the bar at the other end. However good wins over the two Celtics kept us in second place to Linfield at the end of October.

Shelbourne caught us cold in Dublin with two early strikes in a game where we just could not get moving. Roughness crept in during the second half and afterwards the Glentoran committee were advised to tell the players to "cool it". We returned to playing good football and recorded three wins in cold, windy, miserable weather and sodden, slippery pitches. The big Christmas morning clash with the Blues finished inconclusively after we had been 2-1 ahead at half-time. This put Linfield three points ahead with only three games left but a form slump at Windsor left us only needing to beat Bohemians in Dublin to force a test match for the championship. It was not to be however as after we had taken the lead against the breeze the Gypsies piled on the pressure to move 3-1 ahead at the break. The task became hopeless as Rea and McDougall had to retire injured during the second half and Bohemians won comfortably.

Dalymount Park was also to be the Glens' Irish Cup graveyard. After we overcame Derry Celtic in dank weather virtually no-one attended the second round tie with Belfast Celtic. The game was played in a snowstorm and the subsequent state of the pitch reduced it to a travesty. Not surprisingly the only goals came from an early penalty and an own goal following a mis-kick by Smith. McDougall's brilliant shot brightened up our replay success after early and lively Celtic attacks. For the semi-final game special trains were laid on for northern supporters to make the trip to the Metropolis. The game was locked at 0-0 until 15 minutes from time when the Bohs went ahead. Waddell then hit the bar but in 77 minutes the home side went 2-0 up and we could only manage a consolation penalty. Cliftonville won the all-amateur final 2-1.

It was the Reds who dismissed us from the Charity Cup after a marathon semi-final. Rea's sending off hampered us in the deciding game. We pushed Shelbourne all the way in the City Cup but failed to prevent them becoming the first club to take the cup out of Belfast.

Our opening City Cup game was marred by hooliganism. While leading 1-0 Munro claimed a second but the Celtic keeper appeared to scoop out his shot before it crossed the line. The referee consulted the Glentoran linesman and gave a goal. The roughs immediately invaded the pitch with the officials and players heading for the pavilion. Eventually the game was resumed and Celtic too scored a doubtful goal - only being awarded after the referee sought confirmation from the Celtic linesman. This game sparked off calls for "neutral" linesmen as traditionally each club would supply a touchjudge. Indeed the same day Cliftonville had refused to turn out against Linfield as six of their players were under suspension due to dissension over linesmen's decisions.

Worse was to follow for the Reds and Celtic when on the 22nd November these clubs were fined and suspended from football by the Protest and Appeals committee for rough play in an April 1908 Charity Cup game. However after both clubs wrote to the IFA the original decision was cancelled.

Meanwhile the Glens were running into trouble with referees over the state of the Oval pitch. For example at half-time in the Linfield match on 5th December the Scottish referee announced he was abandoning the game. Glentoran officials persuaded him to carry on despite the "pods and troughs." The earlier City Cup tie at Solitude had been declared a 70 minute match by arrangement due to "the drowned pitch."

McDougall and Mitchell gained Irish League representative honours in October against the English League. The same day King and Waddell were in Belfast's team beaten 0-1 in Derry. Alec Macartney appeared for the full Ireland team against all three home nations adding to twelve caps won earlier with Ulster, Linfield, Everton and Belfast Celtic. Macartney played in the inter-pro for Ulster v. Leinster. (Due to lack of interest in the provincial series these games were abandoned after 1909.) The left-back also gained his only inter-league cap against the Scottish League in February.

Results 1908/09

Played 34. Won 15. Drew 11. Lost 8. Goals For 51. Against 43. % 60.3

IL	05/09/08		Cliftonville	A	D	1	1	Smyth
IL	12/09/08		Distillery	H	W	2	1	Smyth, McKnight
IL	19/09/08		Bohemians	H	W	4	2	McDougall, Munro, Mitchell 2
IL	26/09/08		Linfield	A	L	1	4	McDougall
IL	03/10/08		Derry Celtic	A	W	1	0	Davidson
IL	24/10/08		Belfast Celtic	H	W	6	0	Mitchell 2, Carrick 2, McDougall, Munro
IL	07/11/08		Shelbourne	A	L	0	2	-
IL	14/11/08		Cliftonville	H	W	4	1	McKnight 2, Munro, Carrick
IL	28/11/08		Distillery	A	W	1	0	McKnight
IL	25/12/08		Linfield	H	D	2	2	Carrick, Davidson
IL	26/12/08		Derry Celtic	H	W	3	1	Munro 2, Davidson
IL	02/01/09		Shelbourne	H	W	2	1	Davidson 2
IL	13/02/09		Belfast Celtic	A	D	1	1	Munro
IL	13/03/09		Bohemians	A	L	1	6	Carrick
CC	17/10/08		Belfast Celtic	A	D	3	3	Munro 2, Davidson
CC	31/10/08		Distillery	A	D	1	1	Bennett
CC	21/11/08		Cliftonville	A	D	1	1	McDougall
CC	05/12/08		Linfield	H	W	2	0	Carrick, McKnight
CC	09/01/09		Belfast Celtic	H	W	2	1	Munro 2
CC	Unknown		Distillery	H	W	1	0	Unknown
CC	20/03/09		Shelbourne	A	L	0	3	-
CC	12/04/09		Linfield	A	W	2	1	Mitchell, Munro
CC	24/04/09		Shelbourne	H	L	0	3	-
CC	26/04/09		Cliftonville	H	D	1	1	Unknown
IC	12/12/08	1	Derry Celtic	H	D	1	1	Wattie
IC	19/12/08	1R	Derry Celtic	A	W	1	0	McKnight
IC	16/01/09	2	Belfast Celtic	H	D	1	1	McDougall (p)
IC	23/01/09	2R	Belfast Celtic	A	W	2	0	Carrick, McDougall
IC	06/02/09	SF	Bohemians	A	L	1	2	McDougall (p)
CAS	30/01/09	1	Linfield	A	W	2	0	Mitchell, Wattie
CAS	10/03/09	SF	Glentoran II	GP	L	0	1	-
ChC	17/04/09	SF	Cliftonville	GP	D	0	0	aet
ChC	21/04/09	SFR	Cliftonville	GP	D	1	1	Lyner
ChC	28/04/09	SFR2	Cliftonville	GP	L	0	1	-
F	29/08/08		Belfast Celtic	A	D	0	0	-

Appearances and Goals

	App.	Goals		App.	Goals		App.	Goals
Lawrie	31		Wattie	14	2	Harrison	1	
Munro	30	11	McKnight, James	10	6	Watson	1	
Rea F.	29		King R.	8		James	1	
Carrick	28	7	Lyner R.	8	1	Makepeace	1	
Kane	27		Bennett	5	1	Gillespie	1	
Mitchell	26	6	Brown	4		Fullerton	1	
McDougall	25	7	Black	4		Lewis	1	
Macartney	23		Whitten	4		Lillie	1	
Smyth	23	2	Hunter	3		Unknown	22	2
Davidson	20	6	Ritchie	3		TOTAL	374	51
Waddell	16		Mears	3				

1909/10

*A game played on two days - Death of Monarch thwarts cup hopes –
Oval Carnival*

After the Oval had spent a summer hosting major cycling events Glentoran and football returned in September. The Glens appeared to have abandoned their policy of "foreign" players. Out of the previously large Scottish contingent only left winger Davy McDougall and centre-half R.Lawrie remained. Many of the previous season's successful 2nd XI were given a chance in the first team.

In terms of participating senior clubs Irish soccer had remained unchanged for the past six years and in 1909 the league committee experimented with a new format. It was decided to play off half the league fixtures then switch to the first half of the City Cup games. The league would subsequently resume with the City Cup competition completed in March or April. The Irish Cup was not due to begin until the first Saturday in February.

GALLAHER'S CIGARETTES.

R. LAWRIE,
GLENTORAN, 1909-10.

Glentoran were one of a series of Irish clubs featured in this cigarette card set.

Our league campaign was unsuccessful and we finished joint bottom with Shelbourne and Bohemians on 11 points with all three clubs having to apply for re-election. Cliftonville emerged as the early league leaders and we visited Solitude in mid-October. The game was played in heavy non-stop rain until it was abandoned after 55 minutes, as the pitch was an utter quagmire. McAuley had scored the only goal for the Reds via a twice taken penalty. The league committee met and ruled that the remaining 35 minutes would be played out on Monday 8th November with the original line-ups. This duly happened and despite forcing a number of corners we were unable to equalise.

Sam Napier came into the Glens' team in December and he celebrated by scoring four in the first half of a 6-1 drubbing of Bohemians. J.Kane also saved a penalty in this match. After holding a 2-1 interval lead at Derry goals came with "bewildering rapidity" in the second half, mostly in the home side's favour! Despite this defeat a huge crowd attended the Oval for the Christmas morning visit of Linfield. They witnessed a bombardment on the Blues' goal and after securing victory our half-backs and forwards ran rings around the Windsor men. It was not so against Celtic, our only goal coming when Leslie Murphy punched McDougall's corner into his own net. Murphy made amends, however, when he saved a second-half penalty from the same player. Our last league match meant much more to league leaders Cliftonville than to us. They required a point for the title but made sure with a persistent performance on a frost-bound pitch. Another 88 years would pass before they repeated this feat.

Glentoran's City Cup performances showed a marked improvement on the league. After losing the first two fixtures we put together an eight match unbeaten run to finish joint second with Cliftonville. The play-off for the gold medals on 7th May 1910 was postponed due to the sudden death of King Edward VII the previous day. George V was sworn in as the new monarch but no details of any re-arranged test match have been traced.

The initial City Cup meeting with Cliftonville involved some very rough play. There were calls upon various committees to stamp this behaviour out by admonishing lengthy suspensions as the Northern Whig surmised that, "Angels at football matches are as rare as snowballs in Hades." James McKnight ran into form, dribbling half the length of the pitch to finish with a scorching shot for his second goal against Belfast Celtic in November. The same day Ireland drew 4-4 with England in an Amateur international and this result was put into context when the English Amateurs trounced their French counterparts 20-0 at Ipswich a few months later! Back to Glentoran and despite the goals of Napier and James McKnight many supporters felt that their styles of play were not compatible in the same eleven.

We reached the final of the Shield overcoming Steel and Sons Cup finalists Larne on the way. A very workmanlike display saw off Cliftonville in the semi-final and it looked at one stage as if we would win the Shield by default. The reason - Belfast Celtic (who had beaten Linfield 3-2 in the other semi) had their ground closed down by the IFA following numerous pitch invasions. The Celtic directors, already agitated by long suspensions on

---

Results 1909/10

Played 32. Won 12. Drew 6. Lost 14 Goals For 55. Against 50. % 46.9

IL*	20/08/09	RUTM	Cliftonville	GP	L	2	3	Unknown
IL	04/09/09		Distillery	H	L	1	2	McDougall
IL	11/09/09		Bohemians	A	L	1	2	McKnight
IL	18/09/09		Derry Celtic	H	W	1	0	McDougall (p)
IL	25/09/09		Linfield	A	L	1	2	McKnight
IL	02/10/09		Belfast Celtic	A	L	0	2	-
IL	16/10/09		Shelbourne	H	W	2	0	Lyner, McKnight
IL	23/10/09		Cliftonville	A	L	0	1	- Last 35 minutes played 8/11/1909
IL	04/12/09		Distillery	A	W	1	0	Munro
IL	11/12/09		Bohemians	H	W	6	1	Napier 4, McDougall (p), Lewis
IL	18/12/09		Derry Celtic	A	L	4	5	Munro 3, Napier
IL	25/12/09		Linfield	H	W	4	0	Munro, McDougall (p), Napier, Hannah og
IL	08/01/10		Belfast Celtic	H	L	1	4	Murphy og
IL	15/01/10		Shelbourne	A	D	0	0	-
IL	22/01/10		Cliftonville	H	L	1	4	McKee og
CC	30/10/09		Cliftonville	A	L	1	2	McDougall (p)
CC	06/11/09		Linfield	A	L	1	2	McKnight
CC	13/11/09		Distillery	H	W	4	1	Lawrie, McKnight 2, McDougall
CC	20/11/09		Belfast Celtic	H	W	3	1	McKnight 2, McDougall
CC	27/11/09		Shelbourne	A	W	1	0	McKnight
CC	12/03/10		Cliftonville	H	D	1	1	Lyner
CC	28/03/10		Linfield	H	D	1	1	Munro
CC	09/04/10		Distillery	A	D	1	1	Napier
CC	16/04/10		Belfast Celtic	A	D	2	2	McKnight, Napier
CC	23/04/10		Shelbourne	H	W	3	0	Lyner, Lawrie, McKnight
CAS	29/01/10	1	Larne	H	W	4	1	McKnight 2, Munro, Lawrie
CAS	26/02/10	SF	Cliftonville	CP	W	3	1	Munro, Napier, Rea (p)
CAS	02/04/10	F	Belfast Celtic	Solt	L	1	3	Napier
IC	05/02/10	1	Linfield	A	D	2	2	McKnight 2
IC	09/02/10	1R	Linfield	H	W	2	1	Lawrie, McKnight Bye in Round 2
IC	05/03/10	SF	Distillery	WP	L	0	4	-
ChC	13/04/10	1	Distillery	A	L	0	1	-
F	27/12/09		Distillery	H	W	2	0	Napier, Munro Davy McDougall Benefit

* = held over from 1907/8

Team Group 1909/10 Back Row: J.McCarey, A.Waddell, J.Flannigan, F.Rea, J.Kane, R.Bennett, S.Ritchie Front Row: T.D.Reid, R.Lyner, R.Lawrie, J.McKnight, T.Lewis, D.McDougall, F.Dawson .

some of their players, believed this punishment to be harsh in relation to other clubs and decided to abandon football. However, on hearing of this decision, the IFA Council rescinded a suspension on one of their players and Celtic played on. The final itself was unremarkable, Celtic lifting the trophy in the first meeting of the two clubs in Shield competition.

Inclement weather kept the attendance down to 5,000 for our Irish Cup tie versus Linfield at Windsor Park. We built up a 2-0 lead helped by a first half gale, but goals by the Blues in the 84th and 90th minutes forced a replay. That time it was the Glens' turn to come from behind and win. However Distillery proved much superior in the semi-final and went on to capture the Cup with a 1-0 Oval win over Cliftonville.

The Whites had provided the opposition in Davy McDougall's benefit match in December. The Glens, assisted by Linfield's inside-left Dodds and Belfast Celtic's left-back Paddy McCann, won 2-0. But it was hardly a full Whites team who lost as in the morning Distillery had beaten Aberdeen 7-2 in a friendly at Grosvenor Park.

Fred Rea brought the only representative honour to the club playing left-back in the Irish League team humbled 8-1 at Oldham by the English League in October. Sam Napier, though, appeared for a United Belfast team defeated 4-0 by Glasgow Celtic in a money raising effort for the Lough Neagh fishermen's fund.

As the soccer season drew to a close plans were well in hand for the Glentoran Carnival at the Oval in June. One interesting advert in the carnival programme mentioned dental treatment. A "painless" tooth extraction would cost 1/-, while for the more masochistic a normal one could be had for 9d.

Appearances and Goals

	App.	Goals		App.	Goals		App.	Goals
Kane	30		McKnight, James	22	16	Brown	1	
Lawrie	30	4	Munro	19	8	Scraggs	1	
Lyner R.	30	3	Napier	15	10	Lillie	1	
Bennett	29		Smyth	5		Holmes	1	
Ritchie	27		Jamieson	4		Wilson	1	
Lewis	27	1	Flanaghan	4		Unknown	22	2
McDougall	26	7	Cooper	4		Own Goals		3
Waddell	25		Watters	3		TOTAL	322	55
Rea F.	23	1	McKnight, John	2				

1910/11

A hat-trick of trophies - Irish Cup controversy – New programme

Glentoran came very close to completing a clean sweep of all five trophies on offer. Only a play-off defeat against Linfield for the league and a protest from Bohemians in the elusive Irish Cup foiled our ambitions. T.Lewis' name had been omitted from the team when secretary A.McRoberts submitted the list of registered players for the cup tie. He later added the name by telegram but Bohemians refused to accept this and appealed. Many felt it an act of "sour grapes" as Hunter's fine shot had beaten them and two seasons earlier the Glens had unsuccessfully protested about the inclusion of a Cheshire Regiment player, Webb, in Bohemians cup semi-final line-up. Glentoran were removed from the competition and the Dubliners allowed to progress.

With the return of former players Billy Andrews and J.Reid Glentoran had a strong outfield side and were further bolstered by the arrival of Scottish international goalkeeper, Dr. Leslie H. Skene. Skene, who came to Belfast to study at Queen's University, had played for Scotland against Wales in 1904.

In his debut against Belfast Celtic on 3rd September Skene was invincible. The team rattled off five wins to earn the description of "the bounding boys of Ballymacarrett." The 12,000 crowd against Linfield produced record gate receipts of £346. At this game the club launched a new magazine named the "Glentoran Official Observer", a forerunner to the match programme concept. We then faced two long difficult away trips in mid-October. McKnight gave us a second minute lead against Shelbourne at Sandymount but we fell away and had Skene to thank for a draw. Shels' Kelly broke his leg in an accidental clash. Worse was to follow at Celtic Park, Derry when the home side went 2-0 up in seven minutes. Andy Hunter was then sent off before the interval and after we pulled one back Keeley had an effort disallowed. Derry sealed their victory near the end.

Dr. Leslie Skene.

More trouble accompanied the Oval game with Belfast Celtic. The Celts' winning goal came only after confirmation from a linesman, who was then physically assaulted by members of the crowd.

After overcoming Cliftonville in drenching rain we closed the deficit on Linfield to a single point as the Blues were held 2-2 by Derry Celtic. This set up a potential league decider at Windsor but after we had led 2-1 and missed a penalty the Blues equalised with five minutes to go. We annihilated our last two opponents while Linfield were held 1-1 by Belfast Celtic, leaving themselves level with us on 22 points.

Entering the test match as slight favourites we led 2-1 at half-time in front of 10,000. Our second goal came when Napier had a fierce shot initially saved by Hanna. The force of the shot, however, caused the keeper to lose his balance and while he was trying to regain it

Hunter ran in and bundled both him and the ball into the net! Linfield gained the upper hand after the interval, scoring the decisive goal to win the Gibson Cup with ten minutes remaining.

Results 1910/11

Played 31. Won 24. Drew 4. Lost 3. For 82. Against 27. % 83.9.
Honours: City Cup, County Antrim Shield, Charity Cup

IL	03/09/10		Belfast Celtic	A	W	3	1	McKnight 2, Andrews
IL	10/09/10		Bohemians	H	W	2	0	Ritchie, McKnight
IL	17/09/10		Cliftonville	A	W	4	1	Andrews 3, Napier
IL	24/09/10		Linfield	H	W	3	0	Napier (p), Hunter, Andrews
IL	01/10/10		Distillery	H	W	2	1	Hunter, Napier (p)
IL	15/10/10		Shelbourne	A	D	1	1	McKnight
IL	22/10/10		Derry Celtic	A	L	1	3	McKnight
IL	29/10/10		Belfast Celtic	H	L	1	2	Lyner
IL	05/11/10		Bohemians	A	W	1	0	Gough
IL	12/11/10		Cliftonville	H	W	4	0	Andrews 2, Keeley 2
IL	26/11/10		Linfield	A	D	2	2	Napier, Mitchell
IL	03/12/10		Distillery	A	W	2	1	McKnight, Napier (p)
IL	10/12/10		Shelbourne	H	W	4	0	Napier 2, Hunter, Mitchell
IL	17/12/10		Derry Celtic	H	W	9	0	Mitchell, Napier 3, Reid, Hunter 3, Lyner
IL	23/01/11	TM	Linfield	Solt	L	2	3	McKnight, "A Charge"
CC	24/12/10		Cliftonville	A	W	1	0	Napier
CC	26/12/10		Linfield	H	W	4	1	McKnight 2, Lyner, Napier
CC	31/12/10		Belfast Celtic	A	D	1	1	Hunter
CC	07/01/11		Shelbourne	H	W	3	1	Napier, Andrews, McKnight
CC	14/01/11		Distillery	H	W	4	2	Lyner, Hunter, McKnight, Mitchell
CC	21/01/11		Cliftonville	H	W	1	0	Napier (p)
CC	17/03/11		Shelbourne	A	W	3	1	Napier 3
CC	01/04/11		Linfield	A	D	1	1	Mitchell
CC	15/04/11		Belfast Celtic	H	W	4	0	Mitchell, Hunter 2, Reid
CC	22/04/11		Distillery	A	W	2	1	Napier, McKnight
IC	04/02/11	1	Bohemians	A	W	1	0	Hunter Eliminated for playing an unregistered player
CAS	25/02/11	1	Linfield	A	W	3	1	McKnight, Napier 2
CAS	11/03/11	SF	Belfast Celtic	WP	W	1	0	McKnight
CAS	08/04/11	F	Cliftonville	CP	W	2	0	Hunter 2
ChC	29/04/11	SF	Cliftonville	GP	W	6	1	McKnight 2, Mitchell 2, Napier (p), Hunter
ChC	13/05/11	F	Belfast Celtic	Solt	W	4	2	Mitchell 2, Napier 2
F	20/08/10		Linfield	A	D	1	1	Gough In aid of orphans of the drowned Donaldson brothers
F	27/08/10		Derry Celtic	H	W	4	1	McKnight 3, Mitchell
F	14/12/10		Queen's University	H	W	6	2	Napier 4, Weir 2
F	04/03/11		Belfast Celtic	H	W	5	2	McKnight 2, Napier, Mitchell, Ritchie
F	21/03/11		Fulham	A	L	0	2	-
F	17/04/11		Linfield	A	W	1	0	Napier Challenge for Gold Medals
F	18/04/11		St. Mirren	H	W	3	1	Napier, Mitchell, Unknown
F	06/05/11		Shelbourne	A	W	6	1	Napier 2, McKnight 2, Hunter, Mitchell (p) – In aid of local school building fund

The City Cup proved to be something of a walkover, as we cruised through the ten match series unbeaten, finishing seven points ahead of runners-up Belfast Celtic. Paddy McCann, signed from Celtic, made his debut in the opening fixture against Cliftonville. Bumper holiday crowds of 12,000 and 8,000 watched us pick up three points from the two big games and eventually the City Cup was brought to the Oval for the first time in twelve years after we outplayed Belfast Celtic in the return game.

We quickly gained revenge on the Blues for the league play-off defeat by knocking them out of the County Antrim Shield. However our Seconds also fell at this hurdle, beaten 1-0 by Cliftonville. The Seconds had captured the Steel and Sons Cup again beating KOSB 2-1 after a Boxing Day 1-1 draw at Grosvenor Park. Their winning line-up read: Gibb, McAlpine, Ferguson, Smyth, Scraggs, Ferritt, Thompson, Gough, Beggs, Stitt, Waugh. Note two names among the half-backs.

Skene made many remarkable saves in the Shield semi-final against Celtic. When asked his opinion on standards within the Irish League he pointed out two problems. The game in Ireland suffered from a lack of training time plus teams had virtually no opportunity to study the methods of the other British leagues. The Glens had just that chance when they travelled to London to meet Fulham. A "pleasant" game was marred by an injury to Skene himself which kept him out for two weeks. He returned for the Shield final but was a spectator as his opposite number McKee battled to keep the score down to two.

The goals rained in during the Charity competition as we lifted our third trophy of the season. Also many friendlies were played with our best result the win against St.Mirren. Their keeper Duncan had to temporarily retire when he collided with an upright in trying to save our second goal. Queen's University began their first ever association football team but did not help their cause by turning up short against us and also missing a penalty. (Skene maintained his neutrality by refereeing this match.)

The first friendly against Linfield in August was in aid of the orphans of the Donaldson brothers, who had drowned in the River Lagan on 3rd July 1910. We won the gold medals at stake on 17th April and then visited Dublin to play Shelbourne in a game for a local school building fund.

A summary of the season on 8th May said Glentoran had played the best football during the past seven months and all players had re-signed for 1911/2.

Paddy McCann gained his fifth and sixth international caps versus England and Scotland while there were many Inter-League honours for Glentoran players. Two, four and five Glenmen were in the teams against the English, Scottish and Southern Leagues respectively. Andrews played in all three, Napier and Hunter in two each.

Appearances and Goals

	App.	Goals		App.	Goals		App.	Goals
Napier	31	23	Mitchell	25	10	Scraggs	2	
Watters	30		Reid	23	2	Ferritt	2	
Skene L.	29		McCann	16		Norton	1	
McKnight, James	29	16	Lewis	15		McAlpine	1	
Andrews	28	8	Rea F.	13		Gray	1	
Lyner R.	27	4	Keeley	9	2	Munro	1	
Hunter	27	14	Gough	3	1	"Charge"		1
Ritchie	26	1	Gibb	2		TOTAL	341	82

1911/12

The Gibson Cup is captured – Paddy McCann loses his cool - IFA Split

Glentoran went one better in 1911/2, winning the Irish League for the fourth time and retaining the City Cup. Our attempts to add the other trophies were frustrated by Belfast Celtic and a split between the IFA and the league clubs in February 1912.

Bohemians had resigned from the senior league and were replaced by Glenavon. Before our opening fixture with Cliftonville Sam Napier was presented with a special gold medal for finishing top scorer for the club in 1910/1. He soon resumed scoring form with a hat-trick as we raced into a 7-0 half-time lead. We were unable to offset the absence of Skene and Ritchie against Linfield in the third league game despite taking the lead. The "Loyalty to Britain" demonstration affected the gate against Belfast Celtic on 23rd September when the Celts gained a point courtesy of a last minute equaliser.

Belfast's Lady Mayoress, Mrs. McMordie, officially opened our new grandstand before the game against Shelbourne in October. Do Mitchell, sent off in a pre-season friendly against Distillery, found his shooting boots again in this match and also against Glenavon. The newcomers had threatened to shock us in our initial encounter, taking a 2-1 interval lead. Despite this win we still trailed Distillery by a point at the league's half-way stage, sharing second spot with Belfast Celtic.

Three close vital wins, including one over the Whites, followed to leave ourselves and Celtic joint top with four games remaining. Unfortunately the big clash between the two clubs on 18th November was postponed due to the England-Ireland Amateur international. Four Celtic players plus our own Paddy McCann were in the Irish team which went down 0-2. After defeating Derry Celtic in a scrambling match our trip to Shelbourne was also postponed as their ground was under suspension. The decisive result came on Monday 4th December when a workmanlike performance saw off Belfast Celtic's challenge. The league was wrapped up the following Saturday at Lurgan and in the final fixture we even afforded the luxury of giving Shelbourne a two goal start. Throughout the championship the star players were Hunter, Mitchell, Napier and McKnight (who was to be transferred to Preston North End in March) while both our keepers, Skene and Gibb, turned in excellent displays.

Full-back McCann lost his cool in the opening City Cup fixture against his old club Belfast Celtic. Having received a lot of verbal abuse from a spectator, he ran off the pitch, up the bank into the crowd, grabbed his heckler and handed him to a policeman to eject from the ground! The goals flowed over Christmas with Andy Hunter's two against Glenavon involving fine dribbling runs.

An unusual story appeared in the News Letter on 27th December under the headline of "Footballers in a Fix". Glentoran II travelled to play Limavady for a friendly on Boxing Day. In error the Seconds' playing baggage was taken off the train at Cookstown and forwarded to Derry. There appeared to be no way of getting it back until a Mr. Joe Sherrard placed his motor car at the disposal of the Limavady club. A volunteer set off for Coleraine where the baggage had ended up and the teams were able to start the game one hour late. The pitch at Roepark was virtually flooded and Glentoran II went on to win "a ludicrous match" by 8-4.

Over 14,000 attended the Oval on 13th January to see Mitchell head in Hunter's corner and defeat the Blues. Next Linfield beat Distillery 2-0 and after we dropped a point at Lonemoor Road (Derry) only two points separated ourselves, the Blues, Whites and Cliftonville at the top of the table.

Attention then turned to a badly organised Irish Cup. For some reason five first round ties were played with the result that there would be only one game in Round 2 with the three other qualifiers receiving byes to the semi-final! As luck would have it we had to face

Derry Celtic after James McKnight's hat-trick had seen off the dangerous Distillery. With only five minutes to go, and the game sewn up in the Glens' favour, Derry player Duddy kicked out viciously at Lyner. Duddy was promptly ordered off as the crowd had to be restrained. After the final whistle Duddy was smuggled out of the ground for his own safety. The semi-final draw paired us with Linfield but this eagerly awaited fixture was never to take place.

The Irish League clubs were unhappy about the allocation of money from Irish Cup ties and on 19th February Derry Celtic, Shelbourne and Distillery resigned from the IFA. They were soon joined by Glentoran, Cliftonville and Belfast Celtic and together with Glenavon

Results 1911/12

Played 35. Won 25. Drew 7. Lost 3. Goals For 94. Against 33. % 81.4.
Honours: Irish League, City Cup

IL	02/09/11		Cliftonville	H	W	10 0	Ritchie, Mitchell 3, Napier 3, McKnight 3(1p)
IL	09/09/11		Distillery	A	W	3 2	Munro, McKnight, Hunter
IL	16/09/11		Linfield	A	L	1 2	Napier
IL	23/09/11		Belfast Celtic	H	D	1 1	McKnight
IL	07/10/11		Derry Celtic	A	D	1 1	Napier
IL	14/10/11		Shelbourne	H	W	7 0	Mitchell 3, McKnight 2, Lyner, Napier
IL	21/10/11		Glenavon	H	W	3 2	Hunter, Mitchell 2
IL	28/10/11		Cliftonville	A	W	1 0	McKnight
IL	04/11/11		Distillery	H	W	2 1	Lyner, McKnight
IL	11/11/11		Linfield	H	W	1 0	Lyner
IL	25/11/11		Derry Celtic	H	W	2 0	Hunter, Lyner
IL	04/12/11		Belfast Celtic	A	W	3 1	McKnight, Mitchell, Hunter
IL	09/12/11		Glenavon	A	W	5 1	Napier 2, McKnight 2, Hunter
IL	23/12/11		Shelbourne	A	W	5 2	McKnight 2, Munro 2, Mitchell
CC	16/12/11		Belfast Celtic	H	D	0 0	-
CC	25/12/11		Shelbourne	H	W	5 1	Napier 3, Munro, McKnight
CC	26/12/11		Glenavon	A	W	6 3	McKnight 3, Hunter 2, Andrews
CC	30/12/11		Cliftonville	H	D	2 2	McKnight, Napier
CC	06/01/12		Distillery	A	D	1 1	Napier
CC	13/01/12		Linfield	H	W	1 0	Mitchell
CC	20/01/12		Derry Celtic	A	D	1 1	Munro
CC	27/01/12		Belfast Celtic	A	W	2 1	Hunter, Lyner
CC	02/03/12		Cliftonville	A	W	2 1	Hunter, Mitchell
CC	09/03/12		Derry Celtic	H	W	3 0	Munro 2, Napier
CC	30/03/12		Distillery	H	W	5 2	Mitchell 3, Munro, Napier
CC	08/04/12		Glenavon	H	W	2 0	Unknown 2
CC	13/04/12		Shelbourne	A	W	1 0	Munro
CC	27/04/12		"Belfast Blues"	H	W	2 0	Napier, Munro
IC	03/02/12	1	Distillery	H	W	3 2	McKnight 3
IC	17/02/12	2	Derry Celtic	H	W	4 0	Napier 2(1p), Hunter, McKnight
NIC	23/03/12	1	Shelbourne	H	W	4 1	Mitchell 2, Napier 2
NIC	06/04/12	SF	Cliftonville	GP	W	4 0	Hunter, Munro 2, Napier
NIC	20/04/12	F	Belfast Celtic	GP	L	0 2	-
ChC	15/04/12	SF	Belfast Celtic	GP	D	0 0	-
ChC	29/04/12	SFR	Belfast Celtic	GP	L	1 3	Munro
F	26/08/11		Distillery	A	W	2 1	Unknown 2
F	16/03/12		Rest of the League	GP	L	0 1	aet Benefit for Shelbourne
F	10/04/12		Distillery	H	L	2 4	Napier, Hunter Lady Mayoress' Stall at Ulster Hospital Fete

these seven clubs formed a "new" IFA. The "old" IFA still claimed to be the premier body and they intended to continue running with Linfield, Bohemians, Derry Guilds, St. James' Gate, Portadown, Lurgan Celtic, Ulster and Forth River to compete in a new league set-up. The Linfield club was involved in a simultaneous financial dispute over ground levies for the use of Windsor Park for international games. In the end their split membership created two clubs, an official Linfield staying with the old IFA while another team, mainly composed of Swifts' players, joined the new IFA. The latter side was dubbed the new "Belfast Blues" by the press and they fulfilled Linfield's remaining City Cup fixtures while the official XI played friendlies.

The new IFA, formed on 13th March with T.D.Reid of Glentoran as Chairman, had a golden cup struck for their version of the Irish Cup. This trophy was later to become the Gold Cup. Glentoran battled through to the final but lost 0-2 to Celtic in front of 9,500. The teams wore black armbands as a mark of respect to those killed when the Titanic had sunk five days earlier. Football itself had generally taken a back seat in April in Belfast life as 240,000 demonstrated against the Home Rule bill.

Celtic were also our conquerors in the Charity Cup and the County Antrim Shield was not played due to the IFA split. It is interesting to note the punters' reaction to events. On the day that 10,000 watched Ireland lose 1-4 to Scotland at Windsor Park, 12,000 went to Grosvenor Park to see the Glens lose to a League XI in a benefit match for Shelbourne. Peace eventually reigned in the IFA dispute with some concessions made on both sides and a return to normality was expected in 1912/3.

We duly completed our City Cup fixtures, winning a rather devalued tournament. On the representative front the following players gained inter-league caps in the trio of games against the Southern, English and Scottish leagues. Three caps: P.McCann, J.Reid, A. Hunter, S.Napier. Two caps: W.Andrews. One cap: L.Skene, J.Mitchell.

Paddy McCann played for Ireland against England, the English winning 6-1 to knock up 150 goals in 31 meetings. Napier guested for Linfield against Nottingham Forest on New Year's Day 1912 and scored one of the goals in the Blues' 2-1 win.

Appearances and Goals

	App.	Goals		App.	Goals		App.	Goals
Napier	33	21	Gibb	23		Ferguson	3	
Lyner R.	33	5	McKnight, James	23	23	Garrett	1	
Hunter	33	11	Ferritt	19		Smith	1	
Andrews	31	1	Munro	17	13	Heron	1	
McCann	30		Reid	15		Unknown	22	2
Mitchell	28	17	Skene L.	10		TOTAL	385	94
Watters	27		McAlpine	5				
Ritchie	27	1	Scraggs	3				

1912/13

League Championship retained – Gunshots at games

The re-admission of Bohemians and the inclusion of a third Dublin side, Tritonville, increased the Irish League membership to ten clubs. Reigning champions Glentoran warmed up for the season with a couple of eventful friendlies. Against Distillery we led 2-0 at the interval but allowed the Whites to force a draw despite Leslie Murphy saving two penalties.

Chairman Brice McIlroy unfurled the League flag before our opening competitive fixture but Distillery took the honours on the day as too often the Glens' forwards fell into the off-side trap. The early games were low scoring but this did not prevent a large crowd turning up to see us take on the unbeaten Celtic XI on 2nd October. The Glens won 2-0 to go top of the table but at the final whistle a revolver shot was fired off in the crowd, the beginning of an irritating and potentially dangerous practice at grounds this season.

Around 21,000 were at Windsor Park for the goalless draw with Linfield when Clydesdale Skene, brother of ex-keeper Leslie, made an ineffective, solitary appearance. Such was the interest generated in this game that a scribe remarked, "If the battle of Armageddon was being fought at Lisburn while Linfield and Glentoran were playing, I would back the football match to draw the bigger crowd!"

Davy Lyner.

We consolidated our position as league leaders with an easy win over Tritonville and a hard fought victory at a windy Glenavon before drawing with Belfast Celtic on a Wednesday afternoon in the City Cup. For this season the League Committee experimented by playing out a City Cup tie every Wednesday for the opening few months - however the idea drew criticism from most quarters. The knockers claimed it impinged too much on the spectator's pocket and the players' stamina, arguing that Wednesday afternoon football should be left for the shopkeepers for whom the half-day holiday had been brought in.

November began badly and three league defeats saw us slip to joint fifth position, four points behind pacesetters Distillery. The press began a campaign against the "ladies free" rule, referencing an example whereby a man turned up with a coachload of females who occupied all the best seats in the stand. One writer surmised that theses ladies "knew as much about football as a pig knows about packing delf!"

As the dark winter approached Glentoran got back to form thanks to an easy win over a poor Derry Celtic side. James McKnight returned from Preston to play against Shelbourne, for whom goalkeeper Walter Scott was outstanding. More revolver firing at the Linfield-Belfast Celtic fixture increased calls for these two clubs to meet on neutral grounds.

The crowd were on their best behaviour when we visited Celtic Park in early December but not so "Jap" Walker and Celtic's Robinson who were sent off in separate first half incidents. Paddy McCann had a sound game at the back but it was the forwards who earned victory over the Blues a week later. McKnight's return had certainly geed up our front line but with only three games remaining Distillery led us by 23 points to 20.

We visited Tritonville (who were sharing Shelbourne's Serpentine Avenue ground) on the Saturday before Christmas and sneaked a win while Distillery were drawing 1-1 with Shelbourne at Grosvenor Park. On Christmas morning, minus the injured Watters and Reid, Glenavon were beaten in a scrappy encounter. Meanwhile at Solitude 5,000 saw the Whites go down 0-1 to Cliftonville meaning it was all square with one game to go. Solitude housed another large crowd on Boxing Day when the most significant event of an exciting 90 minutes came when McCann punted long upfield and McKnight scored with a sharp shot. Linfield beat Distillery 2-1 and so we retained the championship!

Reid, Walker and Napier arrange a goats' derby!

The only sad Xmas note for the club was the 3-1 defeat of the Seconds by Celtic II in the Steel and Sons Cup final on Christmas morning. However our reserves recovered to capture the Intermediate Cup, defeating St. James' Gate II 3-0 in the St. Patrick's day final, courtesy of a hat-trick from Johnny Mercer.

As 1913 dawned thoughts turned to the knockout competitions and the City Cup. Constant rain caused the postponement of our City Cup game with Linfield on 11th January and when the match was played on the Wednesday the Oval was described as "a veritable slough of despond." No shortage of action though as we went four up after an hour before the Blues staged a fruitless comeback.

With McCann and Watters insurmountable at the back we saw off Celtic II and Glenavon in the Shield and Irish Cup respectively. Despite the heavy snow trainloads of Glens fans made the trip to Lurgan and loudly cheered Sam "Yummy" Napier's winning penalty. A Victor McConnell-inspired Cliftonville ended our Shield hopes as an injured Paddy McCann hobbled on the left wing. The 9,000 who watched Shelbourne draw at the Oval must have thought our Irish Cup aspirations were also about to be curtailed but Jimmy Lindsay did the trick in the replay.

Thanks to a hesitant Oscar Traynor in Celtic's goal we won the cup semi-final rehersal on 1st March at Celtic Park. All parts of the Solitude enclosure were packed (estimated crowd 17,000) a week later. Sam Napier opened the scoring with a stinging shot as the Glentoran forward line of Lyner, Lindsay, Napier, McKnight and Munro played like demons. At half-time it was 2-0 to us, both goals having been celebrated with revolver charges by a spectator only a few yards from the pressbox! Play became slack in the second half and at the conclusion only Linfield (4-1 conquerors of Tritonville) stood in the way of our first Irish Cup success. Before the final the Blues gained a physchological edge by defeating us in the City Cup (although both sides were decimated due to representative demands) and in a benefit match for their right-half Charlie Stewart. Murphy had the pleasure of saving a Willis penalty in the latter game.

Sixteen turnstiles were on active service for the Celtic Park final and over 20,000 crammed in. Despite lacking McCann Glentoran began as slight favourites but could not settle. In the scoreless first half the revolver fiends made themselves heard as they performed their usual "Wild West" antics. Following a scrimmage the Blues went ahead and then a magnificent shot from Marshall McEwan ensured the cup would elude us again.

After that Glentoran's season petered out but Linfield showed their appetite for the knockout tournaments by defeating Cliftonville 1-0 at the Oval in the Shield (after two scoreless draws) and Celtic 3-1 in the Charity Cup final. Distillery, who vied with the Glens for the "team of the season" award, lifted the City Cup by a comfortable margin.

Results 1912/13

Played 39. Won 22. Drew 5. Lost 12. Goals For 73. Against 43. % 62.8.
Honours: Irish League

IL	07/09/12		Distillery	H	L	0	1	-
IL	14/09/12		Bohemians	H	W	2	1	Walker, Lyner
IL	21/09/12		Derry Celtic	A	D	0	0	-
IL	28/09/12		Shelbourne	A	W	2	0	Mitchell, Napier
IL	02/10/12		Belfast Celtic	H	W	2	0	Munro, Walker
IL	12/10/12		Linfield	A	D	0	0	-
IL	19/10/12		Tritonville	H	W	8	0	Lindsay 2, Napier 2, Walker 2, Munro, Ritchie
IL	26/10/12		Glenavon	A	W	3	2	Ferritt, Lindsay, McCullough og
IL	02/11/12		Cliftonville	H	L	0	2	-
IL	09/11/12		Distillery	A	L	0	1	-
IL	16/11/12		Bohemians	A	L	1	4	Lindsay
IL	23/11/12		Derry Celtic	H	W	5	0	Emerson 2, Lyner, Lindsay, Munro
IL	30/11/12		Shelbourne	H	W	2	0	Emerson, Lindsay
IL	07/12/12		Belfast Celtic	A	W	3	2	Ritchie, McKnight, Lindsay
IL	14/12/12		Linfield	H	W	4	2	Lindsay 2, McKnight, Napier
IL	21/12/12		Tritonville	A	W	2	1	McKnight, Napier (p)
IL	25/12/12		Glenavon	H	W	2	0	Lindsay, Napier
IL	26/12/12		Cliftonville	A	W	1	0	McKnight
CC	30/10/12		Belfast Celtic	H	D	2	2	Napier, Reid
CC	28/12/12		Glenavon	H	W	3	1	Lindsay 2, Napier
CC	04/01/13		Cliftonville	A	L	1	3	Napier
CC	15/01/13		Linfield	H	W	4	3	Napier 2, McKnight, Walker
CC	01/03/13		Belfast Celtic	A	W	2	0	McKnight 2
CC	15/03/13		Linfield	A	L	0	1	-
CC	24/03/13		Distillery	H	L	0	2	-
CC	12/04/13		Shelbourne	A	L	1	2	Lewis
CC	16/04/13		Distillery	A	D	1	1	Ritchie
CC	19/04/13		Glenavon	A	L	0	2	-
CC	26/04/13		Shelbourne	H	W	1	0	Lindsay
CC	30/04/13		Cliftonville	H	W	4	1	McKnight 2, Munro, Reid
CAS	25/01/13	1	Belfast Celtic II	H	W	3	0	Lyner, Lindsay, Napier
CAS	08/02/13	SF	Cliftonville	CP	L	1	2	Grainger o.g.
IC	01/02/13	1	Glenavon	A	W	2	1	Lindsay, Napier (p)
IC	22/02/13	2	Shelbourne	H	D	0	0	-
IC	26/02/13	2R	Shelbourne	A	W	1	0	Lindsay
IC	08/03/13	SF	Belfast Celtic	Solt	W	5	1	Napier 3, Lindsay, McKnight
IC	29/03/13	F	Linfield	CP	L	0	2	-
ChC	23/04/13	1	Distillery	H	W	4	1	Napier 3, McKnight
ChC	03/05/13	SF	Belfast Celtic	Solt	L	1	2	Mitchell
F	24/08/12		Belfast Celtic	A	L	2	4	Lindsay, Lyner
F	31/08/12		Distillery	A	D	2	2	Walker, Mitchell
F	25/03/13		Linfield	A	L	1	2	Mitchell Charlie Stewart Benefit
F	02/04/13		Linfield	H	W	2	1	Lindsay, Napier John Mitchell Benefit

An important event was John Mitchell's benefit game in April. Impartial's appraisal of "Do", as he was widely known, was affectionately penned thus:

"Possessed of enormous vitality he does three men's work. Though the covering of his dome of thought is somewhat scanty, it is not due to the advance of old age but rather to concentration of brain-power in developing plans to compose the downfall of his footballing enemies. He has provided yeoman service for Glentoran in the past and has many more years left."

Napier's winner ensured the gold pins on offer came the way of the Ovalites.

During the season many Glentoran players received representative honours. McKnight featured in the Irish team against Scotland at Dalymount Park while Paddy McCann appeared against Wales and also in the Irish Amateur XI's 3-2 win over England. Only injury prevented him

Team Group 1912/13.

playing in the full international win over the English. The lion-hearted, burly amateur was in excellent form for the Irish League in the 0-0 draw with the English League at the Oval in October when he was assisted by fellow Glenmen Murphy, Ritchie and Davy Lyner. Many of the 12,000 crowd for this game had taken "French leave" as they appeared in their working clothes. Murphy, McCann and Ritchie were joined by Mitchell for the game against the Scottish League while Ritchie, Davy Lyner and Jimmy Lindsay played in the 1-1 draw with the Southern League at the Den, Millwall.

At the end of the season three players left the club. Ritchie and McKnight signed forms for Nottingham Forest while Walker decided to try his luck with Belfast Celtic. Derry Celtic (by 12 votes to 11) and Tritonville (by 14 to 7) were not re-elected to the Irish League for 1913/4.

Appearances and Goals

	App.	Goals		App.	Goals		App.	Goals
Murphy	38		McCann	26		Bailie	1	
Reid	37	2	McKnight, James	24	11	Patterson	1	
Lyner D.	37	3	Walker	23	5	Dunwoody	1	
Ferritt	36	1	McAlpine	17		Skene C.	1	
Lindsay J.	34	17	Mitchell	14	2	Hatton	1	
Ritchie	33	3	Scraggs	8		Finaly	1	
Watters	31		Emerson	5	3	Own Goals		2
Napier	27	19	Lewis	4	1	TOTAL	429	73
Munro	27	4	Bennett	2				

1913/14

Distillery marathon - Irish Cup lifted at last - The Vienna Cup

By the time the new season came along Glentoran had undergone further personnel changes. "Do" Mitchell did not re-sign, eventually he joined Shelbourne, while Roly Lyner moved to Linfield. Roly's younger brother Davy now had the right-wing berth to himself. Over on the other flank Willie Lindsay, younger brother of Jimmy, came into the squad. Cross-channel forwards in the form of Hugh Bolton and John Smith were signed prompting shouts that English and Scottish discards were now taking places in local elevens while the best Irish players were moving across the water. Paddy McCann was recovering from an operation following an injury received in the previous season's County Antrim Shield semi-final and it was feared he may never play again. As cover Austin Donnelly was signed from Manchester United.

Off the field new trainer "Punter" Bennett replaced the retiring Ching Morrison. News from Dublin arrived regarding the disbandment of the Tritonville club, whose members did not wish to continue playing in a Leinster junior league.

The new forward line shaped up well in the August friendlies. We came from behind to beat Linfield and Murphy enjoyed a penalty save from McDevitt in the Glenavon game.

A long and momentous season began with a convincing home win over Belfast Celtic whose defence and keeper Fred McKee were kept under constant pressure. However we were to suffer defeat twice in September, firstly at the hands of Shelbourne when a Donnelly o.g. sent the Dubliners on their way. Then after Davy Lyner gave us the lead against Linfield, his brother equalised and a hat-trick from Hamilton sewed the game up for the Blues.

McCann returned as captain for the Distillery fixture when Whites' keeper Hugh Edmonds often saved in great style. Glentoran, known in the press as "the Greenshirts", forced a City Cup draw with the Blues and two weeks later really came to life with four goals in a five minute spell versus Bohemians. At the half-way stage of the championship Linfield held a three point lead over ourselves and Distillery.

Glentoran's hopes of a hat-trick of titles evaporated with a defeat to a late Nixon goal for Belfast Celtic as Billy Emerson was left to rue early missed chances. Hugh Annesley (ex-Cliftonville) replaced McAlpine at left-back forming a repelling defensive partnership with McCann. Emerson, George Ferritt, John Scraggs and James Reid shared the half-back duties and they provided the basis of a good solid run to secure the runners-up spot and medals in the league. Around 14,000 saw us come back from another Roly Lyner goal to draw with the Blues while the Lindsay brothers ended Glenavon's unbeaten home record.

The team's excellent form continued with three wins on consecutive days as the City Cup got under way seriously over Christmas. As John Smith went home for Hogmany, a new signing from junior outfit Broadway, Jack Boyd, was thrown into first team action. Boyd made a tremendous impact scoring in each of his first six appearances. The side's fast style tended to hem opponents into their own half with the goals coming consistently. At the end of the first half of the City Cup we had built up a commanding four point lead over Linfield and Belfast Celtic.

Attentions now became focussed on the Shield and Irish Cup with Distillery the initial obstacle in both cases. Boyd gave a superb exhibition in the Shield game, being described as a born footballer with a lovely feint. In the Cup meeting he was tightly shackled by Burnison and many chances were missed at both ends. The first round tie developed into a saga. In replay number one Boyd gave us the lead but the Whites levelled through Nichol. Another draw forced the postponement of our first round tie in the inaugural Gold Cup against, yes, Distillery! The third cup meeting was played on a Grosvenor Park quagmire with the Glens' forwards making the mistake of playing the ball too close. So it was on to an equally heavy Oval two days later and not surprisingly some very poor football was served up in a scoreless encounter. The players were feeling the effects of all these games but we did manage to squeeze in a County Antrim Shield semi-final which was also inconclusive.

Therefore it came as no surprise when, with the exception of Murphy in goals, Glentoran fielded a 2nd XI against Linfield in the City Cup on the Saturday. The Blues took full advantage to open up that tournament again. Finally, with the public and the players sick of the sight of each other we saw off Distillery at the fifth time of asking after playing seven game in 17 days! The game itself was poor but the result reflected the balance of play. Celtic took a point of us in the City Cup after Boyd had opened up a 2-0 lead. Scraggs own goal helped the Stripes come back.

When the team ran out for the Irish Cup semi-final at Dalymount Park they would have

Team Group 1913/14 Back Row: Telford, Annesley, Scraggs, Murphy, Ferritt, Emerson, Napier, Bennett. Front Row: Lyner, J.Lindsay, McCann (captain), Boyd, Reid, W.Lindsay.

baulked at the thought of another marathon tie. In that match we came from behind, with Willie Lindsay particularly dangerous but Shelbourne held out. On the Monday evening Davy Lyner's late winner knocked Cliftonville out of the Shield but two nights later, just when we looked to have the Dubliners beaten, "Do" Mitchell popped up with an 83rd minute equaliser. After another draw in Dublin two goals from Boyd in a stale mediocre display put us through to the Cup final against the Blues.

The players had to somehow recharge their batteries for the Shield final with Linfield three days later. Young scored twice for the Blues in the first half but after Clifford made it 3-0 the Glens quickly scored and for the remainder of the game held the upper hand but failed to draw level. Despite tasting defeat confidence was sky-high for the Irish Cup final a week later.

Glentoran's directors really decided to go for it in the attempt to bring the Cup to the Oval for the first time. The club scratched its scheduled Gold Cup tie on the Monday against Distillery, instead taking the players to Newcastle, County Down for a full week's relaxation and preparation. This took a leaf out of the Irish FA's book, whom had done the same thing, albeit for only a couple of days, with the Irish international team. Ireland got the draw they wanted against Scotland to become British Champions for the first time - would it work for the Glens?

A rumour in midweek hit Belfast that two of the players had drowned while bathing, but this was totally unfounded and the same eleven who had played in the Shield final were selected. Linfield made one change, bringing in Rollo for Sterling at right-back. Over 20,000 crammed into Grosvenor Park and despite the Glens having most of the early play McEwan gave the Blues the lead. Before the break Jimmy Lindsay had equalised and then into the second half the Glens went ahead. McCann's free-kick was dropped by the Linfield keeper Kelly, and Willie Lindsay nipped in to tap the ball home. Ferritt had to retire through injury but with Paddy McCann outstanding in a stout defence the younger Lindsay made it 3-1 and the Blue Riband of Irish soccer had finally been won after 32 seasons of trying. The celebrations were long and loud in East Belfast.

When the dust had settled there was the almost forgotten City Cup to resume. Shelbourne were tough opponents in Dublin and the small crowd continually jeered the Belfast team. The Irish Cup, decorated in red, green and black ribbons, was formally handed over to Paddy McCann by East Belfast M.P. Colonel Sherman-Crawford at the conclusion of the Distillery game on 11th April. Another tough trip to Dublin finished 1-1 and when the Glens and the Blues both decisively won their last two City Cup games it necessitated a play-off to decide the destination of that competition.

In between we had qualified for the Charity Cup final, coming from behind to beat Distillery, who later gained consolation by defeating Shelbourne in the Gold Cup final. To round off the season we would face the Blues three more times on successive Saturdays.

The Windsor men drew first blood in the Charity final, Roly Lyner the marksman, as Smith was just wide twice with good shots. Then an 87th minute penalty miss meant we had to settle for a draw in a game to raise funds for the Queen's Island Unionist Recreation Fund. However we finished on a high note, defeating an under strength Linfield in the City Cup test match.

In a hectic season, when we played about 30% more games than normal, Napier, Scraggs, Ferritt and Smith gained inter-league honours, while McCann was in his usual right-back spot in the Amateur International with England. One would have thought that the players were due a long rest as summer approached but that pleasure was to be delayed a little longer as Glentoran set out on an historic, globetrotting tour of Europe at the end of 1913/4 as guests of the Vienna football club.

THE 1914 EUROPEAN TOUR AND THE VIENNA CUP

At 6.30 pm on Monday 18th May the Glentoran party sailed on the Larne-Stranraer ferry, to break new ground on the continent of Europe. The regular playing party was strengthened by guest Roly Lyner while Mr. Adam McCann, a well known Ballymacarrett personality, also made the trip.

By Wednesday afternoon the group was travelling by train from Dresden to Prague. The original plan was to hit Prague at 3.30 in the afternoon but due to a misunderstanding the party were over seven hours behind schedule. The North Sea crossing had apparently been delightful with the weather experienced so far beautifully sunny.

Glentoran met Deutsche before a large crowd at Prague in 82 degree heat on the Thursday afternoon. The home side were aided by a couple of Berlin players plus Lee, an Englishman. The Glens took a second minute lead but by half-time it was 3-3 and despite many of our attacks in the second half Deutsche snatched a late winner.

The party left Prague at noon on Saturday bound for Berlin, again by rail. On arrival representatives of the Hertha club met the players and officials. The temperature had soared to over 90 degrees in the shade in mid-afternoon but had dropped to the seventies by the 6.30 pm kick-off time. Playing with the wind Sam Napier put us ahead in the third minute and our interval lead of 2-0 became 4-1 by the end. A crowd of 6,000 watched what was considered to be the best display of football seen in Berlin to date. The off the field hospitality extended to Glentoran had been excellent.

After this match it was onto Vienna where the party was housed in the Hotel Continental. During the week in the capital two fixtures were played against Vienna Select XIs, made up of players from local leagues. The first, again attended by around 6,000, saw the Glens well on top and ahead through Reid when the locals equalised late on. For the Saturday game a silver trophy was available to the winners and when Glentoran won easily the Vienna Cup was won. In the eyes of many, therefore, the Glens became the first British

Results 1913/14

Played 45. Won 24. Drew 15. Lost 6. Goals For 90, Against 45. % 70.0.
Honours: Irish Cup, City Cup, Vienna Cup

IL	06/09/13		Belfast Celtic	H	W	4	0	Napier, Bolton, Smith, Lyner
IL	13/09/13		Shelbourne	A	L	1	3	Lyner
IL	20/09/13		Cliftonville	H	W	3	1	Lyner, Smith, J.Lindsay
IL	27/09/13		Linfield	A	L	2	4	Lyner, W.Lindsay
IL	04/10/13		Distillery	H	D	0	0	-
IL	18/10/13		Glenavon	H	W	1	0	J.Lindsay
IL	25/10/13		Bohemians	A	W	5	2	Napier 2, J.Lindsay 2, Lyner
IL	01/11/13		Belfast Celtic	A	L	0	1	-
IL	15/11/13		Shelbourne	H	W	3	2	Napier 2, Smith
IL	22/11/13		Cliftonville	A	W	3	0	Smith 2, W.Lindsay
IL	29/11/13		Linfield	H	D	2	2	Smith, Napier
IL	06/12/13		Distillery	A	D	0	0	-
IL	13/12/13		Glenavon	A	W	3	2	W.Lindsay 2, J.Lindsay
IL	20/12/13		Bohemians	H	W	5	1	J.Lindsay, Napier, W.Lindsay, Smith, Smith og
CC	11/10/13		Linfield	H	D	2	2	J.Lindsay, Smith
CC	25/12/13		Beltast Celtic	H	W	2	1	Napier, J.Lindsay
CC	26/12/13		Shelbourne	H	W	3	0	Boyd 2, Bolton
CC	27/12/13		Distillery	A	W	3	0	Napier, Boyd, J.Lindsay
CC	03/01/14		Cliftonville	H	W	3	0	Boyd, Lyner, Napier
CC	10/01/14		Bohemians	H	W	3	1	W.Lindsay, Boyd, Smith
CC	17/01/14		Glenavon	A	W	3	0	Boyd 2, Napier (p)
CC	14/02/14		Linfield	A	L	1	4	Smith
CC	28/02/14		Belfast Celtic	A	D	3	3	Boyd 2, Lyner
CC	04/04/14		Shelbourne	A	D	1	1	Boyd
CC	11/04/14		Distillery	H	W	2	1	Napier, J.Lindsay
CC	14/04/14		Bohemians	A	D	1	1	Napier
CC	18/04/14		Glenavon	H	W	5	0	Lyner, Napier, J.Lindsay, Scraggs, Boyd
CC	27/04/14		Cliftonville	A	W	3	0	J.Lindsay 2, Lyner
CC	16/05/14	TM	Linfield	Solt	W	2	0	W.Lindsay, Emerson
CAS	24/01/14	2	Distillery	A	W	2	1	Boyd 2
CAS	07/02/14	SF	Cliftonville	WP	D	1	1	Napier
CAS	09/03/14	SFR	Cliftonville	CP	W	2	1	Boyd, Lyner
CAS	21/03/14	F	Linfield	GP	L	2	3	Napier, W.Lindsay
IC	31/01/14	1	Distillery	A	D	0	0	-
IC	04/02/14	1R	Distillery	H	D	1	1	Boyd
IC	09/02/14	1R2	Distillery	A	D	1	1	Boyd
IC	11/02/14	1R3	Distillery	H	D	0	0	-
IC	16/02/14	1R4	Distillery	A	W	2	1	Boyd, Napier (p)
IC	07/03/14	SF	Shelbourne	DP	D	1	1	Lyner
IC	11/03/14	SFR	Shelbourne	GP	D	1	1	W.Lindsay
IC	14/03/14	SFR2	Shelbourne	A	D	0	0	-
IC	18/03/14	SFR3	Shelbourne	CP	W	2	1	Boyd 2
IC	28/03/14	F	Linfield	GP	W	3	1	W.Lindsay 2, J.Lindsay
ChC	25/04/14	SF	Distillery	WP	W	3	1	Boyd 2, Smith
ChC	02/05/14	F	Linfield	Solt	L	0	1	-
F	21/05/14		Deutsche	A	L	3	4	Unknown
F	23/05/14		Hertha Berlin	A	W	4	1	Unknown
F	27/05/14		Vienna Select	A	D	1	1	Reid
VC	30/05/14		Vienna Select	A	W	5	0	Unknown
F	31/05/14		Pressburg	A	W	3	0	Unknown
F	01/06/14		Hungary	A	L	0	7	-
F	23/08/13		Linfield	A	W	2	1	Smith, Bolton
F	30/08/13		Glenavon	H	W	6	2	Smith 4, Lyner, J.Lindsay
F	09/05/14		Linfield	GP	D	1	1	Napier
								Queen's Island Recreation Club

winners of a European trophy! That evening the party were guests of the president of the Austro-Hungarian FA. An enjoyable night was wound up with a rendition of "Auld Lang Syne."

Sunday morning was given over to a three hour sailing up the River Danube for a fixture at Pressburg. Prince Albrecht attended this match and at a great reception afterwards, he extended his appreciation of Glentoran's play. The following day the full Hungarian international XI proved far too strong but the party set off for home with many happy memories of an interesting and enjoyable tour.

The party arrived safely back in Belfast on Thursday 4th June.

Appearances and Goals

	App.	Goals		App.	Goals		App.	Goals
Murphy	45		Smith	30	10	McMinn	1	
Lindsay J.	43	14	Boyd, Jack	26	21	Bennett	1	
Lindsay W.	43	11	Annesley	24		Young	1	
Napier	41	18	Reid	16		Heron	1	
Scraggs	40	1	McAlpine	10		Potter	1	
McCann	39		Bolton	10	2	Own Goal		1
Emerson	38	1	Donnelly	4		TOTAL	495	90
Ferritt	38		Garrett	3				
Lyner D.	37	11	Bailie	3				

1914/15

Davy Lyner on form – The onset of World War – City Cup captured

When Britain declared war on Germany on 4th August the accompanying euphoria led to a general consensus that hostilities would be finished by Christmas. The FA decided to carry on with normal football in England and when this received official War Office approval the Irish League and IFA followed suit. The only changes to the Glentoran 1st XI squad were the addition of Davy Duff, G.Kitchen (ex-Belfast Celtic II) and Heron, all inside forwards, offsetting the departure of Jimmy Lindsay.

A collection was taken up at half-time during the friendly with Linfield for the Lord Mayor's War Fund and a week later Glens fans had an early chance to view Belfast Celtic's new strip of green and white hoops, which replaced the old green and white stripes.

Johnny Scraggs.

Glentoran got off to a shaky start in the league but after six games were joint leaders with Celtic. Roly Lyner, now at Distillery, scored against us again on 26th September but Sam Napier's hat-trick and Jack Boyd's 84th minute winner gave us the points. Davy Lyner with many scintillating runs outshone his brother on that occasion and Davy's general form over the first few months of the season prompted Impartial to write:

"Davy Lyner has no compeer in Irish football. Without doubt he is the class article as an outside-right. I think he must take a huge enjoyment out of fooling a man. He slips the ball past him, goes round him, gets it again - a dexterous little shove to his partner - it comes back again and Davy sends it sailing perilously near the posts."

A disappointing display against Linfield rounded off the first half of league matches. Then, when Duff gave us the lead after only five minutes at Shelbourne things looked well, but we had to rely on two penalty misses by the Dubliners to gain a point. Devine drove wide in the first moiety and Chalmers placed his kick straight at Murphy midway through the second half.

We therefore entered the home fixture versus Celtic three points behind the unbeaten Falls Road team. It was a great day for Glentoran though, and there was no denying our superiority in a 2-0 win. To complete Celtic's misery their mainstay half-back Mickey Hamill went off injured after 70 minutes.

Another excellent victory was recorded over third-placed Distillery a week later. We had to come from behind in this one, Robinson putting the Whites ahead with a shot from near the corner flag! Impartial's report on the game was marred by the descending gloom and he wrote of our winner:

"I was behind the pavilion goal and away far in the dim vista of the whisky making end of the ground I could discern men jumping about. Then came a big cheer and Annesley and McCann danced down the field like a couple of schoolboys who had been given a half-holiday. Someone at the Dunville end sent wireless that Lindsay had done the trick again."

Celtic recovered from their Oval defeat seeing off Cliftonville (5-0), Glenavon (3-0) and Shelbourne (1-0) to maintain that one point lead going into the final round of fixtures. Despite coming back against Linfield we just could not get the winning goal and had to settle for second place in the championship as Celtic beat Distillery 1-0.

The War had now assumed great proportions and sporting interest and coverage dropped off. The 1915 English cricket season was cancelled and the young men of Britain were being encouraged to enlist in the armed forces rather than watch football!

Willie Moore became a Christmas Day hero when he opened the scoring with a clean drive from 30 yards against Celtic. His effort deserved all the kissing, hugging and handshaking received from his colleagues. The respective 2nd XIs of the two clubs met in the afternoon in the Steel and Sons Cup final at Windsor Park in front of 15,000. The game finished 1-1 with the Wee Glens missing a penalty. Our second string eventually gained

Results 1914/15

Played 35. Won 21. Drew 6. Lost 8. Goals For 61. Against 34. % 68.6.
Honours: City Cup

IL	05/09/14		Glenavon	A	D	0	0	-
IL	12/09/14		Shelbourne	H	W	1	0	Napier
IL	19/09/14		Belfast Celtic	A	L	0	1	-
IL	26/09/14		Distillery	H	W	4	3	Napier 3, Boyd
IL	03/10/14		Bohemians	H	W	3	0	Napier 2, Lyner
IL	10/10/14		Cliftonville	A	W	3	0	Napier 3
IL	17/10/14		Linfield	A	L	0	3	-
IL	24/10/14		Glenavon	H	W	5	0	Duff 2, Boyd, Ferritt (p), Young
IL	07/11/14		Shelbourne	A	D	1	1	Duff
IL	14/11/14		Belfast Celtic	H	W	2	0	W.Lindsay, Ferritt (p)
IL	21/11/14		Distillery	A	W	2	1	W.Lindsay 2
IL	28/11/14		Bohemians	A	W	3	0	Scraggs, Ferritt, W.Lindsay
IL	05/12/14		Cliftonville	H	W	2	0	W.Lindsay, Boyd
IL	12/12/14		Linfield	H	D	1	1	Napier
CC	19/12/14		Bohemians	A	W	3	1	Boyd 2, Moore
CC	25/12/14		Belfast Celtic	H	W	3	0	Moore 2, Napier
CC	26/12/14		Shelbourne	H	W	2	0	Scraggs, W.Lindsay
CC	02/01/15		Cliftonville	A	W	3	2	Boyd 2, Moore
CC	23/01/15		Distillery	H	W	1	0	Boyd
CC	03/04/15		Linfield	H	L	1	3	Moore
CC	05/04/15		Bohemians	H	W	4	1	Moore 2, Boyd, McCann (p)
CC	06/04/15		Belfast Celtic	A	L	1	3	Lyner
CC	10/04/15		Shelbourne	A	W	1	0	Napier
CC	17/04/15		Cliftonville	H	W	4	1	Napier 2, Moore, Emerson
CC	24/04/15		Distillery	A	D	0	0	-
CC	26/04/15		Glenavon	H	W	1	0	Napier
CC	01/05/15		Glenavon	A	W	3	2	Lyner, Boyd, Moore
CC	12/05/15		Linfield	A	D	0	0	-
CAS	13/01/15	1	Linfield	H	W	2	1	Moore 2
CAS	27/01/15	SF	Belfast Celtic	Solt	W	1	0	Boyd
CAS	20/03/15	F	Distillery	WP	L	0	1	-
IC	30/01/15	1	Shelbourne	H	L	1	2	Ferritt
GC	13/02/15	1	Distillery	H	L	1	2	Ferritt
ChC	21/04/15	1	Belfast Celtic	GP	D	2	2	Ferritt (p), Lyner
ChC	03/05/15	1R	Belfast Celtic	GP	L	0	3	-
F	22/08/14		Linfield	H	L	0	1	-
F	29/08/14		Belfast Celtic	H	L	0	3	-
F	13/03/15		Glasgow Celtic	A	L	0	3	-

revenge over the young Celts after the replay had twice been postponed due to frost. Bailie got the only goal at Grosvenor Park on 6th January.

Nixon's hat-trick for Linfield ended our 100% City Cup record but we got back on the rails over the Easter week. After Napier had given us the lead with 20 minutes to go Shelbourne again missed two penalties on their Ringsend Park pitch, Leslie Murphy saving both times. We did well to draw with Distillery, missing Murphy, McCann and Lyner, but Billy Liddell was an excellent replacement in goals.

Two exciting wins over Glenavon allowed us to stay one point ahead of the Blues before meeting them in our last match of the season at Windsor Park. With Murphy and Liddell both injured regular left-back Hugh Annesley donned the keepers jersey, proceeded to keep a clean sheet, and so the City Cup was ours.

This trophy made up for indifferent displays in the knockout competitions. First round exits were suffered in the Irish, Gold and Charity Cups. In the first Charity game against Celtic Murphy sustained his serious injury while Davy Lyner and Norwood of Celtic were sent off. At least we reached the Shield final, going down to Distillery who had beaten our Seconds 4-1 in Round One. (Scorer: Heron).

The state of the Oval pitch had caused concern in January 1915. For the Shield encounter with the Blues it resembled a swimming pool, the players pantomime like antics causing laughter amongst the crowd. The Gold Cup tie with the Whites was oft postponed. Indeed one reporter joked that the referee once had to inspect the pitch from a canoe, and being unable to touch the bottom with his oar, called the game off!

The team had free Saturdays as a result of the cup knockouts and one of these was utilised for a trip to Scotland to meet Glasgow Celtic at Parkhead. The party endured a "fearfully stormy passage" on the ferry over and lost 0-3. Christie Grainger (ex-Cliftonville) made his debut for the Glens in this match.

McCann, Emerson, Scraggs, Lyner and Napier were Glentoran's representatives in the last series of inter-league fixtures for five seasons. Heron of the Seconds appeared in the Junior International at Windsor Park in March when Scotland and Ireland drew 1-1.

Football administrators did their best to raise funds for the War effort. The gate receipts from the trial inter-league game in September were donated to the Prince of Wales fund. The Probables and Possibles drew 2-2 with three Glenmen on each side. The season was finally brought to a close on 15th May when a combined Linfield/Belfast Celtic team beat a Rest of the League XI (including six of our players) 4-2 at Grosvenor Park. The proceeds went to the Wounded Soldiers' Fund.

Appearances and Goals

	App.	Goals		App.	Goals		App.	Goals
Scraggs	34	2	Napier	25	15	McAlpine	2	
Emerson	34	1	Moore W.	25	11	Garrett	2	
Lyner D.	32	4	Duff	16	3	Young	2	1
Boyd, Jack	32	11	Heron	7		O'Neill	2	
Murphy	31		Grainger	6		Reid	2	
McCann	31	1	Bennett	5		Kitchen	1	
Lindsay W.	28	6	Devlin	4		McDevitt	1	
Annsley	28		Cunningham	4				
Ferritt	28	6	Liddle	3		TOTAL	385	61

1915/16

*Football goes on during the war – Glentoran win the Belfast Cup
and the Shield*

While the War raged at Gallipolli and in Europe the IFA Council convened on 10th August 1915 to discuss the options for senior football in Ireland. It was decided that players should get £1 a game with the clubs having to donate a sum at the end of the season to the War Effort. Belfast Celtic stood against this, requesting that professional football be suspended for the season. This was rejected and Celtic decided not to play games against professional opposition. One night later the senior clubs committee met to thrash out the format for the season. With regular travel to Dublin out of the question it was agreed to form a Belfast and District League with Glenavon to travel to Belfast for all their games. An invitation was offered to Celtic but they declined, their directors electing to compete in the Intermediate League.

The new Management Committee of the Belfast League drew up a fixture list two weeks later and set members' season ticket prices at 10/-. However with only five clubs involved Glentoran's Mr. Adams put forward the name of a new team, Belfast United, who were accepted into the league only three days before the opening round of matches. United, under secretary James McGowan, would play all games away from home.

Most of the players attached to senior clubs were involved in munition work for the government. On the other hand Rugby in Ulster had become temporarily extinct as nearly all of the oval ball sportsmen were on active war service.

The crowd at our opening league fixture was swelled by a party of injured soldiers, while the pipe band of the 4th Inniskilling Dragoons supplied interval entertainment. The Reds equalised with five minutes remaining on that day. Roly Lyner had returned to the Oval to join fellow winger and brother Davy, but it was Billy Emerson who shone in the early season games.

Our first meeting with Belfast United saw them take the lead, and it was not until the 81st minute, when Ferritt's penalty gave Elisha Scott no chance, that we overwhelmed them. Sgt. Sommers, a recent recipient of the Victoria Cross, kicked off the game at Distillery on 16th October. There were over 100 injured troops among the 6,000 crowd and they watched Louis Bookman, who had gained an Irish international cap while with Bradford City, make a losing debut on the left wing. After the War Bookman moved to Luton Town gaining three more caps in the early 1920s. Bookman had actually been born in Russia as the son of a Jewish immigrant.

Roly Lyner had a trial in goals and kept a clean sheet against Cliftonville at the end of October. We used four different goalkeepers in the ten league games and a fifth, Steele (signed from the Reds), made the position his own for the second half of the season. After a vigourous and forceful goalless draw with Linfield (who had Houston sent off) the table read thus with three games remaining:

Linfield 12 points, Distillery 10, Glentoran 9.

Our hopes were raised a week later when United beat Linfield 1-0 and we overcame Glenavon before a meagre crowd on a miserable afternoon. Then, in the penultimate fixtures, Duff and Davy Lyner brought us back from a two goal deficit to draw with United. However the Blues saw off the Whites by 1-0 to create a two point gap over both ourselves and Distillery. Linfield duly defeated Cliftonville (2-0) but we overcame Distillery to finish as runners-up in the initial Belfast League.

Next it was the turn of the City Cup - now renamed the Belfast Cup. Davy Lyner and Bookman put in exceptional performances as we raced into joint top position at the end of the year.

The team was strengthened by the inclusion of three Dubliners - Lacey, Seymour and West. Ted Seymour had arrived from Cardiff City while inside-left Johnny West had aspirations outside football. West, who later moved to Linfield, was a baritone vocalist who toured and sang all over Ireland.

The only point we dropped in the first half of the Belfast Cup was to United on Christmas morning. On a sodden pitch Heggarty missed a penalty for the visitors and in the last twenty minutes Glentoran bombarded Scott with 15 shots but he was equal to them all!

Later in the afternoon Glentoran II and Linfield Swifts met in the Steel and Sons Cup final at Solitude. The Seconds had battled through with victories over Brantwood (7-3), Barn (1-0 after two scoreless draws) and Forth River (1-0 in the semi-final). The big crowd were disappointed with another scoreless draw and the New Year's Day replay also failed to divide the teams. Garrett was our scorer in a 1-1 draw before the Swifts won the second replay 2-0 at Celtic Park. The Seconds did pick up the Intermediate Cup, knocking out the Wee Blues 3-0 at the semi-final stage, thanks to a Fitzpatrick hat-trick, and the Intermediate League.

"The worst conditions ever", heralded in 1916. Despite incessant rain and a howling gale the players put on a show to defeat Glenavon 5-4 after we had twice held a four goal lead. George Ferritt put a penalty yards wide but the win kept us neck and neck with Belfast United on 11 points. Rollo's penalty was enough to hand us defeat against Linfield but a week later the Blues did us a favour when defeating United 3-1. Our win over Cliftonville was achieved despite being down to eight men for a 15 minute period in the second half. Grainger had been sent-off while Boyd and Emerson left the field due to injury. The Belfast Cup was more or less secured on 5th February when we hammered Belfast United. Their only moment of glory came when Walker equalised Lyner's third minute opener.

Our last game against Distillery was originally played at the Oval as Grosvenor Park was being used for a Linfield-Celtic Irish Cup semi-final. After our win the match was declared a friendly so we had to do it all again on a Monday evening at the end of the season. The point gained won the Belfast Cup, obviating the need for a play-off with United.

The rest of January through to the beginning of April was given over to our Irish Cup and County Antrim Shield campaigns. With Steele excelling in goals we knocked out United in the Shield and then whenever goals from Kitchen and McLaughlan enabled the Seconds to knock out Linfield Swifts an all-Glentoran semi-final was set up.

Torrential rain kept the crowd to small proportions but those present witnessed a good display from our juniors with Liddell, McLaughlan and Alfie Snape catching the eye. The firsts had only a single goal to show from continuous attacks over the two games. About 8,000 attended the final when we reversed the result of the previous season after an evenly contested game against Distillery.

We did fall, however, at the final hurdle of the Irish Cup. Linfield were rather fortunate on two counts. Firstly they had been "beaten" 1-0 by Belfast United in Round Two. United though were removed from the competition for playing unregistered players. Then in the replay of the final Glens' left-back Grainger injured himself following a tackle on Bovill two minutes before half-time. He took no further part and our defence was disorganised when Nixon netted the only goal.

The Gold Cup was played off on a mini-league basis with all games taking place at neutral venues in Belfast. Generally the matches had an end of season feel to them with the country's interest being distracted to the Easter Rising in Dublin. A large crowd did attend the last fixture when we took a point off the Blues forcing them into a play-off with Distillery for the Cup.

Our Charity Cup tie virtually became an army recruiting campaign. Military pipe and bugle bands played while various patriotic speeches could be heard in different corners of the ground. Linfield won but lost the final 0-1 to Distillery.

Glentoran's final game of the season was against Linfield in a friendly. The East Belfast Women's Committee arranged the fixture so that the gate receipts could be used to help provide comfort for soldiers and prisoners of war in Ireland. This time the Glens won and so received diamond pins with the Bluemen having to be content with silver matchboxes as runners-up. Footballing events were finally wound up a week later when a match between a Distillery/Linfield XI and the Rest of the League (who included Steele, Scraggs and Seymour) raised £42 for the Lord Roberts Workshop Memorial Fund. The Rest won 2-1.

Bennett of the Seconds appeared for the Intermediate League in the season's only representative fixture against the Scottish Junior League. It finished 2-2.

Results 1915/16

Played 34. Won 18. Drew 11. Lost 5. Goals For 65. Against 31. % 69.1
Honours: Belfast Cup, County Antrim Shield

BDL	18/09/15		Cliftonville	A	D	1	1	Duff
BDL	25/09/15		Linfield	H	D	0	0	-
BDL	02/10/15		Glenavon	H	W	5	2	Moore 2, Lyner 2, Boyd
BDL	09/10/15		Belfast United	H	W	2	1	Moore, Ferritt (p)
BDL	16/10/15		Distillery	A	L	0	1	-
BDL	30/10/15		Cliftonville	H	W	4	0	Duff, Boyd, Moore, Ferritt (p)
BDL	06/11/15		Linfield	A	D	0	0	-
BDL	13/11/15		Glenavon	H	W	2	1	Boyd, Moore
BDL	20/11/15		Belfast United	H	D	2	2	Lyner 2
BDL	27/11/15		Distillery	H	W	4	2	Boyd 2, Duff 2
BCC	04/12/15		Glenavon	H	W	5	1	Boyd 2, Moore, Ferritt, Scraggs
BCC	11/12/15		Linfield	H	W	3	0	Ferritt 2(2p), Boyd
BCC	18/12/15		Cliftonville	H	W	4	1	Seymour 2, West 2
BCC	25/12/15		Belfast United	H	D	0	0	-
BCC	28/12/15		Distillery	H	W	2	1	Moore, West
BCC	01/01/16		Glenavon	H	W	5	4	Seymour 2, Boyd 2, West
BCC	08/01/16		Linfield	A	L	0	1	-
BCC	15/01/16		Cliftonville	A	W	3	1	Boyd 3
BCC	05/02/16		Belfast United	H	W	5	1	Boyd 2, Duff, West, Lyner
BCC	08/05/16		Distillery	A	D	1	1	Seymour
CAS	22/01/16	1	Belfast United	H	W	1	0	Boyd
CAS	12/02/16	SF	Glentoran II	GP	D	0	0	-
CAS	26/02/16	SFR	Glentoran II	Solt	W	1	0	Duff
CAS	18/03/16	F	Distillery	Solt	W	1	0	Boyd
IC	19/02/16	2	Distillery	A	W	3	0	Boyd, Lyner, McLaughlan
IC	11/03/16	SF	Bohemians	Solt	W	4	2	Boyd, Bookman, West 2
IC	25/03/16	F	Linfield	CP	D	1	1	Ferritt (p)
IC	01/04/16	FR	Linfield	GP	L	0	1	-
GC	08/04/16		Belfast United	WP	D	2	2	Duff, Boyd
GC	22/04/16		Distillery	Solt	D	0	0	-
GC	24/04/16		Glenavon	WP	W	3	1	Boyd 2, West
GC	25/04/16		Cliftonville	WP	L	0	1	-
GC	06/05/16		Linfield	GP	D	1	1	West
ChC	15/04/16	SF	Linfield	GP	L	0	2	-
F	04/09/15		Linfield	A	W	3	1	Duff, Lyner, Moore
F	11/09/15		Cliftonville	H	W	5	1	Boyd 2, Moore, Scraggs, Redman og
F	04/03/16		Distillery	H	W	1	0	Seymour
F	13/05/16		Linfield	H	W	2	1	Lyner, Seymour Soldiers' Fund

Appearances and Goals

	App.	Goals		App.	Goals		App.	Goals
Ferritt	34	6	Duff	18	7	Snape	3	
Boyd, Jack	33	22	Seymour	18	5	Murphy	3	
Emerson	32		Moore W.	17	7	Brady	1	
Stafford	30		West	17	9	Fitzpatrick	1	
Scraggs	30	1	Lyner R.	15		McLaughlan	1	1
Lyner D.	29	6	McCann	5		Young	1	
Grainger	27		Matthews	4		Bennett	1	
Bookman	23	1	Liddle	4		Hendry	1	
Steele	22		McAlpine	4		TOTAL	374	65

1916/17

A four-trophy season – Ferritt, Scraggs and Emerson – Glentoran Olympic

With largely the same playing panel as the season before Glentoran had one of their best ever years, returning an 86% playing record. Indeed only defeats at the hands of Linfield in the County Antrim Shield and Charity Cup denied us of a clean sweep. Ferritt, Scraggs and Emerson, the half-back trio were the backbone of the team while the forward line of Lyner, Seymour, Boyd, Clarke (signed from St.Mirren) and Willie Moore developed into an excellent combination. With the departure of Paddy McCann Christie Grainger had many partners at full-back, but the infallible left back was a thorn in all opponents attacks.

Early progress in the Belfast League was solid rather than spectacular. Just after half time in the Belfast United game the ball was kicked onto the roof of the Oval pavilion and was unable to be retrieved. Private Clarke enjoyed a scoring debut in that match and was also on target a week later when Hamilton snatched a draw for Linfield in the 88th minute.

Alfie Snape.

When Distillery visited us all seven goals came in the first half. Davy Lyner's accurate crossing led to our four. After two rousing wins over Glenavon and Cliftonville we were locked on 12 points alongside Linfield with three games remaining. The 4th November was a good day for us and Lyner in particular. His lovely centre set up Ted Seymour for the first goal and then Davy grabbed two himself as the Blues lost 0-2 to Distillery at Grosvenor Park.

The title was wrapped up in convincing style at the Oval the following Saturday when an exceptionally large crowd for the time of around 12,000 attended. The game kicked off twenty minutes late and, despite the early darkness, reporters had no doubt of Glentoran's superiority. Although they were missing four regulars the Whites gave us the hardest match of the season so far, but the 3-3 draw ensured we finished the 1916/7 Belfast League as unbeaten champions.

G.Moore came into the side at right-back for the Belfast Cup while Flockhart replaced Clarke at centre-forward, as a consequence of a dispute over the Scottish soldier's registration. The Glens just went from strength to strength, completing the competition with a 100% record. Bennett's solid displays at right-half deserve a mention while Grainger and Moore were too clever for opposing forward lines. The only bad note during the tournament was the dismissal of Emerson and T.Molyneaux (Cliftonville) after a nasty incident between the two at Solitude.

Possibly our best performance of the season was reserved to the last when Linfield were hammered 6-1 at the Oval. Boyd and Seymour had put us 2-0 up after only five minutes.

Glentoran II's failed to reach the final of the Steel and Sons Cup, bowing out 0-1 to Belfast Celtic in the semis. They had recorded wins over St.Mary's Swifts (8-0), Ormiston (4-0) and Forth River (2-0) to reach that stage. Further disappointment came with a first round Intermediate Cup exit (1-2 to Linfield Swifts) and defeat in the McElroy Cup semi-final (0-1 to the Blues' juniors). Individually, Liddell, Brady, Bennett and Snape of the Seconds

100

brought distinction to the club, appearing for Ireland in their 2-0 win over Scotland in the Junior International at Grosvenor Park.

This was the first season in which we formally fielded a third XI, Glentoran Olympic. They played in the second division of the Belfast Combination, and despite suffering a 0-2 Junior Shield loss to first division Glencairn, the Olympic had a very encouraging debut (see the table on the next page).

Results 1916/17

Played 32. Won 25. Drew 5. Lost 2. Goals For 82. Against 31. % 85.9.
Honours: Belfast and District League, Irish Cup, Belfast Cup, Gold Cup

BDL	09/09/16		Glenavon	H	W	4	3	Boyd 2, Seymour, Lyner
BDL	16/09/16		Cliftonville	A	D	1	1	Lyner
BDL	23/09/16		Belfast United	H	W	2	1	Emerson, Clarke
BDL	30/09/16		Linfield	A	D	2	2	Clarke, Boyd
BDL	07/10/16		Distillery	H	W	4	3	Clarke 3, Boyd
BDL	21/10/16		Glenavon	H	W	3	2	Boyd 2, Ferritt
BDL	28/10/16		Cliftonville	H	W	2	0	Ferritt (p), Boyd
BDL	04/11/16		Belfast United	H	W	3	1	Lyner 2, Seymour
BDL	11/11/16		Linfield	H	W	4	0	Seymour 2, Boyd 2
BDL	18/11/16		Distillery	A	D	3	3	Boyd, Seymour, Clarke
BCC	02/12/16		Distillery	A	W	1	0	Lyner
BCC	16/12/16		Glenavon	H	W	7	0	Seymour 3, McLaughlan 2 Kitchen, W.Moore
BCC	23/12/16		Cliftonville	A	W	3	1	Boyd 3
BCC	25/12/16		Belfast United	WP	W	5	2	Lyner 2, Seymour, Boyd, Flockhart
BCC	26/12/16		Distillery	H	W	3	0	W.Moore, Seymour, Flockhart
BCC	30/12/16		Linfield	A	W	2	0	Lyner 2
BCC	06/01/17		Glenavon	H	W	3	1	W.Moore 2, Boyd
BCC	20/01/17		Cliftonville	H	W	1	0	Seymour
BCC	27/01/17		Belfast United	H	W	3	2	Boyd, Ferritt (p), Bennett
BCC	11/05/17		Linfield	H	W	6	1	Boyd 2, Seymour 2, Kitchen, W.Moore
IC	03/02/17	1	Cliftonville	H	W	2	0	Boyd 2 – Round Two Bye
IC	10/03/17	SF	Distillery	Solt	D	1	1	Boyd
IC	17/03/17	SFR	Distillery	Solt	W	3	1	Ferritt, Lyner, Boyd
IC	31/03/17	F	Belfast Celtic	WP	W	2	0	Seymour 2
CAS	10/02/17	SF	Distillery	Solt	W	3	2	Young 2, Boyd
CAS	03/03/17	F	Linfield	CP	L	0	3	-
GC	07/04/17		Distillery	H	D	0	0	-
GC	09/04/17		Linfield	A	A	0	1	Abandoned after 63 minutes, snowstorm. Linfield refused to replay, Glentoran awarded the points.
GC	10/04/17		Cliftonville	H	W	1	0	G.Moore
GC	14/04/17		Belfast United	H	W	4	0	Boyd, Seymour 3
GC	21/04/17		Glenavon	H	W	3	0	Boyd, Seymour 2
ChC	28/04/17	SF	Distillery	WP	W	1	0	Boyd
ChC	05/05/17	F	Linfield	Solt	L	0	1	-
F	26/08/16		Linfield	H	L	0	1	-
F	02/09/16		Belfast United	H	W	5	0	Duff 2, Boyd, W.Moore, Snape
F	26/12/16		Rest of the League	GP	L	0	1	Ulster Patriotic Fund
F	17/02/17		Cliftonville	H	W	1	0	W.Moore
F	23/03/17		Belfast United	H	W	2	0	Lyner 2
F	26/05/17		Linfield	GP	W	2	1	Seymour, Kitchen Limbless Soldiers' Fund

Other third XI results were:

09 Sep	Glenfield	(H)	2-1	13 Jan	Dunadry Swifts	(A)	1-3
23 Sep	Eastmount	(H)	3-2	20 Jan	G.N.Railway	(H)	1-0
30 Sep	Stanley	(A)	0-4	27 Jan	Glenfield	(A)	1-2
07 Oct	Avoneil	(H)	1-0	03 Feb	Vulcan Rovers	(H)	6-2
14 Oct	Willowfield II	(H)	1-0	10 Feb	Oldpark II	(H)	4-2
21 Oct	Vulcan Rovers	(A)	0-1	24 Feb	Cliftonville United	(H)	5-2
28 Oct	St.Paul's Swifts	(A)	1-1	10 Mar	St.Paul's Swifts	(H)	2-2
23 Dec	Cliftonville United	(H)	3-0	19 May	Oldpark II	(H)	3-2
30 Dec	Eastmount	(H)	2-0				

Record Traced: Played 18, Won 11, Drew 2, Lost 5, Goals For 36, Against 26.

The first XI's attention was occupied by the Irish Cup and County Antrim Shield in February and March 1917. A superior all-round display against Cliftonville saw us through to meet Distillery, the 2-0 conquerors of Dundela, in the cup semi-final. After we had led in the first game the Whites took us to a replay but George Ferritt engineered a fine Glentoran win. Old foes Belfast Celtic, now playing as a junior club, awaited us in the final. Over 20,000 flocked to Windsor Park at the end of March, the unexpectedly high gate delaying the kick-off by 15 minutes. After half an hour a heavy snowfall descended but this failed to damage the pitch, which had been excellently prepared by groundsman Campbell. Seymour nodded us ahead just before the break and then shot past Scott on the hour having turned McIlroy inside out. Glentoran supporters did not mind the wind and snow, the Cup had been won again!

This result made up for our abysmal Shield final display when the backs let the side down badly. McEwan (2) and Houston capitalised for Linfield.

The Gold Cup was packed into a two-week spell around Easter. Controversy arose when the match against Linfield at Windsor was "snowed off" after 63 minutes with the Blues ahead. If the result stood the Cup was Linfield's but the Gold Cup committee ordered a replay. Linfield refused and their secretary Sam Close explained why in a letter to the News Letter on 21st May. Apparently Linfield would only agree to play if the gate receipts were donated to the UVF Limbless Hospital. The Gold Cup committee voted 6-4 against this and so the points and the cup came Glentoran's way.

The teams did meet in a game for the above fund in late May. About 10,000 attended to produce a sum of £198. Injured soldiers, provided they were dressed in hospital blue, gained free entry. Kitchen netted the winner with an "unsaveable shot." The Glens had also been involved in a Charity match on Boxing Day. £208 was raised for the Ulster Patriotic Fund when the Champions met the Rest of the League at Grosvenor Park. Lady Liddell kicked off and later awarded gold breastpins to the winners.

Appearances and Goals

	App.	Goals		App.	Goals		App.	Goals
Ferritt	31	4	Clarke	9	6	Liddle	2	
Boyd, Jack	31	26	Kitchen	6	2	Lismore	1	
Moore W.	31	5	Young	6	2	McDevitt	1	
Steele	30		Kirkwood	6		Cowan	1	
Grainger	30		Flockhart	4	2	Garrett	1	
Seymour	29	20	Snape	4		Williamson	1	
Emerson	26	1	Brady	4		Mitchell	1	
Lyner D.	24	10	Duff	4		McMinn	1	
Moore G.	22	1	McCann	4				
Scraggs	22		McLaughlan	3	2	TOTAL	352	82
Bennett	14	1	Taylor	3				

1917/18

Interest in football wanes - A strong Second XI – Scott impassable

The priority of life in 1917 was such that public interest and newspaper coverage of football took a backseat. The pages of the papers themselves became thinner and both the News Letter and Northern Whig dropped to four page issues in April 1918. This coincided with the government passing legislation to make the wasting of paper a criminal offence.

Just prior to the pre-season friendlies Belfast United announced that they would be merging with Intermediate League team Ulster United and play their home fixtures at the old Ulster grounds at Ballynafeigh. Glentoran visited in September, winning 2-1, even with centre-forward Kitchen sent off. Cliftonville's goalkeeper Dan Peck was an adversary in the early games, twice denying us from scoring in friendly and league.

The settled nature of the side was a factor in our conceding only one goal in the opening six league games. Then a 3-1 win (Duff's goal was great) over United left us only a point behind leaders Linfield with three matches left.

As the outcome of our encounter with Glenavon was assumed to be a foregone conclusion a low crowd turned out on a damp day. However spirits were lifted when it transpired that Distillery and Linfield had drawn 2-2 at Grosvenor Park. The crowds flocked to the Oval a week later and Willie Moore gave us an early lead. The Whites made desperate efforts to get level but our defence played in fine style and Ted Seymour wrapped up the two points in the last minute. The Blues overcame Cliftonville 3-1 to set up a Belfast League showdown at Windsor Park on 17th November.

WILLIAM MOORE
GLENTORAN

William Moore.

An estimated 14,000 turned up for the game. Linfield looked the more dangerous early on and Billy Liddell had to be alert in the Glens' goal. Up front Glentoran missed the injured Boyd and George Ferritt was never comfortable in the centre-forward role. Schofield gave the Blues the lead on 40 minutes but after the break Glentoran controlled the game and an equaliser appeared certain. However it was not forthcoming and a late McEwan goal, when Campbell was in an off-side position, allowed the Windsor men to regain the Belfast League.

Possibly frustrated by this defeat the Oval forward line began the City Cup by knocking in 13 goals in the first three fixtures. Emerson and Moore displayed nice touches and we were helped by an injury to Storey, Belfast United's keeper, in the second game. December brought heavy grounds and many complaints from clubs on the state of the pitches. The problems came about after firstly periods of torrential rain, then maybe a week of frost, then a quick thaw leading to quagmires.

Glentoran's performances and results suffered until a Billy Crone goal got us back to winning ways on Christmas Day. The same afternoon Distillery beat Linfield 3-2, allowing us to close the gap at the top of the table to a single point. Both clubs won their eighth and

103

ninth fixtures (a single goal was enough for Linfield on each occasion) leaving a similar situation to the Belfast League.

This time the decider was at the Oval in early March and attracted around 12,000 spectators. The only goal of the game was scored by our ex-forward West for Linfield and the wildness of the Glens forwards' shooting prevented any equaliser.

Elisha Scott must have set some sort of record in February 1918. For, on four successive Saturday afternoons, he prevented a Glentoran forward line from scoring in the Irish Cup. Our first XI perished in Round One, again the forwards missing many chances. Then, in the second round, the Glentoran 2nd XI drew 0-0 at Celtic Park before capitulating in the second half of the replay. Celtic went on to win the Cup for the first time in their history, defeating the Blues 2-0 in the final after two scoreless draws.

The Glens exacted revenge on Belfast Celtic in the County Antrim Shield, and in so doing reached the final for the fifth consecutive season. We were not to be denied a trophy by the Blues this time although it must be said that the Windsor XI were under strength.

Linfield did have the last say, a McBean goal being enough for them in the Charity Cup final. Although the Charity games lacked the usual fire and enthusiasm of the regular fixtures, Glentoran did lodge a protest with the Charity committee over the eligibility of the Linfield centre-half Percy Smith, guesting from Blackburn Rovers. The committee ordered a replay to take place at the start of the 1918/9 season but a subsequent appeal from Linfield was upheld and the initial result stood.

We had to beat the Blues in the last Gold Cup fixture, but a 0-0 draw left us as runners-up, one point behind.

Football again did its bit for the War Effort. On 6th April 1918 there was a gala at Windsor Park in aid of Flag Day. Over 20,000 attended and the £932 raised was presented to the UVF Hospital on behalf of the British Red Cross fund. Various athletic events took place with the main feature a 100 yard challenge sprint. The race was won by Glentoran's left-wing Willie Moore in 10.2 seconds, with Distillery's right-winger Jack Brown in second, three yards behind. Moore also took part and scored in the soccer attraction as Messrs. Workman and Clark and Co. defeated Messrs. Harland and Wolff 3-1, with nine Glentoran players involved in the game.

Women's soccer also featured significantly during the season. There were many organised games and in one at Celtic Park, Lurgan in February, Lurgan Ladies eclipsed Portadown Ladies by 10-3.

An aspect of Junior Football during World War One was the strength of Glentoran II. Their results for 1917/8 are given here as evidence, matches are in the Intermediate League unless stated.

(SC=Steel and Sons Cup, IC=Intermediate Cup, IR=Irish Cup, MC=McElroy Cup)

Date	Opponent		Score			Date	Opponent		Score	
25 Aug	Whitehead	H	1-0			25 Dec	Belfast Celtic	WP	0-1	SCF
08 Sep	Oldpark Corinthians	A	1-1			29 Dec	Willowfield United	H	6-2	ICSF
15 Sep	Ormiston	H	4-2			05 Jan	Ormiston	H	4-0	
22 Sep	Cliftonville Olympic	A	0-0			12 Jan	Whitehead	H	3-0	
29 Sep	Belfast Celtic	A	0-1			02 Feb	Dunmurray	H	6-0	
06 Oct	Bloomfield United	A	6-0	SC1		16 Feb	Belfast Celtic	A	0-0	IR1
20 Oct	Belfast Celtic	H	2-2			23 Feb	Belfast Celtic	A	0-4	IR1R
27 Oct	Summerfield	H	7-0			09 Mar	Distillery II	H	2-1	
03 Nov	Whitehead	H	4-1	IC1		16 Mar	Linfield Swifts	Sol	1-0	ICF
10 Nov	Forth River	H	2-1	SC2		23 Mar	Oldpark Corinthians	H	3-0	
17 Nov	Distillery II	H	4-1	IC2		20 Apr	Linfield Swifts	H	3-0	MCSF
01 Dec	Dundela	H	2-0	IC3		27 Apr	Forth River	A	1-0	
15 Dec	Distillery II	WP	2-0 aet	SCSF		18 May	Ormiston	Sol	2-0	MCF
22 Dec	Cliftonville Olympic	H	5-0							

The only representative fixtures undertaken in this season were the Intermediate League's matches against the Irish Alliance, the Glasgow League and the Lanarkshire Junior League. J.Kirkwood, W.Liddell, F.Brady, D.Lemon and A.Snape of the Seconds appeared in these games.

Results 1917/18

Played 31. Won 19. Drew 7. Lost 5. Goals For 54. Against 18. % 72.6.
Honours: County Antrim Shield

BDL	08/09/17		Cliftonville	H	D	0	0	-
BDL	15/09/17		Belfast United	A	W	2	1	Boyd, W.Moore (p)
BDL	22/09/17		Glenavon	H	W	1	0	Seymour
BDL	29/09/17		Distillery	A	W	2	0	Seymour 2
BDL	06/10/17		Linfield	H	D	0	0	-
BDL	20/10/17		Cliftonville	A	W	4	0	W.Moore 2, Seymour, Lyner
BDL	27/10/17		Belfast United	H	W	3	1	W.Moore (p), Duff, Emerson
BDL	03/11/17		Glenavon	H	W	4	1	W.Moore 2, Boyd, Crone
BDL	10/11/17		Distillery	H	W	2	0	W.Moore, Seymour
BDL	17/11/17		Linfield	A	L	0	2	-
BCC	24/11/17		Glenavon	H	W	4	1	Lemon 2, Seymour, Ferritt
BCC	01/12/17		Belfast United	A	W	5	1	Boyd 3, Lemon 2
BCC	08/12/17		Cliftonville	H	W	4	0	Boyd 4
BCC	15/12/17		Distillery	A	D	1	1	W.Moore
BCC	22/12/17		Linfield	A	L	0	1	-
BCC	24/12/17		Belfast United	H	D	0	0	-
BCC	25/12/17		Glenavon	H	W	1	0	Crone
BCC	29/12/17		Cliftonville	A	W	2	0	W.Moore, Boyd
BCC	05/01/18		Distillery	H	W	3	1	W.Moore 2, Boyd
BCC	02/03/18		Linfield	H	L	0	1	-
IC	02/02/18	1	Belfast Celtic	A	D	0	0	-
IC	09/02/18	1R	Belfast Celtic	H	L	0	1	-
GC	23/02/18		Belfast United	A	D	2	2	Boyd, Scraggs
GC	01/04/18		Cliftonville	A	W	1	0	Connor
GC	02/04/18		Distillery	H	W	3	1	Connor, W.Moore 2(1p)
GC	12/04/18		Glenavon	H	W	3	1	Lyner, Connor, Boyd
GC	11/05/18		Linfield	H	D	0	0	-
CAS	23/03/18	SF	Belfast Celtic	Solt	W	2	1	W.Moore (p), Connor
CAS	20/04/18	F	Linfield	GP	W	2	0	Connor, Crone
ChC	27/04/18	SF	Distillery	Solt	W	3	0	Boyd, Lyner, Connor
ChC	04/05/18	F	Linfield	Solt	L	0	1	-
F	25/08/17		Linfield	A	D	1	1	Smith
F	01/09/17		Cliftonville	H	D	0	0	-
F	26/01/18		Distillery	H	D	2	2	Duff, McDonald

Appearances and Goals

	App.	Goals		App.	Goals		App.	Goals
Moore W.	31	14	Duff	19	1	Lemon	4	4
Grainger	30		Bennett	18		Stewart	3	
Scraggs	30	1	Moore G.	16		Johnston	2	
Ferritt	28	1	Steele	15		Kitchen	2	
Emerson	28	1	Liddle	15		Ferguson	1	
Lyner D.	25	3	Crone	12	3	Mehaffey	1	
Seymour	23	6	Connor	10	6	TOTAL	341	54
Boyd, Jack	23	14	Brady	5				

1918/19

Belfast Celtic return – Many transfers – George Ferritt's Benefit

As the Allies began their final push on the Western Front the football season returned once again in Ireland in August 1918. The newspapers had reverted to their pre-war quality and a reporter previewed - "Football will come as a welcome relief to those whose thoughts are seldom allowed to get away from the war. It affords a pleasant afternoon to thousands of shipyard workers, while it must not be forgotten that the majority of players themselves are deployed at one or other of the yards."

There were hints at a general return to normality with the re-appearance of Belfast Celtic in senior circles, at the expense of Glenavon. However Celtic brought with them an element of "support" which led to probably the worst ever sustained violence at football matches in Belfast, involving weekly rioting, stone throwing and attacks on officials.

Alan Mathieson.

There was a new face in the secretary's post at the Oval, Mr. Walter Scott (ex-Distillery) succeeding Joseph Shaw who had resigned for business reasons. On the playing side Hughie Ferguson and Ernie Dunwoody arrived from Cliftonville, the latter as goalkeeping cover for Liddell. Ted Seymour and Billy Bennett moved to Linfield but Bennett was transferred back to Glentoran before the season commenced! In mid-September the Newby brothers, Harry and Willie, came across from England to play, offsetting the departure of Jack Connor to Distillery. The Glens also obtained permission to field Harry Chambers, the Liverpool centre-forward, while he was stationed in Belfast. The Belfast and District League rescinded the maximum wage of £1 a game rule.

After being involved in two hard friendlies the Glens began their league campaign with a visit from Linfield. With Moore, Lyner and Bennett prominent we got off to a winning start but then fell into a bad run. Peck saved Moore's penalty, then Spence scored for Cliftonville in the last minute. Jack Boyd was lacking support up front and only three goals had been registered at the half way stage of the league. Liddell had a blinder against Distillery, including one marvellous save from Harry Hafekost.

On 12th October Windsor Park hosted the first "War" International when Ireland and England drew 0-0. Glentoran had Scraggs, Emerson and Lyner on the Irish team and immediately after the game the directors permanently secured the services of Chambers, England's centre-forward. Although he did not get on the scoresheet on his debut, Chambers did feature in an excellent win in the return match with the Blues. The result left Glentoran in fourth place, four points behind Celtic, who led Linfield and Distillery by three.

Despite a 0-2 defeat at Celtic Park the Glens began to get it together with Johnny McCullough having a good spell at inside-left. Third place was secured but all attention

106

was focused on the Celtic-Linfield clash on 16th November. The Blues had to win to force a play-off and this they did 1-0. "Justice", the News Letter's footballing columnist added an interesting footnote to the game, but some may doubt the authenticity of the story; "By far the happiest man to leave Celtic Park was a soldier who prior to Saturday afternoon had been dumb for six months. When Harris scored the soldier became most excited and commenced to cheer. He was greatly surprised at the sound of his voice and afterwards was able to talk as fluently as any man in the enclosure."

Celtic had the last say, however, winning the play-off 1-0 at Grosvenor Park in April. Once again rival followers engaged in stone throwing while the Celtic contingent sang "the Soldier's Song."

Glentoran's improved form continued into the Belfast Cup. We romped to a win over Distillery after falling behind and then Elisha Scott had to be at his very best to keep out our forwards, whom were expertly prompted by the half-backs - Ferritt, Scraggs and Emerson. Frank Brady had developed into an excellent right full-back.

With the War officially over many of the Irish clubs bade farewell to their military men who returned home to mainland Britain. The Glens' loss was McCullough.

A Davy Rollo penalty condemned us to defeat against Linfield but we prepared for the taxing Christmas period with a convincing win over Belfast United. Billy Liddell married and spent Christmas on honeymoon in Scotland so forcing secretary Walter Scott to sign Newcastle United goalkeeper Jimmy Laurence as temporary cover. Gough also had a game in nets before Liddell's return against United on 4th January.

Harry Chambers.

Glentoran Seconds faced Distillery's reserve XI in the Steel and Sons Cup final on Christmas afternoon at Solitude. The Seconds, helped ably by Andy Kennedy (ex-Belfast Celtic) and Jack Brown (Distillery's first team winger who had been refused permission to join the Glens' senior panel), had eliminated Dundela (4-0), Bloomfield United (6-0), Oldpark Corinthians (1-0) and Linfield Swifts (4-1) to reach the final. The junior Whites had beaten us 4-1 in the Intermediate Cup so the 20,000 present were expecting a keen game. It finished 1-1 but in the New Year's Day replay at Celtic Park the "Wee Glens" turned the tables winning 2-1, Crooks and Lemon on target. Distillery II tipped the balance later in the season by knocking Glentoran II out of the McElroy Cup but our reserves redeemed themselves by lifting the Intermediate League title.

The year of 1918 was rounded off by George Ferritt's benefit day at the Oval on 30th December. A strengthened Glens XI, containing Dan Peck and Sam Burnison, went down to a Linfield/Celtic XI in a game reduced to 30 minutes each way due to inclement weather. The other sporting attractions that day included a boxing bout in which Jim Dwyer of Dublin outpointed George Cummings over ten rounds. There was a 100 yards handicap sprint competition involving the swiftest players in the Belfast League. The four heat winners O'Brien (United), Emerson (Glentoran), Barrett (Celtic) and Brown (Distillery) ran in the final when Fred Barrett broke the tape by a yard from Jack Brown. Out of the £400 receipts taken on the day, it was reported that Ferritt pocketed £250.

Back to the Belfast Cup and while we came from behind to see off United, Celtic dropped a point in a 2-2 draw with Distillery at Grosvenor Park. This left ourselves and Celtic level on 13 points and the Celts fans vented their feelings by attacking the Whites' players and smashing the goalposts at the final whistle.

The Glens, parading new right-back Spencer, signed from Brighton and Hove Albion, then overcame Cliftonville 3-1, giving Celtic the challenge of defeating Linfield to force a play-off. This they duly did but the Blues protested vainly to the league as their keeper Fred McKee had been struck by a bottle and continually stoned during the game.

The Glentoran-Celtic play-off at the end of the season was another unfortunate affair. From the word go there were free fights on the terraces and the teams didn't help matters with over robust play. Alan Mathieson and Celtic's Ferriss were ordered off and many others were cautioned. Extra time failed to separate the teams and the cup committee ruled that there were be no replay "due to the unsavoury acts of hooliganism in the first meeting."

Violence had also flared when the Glens and Celtic met in the Irish Cup semi-final. An immense crowd had turned up and the atmosphere was tense. The nearest thing to a goal in the first half came when the Glens were awarded a penalty but Scott turned away Willie Moore's spot-kick. Davy Lyner broke the deadlock and when Moore made it 2-0 on 86 minutes the Celtic following jumped over the unreserved stand and invaded the pitch.

Referee Cowan stopped the game but he was stoned and punched for his trouble. The hooligans then smashed up chairs which had been laid out for injured soldiers and indeed one thug threw a chair at Willie Moore. Belfast Celtic were a fine club but their name was being dragged through the mire by the performances of the rowdy element of their support.

Needless to say Glentoran progressed to the final where old adversaries Linfield awaited. A crowd of 18,000 attended the first meeting, played in a blizzard. Lyner shot us ahead after 20 minutes but within 60 seconds Featherstone equalised and the game deteriorated thereafter. A week later the conditions were much better for the replay but neither team could score, Moore having our best chance but firing over when faced with an open goal! The teams met for the third time of asking, the game kicking off at 6.30 pm the following Monday evening. In an excellent game Marshall McEwan proved the Blues' matchwinner with goals from close range either side of half-time. We pulled one back with 15 minutes to go when a penalty for handball was awarded against Lacey. McKee saved Scraggs effort, Johnny drove home the rebound, but it was not enough.

The remaining three tournaments also ended in frustration for the Glens. In the County Antrim Shield Linfield, aided by ex-Glenmen Jimmy Lindsay (recently signed from Burnley) and Davy Duff, dismissed us in a game which contained much "hacking". Jack Boyd was sent off. After drawing 0-0 with Cliftonville, Glentoran II were eliminated from the competition when the Reds protested over the inclusion of Ellis Kifford of Blackburn Rovers in the Seconds' goal.

It had originally been intended for teams to play each other twice in the Gold Cup but due to the congestion caused by Cup and Shield replays the Belfast and District League Committee decided to halve the fixtures. Christie Grainger had to don the goalkeeper's jersey for the first ten minutes against Linfield as Billy Liddell was late in turning up. The Distillery-Celtic game was abandoned after the Whites' players were again attacked by Celtic supporters.

Liddell was then unable to catch a suitable train from his RAF base for the first round Charity Cup tie with Belfast United and John Mehaffey stood in. It was United's keeper Gray who stole the honours though, until he was beaten by three late goals. The Charity Committee had decided that corners would count in the event of drawn games and it was as well those late goals came as United had forced six corners to the Glens' five. By the time the semi-finals were played Harry Chambers had returned to Liverpool after becoming the latest footballing benedict. Cliftonville were swept aside but Linfield won a poor final in front of 9,413. Lindsay scored while Moore hit the bar for the Glens.

Other fixtures included a visit to Dublin, and a combined Glentoran / Celtic XI beating Linfield 2-1 in Marshall McEwans's benefit. Alfie Snape moved to Airdrie in March and the Scottish club put out their full league team at the Oval in May. The game stood at 2-2 with five minutes remaining when Alan Mathieson popped up to complete his hat-trick and a fine win for the Glens.

The resurgent interest in soccer was reflected by a new weekly publication, "The Football Critic". On sale every Wednesday at 1 and 1/2 d it apparently contained all the latest news and crisp criticism and comment on the local game.

Results 1918/19

Played 36. Won 17. Drew 9. Lost 10. Goals For 55. Against 30. % 59.7.
Honours: Belfast Cup (Shared with Belfast Celtic)

Comp	Date	Rd	Opponent	Venue	Res			Scorers
BDL	07/09/18		Linfield	H	W	1	0	W.Moore
BDL	14/09/18		Cliftonville	A	L	0	1	-
BDL	21/09/18		Belfast Celtic	H	L	1	2	Boyd
BDL	28/09/18		Belfast United	A	L	1	2	Boyd
BDL	05/10/18		Distillery	A	D	0	0	-
BDL	19/10/18		Linfield	A	W	2	0	Lyner 2
BDL	26/10/18		Cliftonville	H	W	2	0	Boyd, Johnston
BDL	02/11/18		Belfast Celtic	A	L	0	2	-
BDL	09/11/18		Belfast United	H	W	1	0	Boyd
BDL	16/11/18		Distillery	H	W	3	2	Scraggs (p), Boyd, W.Moore
BCC	23/11/18		Distillery	A	W	4	1	Boyd 2, Newby, Ferritt (p)
BCC	30/11/18		Belfast Celtic	A	D	0	0	-
BCC	07/12/18		Linfield	A	L	0	1	-
BCC	14/12/18		Belfast United	H	W	3	0	Crone 2, Boyd
BCC	21/12/18		Cliftonville	H	D	2	2	Mathieson, Ferritt
BCC	25/12/18		Distillery	H	D	2	2	Mathieson, Ferritt (p)
BCC	26/12/18		Belfast Celtic	H	W	3	1	W.Moore 2, Ferritt (p)
BCC	28/12/18		Linfield	H	W	2	1	Chambers 2
BCC	04/01/19		Belfast United	A	W	3	1	Chambers, Boyd, Lyner
BCC	15/02/19		Cliftonville	A	W	3	1	Boyd, W.Moore, Chambers
BCC	19/05/19	PO	Belfast Celtic	WP	D	1	1	Lyner
								No replay due to unsavoury acts of hooliganism
CAS	11/01/19	1	Linfield	H	D	0	0	-
CAS	18/01/19	1R	Linfield	A	L	1	3	Chambers
IC	01/02/19	1	Bangor	H	W	4	0	W.Moore, Johnston, Lemon, Chambers
IC	08/03/19	SF	Belfast Celtic	Solt	W	2	0	Lyner, W.Moore
IC	29/03/19	F	Linfield	CP	D	1	1	Lyner
IC	05/04/19	FR	Linfield	GP	D	0	0	-
IC	07/04/19	FR2	Linfield	Solt	L	1	2	Scraggs
GC	22/02/19		Linfield	A	L	1	2	Lemon
GC	12/04/19		Belfast Celtic	A	D	0	0	-
GC	21/04/19		Belfast United	H	W	3	0	Crooks 2, Mathieson
GC	22/04/19		Distillery	H	W	2	0	W.Moore, Chambers
GC	17/05/19		Cliftonville	H	L	0	1	-
ChC	14/04/19	1	Belfast United	GP	W	3	0	Mathieson 2, Boyd
ChC	26/04/19	SF	Cliftonville	GP	W	3	0	Croft, W.Moore, Boyd
ChC	03/05/19	F	Linfield	Solt	L	0	1	-
F	24/08/18		Linfield	H	D	1	1	W.Moore
F	31/08/18		Belfast Celtic	H	D	1	1	Brady
F	30/12/18		Linfield/Celtic	H	L	0	3	George Ferritt Benefit
F	19/04/19		Bohemians	A	L	0	2	-
F	23/04/19		Linfield XI 1 Glentoran / Celtic XI 2					Unknown, Marshall McEwan Benefit
F	05/05/19		Airdrieonians	H	W	4	2	Mathieson 3, Croft

Two "Victory" Internationals were played against Scotland. The Scots won 2-1 at Ibrox and then drew 0-0 at Windsor Park. Emerson, Lyner, Moore and Scraggs represented the Glens in these games. An Irish XI played an Anglo-Scots XI at Grosvenor Park on 27th December, meaning the six Glenmen involved had four games on consecutive days! Lemon, Snape and Kirkwood of the Seconds appeared for the Intermediate League against the Birmingham League (0-1) and Glasgow Junior League (1-2) with Lemon also playing in the Junior International between Ireland and Scotland which finished 1-1.

At the Irish League's AGM on 30th May 1919 it was decided to resume the Irish League, City Cup and Gold Cup and commute the transient Belfast and District competitions. Belfast United's application for League membership was rejected.

Appearances and Goals								
	App.	Goals		App.	Goals		App.	Goals
Emerson	35		Chambers	18	7	Johnston	3	2
Moore W.	33	9	Mathieson	16	5	Snape	2	
Lyner D.	32	6	Crone	14	2	Crooks	2	2
Scraggs	32	2	Spencer	10		Connor	2	
Liddle	31		Ferguson H.	9		Gough	1	
Bennett	31		McCullough	9		McDevitt	1	
Ferritt	28	4	Lemon	5	2	Kennedy	1	
Boyd, Jack	25	12	Croft	5	1	Mehaffey	1	
Brady	22		Newby	4	1	TOTAL	396	55
Grainger	21		Laurence	3				

1919/20

Resumption of League football – A walk-off in Dublin - Shots fired at Solitude

Glenavon, Bohemians and Shelbourne returned as the Irish League resumed with the same membership and format as in season 1914/5. Our pre-season friendlies gave mixed results, Alan Mathieson in fine scoring form against Celtic, but then we lost to Linfield in a game which had begun with "much wild kicking."

It did not take long to exact revenge for this loss as a week later the Glens got off to an excellent league start with a 2-0 Oval win over the Blues. Only the keeping of Murphy kept the Windsor men in the game. Another custodian, Peck, frustrated our forwards the following Saturday, cancelling out the creativity of our brilliant half-back trio of Bennett, Scraggs and Emerson. Kearney, an ex-Army and Scottish Junior League inside-right, was signed in early September and he made his debut in a comfortable win at Lurgan. Croft's goal in this game was a superb individual effort, described in one quarter as "one of the best ever seen at the ground."

We maintained our unbeaten start up to the half-way stage of the league, culminating in a heavy win over a lamentably weak Bohemians side. Joe Gowdy was a youth of great promise at centre-forward. The league table on the night of 11th October saw us head Distillery and Belfast Celtic by a single point.

Despite having much the better of the first half we tasted competitive defeat for the first time on 18th October at Windsor Park. Only a fine save from Murphy deprived Gowdy of an equaliser. A week later it was the first representative day of the season. Ireland, including Emerson, Lyner and Gowdy, drew 1-1 with England at Windsor while at Dalymount Park, Dublin Ulster defeated Leinster 5-0. Bennett played in the latter fixture which was abandoned after 83 minutes when hooligans attacked one of the Ulster players.

John Wesley Mehaffey, on loan from Belfast Celtic, had a nightmare in goal when we went down to Shelbourne. In the first half he partially stopped a Fullham shot but could not prevent the ball rolling over the line. Then, after the break, he came out to meet Grainger and the full-back put the ball past him for an own goal. How the Glens missed Liddell (work commitments) and Davy Lyner (ankle). Both had had excellent games for the Irish League against the Scottish League three days earlier. Celtic and Distillery drew 0-0, leaving us in third spot, two points behind the Celts and one adrift of the Whites. At the end of October Jack Boyd was transferred to Linfield.

Gowdy, who also played against the Scottish League, was absent from the next two league fixtures. He was most missed against Celtic when our forward line squandered many chances and then Mulholland netted the only goal following a scrimmage near the end. This ended our championship hopes and ironically we handed Celtic the title a week later by defeating Distillery - the returning Gowdy netting the single goal from a Lemon corner. Glentoran had a chance of sharing the runners-up place if we could travel to Dublin and beat Bohemians. However the events of the day prevented that and left a damaging legacy which lasted well into our City Cup campaign.

Things began well enough as we went 1-0 up in two minutes through Moore and then Croft soon added a second. By half-time Bohs had pulled one back, courtesy of Thomas. As the game wore on our players became very frustrated with the referee's decisions; particularly over a penalty appeal when Gowdy was brought down. Then on 88 minutes the referee, Mr.Kelly, awarded a penalty to the home side. The Glens players protested stoutly and captain Emerson found himself sent off. At this point the rest of the team, with the exception of Andy Kennedy and trainer Jimmy Reid who stayed on to argue, left the field. The Bohemians goalkeeper, Byrne, took the kick, placing the ball between the unattended posts and the referee immediately blew the final whistle.

111

The recriminations on the Glens were severe for this collective action. The Senior Protest and Appeals committee met on 18th December and suspended the nine players involved in the walk off. Emerson received a ban for a full calendar month while Liddell, Grainger, Scraggs, Lemon, Croft, Gowdy, Crooks and Moore were suspended for four weeks. Because of the crowded holiday programme this was a heavier blow than normal but the Glentoran board met on the 19th December and decided to go ahead with the fixtures. Naturally a formal appeal was lodged against the suspensions but the committee confirmed their decision on 1st January.

The irony of the situation was compounded when we hammered Bohemians with our full team in the opening round of City Cup matches. However for the Distillery game six enforced changes were too much to handle, despite a plucky display. Subsequent Christmas results were poor and our City Cup hopes ended prematurely.

A contemporary cartoonist depicts events at the 1920 Irish Cup final.

Our fist choice line-up re-appeared on 17th January. Young players Grant from Banbridge and Victor Clarke had impressed during their unexpected run in the first XI. The team did not immediately blend though, George Ferritt's missed spot-kick was the closest we came to finding the net against Cliftonville. Significantly the same day Glentoran II defeated Linfield Swifts 7-0.

Our City Cup visit to Bohemians was much less controversial than the league meeting, Gowdy's early spectacular goal setting us on our way. Then that Cup was put on ice for two months as the knockout competitions took over.

We kicked-off our Irish Cup campaign with a "capital" win over Distillery. Ferritt opened the scoring just before half-time with a tremendous left-foot drive and sealed the win with a second half penalty. The Whites, who claimed they should have had two penalties in that match, gained revenge the following Saturday by knocking us out of the Shield with an 89th minute goal from G.Reid. Cliftonville proved a difficult nut to crack in the Cup, Kennedy often saving the Glens in the first meeting while Gowdy hit the bar with our best chance. Grant gave a splendid display in the replay as we dominated after going 2-0 up early in the second half.

The semi-final paired us with Belfast Celtic and set the scene for probably the most disgraceful incident ever at a football match in Ireland. The first meeting at Windsor was relatively uneventful although Celtic claimed that the ball had gone behind for a goal-kick before Ferritt's equaliser. The replay was fixed for St.Patrick's Day at Cliftonville and gate receipts topped £600. Glentoran entered as favourites having knocked Celtic out of the Gold Cup on the Saturday, although the Celts were missing Hamill and Ferris who were playing along with our Billy Emerson for Ireland against Scotland.

John McIlveen played left-half for the Glens in that match and lined out there again for the semi-final replay. The Mehaffey brothers, John and Bertie, were in the respective goals. McIlveen was hurt in a collision after only two minutes and took no real part in the game. With twenty minutes to go and the game still scoreless Celtic left-back Fred Barrett brought down young Joe Gowdy for the umpteenth time. Referee McLean, having already cautioned Barrett for the same offence, duly sent him off. At this the Belfast Celtic fans invaded the pitch causing the game to be abandoned.

The following day's Northern Whig reported on the horrific events that followed, under the heading of "A Sinn Fein Outbreak." Trouble had been brewing as Celtic fans flew the Sinn Fein flag and waved green, white and orange hankies. They sang the Soldier's Song, Dolly's Brae, Belfast Celtic Will Be There, the Boys of Wexford and A Nation Once Again. When the referee ordered Barrett to the pavilion Mickey Hamill and other Celtic players tried to keep the fans off the field but to no avail. One of the invaders, a well dressed young man, walked over to the Glentoran end, pulled out a revolver and then calmly fired shots into the crowd. The Glentoran fans scattered after every shot, breaking down railings to flee and then jumping a considerable distance to safety at the back of the ground. The man then threw the revolver away as the police gave chase with the crowd attempting to rescue him. Several times the sound of batons on skulls were heard and many Celtic fans were later treated in hospital.

As the crowd eventually filed slowly out of the ground a fresh volley of stones was thrown at the police. The RIC then promptly plunged into the middle of the stone-throwers and "used their batons vigourously". The firer of the shots was detained and named as George Goodman of 15 Quadrant Street off Albert Street. Glentoran players left the ground an hour later without further mishap.

After the dust had settled and the events sunk in the IFA held Belfast Celtic responsible for the outbreak, dismissed them from the Irish Cup and banned them from football until the end of March. The aggrieved Celtic board issued a writ against the IFA for unfair treatment but the matter did not end there. Celtic also complained that McIlveen's name had not been on the list of eligible Glentoran players submitted to them six days before the replay under Rule 3. The IFA agreed and disqualified us from the cup! This left Shelbourne with a walk-over in the final.

Although Shelbourne "lifted" the Irish Cup a challenge match was arranged between them and the Glens to decide the destiny of the winners and runners-up medals. This game was comfortably won by Glentoran (3-1), all our goals coming in the first half, but was again marred by rowdyism. The Dublin fans attacked and kicked the referee, Mr.W.Moore of Belfast, at the conclusion of the match. He was struck on the legs and face, gaining a split lip and was apparently only saved from a worse beating due to a number of the attackers getting in each other's way. A large crowd then waited outside the dressing rooms and when the Glentoran team emerged at 6-40 pm for the 7-30 train they were stoned. John Scraggs received a nasty facial injury - it was thought that he was mistaken for the referee. Shelbourne's punishment for this was the closure of their ground for two weeks.

The remainder of the City Cup was tame by comparison as the Glens failed to register a win in the last five matches. Indeed our dismal form was reflected by the inclusion of trainer Jimmy Reid for the Glenavon game. Scribes judged Reid the best Glenman on the field, saying there was a lot of football left in him yet.

The Charity Cup game versus Cliftonville began at 7.00 pm to enable "the majority of patrons to have their tea before going to the game." We lost out on corners after holding a 2-0 half-time lead. As Celtic were suspended Glentoran arranged a friendly with Motherwell at the Oval on Easter Monday. The visitors, lying third in the Scottish League, took a first half lead through Scotland's leading scorer Hugh Ferguson. The Glens went 2-1 up before Kelly equalised; all in front of a big crowd.

The last hope of a trophy for the season was the Gold Cup. However, after surprisingly

Results 1919/20

Played 38. Won 16. Drew 9. Lost 13. Goals For 55. Against 35. % 53.9

IL	30/08/19		Linfield	H	W	2	0	Lyner 2
IL	06/09/19		Cliftonville	A	D	0	0	-
IL	13/09/19		Shelbourne	H	W	4	0	Gowdy 2, Scraggs (p), Devoy og
IL	20/09/19		Glenavon	A	W	3	1	Gowdy, Croft, Lyner
IL	27/09/19		Belfast Celtic	H	W	2	0	W.Moore, Gowdy
IL	04/10/19		Distillery	A	D	2	2	Gowdy 2
IL	11/10/19		Bohemians	H	W	6	0	Gowdy 3, Croft 2, Bennett
IL	18/10/19		Linfield	A	L	0	1	-
IL	01/11/19		Cliftonville	H	W	3	1	Kearney, Gowdy, Croft
IL	08/11/19		Shelbourne	A	L	0	2	-
IL	15/11/19		Glenavon	H	W	4	0	Bennett 2, Scraggs, Croft
IL	22/11/19		Belfast Celtic	A	L	0	1	-
IL	29/11/19		Distillery	H	W	1	0	Gowdy
IL	06/12/19		Bohemians	A	D	2	2	W.Moore, Croft Glentoran walked off
CC	13/12/19		Bohemians	H	W	7	0	Croft 3, Lyner, Gowdy, Scraggs, Emerson
CC	20/12/19		Distillery	A	L	1	2	Ferritt (p)
CC	25/12/19		Linfield	H	D	0	0	-
CC	26/12/19		Belfast Celtic	A	L	0	3	-
CC	27/12/19		Shelbourne	A	L	0	2	-
CC	03/01/20		Glenavon	H	W	1	0	Gray
CC	17/01/20		Cliftonville	A	L	0	3	-
CC	24/01/20		Bohemians	A	W	2	0	Gowdy 2
CC	20/03/20		Distillery	H	W	1	0	Gowdy
CC	03/04/20		Linfield	A	L	0	3	-
CC	06/04/20		Shelbourne	H	L	1	2	Ferritt (p)
CC	10/04/20		Glenavon	A	L	0	1	-
CC	17/04/20		Cliftonville	H	L	0	2	-
CC	28/04/20		Belfast Celtic	H	D	0	0	-
IC	31/01/20	1	Distillery	A	W	2	0	Ferritt 2 (1p)
IC	21/02/20	2	Cliftonville	A	D	0	0	-
IC	25/02/20	2R	Cliftonville	H	W	2	0	Grant, Gowdy
IC	06/03/20	SF	Belfast Celtic	WP	D	1	1	Ferritt
IC	17/03/20	SFR	Belfast Celtic	Solt	D	0	0	- Abandoned after 70 minutes due to riot. Belfast Celtic dismissed due to the riot, Glentoran dismissed due to an unregistered player. Cup awarded to Shelbourne.
CM*	27/03/20		Shelbourne	A	W	3	1	W.Moore, Gowdy 2
CAS	07/02/20	SF	Distillery	WP	L	0	1	-
GC	13/03/20	1	Belfast Celtic	H	W	2	0	Gowdy, Kearney
GC	08/05/20	SF	Linfield	Solt	W	3	0	Gowdy 3
GC	15/05/20	F	Distillery	WP	L	1	3	Gowdy
ChC	20/04/20	1	Cliftonville	GP	D	2	2	Gowdy 2 Lost 1-3 on corners
F	20/08/20		Belfast Celtic	H	W	4	2	Mathieson 4
F	23/08/20		Linfield	A	L	0	1	-
F	05/04/20		Motherwell	H	D	2	2	Croft, Grant

* = Challenge for Irish Cup medals

hammering Linfield in the semis, we put in a miserable display against Distillery in the final, only Scraggs and Gowdy playing to form.

So a calamitous season came to an end, with even more violence to flare in the streets of Belfast over the summer of 1920 without the catalytic effect of football.

Appearances and Goals								
	App.	Goals		App.	Goals		App.	Goals
Kennedy	35		Bennett	19	3	Crooks	3	
Kearney	32	2	Liddle	17		Mathieson	3	
Scraggs	29	3	Grainger	16		McIlveen	2	
Emerson	29	1	Grant	14	1	Patton	1	
Croft	29	9	Lemon	7		Boyd, Jack	1	
Moore W.	29	2	Kirkwood	6		Gray	1	1
Gowdy	28	23	Bingham	6		Allen	1	
Ferritt	27	5	Clark	6		Vage	1	
Lyner D.	24	4	McBride	3		Own Goals		1
Ferguson J.	22		Reid	3		TOTAL	418	55
Mehaffey	21		Houston	3				

1920/21

Civil unrest affects football – Glentoran do the double – Burnison's temper

Political upheaval in Ireland resulted in daily street riots in Belfast during the summer of 1920. Obviously sport and football suffered a knock-on effect and the Irish League allowed Shelbourne, Bohemians and Belfast Celtic to withdraw. The Dublin clubs did compete in the Irish Cup but Celtic's directors said that the club would not play football again until the situation was resolved. With this uncertainty it was decided to postpone the Irish League to later in the season and commence matters instead with the Gold Cup on a league basis. In fact the season was to continue throughout with only the five senior clubs.

WILLIAM EMERSON
GLENTORAN

Billy Emerson.

Glentoran signed Hugh L. Meek from Cliftonville to play up front and he was to have a big influence on our championship winning campaign. Meek failed to score in only one of the league matches. We had to settle for third place in the Gold Cup as the team took time to settle down. After the drawn game with Glenavon it was reported that Everton were interested in signing Joe Gowdy. However Gowdy eventually moved to Falkirk and played at the Oval again in Johns Scraggs' testimonial.

Our visit to Grosvenor Park on 25th September was our last for a while as Distillery were not allowed to play there due to the nearby street rioting. The Whites were making plans for a new ground anyway, because of the proposed developments for the distillery itself on the Grosvenor Park site, and found a potential new home on the Shore Road.

George Ferritt's missed penalty against Linfield denied us of a share of the points and led to the Blues wrapping up the Gold Cup two weeks later. In the last fixture against Distillery John Mehaffey played his first game of the season in goals, replacing Dan Peck.

As the Gibson Cup began the Belfast newspapers remarked on the total slump in interest in senior football. Offering stagnation and lack of provincial teams as reasons, they reported that the junior game was greatly benefiting. We got off to a bad start against Glenavon despite taking the lead when their keeper Magee threw the ball against Meek's back and saw it rebound into the net. Ferritt then put a penalty over the bar and Peck let in two soft goals. The gate receipts for the game were a meagre £30. Alfie Snape returned on the left wing against homeless Distillery and showed his old sharpness but it was right-wing Sam McGregor who set up victory with a brilliant performance.

In the vital game with Linfield in December Hugh Davey missed a first half penalty. Mehaffey then made amends at the other end, saving Gaw's spot-kick after the break and Meek eventually broke the deadlock in the 83rd minute. Steady defence from Alan McSeveney and James Ferguson kept Glenavon's forwards at bay in the return game and we maintained our two point lead at the top on Christmas Day.

Inside-right Willie Crooks, attracting the attention of Clyde, was man of the match on New Year's Day against an experimental Distillery XI. Glenavon and Linfield drew 1-1 and after the Lurgan men overcame the Whites 1-0 on the 8th we were left requiring a point at Windsor Park to become champions. The crowds flocked again and they were rewarded with an excellent match. Hugh Meek gave us the lead three times and at the end the scenes were reminiscent of "the good old days" as one reporter put it, when more teams competed. Linfield fans had continually barracked the referee but the displays of Scraggs, McGregor, Crooks and Meek made us worthy winners.

The Irish Cup and County Antrim Shield were quickly to follow the league championship to the Oval trophy cabinet. The Shield began with a comfortable win over Steel and Sons Cup finalists Bangor in miserable conditions. A crowd of 6,000 attended the semi-final replay with the Blues at Solitude. In a game where the pitch cup up badly the only goal came in our favour on fifteen minutes. Linfield had a goal disallowed for a foul on Mehaffey and this prompted a section of their fans to threaten the referee at the finish. The final dragged on into April, with the attendance at the second game reduced by the counter attraction of the Downpatrick Races! Even twenty minutes extra time could not produce a goal in the third match when the play of both teams was hopeless. It was suggested after this that the trophy winners be decided on the toss of a coin or even to share the Shield. Eventually the Glens won when Davy Lyner was fouled in the 10th minute of the fourth game and Billy Emerson converted the resultant penalty.

We saw off junior opposition, including Forth River of Edenderry, to reach the final of the Irish Cup. After having led 4-1 against Brantwood we found ourselves down to nine men due to an injury and a sending off. Glens just held on for victory and in the other semi-final Glenavon were allowed to progress, after a 0-0 draw with Shelbourne in Dublin, as the Shels did not fancy the trip to Belfast for a replay.

Needle was added to the Cup final as in the opening City Cup game Glenavon right-back Sam Burnison had been sent off. When referee McGowan awarded the Glens a penalty Burnison shook the official roughly. On receiving his marching orders he kicked the ball out of the ground and it took eight minutes before he finally departed!

A poor final, with the Mehaffey brothers keeping the respective goals, saw Burnison ordered off again. After deliberately kicking Emerson he again manhandled the referee (Saunders) and had to be restrained by his team mates after striking the official. This did Glenavon's cause no good and Snape sealed victory in the 76th minute.

Glenavon did mange to win the City Cup, but not without further controversy. The issue could be traced back to the two games over the Easter period at the end of March. Torrential rain forced the abandonment of our matches with Cliftonville after 79 minutes and Distillery at half-time. When the league met on 27th April to discuss possible outcomes they ordered a replay of the Distillery game but allowed the Cliftonville score to stand. Glentoran were disgusted at this lack of consistency and there was a tense atmosphere when the Whites visited the Oval on 11th May - especially as they had just beaten us in the Charity Cup final with two late Dalrymple goals. The Glens had the better of the exchanges but Irvine kept a fine goal for Distillery. The referee, Mr. W.Moore, upset Glentoran fans with his decisions and he put in a complaint to the league regarding the treatment he received after the game. Apparently Moore had to spend an hour sheltered in the Newtownards Road police station and did not arrive back at his home until well after the military curfew imposed on Belfast!

Hooliganism was by no means confined to the Oval. After our defeat at Glenavon on 9th April, during which their right-wing McMullan had been ordered off for kicking Emerson, a car containing several Glentoran players was attacked. Fortunately no-one was injured. Although we beat the Whites three days after the drawn re-match, Glenavon won 2-1 over the Reds and took the City Cup by a solitary point.

Full Irish international honours came the way of Emerson (v.England), McGregor (v.Scotland) and Scraggs who captained the team against the Welsh. No fewer than seven Glentoran players were in the Irish League team beaten 3-0 by the Scottish League at Ibrox in January. The troubles in Belfast kept the English League from travelling and our friendly

Results 1920/21

Played 39. Won 24. Drew 9. Lost 6. Goals For 68. Against 29. % 73.1.
Honours: Irish League, Irish Cup, County Antrim Shield

GC	04/09/20		Linfield	A	W	1	0	F. Stewart
GC	11/09/20		Cliftonville	H	W	3	0	Gowdy, Lyner, Kirkwood
GC	18/09/20		Glenavon	H	D	2	2	Scraggs, Gowdy
GC	25/09/20		Distillery	A	L	1	2	Davey
GC	09/10/20		Linfield	H	L	0	1	-
GC	16/10/20		Cliftonville	A	W	3	2	Gowdy 2, Meek
GC	23/10/20		Glenavon	A	L	2	3	Gowdy 2
GC	30/10/20		Distillery	H	W	2	0	Gowdy, Scraggs
IL	06/11/20		Glenavon	A	L	1	3	Meek
IL	20/11/20		Cliftonville	H	W	2	0	Davey 2
IL	04/12/20		Distillery	H	W	5	1	Meek 3, Davey, Crooks
IL	11/12/20		Linfield	H	W	1	0	Meek
IL	18/12/20		Glenavon	H	W	3	0	Meek 2, Crooks
IL	25/12/20		Cliftonville	A	W	2	0	Meek, Davey
IL	01/01/21		Distillery	H	W	3	0	Davey, Meek, Crooks
IL	15/01/21		Linfield	A	W	3	2	Meek 3
CAS	08/01/21	1	Bangor	H	W	2	0	Meek 2
CAS	22/01/21	SF	Linfield	Solt	D	1	1	Scraggs
CAS	03/02/21	SFR	Linfield	Solt	W	1	0	Crooks
CAS	19/02/21	F	Distillery	Solt	D	1	1	Lyner
CAS	09/03/21	FR	Distillery	WP	D	0	0	-
CAS	16/03/21	FR2	Distillery	Solt	D	0	0	aet
CAS	13/04/21	FR3	Distillery	WP	W	1	0	Emerson (p)
IC	29/01/21	1	Belfast United	H	W	2	1	Duffy, Scraggs (p)
IC	12/02/21	2	Forth River	H	W	2	1	Crooks 2
IC	05/03/21	SF	Brantwood	Solt	W	4	3	Davey 2, Crooks, Emerson (p)
IC	26/03/21	F	Glenavon	WP	W	2	0	Crooks, Snape
CC	05/02/21		Glenavon	H	W	2	1	Meek, Crooks (p)
CC	28/03/21		Cliftonville	A	D	0	0	Abandoned after 79 minutes - result stood
CC	29/03/21		Distillery	H	W	2	1	Crooks, Emerson (p) Abandoned after 45 minutes - replay ordered
CC	31/03/21		Linfield	A	D	0	0	-
CC	02/04/21		Linfield	H	W	3	0	Meek, Davey 2
CC	09/04/21		Glenavon	A	L	0	1	-
CC	23/04/21		Cliftonville	H	W	2	0	Meek, Crooks
CC	11/05/21		Distillery	H	D	0	0	-
CC	14/05/21		Distillery	H	W	2	0	Faulkner, Myles
ChC	21/04/21	1	Forth River	H	W	5	0	Meek 3, Crooks, Davey
ChC	30/04/21	SF	Belfast United	WP	D	1	1	Snape
ChC	04/05/21	SFR	Belfast United	H	W	3	1	Knocker 2, Meek
ChC	07/05/21	F	Distillery	Solt	L	0	2	-
F	21/08/20		Linfield	H	W	2	0	Gowdy, Meek
F	28/08/20		Ballyclare Comrades	A	W	3	1	Unknown
F	28/12/20		Falkirk	H	W	3	2	Crooks 2, Meek John Scraggs Benefit
F	18/05/21		Glenbank & Ligoneil	A		Unknown			

with Burnley was similarly postponed. Scraggs and Lyner did get a crack at Glasgow Rangers, being guests in the Linfield team which lost 0-2 in front of 12,000 on 30th March 1921.

At the end of the season Queen's Island and Belfast United applied for senior status as Bohemians and Shelbourne indicated in writing that they would be joining the newly formed Free State League.

Appearances and Goals

	App.	Goals		App.	Goals		App.	Goals
Emerson	38	2	Peck	10		Boyd H.	2	
Ferritt	37		Stewart H.	9		Kelly	2	
Meek H.	37	22	Gowdy	7	7	Knocker	2	2
Scraggs	36	4	Meek R.	7		Ward	1	
Ferguson J.	33		Bowman	6		Agnew	1	
McGregor	31		Croft	5		Faulkner	1	1
McSeveney	30		Kirkwood	4	1	Myles	1	1
Mehaffey	29		Bingham	3		Reid	1	
Snape	26	2	Houston	3				
Crooks	23	11	Trotter	3		TOTAL	429	68
Davey	20	11	Duffy	3	1			
Lyner D.	16	2	Stewart F.	2	1			

1921/22

Linfield's clean sweep – An FA reprimand – Meek in Norway

The first season of football in the newly formed Northern Ireland will always be remembered for Linfield's clean sweep of all seven trophies on offer. This included the new "Alhambra" or Irish League Cup. Glentoran could claim to be the only team to beat the Blues in a competitive fixture when, on the morning of Easter Monday, we won a Gold Cup tie 1-0. Our experimental line-up for that match read: Mehaffey; Ferritt, Ferguson; Watson, Campbell, McClure; McGregor, Lyner, Meek, McAnally, Toppin. Mehaffey had an excellent game.

Team Group in the 1920s.

Glentoran's double-winning team broke up during the season with Davy Lyner and Willie Crooks moving to Manchester United, Lyner later transferring again to Kilmarnock. John Scraggs went to Clydebank while on St.Patrick's Day 1922 Billy Emerson signed for Burnley. A benefit match for Davy Lyner was held on 19th April at the Oval when a Belfast and District XI defeated an Anglo-Irish XI 2-0 in front of 4,500.

Admission prices to league games were reduced to 9d and 1/- with ladies free. Referees' fees were fixed at £1 1s with the linesmen receiving 7/6. For matches starting late the clubs would be fined £2 2s and the referee involved struck off the list. Ten minutes was to be the maximum duration of half-time intervals.

Thin crowds attended the opening league games. We enjoyed a win in our first meeting with senior newcomers Queen's Island at Ballynafeigh. New players John Peden and James Boyd made their marks as good results in October set us up for the big clash with Linfield at the Oval on 5th November. Castle Junction witnessed a wild struggle for tramcars as a huge crowd rolled up. The ball in this game became so heavy that heading it caused many players minor injuries! The Blues gained a scoreless draw and retained their one point lead with two games to go. We then produced two bad performances to leave Linfield champions. The referee was barracked when he ordered the teams to turn straight round, sans interval, in the Queen's Island game.

We shared the points again with the Blues in the opening City Cup tie despite having Lyner sent off in the second half for dissent. Hugh Davey came back as centre-forward the following week allowing his namesake Meek to move to a more natural inside-left position. Davey's influence helped us move into a 4-0 half-time lead against the Whites. But the team then suffered two 0-1 defeats in December as our forwards attempted to play a close game that was too fancy against the first time methods of Queen's Island and Linfield. However improved displays after Christmas enabled us to finish as City Cup runners-up.

Results 1921/22

Played 38. Won 18. Drew 8. Lost 12. Goals For 62. Against 51. % 57.9

AC	27/08/21	SF	Linfield	Solt	L	0	1	-	
IL	03/09/21		Glenavon	A	D	1	1	Scraggs (p)	
IL	10/09/21		Cliftonville	H	W	3	1	James Boyd 3	
IL	17/09/21		Linfield	A	L	0	1	-	
IL	24/09/21		Queen's Island	A	W	2	0	Crooks, Davey	
IL	08/10/21		Distillery	H	W	3	1	Meek, Lyner, Davey	
IL	15/10/21		Glenavon	H	W	1	0	Meek	
IL	29/10/21		Cliftonville	A	W	2	0	Meek, Crooks	
IL	05/11/21		Linfield	H	D	0	0	-	
IL	12/11/21		Queen's Island	H	L	0	1	-	
IL	19/11/21		Distillery	H	D	2	2	Meek 2	
CC	26/11/21		Linfield	A	D	1	1	James Boyd	
CC	03/12/21		Distillery	H	W	5	2	Davey 2, Crooks, Meek	
CC	10/12/21		Cliftonville	H	W	2	1	Lyner, Meek	
CC	17/12/21		Queen's Island	A	L	0	1	-	
CC	24/12/21		Glenavon	H	W	3	2	Crooks, Davey, Meek	
CC	26/12/21		Linfield	H	L	0	1	-	
CC	27/12/21		Distillery	H	W	2	1	Thompson, Meek	
CC	31/12/21		Cliftonville	A	W	2	1	Davey 2	
CC	14/01/22		Queen's Island	H	W	2	0	Davey, James Boyd	
CC	21/01/22		Glenavon	A	D	2	2	Thompson 2	
CAS	07/01/22	1	Dundela	H	D	3	3	Davey 2, Crooks	
CAS	11/01/22	1R	Dundela	H	W	3	0	Emerson, Davey, Lyner	
CAS	08/02/22	SF	Distillery	WP	L	4	5	Davey, McClure, Meek 2	
IC	28/01/22	1	Glenavon	A	L	0	1	-	
GC	11/02/22		Queen's Island	A	D	2	2	Davey 2	
GC	11/03/22		Distillery	H	W	2	0	James Boyd 2	
GC	08/04/22		Glenavon	H	W	3	1	James Boyd 2, Campbell	
GC	15/04/22		Cliftonville	A	L	2	4	Lyner, McAnally	
GC	17/04/22		Linfield	H	W	1	0	Meek	
GC	18/04/22		Queen's Island	H	L	0	1	-	
GC	22/04/22		Distillery	H	W	4	1	McGregor, Topping 2, Campbell	
GC	29/04/22		Glenavon	A	L	0	4	-	
GC	10/05/22		Cliftonville	H	D	2	2	Meek 2(1p)	
GC	20/05/22		Linfield	A	L	1	5	McAnally	
ChC	05/04/22	1	Belfast United	H	W	1	0	John Boyd	
ChC	03/05/22	2	Cliftonville	A	W	1	0	Rodgers	
ChC	06/05/22	SF	Cliftonville Olympic	A	L	0	2	-	
F	20/08/21		Linfield	A	L	0	2	-	
F	31/08/21		Linfield	H	W	4	1	James Boyd 2, Crooks, Meek	

With the soccer public crying out for variety in the games the IFA came under attack for only allowing Intermediate Cup finalists Linfield Rangers and Forth River to compete as the juniors in the Irish Cup. Crusaders, Belfast Bohemians, Brantwood and Dundela were among those dismayed by this decision. Our own Irish Cup hopes were extinguished early. Three hundred travelling fans saw the team lose to a deflected goal at Mourneview Park when we were missing the services of McGregor (injured toe) and Meek (flu).

Glentoran found themselves reprimanded by the FA on 21st February 1922 because the club had run a sweepstake on the outcome of the English FA Cup ties.

Arguably the most exciting games of the season for us took place in the County Antrim Shield. Three times we took the lead in the first half against Dundela but on each occasion the juniors, playing typically fast football, equalised. There were thrills galore in the semi-final versus Distillery, played on a Wednesday as the Solitude pitch had been unplayable the previous Saturday. Again the half-time score was 3-3 and when the game stood 4-4 the Whites were awarded a penalty. Mehaffey saved it but could not prevent Distillery's winner later.

New inside-left McAnally from Linfield Rangers had a great debut against Distillery in our second City Cup fixture while Campbell was man of the match against Glenavon. The remainder of this competition was packed in at the end of the season with many clubs turning out "scrap" elevens. Indeed, in our win over the Whites on 22nd April, keeper Mehaffey took (and missed) a penalty. Mehaffey actually played the second half against Linfield a month later outfield due to a damaged shoulder. Ferguson went into goal and performed quite well until a late hat-trick from Savage bloated the scoreline.

To avoid a fixture pile up the Charity Cup committee decreed that the Charity games would be decided on corners if they finished all square. An inept performance saw us disgraced against Cliftonville's second string. As the season drew to a close scribes pointed out that Glentoran could hardly expect to win games or trophies if they transfer half the team.

Before moving to mainland clubs half-backs Scraggs and Emerson played for Ireland against England on 22nd October. Emerson was joined by Davy Lyner for the Scotland game while Lyner was captain in the 1-1 draw versus Wales. Hugh Meek went on the IFA's end of season tour to Norway, playing against the Norwegians in Bergen and Christiansand.

Glens trainer Jimmy Reid was on duty along with players Scraggs, Emerson, McGregor and Crooks against the English League at the Oval on 1st October. Hugh Davey joined this quartet for the Scottish League game with Lyner coming on as a substitute. Emerson and Lyner were due to play against the Welsh League at Merthyr in February but this game was called off due to Cardiff City's FA Cup involvement.

The public were becoming increasingly fed up with the same old faces in senior football so in April the Irish League put out an advert with the aim of attracting new clubs.

Appearances and Goals

	App.	Goals		App.	Goals		App.	Goals
Mehaffey	36		Toppin	16	2	Widdicombe	1	
Meek H.	35	15	McAnally	12	2	Farrell	1	
Ferguson J.	33		McClure	10	1	Tumilson	1	
Ferritt	32		Bruce	10		Richardson	1	
Lyner D.	32	4	Scraggs	8	1	Reid	1	
McGregor	29	1	Boyd, James	8	8	Ferguson H.	1	
Crooks	23	5	Watson	7		Fleck	1	
Peden	23		Thompson R.	6	3	Mills	1	
Campbell	21	2	Johnston	5		Rodgers	1	1
Emerson	20	1	Woodward	4		Silcock	1	
Boyd, John	19	2	McSeveney	1				
Davey	17	14	Rea	1		TOTAL	418	62

1922/23

A new look team – Cup and Shield final losses - Charity Cup success

Glentoran's team rebuilding continued in the late summer of 1922. Goalkeeper John Mehaffey moved to Oldham while winger Sam McGregor made the short trip to Dundela. New faces included goalkeepers McCormick (ex-Sandford) and McClure (ex-Linfield Swifts). William "Tosher" Burns, a centre-half, arrived from Ards while Harry Ferguson, the younger brother of James, vied with his kinsman for the left-back spot along with Tumilson (ex-Lismore).

The month long printing strike in Belfast finished as the second and last Alhambra Cup ushered in the season. Cliftonville defeated Linfield 2-0 in the Oval final. Our opening Irish League fixture marked Distillery's first match at their new ground York Park. There were conflicting reports over the capacity of the enclosure on the shores of the Belfast Lough, estimates ranging from 50,000 to 100,000!

Our new look line-up lost the opening two games narrowly but we gained our first point against the "Hoops" of Queen's Island. The shipyard team were playing their home games at the Oval pending the completion of Pirrie Park. Gradually our young side began to blend with centre-forward Arnold Keenan and outside-left Mahood emerging as leading lights. Evidence came in a fine 1-1 draw against Linfield. James Ferguson picked up an injury in this game, which prevented him playing against both the English and Scottish Leagues. Glentoran finished third in the league, just a point behind runners-up Queen's Island.

Tommy McKeague.

The Glens and Queen's Island were the main City Cup contenders. In the opening encounter we had an off day, missing left-half Jackie Evans who was on Amateur International duty for Ireland against England at Preston. A nasty incident occurred at the end of the Distillery game on 25th November when Gooddall incensed the crowd by deliberately kicking Mahood. Our player had to be carried off.

Police searched spectators for weapons on entering Windsor Park in December. In this game Keenan gave us a 30 second lead before a Linfield player had touched the ball. The team fell apart in the return match with Queen's Island when after an hour's play of the top of the table clash it was still scoreless. Whereupon we were awarded a penalty and George Ferritt missed. Peden then damaged a knee and the Glens were routed by six goals in the last twenty minutes!

We gave a debut to outside-right Strange (ex-Mountpottinger) against Cliftonville a week later. A win here kept us joint top with the Island but poor results in the last three games over Christmas enabled them to take the trophy. We were forced into a runners-up test match despite the trojan efforts of Ferritt.

Glentoran reached the final of all three knockout tournaments in 1923. We had McClure to thank for keeping us in the Irish Cup at Dunmore Park against an eager Brantwood side.

It eventually took four matches to see off the North Belfast junior outfit. Around this time the poor weather had made most of the clubs' playing surfaces resemble "Kerry bogs." Indeed the referee had to take the players off for a short period during the first Antrim

Results 1922/23								
Played 45. Won 16. Drew 13. Lost 16. Goals For 60. Against 61. % 50.0.								
Honours: Charity Cup								
AC	21/08/22	1	Distillery	H	L	2	3	John Boyd, James Boyd
IL	02/09/22		Distillery	A	L	0	1	-
IL	09/09/22		Linfield	H	L	1	2	McAnally
IL	16/09/22		Queen's Island	H	D	1	1	McAnally
IL	23/09/22		Cliftonville	H	W	3	0	McAnally, Harris 2
IL	30/09/22		Glenavon	A	L	1	2	Burns
IL	07/10/22		Distillery	H	W	1	0	Burns
IL	14/10/22		Linfield	A	D	1	1	Keenan
IL	21/10/22		Queen's Island	H	W	2	0	Thompson, Mahood
IL	28/10/22		Cliftonville	A	D	1	1	Keenan
IL	04/11/22		Glenavon	H	W	3	1	Thompson 2, McAnally
CC	11/11/22		Queen's Island	H	L	2	3	McAnally 2
CC	18/11/22		Cliftonville	A	W	1	0	Thompson
CC	25/11/22		Distillery	H	W	4	1	Keenan, McAnally 2, Thompson
CC	02/12/22		Glenavon	A	W	1	0	Ferritt (p)
CC	09/12/22		Linfield	A	W	3	2	Keenan 2, McAnally
CC	16/12/22		Queen's Island	H	L	0	6	-
CC	23/12/22		Cliftonville	H	W	2	0	McAnally 2
CC	25/12/22		Distillery	A	L	1	2	Thompson
CC	26/12/22		Glenavon	H	D	1	1	Keenan
CC	30/12/22		Linfield	H	D	1	1	Keenan
CC	18/05/23	RUTM	Distillery	Solt	L	1	3	Keenan
GC	06/01/23		Queen's Island	H	W	3	1	Thompson 2(1p), McBride
GC	20/01/23		Glenavon	H	W	4	1	McAnally, Keenan 2, Evans Match Declared Void
GC	07/03/23		Glenavon	H	L	1	2	Swindle
GC	02/04/23		Cliftonville	H	L	0	2	-
GC	03/04/23		Queen's Island	H	L	0	2	-
GC	07/04/23		Glenavon	A	L	0	1	-
GC	14/04/23		Linfield	A	D	0	0	-
GC	21/04/23		Distillery	H	D	2	2	Elwood, W.Reid
GC	28/04/23		Cliftonville	A	L	0	2	-
GC	01/05/23		Distillery	A	D	0	0	-
GC	07/05/23		Linfield	H	L	0	2	-
IC	27/01/23	1	Brantwood	A	D	0	0	-
IC	31/01/23	1R	Brantwood	H	D	2	2	James Boyd, Taylor
IC	05/02/23	1R2	Brantwood	A	D	2	2	Ferritt, Keenan
IC	07/02/23	1R3	Brantwood	H	W	4	1	Campbell og, McAnally 2, McBride
IC	24/02/23	SF	Glenavon	WP	W	2	1	Thompson, McAnally
IC	31/03/23	F	Linfield	Solt	L	0	2	-
CAS	03/02/23	SF	Cliftonville	WP	D	1	1	Keenan
CAS	21/02/23	SFR	Cliftonville	WP	W	2	1	James Boyd, McAnally
CAS	10/03/23	F	Linfield	Solt	L	1	4	Keenan
ChC	23/04/23	1	Dunmurry	H	W	2	0	Keenan, Beattie
ChC	10/05/23	SF	Queen's Island	H	D	1	1	Elwood
ChC	12/05/23	SFR	Queen's Island	Solt	W	2	0	Legge, Ferritt
ChC	23/05/23	F	Crusaders	Solt	W	2	1	McAnally, Keenan

Shield semi-final at Windsor Park. All matches scheduled for the 13th January were cancelled to give the grass time to recover.

Linfield proved our undoing in both Shield and Irish Cup finals in March. Peden had a splendid Shield final but our overall Cup final display was lifeless. The games produced receipts of £211 and £300 respectively.

Silverware eventually came Glentoran's way in the Charity Cup. McCormick's penalty save kept our hopes alive in the first meeting with Queen's Island. We had to come from behind to beat a lively Crusaders XI in the final. The Crues had knocked out Linfield 2-0 in the semis.

Our Gold Cup campaign could be best forgotten about. We failed to score in seven out of the ten games. Ironically the Glens' best performance came in the annulled game with Glenavon. Referee J.B.Stark had declared the waterlogged pitch unplayable, but both clubs were determined to go ahead and a voluntary substitute referee was obtained from the crowd! The Irish League committee frowned on this action, declared the game void and fined the clubs the gate money. The Lurgan men won an ill-tempered re-match, having their left-half Harriss ordered off by Stark in the 65th minute. On the Thursday before this game Harry Ferguson had emigrated to the United States. The club presented him with a watch and a travelling rug for his services.

The drawn game at Windsor Park saw the Blues back Arthur Maultsaid finish with a broken knee cap. Cliftonville captured the Gold Cup, going through their ten games undefeated.

A fairly satisfactory season was brought to a close at the League's meeting on 25th May. At this gathering Barn (from Carrick) and Ards were elected to senior membership and later the ranks were extended to ten clubs with the acceptance of teams representing Larne and Newry Town.

During the year George Ferritt played for the Irish League against our Scottish counterparts, nine years after his previous appearance at this level. Only injury prevented McClure from playing in the first ever meeting with the Welsh League on St.Patrick's Day at Solitude.

In August 1922 Glentoran Juniors met Linfield Juniors at Donaghadee in order to raise funds for the building of the Millisle Masonic Hall. Short time was played in the first half and when this was being made up at the end of the second period Linfield equalised. The gold tie pins intended for the winners were then auctioned off for the fund.

Appearances and Goals								
	App.	Goals		App.	Goals		App.	Goals
Evans	44		Clark	10		Toppin	2	
Ferritt	43	3	Ferguson J.	9		Morrison	2	
McAnally	41	16	Boyd, John	6	1	Laird	2	
Keenan	40	13	Taylor	6	1	Thompson A.	1	
Peden	39		Tumilson	5		Woodrow	1	
McClure	27		McBride	5	2	Finlay	1	
Burns	26	2	McKeague	5		McDonald	1	
Ferguson H.	24		Boyd, James	4	2	Mathieson	1	
Thompson R.	23	9	Strange	4		Bowden J.	1	
Mahood	22	1	McCann	4		McKelvey	1	
Harris	19	2	Swindle	4	1	Walton	1	
McCormick	17		Harland	3		Legge	1	1
Reid W.	17	1	Beattie	3	1	Own Goals		1
Boyd, Duker	13	1	Gowdy	3				
Elwood	12	2	McCartney	2		TOTAL	495	60

1923/24

New clubs join the fray – A wretched January – A trip to Lancashire

Both the Irish League and the Glentoran playing panel had a changed look when the season kicked off at the end of August 1923. With the return of John Mehaffey in goals only the half-back line of James Elwood, Tosher Burns and Jack Evans and centre-forward Arnold Keenan remained from 1922/3. Our new players George Bowman (right-back, Dundela), Kirk (left-back, Summerfield), Tommy McKeague (right-wing, Sydenham YM), Rainey (inside-right, Nortonville), and the left wing partnership of Davy Duff and Allen from Glenbank all featured in the club's Possibles v. Probables match on 21st August. Incidentally, the gate receipts from this game were donated to the dependants of the three men who lost their lives in the Musgrave Channel boating disaster.

**WILLIAM BURNS
GLENTORAN**

William "Tosher" Burns .

After an opening victory over Linfield our results were a mixed bag throughout the first half of the league championship. Evans was sent off against Queen's Island at the Oval and referee Mr.Semple pelted by cinders and verbally abused. The Shipyard team were the early pacesetters in the league despite being deducted two points and fined £100 for fielding ex-Glenman Joe Gowdy before formal clearance came through from Falkirk.

George Ferritt, now playing as a steady full-back, returned against Newry when it took an 85th minute goal from Thompson to earn a point. It was felt by many that the Glens held a falsely low league position as the team had generally played well without getting the results. However in mid-November we began to show signs of turning the corner. First Larne were swamped in the Gold Cup when five of our six goals came in the 30 minutes before half-time. Then excellent wins were recorded over the Blues and the Whites in the league. Leaders Queen's Island proved too strong however, two of their three goals at Pirrie Park coming from Gowdy penalties.

With wins over Glenavon (only their second defeat of the season) and Ards, the Glens jumped from ninth in the table to a more respectable sixth as a hectic Christmas week approached. Our much improved form continued with three league victories out of four and a friendly success over Shelbourne in the space of eight days. Glentoran were the first Irish League team to play in Dublin since the partition of Ireland.

Arnold Keenan crowned his fine personal displays with all four goals against Barn. Keenan's judicious distribution skills allied to the strength of the half-back line and the steadying influences of captain Ferritt at the back were the features of the improved performances.

126

January 1924 turned out to be a disastrous month with exits suffered in three knockout competitions. Glenavon knocked us out of the Gold Cup after we had taken a sixth minute lead then it was Cliftonville in the County Antrim Shield as our backs were tortured by Robinson of the Reds. The most humiliating defeat came at the hands of juniors Crusaders in the Irish Cup. The small pitch did not suit the Glens' swinging play but despite losing Burns with a broken nose we looked to be going through by 1-0 after Keenan nodded in Allen's cross. Then, with four minutes left, Smith equalised for the Crues to force a reply at the Oval. Again we held an interval lead but Crusaders' clever play in the second half won the day. It was a season of shocks in the Irish Cup, Crusaders went on to beat Distillery 5-4 before falling to Queen's Island in a semi-final replay. The other juniors, Willowfield, disposed of Linfield, Newry and Larne to reach the final but failed to prevent the Shipyard men doing the double.

The financial stress caused by these cup defeats was eased with the transfer of players to English clubs. Hugh Davey had gone to Boscombe Athletic in October for £100 plus 50% of any future transfer. John Mehaffey joined New Brighton while stalwart right-half Jimmy Elwood went to Man.City for £1,500. Jackie Evans had a month's trial with Arsenal.

Off the field the league appointed a body to liaise with Belfast Celtic with a view to Celtic's return to senior circles. Indeed on 3rd March the Celtic shareholders voted unanimously to rejoin the Irish League for 1924/5. The possibility of Shelbourne or Bohemians returning was ruled out, but war-time team Belfast United were still functioning as a junior club.

The Glens tried out a couple of youngsters in a friendly against Linfield and nothing was lost as we came from 0-2 down at half-time to draw 2-2. James Bowden was now in goals with Alan McSeveney and Hugh Reid the full-backs. Eddie Inch made his debut (at left-half) in the opening City Cup game. Our defeat at Larne was full of thrills as we came back from 0-2 down but just failed to draw. Evans returned from his trial in this match.

April turned out to be an excellent month for the Glens. On the domestic front we won five and drew one of our six games and then headed off to Lancashire as City Cup leaders for what was on paper an extremely difficult tour.

LANCASHIRE TOUR 1924

The tour had been arranged by Glentoran secretary Walter Scott and would feature games against Manchester City, New Brighton and Everton. A party of 25 left Belfast after the Ards game on the Saturday night, setting sail for Liverpool on the S.S.Heroic under the command of Captain Baker. The 15 players were joined by six club officials, a trainer and two stalwarts of the supporters' committee Alex Chambers and S.Anderson.

The steamer arrived in Liverpool in good time and on the Sunday the party visited Seacombe and the resort of New Brighton, staying overnight in the Hotel Victoria. Despite wretched weather on the Monday the party ventured to the old Roman town of Chester, the mode of transport being "char-a-banc." After visiting the historic cathedral club official Mr. Tom Moore handed over a substantial sum towards the restoration fund.

Man. City were our first opponents on Monday evening and although they were without Mitchell (England Amateur international), Sharpe, Barnes and recent Glenman Elwood a tough encounter was expected. Elwood did his best to make sure the tour was a success off the field. City were too fast and clever as they moved into a 4-1 half-time lead. As the pitch cut up in the second half one wag in the party remarked that Moss Side would be better off called Bog Side! Tommy Browell completed a hat-trick for the home XI and the final score of 7-2 to Man. City summed up the difference in class.

There were some fine individual Glentoran performances. Bowden made many fine saves and received a standing ovation at the end while Hugh Meek was crafty and enterprising at centre-forward. But possibly the star of the show was inside-right Davy Duff - the character of the team. At one stage Duff beat round Browell twice and then passed the ball to the English forward saying, "Here Tommy, I'm tired of it. See what you can do!" Then, near the final whistle, Duff set off on a great run towards his own goal. When questioned about this he quipped, "It was easier to run past our fellows that it was theirs!".

Two days later we crossed the Mersey to face Third Division (North) outfit New Brighton. Belfast's Lord Mayor added his support by flying out for this game. New Brighton included no fewer than six ex-Glenmen (among them John Mehaffey, Willie Crooks and Alan Mathieson) but were a poor side. Despite never reaching the heights we won comfortably by 3-1.

The party then used the free time to play golf, relax and some even went to visit our ex-half-back Billy Emerson, then with Burnley.

"Justice" of the Northern Whig accompanied the party throughout the tour and reported many amusing off the field pieces. He remarked that the tour was an unqualified success

Results 1923/24

Played 36. Won 18. Drew 4. Lost 14. Goals For 76. Against 52. % 52.8

IL	25/08/23		Linfield	A	W	2	1	Rainey, Allen
IL	01/09/23		Distillery	H	L	1	2	Duff
IL	08/09/23		Queen's Island	H	L	0	3	-
IL	15/09/23		Glenavon	A	L	1	2	Meek
IL	22/09/23		Ards	A	W	2	1	Elwood, Allen
IL	06/10/23		Cliftonville	H	L	0	1	-
IL	13/10/23		Newry Town	II	D	2	2	McAnally, Thompson
IL	27/10/23		Larne	A	L	1	2	Keenan
IL	03/11/23		Barn	A	L	1	2	Elwood
IL	17/11/23		Linfield	H	W	2	1	Rainey, Elwood
IL	24/11/23		Distillery	A	W	3	0	Keenan 3
IL	01/12/23		Queen's Island	A	L	1	3	Keenan
IL	08/12/23		Glenavon	H	W	4	0	Allen, Keenan 3
IL	15/12/23		Ards	H	W	2	0	Keenan 2
IL	22/12/23		Cliftonville	A	W	1	0	Keenan
IL	25/12/23		Newry Town	A	L	0	1	-
IL	26/12/23		Larne	H	W	5	1	Keenan 2, Meek 2, McKeague
IL	29/12/23		Barn	H	W	4	1	Keenan 4
GC	10/11/23	1	Larne	H	W	6	0	Allen 2, Keenan 2, McKeague, Elwood
GC	05/01/24	2	Glenavon	A	L	1	2	Burns
CAS	12/01/24	1	Cliftonville	A	L	1	3	Keenan
IC	26/01/24	1	Crusaders	A	D	1	1	Keenan
IC	30/01/24	1R	Crusaders	H	L	1	3	McKeague
CC	22/03/24		Distillery	H	D	2	2	Keenan 2
CC	29/03/24		Larne	A	L	3	4	Meek 2, McKeague
CC	05/04/24		Linfield	A	W	3	2	Rainey 2, Allen
CC	12/04/24		Cliftonville	H	W	5	1	Keenan 2, Allen 2, Meek
CC	19/04/24		Glenavon	A	D	0	0	-
CC	21/04/24		Barn	H	W	3	1	Rainey 2, Meek
CC	26/04/24		Ards	H	W	3	1	Meek 3
CC	07/05/24		Newry Town	A	W	4	1	McSeveney (p), Keenan, Rainey, Simpson
CC	10/05/24		Queen's Island	H	W	3	0	Burns (p), Keenan, McKeague
CC	19/05/24	TM	Queen's Island	WPL		2	3	Rainey, Meek
ChC	24/04/24	1	Queen's Island	H	W	2	1	Keenan, Rainey
ChC	14/05/24	2	Linfield	A	W	3	1	Rainey 2, Burns
ChC	20/05/24	SF	Cliftonville	A	L	1	3	Keenan
F	21/08/23		Probables v Possibles		Unknown			Musgrave Channel Boating Disaster Fund
F	27/12/23		Shelbourne	A	W	1	0	McKeague
F	02/02/24		Linfield	A	D	2	2	Rainey 2
F	28/04/24		Manchester City	A	L	2	7	Keenan, Meek
F	30/04/24		New Brighton	A	W	3	1	Meek, Unknown 2
F	03/05/24		Everton	A	W	4	3	Meek, Unknown 3

without a single hitch or bad incident. There were plenty of practical jokes but none in bad taste. Some members lacked etiquette regarding the use of knives and forks at multi-course meals and this was cruelly played upon. One of the team, who knew what he was doing, sensed about four of the others were copying him. He lifted his serviette, twirled it round until it resembled a piece of string and threw it across his left shoulder. The other four followed suit. Then when a waiter asked if the players required sweets one replied, "No thanks, they always give me toothache!"

One morning all the laces were taken from everyone's shoes and then Justice himself fell foul of the pranksters. While asleep he had his face blackened and an empty beer bottle placed in every pocket.

On the Saturday the weather was again unkind when we visited Goodison Park for the only time in our history. Both clubs were hoping for a big gate to make the tour a financial success. This was achieved and all tramcars were packed on their way to the ground. Everton fielded their strongest side with the exception of their famous forward Sam Chedgozy. However the Toffeemen did not burst any blood vessels in their attempts to win and it was to be Glentoran's day and a 4-3 victory made the tour. Glentoran chairman Joseph Shaw and his friend Sam Muldrew came over for the game and joined in the festivities afterwards. The Everton party and officials were described as "good sports" by the Glentoran party which left Liverpool on Saturday night aboard the "Graphic" giving a final rendition of "Auld Lang Syne."

On arrival back in Belfast there was still the City and Charity Cups to play for. After coming from behind to beat Newry we needed to defeat Queen's Island to force a play-off for the City Cup with them. This was duly accomplished with two goals in the last five minutes but we failed to repeat the feat in the play-off despite coming twice from behind. "Tucker" Croft got Queen's Island's winner shortly before time.

In the Charity Cup we overcame Linfield for a record fourth successive time but were knocked out by Cliftonville in a hotly disputed semi-final. The injured James Ferguson had a benefit match at the Oval on Easter Wednesday when an Irish League XI drew 2-2 with an Intermediate League Select. Glenmen to gain inter-league honours this season were Mehaffey and Allen (2). Portadown were elected as the 12th member of the Irish League, in preference to Summerfield.

Appearances and Goals

	App.	Goals		App.	Goals		App.	Goals
McKeague	34	6	Ferritt	20		McSeveney	13	1
Allen	34	8	Elwood	19	4	Reid H.	12	
Keenan	32	29	Bowden J.	19		McAnally	8	1
Burns	28	3	Mehaffey	17		Thompson R.	2	1
Evans	27		Bowman	14		Kirk	2	
Rainey	27	11	Vance	14		Booth	2	
Duff	22	1	Inch	14		Tumilson	1	
Meek H.	22	11	Reid W.	13		TOTAL	396	76

1924/25

An action packed season – Champions again – Rivalry with Queen's Island

Hopes of success were high in 1924/5 after the near misses of the previous year. The team was much that played in the latter half of 1923/4 but we lost Bowman to new club Portadown and Davy Duff who emigrated to the USA to try his luck with a team near the Falls River. He was later joined by Tucker Croft of Queen's Island.

Bowman had an unhappy start as we gave the Ports a miserable debut in senior circles, although at one stage the score was 1-1. Before the game at Larne there was a Black Perceptory demonstration over the Ulster border question with a clear "No Surrender" message. Alfie Snape returned for the Glens at left-wing in this match.

Our early season promise was severely tested in the latter half of September with encounters against Queen's Island, Distillery and the first meeting with Belfast Celtic for over four years. The Island knocked us out of the Gold Cup but we gained a league point three days later when Legge, making his debut following a signing from Ards United, equalised late on. It was a similar story against the Whites. Two-nil down at half-time we looked beaten until two excellent crosses from Snape resulted in goals for Legge and Tosher Burns, "amidst great applause."

Glentoran and Distillery players appear to be taking part in a dance.

September concluded with a splendid display against Celtic who failed to live up to their "sharpshooters" reputation. Burns subdued the dangerous Mahood brothers while Legge nodded the only goal after home keeper Jackson had missed a McKeague cross. Barn proved a difficult hurdle and we surprisingly dropped a point with both sides guilty of a penalty miss.

So after seven games the Glens held a single point lead over challengers Queen's Island and Celtic. This position was consolidated with wins against Glenavon and Newry before we suffered our first league defeat in controversial circumstances at Windsor Park. The Blues took the lead from a hotly disputed penalty awarded for "hand ball" by our left-back Hugh Reid. Bowden saved Frame's kick with his fists but on bouncing out the ball somehow spun back into the net. Legge equalised but McIlreavy got Linfield's winner ten minutes from time. The team was then boosted by the return of Billy Emerson from Burnley.

We defeated bottom of the table Cliftonville and Queen's Island saw off Celtic 2-0 to enable the two East Belfast clubs to share top spot on 17 points at the half-way stage.

The Glens were then faced with back to back trips to Shamrock Park in league and cup with Portadown defending an unbeaten home record in senior soccer. However a large contingent of fans cheered us on to victory in both matches with Keenan and Snape the scoring heroes. Wilson missed a penalty for the Ports in the cup tie when it had stood 0-0.

A convincing second-half display against Larne and then Newry taking a point off Queen's Island made the press dub us title favourites before Christmas. Progress too was made to the Irish cup semi-final with a 5-3 win over Newry before four important league matches were won in the space of five days. These included a vital 1-0 success over Queen's Island on Christmas Morning and a first half pummeling of Celtic on a muddy surface two days later. Indeed the Sydenham corner of our pitch was completely under water. A shock defeat at Glenavon, however, cut our lead over the Shipyard men to two points with four games left.

In mid-January attentions were turned to the County Antrim Shield. The fast play of our forwards was too much for Queen's Island in Round One and then we took full advantage of Larne's lack of a goalkeeper in the semi-final. (Fulton, normally their left back, played in goal.) Back to the league and the return meeting with Linfield. This game coincided with an eclipse of the sun but one wag remarked that it was the Blues who were eclipsed as our forward line ran riot. Only the good keeping of McMeekin kept the score down to four!

The last day of January gave us a chance of revenge on juniors Crusaders when the teams met in the cup semi-final almost a year to the day on which they knocked us out in 1924. A heavy shower turned Solitude into a swamp and despite the determination of the Crues we put in an error-free performance to win 2-0. Alan McSeveney and Hugh Reid were solid backs.

On the following Wednesday a large crowd travelled to Newry to witness Glentoran become league champions. Queen's

Distillery take the lead in the Irish Cup final.

Island had finished their fixture with 32 points while we stood on 31 and had three games in hand. Things began badly, however, as Newry went ahead and then Hugh Meek had to retire with a crushed shoulder. The turning point came when Newry were awarded a penalty and Bowden saved Groom's spot-kick. Goals from William Reid and Arnold Keenan brought the title to the Oval. We won our remaining two academic fixtures, although a 10-man Cliftonville side held us to a single goal.

The action packed season continued as the Glens kicked off the City Cup with victories over Glenavon and Barn. In between these wins a huge crowd (receipts £586) attended the Shield final with Belfast Celtic. Again the Solitude pitch was very sticky but not enough to prevent Smyth giving the Celts an early lead. Then Meek showed the form which was to win him an international cap versus Wales a month later. He set off on a mazy run which ended in a tantalising cross behind the backs for Keenan to force in. Next, just before half time, he drove in what proved to be the winner and Glentoran lifted the Shield for the seventh time.

Another player under the microscope was back Hugh Reid. QPR twice sent scouts over to watch him but at the end of March he too decided his footballing future lay across the Atlantic and he went to join Duff in America.

March was a disappointing month results-wise. It began with a party of 19 making a trip to the Black Country to take on English Second Division outfit Wolverhampton Wanderers. The crowd gave the Glens a rousing welcome but Wolves were too strong, winning 6-3. We were handicapped by an early injury to Snape but could not complain about the margin of defeat, especially as Inch drove over the bar from the penalty spot. The crowd warmed to Tosher Burns, nicknaming him "Ginger", and even jeered when his goal from a free-kick was ruled out because it was indirect. Overall another enjoyable trip was had with a profit of £50 to show after all expenses had been paid.

131

Results 1924/25

Played 48. Won 36. Drew 6. Lost 6. Goals For 112. Against 48. % 81.3.
Honours: Irish League, County Antrim Shield, Charity Cup

IL	23/08/24		Portadown	H	W	5	1	Rainey 2, Meek, Keenan, McKeague
IL	30/08/24		Larne	A	W	2	0	McKeague, Meek
IL	06/09/24		Ards	H	W	2	1	Keenan, Rainey
IL	13/09/24		Queen's Island	A	D	1	1	Legge
IL	20/09/24		Distillery	H	D	2	2	Legge, Burns
IL	27/09/24		Belfast Celtic	A	W	1	0	Legge
IL	04/10/24		Barn	A	D	1	1	Keenan
IL	18/10/24		Glenavon	H	W	1	0	Meek
IL	25/10/24		Newry Town	H	W	6	2	Meek 3, W.Reid 2, Legge
IL	01/11/24		Linfield	A	L	1	2	Legge
IL	15/11/24		Cliftonville	A	W	1	0	Rainey
IL	22/11/24		Portadown	A	W	2	1	Keenan 2
IL	06/12/24		Larne	H	W	7	2	Rainey 4, Keenan, Meek, Burns
IL	25/12/24		Queen's Island	H	W	1	0	Keenan
IL	26/12/24		Distillery	A	W	3	1	Vance, Rainey 2
IL	27/12/24		Belfast Celtic	H	W	4	0	Meek 2, Vance, Rainey
IL	29/12/24		Ards	A	W	3	0	Vance 2, Burns
IL	10/01/25		Glenavon	A	L	1	2	Meek
IL	24/01/25		Linfield	H	W	4	0	Keenan, Burns, McKeague, Rainey
IL	04/02/25		Newry Town	A	W	2	1	W.Reid, Keenan
IL	11/03/25		Barn	H	W	2	1	Legge, Rainey (p)
IL	16/04/25		Cliftonville	H	W	1	0	McKeague
GC	27/08/24	1	Cliftonville	A	W	1	0	Vance og
GC	10/09/24	2	Queen's Island	A	L	0	1	-
IC	29/11/24	1	Portadown	A	W	1	0	Snape
IC	20/12/24	2	Newry Town	H	W	5	3	Rainey 2, McKeague, Keenan, Meek
IC	31/01/25	SF	Crusaders	Sol	W	2	0	Keenan 2
IC	21/03/25	F	Distillery	Sol	L	1	2	Burns
CAS	12/01/25	2	Queen's Island	Sol	W	4	1	Rainey 2, McKeague, Emerson (p)
CAS	17/01/25	SF	Larne	Sol	W	4	0	Keenan 3, Rainey
CAS	14/02/25	F	Belfast Celtic	Sol	W	2	1	Keenan, Meek
CC	07/02/25		Glenavon	H	W	3	2	Rainey, Allen, Keenan
CC	21/02/25		Barn	A	W	2	1	W.Reid, H.Reid
CC	14/03/25		Queen's Island	A	L	0	5	-
CC	28/03/25		Cliftonville	H	W	4	1	Rainey, Meek, Vance, Keenan
CC	04/04/25		Linfield	A	D	2	2	Vance, Meek
CC	11/04/25		Larne	A	W	1	0	Rainey
CC	13/04/25		Portadown	H	W	2	1	Keenan, McKeague
CC	14/04/25		Ards	H	W	4	0	Rainey 2, Burns, Meek
CC	18/04/25		Belfast Celtic	A	L	1	2	Keenan
CC	25/04/25		Distillery	A	W	2	1	Keenan, Rainey
CC	02/05/25		Newry Town	H	W	4	0	Meek 2, Rainey, Burns
CC	14/05/25	TM	Queen's Island	WP	D	0	0	-
CC	20/05/25	TMR	Queen's Island	WP	D	1	1	aet – Keenan Replay held over
ChC	22/04/25	1	Crusaders	H	W	3	2	W.Reid, McKeague, Meek
ChC	04/05/25	2	Willowfield	H	W	5	3	Keenan 2, Rainey 2, Vance
ChC	12/05/25	SF	Barn	Solt	W	3	0	W.Reid, Keenan, Meek
ChC	16/05/25	F	Belfast Celtic	Solt	W	2	1	Keenan, Rainey
F	20/08/24		Distillery	H	W	3	0	Keenan 2, Allen
F	07/03/25		Wolverhampton W.	A	L	3	6	Burns, McKeague, Unknown
F	09/05/25		Shamrock Rovers	H	L	0	2	-

Much less could be said about our shorter venture to Pirrie Park a week later. Only trailing 0-1 to Queen's Island at the interval we fell apart after their second goal and were hammered 0-5. Confidence was affected but we still maintained the favourites tag going into the Irish Cup final against Distillery.

Over 20,000 people saw McKenzie give the Whites a half-time lead but our hopes were lifted when Burns drove in splendidly to equalise. It was not to be our day however, as Harold Burnison scored a penalty to take the Cup across town. The Glens had attacked manfully towards the end as snow began to fall, but we just could not find a way past Arthur Fitzroy.

Somehow the team managed to lift itself and win four of the next five City Cup games. Crowds though had suddenly dropped off - the receipts for the 2-2 draw with Linfield were a paltry £70. The Blues had come back from a 0-2 deficit aided by a strong wind. Our win over Ards on Easter Tuesday gave us a two point cushion over Queen's Island but on the Saturday two late Celtic goals cancelled out Keenan's early solo effort. Both ourselves and Queen's Island won the last two fixtures, meaning a play-off would be necessary to determine the competition winners.

Meantime we comfortably progressed to the final of the Charity Cup with our first half display against Willowfield particularly impressive. Celtic awaited us and we repeated the Shield final scoreline when Rainey breasted in Watson's free-kick. This came after a spectacular dribble by Ferriss enabled Stanley Mahood to equalise Keenan's first half effort.

A challenge game between the champions of the Irish League (Glentoran) and the League of Ireland (Shelbourne) was held at the Oval on 9th May. The Shels had lifted all the Free State trophies on offer and brought a sizeable support to Belfast (the gate was £330). The Dublin side proved better on the day with both their goals coming early in the second half through Farrell and Fulham. Tommy McKeague was the only Glenman to play to form.

The 20th May 1925 was the last day of the football season and had to be utilised as our City Cup Test Match with Queen's Island had finished scoreless. The replay was again inconclusive. Cowan gave Queen's the lead just after half-time but Keenan soon equalised. Watson was sent off but even twenty minutes extra-time failed to produce another goal and so the season ended somewhat in limbo. Hundreds of fans waited on at the final whistle for more football but were eventually persuaded that the match was to be held over until 1925/6.

During the season Tosher Burns played both for the Irish League against the English League and an IFA XI versus South Africa. He was joined by McKeague in the latter. William Reid appeared for the Intermediate League against a Yorkshire League XI who were coached by ex-Glentoran favourite Ralph Leonard. Finally, Arnold Keenan guested for Belfast Celtic in their 0-3 defeat by Glasgow Celtic at the end of April.

Appearances and Goals

	App.	Goals		App.	Goals		App.	Goals
McKeague	48	8	Snape	26	1	McCrudden	5	
Bowden J.	47		Reid W.	25	6	Meek R.	4	
Rainey	44	28	Emerson	23	1	Gray	2	
Inch	43		Vance	15	7	Jordan	1	
Keenan	41	26	Legge	13	6	Thompson (Gk)	1	
McSeveney	40		Watson	11		McKnight	1	
Burns	39	7	Peden	10		Bowden H.	1	
Meek H.	39	19	Allen	9	1	Own Goals		1
Reid H.	33	1	Evans	7		TOTAL	528	112

1925/26

A scoring goalkeeper – Geary's debut – New off-side rule

From their successful squad of 1924/5 Glentoran lost the services of Rainey (to the United States) and Keenan (to Crystal Palace). This was the season in which the new off-side law was tried out. Now two players, including the goalkeeper, had to be behind the forwards.

We suffered two early set-backs. Larne knocked us out of the Gold Cup when Burns missed a penalty and Queen's Island eventually won the third play-off match for the previous season's City Cup. Glens goalkeeper Jimmy Bowden confidently assumed the penalty taking responsibilities from this match onwards.

Vance slides in against Fergie and Thompson of Queen's Island.

The Irish League was the title everyone wanted but we made slow progress initially in trying to retain it. Our forward line was lacking the thrust and sharpness of the 1924/5 team and did not really find their shooting boots until the middle of October. A solid defensive performance enabled us to win at Windsor Park as the Blues slumped to 11th in the table. A goal from debutant G.Laird and a remarkable score from Hunter, when he shot in against the wind from near the touchline, brought us to within one point of leaders Distillery at the half-way stage.

Our performances in the next four games earned us the championship favourites tag. This run included two vital home wins over Distillery in both cup and league in front of splendid crowds.

Although missing key players Hugh Meek and Tosher Burns, who had both been transferred to Wolverhampton Wanderers, we were involved in a brilliant game at Newry on 19th December. As the sleet and fog descended from the Mourne Mountains, Eddie Inch scored the goal of the match with a 30 yard drive. However we then dropped vital points in the two home Christmas fixtures and Celtic's win enabled them to cut our lead to a solitary point with five fixtures to be played. Receipts for the Boxing Day encounter were £423.

Queen's Island centre-forward Fred Roberts was the thorn in our side on Christmas Day, as he netted both their goals to add to the two he had scored in the City Cup play-off.

After easily overcoming lowly Barn we had a mid-week engagement at Cliftonville. Many Belfast Celtic fans attended this game to cheer on the Reds, but after an interval score of 2-2 Hunter got the crucial winner.

The Linfield team were a shadow of their former selves but we still had to fight hard to see them off and maintain our slender one point advantage with two league games remaining.

The emphasis then switched to the Irish Cup and County Antrim Shield as the league was placed on a back burner during February. An 18 year old Johnny Geary made his debut in the last-kick win over the Blues in the Shield on 2nd January 1926. Linfield showed they

Results 1925/26

Played 48. Won 26. Drew 11. Lost 11. Goals For 110. Against 71. % 65.6.
Honours: Charity Cup (shared)

IL	22/08/25		Portadown	A	D	2	2	Meek, McKeague
IL	29/08/25		Larne	H	W	2	1	Meek 2
IL	05/09/25		Distillery	A	L	1	2	J.Bowden (p)
IL	12/09/25		Newry Town	H	W	5	1	McKeague 2, Curry og, Meek, Armstrong
IL	19/09/25		Queen's Island	A	D	1	1	Meek
IL	26/09/25		Belfast Celtic	A	L	1	2	Inch
IL	03/10/25		Cliftonville	H	W	2	1	H.Bowden, Inch
IL	10/10/25		Barn	A	W	6	0	H.Bowden 2, Hunter, Inch, Ralph, Burns
IL	17/10/25		Ards	H	W	4	2	Meek 3, Armstrong
IL	31/10/25		Linfield	A	W	1	0	Meek
IL	07/11/25		Glenavon	H	W	4	1	Hunter, Laird, Meek 2
IL	14/11/25		Portadown	H	W	2	0	Armstrong, Meek
IL	21/11/25		Larne	A	D	1	1	Laird
IL	05/12/25		Distillery	H	W	2	1	Armstrong 2
IL	19/12/25		Newry Town	A	W	3	2	Inch, Ralph 2
IL	25/12/25		Queen's Island	H	D	2	2	Inch, Ralph
IL	26/12/25		Belfast Celtic	H	L	2	3	Kirkwood og, McKeague
IL	09/01/26		Barn	H	W	4	1	Inch 2, McKeague, Laird
IL	20/01/26		Cliftonville	A	W	3	2	Geary, Ralph, Hunter
IL	23/01/26		Linfield	H	W	3	2	Ralph, McKeague, W.Reid
IL	27/02/26		Ards	A	L	1	2	Walker
IL	03/03/26		Glenavon	A	L	1	2	W.Reid
GC	26/08/25	1	Larne	A	L	0	1	-
CC*	02/09/25	TMR2	Queen's Island	Solt	L	2	3	Meek, J.Bowden (p)
IC	28/11/25	1	Distillery	H	W	3	0	Armstrong 2, Meek
IC	16/01/26	2	Belfast United	H	W	2	1	W.Reid, Armstrong
IC	06/02/26	SF	Linfield	Solt	D	2	2	Armstrong, Geary
IC	10/02/26	SFR	Linfield	Solt	D	2	2	Geary, Hunter
IC	17/02/26	SFR2	Linfield	Solt	L	2	3	Armstrong, McKeague
CAS	12/12/25	1	Barn	A	W	4	1	Laird 2, W.Reid, Hunter
CAS	02/01/26	2	Linfield	H	W	3	2	Laird 2, Armstrong
CAS	30/01/26	SF	Queen's Island	WP	D	0	0	-
CAS	03/02/26	SFR	Queen's Island	WP	W	1	0	Armstrong
CAS	20/02/26	F	Cliftonville	WP	L	1	5	Armstrong
CC	06/03/26		Distillery	A	L	1	3	Rainey (p)
CC	13/03/26		Portadown	A	L	3	4	Devlin 2, H.Reid
CC	20/03/26		Ards	H	W	3	2	Devlin, Armstrong, Moore
CC	02/04/26		Queen's Island	A	D	2	2	Devlin, Moore
CC	05/04/26		Belfast Celtic	H	W	3	0	Geary, J.Bowden (p), Moore
CC	06/04/26		Glenavon	H	D	1	1	J.Bowden (p)
CC	10/04/26		Barn	A	D	2	2	W.Reid, Moore
CC	17/04/26		Newry Town	H	W	6	0	Armstrong 4, W.Reid, Walker
CC	21/04/26		Cliftonville	H	W	4	2	Walker, W.Reid, Armstrong, J.Bowden (p)
CC	24/04/26		Linfield	A	W	2	1	Walker, McKeague
CC	08/05/26		Larne	H	W	3	0	Rainey, Armstrong 2
ChC	27/04/26	1	Brantwood	H	W	2	1	Geary, Rainey
ChC	05/05/26	SF	Distillery	Solt	W	2	1	Moore, Rainey
ChC	15/05/26	F	Belfast Celtic	Solt	D	1	1	J.Bowden (p)
F	20/08/25		Brantwood	H	W	2	0	Boyd, Armstrong
F	27/03/26		Birmingham City	A	L	2	8	Devlin, Armstrong
F	19/05/26		Shelbourne	H	W	2	1	Moore, W.Reid

* = hold over from 1924/5

Bowden gathers safely during the County Antrim Shield semi-final.

should not be written off too hastily by gaining revenge in the Irish Cup semi-final. Twice we led in the first game and a 2-0 lead in the replay (Geary heading home in the first minute) was also cancelled out. Admission to the second replay was 1/- and 8d so the gate receipts of £330 would indicate a crowd of around 10,000. The interval arrived with the score 1-1 but soon after Linfield scored twice in a minute to lead 3-1. Tommy McKeague rushed one in straight from the kick-off but later missed chances cost us dear.

The two Shield semi-finals with Queen's Island were monotonous and uninteresting. Armstrong's late winner, when he beat three defenders in a mazy run, was the only noteworthy incident. Glentoran received a big shock in the final when Cliftonville hammered us on a heavy pitch, to record their first Shield success since 1898!

Whether it was this result or all the earlier hard games and replays which caused us to blow up in the league is not clear. Whatever the reasons the outcome was two very poor displays against Ards and Glenavon (the latter in a gale and hailstones), which allowed Belfast Celtic to nip in and snatch the title from our grasp.

The black period continued as our opening two City Cup fixtures were lost, despite twice holding the lead against Portadown. Then we were badly beaten in a friendly at Birmingham. At last the team slowly came back to form in April staging a brilliant second half comeback against Queen's Island, and then handing Celtic their first defeat in fourteen games on Easter Monday. Glentoran went through the rest of the City Cup unbeaten to

McKeague heads for goal against Queen's Island at Pirrie Park.

finish third behind Celtic (who picked up their fourth trophy of the season) and Queen's Island.

The Charity Cup produced some exciting games, none more so than the semi-finals. Belfast Celtic defeated Crusaders 4-2 while in our match Distillery took the lead. It took a last minute winner from the returned Rainey to earn us one last crack at Celtic. A huge crowd (receipts £410) turned up for the final, refereed by J.B.Stark, and they saw the Celts lead at half-time. However after the break goalkeeper Bowden was again accurate from the penalty spot and the popular opinion was for the two clubs to share the trophy.

Some Glenmen gained Inter League caps during the season. Alan McSeveney played against both the English and Scottish Leagues, being joined by Jimmy Bowden in the former at Anfield and Inch in the latter at Solitude. Willie Reid was our only player involved in the first meeting between the Irish League and the League of Ireland at Dalymount Park on 13th March. A gathering of 18,000 watched the Southerners win 3-1.

Appearances and Goals

	App.	Goals		App.	Goals		App.	Goals
Reid W.	45	7	Ralph	17	6	Devlin	6	4
McKeague	43	8	Burns	16	1	Pestrell	3	
Peden	42		Meek H.	16	14	Morrison	3	
Bowden J.	40	6	Moore W.	13	5	Gallagher	2	
McSeveney	39		Vance	12		Boyd	2	
Armstrong	39	21	Reid H.	12	1	Telford	1	
Inch	36	7	Bowden H.	11	3	Lavery	1	
Hunter	36	5	Kirkwood	11		Jordan	1	
Geary J.	23	5	Preston	8		Bruce	1	
Watson	19		Rainey	7	4	Own Goals		2
Laird	17	7	Walker	6	4	TOTAL	528	110

1926/27

Bambrick's goals – McSeveney misses a train – Hassle on the way to Cork

Pre-season departures at the Oval included Jimmy Bowden and Eddie Inch making the short trip to Dundela, with Inch later joining Belfast Celtic. Willie Reid emigrated to the United States while namesake Hugh travelled south to play for Dundalk GNR. The most famous of the replacements was a centre-forward from Ulster Rangers, Joe Bambrick. Other arrivals were Richardson (a goalkeeper from Linfield), Rogers (ex-Sandown Park) and Dinnen (from Portadown). The Irish League fixed admission prices at 1/- (reserved) and 8d (unreserved). Ladies fees were 9d and 5d respectively. Referees pocketed 30/- plus the train fare for their afternoon's work.

Joe Bambrick.

Queen's Island proved a bogey team, being the only side to defeat us in the first three months of the season. Bambrick was quickly into goalscoring form, netting the winner against the Blues, and only a missed penalty at Larne in September stopped him claiming a personal tally of seven!

The top of the table clash versus Belfast Celtic on 23rd October never presented a dull moment. After we had led 3-2 at the interval Richardson made many brilliant saves only to let a ground shot slither under his body for their equaliser. We let a 2-0 lead against Ards slip and this allowed Celtic to open up a one point gap at the league's half-way stage. The Glentoran directors were praised for allowing the same eleven to play from week to week, thus blending the team well.

Our second trip to Inver Park, this time on Irish Cup business, was a nightmare. Larne took a 40 second lead and soon went 3-0 up before Bambrick pulled it back to 2-3. However the home side ruled the roost and consolidated victory in the last half hour.

The Glens' next league setback came when solid left-back Alan McSeveney missed a connecting train from his Coleraine home and was unable to get to Portadown. After Tommy McKeague had put us in front the Ports gave our defence a pounding. Bambrick also failed with a spot-kick in this game but made amends in the home match with Linfield by firing us ahead after only 30 seconds.

The point gained at Pirrie Park on Christmas Day was valuable as twice we had been two goals behind. However two subsequent defeats left us trailing Belfast Celtic by seven points with only five games to play.

Celtic stayed on course and became champions after defeating Glenavon on 29th January. Glentoran's meaningless defeats in the last two games forced us down into fourth place.

February and March were trying times. While the directors vainly attempted to get Joe Bambrick to sign professional forms, team performances and results were disastrous. We were knocked out of the Shield and found our City Cup chances slim, especially after another debacle at Shamrock Park. To add insult to injury, the Glentoran playing shirts were confiscated by customs officials when we crossed the Irish border for a "friendly" with Fordson's in Cork. The Glens took the lead on twelve minutes in front of 5,000 at the Mardyke Grounds in the "Rebel City". However after McSorley had his penalty saved by O'Hagan our defence caved in. The unfavourable comments about this trip probably led to the cancellation of our proposed friendly in Dundalk.

The remainder of the City Cup was full of very inconsistent Glentoran results. We threatened to turn the corner many times, for example when coming from behind to beat Celtic, but could not put a run together. Many young players were tried, including

---

Results 1926/27

Played 39. Won 18. Drew 5. Lost 16. For 93. Against 100. % 52.6

IL	21/08/26		Newry Town	A	D	1	1	Dinnen
IL	04/09/26		Portadown	H	W	3	2	Bambrick 2, Devlin
IL	11/09/26		Linfield	A	W	1	0	Bambrick
IL	18/09/26		Queen's Island	H	L	1	3	McKeague
IL	25/09/26		Larne	A	W	6	2	Bambrick 6
IL	02/10/26		Distillery	H	D	1	1	Bambrick
IL	16/10/26		Glenavon	A	W	3	2	Bambrick, W.Moore, Devlin
IL	23/10/26		Belfast Celtic	H	D	3	3	Geary, Bambrick 2
IL	30/10/26		Barn	H	W	3	2	Bambrick, Morrison, Geary
IL	13/11/26		Cliftonville	A	W	2	0	Bambrick, Morrison
IL	20/11/26		Ards	H	D	2	2	Dinnen, Geary
IL	04/12/26		Newry Town	H	W	3	2	Bambrick 2, W.Moore
IL	11/12/26		Portadown	A	L	2	5	McKeague, Devlin
IL	18/12/26		Linfield	H	W	3	1	Bambrick, W.Moore (p), McKeague
IL	25/12/26		Queen's Island	A	D	3	3	Devlin, Bambrick, Geary
IL	27/12/26		Larne	H	L	2	4	Bambrick, Geary
IL	01/01/27		Distillery	A	L	2	3	Bambrick 2
IL	08/01/27		Glenavon	H	W	3	1	Bambrick, Morrison, Mills
IL	22/01/27		Barn	A	W	6	2	Bambrick 4, McKeague, Geary
IL	29/01/27		Cliftonville	H	W	3	2	Geary, Abraham, McKeague
IL	09/03/27		Belfast Celtic	A	L	1	4	Devlin
IL	30/04/27		Ards	A	L	2	3	W.Moore, Bambrick
GC	28/08/26	1	Queen's Island	A	L	1	6	W.Moore
IC	27/11/26	1	Larne	A	L	2	5	Bambrick 2(1p)
CC	15/01/27		Cliftonville	H	W	2	0	Bambrick 2
CC	12/02/27		Newry Town	H	L	2	3	Dinnen, Abraham
CC	19/02/27		Queen's Island	A	L	1	4	McKeague
CC	12/03/27		Portadown	A	L	1	6	Bambrick
CC	19/03/27		Barn	H	W	5	1	Bambrick 3, Geary, McKeague
CC	02/04/27		Linfield	A	L	0	5	-
CC	09/04/27		Belfast Celtic	H	W	4	3	Bambrick 2, Abraham, Whitley
CC	16/04/27		Distillery	A	L	1	2	Bambrick
CC	18/04/27		Larne	H	W	6	2	W.Moore, McKeague 4, A.Moore
CC	19/04/27		Glenavon	A	W	1	0	W.Moore
CC	23/04/27		Ards	H	L	2	4	Bambrick, A.Moore
CAS	02/03/27	2	Belfast Celtic	H	L	2	4	McKeague 2
ChC	07/05/27	1	Crusaders	H	W	3	1	Bambrick, A.Moore, McKeague
ChC	11/05/27	SF	Queen's Island	H	W	2	1	Bambrick, A.Moore
ChC	14/05/27	F	Linfield	Solt	L	2	5	Bambrick 2
F	26/02/27		Fordson's, Cork	A	L	1	6	Unknown

McDowell, a goalkeeper from BB football. Tommy McKeague was our best player throughout April as we had to settle for fifth place in a City Cup won by Linfield.

The Charity Cup provided a last hope of silverware and we managed to battle through to the final despite falling behind in both the first round and semi-final ties. However the Blues were too strong in the final, in which they had led 5-0 at one stage. This proved to be Joe Bambrick's last game for us as professional terms could not be agreed, and he joined Linfield for 1927/8. Glentoran also missed out on Hugh Meek, who returned to the Irish League from Wolves to Ards.

Bambrick and Geary brought the only representative honours to the club, playing for Amateur Ireland against the English Amateurs.

Appearances and Goals

	App.	Goals		App.	Goals		App.	Goals
Bambrick	37	44	McCormick	16		McCrudden	3	
Kirkwood	32		Devlin	16	5	Gordon	3	
Moore W.	32	7	Morrison	10	3	Craig	3	
Dinnen	30	3	Peden	9		Morton	1	
Richardson	29		Abraham	8	3	Downie	1	
McSeveney	28		McAuley	6		Whiteside	1	
McKeague	28	14	McDowell	5		Coates	1	
Geary J.	26	8	Moore A.	5	4	Wilson	1	
Rodgers	24		Mills	4	1	Unknown	22	
Watson	22		Gray	4				
Whitley	19	1	Hagan	3		TOTAL	429	93

1927/28

An extended league – Financial problems – A lack of Charity

The Irish League was extended to fourteen clubs with the inclusion of Bangor and Coleraine. Distillery vacated York Park and returned to their Grosvenor Road headquarters.

For Glentoran, the loss of Bambrick, who went on to score 81 goals in his first season for Linfield, was partially offset by the return of veteran half-back John Scraggs from Clydebank. Scraggs was immediately appointed captain. Whitley had moved to Barn and Vance to Willowfield but Scarr, Distillery's left-back, came to the Oval. While our financial outlook was very tight, it was thought that this would be overcome by playing in that "hot bed" of football, East Belfast. The league had reduced unreserved admission to 6d.

Glentoran began playing matters disastrously by getting hammered at Windsor Park with Bambrick on target twice. W.McDowell celebrated his seventeenth birthday by keeping a clean sheet against Ards when a new centre-forward from Brantwood, Gill, made his debut. After Belfast Celtic knocked us out of the Gold Cup the old heads of the team, namely Scraggs and Davy Lyner, became very influential. Six wins were recorded in the next seven league matches with only Celtic being able to reveal our suspected defensive frailties.

We moved to fourth in the table as the formation of the team changed. Abraham moved to centre-forward and Gordon came in at left-half. The Moores, Alan and William, formed an effective left-wing, Scraggs controlled play from centre-half with Lyner and Johnny Geary on the right.

On 22nd October 1927 Ireland beat England (2-0) for the last time at Windsor Park to date. A week later we went down to joint leaders Larne, staging an abortive comeback after trailing by three at the interval. November was an inconsistent month as the team struggled to adjust to the heavier grounds. Twice we led against Coleraine but went down to the odd goal in nine. Glentoran "plodded" to victory over Portadown, handicapped by the loss of Lyner who did not appear for the second half due to a leg muscle injury. David Geary came into the side as replacement right-half.

An Irish Cup exit on our first visit to the re-opened Grosvenor Park heralded a run of four consecutive defeats. Meek scored both Distillery goals with penalties. The concession of thirteen goals in those three league defeats ended any lingering title hopes. Our form improved slightly over Christmas and we drew a crowd of 7,000 for the visit of Celtic on December 27th. Despite giving the Celts defence a hot time we failed to prevent them breaking away to score

Johnny Geary.

through Stanley Mahood and Weir.

For spending all his playing career at the Oval right-back Alan McSeveney was awarded a benefit game against Dundalk. Unfortunately the match was tame and dull, neither side wanting to take unnecessary risks on the frozen surface.

Results 1927/28

Played 45. Won 18. Drew 6. Lost 21. Goals For 101. Against 107. % 46.7

IL	20/08/27		Linfield	A	L	1	6	McKeague
IL	27/08/27		Ards	H	D	0	0	-
IL	03/09/27		Barn	H	W	4	0	Gill 2, Scraggs (p), Stewart
IL	10/09/27		Cliftonville	A	W	2	0	A.Moore, Lyner
IL	17/09/27		Glenavon	H	W	3	2	A.Moore, Abraham, Scraggs
IL	24/09/27		Belfast Celtic	A	L	2	6	A.Moore, J.Geary
IL	01/10/27		Distillery	H	W	4	1	Abraham 2, W.Moore, Lyner
IL	08/10/27		Bangor	A	W	2	0	J.Geary, Lyner
IL	15/10/27		Queen's Island	H	W	3	2	Abraham 2, W.Moore
IL	29/10/27		Larne	A	L	2	3	J.Geary, Abraham
IL	05/11/27		Newry Town	H	D	1	1	W.Moore
IL	12/11/27		Coleraine	A	L	4	5	Walker, J.Geary, Scraggs, W.Moore
IL	19/11/27		Portadown	H	W	3	1	Abraham, McKeague, W.Moore
IL	03/12/27		Linfield	H	L	1	5	Abraham
IL	10/12/27		Ards	A	L	2	5	J.Geary, W.Moore
IL	17/12/27		Barn	A	I	?	3	J.Geary, A.Moore
IL	24/12/27		Cliftonville	H	W	5	2	W.Moore 2, A.Moore, J.Geary, Mercer
IL	26/12/27		Glenavon	A	D	2	2	Leathem, McKeague
IL	27/12/27		Belfast Celtic	H	L	0	2	-
IL	31/12/27		Distillery	A	D	1	1	Mercer
IL	07/01/28		Bangor	H	W	5	4	W.Moore 3, J.Geary, D.Geary
IL	14/01/28		Queen's Island	A	D	4	4	Mercer 2, A.Moore, W.Moore
IL	21/01/28		Larne	H	W	2	1	A.Moore, W.Moore
IL	28/01/28		Newry Town	A	L	1	6	Mercer
IL	11/02/28		Coleraine	H	W	3	1	J.Geary, Mercer, McKeague
IL	18/02/28		Portadown	A	W	4	2	Johnston 2, McKeague, W.Moore
GC	29/08/27	1	Belfast Celtic	H	L	1	3	Gill
IC	26/11/27	1	Distillery	A	L	1	2	McKeague
CAS	22/02/28	2	Distillery	H	W	5	3	J.Geary, Mercer, McKeague, W.Moore, Johnston
CAS	14/03/28	SF	Ards	Solt	L	1	2	W.Moore
CC	03/03/28		Larne	A	L	2	3	Mercer, W.Moore
CC	17/03/28		Barn	A	D	2	2	W.Moore, A.Moore
CC	24/03/28		Ards	H	W	5	2	J.Geary, Mercer 2, W.Moore 2
CC	31/03/28		Newry Town	A	L	1	3	McKeague
CC	07/04/28		Cliftonville	A	L	0	1	-
CC	09/04/28		Coleraine	A	L	0	4	-
CC	10/04/28		Glenavon	A	L	1	3	Colvin
CC	14/04/28		Linfield	H	L	0	2	-
CC	21/04/28		Queen's Island	A	W	3	2	McKeague, Mercer, W.Moore
CC	28/04/28		Bangor	H	W	4	2	Colvin 3, Johnston
CC	05/05/28		Distillery	A	L	0	1	-
CC	10/05/28		Belfast Celtic	H	W	4	0	Firth, J.Geary, Colvin 2
CC	12/05/28		Portadown	H	L	2	3	J.Geary 2
ChC	03/05/28	1	Willowfield	H	W	5	1	Colvin 2, J.Geary, McKeague, W.Moore
ChC	16/05/28	SF	Belfast Celtic	GP	L	1	3	Firth
F	28/12/27		Dundalk	H	L	0	1	Alan McSeveney Benefit
F	26/04/28		Kilmarnock	H	L	1	2	J.Geary
F	15/05/28		Dundela XI	H		Unknown		T.McKnight Benefit

Glentoran's interest in the remainder of the league campaign was purely academic as Linfield and Celtic vied for the title. The directors were in a Catch 22 situation - the playing staff were obviously not good enough to win trophies but worse still the club had slipped into a terrible state financially. Indeed matters became so bad by the end of the season that Linfield even made a £20 donation to our club funds. On a brighter note we won four of our last six league games to finish fifth in the table, only a point behind fourth placed Larne but a massive 16 points adrift of the champions, Celtic. The other two matches in the run-in were an exciting 4-4 draw with Queen's Island and a debacle at Newry when we caved in during the second half on a waterlogged pitch.

Johnstone, Mercer, T.Stewart, Tosh and Walker were introduced into the 1st XI in early 1928. We brushed Distillery aside in the County Antrim Shield but then despite going ahead against Ards in the semi-final a miserable performance allowed the Co. Down men to come back to win. Willie Moore could hold his head up as he alone had a splendid game. Ironically just ten days later we thrashed Ards at the Oval in the City Cup with Moore's display emphasising his claim for Glentoran's "Player of the Season". It was another false dawn however as the next five City Cup matches were lost in the space of a fortnight! This sequence culminated with defeat against the Blues when Scraggs had Bambrick in his pocket for 70 minutes but allowed Joe to break away to score twice late on. On-loan keeper from Parkend, H.Beggs, had made a sound debut up until then.

After a scrappy win at Queen's Island the team showed real character in coming back from two down against Bangor with three of our goals coming in the last twelve minutes. Colvin, the ex-Belvoir centre-forward, began to show goalscoring form. In between these two wins Kilmarnock visited the Oval for a friendly. Glentoran included guest players Ward (St.Mary's goalkeeper), David Reid (Distillery) and Fred Roberts (Broadway United) but lost a good game narrowly with Scraggs missing a penalty.

We produced a flash in the pan win over eventual City Cup winners Celtic, all the goals coming in the last 25 minutes, but had to settle for tenth place in the final table.

The first round of the Charity Cup gave the Glens a chance to boost their goals tally as juniors Willowfield decided to field their second XI. No fewer than 20 shots on target produced a single goal in the first half but we added four more after the interval and even afforded missed penalties from Willie Moore and Colvin. After a benefit game for T.McKnight against Dundela the season was wound up with the Charity semi-final against a Celtic XI eager for revenge. There was little charity on the terraces as our keeper McDowell was struck by a stone and police frequently had to break up scrimmages with baton charges. All the goals came in the first half.

So an unsatisfactory season came to an unsavoury end. During the year many directors had resigned and the club also lost the valiant services of secretary Walter Scott who moved to the County of Meath. Maybe the Grand Carnival at the Oval in May and June would help to lift the gloom!

Appearances and Goals

	App.	Goals		App.	Goals		App.	Goals
Stewart R.	44		Johnstone	13	4	Boyd (Gk)	2	
Moore W.	43	22	Abraham	12	8	Matthews	2	
Scarr	42		Geary D.	11	1	Leathem	2	1
Geary J.	42	15	McKeown	11		Hagan	1	
McKeague	33	10	Gordon	10		Henderson	1	
Scraggs	30	3	Thompson, (Gk)	8		Bowers	1	
McDowell	29		Colvin	8	8	Hutton	1	
Walker J.	25	1	Gill	5	3	Malton	1	
Moore A.	24	8	Tosh	4		Richardson	1	
Stewart T.	21	1	Beggs	4		Bunting	1	
McSeveney	18		Anderson	4		McCrudden	1	
Lynor D.	18	3	Firth	3	?			
Mercer	16	11	James	3		TOTAL	495	101

1928/29

The arrival of Fred Roberts – Goals galore – Charity Cup shared

After three or four years in the doldrums Glentoran signalled their intention to emerge as a power again by bringing new faces to the Oval. Forwards Scott and Hutchinson arrived from Queen's Island while Jamison, a centre-half moved from Coleraine. Goalkeeper Ward was signed from St.Mary's and Carleton, a left back from Dundela, but the most significant capture was to be centre-forward Fred Roberts from Broadway United.

In league membership Ballymena replaced Barn, so bringing to an end the Carrickfergus club's perennial struggles in senior circles.

Roberts began on the right foot despite missing a penalty at Newry where 3,000 saw him debut. Although he had scored three hat-tricks by mid-September it was remarked that "Fred was not an ideal leader of the line." However he had the happy knack of finding the net, amply demonstrated to 15,000 fans against Linfield, for whom Joe Bambrick had opened the scoring.

In mid-October we sat unbeaten in second place in the league and were favourites to reach the Gold Cup final. Against Queen's Island we had finished with only eight men, Roberts sent off for retaliation while McKeague and Scott were carried off injured. Things began to go wrong as Ards' last minute winner in the Gold Cup semi-final began a run of four defeats. Belfast Celtic totally overwhelmed us but Roberts' reappearance in the side coincided with a return to winning ways and revenge over Ards.

Willie Crooks rejoined the Glens (from Larne) after an absence of seven years and quickly formed a formidable forward trio with Roberts and Johnny Geary. Disappointment came though with an early Irish Cup exit against new boys Ballymena after two ding-dong encounters. Ward in goals was particularly brilliant, making many point blank saves in the tie.

Glentoran goalkeeper Ward punches clear from a melee.

The goals really began to flow for us in December, 32 being scored in the league, as wingers McKeague, Moore and Hutchinson provided a plentiful supply of crosses. However a last minute defeat against Linfield and another reverse at the hands of Ballymena left us in fourth place, twelve points behind Celtic as 1929 dawned.

Roberts played splendidly towards the end of the league, even scoring directly from a corner versus Ards. By the time Celtic visited the Oval in the last match they had already taken the title but the main interest was whether or not they could complete their campaign unbeaten. A hard match was played out on a pitch partly frozen, partly muddy and with little

Results 1928/29

Played 50. Won 29. Drew 5. Lost 16. Goals For 156. Against 116. % 63.0.
Honours: Charity Cup (Shared)

IL	20/08/28		Newry Town	A	W	1	0	Roberts
IL	25/08/28		Distillery	H	D	2	2	Carleton (p), Hutchinson
IL	01/09/28		Bangor	A	W	3	1	Roberts 3
IL	08/09/28		Linfield	H	W	2	1	Roberts 2
IL	15/09/28		Glenavon	A	W	4	3	Roberts 4
IL	29/09/28		Ballymena	H	D	2	2	Roberts, Scott
IL	06/10/28		Queen's Island	A	W	4	2	McKeague 2(1p), Roberts, Scott
IL	13/10/28		Portadown	H	L	1	2	McKeague
IL	20/10/28		Belfast Celtic	A	L	0	6	-
IL	27/10/28		Larne	H	L	4	5	McKeague, Scott 2, Moore
IL	03/11/28		Coleraine	A	L	2	5	Jamison, Price
IL	14/11/28		Ards	H	W	3	1	Roberts, Geary 2
IL	17/11/28		Cliftonville	A	W	4	2	Roberts 2, Crooks, Moore
IL	01/12/28		Newry Town	H	W	5	1	Roberts 5
IL	08/12/28		Distillery	A	W	3	2	Roberts 2, Jamison
IL	15/12/28		Bangor	H	W	4	0	Roberts, Irvine og, Crooks 2
IL	22/12/28		Linfield	A	L	3	4	Geary, Hutchinson, Roberts
IL	25/12/28		Glenavon	H	W	7	3	Hutchinson 2, Roberts 3, Hare og, Woods
IL	26/12/28		Ballymena	A	L	0	3	-
IL	29/12/28		Queen's Island	H	W	10	3	Crooks 5, Roberts 4, Geary
IL	05/01/29		Portadown	A	W	4	2	Hutchinson, Geary, Roberts, Crooks
IL	19/01/29		Larne	A	W	3	2	Roberts 2, Crooks
IL	26/01/29		Coleraine	H	L	2	3	Roberts, Geary
IL	02/02/29		Ards	A	L	3	4	Roberts 2, Allen (p)
IL	09/02/29		Cliftonville	H	W	4	1	Hutchinson, Roberts 3
IL	27/02/29		Belfast Celtic	H	D	2	2	Hutchinson 2
GC	29/08/28	1	Cliftonville	H	W	6	2	Roberts 3, Scott 3
GC	12/09/28	2	Bangor	H	W	3	1	Carleton (p), Roberts, Scott
GC	10/10/28	SF	Ards	GP	L	1	2	McKeague
IC	24/11/28	1	Ballymena	H	D	3	3	Moore, Geary, McKeague
IC	28/11/28	1R	Ballymena	A	L	1	2	Firth
CAS	23/01/29	1	Bangor	H	W	4	3	McKeague 3, Hutchinson
CAS	20/02/29	2	Queen's Island	H	W	6	3	Geary, Roberts 4, Hutchinson
CAS	20/03/29	SF	Broadway United	GP	L	0	3	-
CC	02/03/29		Distillery	H	W	10	2	Crooks 2, Roberts 5, McKeague, Mellon og, Hutchinson
CC	16/03/29		Newry Town	A	W	2	1	Allen (p), Crooks
CC	23/03/29		Queen's Island	H	W	3	1	Roberts, McKeown, Wilson
CC	30/03/29		Glenavon	A	L	2	4	Hutchinson, McKeague
CC	01/04/29		Bangor	A	W	3	1	Hutchinson, Moore, Allen
CC	02/04/29		Linfield	H	L	0	2	-
CC	06/04/29		Ballymena	A	L	2	4	Roberts, Crooks
CC	13/04/29		Belfast Celtic	H	W	2	1	Allen (p), Roberts
CC	20/04/29		Portadown	A	L	3	4	Roberts, Hutchinson, Geary
CC	27/04/29		Ards	H	L	2	5	Roberts 2
CC	04/05/29		Coleraine	A	W	2	1	McKeague, Hutchinson
CC	11/05/29		Larne	H	W	3	1	Roberts, Geary, McKeown
CC	13/05/29		Cliftonville	A	W	4	1	Roberts 2, Crooks, McKeown

ChC	08/05/29	1	Broadway United	H	W	5	2	Crooks 2, Roberts, Hutchinson, Geary
ChC	16/05/29	SF	Cliftonville	GP	W	4	2	Roberts 2, Hutchinson, Geary
ChC	18/05/29	F	Distillery	Solt	D	3	3	McKeague, Roberts (p), Hutchinson
F	17/10/28		Linfield	H	W	2	1	Quinn, McCleery og Willie Moore Benefit
F	12/01/29		Distillery	H	W	5	1	Roberts 3, Crooks, Gray og
F	30/04/29		Kilmarnock	H	W	1	0	Roberts
F	20/05/29		Shamrock Rovers	H	L	3	4	Geary 2, Lynn

time remaining it was poised at 2-2. Then Celtic's keeper Jack Diffen had to leave the field with concussion and centre-forward Gallagher went into goals. Diffen came back on wearing an outfield jersey and saved a goalbound shot with his hands, leaving the Glens with a penalty to end the run. The drama did not end there as Diffen re-donned the goalkeeping shirt and promptly saved Allen's penalty to preserve the Celts' unbeaten record.

Our occasional inconsistent result did not stop the press from tipping us to lift at least one of the three remaining trophies. This looked justified as we opened the City Cup with a "day out" against Distillery, Roberts knocking in the last five goals. A shock awaited us in the shape of juniors Broadway United in the County Antrim Shield semi-final. Broadway had most of the play as we struggled to make an impression on their defence, and we bowed out.

We continued to progress nice and quietly in the City Cup until defeats against Glenavon, Linfield (attendance 16,000) and Ballymena ruined our hopes. An excellent result came against Belfast Celtic but lack of consistency was still the major problem. The team proved itself totally capable of playing decisive attacking football but too often there would be periods when we just broke down and let the opposition dictate.

Glentoran rallied again in May to finish third in the City Cup and reach the final of the Charity Cup, including a face saving revenge win over Broadway. In the final Distillery raced into a 3-0 lead but we clawed our way back in a terrific second half. No extra time was played and it was decided to share the trophy.

Scottish Cup holders Kilmarnock were beaten by a first minute goal in a friendly. Glentoran fielded four guest players, one of whom, Black, the goalkeeper of Cliftonville Olympic, frustrated Killie's many attempts to equalise. The final fixture of this frustrating season saw us go 3-0 up against Shamrock Rovers; Lynn, a guest from Ards, netting the third. However by half-time a Gaskin hat-trick had made it level and the same player netted the winner after the break.

S.Scott gained our only representative honour, playing inside-right in the Irish League side beaten 5-0 by the English League at Windsor Park in September.

Appearances and Goals

	App.	Goals		App.	Goals		App.	Goals
Geary J.	49	12	Currie	14		Scarr	1	
Stewart R.	46		Stewart T.	12		Colvin	1	
Roberts	44	66	Moore W.	12	4	McDowell	1	
McKeown	42	3	Anderson	11		Rochill	1	
McKeague	40	13	McMahon	8		Price	1	1
Hutchinson	39	18	Reid H.	7		Lowery	1	
Carleton	33	2	Walker J.	6		Hewitt	1	
Ward	32		Firth	6	1	Johnston	1	
Scott	32	8	Woods	5	1	Moore (Gk)	1	
Crooks	32	17	Quinn	3		Casement	1	
Wilson	22	1	Harrison	2		Own Goals		3
Allen	21	4	McHenry	2		TOTAL	550	156
Jamison	19	2	Coates	1				

1929/30

Shipyard team folds – Twelve goals shared – Appalling weather and pitches

The demise of Queen's Island in 1929 had two significant effects on Irish League football. Firstly, coupled with improved transport links, it allowed a new team from Londonderry into senior circles, Derry City. Secondly Glentoran profited by picking up a group of first team players from our neighbours including the likes of Brown, McClements, Montgomery, Burns and Croft. In addition a goalkeeper, McFarlane, was signed from Willowfield.

After our public practice on 15th August we travelled to the North West to open up Derry's senior campaign on a Thursday evening. Despite continuous rain 7,500 turned up and saw Derry take an interval lead. However we overcame this (and an injury to Geary) in the second half. During the evening the Glentoran directors placed a wreath on the Londonderry War Memorial.

The Glens' early season form was excellent and we finished August with a 100% record. Celtic's goalkeeper Bertie Mehaffey kept the score down in the second league fixture and no weak links could be spotted in our team during the two wins over Ards.

Around 20,000 packed the Oval for a thrilling match with the Blues in early September. Fred Roberts gave us a first minute lead but we twice had to come from behind to draw as Joe Bambrick claimed a hat-trick. Three narrow league wins followed as Cliftonville missed a late penalty, Geary's 86th minute header killed off Glenavon and 2,000 saw Tucker Croft sink Larne. Also Glentoran progressed to the Gold Cup

Tucker Croft scores against Distillery goalkeeper Palmer in February.

semi-finals, thanks mainly to Ward's brilliant display at Brandywell.

The 5th October was a disaster in more ways than one. Coleraine inflicted our first defeat of the season and allowed Linfield to move top by one point. Furthermore, right-back Hugh Reid had retired with an injury on 30 minutes, putting us down to ten men and causing him to miss out on Inter League honours against the Scots. Johnny Geary did play in this fixture but the Irish lost 1-4. Reid and Geary had played against the English League at Everton.

Without Reid our defence leaked twelve goals in five days at the end of October. The fans had full value for their money in the home league game against Bangor. We led 4-3 at the interval and later 6-4 but the Seasiders fought back and the final scoreline of 6-6 provided the highest scoring draw in Glentoran history. After we had taken the lead in the Gold Cup semi-final Distillery's delightful football put them 6-2 up at the break and the tie out of our reach.

Eight different right-backs were tried in nine games as the question was asked, "What is wrong at the Oval?" Only one win was recorded in November but at least the side fought back well after trailing 1-4 at Portadown. The new boardroom was formally opened at the end of the month.

New signing James Alexander (Sandy) McNeill made his debut at centre-forward on a storm-drenched Celtic Park on 7th December. He soon found his shooting boots as we saw off juniors Dunmurry at the third time of asking in the Irish Cup and moved to within three points of Linfield as they lost 0-1 at Bangor on 14th December. However Joe Bambrick's hat-trick put paid to the Glens temporary revival a week later.

The weather had turned many pitches into quagmires and on Christmas Day, after we had made the game secure, it was reported that, "the antics of Crooks and Geary in the mud made the crowd and referee rock with laughter." Alan McSeveney's return against Larne on 28th December was cut short when referee Bunting of Manchester abandoned the game after 48 minutes. The Glentoran players complained over this and maybe the fact that we had changed into a clean strip at half-time and Larne could not influenced his decision.

As the 1930s dawned the appalling weather continued. After the train carrying the team to Coleraine had been delayed by 50 minutes due to the drenching rain this game was also abandoned. Our first Cup game with Larne was played out on a surface covered by three inches of snow. A big crowd attended the replay when after the visitors had taken a 30 second lead we woke up to win with Croft particularly impressive on the left-wing.

Sandy McNeill's good form forced Fred Roberts to move to outside right to get a game and he scored twice from the wing against Newry. We replayed our league match at Coleraine on 1st February and the 2-1 win assured us of the runners-up spot. The News Letter's reporter, "One of the Crowd", could not attend this match due to illness. "One of the Crowd" had supplied excellent and lengthy reports on Glentoran's progress during the season. The same day at Celtic Park Ireland beat Wales 7-0 with Bambrick's six goals setting up a still standing record for the highest number of individual goals in a game for a British International player.

Programme Cover.

Linfield became league champions two days later and the following Saturday witnessed the Irish Cup semi-final showdown at Celtic Park. Before kick-off a black cat wearing a red, green and black rosette was handed to the Glentoran captain. McNeill gave us the lead but we missed many game sealing chances. In the last ten minutes our half-back line of Wilson, Montgomery and McClements began to tire and goals from Bambrick and McCaw allowed the Blues to sneak victory.

Off the field activities in 1930 were geared towards fund raising for the building of a new pavilion at the Oval. Many supporters' rallies were held while the active Ladies Committee organised carnivals and a roller skating event. Glentoran secretary Mr.J.A.McDade urged fans to buy the News Letter as he intended to advertise club events in there.

Harry Thoms, ex-Derby and Crystal Palace, made his debut in the opening City Cup game. Using his 6'3" frame to advantage, he dominated the match from centre-half. Mistakes from McFarlane allowed Derry City to claim their first win in Belfast but then the team put together a great run of seven consecutive City Cup wins, also qualifying for the County Antrim Shield final. However a deplorable performance from our forward line allowed the Blues to lift the Shield.

148

Results 1929/30

Played 56. Won 32. Drew 11. Lost 13. Goals For 164. Against 111. % 67.0

IL	22/08/29		Derry City	A	W	2	1	Roberts 2
IL	24/08/29		Belfast Celtic	H	W	4	0	Roberts 2, Croft, Reid
IL	31/08/29		Ards	A	W	5	1	Roberts 4, Croft
IL	07/09/29		Linfield	H	D	3	3	Roberts 2, Hutchinson
IL	14/09/29		Cliftonville	A	W	3	2	Roberts 3
IL	21/09/29		Glenavon	H	W	2	1	Geary 2
IL	28/09/29		Larne	A	W	1	0	Croft
IL	05/10/29		Coleraine	H	L	2	3	McKeague, Allen (p)
IL	12/10/29		Distillery	A	W	5	2	Hutchinson 2, Roberts 3
IL	26/10/29		Bangor	H	D	6	6	Roberts 5, Geary
IL	02/11/29		Newry Town	H	L	2	3	Geary, Casey
IL	09/11/29		Portadown	A	D	4	4	Roberts, McKeague, Crooks, Geary
IL	16/11/29		Ballymena	H	L	1	2	Geary
IL	23/11/29		Derry City	H	W	2	0	Roberts, Crooks
IL	07/12/29		Belfast Celtic	A	W	2	1	Geary, Crooks
IL	14/12/29		Ards	H	W	6	1	McNeill 3, Hutchinson, Geary, Crooks
IL	21/12/29		Linfield	A	L	1	3	McNeill
IL	25/12/29		Cliftonville	H	W	5	2	McNeill 3, Crooks 2
IL	26/12/29		Glenavon	A	L	1	2	Allen (p)
IL	28/12/29		Larne	H	A	2	0	Crooks, Geary Abandoned after 48 minutes
IL	04/01/30		Coleraine	A	A	1	0	McNeill Abandoned after 79 minutes
IL	18/01/30		Bangor	A	W	3	2	Geary, Cooke, McNeill
IL	22/01/30		Distillery	H	W	4	3	McNeill 2, Geary, Allen (p)
IL	25/01/30		Newry Town	A	W	5	2	Roberts 2, McNeill 2, Crooks
IL	01/02/30		Coleraine	A	W	2	1	Geary, McNeill
IL	05/02/30		Larne	H	W	4	3	Roberts 2, McNeill 2
IL	12/02/30		Portadown	H	D	3	3	Morris, Roberts, Hutchinson
IL	15/02/30		Ballymena	A	L	1	2	McKeague
GC	28/08/29	1	Ards	A	W	3	0	Roberts 2, Geary
GC	18/09/29	2	Derry City	A	W	1	0	Roberts
GC	23/10/29	SF	Distillery	CP	D	1	1	Roberts
GC	30/10/29	SFR	Distillery	CP	L	3	6	Crooks, Roberts, Hutchinson
IC	30/11/29	1	Dunmurry	A	D	1	1	Hutchinson
IC	03/12/29	1R	Dunmurry	H	D	1	1	Hutchinson
IC	09/12/29	1R2	Dunmurry	A	W	4	1	McNeill 2, Geary, Crooks
IC	11/01/30	2	Larne	A	D	2	2	McNeill 2
IC	15/01/30	2R	Larne	H	W	4	2	McKeague, McNeill 3
IC	08/02/30	SF	Linfield	CP	L	1	2	McNeill
CAS	19/02/30	2	Distillery	A	D	2	2	McNeill, Croft
CAS	24/02/30	2R	Distillery	H	W	3	1	Croft, Crooks, Geary
CAS	12/03/30	SF	Ards	Solt	W	2	1	Geary 2
CAS	09/04/30	F	Linfield	Solt	L	1	3	Geary
CC	22/02/30		Glenavon	A	W	6	1	Hoy og, Crooks, Reid, Geary, Roberts 2
CC	08/03/30		Derry City	H	L	3	4	Crooks, Geary, Croft
CC	15/03/30		Portadown	H	W	1	0	Roberts
CC	22/03/30		Larne	A	W	6	3	Hutchinson 2, Crooks 2, Roberts 2
CC	05/04/30		Bangor	H	W	7	1	Roberts 5, McNeill 2
CC	12/04/30		Distillery	A	W	4	3	Cooke 3, McNeill

CC	19/04/30		Cliftonville	H	W	5	0	Roberts, Hutchinson, Reid, Cooke, Morrison
CC	21/04/30		Coleraine	A	W	1	0	Roberts
CC	22/04/30		Linfield	H	W	2	1	Roberts 2
CC	26/04/30		Ballymena	A	D	4	4	Cooke 2, Hutchinson, McNeill
CC	03/05/30		Ards	H	D	1	1	Montgomery
CC	10/05/30		Belfast Celtic	A	L	1	5	Geary
CC	13/05/30		Newry Town	H	W	5	3	Roberts 3, McKeague, Cooke
CC	19/05/30	TM	Belfast Celtic	GP	L	1	3	Roberts
ChC	06/05/30	1	Linfield Rangers	H	W	7	2	Roberts 5, McKeague 2
ChC	14/05/30	SF	Belfast Celtic	Solt	L	2	4	Roberts, Hutchinson
F	15/08/29		Public Practice					-
F	02/05/30		Dundalk	H	L	1	4	Hall
F	16/05/30		Shamrock Rovers	H	W	2	1	McDonald, Roberts

The City Cup win over Larne was marred by the ordering off of Tommy McKeague and the home left-back Anderson. Our determination to win a trophy was highlighted against Distillery. With five regulars missing injured we found ourselves 1-3 down but still fought back to win. The game against the Reds was considerably easier a week later especially as two of their players failed to turn up. Two Cliftonville Olympic players joined the game after 25 minutes.

Going into the Easter fixtures we held a one point lead over Belfast Celtic and Derry City, who had played a game more. Things looked good as we recorded two wins and Celtic lost at Portadown. However we drew our next two games and when Celtic drew 0-0 at Derry the gap was still only two points with two matches remaining.

For some reason Glentoran dropped Fred Roberts after he had scored five in a midweek Charity Cup win over Linfield Rangers. McNeill moved to centre-forward but neither he nor his colleagues could capitalise as we forced ten corners in the first half against Celtic. Then at the start of the second period Belfast Celtic rattled in four goals and we never recovered. Roberts returned with a hat-trick against Newry and Celtic beat Larne to ensure a City Cup Test Match.

The two teams first had to meet on Charity Cup business and a spiritless performance from the Glens allowed Celtic to win a poor game. The same evening Glentoran II brought cheer to the club, defeating Brantwood 2-1 at Dunmore Park to win the Intermediate League.

The Test Match drew 15,000 (Receipts £423) to Grosvenor Park. Celtic took the lead, Roberts equalised, but Coulter was the Stripes' hero completing a hat-trick. The Glens were left to reflect on a season of progress and promise but no trophies.

Joe Bambrick of Linfield finished the season on 94 goals, a new Irish record.

Appearances and Goals

	App.	Goals		App.	Goals		App.	Goals
Geary J.	55	20	Ward	19		Walker H.	2	
Allen	48	3	Cooke	18	8	Kelly	2	
Montgomery	47	1	Thoms	8		Hewitt	2	
Roberts	42	57	Morris	7	1	Bowden	1	
Hutchinson	40	13	Firth	7		Burnside	1	
McFarland	36		Brown	7		Kennedy	1	
Reid H.	35	3	McSeveney	7		Spencer	1	
McClements	34		Casey	6	1	Dunn	1	
Stewart R.	33		Harrison	6		McDonald	1	
McKeague	31	7	McKeown	5		Neely	1	
Croft	27	6	Morrison	3	1	Own Goals		1
Crooks	27	14	Stewart D.	3				
Wilson	24		Vance	2		TOTAL	616	164
McNeil	24	28	Mallon	2				

1930/31

Roberts sets all-time scoring records – League won in a canter –
A visit to the Granite city

Glentoran's 49th season proved a remarkable one. Not only was the Irish League won by nine clear points but Fred Roberts smashed the individual scoring record for a season with 96 goals, including 55 in the league itself - another record. In the 1930 close season we lost Hugh Reid to Hearts but welcomed the arrival of goalkeeper Arthur Fitzroy and Scottish full-backs Billy Gibson and Matt McMeekin. The left and right wings were strengthened by Johnny Burke and J.Gwynne respectively. Glentoran's chairman in 1930/1 was Joe Shaw M.P., with W.H.McKittrick as secretary and Thomas Galbraith as treasurer. The board of directors included J.T.Mercer and R.McIndoe while Billy Ritchie was first team trainer.

Fitzroy had a marvellous debut at Coleraine when Roberts' last minute strike ensured victory and sent a large visiting contingent home happy. The second league fixture was switched to a Friday night to avoid a clash with the Ulster TT races at Newtownards. Roberts was both hero and villain, netting an 88th minute winner after missing a penalty. The team then faltered in front of 17,000 against the Blues and also at Portadown after doing three-quarters of the attacking. Harry Johnston had got all four for the Ports when, near the end, a youth came onto the pitch and struck the referee with a stick. The invader was immediately arrested.

The months of September and October then set the scene for the rest of the season as 36 goals were scored in the eight league games. The feature of Glentoran's intricate forward play was the overwhelming skill of Crooks and Geary. The crowds rolled up to watch; record gates were set at Ballymena, Bangor, and Ards while 22,500 flocked to Windsor on 11th October. This win, inspired by Burke's first minute goal, saw the Glens prove themselves a fine all-round team with Gibson and McMeekin especially strong at the back. Centre-half and captain, Jock Mitchell, signed from Third Lanark, completely blotted out the threat of Joe Bambrick.

Despite these displays and a three point lead in the league by the end of October only Gibson could force his way into the Irish League team. He appeared at Firhill Park against the Scottish League but there were no Glenmen in the line-up for the 2-2 draw with the English League at Windsor Park.

Fred Roberts.

Mitchell showed his character against second-placed Distillery on 1st November. All week he had been confined to bed with a heavy cold but went out to have a brilliant game before collapsing from exhaustion in the dressing room afterwards. The Oval became flooded over the next few days causing the postponement of the Linfield-Portadown Gold Cup semi-final for which the Glens were fined for failing to notify the referee.

Roberts showed masterly scoring form against Derry and Coleraine while Crooks was the star when we inflicted Glenavon's second home defeat of the season. Our lead had been extended to five points over Linfield when attention turned to the Irish Cup at the end of November.

Both our 1sts and 2nds were involved. The Seconds travelled to Derry three days after beating Carrick 5-0 in the R.Clements Lyttle Cup (McNeill 5). Despite a good performance, particularly from Alfie Allen at the back, the "Stiffs" went down to goals in the 37th and 82nd minutes. Meanwhile the Oval witnessed an 11-goal thriller. At one stage versus Ards in the second half it stood 4-4 but then our forward line really clicked. Spare a thought for J.Davidson who netted four times for the visitors.

In the win over Portadown Arthur Fitzroy dislocated his shoulder after a fall. International referee Mr.W.McClean allowed the game to continue but after crowd hooting and jeering, he permitted the keeper to receive treatment. Fitzroy played on but conceded two soft goals. The injury gave Livingstone, the Seconds' keeper, a chance to impress at senior level.

Roberts now began a purple patch of goalscoring. During December he netted 19 times in six games as our lead over Linfield and Belfast Celtic stretched to eight points by the end of the year. Larne were knocked for six despite their keeper Irvine saving two penalties.

A copy of William Reid's contract.

Glentoran had protested to the league over McClean's refereeing and requested that he never again take charge of a game at the Oval. However this was refused and he duly appeared with the whistle for the visit of Ballymena when only Roberts' last minute goal prevented defeat. The Braidmen had brought our run of fourteen successive league wins to an end. December had a black note when our old forward of the 1909-14 period, Sam Napier, passed away.

The frozen pitch hampered the players in the 1-1 draw with Linfield when 17,500 attended. A week later the Glentoran forwards played "shooty-in" against Coleraine in the Cup, as the Bannsiders' keeper had to retire at half-time. Glentoran II had brought the first trophy of the season to the Oval on New Year's Day when a Herbie Hall goal was enough to defeat Broadway United in the Intermediate Cup final replay. The firsts had a chance to add to this when they visited a George Ferritt managed Cliftonville, needing only a point for the title. Despite a treacherous surface a win was easily achieved and the Glens became champions. Roberts' two goals made it 48 in the league, just two behind Bambrick's record of 50 the previous season.

Big Fred passed that total three days later against a financially struggling Newry Town. The Glentoran directors suggested a challenge match between the newly crowned champions and the rest of the league in order to raise funds for the Frontiermen. This game came off in February when gate receipts totalled £88 16/- and the teams lined out:

Glentoran: Fitzroy; McMeekin, Gibson; Mathieson, Mitchell, Allen; Burke, Neely, Good, Hewitt, Callaghan.

The Rest: Sammy Moore (Bangor); McGinnigle (Coleraine), Hoy (Glenavon); Hilley (Derry C.), Edwards (Portadown), Mitchell (Distillery); R.E.Mitchell (Cliftonville), Cassidy (Ballymena), Gilmour (Ballymena), Connolly (Newry T.), Kelly (Derry C.). Referee: W.McClean.

The only target left for Glentoran in the Gibson Cup was to win their last two games and thus equal Belfast Celtic's points record of 48 set in 1928/9. The winning goal against the Whites came in the 86th minute so it was all down to the trip to Derry. This match was played at a furious pace on a heavy pitch and at half-time we led 3-2. After the break Dubois and McClements were ordered off and in the last minute Hilley equalised, so denying us a share of the record!

Our league and cup double hopes evaporated during the first 24 minutes at Celtic Park the following Saturday. The Blues were 4-1 up by then and second half injuries to McClure and Callaghan left us down to nine men and outclassed.

The hangover continued in the opening City Cup game as Glenavon scored four times in the fifteen minutes before half-time, and then Gibson missed a penalty during our comeback attempt. Fred Roberts gobbled up the chances against Larne a week before he and Johnny Geary made their Irish International debuts against Scotland at Windsor Park. Around 40,000 turned up to witness a scoreless draw with Roberts almost breaking the deadlock when a header was well saved by Thompson.

Roberts' return to club football was more successful as he netted the winner against Distillery in the Shield and followed that up with hat-tricks in the easy wins over Bangor and Coleraine. Prior to kick-off against Bangor the Gibson Cup was presented and the league championship flag unfurled by Thomas Hall.

We were "humbled at Paradise" on 14th March but four days later Roberts single-handedly carried us into the County Antrim Shield final. The 3-0 win over Cliftonville provided some disgraceful tackling as Reds' players McGuire and McClelland were sent off. A large crowd gathered at the final whistle to protest about the rough play and the display of the referee, Mr.P.Snape of Blackpool.

With Glentoran having a free Saturday on Irish Cup final day the club arranged a friendly at Aberdeen, setting off on Thursday night, the 26th March. We acquitted ourselves well on and off the pitch and "the party was subject to superb hospitality from the people of the granite city."

Our good Easter results enabled us to move into fourth place in the City Cup, just two points behind leaders Celtic. Against Ards Roberts took his season's goal tally to 87, just seven short of Bambrick's record. Meanwhile the Reserves visited Omagh United, to promote the game in that area, and won 4-2. George McMaster, Glentoran centre-half of the 1890's and the first player to be awarded a benefit by the club, passed away.

Linfield ended our outside City Cup hopes by routing us 6-1 but we had the consolation of lifting the Shield four days later after a poor game with Cliftonville. Roberts four goals against hapless Newry took him to 93 with at least two games against Distillery to go. In the City Cup tie Bambrick's record was equalled when Fred scored the winner on 70 minutes and apparently the cheers could be heard at Castle Junction!

So the scene was set for the following Monday and on the half-hour the record went like this. Callaghan received a perfect pass from Geary, centred and, despite being hampered by Burnison, Big Fred nodded in for number 95. He added one more for good measure and was chaired off the pitch at the end by jubilant Glentoran supporters despite the team's defeat.

Billy Ritchie, Glentoran's trainer for many years.

The Glens played out the remainder of the season with friendlies. We drew a challenge match at Derry and then won the prizes of pocket wallets on the toss of a coin. The proceeds from the RUC game went to the Ulster Hospital on Templemore Avenue. Linfield took the gold scarf pins on offer in Tommy McKeague's benefit when the Glens fielded seven guests. The Irish League prohibited us from playing an All-Ireland championship game with Shelbourne but we did meet another Free State League team in Dolphin. Glentoran II failed to lift their third trophy of the season when Newington Rangers beat them 1-0 in the McElroy Cup final on 18th May.

Captain Harry Borland with our canine mascot before the 1932 Irish Cup final.

Throughout 1930/1 the Pavilion Fund Committee published the official programme known as "Glentoran and Who's Who at the Oval", costing 1d. It reported on the fund raising events for the pavilion which included the 2nd XI whist drive every Saturday night at the Labour Hall on Albertbridge Road, the fireworks display (attended by 3,000), and various concerts, dances and jumble sales. Souvenirs available included team handkerchiefs, photographs and poems. The programme reported that there were plans to erect a scoreboard at the ground to enable spectators to follow cross-channel games. It also gave space to the G.W.Wolff Glentoran supporters band which travelled and played on the terraces at away grounds. The range of instruments were expanded by supporters' donations. During the season the following players were featured in profile by "Right Ho" with accompanying poetry by others:

TOM CALLAGHAN (Outside Left) BORN: Govan, Glasgow
Height: 5'6" Weight: 10st
Previous Clubs: Middlesbrough and Third Lanark
It does not require the second thoughts of keen football fans to describe your play as "Scottish". This is indeed complimentary when one considers the masterly artistic movements associated with Scottish football. The clean, clever manner in which you can draw and elude opponents has made you a very prominent figure in our club's attack. Your sociable personality both on and off the field has gained you extreme popularity which is very praiseworthy for one who was practically unknown a few months ago in Irish football circles. Although yet in your early twenties you have sampled football in England, Ireland and Scotland so coupling that experience with a "levelhead" we have little doubt you will become even yet a greater power in football.

FRED ROBERTS (Centre-Forward) Height: 6'1" Weight: 12st 10lbs
Big Fred came into prominence with Newington Rangers, for whom he scored goals with such regularity as to lead Queen's Island to persuade him to join them in the senior league. The experience gained with them was all to the good as he proved when he returned to juniors Broadway United, his consistent play with the later club led to his selection against Wales, an honour fully merited. Fred is now in his third season at the Oval and has scored over 100 goals, a truly wonderful performance when one considers his unselfish play each week. A clean player on the field and of a quiet unassuming nature off it, his popularity knows no bounds with the club supporters. May you long remain at the Oval, Fred, and may success always be yours.

> We have a class centre, a tall lad called Fred,
> A most dangerous player near goal with his head;
> The goals he has scored since the season begun,
> Has made him a favourite with everyone.
> With a tiger-like spring he gets up to the ball,
> I'm sometimes surprised how he gets at it at all;
> Big Fred has the knack for doing things right,
> He has speed, the dash and also the height.
> For a while we heard nothing but "slip it to Joe",
> Fred's name wasn't mentioned, he's not in the know;
> I can judge a good player, although I'm no tout,
> But there's not any better than Freddy about.
> To barrack a player puts him off his game,
> I heard it last season, he wasn't to blame;
> So let us be Sportsmen, and play the game clean,
> And you'll help the Directors who manage the team. J.S.W.

WILLIAM GIBSON (Left-Back) Height: 5'8" Weight: 11st 7lbs
Gibson is one of several cross-channel players at the Oval. Born in Scotland his clubs there were Morton FC and Dumbarton FC. After gaining experience in his native land he paid a visit to the USA where he gave his services to New Bedford, also Boston and Bethlehem Steel. On arrival at the Oval Gibson struck the top of his form and with McMeekin, they are in opinion the best pair of backs in the league.

JOHN GEARY (Inside Left)
Dundela, the Intermediate League club, have given many good players to Irish football, but we question if they have produced a better one than John Geary. From his first match, "Chit" proved a success and was honoured by the selectors against England as an amateur. A real "bunch of tricks" he often has the opposing backs in "Queer Street" as to what he is going to do next. John has been with the Glens for almost six years now and is due for a benefit soon. The followers of the club will see that he gets a bumper one.

How often have we heard this tale
From folks older than we,
Of famous forwards long ago,
When we weren't born to see.

When luck was dead against us
And fortune then did frown,
Johnny played his hardest
And never let us down.

There were famous forwards long ago,
Of that we have no doubt;
But for loyalty we have got one
Of whom we'll sing and shout.

He's always in the thickest fray;
For chances ever ready;
A feint, a push between the backs,
'Tis easy then for Freddy.

The Glens most loyal player,
Must surely be Johnny Geary,
He has stood by the team
Through days both dark and dreary.

The praises of John Geary,
We can sing aloud;
Long at the Oval may he be
The Idol of the crowd.

HUGH GOOD (Centre-Forward) Height: 5'10" Weight: 11st 10lbs
Hugh claims Motherwell as his home town and first played for Wishaw YMCA. As a junior he gained International and County honours as left-half and as centre-half. He afterwards joined Middlesboro' and was with them for three seasons, when he was transferred to Bristol City and later to Raith Rovers. Previous to coming to the Oval Good returned into business life for a short time, but the call of the game was too strong and so he found his way to Belfast. His display for the 2nd XI at Derry last Saturday let us know that he will soon be back in the senior team, fit and well once more.

ARTHUR FITZROY
Our goalkeeper has a long experience with the game, having first come into the limelight with Palmerston FC. As a senior however it was with Distillery that his splendid qualities were brought before the football public, indeed his performances with the Whites proved him to be a goalkeeper of first class ability and one who was absolutely fearless. A few seasons ago Arthur met with a severe injury which put him into hospital for a considerable time - it was said that he would never play again. Not only is he in the game again, but he is playing with all the brilliance of his former days. Of his courage there can be no doubt, as at the recent match against Portadown he played most of the game with an injured shoulder. We all wish him a speedy recovery.

JOHN BURKE (Outside-Right) Born: West Hartlepool Weight: 11st 7 lbs Height: 5'10"
It was with Stratton Colliery that our whole-hearted winger first came into the limelight. His displays there brought him to the notice of Huddersfield Town, from there to Birmingham and West Ham United, from where he migrated to his present position on our flank. The all-for-club spirit which dominates Johnny Burke has made him a warm favourite with the Glens followers.

HUGH McCLEMENTS (Right-Half) Height: 5'9" Weight: 11st 6lbs
Hugh McClements is a product of a military team, the 2nd Light Brigade. His first club on his return to civil life was Portaferry, for whom he played in the Belfast Combination,

Results 1930/31

Played 47. Won 36. Drew 4. Lost 7. Goals For 172. Against 80. % 80.9.
Honours: Irish League, County Antrim Shield

IL	20/08/30		Coleraine	A	W	2	0	Roberts 2
IL	22/08/30		Glenavon	H	W	3	2	Crooks, Callaghan, Roberts
IL	30/08/30		Portadown	A	L	1	4	Crooks
IL	06/09/30		Larne	H	W	9	0	Roberts 4, Crooks 3, Mitchell (p), Callaghan
IL	13/09/30		Ballymena	A	W	4	2	Roberts 3, Crooks
IL	20/09/30		Bangor	H	W	3	1	Roberts 2, Crooks
IL	27/09/30		Ards	A	W	4	1	Callaghan 2, Burke, Geary
IL	04/10/30		Belfast Celtic	H	W	4	3	Roberts 2, Crooks, Mitchell
IL	11/10/30		Linfield	A	W	2	0	Burke, Roberts
IL	18/10/30		Cliftonville	H	W	5	2	Crooks 2, Geary 2, Roberts
IL	25/10/30		Newry Town	A	W	5	1	Roberts 4, Crooks
IL	01/11/30		Distillery	H	W	2	0	Callaghan, Roberts
IL	08/11/30		Derry City	H	W	4	1	Crooks 2, Roberts 2
IL	15/11/30		Coleraine	H	W	2	0	Roberts 2
IL	22/11/30		Glenavon	A	W	5	1	Crooks 3, Roberts 2
IL	06/12/30		Portadown	H	W	4	3	Roberts 3, Crooks
IL	13/12/30		Larne	A	W	6	2	Roberts 4, Crooks, Burke
IL	20/12/30		Ballymena	H	D	2	2	Roberts 2
IL	25/12/30		Bangor	A	W	3	0	Roberts 3
IL	26/12/30		Ards	H	W	4	2	Roberts 4
IL	27/12/30		Belfast Celtic	A	W	4	2	Roberts 3, Burke
IL	03/01/31		Linfield	H	D	1	1	Crooks
IL	14/01/31		Cliftonville	A	W	5	0	Roberts 2, Callaghan, Crooks, Geary
IL	17/01/31		Newry Town	H	W	5	3	Roberts 3, Crooks, Mathieson
IL	24/01/31		Distillery	A	W	3	2	Roberts 2, Burke
IL	31/01/31		Derry City	A	D	4	4	Roberts 2, Geary 2
GC	27/08/30	1	Linfield	H	L	1	2	Crooks
IC	29/11/30	1	Ards	H	W	7	4	Roberts 2, Geary, Mitchell (p), Burke, Crooks 2
IC	10/01/31	2	Coleraine	H	W	6	2	Roberts 2, Crooks, Burke, Callaghan, Geary
IC	07/02/31	SF	Linfield	CP	L	1	5	Roberts
CC	11/02/31		Glenavon	H	L	2	4	Roberts 2
CC	14/02/31		Larne	A	W	7	1	Roberts 6 (1p), Crooks
CC	28/02/31		Bangor	H	W	6	1	Roberts 3, Crooks, Geary, Callaghan
CC	07/03/31		Coleraine	A	W	6	1	Roberts 3, Callaghan 2, Geary
CC	14/03/31		Belfast Celtic	A	L	1	5	Crooks
CC	21/03/31		Cliftonville	H	W	3	0	Geary, Roberts (p), Mathieson
CC	04/04/31		Derry City	A	D	1	1	Good
CC	06/04/31		Portadown	H	W	5	0	Roberts 2, Burke, McNeill 2
CC	07/04/31		Ballymena	A	W	5	1	Roberts 2, Crooks 2, McNeill
CC	11/04/31		Ards	H	W	4	1	Roberts 2, McNeill, Geary
CC	18/04/31		Linfield	A	L	1	6	Crooks
CC	25/04/31		Newry Town	H	W	7	1	Roberts 4, Mathieson 2, Crooks
CC	02/05/31		Distillery	A	W	2	1	Burke, Roberts
CAS	25/02/31	2	Distillery	H	W	2	1	Callaghan, Roberts
CAS	18/03/31	SF	Bangor	GP	W	5	0	Roberts 5
CAS	22/04/31	F	Cliftonville	GP	W	2	1	Roberts 2
ChC	04/05/31	1	Distillery	A	L	2	3	Roberts 2
F	03/09/30		Shamrock Rovers	A	L	0	2	-
F	18/02/31		Rest of the League	GP	L	2	3	Good 2
F	28/03/31		Aberdeen	A	D	1	1	Roberts
F	09/05/31		Derry City	A	D	2	2	McNeill, Roberts

F	12/05/31	R.U.C.	H L 1 2	Roberts
F	15/05/31	Dundalk	H L 3 4	Roberts 2, Burns
F	18/05/31	Linfield	GP L 3 5	Roberts 3
F	19/05/31	Dolphin	H L 2 5	Roberts 2

afterwards going to Ards United. It was with the latter that he came under the notice of Queen's Island, and for a long time he gave them splendid service. When the Island failed to gain re-election to the league, McClements was transferred to the Oval camp. A bustling player who, if he has not all the artistic qualities of some half-backs, nevertheless, knows his job, and goes about it in no half-hearted manner. No matter what ground or weather conditions are like he can come off at the finish of a match almost as fresh as when he started.

ALFIE ALLEN (Left-Back)
Alfie Allen is a much travelled player. His career as a player began with 39th BB. His next club of note was the 8th Batt. RIR team during the war days. On leaving the Army, he took up the game with Ravenscroft, thence to Ormiston, and later made his debut as a senior with Queen's Island. We next find him at Portadown, from whom he came to the Glens. Although he is not playing in our 1st XI as often as last season, he is a tower of strength in the Intermediate League team and his experience was in no small way the means of their winning the Intermediate Cup.

WILLIE CROOKS (Inside-Right)
Crooks, our clever inside-right, first came into prominence with the Glentoran 2nd XI, and soon secured his place in the senior team. Most of our followers will remember the famous Crooks and McGregor right wing of the 1920s. Each of them, to use an old saying, was "a terror for his size", and together they made an opposing half-back often wish he had never been born. Since those days Crooks had had cross-channel experience with Manchester United and New Brighton. He came back to Irish football with Belfast Celtic, and after a spell with Larne he returned to the Oval, where he is now playing with all the brilliance of the days when he first donned the Glentoran colours.

> To Willie Crooks, our inside-right, a star at present shining bright,
> Your form this season can't be beat, at making openings you're a treat.
> Every week you make us laugh, how simply you can slip the half,
> Your brainy play when on the ball, makes football simple to us all.
> I'll finish Bill, so here's "Good luck", that Glentoran win the Irish Cup,
> No doubt you are the mastermind, in our goal scoring forward line.

CHARLIE McCLURE (Left-Half)
McClure began his football with Altmore FC from whom he came to the Oval with our 2nd XI. After a spell here, he moved to Willowfield FC and gave yeoman service. While with them he gained his junior cap, and was one of the team that took the Irish Cup to Gibson Park. On returning to the Oval he soon fell into the lines of the senior game, and by consistent play has held his place in the 1st XI. There are few players in Irish football who can place a ball to greater advantage than he can. May he long remain in the game.

Appearances and Goals

	App.	Goals		App.	Goals		App.	Goals
Roberts	47	96	Gibson	28		Hewitt	2	
Burke	46	9	Fitzroy	26		Burns	2	
McMeekin	45		Mathieson, John	23	4	Hall	1	
Geary J.	45	12	Allen	20		Patterson	1	
Callaghan	42	11	Good	16	1	Gwynne	1	
Mitchell	41	3	Bennett	12				
Crooks	38	32	Livingstone	9		TOTAL	517	172
McClements	34		McNeill	1	1			
McClure	32		Neely	2				

1931/32

Fifty years reached – A memorable Irish Cup final win – A broken cross-bar

Glentoran began their Golden Jubilee season with a few new faces on the playing staff. Alex McMinn, ex-goalkeeper of Newry Town, was joined by Frank Lucas (ex-Barrow and Lancaster Town), Joe Penderleith (ex-Carlisle and Preston) and Harry Borland from Clyde. Off the field the concerts continued for the new Pavilion Fund while the exits for the unreserved enclosure were improved. This covered enclosure had room for 5,000 spectators with the grandstand boasting 1,150 seats. The directors initiated a project to improve the ground drainage at the Oval. In October a new directors' stand and press box was opened for the visit of Distillery.

Frankie Bennett makes a save against Ballymena in the Irish Cup replay.

Over 20,000 turned up to see us begin our championship defence but a Bambrick hat-trick allowed the Blues to turn round 4-0 up. Morgan and Roberts were the pick of the forwards against Ards (TT races imposing a 7pm kick-off) but Crooks tended to hold onto the ball too long. Our Gold Cup exit at Coleraine saw us fail to score for the first time in 116 competitive games, despite having plenty of the play.

The next four league games produced brilliant, open football. Roberts had a spell in goals at Newry when Payne went off injured and kept a personal clean sheet. Bangor's right-back Lamont had a nightmare on 19th September scoring an own goal and then being sent off. The same day Johnny Geary gained his second International cap as Ireland lost 1-3 to Scotland at Ibrox.

The Glens failed their second big league test when decisively going down to Belfast Celtic. The press wrote the team off as no comparison to the 1930/1 side, but this stung our players, particularly Fred Roberts, into action. Roberts knocked in eleven goals in four days, including a hat-trick of headers against the Whites. Inside-left Borland was proving to be the general of the team, surpassing even Crooks and Geary, and he was rewarded with Inter-League honours against the English and Scottish Leagues. The latter game was won 3-2 in front of 14,584 at Windsor Park, the Irish League's first win in this fixture for 28 years.

The end of October saw us inflict Derry's first defeat of the season and then score late twice to see off Portadown. We sat in second place three points behind leaders Linfield. Peter Doherty, a Coleraine youth, made his debut against Cliftonville and immediately showed off clever ball control and deadly finishing. Our ex-forward Alfie Snape died on the Friday before the Ballymena game and the flags at the Oval were flown at half-mast. At the half way

Johnny Geary scores against Ards.

Alfie Allen tackles Linfield's Harry McCracken in the Irish Cup final as Bennett looks on.

stage of the league the table stood thus:
1. Linfield 22 pts, 2. Glentoran 21, 3. Celtic 20, 4. Derry City 18.

The large crowd at the top of the table clash witnessed Pyper break up many of our attacks and Bambrick's great goal gave the Blues the points. Belfast Celtic's reserve XI put up a lot less resistance in the Irish Cup, as Roberts went past 30 goals for the season.

Glentoran's form during December was erratic, and four points from five games signalled the end of our title challenge. For the visit to Ards a special train was led on with the third class return journey costing a shilling. The service left at 1.25 pm returning at 4.30 pm with a Bloomfield stop. Those who went could have rejoiced at a 25 yard beauty from Doherty. The Ards club had fallen on hard times and the Glens took on a League XI in an exhibition game for the benefit of their coffers. Then, despite being involved in "the best game at Ballyholme this season" we were still unable to take both points off bottom club Bangor.

After defeating Belfast Celtic our 1932 league results fell away badly and we finished an embarrassing fifth in the table. The hard earned point against runners-up Derry maintained our unbeaten record against the men from the Maiden City.

The Irish Cup was to be the big fish Glentoran managed to catch. In the first game with Ballymena Borland's goal was a repeat of his winner against Celtic a week earlier. His shot hit the bar, and then rebounded into the net via the back of the goalkeeper's head! John Mathieson's 20 yard free-kick was the highlight of the replay win, when visiting right-back McNinch scored for both teams within 60 seconds.

When the IFA increased admission prices drastically for the semi-finals they received two protests from the Glens. Firstly the club registered its disapproval formally and then supporters voted with their feet as only 5,500 attended. We got through a poor game with the Ports, even affording a missed penalty.

The final was switched from Grosvenor Park to Celtic Park when Linfield defeated the Celts in the other semi-final after two replays. Bambrick drew first blood but the Glens played the better football

Goalmouth action in the Irish Cup final as Jack Curran heads clear from Roberts.

and gradually took over. Lucas equalised and a loopy Roberts' header from an acute angle took the cup to the Oval for only the fourth time in our 50-year history.

Our City Cup got off to a cracking start at Ards - literally! With twelve minutes remaining Roberts challenged home goalkeeper McMullan for a crossball. The two players became entangled with each other and the goalnet and both posts and the crossbar were snapped. The woodwork was beyond repair and referee S.Thompson had to abandon the contest. At the Irish League Management Committee meeting two weeks later Glentoran requested a replay, and offered to donate our share of the original gate money to Ards. Belfast Celtic's representative condemned this as "trying to buy a rematch" and the vote finished 10-9 in favour of letting the result stand.

Meantime easy wins had been recorded over Linfield and Newry. The excellent result against the Blues had been obtained without the assistance of Roberts, Morgan, Pitt and Crooks but the Windsor men soon took revenge in the Shield, with their centre-half Jack Jones

Results 1931/32

Played 49. Won 29. Drew 9. Lost 11. Goals For 137. Against 84. % 68.4.
Honours: Irish Cup, City Cup

IL	20/08/31		Linfield	A	L	3	4	Crooks, Millar, Lucas
IL	22/08/31		Ards	H	W	6	2	Roberts 2, Borland 2, Millar, Morgan
IL	29/08/31		Newry Town	A	W	5	2	Roberts 3, Burns, Crooks
IL	05/09/31		Coleraine	H	W	3	2	Roberts, Burns, Morgan (p)
IL	12/09/31		Glenavon	A	D	2	2	Geary, Roberts
IL	19/09/31		Bangor	H	W	3	1	Lamont og, Roberts, Borland
IL	26/09/31		Belfast Celtic	A	L	0	4	-
IL	07/10/31		Distillery	H	W	5	2	Roberts 5
IL	10/10/31		Larne	H	W	8	2	Roberts 6, Borland, Crooks
IL	24/10/31		Derry City	A	W	2	1	Roberts 2
IL	31/10/31		Portadown	H	W	3	1	Borland, Burns, Crooks
IL	07/11/31		Cliftonville	A	W	5	0	Doherty 2, Morgan 2(1p), Roberts
IL	14/11/31		Ballymena	H	W	3	0	Roberts 2, Crooks
IL	21/11/31		Linfield	H	L	0	1	-
IL	12/12/31		Ards	A	L	2	3	Morgan (p), Doherty
IL	19/12/31		Newry Town	H	L	2	3	Roberts, Borland
IL	25/12/31		Coleraine	A	D	3	3	Lucas 2, Lyness og
IL	26/12/31		Glenavon	H	W	3	1	Roberts 2, Doherty
IL	28/12/31		Bangor	A	D	3	3	Roberts 3(1p)
IL	02/01/32		Belfast Celtic	H	W	2	1	Geary, Borland
IL	16/01/32		Larne	A	D	2	2	Lucas, Roberts
IL	20/01/32		Distillery	A	D	3	3	Roberts 2, Borland
IL	23/01/32		Derry City	H	D	1	1	Roberts
IL	30/01/32		Portadown	A	L	3	4	Roberts 2, Crooks
IL	08/02/32		Cliftonville	H	D	1	1	Doherty
IL	13/02/32		Ballymena	A	L	0	5	-
GC	27/08/31	1	Coleraine	A	L	0	3	-
IC	28/11/31	1	Belfast Celtic II	H	W	6	1	Roberts 5, Crooks
IC	09/01/32	2	Ballymena	A	D	2	2	Roberts, Borland
IC	13/01/32	2R	Ballymena	H	W	3	1	Mathieson, Roberts, McNinch og
IC	06/02/32	SF	Portadown	WP	W	2	1	Geary, Roberts
IC	26/03/32	F	Linfield	CP	W	2	1	Lucas, Roberts
CC	20/02/32		Ards	A	D	1	1	Roberts – Abandoned after 78 minutes - result stood
CC	27/02/32		Linfield	H	W	5	2	Geary 2(1p), Burns, Doherty, Borland
CC	05/03/32		Newry Town	A	W	4	1	Borland 2, Lucas, Roberts
CC	12/03/32		Ballymena	H	L	2	3	Doherty, Lucas
CC	19/03/32		Portadown	A	W	3	1	Roberts 3
CC	28/03/32		Belfast Celtic	H	W	2	1	Borland, Morgan
CC	29/03/32		Bangor	A	W	4	0	Borland 2, Geary, Roberts
CC	02/04/32		Coleraine	H	W	3	0	Burns 2, Geary
CC	09/04/32		Distillery	H	W	5	3	Roberts 3, Lucas, Geary
CC	16/04/32		Larne	A	W	1	0	McClements
CC	23/04/32		Glenavon	H	W	5	0	Roberts 2, McClements (p), Lucas, Borland
CC	30/04/32		Derry City	A	W	3	1	Roberts 3
CC	07/05/32		Cliftonville	H	W	4	0	Lucas, Borland, Allen, Roberts
CAS	24/02/32	2	Dunmurry	H	W	1	0	Doherty
CAS	09/03/32	SF	Linfield	Solt	L	0	2	-
ChC	03/05/32	1	Brantwood	H	W	5	1	Roberts 3, Lucas, Borland
ChC	14/05/32	SF	Belfast Celtic	GP	L	1	5	Roberts
F	11/11/31		Irish League Select	H	L	2	3	Lucas, Doherty Benefit for Ards

F	19/04/32	St. Mirren	H	D	1	1	McClements (p)
F	21/04/32	Aberdeen	H	L	1	2	Roberts
F	27/04/32	Dundalk	H	W	3	0	Lucas 2, McClure
F	09/05/32	Dolphin	H	W	7	1	Borland, Roberts 4, Priestly, Lucas
							Johnny Geary Benefit

totally dominating Roberts.

Ballymena's brilliant defensive performance on 12th March was crowned by their keeper King's two penalty saves from Geary and Mathieson, but a week later we bounced back from behind against Portadown. This, plus the Easter Monday holiday, drew a

Fred Roberts heads home versus Ards.

large crowd to the Oval to watch the new Irish Cup holders play the City Cup leaders, Belfast Celtic. The Glens were always in command although the Celts could have snatched a point had Wright not driven a penalty wide.

Many coachloads of fans travelled to Bangor the next day and saw us move into joint second in the table, just a point behind Derry who drew at Ballymena. Burns successfully deputised for Roberts against Coleraine, and in this game the visitors' expert penalty taker, Williams, missed his first ever spot-kick when Frankie Bennett saved. Distillery, with only two points from nine games were easily swept aside leaving ourselves and Derry level on 15 points with four matches remaining.

The "Candystripes" came from two goals down to beat Bangor 7-4 while we sneaked a win at Larne with a disputed goal in the 40th minute. Four games at the Oval in nine days was hardly ideal preparation for the City Cup decider at Brandywell. The return meeting with Aberdeen was played like a cup tie with many players spoken to by referee McClean. Geary hobbled off injured and the Dons netted their winner when we had only nine men on the field.

In the vital game Don Shearer's goal put Derry ahead but the cool confidence of Borland and the clinical finish of Roberts (he had a fourth goal disallowed for offside) enabled us to win the City Cup for the first time since 1915. League President J.Ferguson presented the trophy to captain Harry Borland prior to the Cliftonville game.

Injury prevented Johnny Geary from playing in his own benefit match with Free State League runners-up Dolphin. The only meritorious aspect of a one-sided affair was the experiment of officiating with two referees, one in each half of the field!

The season finished with Belfast Celtic lifting the Charity Cup after they had outclassed a disorganised Glentoran side, which was missing six regulars, in the semi-final.

Appearances and Goals

	App.	Goals		App.	Goals		App.	Goals
Borland	43	18	McMeekin	25		Peters	3	
Roberts	43	64	Gibson	22		Mills	3	
Geary J.	40	8	McClements	21	2	McMinn	3	
Bennett	38		Doherty	18	8	Agnew	2	
Mathieson, John	38	1	Pitt	14		Penderleith	1	
McClure	37		Turnbull	10		Wilkins	1	
Allen	36	1	Kennedy	8		Kilpatrick	1	
Lucas	31	11	Burke	6		Williams	1	
Morgan	29	6	Miller	4	2	Burton	1	
Burns	27	6	Anderson	4		Own Goals		3
Crooks	26	7	Payne	3		TOTAL	539	137

1932/33

The heroics of Peter Doherty – Irish Cup retained – Free transfer for Roberts

Team captain Harry Borland did not return to the Oval, instead signing for Greenock Morton. The Glens also changed chairman, R.S.Jefferson replacing Joe Shaw, and the club's first manager, Billy McStay, the ex-Glasgow Celtic and Scotland full-back, was appointed. The Irish League Committee, as well as prohibiting begging and singing (busking) at matches, also decreed that "the selling of ballot tickets at grounds was a nuisance and should be frowned upon by clubs." A proposal to allow the unemployed free admittance to games was also disallowed.

After a public practice on 13th August the League began with a 7 pm visit from the Reds the following Saturday. Lucas' terrific volley sealed victory after Cliftonville had missed early chances. A fine sporting win at Newry was spoilt when referee McClean was struck on the head by a stone thrown from the crowd at the finish.

Glentoran Seconds keeper Campbell can only watch Connolly score for Celtic Seconds in the Steel and Sons Cup final.

The decision to play off the first round of the Charity Cup at the start of the season enabled us to make early progress on two knockout fronts. However a shock awaited us in the league in the form of Coleraine, for whom keeper Magee played a blinder.

Our defence looked shaky in the games with Glenavon and Derry, but in the latter match we suffered a devastating loss of a different kind. Johnny Geary sustained a knee injury in a tackle with visiting left back Joe Harkin and limped off. After playing him versus Distillery, manager McStay forced Geary into a second premature comeback against the Whites on New Year's Eve but he had to be carried off after only 20 minutes. A specialist advised him to quit football and he did, thus ending a brilliant career at 25 years of age. Tommy Leeman took his place in the team.

How this affected the Glens' success is not measurable but the defence clearly needed tightening up. By the time Bangor became the fourth consecutive team to score five at the Oval we had slipped from joint second in the league to seventh. Moreover, Cliftonville outclassed us in the Gold Cup semi-final when the Amateurs also had two more goals disallowed. Fred Roberts was doing his bit, scoring a whirlwind 25 yarder in this game but the defence, strangely in particular "Hookie" Gibson, was making many woeful mistakes.

H.C.Hewitt, a recent convert from Rugby, got his third hat-trick in successive games for the Reds on 19th November, after netting twice in the Gold Cup semi. Peter Doherty, filling in at centre-forward, scored twice but was somewhat harshly described as "not a Roberts." Then, for some reason, we put an impressive run together up until Christmas. Confidence flooded back as Allen and Craig proved themselves fine backs and we inflicted Coleraine's first home defeat for over a year. Even the Seconds got in on the goalscoring act, hammering Dundela 7-1 in the Steel and Sons Cup semi-final.

Team Group 1932/3 Back Row: Billy Ritchie (Trainer), Hugh McClements, Matt McMeekin, Arthur Fitzroy, Willie Gibson, Charlie McClure, Hugh Good. Front Row: John Shaw (Chairman), Jack Burke, Willie Crooks, Jock Mitchell, Fred Roberts, Johnny Geary, Tom Callaghan, Harry McKitterick (Secretary).

The Blues put paid to our last lingering league hopes as Bambrick recorded his customary hat-trick against us on 27th December. We retained the mantle of the only unbeaten Irish team at Brandywell, preserving the honour by coming twice from behind. Glentoran still had a say in the Gibson Cup's destination as we met leaders Celtic in the last fixture. The West Belfast men held a two point advantage over Linfield and Distillery and made sure of the title by winning 4-2 before 15,000.

After we were surprisingly held to a draw in the Cup by Amateur League outfit Dunvilles, Doherty's magic settled the replay. We progressed to the final via our "lucky" Brandywell thanks to an 83rd minute strike from Willie Crooks. The final with Distillery was dominated by the defences with only Harris' mistake in the 25th minute allowing the Whites to take the lead. Distillery held on until the 87th minute when the story goes that the Cup was bedecked in their ribbons and placed ready for presentation. "Too soon", thought Fred Roberts as he drove in an unstoppable equaliser to leave the 33,000 crowd with mixed emotions. A further 25,000 attended the replay and the goals this time came early. McNeill's picturesque header gave us a fourth minute lead but two minute later Kirby levelled. Both sides strove for the winner, Harris made many remarkable saves, McNeill hit a post and Doherty strained his ankle badly, having to retire. Glens' trainer Billy Ritchie performed miracles on the ankle and Peter was able to take his place at outside-right in the second replay.

Despite going a goal down on that occasion we played the better football and Doherty became a hero when he drove home our second goal and then hobbled on for the rest of the game. The Glens had retained the Irish Cup with combined gate receipts for the three games just under £2,400.

Glentoran IIs also annexed silverware when they overcame Belfast Celtic Reserves 3-1 in the replay of the Steel and Sons Cup final. This qualified them for the County Antrim Shield and they disposed of Bangor (even missing a penalty) and Cliftonville before finding Celtic's senior XI too strong in the semi-final. Missed open goals by Doherty and McNeill cost us dearly against the Blues when Joe Bambrick again sealed our fate.

Meanwhile the City Cup was boiling up into an exciting climax. Despite fielding many new and young players we rattled in the goals and right-half Tommy Arrigan made effective contributions. Doherty was head and shoulders above the rest against Ballymena

Results 1932/33

Played 52. Won 28. Drew 12. Lost 12. Goals For 150. Against 102. % 65.3.
Honours: Irish Cup

IL	20/08/32		Cliftonville	H	W	4	0	Roberts 2, Geary, Lucas
IL	24/08/32		Ballymena	A	W	3	2	Roberts 3
IL	27/08/32		Newry Town	A	W	2	1	McAllister (p), Geary
IL	03/09/32		Coleraine	H	L	0	2	-
IL	10/09/32		Glenavon	A	D	1	1	Roberts
IL	24/09/32		Ards	H	W	7	5	Roberts 6, Lucas
IL	08/10/32		Larne	A	W	4	2	Roberts 2(1p), Lucas, Crooks
IL	15/10/32		Linfield	H	L	1	5	Mathieson
IL	22/10/32		Distillery	A	W	4	3	Roberts 2, Geary, Lucas
IL	26/10/32		Derry City	H	L	3	5	Roberts 2(1p), McGonigle
IL	29/10/32		Portadown	A	W	2	1	Roberts, McClure og
IL	05/11/32		Bangor	H	L	2	5	Roberts, Wilkins
IL	12/11/32		Belfast Celtic	A	L	1	4	Roberts
IL	19/11/32		Cliftonville	A	L	2	5	Doherty 2
IL	26/11/32		Ballymena	H	W	6	1	Crooks 2, Doherty 2, Lucas 2
IL	03/12/32		Newry Town	H	W	7	1	Roberts 3, Crooks 2, Doherty, Lucas
IL	10/12/32		Coleraine	A	W	2	1	Rafferty, Roberts
IL	17/12/32		Glenavon	H	W	2	1	Crooks, Doherty
IL	24/12/32		Ards	A	D	4	4	McNeill, Roberts, Lyttle, Doherty
IL	26/12/32		Larne	H	W	5	0	Roberts, Lyttle (p), Crooks 2, Mathieson
IL	27/12/32		Linfield	A	L	2	4	Roberts, Crooks
IL	31/12/32		Distillery	H	D	1	1	Crooks
IL	07/01/33		Derry City	A	D	2	2	Doherty, Lyttle (p)
IL	21/01/33		Portadown	H	W	2	1	Gourley, Roberts
IL	28/01/33		Bangor	A	W	3	0	Lyttle (p), Doherty, McNeill
IL	04/02/33		Belfast Celtic	H	L	2	4	Craig, Doherty
GC	01/09/32	1	Ards	A	W	3	1	Crooks, Roberts, Geary
GC	21/09/32	2	Derry City	H	W	2	1	Roberts 2
GC	02/11/32	SF	Cliftonville	CP	L	2	4	Roberts, Crooks
ChC	07/09/32	1	Crusaders	H	W	4	0	Crooks, Geary, Roberts, Lucas
ChC	09/05/33	SF	Distillery	Solt	L	3	4	Sproule, Fitzsimmons 2
IC	14/01/33	1	Dunvilles	H	D	4	4	Agnew 2, Doherty, Roberts
IC	18/01/33	1R	Dunvilles	H	W	6	1	McCusker og, Doherty 2, Roberts, Craig 2
IC	11/02/33	2	Portadown	H	W	4	1	Doherty 2, Roberts, McNeill
IC	11/03/33	SF	Coleraine	Bw	W	2	1	Lucas, Crooks
IC	08/04/33	F	Distillery	WP	D	1	1	Roberts
IC	12/04/33	FR	Distillery	WP	D	1	1	McNeill
IC	28/04/33	FR2	Distillery	WP	W	3	1	Roberts, Doherty, Crooks
CC	18/02/33		Glenavon	A	W	7	2	McNeill 4, Doherty, Lyttle, Crooks
CC	21/02/33		Coleraine	H	D	1	1	Gourley
CC	04/03/33		Larne	A	D	5	5	Roberts 3, Crooks, Campbell
CC	08/03/33		Portadown	H	W	4	1	McNeill 4
CC	18/03/33		Bangor	A	W	4	1	McNeill 2, Hutchinson, Doherty
CC	20/03/33		Ballymena	H	W	4	0	Roberts, Doherty 3
CC	25/03/33		Ards	H	W	2	1	McNeill, Roberts
CC	01/04/33		Belfast Celtic	A	L	1	2	Roberts
CC	15/04/33		Linfield	H	D	1	1	Roberts
CC	17/04/33		Cliftonville	A	W	5	2	Crooks 3, Turnbull, McClure (p)

CC	18/04/33		Newry Town	H	W	4	1	Roberts 3, McClure (p)
CC	22/04/33		Distillery	A	D	2	2	Craig, Fitzsimmons
CC	29/04/33		Derry City	A	D	1	1	Fitzsimmons
CAS	15/03/33	2	Linfield	H	L	0	1	-
F	13/08/32		Public Practice					-
F	24/04/33		Partick Thistle	H	D	1	1	Roberts

when he scored three and "could have had a dozen!" With two game remaining the table read:

1. Celtic 18 pts, 2. Glentoran 17, 3. Linfield 16.

Celtic went down at Portadown, Linfield beat Glenavon and we looked to be overcoming Distillery until their 87th minute penalty equaliser left the City Cup a three way tie. It was, perhaps, asking too much of the Glens to win at Derry the day after lifting the Irish Cup and so it proved. Celtic and Linfield duly won their last two games, and the former took the trophy with a 2-1 test match victory.

Obviously performances and results over the season were not good enough for the board and they dropped a bombshell on 4th May 1933 when four first teamers were handed free transfers. Among them was Fred Roberts, scorer of 332 of our 779 goals in 221 appearances over five seasons - an abrupt end to an illustrious Oval career. Distillery expressed an interest in him as the Whites beat us in our final game of the season in the Charity Cup. The directors also had to face the wrath of Cliftonville, as the Reds claimed that we had illegally approached and signed without permission their international outside-right, E.J.Mitchell. Mitchell had guested for us against Partick Thistle.

The Glens entered a team in the RUC five-a-sides on 27th May but we went out early to Hamilton Academicals by 3 goals to 2 corners. Belfast Celtic beat Linfield after extra time in the final.

Appearances and Goals

	App.	Goals		App.	Goals		App.	Goals
Roberts	45	49	Geary J.	10	5	Kirkpatrick	3	
Craig	42	4	McGonigle	9	1	Rodgers	3	
Crooks	38	19	Leeman	8		Wilkins	3	1
Gibson	37		McClure	8	2	Beattie	3	
Turnbull	37	1	Peters	7		Walker	3	
McClements	31		Coates	7		Moody	2	
Doherty	29	21	Rafferty	7	1	Woods	2	
Bennett	26		Agnew	7	2	Yeates	2	
Lucas	25	9	Fitzsimmons	7	4	McCormick	1	
Allen	22		Arrigan	7		Irvine	1	
Lyttle	22	5	Crombie	5		Sproule	1	1
McNeill A.	19	15	Matier	5		Wilson	1	
Gourley	15	2	Hutchinson	5	1	McCallum	1	
McAllister	12	1	Weldon	5		Stitt	1	
Leathem	12		Anderson	4		Hanna	1	
Harris	12		Campbell (Gk)	4		Own Goals		3
Mathieson, John	11	2	Campbell, (RW)	4	1	TOTAL	572	150

1933/34

South American visitors – Harris and the heckler - Another clear-out

William McStay put his resignation in writing to the board of directors in the close season but by the start of August 1933 they had asked him to withdraw it and he remained as manager. Tommy Walker would train the first team. The Irish League announced that referees who failed to hand in their match reports within 48 hours of the conclusion would be fined 10s 6d. Admission to the Oval was 6d and 1/- with a seat in the stand costing 6d extra.

Jimmy Duncan had arrived from Kilmarnock to replace Roberts at centre-forward but his debut was put back two days to avoid a clash with the Ulster Grand Prix. After opening his account with a hat-trick against Bangor it was remarked that although the Scot did not have the height of his predecessor he certainly had the scoring ability. Meanwhile Fred found the net on his debut for Distillery.

The second league fixture was our only early season defeat and even then there was doubt over the legitimacy of three of Celtic's goals. Nixon had a great game in the Glenavon goal on 2nd September. Up front Duncan and Peter Doherty were the early eye-catchers while Tommy Arrigan was outstanding at right-half. We entered the Linfield match as firm underdogs but Duncan's header from Mitchell's beautiful centre startled the confident Blues. Five days later Willie McStay resigned for good and the directors immediately launched a search for a successor with cross-channel experience.

Tommy Arrigan clears from Kelly against Derry City.

The new pavilion was finally officially opened in early October with a match against a touring team from the countries of Peru and Chile. The game had been originally planned for the 25th September but the visitors' boat journey to Liverpool was delayed by four days due to bad weather in the Atlantic Ocean. Before kick-off the Glentoran players received miniature Peruvian and Chilean flags from their opponents. It was remarked that the Oval was now capable of housing crowds of up to 60,000.

One scribe, obviously sampling South American football for the first time, reported, "The visitors played a neat passing game but too often delayed their shots and let the defenders get back. Also their forwards tended to run all over the park." The Glens took the lead four minutes after half-time but a great shot from Alegre on 51 minutes made the game level. Teams:

GLENTORAN: Harris; McClure, Gibson; Arrigan, Craig (injured), Leathem; Mitchell, McKnight, Duncan, McCartney, Doherty.

PERU/CHILE XI: Valdivieso; Saldarriaga, Fernandez; Monterro, D'Arce, Astengo (captain); Pacheco, Alegre, Subiabre, Villanueva, Schneeberger.

The team responded magnificently to McStay's departure, beating Distillery to go top of the league by a point from the Whites and Linfield. Four days later we qualified for the Gold Cup semi-final but this was an achievement due mainly to Harris in goals as Ballymena had most of the play. Glentoran stayed in first position until mid-

November but were knocked off when we suffered our first ever defeat at Brandywell. At the end of this game a spectator verbally abused Harris, who then scaled a 10 foot fence and gave chase to his heckler. Other Glentoran players and the police went after Harris, eventually calming him down and leading him back to the dressing room before the altercation worsened! The side was severely weakened when Peter Doherty was transferred to bigger and better things at Blackpool for £2,000.

Duncan scores against Ballymena despite McNinch's stretch.

Ex-Glens winger Archie Coates grabbed a hat-trick as Bangor shocked us but the return of Arnold Craig at centre-half enabled Glentoran to beat Celtic again. Disappointment manifested itself once more in the Gold Cup final. Portadown were always the livelier team and deserved their win courtesy of an 85th minute goal from Johnstone. The Glens share of the gate receipts was £104.

Defeats in December against Glenavon and especially Linfield (before 20,000) killed the league and by the end of 1933 Celtic and ourselves trailed the Blues by eight points. Two shock reverses in the run in forced us to settle for third place but at least new players Nixon, English and Les Williams showed up well.

By the end of the championship we were well into our bid to lift the Irish Cup for the third successive year. In the excellent first game versus Distillery Fred Roberts scored against us twice and it was stated that referee Mr. Hull never once had to admonish a player. The gale and heavy ground spoiled the replay, Lucas eventually breaking a strong Whites' defence in the 70th minute. Ex-Bangor inside-right J.E.McKnight sunk his old club in Round Two but then disaster struck in the semi-final against Cliftonville. Nixon in goals made a couple of blunders to give the Reds a 2-0 start and despite outplaying the Amateurs in the second half we just could not draw level. Linfield hammered Celtic 7-0 in the other semi and then Cliftonville 5-0 in the final.

Glentoran's season folded after this as we fielded many experimental line-ups in the City and Charity Cups. Our Shield interest had already been curtailed as Joe Bambrick capitalised four times on defensive errors in the last half-hour of our second round tie.

There were some bright spots; particularly new Scottish centre-forward Kerr's display against Ards when one of his four goals was a cheeky backheel. Jimmy Duncan's goal at Newry was a masterpiece. He turned on a sixpence by the touchline, charged infield, and smacked home a shot at terrific speed. Our final City Cup placing of sixth was helped by the award of two points when Ballymena were suspended by the IFA for alleged payments to "amateur" players.

A sparkling victory was recorded in a "mud frolic" against Blackpool, who included Peter Doherty, as captain, in their ranks. Three days later we failed to see off Intermediate League side Crusaders in the 90 minutes as Duncan missed a penalty but then made amends in extra-time. The Blues were too strong for the Glens' skeleton team in the Charity semi-final, our only regulars being Leathem and Duncan.

These two were joined by Dunseith (a goalkeeper signed from Coleraine), Stitt and McKnight in the RUC organised five-a-sides at Windsor Park on 26th May 1934. A crowd of 15,000 turned up to watch teams from the Irish, Scottish and Free State Leagues and the RUC compete. Clyde knocked us out 3-0 in Round One, and Glasgow Rangers defeated Linfield 1-0 in the final.

Results 1933/34

Played 49. Won 26. Drew 8. Lost 15. Goals For 105. Against 80. % 61.2

IL	21/08/33		Bangor	H	W	5	2	Duncan 3, Arrigan, Craig
IL	24/08/33		Belfast Celtic	A	L	0	4	-
IL	26/08/33		Ards	A	W	2	0	Duncan 2
IL	02/09/33		Glenavon	H	W	1	0	Duncan
IL	09/09/33		Newry Town	A	D	1	1	Arrigan (p)
IL	16/09/33		Larne	H	W	4	0	Duncan 3, Doherty
IL	23/09/33		Linfield	A	W	1	0	Duncan
IL	07/10/33		Distillery	A	W	1	0	Duncan
IL	18/10/33		Portadown	H	D	3	3	Doherty 2, Duncan
IL	21/10/33		Cliftonville	A	W	2	0	Duncan 2
IL	28/10/33		Coleraine	H	W	3	1	McKnight, Doherty, Fitzsimmons
IL	11/11/33		Ballymena	H	D	1	1	Mitchell
IL	18/11/33		Derry City	A	L	1	2	Hodder
IL	25/11/33		Bangor	A	L	2	3	Hodder 2
IL	02/12/33		Belfast Celtic	H	W	4	2	McKnight, Mitchell, Fitzsimmons 2
IL	09/12/33		Ards	H	W	6	2	Fitzsimmons 3, Leathem 2, Duncan
IL	16/12/33		Glenavon	A	L	1	2	Leathem
IL	23/12/33		Newry Town	H	W	3	0	Miller, Fitzsimmons, Duncan
IL	25/12/33		Larne	A	W	4	1	Mitchell 2, Leathem, Fitzsimmons 2
IL	26/12/33		Linfield	H	L	0	3	-
IL	30/12/33		Distillery	H	W	3	0	Mitchell, Fitzsimmons, Duncan
IL	06/01/34		Portadown	A	W	4	0	Duncan 2, Leathem 2
IL	20/01/34		Cliftonville	H	L	2	5	Leathem, Lucas
IL	27/01/34		Coleraine	A	W	3	1	Leathem 2, McGhee
IL	03/02/34		Ballymena	A	L	1	3	Duncan
IL	14/02/34		Derry City	H	W	1	0	Stitt
GC	06/09/33	1	Newry Town	A	W	2	0	Doherty, Duncan
GC	11/10/33	2	Ballymena	H	W	2	1	Duncan, McKnight
GC	08/11/33	SF	Belfast Celtic	WP	W	3	1	Arrigan (p), Miller, McKnight
GC	06/12/33	F	Portadown	Solt	L	0	1	-
IC	13/01/34	1	Distillery	A	D	2	2	Duncan, McKnight
IC	17/01/34	1R	Distillery	H	W	1	0	Lucas
IC	10/02/34	2	Bangor	A	W	2	0	McKnight 2
IC	10/03/34	SF	Cliftonville	GP	L	2	4	McCartney, McKnight
CC	17/02/34		Belfast Celtic	A	L	1	2	McGhee
CC	24/02/34		Cliftonville	H	D	0	0	-
CC	03/03/34		Glenavon	A	L	1	7	Williams (p)
CC	12/03/34		Coleraine	H	W	6	3	Duncan 4, Fitzsimmons, Leathem
CC	17/03/34		Ards	H	W	7	2	Kerr 4, McKnight 3
CC	24/03/34		Linfield	A	L	0	3	-
CC	31/03/34		Newry Town	H	L	1	2	Duncan
CC	02/04/34		Larne	A	D	1	1	Agnew
CC	03/04/34		Distillery	H	D	1	1	Fitzsimmons
CC	07/04/34		Derry City	A	W	2	1	McKnight, Kerr
CC	21/04/34		Portadown	H	W	4	1	Wilson, Kerr, Duncan, Fitzsimmons
CC	28/04/34		Bangor	A	D	1	1	Kerr
CAS	21/02/34	2	Linfield	A	L	1	5	Mitchell
ChC	26/04/34	1	Crusaders	H	W	6	2	aet – Hood og, Duncan 2, Kerr, Fitzsimmons 2

ChC	12/05/34	SF	Linfield	GP	L	0	4	-
F	12/08/33		Public Practice					
F	28/08/33		Linfield	H	D	1	1	Wallace
								Ching Morrison Benefit
F	13/09/33		Portadown	H	L	2	4	Doherty, Moore
								Portadown Club Funds
F	02/10/33		Peruvian & Chilean XI	H	D	1	1	Arrigan (p)
								Opening of New Pavilion
F	23/04/34		Blackpool	H	W	3	1	Kerr 2, Brown

The only silverware brought to the club this season was the R.Clements Lyttle Cup won when the Seconds defeated Linfield Swifts 4-0 on 30th March. The directors' actions were quick and drastic. Free transfers were given to Gibson, Allen, Craig, Harris, Agnew, Mitchell, Wilson, Fitzsimmons, the injured Geary, English, McClure, McKinny and McGhee as we intended to build a new team from scratch to challenge for the major honours.

Appearances and Goals

	App.	Goals		App.	Goals		App.	Goals
Gibson	46		Miller N.	13	2	Weir	2	
Leathem	44	10	Wilson	13	1	Wallace	2	
Harris	43		English	12		McKinny	2	
Duncan	43	31	Yeates	10		Connolly	1	
Fitzsimmons	40	14	McGhee	10	2	McIntosh	1	
Arrigan	38	3	Kerr	8	8	McFerran	1	
McCartney	35	1	Hodder	4	3	Phillips	1	
McKnight	31	12	Stitt	4	1	Payne	1	
Mitchell	30	6	Wilkins	4		Dunseith	1	
McClure	20		Lucas	3	2	Adams	1	
Agnew	18	1	Allen	3		McIlroy	1	
Williams	18	1	McFadyen	3		Own goals		1
Doherty	14	5	Drain	3		TOTAL	539	105
Craig	13	1	Nixon	2				

Peter Doherty.

1934/35

A new Ballymena club – A marathon Irish Cup final –
Shock Shield defeat by juniors

Glentoran's new coach for the season was David Reid, with P.Dewley-Bull as first team trainer. On the playing front new faces abounded to replace those released at the end of 1933/4. Lewis, a keeper, arrived from Merthyr, while Gordon McDairmid was the new left-back. The half-back line was strengthened by Harold McCaw (ex-Linfield) and Jerry Kelly from Dolphin. New winger were H.Goodwin (ex-Reading), A.Smith (ex-Rangers, Aberdeen and Shamrock Rovers) and W.Tyson.

There were other changes around the league. Ballymena United were formed to replace the expelled Ballymena, and Elisha Scott joined Belfast Celtic as goalkeeper-manager. Bangor were ordered out of their Ballyholme Showgrounds, playing their home matches for the first half of the season at Castlereagh Park, Newtownards, and then fulfilling all remaining games away.

Ballymena United got off to an encouraging start, gaining a useful draw at the Oval. Glentoran then put in four below par performances, the only bright spot coming when we turned around Newry's three goal lead. The Lurgan Glens knocked us out of the Gold Cup with all their goals coming in the last fifteen minutes as Duncan fought our lost cause up front.

McNeill's shot is saved by Crusaders keeper Penny in the County Antrim Shield tie.

At Brandywell on 15th September a second half thunderstorm sent most of the crowd home! The Glens hung on for a draw despite being outplayed. Then we reeled off three wins including one over the strong Belfast Celtic to move up to fourth place, four points behind Linfield. A reporter at the Celtic game remarked, "Elisha Scott is far from being a spent force as he made magnificent saves from Wallace, Duncan and Kelly." Tyson got the better of him, netting the winner in the 81st minute after we had earlier been two down.

The 10th October dealt the club a double blow. Chairman R.S.Jefferson resigned and then in the afternoon the Seconds went down 1-3 to Belfast Celtic 2nds in the R.Clements Lyttle Cup final. After losing to Cliftonville we found some consistency and managed an excellent home draw with Linfield. The respective captains, McCaw and Jones, were outstanding in this match. The Newry game developed into a "roughhouse" with Arrigan and Hall (Newry) sent off. The dismissal of these two came as a surprise as up until their clash their conduct had been exemplary.

Both our unbeaten home run (ten games) and our league hopes were ended by Distillery on 8th December. Nine points behind the Blues with the same number of fixtures remaining was too much of a gap. The weather on Boxing Day was so bad that referee J.McKay of Glasgow had the touchline on the unreserved side moved three yards in. The game started twenty minutes late but Duncan was soon on target in front of Dundee's watching scout

Results 1934/35

Played 50. Won 30. Drew 8. Lost 12. Goals For 127. Against 78, % 68.0.
Honours: Irish Cup

IL	18/08/34		Ballymena United	H	D	1	1	Kerr
IL	22/08/34		Linfield	A	L	0	1	-
IL	25/08/34		Newry Town	H	W	4	3	Goodwin 2, McCaw, Kerr
IL	01/09/34		Distillery	A	L	0	2	-
IL	08/09/34		Ards	H	W	6	0	Kerr 3, Tyson 2, Smith
IL	15/09/34		Derry City	A	D	2	2	Smith 2
IL	22/09/34		Portadown	H	W	2	1	Tyson, Smith
IL	29/09/34		Larne	A	W	4	0	Duncan 3, Tyson
IL	06/10/34		Belfast Celtic	H	W	3	2	Tyson 3
IL	13/10/34		Cliftonville	A	L	2	3	Kelly, Wallace
IL	27/10/34		Bangor	CrP	W	7	2	McNeill 3, Tyson 2, Duncan, Smith
IL	03/11/34		Coleraine	H	W	2	1	McNeill, Beck
IL	10/11/34		Glenavon	A	D	2	2	Smith (p), Wallace
IL	17/11/34		Ballymena United	A	W	3	0	Wallace, Duncan, McNeill
IL	24/11/34		Linfield	H	D	2	2	Goodwin, Smith
IL	01/12/34		Newry Town	A	W	3	1	McNeill, Leathem, Goodwin
IL	08/12/34		Distillery	H	L	1	3	McNeill
IL	15/12/34		Ards	A	W	4	3	McNeill 2, Leathem, Goodwin
IL	22/12/34		Derry City	H	W	2	1	McNeill 2
IL	25/12/34		Portadown	A	L	1	3	Smith
IL	26/12/34		Larne	H	W	4	1	Duncan, Reid 2, Wallace
IL	29/12/34		Belfast Celtic	A	L	1	3	Smith (p)
IL	05/01/35		Cliftonville	H	W	4	1	Tyson 2, Smith, McNeill
IL	12/01/35		Bangor	H	W	5	3	Goodwin 2, McNeill 2, Smith
IL	26/01/35		Coleraine	A	W	2	0	Tyson 2
IL	02/02/35		Glenavon	H	W	3	1	Duncan, McNeill, Goodwin
GC	05/09/34	1	Glenavon	A	L	0	3	-
IC	19/01/35	1	Ards	H	W	3	1	Tyson 2, McNeill
IC	23/02/35	2	Linfield	H	W	4	2	McNeill, McDiarmid, Goodwin, Smith
IC	16/03/35	SF	Ballymena United	Solt	W	3	0	McNeill 2, Tyson
IC	06/04/35	F	Larne	WP	D	0	0	-
IC	10/04/35	FR	Larne	WP	D	0	0	-
IC	30/04/35	FR2	Larne	WP	W	1	0	Goodwin
CAS	23/01/35	1	Crusaders	H	W	5	0	Smith, Tyson 2, Goodwin, McNeill
CAS	06/02/35	2	Bangor	H	W	5	0	Goodwin, Duncan 2, Leathem, Beck
CAS	27/03/35	SF	Belfast Celtic II	Solt	L	0	5	-
CC	09/02/35		Newry Town	A	L	1	2	Leathem
CC	16/02/35		Linfield	H	W	3	1	McNeill 2, Goodwin
CC	27/02/35		Ards	A	W	4	1	Tyson, McNeill 3
CC	02/03/35		Coleraine	H	W	5	1	Tyson 2, Smith, Aicken 2
CC	09/03/35		Ballymena United	A	W	3	2	McNeill 2, Goodwin
CC	18/03/35		Glenavon	H	W	3	1	McNeill 3
CC	23/03/35		Cliftonville	A	D	4	4	McNeill 2, Goodwin, Aicken
CC	30/03/35		Belfast Celtic	H	L	0	3	-
CC	13/04/35		Bangor	H	W	3	0	Leathem 2(1p), Duncan
CC	20/04/35		Derry City	H	L	0	3	-
CC	22/04/35		Larne	A	W	4	3	Wallace 2, McNeill, Goodwin
CC	23/04/35		Distillery	H	D	2	2	Arrigan, Duncan
CC	27/04/35		Portadown	H	W	3	0	Goodwin 2, Tyson
ChC	11/05/35	SF	Belfast Celtic	Solt	L	1	2	McNeill
F	08/08/34		Public Practice					
F	11/08/34		Public Practice					
F	20/10/34		Derry City	A	L	2	6	McNeill, Smith (p)

Billy McCandless. Winning the last four leagues games not only assured us of fourth place but built confidence for the forthcoming competitions.

Easy wins were recorded in the early rounds of the Irish Cup and County Antrim Shield but in mid-February Linfield provided a double obstacle to us. The teams firstly met at the Oval in the City Cup when a heavy pitch hampered the players' skill. Sandy McNeill sealed our victory with a "carpet shot" from 20 yards. The 12,000 for this "dress rehearsal" doubled when the two teams met on Cup business at the same venue a week later. Glentoran fielded an identical XI, namely: Lewis; Miller, McDairmid; Arrigan, Beck, Leathem; Goodwin, Aicken, McNeill, Tyson, Smith; whereas the Blues made five changes. The Glens raced into a 3-1 half-time lead but had to withstand an onslaught from Linfield after the break during which they scored once. However, in the last minute, Smith raced away, beat round two defenders, and shot past Eckersley to send the crowd into raptures. The champions had been beaten on consecutive Saturdays.

Soon afterwards Smith became Glentoran's player-coach and the team went from strength to strength during March, playing pretty football with the long, swinging passes from the middle invariably finding their men. Ballymena United were also beaten on successive Saturdays. In the City Cup we came from 0-2 down to win and then 20,000 at the Irish Cup semi-final saw United's keeper McDowell fumble three shots allowing McNeill (twice) and Tyson to net the rebounds.

However the team was brought back down to earth by Belfast Celtic's 2nd XI who hammered us in the Shield semi-final. We took our opponents too lightly early on and just made too many mistakes, never threatening their goal. Celtic's senior team then virtually ended our City Cup hopes three days later. Jimmy McAlinden tortured us in both games - "a youngster who will go far in the game", wrote one scribe.

There was still the Irish Cup to be won and 15,000 attended Windsor Park for the final versus Larne in early April. A poor game finished scoreless, not even Glentoran's new shirts by "Viyella" could brighten up the occasion. Larne had the better of a dour replay as the Glens failed to find the net for the fourth game running. On Easter Monday we gained a psychological advantage over the Inver men, defeating them in the City Cup after trailing 1-3 at the interval. On the last day of April 10,545 witnessed us lift the Cup for the third time in four seasons thanks to a 20th minute goal from Goodwin. The consistency and accuracy of passing by our half-back line of Arrigan, Beck and Leathem was cited as the main reason for success.

The rest of Glentoran's season petered out but Derry City kept going to claim both the City and North-West Cups. After winning the latter, the Derry team turned down the prizes of wristwatches and instead requested eleven pairs of grey flannel trousers! The North-West association duly granted their wish.

Johnny Leathem gained our only representative honour of the season, playing left-half in the Irish League XI which went down 1-6 to the Football League at the Oval on 19th September.

Appearances and Goals

	App.	Goals		App.	Goals		App.	Goals
Lewis	46		Aicken	18	3	Walsh	2	
Arrigan	46	1	Johnstone	17		McFarland	2	
Smith	40	14	Wallace	17	6	Adams	2	
Leathem	37	6	Kelly	10	1	Dunseith	1	
Goodwin	37	18	McMaster	6		Stitt	1	
McDiarmid	36	1	Kerr	6	5	Wilson	1	
Tyson	36	22	Yeates	5		Brownlow	1	
Duncan	36	11	McCartney	5		Dornan	1	
McCaw	33	1	Buchanan	4				
Beck	33	2	McIlroy	3		TOTAL	550	127
McNeill A.	33	34	Reid	3	2			
Miller N.	30		Salmond	2				

1935/36

Start of a barren period – McCrae's double hat-trick – Seconds' Irish Cup run

The arrival of new blood in the shape of F.Wilson (outside-right from Falkirk), G.Blayney (inside-right from Motherwell), Deacon (outside-left from Chelsea) combined with local players R. and J.Mathieson (ex-R.U.R. and Larne respectively), S.B.Leckey (Cliftonville) and Hanna (Bangor) prompted a previewer to predict, "The Oval should see a successful season." Little was he to know that Glentoran were about to embark on one of the least productive five year spells in terms of trophy winning. Belfast Celtic, Derry City and Linfield proved to be the leading lights of the Irish League in the latter 1930's.

Our early season league defeats against these three clubs bore this out. Around 25,000 had attended the Blues game when our consolation goal was an 88th minute Norman Miller penalty. It was Miller's right-back duties however, which drew scouts from Motherwell and several London clubs to the Glenavon game three days later. Celtic's Elisha Scott kept us at bay on 7th September in a match where our forwards hit the woodwork twice but could not score. Injuries hampered our progress and were partly to blame for shock defeats at the hands of Ballymena (Gold Cup) and Bangor.

Boyd and NcNeill had shared the centre-forward position but McCrae, signed from St.Mirren, fulfilled this role from his scoring debut at Portadown. Fellow Scot, Marshall (ex-Clyde), also made his first appearance on that day.

McCrae really made his mark in the amazing game with Ards, finding the net on six occasions! The first half was a scoring spree as we turned round 6-3 up. Boyce, making only his second appearance deputising for injured keeper Lewis, was beaten

Glentoran and Cliftonville players observe a minute's silence for the death of the King.

three more times but Ards' defence was woefully weak and we finished with nine. The team then found form and reeled off six successive league wins to move into third place, still six points behind pace-setters Celtic.

During this run we inflicted Linfield's first home defeat of the season killing off their league hopes in the process. McCaw and Boyce were in particularly good form, spurred on by playing against their old team mates. Marshall and Hoy (Glenavon) received their marching orders in the next game. Maybe this was a blessing in disguise for them as the rest of the players were reduced to "indistinguishable silhouettes" by the relentless rain and Mourneview mud.

Our undefeated streak was decisively brought to an end by Belfast Celtic on 14th December. Glens' close passing game was useless on a heavy Celtic Park and the champions elect ruthlessly exposed the team's weaknesses. The dismal weather continued throughout the month and we experienced further adverse results. Indeed Glentoran only

Results 1935/36

Played 46. Won 19. Drew 9. Lost 18. Goals For 105. Against 93. % 51.1

IL	17/08/35		Coleraine	A	W	1	0	McNeill
IL	21/08/35		Linfield	H	L	1	2	Miller (p)
IL	24/08/35		Glenavon	H	W	1	0	McNeill
IL	31/08/35		Larne	A	W	2	1	Boyd 2
IL	07/09/35		Belfast Celtic	H	L	0	1	-
IL	14/09/35		Newry Town	A	W	3	2	Boyd, Wallace, Deacon
IL	21/09/35		Distillery	H	D	1	1	Hanna
IL	28/09/35		Derry City	A	L	0	3	-
IL	05/10/35		Bangor	H	L	1	2	Aicken
IL	12/10/35		Portadown	A	W	4	0	McCrae 2, Marshall, Blayney
IL	26/10/35		Ballymena United	H	D	2	2	Blayney, McNeill
IL	02/11/35		Cliftonville	A	W	4	2	McNeill, Marshall (p), Blayney, McCrae
IL	09/11/35		Ards	H	W	9	6	McCrae 6, McNeill, Miller (p), Aicken
IL	16/11/35		Coleraine	H	W	4	0	McCrae 2, McNeill, Grey
IL	23/11/35		Linfield	A	W	1	0	Jones og
IL	30/11/35		Glenavon	A	W	2	1	McCrae 2
IL	07/12/35		Larne	H	W	6	0	Loughlin 3, McCrae 3
IL	14/12/35		Belfast Celtic	A	L	0	4	-
IL	21/12/35		Newry Town	H	L	2	5	McNeill, Miller (p)
IL	25/12/35		Distillery	A	L	2	4	Blayney, Miller (p)
IL	26/12/35		Derry City	H	L	2	3	Aicken, McCrae
IL	28/12/35		Bangor	A	L	2	3	Grey, McNeill
IL	04/01/36		Portadown	H	D	1	1	McCrae
IL	18/01/36		Ballymena United	A	W	4	2	McNinch og, McCrae 2, Aicken
IL	25/01/36		Cliftonville	H	L	1	3	McCrae
IL	01/02/36		Ards	A	L	1	2	McNeill
GC	04/09/35	1	Glenavon	H	W	5	0	Boyd 3, Wilson, McFarlane
GC	18/09/35	2	Ballymena United	A	L	2	3	McNeill 2
IC	11/01/36	1	Cliftonville	H	D	1	1	Hanna
IC	15/01/36	1R	Cliftonville	A	W	2	1	McNeill, McFarlane
IC	19/02/36	2	Derry City	H	L	0	4	-
CC	08/02/36		Linfield	A	L	1	3	McNeill
CC	15/02/36		Newry Town	H	D	5	5	Grey, McNeill, Yeates, McIndoe, Loughlin
CC	22/02/36		Ards	A	W	7	2	McNeill, McIndoe, McCrae 2, Grey, Loughlin, Blayney
CC	29/02/36		Portadown	H	D	3	3	McNeill 2, McIndoe
CC	07/03/36		Derry City	A	L	1	5	McNeill
CC	14/03/36		Cliftonville	H	W	3	1	Barr 3
CC	28/03/36		Ballymena United	H	W	4	0	Barr 3, Grey
CC	30/03/36		Belfast Celtic	A	D	0	0	-
CC	11/04/36		Bangor	H	W	6	3	Boyd 4, McIndoe, McFarlane
CC	13/04/36		Larne	A	W	3	0	Loughlin, McIndoe, Boyd
CC	14/04/36		Glenavon	H	D	2	2	Loughlin, McIndoe
CC	18/04/36		Coleraine	A	D	2	2	McDaid og, Smith
CC	25/04/36		Distillery	H	L	0	1	-
CAS	12/02/36	2	Belfast Celtic II	A	L	1	2	McCrae
ChC	09/05/36	SF	Belfast Celtic	GP	L	0	5	-
F	28/08/35		Derry City	A	L	0	6	Jimmy Kelly Benefit
F	21/04/36		Glentoran II	H	W	2	0	Grey, McIndoe

managed to win one of their last nine league games, finishing fifth. This lone bright spot was overcoming Ballymena United after the Braidmen had been 2-0 up in 12 minutes.

The flags at the Oval were flown at half-mast on 25th January and the players wore black armbands to mourn the death of King George V. Miller and the Reds' keeper Lillie were sent off on this day.

The remainder of the season offered little solace for Glentoran followers. Belfast Celtic II's outplayed us in the County Antrim Shield again and although we had taken the lead a scoreline of seven or eight to the juniors would have better reflected the play. Six changes were made for the next game in the City Cup versus Newry when Redfern got all five for the visitors in a hard fought draw.

Glentoran II also took part in the Shield, losing 0-4 to Linfield. The Seconds performed heroically in the Irish Cup, reaching the semi-final. Ards were beaten 3-2 at Castlereagh Park in Round One, then a display of teamwork saw off Distillery at the Oval by 3-1. Smith was in tremendous form scoring twice. The 1st XI fell 0-4 to Derry in the quarter-finals but were unlucky, hitting the post three times and also seeing the ball get stuck on the goalline once. Derry then overcame Glentoran II 3-0 in the semis at Grosvenor Park.

The Seconds also had the disappointment of losing the two major junior finals to Celtic II. The Christmas Day Steel and Sons Cup final finished 1-1 and then two days later the Celts won the Intermediate Cup 1-0 courtesy of a penalty. The Steel final was replayed on St.Patrick's Day and at the end of Celtic's 2-1 victory opposing players came to blows with the police having to step in. Celtic II went on to reach the Antrim Shield final, going down 0-1 to their own senior XI.

Back to the Glens' first team and the City Cup contained many poor, inconsistent displays watched by small crowds. The pick of the games was a 6-3 win over Bangor when Boyd notched a first half hat-trick. Two of the Seasiders' goals were in the last two minutes. Linfield lifted the City Cup as the Glens languished in sixth position.

May brought further defeats against Belfast Celtic. Livingstone (goals) and Duncan (inside-left) were our only performers in an unrecognisable line-up in the Charity Cup semi-final. Two weeks later we obtained a bye in the first round of the RUC Fives but then went down 0-3 to Belfast Celtic. Glasgow Celtic won the tournament, defeating their Belfast namesakes 2-0 in the final.

Norman Miller earned Inter League honours against the Scottish and English Leagues.

Appearances and Goals

	App.	Goals		App.	Goals		App.	Goals
Hanna	40	2	King	11		Leckey	2	
Blayney	37	5	Boyd	10	11	Brown	1	
McCaw	35		Barr	10	6	Gorman	1	
Miller N.	33	4	Deacon	9	1	Livingstone	1	
McNeill A.	32	18	Yeates	9	1	Mellon	1	
Grey	29	5	Martin	9		Wilkinson	1	
McCrae	24	23	Marshall	8	2	Strutt	1	
McFarland	22	3	Wilkin	6		Duncan	1	
Lewis	20		Mathieson J.	5		Whan	1	
Aicken	20	5	Stitt	4		Stewart	1	
Leathem	18		Williamson	4		Mitchell	1	
Wilson	16	1	Smith	4	1	Montgomery	1	
Loughlin	14	7	McKay	3		Bell	1	
McIndoe	14	6	Gray C.	3		Own Goals		3
Boyce	13		Coulter	3		TOTAL	506	105
Mathieson R.	12		Weir	2				
Wallace	11	1	McCready	2				

1936/37

New Chairman Toby Mercer – An unsettled team –
Navy submarine team sunk

Glentoran began 1936/7 with a new regime, full of hope. Sir Dawson Bates was club president with John "Toby" Mercer as Chairman of the board of directors. Mercer's playing career included service at Derby County, Distillery, Linfield and Belfast Celtic. Sam Jennings came from Middlesbrough to take up the first team coaching duties and Ching Morrison was appointed as his assistant. The new faces on the playing panel included Freddie Lee, left-back, ex-Wisbech Jock Miller, outside-left, ex-Lancaster, McNulty, outside-right, ex-Motherwell J.McNeill, half-back, ex-Cliftonville, McCarthy, centre-forward, ex-Lancaster A.McGivern, outside-left, ex-Celtic.

Things began well with three league wins. McCarthy was carried off on his debut against Glenavon when Miller's winning goal on 84 minutes freakishly bounced over visiting keeper Murray, who had appeared to have the shot covered. Celtic knocked us out of the Gold Cup after we had held an interval lead but the team showed immense character four days later against Derry City. Defensive blunders left us 0-4 down at one stage but our rally was all in vain as Derry triumphed 5-4 on a sweltering afternoon.

We forced a draw in the league game at Celtic Park but then turned in three dismal displays. Supporters criticised the chopping and changing of the forward line while the press thought that the defence needed strengthening urgently. Lillie (ex-Cliftonville) took over in goals from the hapless Cranston for the visit of Newry Town. Lillie had a stinking first half against the Blues but then a powerful forward display overcame Coleraine.

November saw the goals rain in with Jock Miller and McIndoe the livewires of the attack. We confidently went to the Brandywell and when McIndoe put us ahead just into the second half Derry's 32 game unbeaten home record was threatened. However, after a hailstorm, the home side won comfortably. The day before we played Belfast Celtic at the Oval King Edward abdicated and King George VI was placed on the throne.

Poor results over Christmas forced us to drop into the bottom half of the table. Victor Aicken and Norman Miller worked hard at the back, and the early displays of 1937 were very promising. We inflicted Coleraine's first home defeat in four months, ended our hoodoo against Belfast Celtic 2nds and qualified for the semi-finals of the County Antrim Shield. In the Shield match with Ballymena we toyed with the opposition and as well as notching a hat-trick Sandy McNeill hit the crossbar four times!

It was a different story when United got us at the Showgrounds in the league. The Glens went down to ten men when goalkeeper Moore had to retire and Ballymena romped into a 4-0 lead with half an hour remaining. Within five minutes we had rattled in three goals and then equalised in the 76th minute. The drama still had not finished as, in the last minute, Ballymena's Fisher had his penalty saved by stand-in keeper J.McNeill. United finished bottom of the league and Glentoran seventh.

During February the Royal Navy's 2nd Submarine Flotilla was lying in Belfast Harbour. The sailors requested a football friendly and the Glens, not knowing what to expect, obliged and put out the regular 1st XI. By half-time the standard of the opposition was clear as we led 7-0. Despite easing up in the second half we still recorded our biggest win of the 20th Century.

Our weak display at Windsor in the Irish Cup was depressing after the team had "worked like Trojans" at a muddy Oval in the first game. All the Linfield forwards were on target and Aicken put the ball into his own net for the sixth.

The IFA Amateur team wore numbers for the first time against their English counterparts on 13th February. This was soon adopted for all games to reduce confusion for supporters and media alike.

Billy Rigby (ex-Peterborough and Southport) shone against Ards as the City Cup got underway. Also in this fixture a schoolboy international, Johnny Lavery (not to be mixed up with outside-left Laverty), made a scoring debut at inside-left. Two further wins followed during the week but the Portadown game produced gate receipts of only £9 on a Thursday afternoon.

New goalkeeper Andrew Jelly played well on his debut in the Shield semi-final success over Larne. It was good to see the Glens come from behind to win after Ballymena had done that to us four days earlier.

A heavy snowfall caused the postponement of our game with Celtic on 13th March. Under league rules the match had to be played off within 17 days but because of the Glens' heavy Easter programme and Celtic's Irish Cup commitments an appeal was lodged to the management committee to play off the fixture on 14th April. This cut no ice and the match was annulled - i.e. not played with neither team receiving points.

The ruling did not matter much to Glentoran as our City Cup hopes collapsed anyway with defeats at Coleraine and Glenavon, for whom Prince went nap. Easter brought a mixed bag; Bangor were hammered on Monday but Redfern got four when Newry thrashed us a day later. The Glens performed feebly in the remainder of the competition finishing a lowly 12th as the Cup went to Derry.

With a minute remaining in the County Antrim Shield final Glentoran led Belfast Celtic 2-1. Our "kick and rush" tactics looked like winning the day but it was not to be as the Hoops equalised. The only goal of the replay came from a Turnbull free-kick on the hour so we were again left empty handed.

On 3rd May the directors announced that the only way forward was to build from scratch again and they cleared out the cross-channel players. In addition, Norman Miller was transferred to Bournemouth, who had just finished sixth in the Third Division (South). Miller had again appeared in both fixtures against the Scottish and Football Leagues, being joined by J.McNeill in the former.

There was still some playing to be done although the side which met Distillery in the Charity Cup showed nine changes from the corresponding fixture the previous Saturday. (The Whites made seven changes.) The final note of the season is to record that we lost 0-2 to Ards in the first round of the RUC Fives at Grosvenor Park on 22nd May with the following line-up: Miller, Williamson, Duncan (guest from Sligo Rovers), Crossett, McGurk. Glasgow Celtic triumphed for the third consecutive year, this time defeating Cliftonville 2-1 in the final.

Victor Aicken.

Results 1936/37

Played 48. Won 19. Drew 6. Lost 23. Goals For 123. Against 121. % 45.8

IL	15/08/36		Glenavon	A	W	1	0	J.Miller
IL	19/08/36		Cliftonville	H	W	1	0	J.Miller
IL	22/08/36		Bangor	A	W	4	1	Williamson 2, McIndoe, Johnston
IL	29/08/36		Derry City	H	L	4	5	McGivern, McAnulty, McIndoe, J.Miller
IL	05/09/36		Belfast Celtic	A	D	2	2	Johnston, J.Miller (p)
IL	12/09/36		Larne	H	L	2	4	Aicken, McKay
IL	19/09/36		Portadown	A	L	1	3	McGivern
IL	26/09/36		Distillery	H	L	0	5	-
IL	03/10/36		Newry Town	H	W	4	2	McIndoe 2, Stitt, J.Miller
IL	10/10/36		Linfield	A	L	1	5	J.Miller
IL	17/10/36		Coleraine	H	W	5	3	McIndoe 2(1p), J.Miller, McGivern, Johnston
IL	24/10/36		Ards	A	L	0	2	-
IL	07/11/36		Ballymena United	H	W	8	2	McIndoe 4, J.Miller 4
IL	14/11/36		Glenavon	H	W	5	2	J.Miller 3, McIndoe, Williamson
IL	21/11/36		Cliftonville	A	D	3	3	McIndoe, Aicken, J.Miller
IL	28/11/36		Bangor	H	W	6	1	McGivern 2, J.Miller 2, McIndoe, McKay
IL	05/12/36		Derry City	A	L	1	4	McIndoe
IL	12/12/36		Belfast Celtic	H	L	2	4	J.Miller, McGivern
IL	19/12/36		Larne	A	L	2	4	McGivern 2
IL	25/12/36		Portadown	H	L	2	3	Williamson, Cooper
IL	26/12/36		Distillery	A	L	0	1	-
IL	02/01/37		Newry Town	A	W	2	1	McAnulty, McGivern
IL	16/01/37		Linfield	H	L	2	3	McNeill, J.Miller
IL	23/01/37		Coleraine	A	W	1	0	McGivern
IL	30/01/37		Ards	H	W	2	1	McKay, McNeill
IL	06/02/37		Ballymena United	A	D	4	4	Laverty, J.Miller, McIndoe, McNeill
GC	25/08/36	1	Belfast Celtic	A	L	1	2	Johnston
IC	09/01/37	1	Belfast Celtic II	H	W	3	0	McGivern, McIndoe, J.Miller
IC	20/02/37	2	Linfield	H	D	0	0	-
IC	24/02/37	2R	Linfield	A	L	1	6	N.Miller (p)
CAS	20/01/37	1	Glentoran II	H	W	6	2	McNeill 4, Smith, J.Miller
CAS	27/01/37	2	Ballymena United	H	W	5	1	Gorman 2, McNeill 3
CAS	10/03/37	SF	Larne	GP	W	4	1	J.Miller 2, Laverty 2
CAS	21/04/37	F	Belfast Celtic	GP	D	2	2	J.Miller 2(1p)
CAS	30/04/37	FR	Belfast Celtic	GP	L	0	1	-
CC	27/02/37		Ards	H	W	7	2	Stitt 3, Rigby 2, Lavery, Williamson
CC	01/03/37		Cliftonville	H	W	6	1	Rigby, Williamson, Stitt 2, J.Miller 2
CC	04/03/37		Portadown	A	W	4	1	J.Miller, Stitt 2, N.Miller (p)
CC	06/03/37		Ballymena United	A	L	1	2	Laverty
CC	20/03/37		Coleraine	A	L	1	2	McKay
CC	27/03/37		Glenavon	A	L	2	6	J.Miller, Rigby
CC	29/03/37		Bangor	H	W	7	1	Laverty 3, Rigby 3, Lavery
CC	30/03/37		Newry Town	A	L	3	7	Rigby, McNeill, N.Miller (p)
CC	03/04/37		Larne	H	D	3	3	Rigby, Aicken, McAnulty
CC	17/04/37		Linfield	A	L	0	3	-
CC	24/04/37		Derry City	H	L	1	3	McIndoe
CC	01/05/37		Distillery	A	L	0	6	-
ChC	08/05/37	SF	Distillery	Sol	L	1	4	McGurk
F	10/02/37		2nd Subm'ine Flotilla	H	W	11	0	J.Miller 3, McGivern 5, McIndoe 2, Laverty

Appearances and Goals

Name	App.	Goals	Name	App.	Goals	Name	App.	Goals
Miller N.	46	3	Gray C.	12		O'Neill	1	
Aicken	45	3	Martin	12		Surgenor	1	
McNeill J.	43		McAnulty	11	3	Brown	1	
McIndoe	38	17	Cranston	10		Heggarty	1	
McGiven	33	11	McNeill A.	10	11	Currie	1	
Miller J.	32	30	Jelly	9		Duncan	1	
Lillie	25		Johnstone	8	4	Moorfield	1	
McKay	24	4	McCarthy	5		McGurk	1	1
Blayney	24		Smith	4	1	Bailie	1	
Lee	23		Lavery	4	4	Hillen	1	
Williamson	23	6	Cooper	4	1	Busby	1	
Wilkin	16		Gorman	3	2	McCready	1	
Laverty	16	5	Buckley	3		Moore	1	
Rigby	15	9	Patterson	2		**TOTAL**	**528**	**123**
Stitt	14	8	McAnally	1				

1937/38

Jennings brings in the English – Inconsistent displays – Referee pelted

Sam Jennings had cast his net far in the search for new players in the summer of 1937. Billy Wright and Sydney Goodfellow arrived from Port Vale and they were soon joined by Arthur Griffiths (ex-Torquay), A.Horton (ex-Bournemouth), James Dodds (ex-Fulham and Gillingham) and a six foot goalkeeper, Thomas Pearson, who had been with Hull City and Derby County. Two years previously Glentoran supporters were complaining about the high number of Scottish players in the team, now many English accents could be heard in the dressing room. In fact, for the club's practice match on 11th August the 1st XI included only one player, Dodds, who had been born in Ireland. This game was a personal triumph for Litherland, a centre-forward signed from Sligo Rovers, who netted five times in the 1st's 7-2 win.

The team blended well early on with Pearson and Litherland outstanding. Celtic showed us we still had a long way to go but Linfield were defeated in an exciting Gold Cup tie. Our defence played robustly and a lovely run and cross from Griffiths set up Litherland's eighth minute winner. Our attacking game was based around the pace of wingers Dodds and Griffiths. When we visited Windsor in the league only one point separated the leading five teams. Revenge was sweet for the Blues, the turning point of this game coming after half-an-hour when Doak saved Goodfellow's penalty.

Pearson about to claim the ball at Glenavon in the Irish Cup.

Litherland was lacking support up front and we were fortunate to gain both points off Larne when their left-winger Mitchell blew his chance of a hat-trick by missing a late penalty. Peter Casciani (ex-East Fife and Dundee) arrived to strengthen the half-back line, but a bad patch in October saw us lose three times in a week. We took the lead against Portadown but visiting keeper O'Hare was thereafter in unbeatable form. Celtic's right side partnership of Kernoghan and McAlinden was our undoing in the Gold Cup with ex-Glenman Leathem getting on the scoresheet. Defeat at Bangor knocked us down to fifth place in the league, seven points behind new leaders Portadown.

The Supporters Committee presented a new set of jerseys for the Distillery game and fans were rewarded with a fine win. A week later we had to come back from two down to earn a point against Derry City. Litherland missed many good chances in this game and when he repeated this form against Ballymena he found himself replaced by Cyril Browne (ex-Ashington) at centre-forward.

Celtic's neat football, as opposed to our aimless kicking, left us well beaten on 27th November but following this we put together a run of eight successive wins. Stitt was solid at right-back while young George Lonsdale began to impress at centre-half. Christmas Day brought a double celebration. The first team overcame Linfield while the Seconds defeated Summerfield 2-1 at Grosvenor Park to bring the Steel and Sons Cup to the Oval for the seventh time. Two days later we routed Larne in the second half after the game had stood 2-2 at the interval.

180

Our best display of the season came on 15th January when we smashed Portadown's unbeaten run and their league aspirations. On a rain-soaked surface we made the best of the 25% possession we had. The remainder of January, however, was disastrous. Bangor brought our winning streak to an end at the Oval. Goodfellow did not live up to his name and was ordered off after 17 minutes

Glentoran Seconds team group 1937/8.

and eventually the Seasiders made the extra man tell despite the many saves of Pearson.

Crawford became a Cliftonville hero in the County Antrim Shield. He sustained a head wound early in the game and played on heavily bandaged. At half-time he made a quick visit to an East Belfast doctor and then resumed at centre-half! Two further inept league displays meant we finished sixth. Celtic won the Gibson Cup, defeating Derry after two test matches.

With poor City Cup form bringing only one point from five games the Irish Cup provided our main interest in the second half of the season. The second round tie with Glenavon was gruelling. When 0-1 down in the first meeting we appeared to equalise in the 75th minute with a shot going in via the crossbar, but the referee McKay said no. He did award a penalty two minutes from time to enable us to draw. The Lurgan men had the better of a scoreless replay but then a scintillating wing display from Griffiths and two excellent Lavery goals got us through to face Belfast Celtic in the semis. The first meeting was a tale of missed chances for the Celts as Pearson defied them many times. In the replay a fluke goal from Griffiths put us ahead. His high cross from the wing was blown in by the wind but our overall display was disappointing and Celtic won in a canter. The Glens' cause was not helped by the dismissal of young inside-right Best.

The fans' frustration had boiled over during the City Cup fixture with Portadown. Two of the Ports five goals were extremely doubtful and a small section of the crowd pelted the referee, Mr.Nattrass of Durham, with missiles. The League closed down the Oval for 14 days and ordered our home game with Larne to be played at their Legion Park ground on 19th March. Glentoran refused and appealed for the match to take place at Grosvenor Park to reduce our travelling costs but this appeal was dismissed by six votes to two.

We did win a City Cup game but the main aim now was to experiment and build for 1938/9. The Distillery game was an angry affair culminating in the sending-off of Glens' right-back S.Todd and the Whites' Reid. Patton of Distillery dislocated an ankle while another player had his face badly cut up. The remainder of the competition was played out in a lifeless manner and we finished joint bottom with Cliftonville and Coleraine on six points.

Sam Jennings and Goodfellow moved to Rochdale but a proposed visit to Lancashire for a friendly with "The Dale" on 12th April does not appear to have taken place. Luton Town did visit the Oval in May. The Hatters were an excellent combination and four of their goals came from Redfern, who had haunted Glentoran in his Newry Town days.

An unrecognisable team, including four guest players, lined out against the Reds in the Charity Cup semi-final. The very small crowd saw us win 5-1 but Linfield had too much experience for the young Glens team in the final.

Gray, Stitt, Robinson, Lavery and McKeown formed our squad in the RUC Five-a-Sides at Windsor Park two days later. They suffered a 0-2 defeat at the hands of Partick Thistle in Round One and later watched Belfast Celtic defeat Shelbourne 3-0 in the final.

Results 1937/38

Played 51. Won 21. Drew 9. Lost 21. Goals For 105. Against 113. % 50.0

IL	21/08/37		Ballymena United	A	W	1	0	Litherland
IL	23/08/37		Newry Town	H	W	4	2	Litherland 3, Griffiths
IL	26/08/37		Belfast Celtic	A	L	1	6	Litherland
IL	28/08/37		Ards	H	W	2	0	John (p), Griffiths
IL	04/09/37		Glenavon	A	W	4	0	Dodds 2, Rigby, Griffiths
IL	11/09/37		Coleraine	H	D	1	1	Goodfellow
IL	18/09/37		Linfield	A	L	2	5	Litherland 2
IL	25/09/37		Larne	H	W	3	2	Litherland 3(1p)
IL	02/10/37		Cliftonville	A	W	3	1	Litherland 2, Lavery
IL	09/10/37		Portadown	H	L	1	2	Lavery
IL	16/10/37		Bangor	A	L	1	2	Dodds
IL	30/10/37		Distillery	H	W	5	3	Griffiths 2, Lavery, Gotham, Goodfellow
IL	06/11/37		Derry City	H	D	3	3	Foster, Griffiths, Lavery
IL	13/11/37		Ballymena United	H	L	1	2	Dodds
IL	20/11/37		Newry Town	A	W	3	2	Browne 2, Goodfellow
IL	27/11/37		Belfast Celtic	H	L	1	4	Dodds
IL	04/12/37		Ards	A	W	4	3	Browne 2, Lavery, Rigby
IL	11/12/37		Glenavon	H	W	2	0	Goodfellow 2(1p)
IL	18/12/37		Coleraine	A	W	4	2	Lavery 2, Browne, Griffiths
IL	25/12/37		Linfield	H	W	2	0	Browne, Griffiths
IL	27/12/37		Larne	A	W	8	3	Browne 4, Griffiths, Goodfellow (p), Dodds, Lavery
IL	01/01/38		Cliftonville	H	W	3	2	Lavery 2, Dodds
IL	15/01/38		Portadown	A	W	3	1	Wallace, Browne, Griffiths
IL	22/01/38		Bangor	H	L	1	5	Lavery
IL	29/01/38		Distillery	A	L	1	3	Lavery
IL	05/02/38		Derry City	A	L	0	3	-
GC	08/09/37	1	Linfield	A	W	1	0	Litherland
GC	13/10/37	2	Belfast Celtic	A	L	0	5	-
IC	08/01/38	1	Crusaders	A	W	2	1	Griffiths, Lavery
IC	26/02/38	2	Glenavon	H	D	1	1	Blayney (p)
IC	02/03/38	2R	Glenavon	A	D	0	0	-
IC	07/03/38	2R2	Glenavon	H	W	2	1	Lavery 2
IC	26/03/38	SF	Belfast Celtic	WP	D	1	1	Lavery
IC	30/03/38	SFR	Belfast Celtic	WP	L	1	3	Griffiths
CAS	12/01/38	1	Glentoran II	H	W	6	1	Goodfellow 2, Browne 2, Griffiths, Owen
CAS	26/01/38	2	Cliftonville	H	L	2	4	Wallace, Goodfellow
CC	12/02/38		Derry City	H	L	2	3	McKeown, Owens
CC	19/02/38		Ballymena United	A	L	2	4	Browne, Best
CC	05/03/38		Portadown	H	L	0	5	-
CC	12/03/38		Cliftonville	A	D	1	1	Browne
CC	17/03/38		Bangor	A	L	0	1	-
CC	02/04/38		Coleraine	H	W	3	0	Browne, Lavery, Griffiths
CC	06/04/38		Linfield	A	L	1	4	Rosbotham
CC	09/04/38		Larne	A	D	1	1	McKeown
CC	16/04/38		Distillery	A	D	2	2	Griffiths, Browne
CC	18/04/38		Glenavon	H	L	2	4	Browne, Griffiths
CC	19/04/38		Ards	A	D	1	1	Browne
CC	23/04/38		Belfast Celtic	H	L	0	2	-
CC	30/04/38		Newry Town	A	L	4	7	Griffiths 2, Goodfellow, Browne
ChC	13/05/38	SF	Cliftonville	GP	W	5	1	Robinson 4, McWilliams
ChC	19/05/38	F	Linfield	Solt	L	1	3	Stitt
F	11/08/37		Practice Match: 1st XI 7 (Litherland 5) 2nd XI 2					
F	04/05/38		Luton Town	H	L	2	5	Lavery, Bell

Appearances and Goals

	App.	Goals		App.	Goals		App.	Goals
Pearson	48		Wallace	13	2	McWilliams	3	1
Wright W.	48		Best	12	1	Craig	2	
Griffiths	42	18	Todd S.	12		Wright S.	2	
Goodfellow	41	10	Lee	10		Todd E.	2	
Dodds	32	7	Lonsdale	10		Smith	2	
Blayney	31	1	McKeown	8	2	Morrow	1	
Lavery	31	17	Gray C.	7		Carser	1	
Browne	29	20	Casciani	5		Fitzsimmons	1	
Robinson	20	4	Laverty	5		Scott	1	
Rigby	18	2	Gotham	4	1	Railton	1	
Foster	16	1	Patton	4		McClure	1	
Wright J.	15		McHurk	4		Unknown	11	
Stitt	14	1	Heggarty	4		Own Goals		1
Owens	14	2	John	4	1	TOTAL	561	105
Hooton	13		McCune	3				
Litherland	13	13	Irvine	3				

Turnbull scores Celtic's second goal in the Irish Cup semi-final replay.

183

1938/39

Louis Page appointed – A free-scoring Taylor - Hannigan Cup

At the request of Glentoran kick-off times for Irish League matches were re-scheduled for 3 pm instead of 3.30 pm. The League itself made the stamping out of bad language at club grandstands a priority. The directors could not quite obtain the players they wanted to come to the Oval but nevertheless many signings were made. The most significant of these were Artie Douglas (outside-left from Clyde), Moorhead (left-back from Cliftonville),

Joseph Stitt.

McCready (left-half from Coleraine) and A.Taylor, a centre-forward. T.McCandless came into the side, mainly at outside-right, as the season progressed. The 1sts v. 2nds practice match on 13th August resulted in an attractive 4-2 win for the seniors. Any gate receipts from these games were usually handed to the IFA for donation to charity.

Glentoran's results over the first two months were extremely inconsistent. We began well with a win over Larne despite a penalty miss from centre-half Jerry Murray. Then, after trailing 1-3 at half-time we "swung the ball from wing to wing" at Coleraine in a masterly second half display with Taylor adding the goalscoring punch. Gibb's hat-trick spoiled our trip to Newry but then Linfield were overcome in an exciting Friday night encounter. Right-wing Jimmy Todd was in great form against his old team, setting up two of the goals, while Tom Pearson was safe on his return to goals.

With four minutes to go at Celtic Park on 17th September we led 3-2 and many spectators had left the ground. However Belfast Celtic "fought like demons" to avoid defeat and were rewarded with two very late goals. Undaunted, the Glens put in a splendid display to see off Derry a week later with Johnny Lavery showing breathtaking individual skill. New right-back W.Todd was solid.

Glenavon's goalkeeper Kelly was the main reason for our Gold Cup exit. In fact, straight after the second round tie Kelly was transferred to Chesterfield. By mid-October the team had begun picking itself and six consecutive league wins saw us move into second place, two points behind Celtic. Pearson's good keeping was a major factor in this. The run included comebacks from two goals down to both Cliftonville and Distillery. James Connor's 85th minute header did the trick against the Whites.

Then things started to go wrong. Numerous easy chances, including two penalties, were missed against Newry and then the half-backs had an off day against the Blues. Much worse was to follow though on 10th December. After Douglas had given us the lead against the Ports, Moorhead had to retire through injury. By half-time we were 1-4 down and when right back Cameron Gray was sent off early in the second period our defence was just totally overwhelmed as the visitors knocked in nine!

184

Although we beat Bangor confidence was drained from the team. Heavy defeats at the hands of Derry City and Belfast Celtic were coupled by Ballymena's inter-league forward Sclater helping himself to a hat-trick in the league and then knocking us out of the Irish Cup. We even struggled to overcome "kick and rush" juniors Crusaders in the County Antrim Shield, having to come from 1-2 down with McCandless sent off. The battling attitude of the team could not be faulted but our final league placing of sixth, eleven points behind Celtic, did not do the side justice.

The gloom was brought to a head at a special meeting of shareholders in early February and Louis Page was appointed trainer-coach. The club was also in financial difficulties and welcomed a £200 donation from the Supporters Committee to improve the draining facilities in the popular enclosure.

Early results under Page were promising. Glentoran reached the Shield semi-finals and then ran up double figures against Coleraine. Left-half Murray prompted the attack for these goals but it was one thing defeating weaker sides but then failing when coming up against the big guns of Celtic, Derry and Linfield. McCandless found

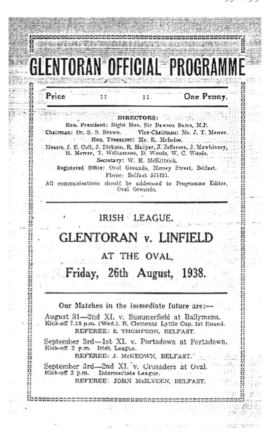

Programme Cover.

scoring form in March as Cliftonville were easily brushed aside in the Shield and Newry in the City Cup. However our search for a first trophy since the Irish Cup of 1935 was thwarted by Celtic in the Shield final. The Glens missed Robinson, who had been transferred to Birmingham just before the game, and Taylor had the misfortune of missing a penalty. A good all-round performance against Distillery, with Connor superb at centre-half, ensured us of fourth position in the City Cup.

Later in that week we entertained two League of Ireland sides. Southern champions Shamrock Rovers won the Hannigan Cup in a lively game and then Dundalk threatened to outclass us but we fought back to almost draw from three goals down. Trialists Kane and Davis impressed in the latter fixture.

There was little interest in the Charity Cup game versus Distillery but plenty of goals as we turned round 4-3 ahead, Connor snatching a late winner. The semi-final with Linfield was fiercely contested. Lavery put us ahead after only two minutes but a Rosbotham penalty brought he Blues level. The excitement level was high when White netted Linfield's winner in extra-time.

Glentoran made the usual early exit when the RUC staged their five-a-side tournament at Windsor Park on 27th May. Our team of Murray, Gray, McCandless, Irvine and Wilkin lost 1-2 to Belfast Celtic. The final turned out to be an all-Glasgow affair, Celtic beating Rangers 2-0.

On the season's representative front Jimmy Todd played for the Irish League against the Scottish and Football Leagues in September, being joined by Taylor in the former. Todd scored against the Scots. Douglas was the sole Glenman against the League of Ireland in March.

Results 1938/39

Played 48. Won 27. Drew 2. Lost 19. Goals For 123. Against 101. % 58.3

IL	20/08/38		Larne	H	W	3 1	Taylor 2, Todd
IL	22/08/38		Coleraine	A	W	5 3	Taylor 3, Connor, Douglas
IL	24/08/38		Newry Town	A	L	1 5	Todd (p)
IL	26/08/38		Linfield	H	W	3 2	Taylor 3
IL	03/09/38		Portadown	A	L	1 3	Todd (p)
IL	10/09/38		Bangor	H	W	3 2	Todd, Lavery, Connor
IL	17/09/38		Belfast Celtic	A	L	3 4	Douglas, Taylor, Best
IL	24/09/38		Derry City	H	W	4 2	Taylor 3, Todd
IL	01/10/38		Ballymena United	A	L	0 1	-
IL	15/10/38		Cliftonville	H	W	4 2	Taylor 2, Thain, Todd
IL	22/10/38		Glenavon	A	W	3 2	Douglas, Connor, Taylor
IL	29/10/38		Ards	H	W	2 1	Lavery, Todd
IL	05/11/38		Distillery	A	W	5 4	McCready, Connor 2, Lavery, Taylor
IL	12/11/38		Larne	A	W	5 2	Connor, McCready, Douglas (p), Best 2
IL	19/11/38		Coleraine	H	W	4 0	Best 2, Lavery, Connor
IL	26/11/38		Newry Town	H	D	0 0	-
IL	03/12/38		Linfield	A	L	1 2	Taylor
IL	10/12/38		Portadown	H	L	2 9	Douglas, Taylor
IL	17/12/38		Bangor	A	W	4 2	Taylor 2, Douglas, Lavery
IL	26/12/38		Derry City	A	L	0 4	-
IL	27/12/38		Ballymena United	H	L	1 3	Douglas
IL	31/12/38		Cliftonville	A	L	3 4	Connor 2, Wilkin
IL	04/01/39		Belfast Celtic	H	L	1 6	Taylor
IL	07/01/39		Glenavon	H	W	4 3	Taylor 2(1p), Douglas, McCandless
IL	14/01/39		Ards	A	L	1 2	Taylor (p)
IL	28/01/39		Distillery	H	W	2 0	Taylor, Connor
GC	13/09/38	1	Larne	H	W	1 0	Todd
GC	28/09/38	2	Glenavon	A	L	1 2	Taylor
CAS	11/01/39	1	Crusaders	A	W	5 2	Taylor 4, Connor
CAS	01/02/39	2	Ards	H	W	3 2	Taylor 2(1p), Connor
CAS	15/03/39	SF	Cliftonville	GP	W	4 0	McCandless 3, Taylor
CAS	19/04/39	F	Belfast Celtic	GP	L	1 2	Lavery
IC	21/01/39	1	Ballymena United	A	L	0 1	-
CC	04/02/39		Cliftonville	A	W	3 1	Taylor 2, Allen og
CC	11/02/39		Coleraine	H	W	10 1	Taylor 4(1p), Douglas 2, Connor 3, McCandless
CC	18/02/39		Linfield	A	L	0 2	-
CC	25/02/39		Ards	H	W	1 0	McCandless
CC	04/03/39		Portadown	A	L	1 2	Taylor
CC	18/03/39		Larne	H	D	1 1	Connor
CC	25/03/39		Newry Town	H	W	4 0	McCandless, Robinson, Connor, Lavery
CC	01/04/39		Derry City	A	L	1 5	Robinson
CC	08/04/39		Ballymena United	H	W	5 1	McCandless 3, Connor 2
CC	10/04/39		Belfast Celtic	A	L	0 2	-
CC	11/04/39		Bangor	H	W	2 1	Irvine, Wilkin
CC	15/04/39		Glenavon	A	W	4 2	Robinson 2, Lavery, Douglas
CC	22/04/39		Distillery	H	W	5 0	Taylor 2, Lavery, McCandless, Irvine (p)
ChC	08/05/39	1	Distillery	H	W	5 4	Wilkin, Stitt 2, Connor 2
ChC	13/05/39	SF	Linfield	Solt	L	1 2	Lavery
F	13/08/38		Practice Match: 1st XI 4 (Lavery 2, Taylor, Todd) 2nd XI 2 (Houston 2)				
F	26/04/39		Shamrock Rovers	H	L	2 3	Douglas, Murray (p)
			Hannigan Cup				
F	28/04/39		Dundalk	H	L	2 3	Lavery, McCandless

Appearances and Goals

	App.	Goals		App.	Goals		App.	Goals
Connor J.	47	21	Moorhead	17		Ritchie	2	
Lavery	44	10	Flynn	16		Wright S.	1	
Douglas	42	11	Robinson	10	4	McDermott	1	
Pearson	41		Best	10	5	Mahon	1	
Murray	41		Patton	5		Walsh	1	
Taylor	41	42	Magee	4		Price	1	
Todd W.	38		Connor W.	3		Hull	1	
Gray C.	38		Wright J.	3		Fitzsimmons	1	
Wilkin	26	3	Thain	3	1	Own Goals		1
McCready	22	2	McVeigh	3				
Irvine	20	2	Black	2		TOTAL	528	123
McCandless	20	11	Nixon	2				
Todd J.	19	8	Stitt	2	2			

1939/40

Attractive new jerseys – The goals of Henry Smith – A trophy again at last

Few new faces came to the Oval in the close season due to the club's financial hardship - indeed 70% of our playing staff were amateurs. The panel read: E.Martin, P.Johnstone(ex-Southport and Runcorn), R.Irvine, C.Fitzsimmons, R.McGorman(Sirocco Works), J.Uprichard, C.Gray, I.Stitt, R.Butler(ex-Birmingham), J.Murray(captain), H.Smith, T.McCandless, J.Mills, J.McDermott, J.Connor, J.Lavery, A.Douglas, R.Corbett, C.Black, T.Pearson, C.O'Flynn and A.Wilkin.

Team Group 1939/40 Back Row: T.Wilkins, H.Johnstone, S.Pearson, C.Gray, R.Irvine Front Row: B.McCandless, R.Connor, H.Smith, G.Murray (captain), J.Cahoon, A.Douglas.

A splendid attendance was at the practice match on 12th August when the "A" team in stripes beat the "B" team in green by 10-5. Smith got five and Connor notched a hat-trick for the "A"s while Shannon claimed three for the "B" team. Jerry Murray scored for both sides, putting through an own goal for the "B"s in the second half. The press were confident that Glentoran were to have a successful season.

The City Cup began with war imminent in Europe. The Glens paraded their new green jerseys, complete with Lord Glentoran's coat of arms, at Coleraine. A hectic game was settled in favour of the home side by a 75 yard run and drive by Green. Our next four games all ended 1-1, Smith equalising against Linfield with a last minute lob. As France and Britain declared War on Germany in early September it became customary to play the National Anthem before games to whip up patriotism and loyalism.

The early games were blessed with glorious weather and that was the case on 9th September when we finally gained our first win of the season. Over gave Cliftonville the lead but the Reds fell away badly as we helped ourselves in the second half. Early City Cup pacesetters Derry City were too much for us a week later as we showed a hangover from our Gold Cup defeat by Portadown. More chances went a-begging against Celtic and it was

188

after this match that the directors had a meeting with the senior players to discuss the club's immediate future.

The club chairman, Dr.Brown, outlined the recessionary conditions and requested the players to take a drop in wages to £1 10s per week. As could be expected some players agreed and others did not and the latter subsequently departed.

Back on the field three victories were obtained from the final four City Cup games but this still only ensured eighth place with a 50% record. Matches in October kicked-off at 4.30 pm to enable as much daylight work as possible to be done in aid of the War Effort. B.Martin (Spurs' right back) and Walter McMillen (Millwall's half-back) "guested" against Newry and this was the beginning of a trend, which lasted during the war-time days, of professionals with English and Scottish clubs sent to Northern Ireland on military duty being snapped up to play in the local game.

Frank Grice began his association with the club in the opening league game and claimed our first goal but Celtic proved too strong on the day. Then, after Portadown had continued their good Oval form, the team settled down and rattled off nine successive wins to see out the 1930's. Our usual line-up in these matches was: Hinton; Gray, Martin; McMillen, Irvine, Wilkin; Robinson, Grice, Smith, Lavery, Douglas.

The goals came thick and fast despite the heavy pitches with the only slight hiccup coming on Boxing Day at Ballymena when we trailed 0-2 at half-time. However in a dramatic second half we were reduced to ten men, Ted

Dave "Boy" Martin.

Hinton saved a penalty, and eventually Jackie Robinson sent us on our way to victory.

The bubble finally burst at Derry, where defeat left us four points behind Belfast Celtic, and then at Glenavon, when Duffy's 78th minute strike knocked us out of the Irish Cup at the first hurdle.

Ards and Larne felt the backlash but our big test came with the visit of Celtic on 3rd February. It was not to be the Glens' day as Tommy Breen saved everything we fired at him and Celtic's 3-0 win put them six points clear of us with twelve games to go.

Goalkeeper Charlie Tizard and full-back O'Neill (ex-Dundalk) came into the side as we put together another unbeaten run of seven games. The feature of our win over Distillery came when Henry Smith directly headed back into goal a free-kick taken by Whites' keeper Galway!

The War began to take a deeper effect on the public and in early March meat rationing was introduced. Petrol prices shot up too to further reduce attendances at matches although 16,000 came to the Oval for the meeting with Linfield on 16th March. Robinson netted our winner six minutes from time. This good form took us to within three points of Celtic who had faltered against Portadown and Larne. However Mourneview Park again proved a bogey ground after a terrific struggle which saw us draw level three times but eventually lose.

An Easter Tuesday trip to Newry would have cost you 3/- return on the train. Those who travelled got full value as the Glens had knocked in seven by half-time. This win was to no avail as the following Saturday Celtic beat Linfield 5-0 to claim a fifth successive championship.

Further bad news came with the death of Tommy "Ching" Morrison and the players wore black armbands in respect against Cliftonville. Then defeat at Ards allowed Portadown to sneak into second place in the final league table.

However there was opportunity for consolation in the County Antrim Shield and the Charity Cup. Over 20,000 people flocked to Solitude for the Shield final with the Blues and they witnessed some of the fastest and finest football played by Glentoran that season.

Results 1939/40

Played 46. Won 27. Drew 6. Lost 13. Goals For 156. Against 79. % 65.2.
Honours: County Antrim Shield

CC	19/08/39		Coleraine	A	L	2	3	Smith, Douglas
CC	23/08/39		Linfield	H	D	1	1	Smith
CC	26/08/39		Portadown	A	D	1	1	Douglas
CC	02/09/39		Distillery	H	D	1	1	Smith
CC	06/09/39		Larne	A	D	1	1	Murray (p)
CC	09/09/39		Cliftonville	H	W	7	1	Douglas, Smith 4, Russell, McCurry og
CC	16/09/39		Derry City	A	L	1	3	Smith
CC	23/09/39		Belfast Celtic	H	L	0	2	-
CC	30/09/39		Glenavon	A	D	1	1	Lavery
CC	07/10/39		Ards	H	W	5	3	Douglas 2, Smith 2, Lavery
CC	14/10/39		Bangor	H	W	6	0	Douglas 3, Smith 2, Gray
CC	21/10/39		Ballymena United	A	L	1	4	Robinson
CC	04/11/39		Newry Town	H	W	6	1	Smith 4, Robinson, Lavery
GC	13/09/39	1	Portadown	H	L	3	4	Smith 2, Russell
IL	11/11/39		Belfast Celtic	A	L	2	4	Grice, Lavery
IL	18/11/39		Portadown	H	L	0	3	-
IL	25/11/39		Larne	A	W	2	0	Smith, Robinson
IL	02/12/39		Distillery	H	W	6	2	Lavery, Robinson 2, Smith 2, Grice
IL	09/12/39		Coleraine	A	W	7	3	Lavery, Robinson, Smith 3, Douglas, McMillen
IL	16/12/39		Bangor	H	W	5	1	Grice 2, Smith, Robinson, Gray (p)
IL	23/12/39		Linfield	A	W	2	1	Robinson, Grice
IL	25/12/39		Glenavon	H	W	6	1	Douglas 2, McMillen, Smith 3
IL	26/12/39		Ballymena United	A	W	3	2	Robinson 2, Grice
IL	30/12/39		Newry Town	H	W	6	1	Smith 3, Douglas, Grice, Robinson
IL	06/01/40		Cliftonville	H	W	8	2	Douglas, McMillen, Smith 4, Robinson 2
IL	13/01/40		Derry City	A	L	2	3	Robinson, Smith
IL	27/01/40		Ards	H	W	8	1	McMillen 2, Grice 2, Lavery, Smith 2, Robinson
IL	03/02/40		Belfast Celtic	H	L	0	3	-
IL	10/02/40		Portadown	A	D	2	2	Grice 2(1p)
IL	17/02/40		Larne	H	W	6	2	Smith 2, Lavery 2, McMillen, Grice
IL	24/02/40		Distillery	A	W	3	2	Smith 2, Robinson
IL	02/03/40		Coleraine	H	W	4	1	Smith 3, McMillen
IL	09/03/40		Bangor	A	W	4	0	Smith 2, Robinson, Grice
IL	16/03/40		Linfield	H	W	3	2	Smith, McMillen, Robinson
IL	23/03/40		Glenavon	A	L	3	4	Smith 2, Lavery
IL	25/03/40		Ballymena United	H	W	4	2	McMillen, Smith, Grice, Robinson
IL	26/03/40		Newry Town	A	W	9	1	Grice 5, Smith 2, Lavery, Gray
IL	30/03/40		Cliftonville	A	W	2	0	Lavery, Grice
IL	06/04/40		Derry City	H	W	6	1	Smith, Robinson, Lavery 2, McMillen 2
IL	13/04/40		Ards	A	L	1	2	Smith
IC	20/01/40	1	Glenavon	A	L	1	2	Smith
CAS	31/01/40	2	Larne	H	W	4	0	Lavery, Douglas 2, Grice (p)
CAS	13/03/40	SF	Ballymena United	WP	W	2	0	Robinson, Smith

CAS	24/04/40	F	Linfield	Sol	W	4	0	Robinson 2, Grice, Smith
ChC	11/05/40	SF	Cliftonville	GP	W	5	2	Smith 3, Sloan 2
ChC	18/05/40	F	Belfast Celtic	Sol	L	0	3	-
F	12/08/39		Practice Match: A Team 10 (Smith 5, Murray, Connor 3, Douglas)					
			B Team 5 (Shannon 3, Russell, Murray og)					
F	12/04/40		St. James' Gate	H	W	3	1	Smith, Grice 2
F	19/04/40		Dundalk XI	H	D	2	2	Grice, Lavery

Linfield were handicapped by an injury to their keeper Doak but this had little bearing on the end result. The Glens had lifted their first trophy in five years.

A couple of friendlies were arranged against Free State League teams. St.James's Gate (complete with six internationals) had a losing first visit to Ulster whereas the game with Dundalk was curtailed after 65 minutes due to the failing light.

New players Bryson, Duffy and Sloan were tried out in the Charity Cup with the most impressive, Bryson, offered a contract. In the semi-final Jackie Robinson and Cliftonville's full-back Fleck were ordered off after a scuffle as we triumphed 5-2. The season finished on a disappointing note with defeat by Celtic in the final - again Breen proved to be our major stumbling block.

So a difficult year was completed but this was to be the last season of normal Irish League football for seven years due to the continuation of the Second World War.

Appearances and Goals

	App.	Goals		App.	Goals		App.	Goals
Douglas	46	15	O'Neill	14		Sloan	2	2
Smith	46	61	Pearson	9		Shannon	1	
Irvine	44		Murray	9	1	McLean	1	
Wilkin	43		Stitt	9		Atkinson	1	
Lavery	42	15	Johnstone P.	8		Wright S.	1	
Gray C.	40	3	McCandless	6		Duffy	1	
Robinson	31	23	Connor J.	5		McDermott	1	
Grice	30	22	Pollock	4		Thompson	1	
McMillen	28	11	Butler	3		Fitzsimmons	1	
Hinton	20		McAleer	3		Own Goals		1
Martin B.	19		McGorman	3		TOTAL	506	156
Tizard	16		Heggarty	2				
Russell	14	2	Bryson	2				

1940/41

*War again reorganises league – Grice goal retains Shield -
The Oval is bombed*

The War situation forced radical changes upon football in Northern Ireland in 1940/1. During the summer the grounds of Ballymena and Bangor were used for military work, forcing these clubs to resign from the league. Juniors Summerfield and Crusaders were mooted as possible replacements but on 2nd August an even bigger bombshell was thrown into Irish League circles. The four major Belfast clubs, Linfield, Celtic, Glentoran and Distillery announced that they no longer wanted to participate in the league but preferred to set up new competitions more suited to the current emergency. Finance was a major motivation for this stance as costs were increasing due to travelling to provincial grounds and gate receipts were relatively low against the poorer opposition.

Many frantic meetings took place in the first two weeks of August in an attempt to resolve the situation and by the 15th a new set up had emerged and gained the necessary formal approval from the IFA. So the Irish League was suspended and a new body "the Northern Ireland Football League" was its replacement. The joining fee was £5 5s with visiting teams guaranteed £20 instead of the £10 under the previous arrangement. The initial membership composed of the big Belfast four plus Cliftonville, Derry City, Glenavon and Portadown. The remaining clubs were left to apply to the Intermediate League but would still be eligible to compete in the Irish Cup and County Antrim Shield.

Frank Grice.

The City Cup and Charity Cup were abandoned and the format of the "Substitute" Gold Cup and Regional League altered. Teams would play each other twice in the former and four times in the latter.

During all this off-field activity Glentoran fitted in a practice game at the Oval on 9th August. The "Seniors" defeated the "Reserves" 6-4, McCartney and Smith getting two each for the Seniors, Bunting two for the Reserves. The following playing panel was established: Tizard, Hinton, Gray, B.Martin, Morrison, McMillen, Bryson, Wilkin, Irvine, Johnston, Lyness, Robinson, Grice, Smith, Douglas, Lavery, McCartney, Bunting, Thompson, Hamilton, Crosby. Trainer: Billy Ritchie.

The early matches of the season hinted at a pattern that was to last right throughout wartime football. Celtic and Linfield were the strongest sides, Glentoran on a par with Distillery, while Derry and Cliftonville brought up the rear. Two mistakes from Tizard allowed Celtic to win our pre-season friendly but when we met them ten days later on Gold Cup business their forwards toyed with us, and we conceded seven! Henry Smith, scorer of the first ever goal in Regional League football, was on form a week later scoring five in a row as we knocked in seven against Derry City.

Despite taking the lead against Linfield we lost 1-2, but then put together four wins on the trot to move into second place in the Gold Cup, three points behind Celtic. Peter

McKennan (Partick Thistle) came into the side at inside-right and his second goal against Portadown was a lovely lob. The Gold Cup crunch match came when Celtic visited the Oval on 12th October. It was a furious game watched by a gate of £234 but the draw did more for Celtic's cause than ours. Indeed the Celts sewed up the cup two weeks later after we lost at Derry and drew at home to Linfield. Jackie Robinson inspired the Glens to come back against the Blues after we had been 0-2 down. Meagre crowds populated our last two games but two wins gave us the Gold Cup runners-up spot as Linfield slipped up at Glenavon. Glentoran's most influential player in the series was Walter McMillen at right-half.

By the completion of the first quarter of Regional League fixtures the Glens shared top spot with Celtic on eleven points. Our only reverse had been surprisingly at Glenavon. We opened with an excellent 4-1 success at Windsor Park when Albert Young of Arsenal made his debut at right-back. This was followed by another draw at the Oval versus Celtic when our equaliser arrived in the 88th minute after constant pressure on Breen's goal.

P. McKENNAN

Peter McKennan.

By Christmas the team had really settled down, especially Tizard in goals, but we had a Boxing Day disappointment going down at home to Linfield. However the Glens bounced back two days later with our first win over Belfast Celtic for six years in a thriller at Celtic Park and on 4th January we moved to the top of the table after overcoming a lamentable Derry City outfit.

In early 1941 goals came a-plenty at both ends as football teams felt duty bound to entertain the long suffering public. McKennan ran riot scoring five against Glenavon but the Lurgan men gained some sort of revenge a week later by beating our Seconds 5-0 in the Irish Cup. Then we were involved in the most exciting game at Shamrock Park all season, going down 5-6 after holding an early 2-0 lead. The high scoring was by no means confined to Glentoran games as the same day Celtic defeated Glenavon 13-0 with Peter O'Connor setting the Irish individual scoring record of eleven goals.

February was a bad month for the Glens. We only managed one win, slipped to third in the league and were knocked out of the Irish Cup by Distillery after the tie had twice been postponed. The team though had a fighting quality, never more aptly demonstrated than at Windsor Park on the 15th of the month. A Marshall hat-trick allowed the Blues to lead 3-0 and then Tony Wilkin broke his leg in the 65th minute after a collision with Linfield's left-half Tommy Brolly. Undeterred the Glens applied tremendous pressure and brought off a 3-3 draw. Wilkin was out of football for almost two years.

In the County Antrim Shield we stuttered to the semi-finals after needing a late penalty to overcome Distillery's second string in the first round. Frank Grice's spectacular overhead kick set up the win over Larne for whom keeper Ross pulled off many brilliant saves. The arrival of Dave "Boy" Martin to the Oval coincided with a upturn in scoring form in the Regional League. Martin had been a deadly marksman at Belfast Celtic and Wolves and his nine goals in his first four games showed nothing had changed.

Glentoran defeated Bangor at Celtic Park to qualify for the Shield final but we met our Armageddon at that same venue four days later in the league. We went into the game four points behind Celtic and completely dominated for 20 minutes as goals from Martin and McMillen put us 2-0 up. However Celtic countered and our defence disintegrated as eight goals were conceded, including four in a six minute spell. O'Connor got a hat-trick and the title was now destined for Celtic Park for the sixth time in succession.

With interest in the league now over the Glens tried out some new faces, notably Clancy McDermott, in the remaining matches. Before the game with Portadown a two minute silence was observed for those killed in the air raids on Belfast but three weeks later another raid was to have a much more significant effect on the club. The Oval had witnessed two

Results 1940/41

Played 47. Won 28. Drew 8. Lost 11. Goals For 149. Against 95. % 68.1.
Honours: County Antrim Shield

SGC	20/08/40		Distillery	H	D	1	1	Smith
SGC	24/08/40		Glenavon	A	W	2	0	Johnston 2
SGC	27/08/40		Belfast Celtic	A	L	1	7	Smith
SGC	31/08/40		Derry City	H	W	7	3	Smith 5, Robinson 2
SGC	07/09/40		Linfield	A	L	1	2	Smith
SGC	14/09/40		Cliftonville	H	W	3	1	Smith 2, Grice
SGC	21/09/40		Portadown	A	W	4	2	McKennan 2, Robinson, Smith
SGC	28/09/40		Distillery	A	W	3	2	Grice, McMillen, Smith
SGC	05/10/40		Glenavon	H	W	1	0	Robinson
SGC	12/10/40		Belfast Celtic	H	D	1	1	Robinson
SGC	19/10/40		Derry City	A	L	2	5	Douglas, Robinson
SGC	26/10/40		Linfield	H	D	3	3	Robinson 2, McKennan
SGC	02/11/40		Cliftonville	A	W	8	3	McKennan 2, McCartney 2, McMillen, Lavery, Robinson, Douglas
SGC	09/11/40		Portadown	H	W	4	2	McMillen 2, McKennan, Douglas
RL	16/11/40		Linfield	A	W	4	1	Smith 2, Lavery, McKennan
RL	23/11/40		Belfast Celtic	H	D	1	1	McMillen
RL	30/11/40		Derry City	A	W	4	0	Smith 3, Douglas
RL	07/12/40		Glenavon	A	L	0	1	-
RL	14/12/40		Portadown	H	W	4	2	McKennan 2, Lavery, Smith
RL	21/12/40		Cliftonville	A	W	3	1	Smith, Lavery, Duke
RL	25/12/40		Distillery	H	W	5	0	McKennan 3(1p), Lavery 2
RL	26/12/40		Linfield	H	L	1	2	Duke
RL	28/12/40		Belfast Celtic	A	W	2	1	Smith, Grice
RL	04/01/41		Derry City	H	W	5	0	Grice 2, Smith 2, Douglas
RL	11/01/41		Glenavon	H	W	8	0	McKennan 5, Smith, Lavery, Douglas
RL	25/01/41		Portadown	A	L	5	6	Lavery 2, McKennan, Grice, Smith
RL	01/02/41		Cliftonville	H	W	6	2	McKennan 4, Douglas, Grice
RL	08/02/41		Distillery	A	L	3	6	Lavery, McKennan, Douglas
RL	15/02/41		Linfield	A	D	3	3	Smith 2, McKennan
RL	01/03/41		Derry City	A	D	2	2	Smith, Robinson
RL	08/03/41		Glenavon	A	D	1	1	McKennan
RL	22/03/41		Cliftonville	A	W	4	0	Robinson, McKennan 2, Douglas
RL	26/03/41		Portadown	H	W	7	4	Martin 4, McKennan, Grice, Robinson
RL	29/03/41		Distillery	H	W	6	1	Bradley og, McKennan 2, Douglas, Grice, Martin
RL	12/04/41		Belfast Celtic	A	L	2	8	Martin, McMillen
RL	14/04/41		Derry City	H	W	4	0	Martin 3, Grice
RL	15/04/41		Glenavon	H	L	1	2	Smith
RL	19/04/41		Portadown	A	L	3	4	Smith 2, Lavery
RL	02/05/41		Belfast Celtic	H	D	3	3	McKennan 2(1p), Grice
RL	03/05/41		Cliftonville	H	W	6	3	Weir 2, Robinson 2, McKennan 2
RL	10/05/41		Distillery	A	W	3	2	Martin, Lavery, McKennan
RL	17/05/41		Linfield	A	W	3	1	Martin 2, Grice
IC	22/02/41	1	Distillery	A	L	0	3	-

CAS	05/03/41	1	Distillery II	A	W	3	2	Douglas, Smith, Gray (p)
CAS	15/03/41	2	Larne	H	W	2	0	Grice, Robinson
CAS	08/04/41	SF	Bangor	CP	W	3	1	Smith, Lavery, McKennan
CAS	14/05/41	F	Distillery	WP	W	1	0	Grice
F	09/08/40		Trial Game: Seniors 6 (McCartney 2, Smith 2, Grice, Douglas) Reserves 4 (Bunting 2, Johnston, Thompson)					
F	17/08/40		Belfast Celtic	H	L	3	5	Grice, Smith, McMillen War Effort
F	04/04/41		St. James's Gate	A	L	3	4	Lavery 3
F	25/04/41		St. James's Gate	H	W	6	3	Smith, Martin 2, McKennan, Lavery 2 – Air Raid Fund
F	Unknown		Belfast Celtic	H	W	3	0	Lynass 3 Tony Wilkin Benefit

games on consecutive days as we gained a creditable draw against Celtic and cantered to a 6-3 win over the Reds. Just over 24 hours later the ground was a shattered wreck, reduced to rubble by an attack of German Heinkel and Dornier bombers whose main target was the nearby Harland and Wolff shipyard. Everything was destroyed - the pitch, the terracing, stands and offices - the playing kit, the players' boots and all the club's records. Belfast itself was in a state of shock due to the effects of the air raids in general and little importance was placed on the loss of the ground when compared with the loss of human life elsewhere.

However the show went on as other local clubs came quickly to Glentoran's aid. Linfield, Distillery and Crusaders offered the loan of a strip. With two of the remaining three fixtures against Distillery the Glens turned out in the Crues' red and black stripes against the Whites and then wore white against the Blues in the league game switched to Windsor Park. All three games were won ensuring we finished third in the league and retained the Shield but there was a hollowness to victory caused by the War.

Ironically Glentoran had met Dublin side St.James's Gate in a return friendly in April with the gate receipts handed over to the Belfast Air Raid Fund. Now it was the Glens themselves who faced extinction.

The season was brought to a close with Belfast Celtic losing to a League Select 3-1 in a Charity match to replace the Charity Cup competition. But for Glentoran there was a lot of sorting out to do before the resumption of football in August.

Appearances and Goals

	App.	Goals		App.	Goals		App.	Goals
Irvine	42		Young	16		Duke	2	2
Douglas	42	11	Hamilton	13		O'Boyle	2	
McMillen	38	6	Elliott	10		Crosby	1	
Grice	38	14	McCartney	9	2	Sherry	1	
Martin B.	36		Keddie	7		Corry	1	
McKennan	36	36	Martin D.	7	12	Miller	1	
Gray C.	35	1	McDermott	6		Mathieson	1	
Tizard	33		Cooper	5		Own Goals		1
Smith	32	32	Hinton	4		TOTAL	517	149
Robinson	32	15	Weir	4	2			
Lavery J.	30	13	Johnston	3	2			
Wilkin	27		Bryson	3				

1941/42

The Glens decide to carry on – A temporary home at Grosvenor Park –
Boy Martin on form

Glentoran's shareholders and directors faced a critical dilemma in the 1941 close season. Without a home ground the options to the club ranged from sharing accommodation with another Regional League club to joining the Intermediate League or resigning from football altogether for the duration of the War. The board of directors were split on a resolution passed by the shareholders that the club should consider joining the Intermediate League and at an extraordinary general meeting it took the casting vote of the chairman, Johnny Mercer, to continue in senior football. Distillery were approached for the use of Grosvenor Park for offices and home fixtures. Their chairman duly consented and so by early August the club was alive again.

It was a much reduced Gold Cup and Regional League awaiting the Glens as Portadown and Glenavon had resigned to leave only six senior clubs. After all the fuss off the field a much changed line-up faced Cliftonville in the first friendly of the season in mid-August. It read: Hinton, Mathieson, Gray, O'Boyle, Irvine, McDermott, Harris, McKennan, Sloan, Hamilton, Scattergood.

Ted Hinton.

A win was recorded despite falling behind but the following Friday we went down to St.James's Gate at Dalymount Park in a return match for the Unity Cup.

The season proper began with our first home match at Grosvenor Park in the Gold Cup with the Reds again our opponents. A moderate attendance witnessed a pleasant game and "Boy" Martin's second hat-trick in two days was the main reason for the large victory margin. A week later hosts met lodgers and we showed no amiability by winning 3-2. Peter McKennan was a class apart in this game, however he was forced to miss the next match versus Celtic due to military service. A "ding-dong" battle finished in favour of Glentoran with defenders Albert Young and Victor Aiken outstanding.

After overcoming Derry at Brandywell, the home side missing two penalties, we suffered our first defeat of the competition against the Blues. Without Elliott (ex-Wolves goalkeeper) and Young our defence was completely disorganised as we conceded five goals in the first half-hour. It was a feature of war-time football for line-ups never to be the same two weeks running as players were pressed into military duty and occasionally the final eleven was not decided until the morning of a match.

Ted Sagar (ex-Everton and England) made his debut against Cliftonville as Martin and McKennan kept knocking the goals in. The vital Gold Cup fixture was the return with Distillery at "home." We went into the match just a point ahead of the Whites and things looked bleak when Distillery went 2-0 up. However wave after wave of Glentoran attack eventually broke the Whites' rearguard and we earned a draw. A weak Belfast Celtic side were beaten seven days later and then in the penultimate series of matches Distillery lost to Celtic to leave us Gold Cup winners.

The only remaining interest in the last match against Linfield was the completion of Boy Martin's scoring in every Gold Cup fixture. However despite achieving this he was beaten to the honour of the competition's leading goalscorer by Davis of Distillery, 16 goals to 15. It was a poignant sign of the times that the Glens received no medals on winning the Gold Cup, merely congratulations on the team's performances in such difficult times. Special mention was made of the fans who gave magnificent support despite having to travel for every single game.

Before the commencement of the Regional League the committee met to discuss admission prices. The War had increased equipment costs dramatically; for example the price of a pair of boots had risen from 15/6 in 1939 to 37s while a football had gone up from 7/9 to 30s in the same period. All clubs agreed on the proposed increases from 6d to 9d for the "popular" side and 1/6 to 2s for the grandstand. At the same meeting the Glens complained that Linfield had "poached" Walter McMillen from them and he was therefore ineligible. The league secretary retorted that while no form had been received for McMillen's registration no action would be taken against Linfield. Derry City criticised the Regional League referees, suggesting that they were afraid to order players off as they may not be chosen to officiate by that man's club again. Derry proposed that referees' names should be drawn out of a hat for the match allocations.

Glentoran began the Regional League where we had left off in the Gold Cup. In the opening fixture against Linfield we raced into a 6-0 half-time lead and then knocked in another seven against hapless Derry two weeks later. However Belfast Celtic had rediscovered their winning ways and after trouncing us they emerged as the early league pacesetters, opening up a four point gap by mid-

John "Toby" Mercer.

December. Linfield gained quick revenge over us as we paid dearly for an early penalty miss by Keddie. Ted Hinton was displaying marvellous form in goals and his penalty save against Celtic on Boxing Day helped us close the gap at the top of the table to two points.

The Celtic club secretary announced an amazing tale of honesty that day. The Christmas Day Celtic-Linfield fixture produced massive receipts of £925, but had ended scoreless. However the secretary had received a postal order for 1/6 from a Linfield supporter who had obtained free entry to Celtic Park when a gate collapsed. The punter felt obliged to pay for his entertainment!

However Glentoran had arguably a more remarkable Christmas Day story to relate. The team travelled to Londonderry by train including Fields in his soldier's uniform. When the train pulled in at Strabane someone realised that the next stop came at Carrigan, which was actually on the Irish Republic side of the border. In order to avoid possible capture and internment Fields had to leave the train and attempt to make his own way to Brandywell. Fortunately he managed to flag down a car carrying two Derry supporters who managed to get him to the game twenty minutes before kick-off. Fields apparently had not eaten since seven o'clock that morning but after a quick snack was able to take his place in the side and play in the 1-1 draw!

The year of 1942 kicked-off with "the finest game at Windsor Park for a long time", according to the News Letter. The Glens trailed 1-2 at half-time but after the break Martin completed his hat-trick to put us ahead only for Pemberton to square matters via a late penalty. This result allowed Celtic to move three points clear and when Jimmy McAlinden's superb solo goal defeated us at Celtic Park in early February the gap was stretched to five and the race looked over.

Glentoran were doing remarkably well to stay in the title race as only three of our winning Gold Cup squad were still regulars. Against Cliftonville at Grosvenor Park we introduced four more players namely O'Rourke, Matthias, Chalmers and Allchorne. Indeed in the 20 Regional League games we fielded more than 35 players - compare this with 17 players used in 26 games just two seasons previously.

The Glens also progressed smoothly in the Irish Cup, which had its early rounds played on a two-legged basis for the first time ever. We were never extended in seeing off Larne in Round One and that set up an interesting clash with the Royal Irish Fusiliers. Three military teams had been invited to compete in the cup, the other two being the Royal Inniskilling Fusiliers and the Royal Irish Rifles. In the first leg the "Foughs" never looked up to senior standard and our new centre-forward from Woking, Barrie, scored twice in a 4-0 win. However a week later we needed the cushion of this lead as the Fusiliers surprisingly beat us 2-0 at Solitude in the return. One of their goals came from Scattergood, a player who had been with the Glens in the early part of the season.

Results 1941/42

Played 39. Won 24. Drew 4. Lost 11. Goals For 109. Against 72. % 66.7
Honours: Substitute Gold Cup

SGC	23/08/41		Cliftonville	GP	W	5	1	Martin 3, Aicken, McKennan
SGC	30/08/41		Distillery	A	W	3	2	McKennan 2, Martin
SGC	06/09/41		Belfast Celtic	GP	W	2	1	Martin, Fulton og
SGC	20/09/41		Derry City	A	W	3	0	McKennan 2, Martin
SGC	27/09/41		Linfield	GP	L	4	6	Martin, McKennan 2(1p), Wright
SGC	04/10/41		Cliftonville	A	W	5	3	Martin 2, McKennan 2, Wright
SGC	11/10/41		Distillery	GP	D	2	2	Martin, Jackson
SGC	18/10/41		Belfast Celtic	A	W	3	1	Martin 2, McKennan
SGC	25/10/41		Derry City	GP	W	5	4	McKennan 2, Saunders, Douglas, Martin
SGC	01/11/41		Linfield	A	W	3	1	Martin 2, Douglas
RL	08/11/41		Linfield	A	W	7	3	Martin 4, Wright, Douglas, Reid
RL	15/11/41		Distillery	GP	W	2	1	Douglas, Martin
RL	22/11/41		Derry City	GP	W	7	0	Martin 3, Wright, Keddie, McCartney, Corbett
RL	29/11/41		Belfast Celtic	A	L	0	4	-
RL	06/12/41		Cliftonville	GP	W	3	1	Keddie 2, Martin
RL	13/12/41		Linfield	GP	L	0	3	-
RL	20/12/41		Distillery	A	L	1	5	Martin
RL	25/12/41		Derry City	A	D	1	1	Martin
RL	26/12/41		Belfast Celtic	GP	W	4	1	Martin 2, Douglas, Smith
RL	27/12/41		Cliftonville	A	W	5	0	Martin 2, Douglas 2, Smith
RL	03/01/42		Linfield	A	D	3	3	Martin 3
RL	10/01/42		Distillery	GP	W	4	2	Keddie 3, Martin
RL	31/01/42		Derry City	GP	W	7	1	Martin 4, Douglas 2, Allchorne
RL	07/02/42		Belfast Celtic	A	L	1	2	Douglas
RL	14/02/42		Cliftonville	GP	W	4	1	Keddie 2, Martin 2
RL	14/03/42		Distillery	A	D	1	1	Martin (p)
RL	28/03/42		Derry City	A	W	2	0	Gorman, Carlyle og
RL	04/04/42		Belfast Celtic	GP	L	1	3	Martin (p)
RL	07/04/42		Cliftonville	A	W	3	1	Robinson, Martin 2(1p)
RL	11/04/42		Linfield	GP	L	3	4	Wright, Douglas, Keddie
IC	17/01/42	1.1	Larne	A	W	3	1	Keddie 2, Woodburn
IC	24/01/42	1.2	Larne	GP	W	2	0	Wright, Crosby
IC	21/02/42	2.1	Royal Irish Fusiliers	GP	W	4	0	Barrie 2, Wright, Gager
IC	28/02/42	2.2	Royal Irish Fusiliers	Solt	L	0	2	-
IC	21/03/42	SF	Ards	Solt	W	2	0	Barrie, Keddie
IC	18/04/42	F	Linfield	CP	L	1	3	Keddie
CAS	12/03/42	1	Belfast Celtic II	A	L	0	2	-
ICC	04/05/42	1.1	Dundalk	GP	L	1	5	Keddie
ICC	09/05/42	1.2	Dundalk	*	W	2	1	Gager 2(1p)
F	16/08/41		Cliftonville	A	W	4	1	McKennan, Scattergood, Sloan, Henderson og
F	22/08/41		St. James's Gate	A	L	3	5	Martin 3 – Unity Cup

* = played in Dublin

It was around this time that the Regional League clubs met with representatives from Dublin clubs with a view to establishing an All-Ireland Cup at the end of the season. The principle was agreed, six teams from each country would compete over two-legged ties to be played one each in Belfast and Dublin. The IFA gave formal approval for the tournament on 24th March.

A big surprise came our way in the County Antrim Shield when Celtic's 2nd XI knocked us out, Cairns getting both goals in the juniors' 2-0 win. However we made up for this with an Irish Cup semi-final success over Ards when only Hinton stood between ourselves and defeat.

Back to the Regional League and when Linfield defeated Celtic 3-0 at Celtic Park on 28th March the title was thrown back into the melting pot. Only three games remained as Celtic stood on 25 points with Linfield and Glentoran joint second on 23.

Celtic visited Grosvenor Park on Easter Saturday. It was a bad day for us as despite putting a lot of pressure on the Celts, they took the chances that came their way to triumph 3-1. In truth they had keeper Wright to thank for this victory.

Although our hopes were dashed we still had a part to play in the destination of the championship. Celtic returned to Grosvenor three days later to draw 1-1 with Distillery meaning they held a single point lead over the Blues going into the last game. We entertained Linfield in a Cup final rehearsal and despite a late rally went down 3-4. Over at Solitude Celtic held their nerve, winning 2-0 to become champions for the seventh year in a row.

The Irish Cup final the following weekend was a big disappointment to us. Glentoran, minus Dave Martin up front, missed chance after chance in the second half. Thompson put Linfield ahead after ten minutes but within 60 seconds Keddie had equalised. Five minutes later Peppitt made it 2-1 in the Windsor men's favour and ten minutes before the interval Thompson netted his second and completed the scoring.

All that was left to play for was the inaugural Inter-City Cup. Each of the six Northern teams would meet a Southern team in the first round with the six tie winners being joined by a "best loser" from each country in an open quarter-final draw. We were paired with Dundalk and Grosvenor Park witnessed a magnificent display as the Southerners tore us apart in the first leg by 5-1. Our only score was an 82nd minute consolation. Remarkably we won the return leg in Dublin, when Hinton and Gager were outstanding, but our 3-6 aggregate defeat was not quite enough to qualify as Cliftonville only went down 3-5 to Bohemians. Dundalk went on to win the trophy, pipping Shamrock Rovers 1-0 in the final in front of 20,000 at Dalymount Park.

Appearances

Name	App.	Goals	Name	App.	Goals	Name	App.	Goals
McDermott	36		Hamilton	6		McCune	1	
Douglas	36	11	Sager	5		O'Boyle	1	
Keddie	28	14	Bray	5		Morgan	1	
Wright F.	28	7	Cooper	4		Crawford	1	
Martin D.	27	44	Barrie	4	3	Chambers	1	
Gray C.	23		Wright B.	3		Kennedy	1	
Elliott	16		Crosby	3	1	Best	1	
Woodburn	16	1	Robinson	3	1	Bradford	1	
Hinton	15		Smith	3	2	O'Neill	1	
Gager	15	3	Jackson	3	1	Clewlew	1	
Aston	14		Reid	3	1	Walsh	1	
McCartney	13	1	Corbett	3	1	Dunlop	1	
Fields	13		Irvine	2		O'Rourke	1	
Hughes	11		McGowan	2		Gorman	1	1
McKennan	9	12	Harris	2		Hanford	1	
Young	8		Scattergood	2		Allchorne	1	1
Matthias	8		Bentley	1		Unknown	22	
Kirkham	7		Mitchell	1		Own Goals		2
Saunderson	0	1	Doherty	1				
Aicken	6	1				TOTAL	429	109

1942/43

Soldiers sign up - Artie Kelly's scoring feat - Death of a hero

Despite initial doubts the Regional League had operated smoothly over its two year history, with the inclusion of the Scottish and English military players giving the local game a fillip. When the fixtures for 1942/3 were drawn up on the 5th August Glentoran objected to the Linfield-Celtic match being played on Christmas Day as it gave these two clubs substantially extra gate money. The League overruled us and also forbade our planned match with St.James's Gate on 8th August, stating that it was too early for football. The game, doubling as the Unity Cup and Gate's Joe O'Reilly benefit, took place a week later and finished in a draw after Clarke had given us an early lead.

Before this though the annual practice match had resumed with the "Greens" defeating the "Stripes" 7-2. Line-ups and scorers as follows with Clancy McDermott and "Boy" Martin the outstanding players.

GREENS: Hinton, Taylor, Henderson, McDermott, Irvine, McNeilly(1), Wright(2), Radford, Martin(3), Patrick(1), Douglas.

STRIPES: Millar, Black, Simms, McKeown, Walker, Goodall, Kearney, Clarke(1), Stokes, Ferguson(1), Campbell.

Our attempt at retaining the Gold Cup floundered as frequent team changes never allowed a pattern of play to be established. Every week it was a new style line-up taking the field and although players showed individual touch and class it never really came together. One bright spot was the form of Southern Irelander Artie Kelly while McDermott continued to be the lion of the half-back line.

Glentoran's best display came undoubtedly in the win at Celtic Park when Kelly enjoyed a hat-trick against his old team-mates. Celtic gained revenge in the Grosvenor Park return when McNeilly missed a crucial second half-penalty. There was some early season silverware, though, in the form of the Unity Cup. St.James's Gate were hammered 6-2 after a goalless first half. The Glentoran players received gold medals from the Guinness Athletic Union. Meanwhile Linfield pipped Celtic by a point for the Gold Cup (after they drew 3-3 with each other in the final game) with the Glens a further nine points behind in third.

Before the Regional League commenced Glentoran were involved in another off-field dispute, this time with the IFA. The protest centred around the IFA taking a 5% levy from gate receipts for the first two rounds of the Irish Cup. The Glens did not want to pay but when threatened with expulsion from the Cup reluctantly agreed.

Our league campaign began indifferently. The opening match with Celtic was brilliant but ended in defeat when the visitors nicked the winner towards the end. Hugh Kelly had been superb in the Celtic goal. Then we inflicted Linfield's first defeat of the season with Glentoran supporters having to be escorted off the field after over exuberance in celebrating Kelly's winning goal. Hopes were high of a win over Distillery as their centre-forward Rowley, who had scored all three goals against us in the Gold Cup, had gone home on leave. However the Whites ran out winners inspired by their other English stars Drury (Arsenal) and Bennett (Spurs). Vaux (ex-Chelsea) made his Glens debut at right-back. Incidentally Rowley scored eight goals for Wolves against Derby the same day.

Artie Kelly performed the Irish individual feat of the season by scoring a double hat-trick against Cliftonville in early December. The half-time score had been only 4-3 in our favour but we pulled away netting a further five in the second period.

A 6'3" centre-half from Hearts by the name of Jimmy Dykes made his debut against Celtic a week later but was powerless to stop defeat. However by the end of the month he had become a dominating pivot to build our defence around. "Boy" Martin, now a sergeant in the Royal Ulster Rifles, returned on Christmas leave to score two against Derry City.

Results 1942/43

Played 40. Won 16. Drew 4. Lost 20. Goals For 110. Against 100. % 45.0

SGC	22/08/42		Cliftonville	GP	W	4	1	Martin, Richards, Kelly, Douglas
SGC	29/08/42		Linfield	A	L	1	6	Douglas
SGC	05/09/42		Distillery	GP	D	2	2	Martin 2
SGC	19/09/42		Belfast Celtic	A	W	4	2	Kelly 3, Roberts
SGC	26/09/42		Derry City	GP	W	4	2	Roberts 2, McNeilly (p), Dykes
SGC	03/10/42		Cliftonville	A	L	1	3	Livingstone
SGC	10/10/42		Linfield	GP	L	1	4	Roberts
SGC	17/10/42		Distillery	A	W	3	1	McNeilly, Kelly, Wright
SGC	24/10/42		Belfast Celtic	GP	L	1	2	McNeilly (p)
SGC	31/10/42		Derry City	A	L	2	4	Ferguson, Kelly
RL	07/11/42		Belfast Celtic	GP	L	3	4	Kelly 2, Bunting
RL	14/11/42		Linfield	GP	W	2	1	Josephs, Kelly
RL	21/11/42		Distillery	A	L	1	2	Kelly
RL	28/11/42		Derry City	A	L	2	4	Josephs, Kelly
RL	05/12/42		Cliftonville	GP	W	9	3	Kelly 6, Kirkham 2, Wright
RL	12/12/42		Belfast Celtic	A	L	0	3	-
RL	19/12/42		Linfield	A	L	3	4	Watson 2, Wright
RL	25/12/42		Distillery	GP	W	2	1	Kelly 2
RL	26/12/42		Derry City	GP	D	3	3	Martin 2(1p), Kelly
RL	02/01/43		Cliftonville	A	L	2	4	Douglas, Dykes
RL	09/01/43		Belfast Celtic	GP	W	2	1	Wright, McMullan og
RL	30/01/43		Linfield	GP	L	1	3	Kelly
RL	06/02/43		Distillery	A	L	2	5	Wright, Dykes (p)
RL	13/02/43		Derry City	A	W	6	2	Kelly 2, Dykes 2, Carson, McKeown
RL	06/03/43		Cliftonville	GP	W	6	2	Kelly 4, Wright, Carson
RL	13/03/43		Belfast Celtic	A	L	1	2	McKeown
RL	20/03/43		Linfield	A	L	3	5	Patrick 2, Beattie
RL	03/04/43		Distillery	GP	L	1	3	Collis
RL	10/04/43		Derry City	GP	W	3	2	Martin 2, Ferguson
RL	24/04/43		Cliftonville	A	D	2	2	McKeown, Kelly
IC	16/01/43	1.1	Bangor	A	W	3	2	Kelly 2, Douglas
IC	23/01/43	1.2	Bangor	GP	W	8	2	Kelly 2, Wright 2, Douglas 2, Watson, McKeown
IC	20/02/43	2.1	Royal Irish Fusiliers	GP	W	7	2	Kelly 3, Douglas 2, Wright, Carson
IC	27/02/43	2.2	Royal Irish Fusiliers	GP	W	8	0	Kelly 4, Watson, Douglas, McDermott, Wright
IC	27/03/43	SF	Ards	Solt	W	4	2	Kelly 2, Wright 2
IC	17/04/43	F	Belfast Celtic	WP	L	0	1	-
CAS	06/04/43	2	Belfast Celtic	A	D	2	2	Ferguson, Wright
CAS	12/04/43	2R	Belfast Celtic	GP	L	1	3	Stevenson
ICC	01/05/43	1.1	Shelbourne	A	L	0	1	-
ICC	07/05/43	1.2	Shelbourne	GP	L	0	2	-
F	10/08/42		Practice Match: Greens 7 (Martin 3, Wright 2, Patrick, McNeilly) Stripes 2 (Clark, Ferguson)					
F	15/08/42		St. James's Gate	A	D	2	2	Clarke 2 – Unity Cup Joe O'Reilly Benefit
F	11/09/42		St. James's Gate	GP	W	6	2	McNeilly 3, McAusland, Roberts, Kelly Unity Cup Replay
F	28/04/43		Linfield	GP	L	4	5	Dykes 2(2p), Kelly, Lavery Billy Ritchie Benefit
F	28/05/43		Linfield	A	L	0	1	Charity Match

After losing at Solitude we entered 1943 at fourth in the league, eight points behind joint leaders Linfield and Celtic. However we showed we were capable of competing with the best by defeating Celtic 2-1 with Dykes outstanding.

The Irish Cup provided a change of opponents and plenty of goals as we beat Bangor 11-4 and the Royal Irish Fusiliers 15-2 on aggregate in the early rounds. We even afforded the luxury of two missed penalties in the second leg against the "Foughs".

After defeats against Linfield and Distillery our league hopes became academic with many of the fixtures producing little football. Attendances became sparse and we eventually finished a miserable fourth with 16 points from the 20 games. The Blues managed to break Celtic's stranglehold on the league by a solitary point and when the final analysis was performed Linfield could possibly have looked back on their match with us at Windsor Park on 19th December as being vital. With only 20 minutes to go we led 3-1. The Blues were down to nine men with an outfield player in goals and another virtually a passenger, but still clawed back to victory inspired mainly by Cochrane and Peppitt.

There was still plenty to play for in the knockout cups, especially as we repeated our Irish Cup semi-final win of 1941/2 over Ards. The game had a 6.30 pm kick-off to avoid a clash with the other semi between Celtic (4) and Larne (2). In an attractive encounter the Glens went three up before a plucky Ards fightback, but we emerged 4-2 victors.

Belfast Celtic now presented us with a double hurdle in the Cup and County Antrim Shield, and it was one we failed to surmount on either occasion. In the Shield tie two Len Townsend goals put Celtic ahead but Ferguson pulled one back before half-time. Wright equalised in the second half to force a replay and that time it was the Glens who held the interval lead thanks to a goal from ex-Third Lanark centre-forward Stevenson. However we finished well beaten following a thrustful second half display from Celtic with only Hickman at right-back able to cope with the home attacks.

The Irish Cup final in April was described as the dullest for many years. Both sides produced very ordinary football, Hollinger getting the only goal for Celtic, as we rarely troubled Kelly in goals. At least any soldiers who attended the game in uniform only had to pay half the admission prices, which ranged from 1/- to 4/-.

Old-timer Joe Bambrick was in fine form for Linfield in Billy Ritchie's benefit game, netting four times in the Blues' 5-4 win. Around 4,000 paid tribute to the trainer's services to the club over the years. Bambrick was also on target against us in a charity game at the end of May.

The competitive season ended with an acrimonious Inter City Cup tie with Shelbourne. In the first leg in Dublin tempers became frayed late on and Glentoran players Stevenson and Wright received their marching orders. The return leg also finished in favour of the Southerners with ex-Glens keeper Tizard keeping a clean sheet in both matches. The Cup stayed in the South, Shamrock Rovers defeating Bohemians 19-9 on a corner count after both teams had won a leg by 2-0. The first game had been played in Belfast.

The IFA rejected a proposal by Belfast Celtic for football to be played on Sundays in 1943/4.

Some bad news came to the club on 14th May when our goalkeeper of 1937-39, Thomas Pearson, was killed in action in North Africa. Pearson had been awarded the Military Medal for gallant service during the War.

Appearances

For this season's appearances see page 206.

1943/44

Christmas fixture disputes – Seconds move to Wilgar Park –
All-Ireland Champions

Once again Glentoran introduced many new players at the club's annual practice match on 16th August. However on this occasion the "Reserves" defeated the "Probables" 4-2 and a week later our strength in depth was emphasised when our Seconds defeated a Linfield XI 6-2 at Wilgar Park. The scorers in this match to open the Seconds' new headquarters were Magee(2), Thompson o.g., Ferguson and Sammy Nimmick(2).

Glentoran had a reasonable Gold Cup campaign, finishing joint second with Distillery, but three points behind Celtic. Our line-up against Linfield in the first fixture of the season was: Vernon, Noonan, Cathcart, McDermott, Dykes, Creevey, Kennedy, Battersby, Nimmick, Currie, Douglas.

Vernon, Noonan and Creevey were from the south of Ireland, the latter two both ex-St.James's Gate players. Results in August and September were good, in particular two wins over Celtic and Shamrock Rovers in four days. Against Celtic we opened the game up well with long accurate passing and gave the Celts defence a gruelling time. Weir and Paddy Gregg were the most prominent players but Bertie Wright claimed the goal of the game against Shamrock when his 20 yard drive went in off the underside of the bar. We were awarded the Hannigan Cup for this win but had to settle for a share of the Unity Cup when coming from behind to draw 3-3 with St.James's Gate. Dunn could have had a hat-trick of penalties for Gate but after putting two away he blazed the third over the bar.

On the morning of 9th October four teams shared top spot in the Gold Cup table but from then on Celtic moved into overdrive, commencing with a 5-1 win over us. The Glens were left to play for second place and with wingers Kennedy and Douglas in top

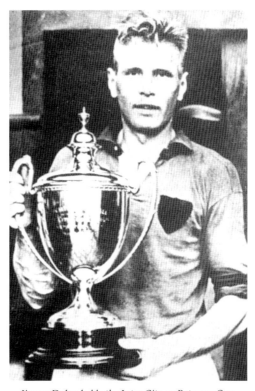

Jimmy Dykes holds the Inter City or Bateman Cup.

form we saw off Cliftonville and Derry City comfortably. Vernon saved a penalty against the Reds, but it was ex-Glens keeper Ted Hinton whose brilliant display prevented us from scoring against Distillery and claiming second place outright. In fact this was Glentoran's first scoreless draw in just under five years - a period covering 226 matches!

The issue of who would play who over Christmas threatened to turn the Regional League into a farce this season. After complaints from many other clubs over the previous two to three years the League committee ruled that Linfield and Celtic could not meet on Christmas Day - the rationale being that the massive receipts generated would give these two clubs an unfair financial advantage. Naturally Linfield and Celtic were furious and they refused to play any league fixtures until the date of the fixture was re-instated as December 25th. An Emergency committee imposed a £10 fine on each but both Celtic and

Linfield refused to pay. There was talk of Bangor and Ards replacing the two Belfast clubs or even completing the competition with only four teams. Glentoran and the other Regional League clubs were becoming agitated as the situation dragged on into early December. Eventually at a meeting of all clubs a compromise was reached whereby the Linfield-Celtic fixture would take place on Boxing Day, falling on the 27th December. (Incidentally 27,000 people attended the game.)

The two clubs showed that their month lay-off had not affected them much as we lost our next two games against them on the first two Saturdays in December. Glentoran lay at the bottom of the Regional League table despite having played more games than anyone else. Local experts agreed that our problem was the lack of two good inside forwards.

Christmas brought little cheer with defeats against Distillery and Derry but there was one bright spot when we fought back to gain a draw with the Blues on New Year's Day after being 0-2 down in 70 minutes. Banks, Bolton's full-back, had a sound debut for the Glens in this one. Things reached rock-bottom following defeats against Celtic on three successive Saturdays. In the league fixture we held them to a single goal but Banks, McDermott, Cathcart and Wright apart, it was felt that this was the worst ever side to represent Glentoran. Our Irish Cup display backed up this claim as the Celts completely overwhelmed us 16-3 on aggregate. The team lacked fight but what could be done mid-season in the middle of a war?

Changes were made against Cliftonville. Shuck replaced the unfortunate McNulty in goal and Smith (Aberdeen) and Baldwin (London Athenians) came in up front. Displays improved and morale was lifted by four successive victories featuring 17 goals for. Jimmy Dykes began to show his true form at centre-half and even found the time to score with a 25 yard shot against Derry. The only reverse for the club in February was the Seconds 0-5 defeat at Larne in the County Antrim Shield.

Our excellent mini-run came to an end at Windsor Park on 4th March, with a 4-5 defeat versus Linfield. McNulty had been knocked out in a collision with Davy Walsh but recovered to take his place in goal against Celtic a week later. Despite a grand display from him Celtic built up a 4-0 lead after 65 minutes but we refused to lie down and die, instead fighting back to reduce the final deficit to 3-5. In league games this season the Glens used six different goalkeepers.

Scot Johnny Deakin (St.Mirren) signed for the Glens and his tricky wing play was a major factor in our winning of four of the last six league games to earn a final placing of fourth. Celtic finished top of an "uncompleted" league table.

Meantime we had progressed to the final of the County Antrim Shield via successes over Cliftonville and Larne. Strongly fancied Celtic awaited us in the final but a magnificent display from Dykes and his defence prevented the Celts from scoring. At the other end Frank Neary (QPR) found the net twice in our 3-0 win. The final whistle brought scenes of wild jubilation among the Glentoran support - many unable to believe the turnaround since the Irish Cup exit. Over the next few days the team received numerous telegrams and letters of congratulation.

Following this unexpected success thoughts turned to the Inter City (Bateman) Cup. After our win in Dublin St.James's Gate sent a weak team containing seven guests to face us at Grosvenor Park. The first half was scoreless then Paddy Gregg opened the floodgates and we finally went through 7-2 on aggregate. It was much tighter in Round Two against old foes Shelbourne. Late on in the second leg the score was still level on aggregate and no further scoring meant the tie would be decided on a corner count. The Shels led 9-8 over the two legs but tremendous Glentoran pressure brought two more corners and so we sneaked through.

The chances of the cup coming North for the first time were bright as the Regional League provided three of the four semi-finalists. We were drawn against Distillery and the Whites returned from the first leg at Dalymount Park with two slender advantages, 2-1 on goals, 7-6 on corners. However only two days later Neary destroyed them on home soil, netting four times in front of a large crowd, as the Glens went through 7-3 overall. Celtic overcame Bohemians 2-1 in the other semi and there was huge public interest in the meetings of the two Belfast clubs at the end of May.

Results 1943/44

Played 44. Won 21. Drew 6. Lost 17. Goals For 105. Against 97. % 54.5.
Honours: County Antrim Shield, Inter City Cup

SGC	21/08/43		Linfield	A	L	1	3	Kennedy
SGC	28/08/43		Belfast Celtic	GP	W	1	0	Gregg
SGC	04/09/43		Cliftonville	A	W	3	1	Dykes (p), Kennedy, Gregg
SGC	18/09/43		Derry City	GP	W	6	2	Currie 3, Gregg 2, Kennedy
SGC	25/09/43		Distillery	GP	L	2	3	Gregg 2
SGC	02/10/43		Linfield	GP	D	1	1	Kennedy
SGC	09/10/43		Belfast Celtic	A	L	1	5	Gregg
SGC	16/10/43		Cliftonville	GP	W	2	0	Cathcart (p), Weir
SGC	23/10/43		Derry City	A	W	2	1	Weir, Dykes
SGC	30/10/43		Distillery	A	D	0	0	-
RL	06/11/43		Derry City	A	L	1	2	Carlyle
RL	13/11/43		Cliftonville	A	L	2	4	Gregg 2
RL	20/11/43		Distillery	GP	W	3	1	Nimmick 2, Dykes
RL	04/12/43		Linfield	A	L	1	4	Wright
RL	11/12/43		Belfast Celtic	A	L	1	3	Dykes (p)
RL	18/12/43		Cliftonville	GP	A	1	2	Weir – Abandoned at half-time
RL	25/12/43		Distillery	A	L	1	3	Douglas
RL	27/12/43		Derry City	A	L	2	4	Nimmick, Wright
RL	01/01/44		Linfield	GP	D	2	2	Gregg 2
RL	08/01/44		Belfast Celtic	GP	L	0	1	-
RL	29/01/44		Cliftonville	A	W	5	3	Gregg 3, Bailey, Wright
RL	05/02/44		Distillery	GP	W	3	1	Gregg, Neary 2
RL	12/02/44		Derry City	GP	W	5	0	Neary 2, Gregg, Dykes, Baldwin
RL	04/03/44		Linfield	A	L	4	5	Gregg 2, McDermott, Nimmick
RL	11/03/44		Belfast Celtic	A	L	3	5	Nimmick, Ramscar, McMillan og
RL	18/03/44		Cliftonville	GP	W	3	1	Neary 2, Gregg
RL	28/03/44		Belfast Celtic	GP	L	0	1	-
RL	01/04/44		Distillery	A	W	4	2	Neary 2, Ramscar, Nimmick
RL	08/04/44		Derry City	GP	W	5	4	Frost 2, Deakin, Mackin, Ross og
RL	11/04/44		Linfield	GP	L	1	3	Wright
RL	15/04/44		Cliftonville	GP	W	3	1	Gregg, Deakin, Wright
IC	15/01/44	1.1	Belfast Celtic	GP	L	1	7	Gregg
IC	22/01/44	1.2	Belfast Celtic	A	L	2	9	Gregg 2
CAS	26/02/44	1	Ballyclare Comrades	A	W	4	2	Gregg 2, Neary, Wright
CAS	04/04/44	2	Cliftonville	GP	W	2	1	Gregg 2
CAS	19/04/44	SF	Larne	Solt	W	4	1	Gregg 3, Frost
CAS	02/05/44	F	Belfast Celtic	Solt	W	3	0	Tyrie, Neary 2
ICC	28/04/44	1.1	St. James's Gate	DP	W	2	1	Gregg, McAuley
ICC	08/05/44	1.2	St. James's Gate	GP	W	5	1	Gregg 3, Dykes (p), Frost
ICC	15/05/44	2.1	Shelbourne	GP	D	2	2	Deakin, Mackin
ICC	20/05/44	2.2	Shelbourne	A	D	0	0	Won 10-9 on corners
ICC	22/05/44	SF.1	Distillery	DP	L	1	2	Gregg
ICC	24/05/44	SF.2	Distillery	GP	W	6	1	Neary 4, Gregg, Deakin
ICC	27/05/44	F.1	Belfast Celtic	WP	D	3	3	Neary 2(1p), Deakin
ICC	29/05/44	F.2	Belfast Celtic	DP	W	2	1	McIlroy, Bradford
F	16/08/43		Practice Match: Probables 2 Reserves 4					
F	25/08/43		Shamrock Rovers	GP	W	7	1	Weir 2, Douglas 2, Wright, Collins og, McDermott Hannigan Cup
F	10/09/43		St. James's Gate	A	D	3	3	Weir, Dykes, Graham Unity Cup

Windsor Park was the first venue and an exciting game finished 3-3. Again Neary was a continual threat to Celtic, Deakin stamped his class and our backs Tyrie and Lavery were sound. However we faced a major political problem for the second leg in Dublin two days later, our fifth game in the competition in ten days and the eleventh of the season versus Celtic. Because Deakin, Neary, Ramscar and Mackin were regulars in the British Army they were forbidden to travel to the Irish Free State. Replacements had to be found at short notice and Jimmy Todd (Ards), Syd McIlroy (Ballymena) and Billy Bradford (Bangor) were signed for the game. Celtic were again hot favourites but the Glens sprung another surprise. Goals from McIlroy in the 19th minute and Bradford, a header in the 79th, put us 2-0 up and Celtic could only muster a late consolation from O'Neill. Jimmy Dykes had been the best player on the field and had the honour of receiving the Bateman Cup.

At a joyous annual meeting three days later praise was heaped on the players for their recent displays and a profit of £509 for the season was announced.

Appearances and Goals

	App.	Goals		App.	Goals		App.	Goals
Wright B.	37	6	Mackin	11	2	Mahon	2	
Gregg	37	36	Noonan	10		Todd	1	
Dykes J.	35	6	Neary	9	17	Battersby	1	
Douglas	34	1	Deakin	9	5	McIlroy S.	1	1
Vernon	30		McNulty	7		Bradford	1	1
Lavery T.	23		Beattie	7		Graham	1	
McDermott	23	1	Currie	7	3	Greer	1	
Nimmick	23	6	Smith	5		Robinson	1	
Cathcart	21	1	Banks	3		Shuck	1	
Tyrie	20	1	Frost	3	4	Potter	1	
Creevey	17		Taylor	2		Bailey	1	1
Carlyle	15	1	Gooddall	2		McComish	1	
Ramscar	15	2	McAuley	2	1	Davison	1	
Doherty K.	12		Cowley	2		Unknown	22	
Weir	12	2	Hill	2		Own Goals		2
Kennedy	11	4	Baldwin	2	1	TOTAL	484	105

Appearances and Goals 1942/43 Season

	App.	Goals		App.	Goals		App.	Goals
Douglas	39	9	Martin D.	7	7	Weir	2	
Kelly	36	41	Bray	7		Hayden	1	
McDermott	33	1	Josephs	7	2	Aston	1	
Wright B.	32	13	Roberts	6	4	Clark	1	
Henderson	28		Hickman	6		Irvine	1	
Dykes J.	26	5	Grant	6		Atkinson	1	
Watson	24	4	Bunting	5	1	Livingstone	1	1
Beale	24		Carson	5	3	Drain	1	
Kirkham	18	2	Wright S.	4		Sherry	1	
Marriott	15		Ferguson	4	3	Dykes F.	1	
McKeown	14	4	Richards	3	1	McConell	1	
Vaux	13		Stewart	3		Collis	1	1
Beattie	11	1	Patrick	3	2	Milligan	1	
Hinton	10		Meek	3		Own Goals		1
McNeilly	10	3	Radford	2		TOTAL	440	110
Hill	10		Croxen	2				
Stevenson	8	1	McCurry	2				

1944/45

Back to the Oval plans – Heavy defeats to Linfield –
A poor pre-Christmas run

As World War II began to draw to a close Glentoran reported back for the new season with virtually the same playing panel that had finished 1943/4. Off the field it was a time where real feeling for going back to the Oval became obvious. New offices were secured on the Albertbridge Road and an official "Back to the Oval Committee" was set up in February 1945.

Firstly though it was the Glens' turn to help a couple of other causes. The season opened up with a benefit match for Norman Rae, who had broken his leg a year ago, and on 11th August an Old Glentoran XI beat an Old Linfield XI 4-1 at Windsor Park. Fred Roberts(2), Geary and Jordan scored for the Old Glens with Joe Bambrick replying. Then, on a Monday night, we marked Dundela's re-entrance to the Intermediate League with a friendly at Wilgar Park. It resulted in a comfortable 7-4 win although we had twice been behind and Dykes missed a penalty.

The first half of the Gold Cup was reasonably satisfactory for us. Johnny Lavery had come back to the side after a spell with Dundalk but Frank Neary had to return home to England. Easy wins were recorded over Derry and Cliftonville and hard earned points obtained from Distillery and Celtic. Against the Whites Jimmy Dykes had to play most of the game in goals after young reserve keeper McKinstry was concussed.

Then everything went disastrously wrong. We were completely routed 7-0 at Windsor Park but managed a narrow win over Derry with debutant Allder from Tranmere netting twice. As fans left Grosvenor Park that evening little did they know what lay ahead - the worst run in the club's history, eleven successive defeats! The forward line seemed unable to play as a combination with the result that the opposition half-backs were able to get upfield and add to their attack.

Things went from bad to worse as the Regional League commenced in November. Even the mediocre Derry and Cliftonville outfits recorded easy 4-0 wins over Glentoran. Outside-right Danny Williamson broke his leg in the latter.

Sammy Nimmick.

Deakin tried hard but only two goals came in a six match spell, both from Paddy Gregg. A Limerick player, O'Mahoney, was tried in defence but it made no difference. The run continued at Windsor where the Blues hammered us 9-2, meaning they had scored 30 goals in our five meetings to date this season.

Christmas cheer came with 6-2 home wins over Derry and Cliftonville on successive days. Some form had at last been found, with new players Robinson, McIlvenney and Pickering taking a lot of credit. We got off the bottom of the league after beating Distillery in our first match of 1945, but then suffered two narrow defeats against the Blues and Derry City. Gilmore at left-back had a fine game in the former as he totally subdued Davy Cochrane.

The Irish Cup was a welcome relief from the league struggle and we drew Larne in Round Three with revenge in mind. The men from Legion Park had dismissed Glentoran II 10-4 on aggregate (6-0, 4-4) in the previous round. In the away leg we were always the more polished side after Wright's long lob had put us ahead but Larne fought tigerishly at

Results 1944/45

Played 39. Won 15. Drew 3. Lost 21. Goals for 97. Against 115. % 42.3

SGC	19/08/44		Linfield	GP	L	0	4	-
SGC	26/08/44		Derry City	A	W	5	2	Neary 3, Mackin, Lavery
SGC	02/09/44		Distillery	GP	D	2	2	Mackin, Lavery
SGC	16/09/44		Belfast Celtic	A	D	2	2	Gregg, Lavery
SGC	23/09/44		Cliftonville	GP	W	6	1	Gregg 3, Dykes, Lavery, McIlroy
SGC	30/09/44		Linfield	A	L	0	7	-
SGC	07/10/44		Derry City	GP	W	4	3	Allder 2, Dykes, Gregg
SGC	14/10/44		Distillery	A	L	2	3	Douglas, Mackin
SGC	21/10/44		Belfast Celtic	GP	L	0	1	-
SGC	28/10/44		Cliftonville	A	L	0	4	-
RL	04/11/44		Belfast Celtic	GP	L	1	2	Gregg
RL	11/11/44		Distillery	A	L	0	5	-
RL	18/11/44		Linfield	GP	L	1	5	Gregg
RL	25/11/44		Derry City	A	L	0	4	-
RL	02/12/44		Cliftonville	A	L	1	2	Wright
RL	09/12/44		Belfast Celtic	A	L	3	7	Mullen, Wright (p), Lavery
RL	16/12/44		Distillery	GP	L	3	4	Mackay, Wright, Lavery
RL	23/12/44		Linfield	A	L	2	9	Lavery, Wright (p)
RL	25/12/44		Derry City	GP	W	6	2	Nimmick 2, McComish, Lavery, Deakin, Wright
RL	26/12/44		Cliftonville	GP	W	6	2	Lavery 3, McIlvenney 2, Deakin
RL	30/12/44		Belfast Celtic	GP	L	1	2	Lavery
RL	06/01/45		Distillery	A	W	5	3	Deakin 3, Nimmick 2
RL	13/01/45		Linfield	GP	L	1	2	Sterling
RL	03/02/45		Derry City	A	L	1	2	Nimmick
RL	24/02/45		Cliftonville	A	W	3	2	Robinson 3
RL	03/03/45		Belfast Celtic	A	L	1	4	Lavery
RL	10/03/45		Distillery	GP	W	2	1	Langton 2
RL	31/03/45		Linfield	A	D	3	3	Hill, Nimmick, Lavery
RL	03/04/45		Derry City	GP	W	6	3	Sterling 2, Redpath, Wright 2, Nimmick
RL	07/04/45		Cliftonville	GP	W	9	3	Nimmick 4, Deakin 2, Wright 2, Hill
IC	10/02/45	3.1	Larne	A	W	4	3	Wright, Lavery, McIlvenney, Deakin
IC	17/02/45	3.2	Larne	GP	W	5	3	Wright 2, Deakin, Sterling, Nimmick
IC	24/03/45	SF	Distillery	CP	W	3	0	Hill, Deakin, McIlvenney
IC	14/04/45	F	Linfield	CP	L	2	4	Hill, McIlvenney
CAS	13/03/45	1	Belfast Celtic	A	L	1	3	Houston
ICC	28/04/45	1.1	Limerick	GP	W	2	1	Sterling 2
ICC	30/04/45	1.2	Limerick	*	L	1	2	Wright. Lost 8-12 on corners but qualified as best losers
ICC	12/05/45	2.1	Bohemians	GP	W	1	0	Robinson
ICC	19/05/45	2.2	Bohemians	DP	L	2	3	Lavery 2. Lost 9-10 on corners
F	21/08/44		Dundela	A	W	7	4	Deakin 4(1p), McAuley og, Cunningham, Mackin
F	13/09/44		Linfield	GP	L	3	5	Mackin 2, Nimmick. Arthur Douglas Benefit
F	17/03/44		Linfield	A	L	2	4	Langton 2 (1p). Norman Rae Benefit

* = played in Dublin

Grosvenor Park and it was anybody's tie up until fifteen minutes from the end.

Back to the league and despite being on top for a while against Celtic we could not break down their defence enough. The main reason was their big pivot Jackie Vernon who controlled the game by breaking up opponent's attacks and setting Celtic off on forays of their own. He repeated this domination later in the month, knocking us out of the County Antrim Shield. However in between these two games Glentoran had secured a new outside-left, Bobby Langton of Blackburn Rovers. Over 12,000 attended Langton's debut against Distillery when Peter Doherty also put in a re-appearance for the Glens. Langton's two goals were enough to give us victory, although there was some reliance on Black's missed penalty for the Whites.

Langton was again a thorn in Distillery's side in the Irish Cup semi-final. He set up our first two goals with corners as we gave our best display in weeks to win 3-0. Linfield were to be our final opponents and we indicated that we would be no pushover by drawing 3-3 with the Blues in the League a fortnight before the big game.

Admission to the final was 2/- (Reserved) and 1/- (Unreserved) and before kick-off the band played "The Star Spangled Banner" and "God Save the King." Between anthems a two minute silenced was observed to mark the death on the Thursday of American president Franklin Roosevelt. The game itself was a disappointment, never reaching a high standard. Linfield went ahead but Hill equalised on 10 minutes. By half-time the Blues were 3-1 up but excellent work by Langton allowed McIlvenney to pull one back. The Glens applied late pressure but with the last kick of the match Cochrane made it 4-2 as 20,000 people saw the Blues add the Irish Cup to the League and Gold Cup.

We had finished the Regional League on a high, stuffing Cliftonville 9-3 after being 0-2 down on 18 minutes, and now looked forward to defending the Inter City Cup. The opening tie against Limerick in front of 6,000 at Grosvenor Park was another dull and unimpressive affair but at least we took a 2-1 lead to Dublin. The scoreline was reversed in the second leg and a corner count of 12-8 to Limerick allowed them to progress. Glentoran also went through as the best Northern losers but we again fell foul of the corner count against Bohemians. The margin was 10-9 in favour of the Dubliners after a great battle. Goalkeeper Vernon had been a hero for the Glens in the second leg but was wound up concussed in hospital when the Bohs scored their third and decisive goal in the 83rd minute. Vernon had been taken off with 28 minutes to go. Bohemians went on to win the Bateman Cup, beating Celtic 3-2 in the final in early June.

At the end of May the new Oval construction plans were announced. It was envisaged that the revamped ground would be capable of accommodating between 60-70,000 spectators with a two tier stand on the reserved side and unreserved covering for 12,000. The club gymnasium, offices and buffet rooms would be under the main stand. Cost estimates for the work were put at £45,000.

Appearances and Goals

	App.	Goals		App.	Goals		App.	Goals
Nimmick	35	12	Mullen	9	1	Mackay	2	1
Wright B.	33	13	Sterling	8	6	Pinnington	1	
McIlroy W.	32	1	Douglas	6	1	Houston	1	1
Vernon	27		Langton	6	2	Sutcliffe	1	
Deakin	26	10	Pickering	6		Cunningham	1	
McDermott	24		O'Mahoney	5		Girvan	1	
Lavery J.	24	17	Hill	5	4	Steele	1	
Dykes J.	19	2	Neill B.	4		Reddick	1	
Gilmore	18		McKinstry	3		McBurney	1	
Lavery T.	15		Redpath	3	1	Watson	1	
Robinson	15	4	Neary	2	3	Doherty P.	1	
McIllvenney	15	5	Allder	2	2	Lavery W.	1	
Gregg	13	7	McNee	2		Unknown	33	
Tyrie	11		McComish	2	1	TOTAL	429	97
Mackin	11	3	Jukes	2				

1945/46

Normality returns – Frank Thompson appointed manager –
Blanchflower emerges

With the surrender of the Japanese in August 1945 the Second World War ended and "peace-time soccer" resumed. It was decided to continue with the six team Regional League but most clubs' guest players had returned cross-channel. Glentoran's playing panel at the start of the season read (the ex-club is given in brackets):

Goalkeepers: G.Matier (Blackburn), C.W.Moore, Clark (Scotts).

Backs: M.Connor (Shanklin YM), W.S.McIlroy, J.Gilmore, B.Neill, H.Morrow.

Half-Backs: G.McNally (Linfield), W.Kilpatrick (Victoria Works), F.Lunn (Carrick Rangers), J.Robinson, S.Nimmick.

Forwards: J.P.Williamson (Cliftonville), J.Lavery, J.Deakin, R.Langton, W.L.Bingham, A.Corry (Derry).

The squad suffered a mixed start to the season. Despite sound defensive play we lost our opening Gold Cup tie to Celtic and two days later went down 1-2 to Dundela in a friendly. Sammy Nimmick's hat-trick gained a victory over Distillery but we failed to win any of the next four matches despite thrilling games with Linfield and Celtic at Grosvenor Park. The Blues game was attended by 12,000 when Langton had a roaring first half capped by a great left foot shot past Tommy Breen for his goal. But we fell away in the second half and Linfield triumphed 3-1.

Four of our players, Deakin, Langton, Matier and Robinson, were involved in the showpiece game between the Irish League and the Combined Services in September. The local XI won 1-0.

October brought better things with victories over Distillery and Linfield. Nineteen year-old Cecil Moore was brilliant in goals in both these games and gained the distinction of becoming the first goalkeeper of the season to stop Linfield scoring. His miraculous antics between the sticks brought applause not only from spectators but also from bemused opposition forwards! To round off the Gold Cup we suffered a shock defeat against Cliftonville. Outside left Williamson broke his ankle in this game and retired when we were 2-0 up. Third place in the Cup had been assured previously as we finished eight points behind Celtic.

Before starting league matters the futures of our cross-channel players had to be resolved. Johnny Deakin wanted to remain in Belfast after demobilisation and was attempting to gain employment as a P.E.Teacher. Talks between the Glens and St.Mirren were in motion regarding a transfer fee. Gerry Matier got fixed up with a job and continued his battle with Moore for the goalie's jersey.

A battle of a different kind could describe the opening Regional League encounter at Celtic Park. A competitive first half was nearing a close when Celtic, already leading 2-0, were awarded a penalty. Immediately half-a-dozen fist fights broke out with nearly all the players involved in a free for all. The penalty was missed but at half-time District Inspector Murphy and Belfast's Head Constable visited both dressing rooms and warned the players for a breach of the peace. This coupled with advice from directors of both clubs calmed the situation and there was no further trouble. Glentoran fought back to draw as Deakin and Langton often split open the Celtic defence.

Results for the rest of November were somewhat inconsistent. For example against Derry City we came back from an interval deficit to win 9-2, only Langton's poor penalty miss preventing us from reaching double figures. Then we were outclassed by both Distillery and Linfield, in particular the latter when the Blues' young forward line ran us ragged.

The directors appointed Frank Thompson as manager in December but the team had hit a bad patch and in a six match spell only three points were gained. Our league hopes were over at the half-way stage and Thompson attempted to strengthen the side in early 1946 with two Scottish players, Robertson (outside-right from Clyde) and Logan (full-back of Hibernian).

Despite seeing 15 goals in our first two games of the new year the fans were being treated to some featureless fayre and another rut had set in. This was confirmed by our disastrous Irish Cup exit at the hands of Belfast Celtic 2nd XI. We took a slim 3-2 lead into the second leg and by half-time found ourselves 0-3 down. The second half was played at a tremendous pace and soon Robinson and Currie (of Celtic II) were ordered off following a fracas. Bertie Wright pulled one back but two late goals saw the juniors through on a 7-4 aggregate.

Robertson and Logan, along with Clark (ex-Stockport), eventually made their debuts against Linfield on 9th February - a week after 53,000 had attended the Victory

Results 1945/46

Played 37. Won 11. Drew 8. Lost 18. Goals For 79. Against 100. % 40.5

SGC	18/08/45		Belfast Celtic	A	L	1	2	Nimmick
SGC	25/08/45		Derry City	GP	W	4	2	Nimmick 3, Deakin
SGC	01/09/45		Distillery	A	D	0	0	-
SGC	08/09/45		Linfield	GP	L	1	3	Langton
SGC	22/09/45		Cliftonville	A	D	2	2	Lavery 2
SGC	29/09/45		Belfast Celtic	GP	L	3	5	Deakin, Langton, Campbell
SGC	06/10/45		Derry City	A	W	3	2	Langton, Williamson 2
SGC	13/10/45		Distillery	GP	W	2	1	Langton, Lavery
SGC	20/10/45		Linfield	A	W	3	0	Lavery 2, Williamson
SGC	27/10/45		Cliftonville	GP	L	3	4	Dunwoody, Deakin, Lavery
RL	03/11/45		Belfast Celtic	A	D	2	2	Lavery 2
RL	10/11/45		Derry City	GP	W	9	2	Wright 3, Lavery 2, Langton 2, Campbell 2
RL	17/11/45		Distillery	A	L	1	4	Dunwoody
RL	24/11/45		Linfield	GP	L	1	7	Lavery
RL	01/12/45		Cliftonville	A	W	3	2	Lavery 3
RL	08/12/45		Belfast Celtic	GP	D	2	2	Campbell, O'Reilly
RL	15/12/45		Derry City	A	L	3	4	Lavery, Neill, Lunn
RL	22/12/45		Distillery	GP	D	2	2	Campbell, Neill (p)
RL	25/12/45		Linfield	A	L	2	4	Neill (p), Langton
RL	26/12/45		Cliftonville	GP	D	1	1	Langton
RL	29/12/45		Belfast Celtic	A	L	1	3	Langton
RL	05/01/46		Derry City	GP	W	5	4	Campbell 4, Neill
RL	12/01/46		Distillery	A	D	3	3	Langton, Deakin, Lavery
RL	09/02/46		Linfield	GP	L	0	3	-
RL	02/03/46		Cliftonville	A	D	1	1	Roberts
RL	09/03/46		Belfast Celtic	GP	L	2	5	Lavery, Clark
RL	16/03/46		Derry City	A	W	2	1	Lavery, Waters
RL	30/03/46		Cliftonville	GP	W	5	0	Crossan 2, Nimmick, Waters, Serjeant
RL	06/04/46		Linfield	A	L	0	5	-
RL	20/04/46		Distillery	GP	L	1	3	Blanchflower
IC	19/01/46	1.1	Belfast Celtic II	GP	W	3	2	Campbell, Lavery, Deakin
IC	26/01/46	1.2	Belfast Celtic II	A	L	1	5	Wright
CAS	13/03/46	1	Distillery	A	L	0	5	-
ICC	08/05/46	1.1	Bohemians	DP	L	0	1	-
ICC	11/05/46	1.2	Bohemians	GP	W	3	1	Deakin, Lavery 2
ICC	18/05/46	2.1	Shamrock Rovers	DP	L	1	3	Robinson
ICC	22/05/46	2.2	Shamrock Rovers	GP	L	3	4	Blanchflower 2, Deakin
F	20/08/45		Dundela	A	L	1	2	Deakin

International between Ireland and Scotland at Windsor Park. Linfield again proved too strong despite the valiance of Cecil Moore.

The Glens then had two free Saturdays due to our early Cup exit and during this period Thompson signed up three more players - Watters (Bohemians), Hilton (Arbroath) and Sloan (centre-half of Dundee). Still the poor form continued with a draw against the Reds and five goal defeats against Celtic (after Lavery had put us ahead on 12 minutes) and Distillery (in the Shield). Incidentally all five of the Whites' goals were headers.

Joy at last came at the end of March with Regional League wins over Derry and Cliftonville and it was reported that we could have run up double figures in the latter. However the residualness of that display was shown up the following Saturday when Linfield gave us a similar dose as our defence was frequently caught in tangles. The final league match of the campaign had an end of season feel to it but it was notable for the display of our young half-back Danny Blanchflower. One local analyst prophesised, "Although slow at times Blanchflower showed a lot of promise for the future." Linfield won the league with the Glens languishing back in fourth position.

Our Inter-City Cup hopes were not high especially once we were paired with holders Bohemians in Round One. However a brave display at Grosvenor Park in the first leg enabled us to take a two goal lead to Dublin. We played splendid football down there but just lacked the punch up front to score. Bohemians managed only one and ironically that was enough to send both teams into the quarter-finals, Glens as 3-2 aggregate winners and Bohs as best Southern losers. Moore's penalty save in the first leg suddenly became irrelevant.

Shamrock Rovers were a different kettle of fish in Round Two but we only had ourselves to blame for the aggregate defeat. Moore let in a very soft goal in Dublin and in the return leg Deakin missed a penalty and Lavery a sitter. The Glentoran team also received a lecture in the middle of the pitch from the referee after he had turned down frantic claims for another penalty.

During the year the "Back to the Oval" campaign had continued but the club itself reported a small loss of £24 on the season. Income included £7,205 for 1st XI games and £702 for the Seconds' fixtures plus £321 in season ticket sales. The major outgoings were players' wages at £1,785 with signing fees totalling £2,175. A motion to reduce the size of the board from twelve to five was ruled "out of order".

Appearances and Goals

	App.	Goals		App.	Goals		App.	Goals
Gilmore	34		Watters	10	2	Clark	3	1
Lavery J.	30	21	McDermott	8		Mills	3	
Deakin	28	7	Williamson	8	3	Burt	2	
Wright B.	26	4	Dunwoody	7	2	Morgan	2	
Nimmick	25	5	Kilpatrick	6		Serjeant	2	1
Robinson	25	1	Blanchflower	6	3	McIntyre	1	
Moore	23		Robertson	5	1	Greer	1	
McIlroy W.	22		O'Reilly	5	1	Adams	1	
Neill B.	18	4	Glaister	4		Mackin	1	
Campbell	17	10	Hilton	4		Bartlett	1	
Langton	16	10	Logan	4		Tolan	1	
Matier	13		Crossan	4	2	Kelly	1	
Lunn	13	1	Kearney	3		Unknown	11	
Sloan	10		Mulholland	3		TOTAL	407	79

1946/47

Our heaviest ever defeat, then revenge – A penalty jinx – Big crowds return

This was the last season of the Regional League structure and Coleraine and Ballymena United were brought into the set-up to provide more variation. However the re-formed provincial teams would not compete in the Inter-City Cup.

The Back to the Oval Committee made a £1,000 donation to the board on 15th August. Chairman Johnny Mercer remarked that although the ground was still under water it was hoped to play 2nd XI matches there next season with the firsts returning for 1948/9.

Glentoran's playing panel had been strengthened by the arrival of three more Southern Irish players, Noel Kelly (ex-Shamrock Rovers) and, from Drumcondra, Con Martin and Jimmy Lawlor. Manager Frank Thompson and secretary Sandy Chambers signed up these players for nothing under a "no fee" arrangement in existence between clubs on either side of the Irish divide. The move looked a good one as the Glens started the Gold Cup in fine style winning six of the first seven matches including an opening day home win over Belfast Celtic.

Crowds were flocking to the games, there were 20,000 at Windsor for the Linfield match. Against Distillery we went 3-0 up early on, missed a penalty (Ben Neill), hit the woodwork three times and then watched the Whites pull back to 3-3! Tommy McCormick eventually got our winner.

The defence tightened up after this with Shaw solid at right-back and Cecil Moore displaying international form in goals. Our penalty troubles were continuing though, Paddy Watters missing one against Cliftonville and Con Martin versus Ballymena after the ref had ordered a retake.

So we began our return meeting with Celtic on 10th September, holding a one point lead over the Celts at the head of the Gold Cup table. But what a shock awaited us as a fast moving Celtic side inflicted the worst defeat in the club's history, 9-0! The Glens were totally swamped as we had no answer to the teamwork of Celtic. For the record the line-up was:

Moore, Shaw, Neill, Nimmick, Martin, Watters, O'Reilly, Kelly, McCormick, Lawlor, Lavery.

Not surprisingly this experience knocked the stuffing out of the side and the following three games were also lost. Even at home to Coleraine we threw away a two goal lead, McDowell getting a hat-trick for the newcomers. Billy Bradford, who had played for us in the 1944 Inter-City Cup, was signed from Bangor and marked his debut against Cliftonville with a hat-trick.

By the time we entertained Ballymena in the final Gold Cup fixture Celtic had already won the trophy but the match was probably the most incident packed of the tournament. After only five minutes the ball burst and three minutes later McCormick had his penalty saved by Redmond. However Tommy made up for this with a hat-trick but in between Martin drove another penalty against the crossbar. The action continued in the last 15 minutes with the Glens 3-1 up. Ballymena were awarded a penalty but "Tiger" McKee, who had replaced Moore in goals, saved Nelson's effort. Then Lavery scored and appeared to have wrapped the game up for us but the referee was surrounded by six Ballymena players and after a two minute consultation the "goal" was chalked off. There was no further scoring and we thus pipped the Braidmen to third place in the Gold Cup. Cliftonville brought up the rear losing all of their fourteen matches.

Following the Celtic Park humiliation the team had steadied itself in time for the commencement of the last ever Regional League, now extended to 28 matches. Ironically Ballymena were our first opponents but the ding-dong antics of the previous week failed to materialise and a tenacious game finished all-square. Revenge was sweet seven days later when we defeated Celtic 4-2 at Grosvenor Park. Con Martin was a star at centre-half and Danny Blanchflower, brought back into the team at right-half, dictated the midfield matters. At one stage we had led 3-0 but the fans were just happy to see that 9-0 hammering laid to rest.

We suffered disappointment against Distillery, going down to an 88th minute winner (McIlhenney overhead kick) but then showed real character to beat Derry after being three goals behind in the first half-hour. Linfield were still a difficult nut to crack and on a heavy Windsor pitch they overcame us 4-2.

The Glens' half-back line soon caught on to the muddy pitches as the team adopted a policy of playing the ball to the wings, O'Reilly and Lavery. This worked well as eleven goals came in the next two games but Celtic stopped this run on Christmas Day. But 1946 concluded with another two wins and the Regional League table read as follows after eleven games:

1. Belfast Celtic 19 pts, 2. Glentoran 15 pts, 3. Linfield 12 pts.

Con Martin was transferred to Leeds United for £8,000 as we enjoyed a rout of the Reds to kick-off 1947. At half-time the scoreline was 6-0 in our favour and after 80 minutes we had extended this to 9-1 before the sorry Solitude side netted two late consolations. Martin's organisational skills were missed a week later as we trailed 0-4 to the Blues before staging a mini-comeback. A 20 year-old centre forward named Sammy Hughes scored a hat-trick for Linfield but more of him later! Meantime Celtic beat Derry 8-1 to open up a six point lead on us.

Glentoran began a marathon Irish Cup campaign up north at Ballymoney on 18th January. We were always the better team in the first leg but needed two goals in the last eight minutes to really prove it. An 11-3 aggregate win was duly completed in Belfast a week later with Tommy McCormick getting another hat-trick. Two mid-week away wins at Coleraine and Ballymena had set us up nicely for our third league meeting with Celtic. A splendid display by the Glens put the race back into the melting pot as Celtic were humbled 3-0. A young Portadown youth, Tommy Hughes, was impressive at centre-half while Blanchflower fed the forward line well and we even managed to score a penalty through Ben Neill. The rest of February was given over to meeting the double challenge of Distillery in league and cup.

The Whites drew first blood in the Regional League at an icy Grosvenor Park. Neill scored our only goal from the penalty spot but then he missed a vital spot-kick a week later in the second round (first leg) of the Irish Cup. Our half-backs Blanchflower and Len Kane were strangely off-colour and Distillery were disappointed only to have won 1-0.

A huge crowd turned up for the second leg the following Saturday to see if the Glens could turn things round. The Grosvenor Park pitch had been covered in sand, to prevent it freezing, producing a tricky surface. McCormick mastered it though, and forced Whites' keeper Smyth into many saves. The goal eventually came courtesy of an o.g. by Molloy and so we forced a replay, scheduled for the following Wednesday. However the pitch could not stand up to another game so quickly and it was delayed by a week.

In the interim we visited Windsor Park and came away with a fine win. A squad of forty men had swept the snow off the surface before kick-off but the players still slithered around during the game. Fans from rival teams enjoyed a massive snowball fight during the half-time interval. Glens peppered the Linfield defence after the break with Tommy Hughes netting the goal of the game after dribbling past three defenders. When the final whistle blew the score stood at 3-2 to us but 17 more years would pass before Glentoran defeated Linfield in a competitive match at Windsor again.

Two days later the Distillery cup saga resumed. There was more drama as the 90 minutes drew to a close with the score locked at 1-1. The Whites had the ball in the net but the referee ruled that he had blown for full-time before it had crossed the line. The official was surrounded by protesting players and booed by Distillery supporters but extra-time eventually begun. McCormick became the Glens hero with the winner and brought great relief to Ben Neill as he had missed another penalty. We deserved to go through on sheer pressure alone as we had forced eleven corners to the Whites' two.

There was great interest in the run-in to the Regional League. Thankfully two of our games were postponed due to the snow in March and on Easter Tuesday we completed a run of eight wins in a row including qualification for the semi-final of the County Antrim Shield. The most notable of these was our third league win of the season over Celtic, our first at Celtic Park since 1942. Noel Kelly was our two goal hero after Bonnar (Celtic) and O'Reilly had been sent off. So, with only five league games to go we trailed Belfast Celtic by two points but had a game in hand. However the crowded fixture list was then to catch up on us.

Prior to the Irish Cup semi-final versus Ballymena the governing bodies had extended the season to 14th June to cope with the volume of the outstanding fixtures. That game kicked off at 6 pm to avoid a clash with the Linfield (0) - Celtic (1) semi in the afternoon. The crowd of 14,000 braved heavy rain to watch a dour battle finish 1-1. The penalty jinx struck yet again as Neill hit his spot-kick against the post, but in the replay (watched by 16,000) he converted a penalty for the Glens' only goal. Again it finished 1-1 and the second replay was fixed for the Monday after our vital league game with the Blues at Windsor Park.

The team were taking part in their eighth "big" game inside three weeks and many players appeared jaded. Linfield won 2-1 and we really had to lift it for the cup replay. But lift it we did as a "first-time" approach was adopted to knock Ballymena both out of their stride and the cup. Blanchflower was excellent.

Five days later it was off to Coleraine where victory was required to keep the league alive. However defences came out on top and a scoreless draw allowed Celtic (2-1 winners at Cliftonville) to lift the championship.

Now it was down to Glentoran versus Belfast Celtic in the Irish Cup final. Over 25,000 flocked to Windsor Park to watch the Glens create chance after chance but miss them all. Watters was outstanding in defence but made one slip in the 53rd minute and Charlie Tully nipped in to score the only goal of the game. So Celtic completed the "double" but the Glens had only themselves to blame for those countless missed opportunities.

Although May had come round there was still no let up in the number of games to be played. Dundalk, including our former centre-half Jimmy Dykes, were first round opponents in the Inter-City Cup. The first leg was one of the poorest games of the season and we should have had more than Tommy McCormick's hat-trick of goals. Ben Neill suffered yet another penalty miss. Before the return leg Second Division Fulham visited Belfast for a friendly. The Londoners put on a grand exhibition of football and their left-wing Shepherd delighted the crowd with his juggling skills. Fulham had to rely on an own goal for their winner.

We duly qualified for the next round of the Inter-City Cup and attention switched to the conclusion of the Regional League. Runners-up spot was clinched with three convincing wins, as we signed off with a bang at Solitude with five second half goals after Cliftonville had held an interval lead. Kane had taken over the penalties but his spot-kick was brilliantly saved by Reid.

Just two days later we surprisingly folded to Shamrock Rovers at Dalymount Park by six goals to nil, leaving far too much to do in the second leg at Grosvenor Park. We did manage a draw in this one thanks to King's overhead kick five minutes from time after Wright had added his name to the list of Glentoran penalty missers!

At the end of May there was one last chance to earn some silverware as we faced up to Celtic in the County Antrim Shield final. We hung on for a draw at Solitude, young Cleland having a fine game in goals, and then outplayed Celtic in the replay. However it was a similar story to the Irish Cup final - lots of missed chances. The game went into extra-time, Blanchflower failed from the penalty spot (our 12th such miss of the season), and Celtic emerged victorious by 3-1.

A long hard season was brought to a close on 30th May with a 4-0 win over a Lanarkshire XI. The game was actually billed as a 2nd XI fixture but we fielded a virtual full-strength team and the goals came from Neill, McCormick (2) and Wright. In mid-June Kane and Watters were transferred to Preston North End for a combined fee of £5,000 and later Noel Kelly moved to Arsenal. Glens' players donned their boots once more for a benefit game at Portadown.

Results 1946/47

Played 58. Won 36. Drew 7. Lost 15. Goals For 157. Against 94. % 68.1

SGC	17/08/46		Belfast Celtic	GP	W	2	1	Kelly, McCormack
SGC	21/08/46		Linfield	A	L	1	2	Lavery
SGC	24/08/46		Distillery	GP	W	4	3	McCormack 2, Waters, Lavery
SGC	28/08/46		Coleraine	A	W	3	1	Lavery 2, Kelly
SGC	31/08/46		Derry City	GP	W	5	0	Lavery 2, McCormack 2, Kelly
SGC	05/09/46		Cliftonville	A	W	6	0	McCormack 4, Lavery 2
SGC	07/09/46		Ballymena United	A	W	2	1	McCormack, Lavery
SGC	10/09/46		Belfast Celtic	A	L	0	9	-
SGC	14/09/46		Linfield	GP	L	0	2	-
SGC	21/09/46		Distillery	A	L	0	3	-
SGC	05/10/46		Coleraine	GP	L	2	3	Lavery, McCormack
SGC	12/10/46		Derry City	A	W	2	0	Lawlor, McCormack
SGC	19/10/46		Cliftonville	GP	W	5	0	Bradford 3, McCormack. Lawlor
SGC	26/10/46		Ballymena United	GP	W	3	1	McCormack 3
RL	02/11/46		Ballymena United	A	D	1	1	Lavery
RL	09/11/46		Belfast Celtic	GP	W	4	2	Lavery 3, Bradford
RL	16/11/46		Distillery	A	L	1	2	Kelly
RL	23/11/46		Derry City	GP	W	4	3	Bradford 3, Lawlor
RL	30/11/46		Cliftonville	A	W	5	0	Nimmick, Lavery, Wright, Kelly, Martin (p)
RL	07/12/46		Linfield	A	L	2	4	Lawlor, Lavery
RL	14/12/46		Coleraine	GP	W	6	1	Lavery 2, Bradford 2, Blanchflower, Lawlor
RL	21/12/46		Ballymena United	GP	W	5	1	McCormack 3, Lavery, Kelly
RL	25/12/46		Belfast Celtic	A	L	1	3	Bradford
RL	26/12/46		Distillery	GP	W	4	1	Bradford 3, McCormack
RL	28/12/46		Derry City	A	W	3	0	McCormack, Lavery, Bradford
RL	04/01/47		Cliftonville	GP	W	9	3	Bradford 2, Lavery 2, Wright, Kane (p), McCormack, Blanchflower, Nimmick
RL	11/01/47		Linfield	GP	L	2	4	Nimmick, McCormack
RL	23/01/47		Coleraine	A	W	2	0	O'Reilly, McCormack
RL	29/01/47		Ballymena United	A	W	5	3	McCormack 2, Kelly, Lavery, Wright
RL	01/02/47		Belfast Celtic	GP	W	3	0	McCormack 2, Neill (p)
RL	08/02/47		Distillery	A	L	1	2	Neill (p)
RL	01/03/47		Linfield	A	W	3	2	T.Hughes, Neill (p), O'Reilly
RL	08/03/47		Coleraine	GP	W	7	2	McCormack 4, O'Reilly 2, Kelly (p)
RL	22/03/47		Belfast Celtic	A	W	3	1	Kelly 2, Lavery
RL	25/03/47		Derry City	GP	W	2	1	McCormack, Lavery
RL	05/04/47		Derry City	A	W	3	2	Lavery, Kelly, Blanchflower
RL	08/04/47		Cliftonville	GP	W	5	2	McCormack 4, Graham
RL	12/04/47		Linfield	GP	L	1	2	Lawlor
RL	19/04/47		Coleraine	A	D	0	0	-
RL	08/05/47		Distillery	GP	W	3	1	Lavery 2, McCormack
RL	12/05/47		Ballymena United	GP	W	3	1	McCormack 2, King
RL	15/05/47		Cliftonville	A	W	5	2	Kelly 2, McCormack 2, Lawlor
IC	18/01/47	1.1	Ballymoney United	A	W	5	2	McCormack 2, Lavery 2, O'Reilly
IC	25/01/47	1.2	Ballymoney United	GP	W	6	1	McCormack 3, O'Reilly, Lawlor, Wright
IC	15/02/47	2.1	Distillery	A	L	0	1	-
IC	22/02/47	2.2	Distillery	GP	W	1	0	Molloy og
IC	03/03/47	2R	Distillery	GP	W	2	1	aet – Kelly, McCormack

IC	29/03/47	SF	Ballymena United	WP	D	1	1	Kelly
IC	02/04/47	SFR	Ballymena United	WP	D	1	1	Neill (p)
IC	14/04/47	SFR2	Ballymena United	WP	W	2	1	McCormack, Wright
IC	26/04/47	F	Belfast Celtic	WP	L	0	1	-
CAS	19/03/47	1	Cliftonville	A	W	3	0	O'Reilly, Lawlor, McCormack
CAS	22/05/47	SF	Belfast Celtic	Solt	D	0	0	-
CAS	28/05/47	SFR	Belfast Celtic	Solt	L	1	3	Lavery
ICC	02/05/47	1.1	Dundalk	GP	W	3	0	McCormack 3
ICC	10/05/47	1.2	Dundalk	DP	D	2	2	Lavery, Kelly
ICC	17/05/47	2.1	Shamrock Rovers	DP	L	0	6	-
ICC	24/05/47	2.2	Shamrock Rovers	GP	D	2	2	Waters (p), King
F	04/04/47		Shelbourne	GP	W	7	1	Graham 2, Lavery, Smyth 2, O'Reilly, Kinsella Williamson Benefit
F	05/05/47		Fulham	GP	L	3	4	Neill (p), McCormack 2
F	14/06/47		Portadown	A		Unknown		Herbie Rainey Benefit

Appearances and Goals

	App.	Goals		App.	Goals		App.	Goals
McCormick T.	54	53	Lawlor	43	9	Henderson	5	
Neill B.	52	4	Wright B.	36	5	Graham	3	1
Lavery J.	52	32	Nimmick	30	3	Cleland	2	
Watters	50	2	Martin C.	22	1	Mulholland	1	
Blanchflower	49	3	Hughes T.	16	1	Sloan	1	
Kelly	49	16	Bradford	13	16	Ferran	1	
Kane	47	1	Moore	11		Own goals		1
McKee	45		King	7	2			
O'Reilly	43	7	Shaw	6		TOTAL	638	157

At the end of the war many players from Southern Ireland played for the Glens, pictured here are Tommy McCormick, Noel Kelly, Con Martin, Paddy Watters and Jimmy Lawler.

1947/48

The Irish League resumes – More Christmas fixture uncertainty –
Frank Grice appointed

After an absence of seven seasons the Irish League resumed in its normal format. The City Cup returned to be the mini-league competition with the Gold Cup resorting back to its original knock-out formula. The financial arrangements were as follows:- Annual subscription to the league was £25 with gate receipts from all matches split 60% to the home club and 40% to the visitors. No club was allowed to have more than 500 season ticket holders, including women and boys.

The season opened on 16th August with a visit from Derry City in the City Cup. Glentoran's new centre-forward, Frank Coffey, scored the first goal of the season in the first minute and this was enough to give us a winning start. On the following Monday night

Danny Blanchflower.

5,000 crammed into Wilgar Park for the "East End Championship" between ourselves and Dundela. The Duns won a free for all by 5-3.

Celtic again proved a bogey for us as we went down 0-1 at Celtic Park having hit the crossbar in the closing seconds. Both sides wore armbands marking the death of Archie Hegarty. Many of the early season games were poor but at least we were winning and qualified for the semi-final of the Gold Cup with a deserved success over Linfield. Celtic put paid to our hopes in this competition and then Ballymena held us to a goalless draw in the City Cup. Before kick-off in the latter the crowd stood in silence as the band played "Abide With Me" in respect of the twenty people killed by an explosion on board the "Reinna del Pacifico" while she was docked in Belfast the previous Thursday.

The Glens came with a strong run at the end of the City Cup to finish joint second with Linfield, three points behind Celtic. Over 20,000 had attended our second 3-1 success of the season over the Blues at Grosvenor Park. The runners-up test match was arranged for New Year's Eve.

The 8th November 1947 saw the resumption of Irish League matches and Glentoran were the only home team to gain two points. We were unlucky not to win a week later at Windsor after playing well into the breeze. However we did enjoy our first visit to Lurgan in six years by defeating Glenavon 5-0. Coffey grabbed a hat-trick with John "Bap" Dunlop getting the other two. Our first league defeat came at Solitude in a game of frayed tempers. This was the last thing we wanted going into a busy Christmas period which began with a home defeat by Belfast Celtic on Christmas Day. Then controversy arose.

Celtic and Linfield were down to meet at Windsor Park on Boxing Day while the Glens took on Distillery at Grosvenor Park. In order to avoid having four lots of supporters in the same vicinity our match was ordered to start at 11.15 am with the Celtic-Blues game at 2.30 pm. The Glentoran directors were not amused and publicly announced that if our match could not be played in the afternoon then it would not be played at all. Everyone thought that was that but at 10.30 on Boxing morning the directors held an emergency meeting and voted 5-3 in favour of the game going ahead. It was played before 400 spectators producing £34 in gate receipts. This left the Whites out of pocket as it was their home fixture and they had to guarantee the "visitors" £50. The League Committee fined Glentoran £250 for objectionable conduct in the affair.

The next day the Coleraine game kicked off twenty minutes late due to the delayed arrival of the visitors. With three games on successive days Grosvenor Park had become a mud heap but we produced enough good football to win 3-0. After ten league games we stood fifth in the table with 13 points as Belfast Celtic led the way with a 100% record.

The year ended on a high note as we beat Linfield in the City Cup runners-up test match. The ball behaved freakishly on the frozen Solitude surface but the Glens were always on top. We won 3-2 after it had stood 1-1 with just ten minutes remaining.

January 1948 was an extremely depressing month as we recorded only one win in the five games played. That victory came at Derry, John "Danno" Feeney scoring two of the goals against his old team-mates. The league defeats against the Blues and Glenavon had a similar thread - Glens had 75% of the play but could not get the goals. Worst of all, though, was the Irish Cup defeat at home to juniors Brantwood. Once again we monopolised possession, created the chances, but up popped the Brants with an 83rd minute winner.

Something had to be done and five reserves were thrown into the fray at Ballymena. A point was gained and then a Scot Muldoon was given a trial in a friendly at Ards on Irish Cup Round Two day. On 21st February the directors placed a large advert in the Ireland's Saturday Night - "TEAM MANAGER WANTED - GOOD SALARY FOR FULLY QUALIFIED MAN." Frank Grice was the man eventually given the job at the end of the season.

Meantime results improved and we put together a run of three wins in a row. This was nothing however to the form of Belfast Celtic, who had a record 35 consecutive victories under their belts when they entertained the Glens on 13th April. A tremendous display held the Celts to 0-0 and they went on to lose two of their remaining three fixtures. Celtic finished runaway champions (their sixth successive Irish League title) while we had to settle for joint fourth place with Distillery, thirteen points adrift.

The rest of the season was given over to the County Antrim Shield, the Inter-City Cup and various benefit and fund raising games.

Dundalk were again our first round All-Ireland opponents. We were fortunate to earn a draw in Dublin, but dominated the second leg totally, Reggie McKnight getting two of our four goals. Our Shield aspirations were curtailed by Linfield after we had outclassed them at Grosvenor Park but failed to put the chances away. The Blues dominated the replay so much it was remarked that they could have done without a keeper.

After taking the lead on two minutes against Shelbourne (through Dunlop) we kept the game tight and there was no further scoring. In the second half Lavery and Shel's Sheedy were sent off but the latter had a much happier second leg scoring the only goal in Dublin after 23 minutes. Extra-time failed to produce a decisive moment so a third game at Dundalk was hastily arranged. Shelbourne got off on the wrong foot by arriving half an hour late and having to get changed on the bus. During the game they found Moore unbeatable in goals and at the other end ex-Dundalk forward Lavery got both the Glens' goals.

In the all-Northern semi-final with Distillery we put in two poor displays and went out 1-4 on aggregate. Then Peter Doherty and Kevin McAlinden guested for the Glens against Preston while there were no fewer than 15 guests on both sides for the Billy Bradford benefit match.

The curtain was finally brought down on a transitional season with the restoration of the RUC Five-A-Sides at Windsor Park on 29th May. We suffered a first round exit, going down 0-1 on corners to Glasgow Rangers. An estimated 15,000 watched the final when Linfield overcame Rangers.

Although the Oval pitch had been resurfaced the directors decided to remain at Grosvenor Park for one more season as numerous other tasks still needed to be performed at the ground. It was hoped that the Seconds could play at the Oval before the end of 1948.

Results 1947/48

Played 47. Won 23. Drew 11. Lost 13. Goals For 91. Against 51. % 60.6

CC	16/08/47		Derry City	GP	W	1	0	Coffey
CC	23/08/47		Belfast Celtic	A	L	0	1	-
CC	30/08/47		Coleraine	A	W	4	1	Lawlor, Nimmick, Coffey, Wright
CC	06/09/47		Glenavon	GP	W	3	1	Nimmick, McCormack, Reith og
CC	13/09/47		Ballymena United	GP	D	0	0	-
CC	20/09/47		Ards	A	W	3	1	McCormack 3
CC	27/09/47		Distillery	GP	L	1	2	Wright
CC	11/10/47		Portadown	A	W	2	0	McCormack 2
CC	18/10/47		Linfield	GP	W	3	1	Coffey, Wright, Nimmick
CC	25/10/47		Bangor	GP	W	6	0	Feeney 2, Coffey, McCormack, Nimmick, Wright
CC	01/11/47		Cliftonville	A	W	7	0	Dunlop 3, Coffey 2, McCormack, Nimmick
CC	31/12/47	RUTM	Linfield	Solt	W	3	2	T.Hughes (p), Dunlop, Nimmick
GC	27/08/47	1	Cliftonville	GP	W	1	0	T.Hughes (p)
GC	02/09/47	2	Linfield	GP	W	3	1	McCormack, Coffey, Nimmick
GC	09/09/47	SF	Belfast Celtic	Solt	L	0	1	-
IL	08/11/47		Derry City	GP	W	4	0	Coffey 2, Feeney, Dunlop
IL	15/11/47		Linfield	A	D	1	1	Dunlop
IL	22/11/47		Glenavon	A	W	5	0	Coffey 3, Dunlop 2
IL	29/11/47		Ballymena United	GP	D	2	2	T.Hughes, McCormack
IL	06/12/47		Bangor	A	W	3	2	Coffey 2, Dunlop
IL	13/12/47		Portadown	GP	D	1	1	T.Hughes
IL	20/12/47		Cliftonville	A	L	1	2	McCormack
IL	25/12/47		Belfast Celtic	GP	L	1	3	McCormack
IL	26/12/47		Distillery	A	D	2	2	Smart, T.Hughes (p)
IL	27/12/47		Coleraine	GP	W	3	0	T.Hughes, McKnight, Dunlop
IL	03/01/48		Ards	A	D	1	1	McKnight
IL	10/01/48		Derry City	A	W	3	2	Feeney 2, McKnight
IL	17/01/48		Linfield	GP	L	0	2	-
IL	31/01/48		Glenavon	GP	L	1	3	Dunlop
IL	07/02/48		Ballymena United	A	D	1	1	T.Hughes
IL	21/02/48		Bangor	GP	W	4	0	Coffey, Richardson 2, McKnight
IL	28/02/48		Portadown	A	W	2	1	Wright, Richardson
IL	06/03/48		Cliftonville	GP	W	3	1	Dunlop 2, McKnight
IL	13/03/48		Belfast Celtic	A	D	0	0	-
IL	27/03/48		Distillery	GP	L	0	2	-
IL	30/03/48		Coleraine	A	D	2	2	Lavery 2
IL	03/04/48		Ards	GP	W	4	1	McKnight 2, Lavery, Coffey
IC	24/01/48	1	Brantwood	GP	L	1	2	Dunlop
ICC	10/04/48	1.1	Dundalk	A	D	0	0	-
ICC	16/04/48	1.2	Dundalk	GP	W	4	1	Wright, McKnight 2, Lavery
ICC	28/04/48	2.1	Shelbourne	GP	W	1	0	Dunlop
ICC	01/05/48	2.2	Shelbourne	A	L	0	1	aet
ICC	03/05/48	2R	Shelbourne	OP	W	2	0	Lavery 2
ICC	07/05/48	SF.1	Distillery	DP	L	1	3	McKnight
ICC	11/05/48	SF.2	Distillery	GP	L	0	1	-
CAS	14/04/48	1	Linfield	GP	D	1	1	Coffey
CAS	20/04/48	1R	Linfield	A	L	0	2	-
F	11/08/47		Practice Match					-
F	18/08/47		Dundela	A	L	3	5	Bennett, McArthy (p), Smith
F	14/02/48		Ards	A	W	3	1	Muldoon, McKnight, Coffey
F	08/05/48		Preston North End	GP	L	0	2	Back to the Oval Fund

F	12/05/48	St. Mirren	GP	L	2	3	Smith 2
							Bertie Wright Benefit
F	14/05/48	Bangor XI	GP	W	4	3	Nimmick 2, Brennan, McFarlane
							Billy Bradford Benefit
F	17/05/48	Dundela XI	A	W	2	1	T.Hughes, Bingham
							Wilf Stanex Benefit

Appearances and Goals

	App.	Goals		App.	Goals		App.	Goals
Hughes T.	41	7	McCarthy	15		Mulholland	3	
Wright B.	40	6	Breen	14		Cleland	2	
Nimmick	38	7	Lavery J.	13	6	O'Boyle	1	
King	35		Shaw	10		McCormick W.	1	
Blanchflower	35		Feeney	10	5	Kearney	1	
McCormick T.	31	12	Lawlor	8	1	Craig	1	
Neill B.	29		Richardson	7	3	Green	1	
Coffey	29	17	O'Reilly	6		Watson	1	
Moore	28		Smart	5	1	Unknown	33	
Ferran	28		Andrews	3		Own Goals		1
Dunlop	23	15	Cahoon	3				
McKnight	19	10	Bennett	3		TOTAL	517	91

John "Bap" Dunlop.

1948/49

Team re-building - Cup final loss to Derry - Belfast Celtic resign from football

Frank Grice strengthened the playing panel for our last season at Grosvenor Park with a number of shrewd signings. Jackie Greenwood came from Belfast Celtic and two Scots were imported - Jimmy McFarlane (ex-Falkirk and Stenhousemuir) and Jimmy Kerr (ex-Dundee). Noel McCarthy was signed from Gaelic football.

The 10th August 1948 became an historic date as the first game on the new Oval pitch took place. An Intermediate Cup tie between Glentoran II and Carrick Rangers finished 1-1 (Carrick won the replay 3-1) but no spectators were allowed in until a month later when the Seconds entertained Brantwood.

Bertie Peacock.

After the practice match on 16th August the City Cup began. A creditable 1-1 draw was gained at Windsor Park in front of a big crowd in atrocious weather. The drenching rain continued on the Tuesday but 15,000 still turned out to see us suffer an early Gold Cup exit to Celtic. After thrashing Bangor another point was hard earned against Celtic in the City Cup. The post-war attendance boom had materialised and the grandstand was packed out over half an hour before kick-off.

The remainder of the City Cup produced a very mixed bag of results and we had to rely on winning the last three games to finish fifth, seven points behind winners Celtic. This was also the inaugural season of the Ulster Cup but the Glens were not one of the eight sides who took part.

We began the Irish League with another home draw against Celtic in a game of missed chances. McCarthy and Celtic's Haslett took early baths in the second half. Then, after defeat at Ards, the team clicked into gear again knocking in fifteen goals over the next three Saturdays. Dan Lavery and Danno Feeney were forming a devastating wing partnership. Meanwhile Bertie Peacock, Jimmy Ferran and Billy Bingham became regular names on the team sheet and it was not surprising that we won twelve out of our next thirteen league games.

The only blemish on the record came in a 0-2 reverse at Windsor Park which one scribe described as "a somewhat lucky win for Linfield." Twenty thousand had attended that Christmas Day fixture but the game at Windsor one day later was to have a more significant effect on the Irish League. Linfield and Celtic had played in a game of tension and incident with sendings-off, a leg break for a Linfield player and a late Blues' equaliser. At the conclusion the Linfield fans invaded the pitch and managed to trap young Celtic forward Jimmy Jones from reaching the dressing rooms. A crowd of about twenty pushed Jones over the terracing where he too suffered a broken leg. After the dust had settled and the riot discussed in the Northern Ireland parliament, Celtic's directors announced that they could no longer continue to play in the Irish League. Belfast Celtic toured the USA at the end of the season but never returned to football again - a great loss to the local game.

Results 1948/49

Played 44. Won 22. Drew 9. Lost 13. Goals For 86. Against 59. % 60.2

CC	21/08/48		Linfield	A	D	1	1	Feeney
CC	28/08/48		Bangor	GP	W	6	0	Nimmick 2, McFarlane, Blanchflower, Feeney, Richardson
CC	04/09/48		Belfast Celtic	GP	D	1	1	McFarlane
CC	11/09/48		Distillery	A	L	1	2	T.Hughes (p)
CC	18/09/48		Glenavon	GP	D	2	2	Mulholland, Feeney
CC	25/09/48		Ballymena United	A	L	1	2	McFarlane
CC	02/10/48		Derry City	GP	W	5	1	Richardson, Feeney, McFarlane 2, Peacock
CC	16/10/48		Portadown	A	L	1	5	Feeney
CC	23/10/48		Coleraine	GP	W	2	1	Feeney 2
CC	30/10/48		Cliftonville	A	W	3	1	Feeney, Greenwood, Kerr
CC	13/11/48		Ards	A	W	3	1	Lavery 2, og
GC	24/08/48	1	Belfast Celtic	A	L	1	2	Kerr
IL	20/11/48		Belfast Celtic	GP	D	0	0	-
IL	27/11/48		Ards	A	L	1	2	Feeney
IL	04/12/48		Glenavon	GP	W	7	1	Lavery 2, Feeney 2, McKnight, T.Hughes 2(1p)
IL	11/12/48		Portadown	A	W	4	1	Kerr, Feeney, Lavery, McKnight
IL	18/12/48		Ballymena United	GP	W	4	2	Kerr 2, Feeney, Greenwood
IL	25/12/48		Linfield	A	L	0	2	-
IL	27/12/48		Distillery	GP	W	4	1	Lavery, T.Hughes, McFarlane Kerr
IL	01/01/49		Coleraine	A	W	3	1	Peacock, McFarlane, Lavery
IL	08/01/49		Cliftonville	GP	W	2	0	McFarlane 2
IL	15/01/49		Bangor	GP	W	2	1	Feeney, T.Hughes
IL	29/01/49		Derry City	A	W	1	0	Feeney
IL	05/02/49		Belfast Celtic	A	W	3	0	Lavery, McFarlane, Kerr
IL	19/02/49		Ards	GP	W	2	0	Feeney, McFarlane
IL	26/02/49		Glenavon	A	W	2	1	McFarlane, Feeney
IL	05/03/49		Portadown	GP	W	2	1	Lavery, T.Hughes (p)
IL	12/03/49		Ballymena United	A	D	1	1	T.Hughes
IL	19/03/49		Linfield	GP	L	1	4	Lavery
IL	02/04/49		Distillery	GP	L	1	2	Bingham
IL	09/04/49		Coleraine	GP	W	3	2	T.Hughes, McFarlane, Kerr
IL	19/04/49		Cliftonville	A	L	0	1	-
IL	27/04/49		Bangor	A	L	0	3	-
IL	30/04/49		Derry City	GP	D	2	2	McFarlane 2
IC	22/01/49	1	Linfield	Solt	W	2	0	McFarlane, Lavery
IC	12/02/49	2	Cliftonville	A	W	3	1	Kerr, Feeney 2
IC	26/03/49	SF	Portadown	WP	D	2	2	McFarlane, Bingham
IC	30/03/49	SFR	Portadown	WP	D	1	1	Feeney
IC	04/04/49	SFR2	Portadown	WP	W	3	0	Feeney 2, Kerr
IC	16/04/49	F	Derry City	WP	L	1	3	Peacock
CAS	06/04/49	2	Ballymena United	GP	W	1	0	McFarlane
CAS	23/04/49	SF	Bangor	Solt	L	0	3	-
ICC	29/04/49	1	Shamrock Rovers	Solt	D	1	1	Peacock Both teams qualified
ICC	11/05/49	2	Bohemians	A	L	0	1	-
F	16/08/48		Practice Match					
F	25/08/48		Dundela	A	D	2	2	Richardson, McKnight Back to the Oval Fund
F	09/05/49		St. Mirren	GP	D	1	1	T.Hughes (p) Back to the Oval Fund
F	12/05/49		Everton	GP	D	1	1	Ewing Back to the Oval Fund

Windsor Park was closed down for a month meaning our first round Irish Cup tie with the Blues was transferred to Solitude. We emerged victorious (2-0) after a hard fought game in front of over 20,000 fans and then comfortably swept aside Cliftonville at the same venue in Round Two. Meantime we had "whipped" Celtic in the league, after a scoreless first half, in what proved to be our last ever meeting with them. The black spot of February came at Mourneview Park when new boy McComish had to be carried off on a stretcher, never to play again.

Linfield came to Grosvenor Park on 19th March, just one point ahead of us in the title race with six fixtures remaining. It was a bad day for the Glens as we put in a poor display with Tommy Hughes missing a penalty in the 1-4 defeat. However there was still the Irish Cup semi-final to look forward to. Half of Portadown seemed to be at Windsor for the game, including a dog and a goat decked out in red and white. The match itself finished in a draw and the replay the following Wednesday was also inconclusive.

Frank Mulholland.

Before the third meeting our by now outside league hopes were buried by Distillery. When the referee, H.G.Robinson, blew for time we were 1-2 down but the crowd became agitated as they realised that the whistle had gone five minutes too soon. The teams came back on again but there was no further scoring. The remainder of our league results were so poor that Celtic were able to nip in and claim the runners-up spot.

The Windsor pitch was very heavy for the cup semi-final second replay but our forwards adapted well to the conditions and opened Portadown up with fast, direct play. Feeney (2) and Kerr provided the killer punch in front of goal to see us through. A McFarlane goal saw off Ballymena after a close County Antrim Shield tie but the club was gearing itself up for the Irish Cup final.

Derry City were the opposition on a fine day. Before 25,000 the game kicked off and after 25 minutes Bertie Peacock fired us ahead. However it was to be Londonderry's day and goals from Colvin, Hermon and Cannon took the trophy to the Maiden City for the first time ever.

The Glens' season was completely in tatters a week later when Bangor defeated us 3-0 in the Antrim Shield semi-final. Tommy Neill, father of George Neill, made his only appearance for us in goals in this match. The Seasiders then amazingly lost 2-3 to Linfield Swifts in the final. The Swifts qualified after Belfast Celtic had withdrawn from the other semi-final.

The Inter-City Cup brought little cheer although both ourselves and Shamrock Rovers went through after drawing in order to make up for Celtic's withdrawal. Interest in this competition was non-existent following the resumption of normal league football and there was hardly anyone present when Bohemians knocked us out.

Glentoran finished the season with two farewell fund-raising affairs at Grosvenor Park. Ex-Glens star Johnny Deakin scored St.Mirren's goal in a 1-1 draw (attendance 3,000) and then a strengthened home XI had an identical scoreline against Everton's full league team. All that remained was to suffer our usual first round exit in the RUC five-a-sides, this time to hosts Linfield, 0-2 on corners after a scoreless draw. Cliftonville won the tournament.

Two of our best players left to find fame elsewhere, Danny Blanchflower to Barsnley and Bertie Peacock to Glasgow Celtic. Crusaders were admitted to the Irish League to replace Belfast Celtic.

224

Appearances and Goals

	App.	Goals		App.	Goals		App.	Goals
Moore	41		King	14		Wright B.	3	
Feeney	39	22	McKnight	13	2	Proctor	2	
Hughes T.	37	8	Peacock	13	4	Neill T.	1	
McFarlane	36	18	Lewis	11		Newberry	1	
Neill B.	34		Bingham	8	2	Shiells	1	
McCarthy	34		Millar	7		McIlroy	1	
Blanchflower	34	1	Greenwood	7	2	Unknown	22	
Nimmick	33	2	Mullholland	6	1	Own Goals		1
Kerr	32	10	McComish	4				
Lavery D.	23	11	Richardson	4	2	TOTAL	484	86
Ferran	19		Dunlop	4				

Billy Bingham.

1949/50

The return to East Belfast – League just eludes us - Shield success

The time had arrived at last for Glentoran to go back to the Oval. After all the problems with the war years and the draining of the pitch the arena was ready for full-time football once again. The club had spent over £20,000 refurbishing the ground. Most of this cash had been raised through supporters' clubs and various events organised by the "Back to the Oval" committee.

Excitement mounted in East Belfast as the 20th August approached. Many younger supporters had never seen Glentoran play at the Oval and they along with the older fans were anticipating the dawn of a new era. For the coming season the playing panel read as follows:

GOAL: Cecil Moore. FULL-BACKS: Ben Neill, Noel McCarthy, Jim Lewis (Utility), W.A.Macartney. HALF-BACKS: Clancy McDermott, Tommy Hughes, Jimmy Ferran, Frank Mulholland. FORWARDS: Billy Bingham, Jim McFarlane, Jimmy McIlroy, Sandy Lister, Danno Feeney, Tom Dornan.

Jimmy McIlroy.

Appropriately enough, old rivals Linfield were to provide the opposition for the first Oval fixture in the City Cup. A crowd of some 25,000, paying 1/6 (boys 6d.) turned up for the historic game and witnessed a win for the Blues; but it did not seem to matter, the Glens were back home after an eight-year absence. Teams:

GLENTORAN: Moore; Neill, McCarthy; McDermott, Hughes, Mulholland; Bingham, McIlroy, Lewis, Lister, Feeney.

LINFIELD: A.Russell; McCune, McMichael; Currie, Hamill, Walsh; Thompson, J.Russell, Simpson, Hannah, McGrath.

There were still two more historic matches to come that week - our first victory at the new Oval (over the Reds in the Gold Cup) and then we became the first visitors to play at Seaview on a Saturday with our initial meeting with senior newcomers Crusaders. Tommy Hughes ruined the Crues' celebrations with a penalty eight minutes from time on a pitch that was far from the bowling green-like Oval.

The early part of the season had a confusing look to it. In fact our first nine games were spread equally between three different competitions, the City, Gold and Ulster Cups. This was our first time in the latter, which was played on a four groups of four basis (junior teams making the numbers up), with the group winners meeting at the semi-final stage later in the season. We qualified comfortably from our group but the return of only six goals in the three games began to highlight the lack of a centre-forward.

The Gold Cup gave us a chance of quick revenge over the Blues but it was not to be. After a vigourous draw at the Oval we entered the Windsor replay as odds-on favourites but were thrashed 6-0. Worse still Cecil Moore broke a bone in his knee to put him on the sidelines for three weeks. By the end of September the injury crisis had become so pronounced that we fielded six reserves in the City Cup defeat at Ballymena.

Youngsters Sammy Lowry and Sammy Ewing began to figure in the side but results in early October were poor and the best we could hope for in the City Cup was a mid-table

226

placing. We went into the last fixture at Derry with the Brandywell men standing just a point behind Linfield. The Glens fought tooth and nail, and probably deserved a draw, before going down 1-2. However it all became irrelevant when news came through that Linfield had beaten Portadown 10-0 at Windsor to lift the City Cup.

Glentoran's problem was obvious. In order to compete with the Blues we required a goalscoring centre-forward to lead the attack. Frank Grice decided to sign a young man from Larne by the name of Sammy Hughes and gave him his debut straightaway in the opening league fixture versus Glenavon. Hughes did not disappoint his manger as he began his Oval career with a scoring spree. Sammy found the net in thirteen of his first fourteen league appearances and was to go on to score almost 300 goals in his nine seasons with the club.

By the end of 1949 eight Irish League games had been played and we stood second in the table, two points behind Linfield. Our only defeat had been on Boxing Day after leading Distillery 2-0, but our forwards rectified this by scoring fourteen times in three games over the next five days. Billy Bingham was having a field day on the right wing and record gates were being set everywhere we visited. The acid test came with the visit of Linfield for the first match of the 1950's.

Programme Cover 1949/50.

Again over 25,000 fans attended and again the Blues sneaked victory by 3-2 to leave us four points in their wake. However the team continued with its attacking philosophy to record wins over Portadown and Crusaders as the league reached the half-way stage. Coleraine were swept aside in the Irish Cup, all four goals coming in the last 20 minutes, but luck was not with us in the second round tie at Windsor Park. The Blues won the toss and elected to play with a hurricane force gale at their backs. That first half produced three Linfield goals, one direct from a corner by Tommy Dickson, but there was no wind to speak off in our favour in the second half and no further goals.

February was a month which saw our title challenge get back on the rails. The Blues dropped a point at Seaview and then lost at home to Derry City (1-2), who had also become serious championship contenders. We extended our winning sequence to five games and after fourteen fixtures the points situation was as follows:

1=. Glentoran 23, 1=. Linfield 23, 3. Derry City 21.

Scouts of Bolton, Tottenham, Burnley and Sheffield Wednesday viewed our 2-0 win over Derry and a week later Jimmy McIlroy was transferred to Burnley. Derry's challenge had faded as both Belfast clubs won five games in a row to set up a potential title decider at Windsor Park on 11th April 1950. In this match the Blues were the better all-round side but the Glens plucky display earned a 1-1 draw. Both sides won their last two league games meaning a play-off would be necessary to settle the championship.

Meanwhile Glentoran and Linfield had also battled their way through to the County Antrim Shield final to set up two derby meetings at Solitude in the space of four days. To the league play-off first and the Glens opened up like they wanted to play Linfield off the park. However Alex Russell was unbeatable in goals and we missed many chances, the worst offender Bingham, who spooned over the bar from three yards when faced with an open net. The feeling was that it wasn't our night and so it proved when the Blues scored twice in the second half to complete a league and cup double.

Revenge was gained in the Shield final the following Saturday afternoon when the score was 2-0 in our favour. Our superiority in this match was reflected in the first half corner

Results 1949/50

Played 46. Won 31. Drew 4. Lost 11. Goals For 114. Against 56. % 71.7.
Honours: County Antrim Shield

CC	20/08/49		Linfield	H	L	2	3	Mulholland, Feeney
CC	27/08/49		Crusaders	A	W	1	0	T.Hughes (p)
CC	10/09/49		Glenavon	H	W	2	1	Feeney 2
CC	24/09/49		Ballymena United	A	L	1	2	Feeney
CC	08/10/49		Ards	H	L	1	2	T.Hughes (p)
CC	15/10/49		Coleraine	A	L	2	4	T.Hughes (p), McIlroy
CC	22/10/49		Distillery	H	W	2	0	Feeney 2
CC	29/10/49		Cliftonville	A	W	2	0	McFarlane 2
CC	05/11/49		Portadown	H	D	0	0	-
CC	12/11/49		Bangor	H	W	1	0	Ewing
CC	19/11/49		Derry City	A	L	1	2	Lowry
GC	24/08/49	1	Cliftonville	H	W	5	0	Bingham 2, McFarlane 3
GC	31/08/49	2	Linfield	H	D	1	1	Feeney
GC	20/09/49	2R	Linfield	A	L	0	6	-
UC	03/09/49		Ards	H	W	2	1	Feeney, McFarlane
UC	13/09/49		Dundela	A	W	2	0	Mulholland, Lowry
UC	17/09/49		Bangor	H	W	2	0	Turtle, Bingham
UC	19/04/50	SF	Ballymena United	WP	L	1	2	Ewing
IL	26/11/49		Glenavon	H	W	3	1	S.Hughes 2, Feeney
IL	03/12/49		Coleraine	H	W	2	1	S.Hughes, Ewing
IL	17/12/49		Ballymena United	H	W	5	0	T.Hughes, S.Hughes 2, Ewing, Bingham
IL	24/12/49		Derry City	A	D	1	1	S.Hughes
IL	26/12/49		Distillery	H	L	2	3	McIlroy, Ewing
IL	27/12/49		Bangor	A	W	4	0	Feeney 2, S.Hughes, T.Hughes (p)
IL	28/12/49		Cliftonville	A	W	6	0	McIlroy 2, Feeney, S.Hughes 2, McCarthy (p)
IL	31/12/49		Ards	A	W	4	3	Ewing 2, Feeney, S.Hughes
IL	07/01/50		Linfield	H	L	2	3	S.Hughes, Feeney
IL	14/01/50		Portadown	A	W	4	2	S.Hughes 3, Bingham
IL	28/01/50		Crusaders	H	W	4	2	S.Hughes 2, McIlroy 2
IL	04/02/50		Glenavon	A	W	3	2	S.Hughes 2, McCarthy (p)
IL	18/02/50		Coleraine	A	W	5	0	Feeney 2, McFarlane 2, McIlroy
IL	25/02/50		Cliftonville	H	W	4	2	S.Hughes 2, Ewing, Feeney
IL	04/03/50		Ballymena United	A	W	5	1	Ewing, Bingham, S.Hughes, McCarthy (p), Feeney
IL	11/03/50		Derry City	H	W	2	0	Ewing, McIlroy
IL	18/03/50		Distillery	A	W	4	1	Feeney 2, Bingham, McIlroy
IL	01/04/50		Bangor	H	W	1	0	Feeney
IL	08/04/50		Ards	H	W	2	1	Lowry, McCarthy
IL	11/04/50		Linfield	A	D	1	1	S.Hughes
IL	15/04/50		Portadown	H	W	2	1	McFarlane, Bingham
IL	29/04/50		Crusaders	A	W	4	0	Lowry, S.Hughes, Feeney, McCarthy
IL	10/05/50	TM	Linfield	Solt	L	0	2	-
IC	21/01/50	1	Coleraine	H	W	4	0	S.Hughes 2, Feeney 2
IC	11/02/50	2	Linfield	A	L	0	3	-
CAS	05/04/50	2	Ards	H	W	4	2	Feeney, McFarlane 2, Bingham
CAS	04/05/50	SF	Distillery	WP	W	6	0	S.Hughes 3, Bingham, Lowry, Ewing
CAS	13/05/50	F	Linfield	Solt	W	2	0	Feeney, Lowry

F	25/03/50	Ards	A	W	4	0	Napier 2, Ewing, Mulholland
							Oval Reconstruction Fund
F	13/05/50	Doncaster Rovers	H	L	1	3	McGarry
							Oval Reconstruction Fund
F	17/05/50	St. Mirren	H	L	0	5	Oval Reconstruction Fund
F	19/05/50	Arsenal	H	L	2	4	Bingham 2
							Oval Reconstruction Fund

count of 16-3. So we recorded our first victory of the season over the Blues at the eighth attempt, and our first trophy.

Later in the evening a Glentoran Select XI met Peter Doherty's Doncaster Rovers in an "Oval Reconstruction Fund" friendly. Doherty gave a brilliant display, scoring a penalty and setting the other two Doncaster goals. Cliftonville's Kevin McGarry scored the Select XI's goal. A crowd of 10,000 patronised that game, many of whom had been among the 12,000 at Solitude in the afternoon.

The season finished with two other "glamour" friendlies against cross-channel sides. Left-back Noel McCarthy had a nightmare against St. Mirren, scoring two own goals in our 0-5 defeat. We saved one of our best displays of the season for the visit of Arsenal. The Gunners had just lifted the F.A. Cup and had finished sixth in the first division and around 18,000 came to watch them. After a goal-less first half Arsenal ran out 4-2 winners, Bingham netting both our goals.

Appearances and Goals

	App.	Goals		App.	Goals		App.	Goals
Feeney	43	26	McIlroy J.	25	9	Turtle	5	1
McCarthy	42	5	Hughes S.	25	28	Lister	3	
Hughes T.	40	5	Neill B.	22		Cronin	3	
Bingham	39	10	Macartney	16		Duncan	2	
Ewing	35	11	Ferran	15		Jordan	1	
Lewis	31		Lowry S.	14	6	Unknown	33	
Moore	28		McFarlane	14	11			
McDermott	26		Beare	13		TOTAL	506	114
Mulholland	25	2	Milford	6				

1950/51

Halcyon days – Four trophies including the double – Bingham transferred

Hopes were high of trophy success in Frank Grice's third season in charge as following the demise of Belfast Celtic, Glentoran and Linfield had established themselves as Northern Ireland's strongest clubs. Grice's attacking football policy had almost brought the championship to the Oval the previous season and with more or less the same playing panel the pattern of play could be built upon. The squad read:

Moore, Lewis, McCarthy, King, McDermott, W.Neill, T.Hughes, Ferran, Ewing, Mulholland, Thompson, S.Lowry, McFarlane, S.Hughes, Feeney, Taylor, Dunlop, Bingham.

Spectators visiting the Oval in August noticed further development work on the stadium. A new unreserved stand had been built and there was a temporary stand on the reserved side. The season commenced with the Ulster, Gold and City Cups running concurrently. Ards were frequent opponents early doors and gave us a hard fight in our Ulster Cup group. After the 2-2 draw at the Oval Glentoran fans staged a demonstration against the referee, Captain W.Higham. An Ards player appeared to handle the ball before netting their second goal. Higham consulted with a linesman for over a minute before allowing the score to stand. This result forced a play-off between ourselves and the County Down men for a semi-final place. This time the Glens made no mistake despite the heroics of Mick O'Connell in the Ards goal. Referee J.H.Cox of Rutherglen also had an excellent match.

We progressed to the first final of the season (the Gold Cup) after relying on a last minute Danno Feeney goal to defeat Crusaders in an awful semi-final at a sodden Solitude. However we were outclassed by Linfield, who played in Glasgow Rangers jerseys, our only goal coming from the penalty spot.

Sound progress was being made in the City Cup with five consecutive wins after an early 1-1 draw with the Blues at Windsor (attendance: 14,000). Billy Bingham scored the last goal in this run (against Coleraine) and the following Wednesday he was transferred to Sunderland. Bingham received the news after playing for the Irish League against the English League at Blackpool and the move opened the door for a marvellous playing career with the Roker men, Luton, Everton and Port Vale and later international management with Northern Ireland (twice) and Greece.

Four days later Distillery held us to a draw at a misty Oval but we still headed the City Cup by a point from Linfield with four games remaining. We then faced Cliftonville twice in four days and recorded two convincing wins, knocking in ten goals and qualifying for the Ulster Cup final. For the City Cup match with the Reds the scheduled referee was fogbound at Liverpool and linesman Jack Adair took over, giving a competent display.

Alan Thompson had assumed Bingham's right-wing berth and he scored crucial goals at Portadown and Bangor as we captured the City Cup for the first time in 19 years.

The dismal weather of Autumn 1950 came to a head on 18th November when appalling sleet caused the abandonment of our last City Cup game with Derry five minutes into the second half. However, with the destiny of the cup already decided, the results stood in all four games prematurely curtailed that afternoon.

It was the diamond jubilee year of the Irish League and Glentoran were dubbed pre-title favourites by the press. Twenty years had passed since our last success in the days of Fred Roberts but the tag was probably justified given the team's form over the previous nine months. Moore was solid in goals while "Bap" Dunlop had settled in well at right-back. Skipper Noel McCarthy occupied the other defensive flank while up front Lowry and Feeney were twinkle-toed on the left wing. Sammy Hughes continued to find the net while namesake Tommy could read a game brilliantly from centre-half. Frank Mulholland and Jimmy Ferran added the necessary steel at half-back. "I slow the other team down and let our footballers play", was how Ferran described his role. Jimmy "Spanky" McFarlane and Sammy Ewing shared the other inside-forward position.

The league campaign began well and we reeled off five straight wins up to Christmas. Ewing and Bangor's Jim Murdough were sent off after squaring up to each other in the opening game causing the crowd to jeer the referee continually. The Oval was a mass of yellow and white for the Portadown game. The pitch was covered in snow forcing new groundsman Billy Crawford to come up with a different colour for the line markings. Visiting keeper McNeill was kept warm dealing with our forwards' efforts but was beaten three times, the last a terrific shot from Lowry.

Billy Neill.

On Christmas Day Linfield beat us to reduce our lead over them to a solitary point and the Blues moved to the top five days later when we lost to "giantkillers" Coleraine. Grice immediately strengthened the side with the signings of Tommy Williamson and Scot Hugh Cunningham as the heavy grounds began to take their toll on some of our lighter players.

The Ulster Cup final was due ten days later and not only was the trophy at stake between the Blues and ourselves but also the gaining of a vital psychological advantage for the second half of the league. The game had been snowed off on New Year's Day but a large crowd still attended Grosvenor Park for the Wednesday afternoon kick-off. Midway through the first half the Glens went ahead and the event was put to parody, accredited to Bob Young, in a verse still sung with gusto on the terraces to this day,

"In the year of '51, when the Ulster Cup was won,

It was won against the famous Windsor Blues.

With your last bob you can bet, that the first goal in the net,

Was scored by the famous Sammy Hughes!

Sammy who? - Sammy Hughes, Sammy Hughes!"

Within ninety seconds Cunningham had made it 2-0 and although Linfield pulled one back we held on for a deserved win, our second trophy of the season.

Juniors Corgy Mills offered little resistance in the first round of the Irish Cup but the league was still the major priority. Wins over Ballymena and Cliftonville allowed us to go back to the top of the table but Linfield and Glenavon were close behind.

The team, however, was thriving on pressure and February witnessed some of the most brilliant displays of the season. Five goals went past Bangor in the first half at Clandyboye, it was a mystery how we failed to score at least ten against Derry City and the Ards net bulged seven times at the Oval. We reached the Irish Cup semi-finals and with eight league games to go the table read;

1. Glentoran 23, 2. Linfield 21, 3=. Coleraine, Glenavon 19.

Crowds were flocking to the games, it was a real boom-time for football. We fell a goal behind to Distillery but netted three times during a ten minute spell in reply. The Blues dropped a point at Seaview and when the "big two" Oval meeting in front of 25,000 on St. Patrick's Day finished 1-1 it meant we had a three point cushion with only five fixtures left. Both ourselves and Linfield won three games in a row at the end of March to maintain that status quo but league ambitions were placed on one side as the two teams clashed in the Irish Cup semi-final on 7th April.

The gates were closed at Solitude fifteen minutes before kick-off as around 27,000 crammed into the ground. It was an afternoon when the Glens laid the "blue shirt bogey"

Results 1950/51

Played 51. Won 41. Drew 4. Lost 6. Goals For 153. Against 50. % 84.3.
Honours: Irish League, Irish Cup, Ulster Cup, City Cup

UC	19/08/50		Dundela	H	W	4	0	Bingham, Feeney, S.Hughes, Lowry
UC	28/08/50		Ards	H	D	2	2	S.Hughes, Lowry
UC	02/09/50		Bangor	H	W	6	1	S.Hughes 3, McFarlane, Bingham, Feeney
UC	02/10/50	PO	Ards	H	W	2	0	S.Hughes, Bingham
UC	25/10/50	SF	Cliftonville	GP	W	4	1	McCarthy (p), Thompson, S.Hughes 2
UC	10/01/51	F	Linfield	GP	W	2	1	S.Hughes, Cunningham
GC	23/08/50	1	Ards	A	W	3	1	McFarlane, Feeney, Bingham
GC	31/08/50	2	Distillery	H	W	3	1	S.Hughes 2, McCarthy (p)
GC	11/09/50	SF	Crusaders	Solt	W	1	0	Feeney
GC	20/09/50	F	Linfield	Solt	L	1	5	McCarthy (p)
CC	26/08/50		Linfield	A	D	1	1	S.Hughes
CC	09/09/50		Crusaders	H	W	5	2	S.Hughes, Mulholland, McFarlane 2, Bingham
CC	16/09/50		Glenavon	A	W	3	1	Ewing, Feeney, Bingham
CC	23/09/50		Ballymena United	H	W	5	0	S.Hughes, McFarlane, McCarthy (p), Feeney 2
CC	30/09/50		Ards	A	W	4	1	McFarlane 2, Bingham 2
CC	14/10/50		Coleraine	H	W	4	0	S.Hughes, Feeney, Ewing, Bingham
CC	21/10/50		Distillery	H	D	1	1	Feeney
CC	28/10/50		Cliftonville	H	W	6	0	Ewing 2, S.Hughes 2, Feeney 2
CC	04/11/50		Portadown	A	W	1	0	Thompson
CC	11/11/50		Bangor	A	W	3	1	Thompson, Lowry, McCarthy
CC	18/11/50		Derry City	H	W	1	0	Ewing –Abandoned after 50 minutes result stood
IL	25/11/50		Bangor	H	W	2	1	S.Hughes 2
IL	02/12/50		Derry City	A	W	2	1	Feeney, McFarlane
IL	09/12/50		Ards	A	W	5	1	Feeney 2, McCarthy (p), McFarlane, Dunlop
IL	16/12/50		Portadown	H	W	3	0	Dunlop, Feeney, Lowry
IL	23/12/50		Distillery	H	W	2	1	McCarthy (p), S.Hughes
IL	25/12/50		Linfield	A	L	1	2	S.Hughes
IL	26/12/50		Glenavon	H	W	3	0	Dunlop, Feeney, S.Hughes
IL	30/12/50		Coleraine	A	L	0	1	-
IL	13/01/51		Crusaders	A	D	1	1	S.Hughes
IL	27/01/51		Ballymena United	H	W	2	0	S.Hughes, Williamson
IL	31/01/51		Cliftonville	H	W	5	3	Williamson, S.Hughes 2, Dunlop, Ferran
IL	03/02/51		Bangor	A	W	6	1	S.Hughes 3, McFarlane, Ewing, McCarthy (p)
IL	10/02/51		Derry City	H	W	4	1	Cunningham 2, S.Hughes, Williamson
IL	24/02/51		Ards	H	W	7	2	S.Hughes 3, Cunningham 2, Ewing, Williamson
IL	03/03/51		Portadown	A	W	2	0	Dunlop, S.Hughes
IL	10/03/51		Distillery	A	W	4	1	S.Hughes, Feeney, Ewing, McCarthy (p)
IL	17/03/51		Linfield	H	D	1	1	Williamson
IL	24/03/51		Glenavon	A	W	3	1	S.Hughes, Ewing, Williamson
IL	27/03/51		Coleraine	H	W	3	2	Ewing, S.Hughes, Williamson

IL	31/03/51		Cliftonville	A	W	4	0	Wilson og, Feeney, S.Hughes 2
IL	14/04/51		Crusaders	H	W	4	1	Feeney 2, S.Hughes, Dunlop
IL	21/04/51		Ballymena United	A	W	2	0	Walker, Ewing
IC	20/01/51	1	Corgy Mills	H	W	9	0	Feeney 4, S.Hughes 2, Ewing, McFarlane, Ferran
IC	17/02/51	2	Brantwood	H	W	2	0	Ewing, Barnes og
IC	07/04/51	SF	Linfield	Solt	W	3	1	McCarthy (p), Williamson, Ewing
IC	28/04/51	F	Ballymena United	WP	W	3	1	Williamson, S.Hughes 2
CAS	20/03/51	1	Ballymoney United	A	W	1	0	S.Hughes
CAS	18/04/51	2	Ards	H	W	2	1	Ewing, Moore og
CAS	05/05/51	SF	Cliftonville	WP	D	3	3	McCarthy, S.Hughes, Ewing
CAS	09/05/51	SFR	Cliftonville	WP	L	2	4	Feeney, Williamson
F	14/05/51		B.V.V.	H	L	2	4	Cunningham, Feeney Festival of Britain

to rest as we played delightful football, seldom seen against Linfield. McCarthy, Williamson and Ewing were the scorers in a 3-1 win.

The Glentoran celebrations continued a week later when a 4-1 success over Crusaders gave us the league title for the first time since 1931 and the ninth in all. It was a truly deserved honour for Frank Grice and his players. Now only Ballymena United stood between us and a league and cup double.

The Glens won the dress rehearsal at the Showgrounds a week before the cup final but there was little to choose between the teams going into the big game. Ballymena were dealt a cruel blow after only fifteen minutes when full-back Joe Barr was injured in a clash with Cunningham and took no further part. With Moore a virtual spectator we bombarded the Ballymena penalty area but it was not until after the break that Sammy Hughes scored the goals to give us the cup.

His first came when Cunningham picked up the ball on the right wing and lifted over an inviting cross. Up like a bird leapt Hughes and the ball went crashing into the net. For he second Feeney sent over a head-high corner and with a neat flick of the head the ball went

Team Group 1950/1 with trophies.

Team Group 1950/1 Back Row: Ronnie Peden, Sammy Hughes, Sammy Lowry, John Dunlop, Cecil Moore, Noel McCarthy, Frankie Mulholland, Tommy Edgar. Front Row: Alan Thompson, Sammy Ewing, Jimmy Ferran, Tommy Hughes, Jimmy Feeney.

flashing into the top of the net. Final result – Glentoran 3 Ballymena United 1. The crowd was 25,000 with the most expensive tip-up seats costing 7/6.

The County Antrim Shield provided the chance of winning five trophies in a season for the first time in our history. We met a fighting Cliftonville side in the Windsor Park semi-final and twice had to come from behind to force a replay. Sammy Hughes' goal was our 150th of the season. In the replay Danno Feeney put us ahead, but the Reds, inspired by two goal Kevin McGarry, never let us settle and inflicted our first defeat of 1951 to bring our season to a sudden end.

Playing matters were concluded with a Festival of Britain match versus touring Dutch league champions BVV. Cecil Moore had a rare off day letting in four goals while we could only put two past the inspired visiting goalkeeper, Bil. BVV drew their other two games, 0-0 against a strengthened Ards XI and 4-4 with Glenavon.

During 1950/1 two other "Glentoran" teams had been active. An Old Glens XI drew 2-2 with the Old Blues at Grosvenor Park in October in a fund raising match for the NSPCC. The Old Glens lined out: Ward, Mathieson, Allen, Collins, Irvine, Grice, Gamble, Stannex, Hall, Graham, Agnew. Graham got both goals, one from the penalty spot.

A Glentoran Ladies team played a series of games against Ballywalter Ladies with the gate receipts going towards the Oval Reconstruction Fund. The first game finished scoreless, the Glens goalkeeper distinguishing herself by saving a penalty.

Appearances and Goals

	App.	Goals		App.	Goals		App.	Goals
Moore	50		Ewing	41	16	Neill W.	9	
Feeney	50	25	McFarlane	28	11	Lewis	6	
McCarthy	49	11	Cunningham	25	5	McDermott	1	
Ferran	49	2	Williamson	18	10	Walker	1	1
Hughes S.	48	46	Thompson	14	3	Unknown	11	
Hughes T.	44		Bingham	13	9	Own Goals		3
Dunlop	42	6	Lowry S.	12	4			
Mulholland	41	1	King	9		TOTAL	561	153

1951/52

Out of Africa – Gold Cup success – Shock Cup Final defeat to Ards

The first match of the season at the Oval did not involve Glentoran but a visiting team from the Gold Coast who played in bare feet! An IFA XI defeated the flamboyant Africans 4-2 and two days later Cliftonville repeated the feat (5-2).

The more traditional football got underway in mid-August with reigning league champions Glentoran determined to repeat the successes of 1950/1 using virtually the same playing panel. Linfield were again our first opponents in the City Cup and they retained their unbeaten record at the "new" Oval with a 1-1 draw. The atrocious weather restricted the attendance to under 10,000.

The Ulster Cup was mothballed this season to facilitate the one-off Festival of Britain Cup. This tournament ran as four groups of three with each group winner going through to the semi-finals. We recorded early wins over both our group opponents, Bangor and Ards, coming from behind in the latter. The return fixtures were saved until the end of the season.

Meantime the team continued from where it had left off in April with good progress in the City and Gold Cups. In fact from the start of the season up until Boxing Day we only lost one of our 25 games. That reverse came at Coleraine and left us three points behind the Bannsiders in the City Cup. However they cracked, losing two consecutive games in early October and with ourselves and Linfield winning our last five games it meant a Glens-Blues play-off to decide the destination of the trophy. Unfortunately no suitable date could be found and this match was delayed until May 1952. The best game of the City Cup had been our 4-3 win over Ards, Sammy Hughes netting the winner in the 88th minute.

Bangor gave us a shock in the second round of the Gold Cup forcing a draw at the Oval. However two Tom Williamson goals in the first ten minutes of the replay killed the tie. We recorded a routine 2-0 win over the Ports in the semi-final but it was the other semi which captured public interest. The reason, Jimmy Jones, signed by Glenavon from Fulham was playing his first game in Northern Ireland following his infamous leg break on Boxing Day 1948. Ironically Linfield were again the opponents and Jones scored in a 2-0 win.

Jimmy Ferran.

Although it was the free-scoring Glentoran forward line who were taking most of the credit for the team's results mention must be made of youngster Billy Neill. Following the transfer of Frank Mulholland to English First Division Middlesbrough, Neill had slotted into the right-half position and held his place with a series of competent displays.

Scot Jimmy Clarke (ex-Raith Rovers) was in goals for us when the league championship got underway. He had little to do but watch as our forwards knocked in eight against Ards.

235

Results 1951/52

Played 55. Won 32. Drew 11. Lost 12. Goals For 135. Against 76. % 68.1.
Honours: Gold Cup, County Antrim Shield

CC	18/08/51		Linfield	H	D	1	1	Williamson
CC	25/08/51		Crusaders	A	W	4	3	Mulholland, Feeney, Williamson, McFarlane
CC	01/09/51		Glenavon	H	D	3	3	S.Hughes, Feeney 2
CC	08/09/51		Ballymena United	A	D	1	1	Feeney
CC	15/09/51		Ards	H	W	4	3	Ewing, Feeney, Lowry, S.Hughes
CC	22/09/51		Coleraine	A	L	2	4	S.Hughes, McCarthy (p)
CC	29/09/51		Distillery	H	W	5	1	Lewis, Ewing, Williamson, S.Hughes, Lowry
CC	13/10/51		Cliftonville	A	W	4	0	S.Hughes 2, Williamson, McCarthy
CC	20/10/51		Portadown	H	W	4	1	S.Hughes, Feeney, Williamson, Lowry
CC	27/10/51		Bangor	H	W	4	1	Feeney 3, McCarthy (p)
CC	03/11/51		Derry City	A	W	5	2	Ewing, S.Hughes, Feeney 2, Williamson
CC	12/05/52	TM	Linfield	GP	L	2	3	Feeney 2
FBC	21/08/51		Bangor	H	W	6	2	Ewing 2, Feeney, S.Hughes 3
FBC	09/10/51		Ards	A	W	2	1	Feeney 2
FBC	28/04/52		Bangor	A	W	2	1	S.Hughes, McFarlane
FBC	30/04/52		Ards	H	L	1	3	S.Hughes
FBC	05/05/52	SF	Ballymena United	WP	L	0	1	-
GC	28/08/51	1	Distillery	H	W	5	0	Watters og, McFarlane 2, Lowry, Ferran
GC	12/09/51	2	Bangor	H	D	1	1	Williamson
GC	19/09/51	2R	Bangor	A	W	2	0	Williamson 2
GC	31/10/51	SF	Portadown	GP	W	2	0	Ewing, Lowry
GC	09/01/52	F	Glenavon	WP	W	2	1	McFarlane, Ewing
IL	10/11/51		Ards	H	W	8	1	S.Hughes 4, Ferran 2, Lowry, Ewing
IL	17/11/51		Crusaders	A	W	1	0	Feeney
IL	24/11/51		Coleraine	H	W	3	2	Feeney 2, S.Hughes
IL	01/12/51		Bangor	A	D	1	1	Feeney
IL	08/12/51		Portadown	H	D	2	2	Ewing, Lowry
IL	15/12/51		Ballymena United	A	D	2	2	Ewing, Lowry
IL	22/12/51		Cliftonville	A	W	3	2	Lowry, O'Kane, Ewing
IL	25/12/51		Linfield	H	W	4	3	McFarlane 2, Ewing, Feeney
IL	26/12/51		Glenavon	A	L	3	8	Feeney, O'Kane 2
IL	29/12/51		Derry City	H	W	4	0	S.Hughes 2, O'Kane, Lowry
IL	05/01/52		Distillery	H	W	3	0	Simpson og, S.Hughes, Lowry
IL	12/01/52		Ards	A	W	3	1	Williamson, Ewing, Feeney
IL	26/01/52		Crusaders	H	W	4	1	S.Hughes 2, Lowry 2
IL	02/02/52		Coleraine	A	L	1	2	Feeney
IL	09/02/52		Bangor	H	W	6	0	S.Hughes, Feeney 2, Ewing 2, McFarlane
IL	23/02/52		Portadown	A	W	3	1	Feeney. Lowry, S.Hughes
IL	01/03/52		Ballymena United	H	L	1	3	Williamson
IL	08/03/52		Cliftonville	H	W	3	1	S.Hughes 2, Ewing
IL	22/03/52		Linfield	A	L	0	1	-
IL	29/03/52		Glenavon	H	L	1	2	Ewing
IL	05/04/52		Derry City	A	L	1	3	Feeney

IL	12/04/52		Distillery	A	L	0	3	-
IC	19/01/52	1	Bangor	H	W	1	0	Feeney
IC	16/02/52	2	Glenavon	H	W	3	0	Feeney, Williamson, Ewing
IC	15/03/52	SF	Linfield	Solt	D	0	0	-
IC	02/04/52	SFR	Linfield	Solt	D	2	2	Neill, O'Kane
IC	09/04/52	SFR2	Linfield	Solt	D	0	0	aet
IC	17/04/52	SFR3	Linfield	Solt	W	1	0	Ewing
IC	26/04/52	F	Ards	WP	L	0	1	-
CAS	19/04/52	2	Ballymena United	A	D	1	1	Williamson
CAS	22/04/52	2R	Ballymena United	H	W	3	0	Williamson, McKeague 2
CAS	03/05/52	SF	Distillery	WP	W	2	0	Ewing, Lowry
CAS	10/05/52	F	Brantwood	Solt	W	3	0	S.Hughes 2, O'Kane
F	08/05/52		Middlesborough	H	L	0	3	-
F	14/05/52		Luton Town	H	D	1	1	Deakin
F	20/05/52		Doncaster Rovers	H	W	3	2	O'Kane, Ewing, S.Hughes

Jimmy Ferran got two of those but a week later his season was finished as he received a nasty knee injury. Jim McFarlane and Ronnie Giffen shared the left-half spot for the rest of the league but the loss of the tenacious Ferran was a big blow.

The Glens had a run of three consecutive draws in December – all three games were attended by Bolton scouts but no further transfers evolved. Every Glens' match seemed to be exciting, none more so than the Christmas Day victory over Linfield. The damage was done in the first half as we scored three without reply and although the Blues fought back to 3-4 we held on to break the Oval hoodoo. It had been seven games and 12 years since we had last beaten Linfield in East Belfast.

This result set us up nicely for the meting with Glenavon at Mourneview Park on Boxing Day. The Lurgan Blues had won their first eight league games and a record provincial crowd of 12,000 were there to see if they could continue the run. This they did in fine style as the Glens were torn apart to the tune of 8-3. Glenavon now began to believe that they could become the first team from outside Belfast to win the league. However the following Saturday Distillery beat them 1-0 and to complete the triangle we beat Distillery 3-0 in the first game of 1952 to leave the league table looking like this at the half-way stage:

1. Glenavon 20 points, 2=. Glentoran, Distillery 17,..................., 11. Linfield 6.

Sammy Hughes had made a welcome return to the side against Derry after a five match lay-off and this enabled us to field our strongest team for the Gold Cup Final with Glenavon on 9th January. Not surprisingly Glenavon began the game as favourites but we proved the better team on the day and emerged as 2-1 victors to capture the Gold Cup for the first time in our history. Sammy Ewing scored the winner in front of 15,000 people, paying receipts of £1,300.

For our first round Irish Cup tie with Bangor ten days later the Oval was a sea of brown, green and white. Sand had been sprinkled liberally onto the surface to try and counter the effects of a heavy snowfall. Danno Feeney's goal separated the teams that day. Back to the league and sandwiched between fine wins over Crusaders and Bangor was another defeat at Coleraine. This left us two points behind Glenavon but with a game more played.

As fate would have it the top two teams in the league were drawn to meet at the Oval in the second round of the Irish Cup. Over 22,000 passed through the turnstiles to witness a typically fast and furious cup tie. It was probably our best display of the season, reflected in the 3-0 scoreline in our favour. The Ulster, then costing 3d., nominated young full-back Tommy Lucas as the "man of the match" and predicted possible future international caps for him . Lucas was vying with Willie "Flash" King for the right-back shirt.

Glenavon's league form was more determined after this reverse whereas the Glens suffered two defeats in the next three games. Against Ballymena we lost at home for the first time in the season, handicapped by an injury to Clarke which forced McFarlane into goals for the last forty minutes. Then Linfield gained their first home league win on 22nd March – this defeat coming in the middle of a marathon Irish Cup semi-final tie with the men from Windsor.

The "highlight" of the first meeting actually came after the final whistle! At the conclusion a fan, dressed as Charlie Chaplin, walked onto the pitch and shook hands with both captains and the referee. In the first replay the Glens, without Feeney and Ewing, were lucky to earn a 2-2 draw – O'Kane equalising in the 81st minute. Even twenty minutes extra time failed to produce a goal in the second replay and it was left to Sammy Ewing to book our final place with a 51st minute goal in the fourth match. The declining attendances at the games reflected the general dullness of the encounters – they went from 17,700 to 12,000 to 10,000 to 8,000. Overall gate receipts for the four games were in excess of £4,000.

Glenavon came to the Oval on league business at the end of March needing only a point for the championship. The game was vibrant with tension but a weakened Glentoran side were not up to the challenge and went down 1-2. So the title went to Mourneview Park for the first time ever and, with the Glens gaining no more points in our remaining two games, we ended up sharing second place with Distillery and Coleraine. Play-offs for the medals were held over until 1952/3 due to the appalling end of season fixture congestion.

Four days before the Irish Cup final with Ards we became the first Belfast side to defeat Ballymena all season. In doing so we reached the County Antrim Shield semi-final. All roads led to Windsor Park on 26th April as we attempted to retain the Irish Cup. However it was not to be our day as Ards' player-coach Isaac McDowell inspired them to a 1-0 win. It was a miracle that Ards did not by more as they swamped all round our goal in the second half. The crowd figure was 23,000.

The players then had to lift themselves for the completion of three more tournaments and various Oval friendlies. In fact in the last three weeks of the season we took the field on no fewer than nine occasions.

Despite going down to Ards again we qualified for the semi-final of the Festival of Britain Cup. However that was to be Ballymena's cup as they beat Crusaders 3-0 after seeing us off 1-0 in the semi. A great display by our half-back line of Neill, Hughes and McFarlane was the main factor in overcoming Distillery in the Shield semi-final. In the final Brantwood were virtually a pushover but it was the second half before we broke through.

The most disappointing result in May was the City Cup Test Match against Linfield who had finished tenth in the league. For seventy minutes we gave the Blues a footballing lesson but only had two goals to show for it. The Blues pulled it back to 2-2 and then notched the winner in the last minute.

Goals from Wilf Mannion, Delapenha and Spulher gave Middlesbrough a 3-0 win over us but we performed much better in Cecil Moore's benefit game against Luton Town. Inspired by guest player Johnny Deakin we forced a draw, and then went one better defeating Doncaster Rovers (who were without Peter Doherty) by the odd goal in five in a "rousing" game.

The curtain thus came down on a strange season which had promised so much but only realised two relatively minor trophies.

Appearances and Goals

	App.	Goals		App.	Goals		App.	Goals
Clark	50		King	33		Dunlop	4	
Hughes T.	49		McFarlane	31	8	Giffen	4	
Lowry S.	47	15	Lucas	22		McKeague	3	
Ewing	46	20	Cunningham	15		Bond	1	
Hughes S.	45	29	O'Kane	13	6	Corbett	1	
Feeney	44	32	Mulholland	11	1	Unknown	44	
McCarthy	43	3	Ferran	10	3	Own Goals		2
Williamson	40	14	Lewis	8	1	TOTAL	605	135
Neill W.	36	1	Dawson	5				

1952/53

Hughes scores 64 out of a record 183 goals – League regained –
A floodlit cup

The structure of the Irish League season changed for the better in 1952/3. The Ulster Cup returned as the opening competition with the teams split into two groups of six and playing each other twice. This was to be followed by the City Cup in its usual format, then the league itself with the Gold Cup to be played for on a knockout basis In April and May. Oval season ticket prices were as follows: Patrons £2 2s, Members £1 10s, Ladies £1 1s, Boys 10/6.

Fans purchasing these were to witness a momentous season of goalscoring, the highest total in the club's history, and the regaining of the Irish League championship. Sammy Hughes was the leader of the line, netting 64 times for the Glens and being named Ulster Footballer of the Year. Sammy Lowry also had his best ever goalscoring season and set up many from the wing for Hughes and captain Sammy Ewing.

We began in splendid style in the Ulster Cup, knocking in 31 goals in the first seven games. Then a heavy defeat at Coleraine left the Bannsiders just a point behind us in our section. Cliftonville gave us a shock in the penultimate group game when they went 2-0 up after only five minutes but we gradually took control and won 4-2. A commanding win at Seaview took us through to the final against Section I winners Distillery.

Unfortunately for the Whites they were forced to line up without two injured regulars and thanks to a comfortable 3-0 win we brought the Ulster Cup to the Oval for the first time. One of our goals came from Johnny Deakin who had made a welcome return to the club, reviving memories of his guest appearances during the Regional League days.

Jimmy Clark is beaten by a penalty at Windsor Park .

The City Cup had already begun and our opening fixture with Linfield was full of thrills but little good football. The Blues had taken the lead with a penalty but a "picture" goal from Tom Williamson levelled matters and even brought applause from some Linfield supporters. In a second period it was a case of the Glens forward line versus Joe Kinkead in the home goal. The young keeper was equal to everything and his heroics included two brilliant penalty kick saves.

After four games we shared top spot with Ards and this ensured a record crowd when we visited Castlereagh Park a week later. Ards players adopted a "no prisoners" policy and the referee had to intervene frequently in heated scenes following some rough tackling. The Glens skilful fast play won the day, the final victory margin 5-1. The following Saturday we gave probably our most perfect display of the season in thrashing Coleraine 9-0 at the Oval. This opened up a four point lead with five City Cup games remaining.

Distillery proved something of a bogey team as they defeated us twice in November. A last minute goal gave them a win in the City Cup at Grosvenor Park and then an extra-time strike defeated us in the 1951/2 league runners-up play-off match. The latter result gave the Whites the right to meet Coleraine for this honour but when that game finished 1-1 after extra time the two clubs were declared joint second and both received medals.

Results 1952/53

Played 58. Won 39. Drew 9. Lost 10. Goals for 183. Against 77. % 75.0.
Honours: Irish League, Ulster Cup, City Cup

UC	16/08/52		Coleraine	H	W	4	1	Lucas, Neill, Feeney 2
UC	19/08/52		Ballymena United	A	L	2	4	S.Hughes, Ewing
UC	21/08/52		Derry City	H	W	4	1	Williamson, Feeney, Curran og, McFarlane
UC	23/08/52		Cliftonville	A	W	7	3	Ewing 3, S.Hughes 2, Williamson, Feeney
UC	26/08/52		Crusaders	H	W	5	0	S.Hughes 3, Lowry, Williamson
UC	30/08/52		Ballymena United	H	W	5	1	S.Hughes 3, Lowry (p), Williamson
UC	04/09/52		Derry City	A	W	4	1	Lowry 3, Curran og
UC	06/09/52		Coleraine	A	L	1	5	Williamson
UC	11/09/52		Cliftonville	H	W	4	2	S.Hughes, Ewing, Lowry 2
UC	16/09/52		Crusaders	A	W	4	1	Williamson 2, S.Hughes 2
UC	30/09/52	F	Distillery	Solt	W	3	0	Lowry 2, Deakin
CC	13/09/52		Linfield	A	D	1	1	Williamson
CC	20/09/52		Crusaders	H	W	6	1	Williamson, Deakin 2, S.Hughes 2, Lowry
CC	27/09/52		Glenavon	A	W	3	2	Deakin, Lowry 2
CC	11/10/52		Ballymena United	H	W	2	1	S.Hughes, Williamson
CC	18/10/52		Ards	A	W	5	1	Deakin 2, S.Hughes 2, Williamson
CC	25/10/52		Coleraine	H	W	9	0	Ewing 4, S.Hughes 3, Lowry 2
CC	01/11/52		Distillery	A	L	2	3	Lowry, Ewing
CC	08/11/52		Cliftonville	H	W	2	0	Lowry, Deakin
CC	15/11/52		Portadown	A	W	3	0	Williamson, Ewing 2
CC	22/11/52		Bangor	A	W	6	1	S.Hughes 3, Lowry 2, Feeney
CC	29/11/52		Derry City	H	W	9	1	S.Hughes 5, Lowry 3, Williamson
IL*	19/11/52	RUTM	Distillery	Solt	L	1	2	aet S.Hughes
IL	06/12/52		Coleraine	H	D	2	2	S.Hughes, Lowry
IL	13/12/52		Distillery	A	D	1	1	Deakin
IL	20/12/52		Ards	H	W	3	0	Lowry, S.Hughes, Ewing
IL	25/12/52		Linfield	A	D	1	1	S.Hughes
IL	26/12/52		Glenavon	H	D	1	1	S.Hughes
IL	27/12/52		Cliftonville	A	W	4	2	Feeney 2, S.Hughes, Williamson
IL	03/01/53		Crusaders	A	L	2	4	Feeney, Lowry
IL	10/01/53		Portadown	H	W	4	1	McFarlane 2, Lowry, Williamson
IL	17/01/53		Ballymena United	H	W	4	1	S.Hughes 3, Deakin
IL	24/01/53		Derry City	H	W	2	0	S.Hughes, Feeney
IL	31/01/53		Bangor	A	W	2	0	S.Hughes, Williamson
IL	14/02/53		Coleraine	A	W	5	2	S.Hughes 4, Ewing
IL	21/02/53		Distillery	H	L	1	3	Lowry
IL	28/02/53		Portadown	A	L	1	2	S.Hughes
IL	14/03/53		Linfield	H	W	3	1	S.Hughes 2, Lowry
IL	21/03/53		Glenavon	A	W	3	0	S.Hughes 3
IL	04/04/53		Cliftonville	H	W	7	1	Ewing, S.Hughes 2, Lowry 2, Cunningham 2
IL	06/04/53		Crusaders	H	W	2	0	Deakin, S.Hughes
IL	07/04/53		Ballymena United	A	W	1	0	S.Hughes
IL	11/04/53		Bangor	H	W	6	0	S.Hughes 3, McFarlane, Cunningham, Lowry

IL	18/04/53		Derry City	A	W	3	2	Ewing 2, Cunningham
IL	20/05/53		Ards	A	D	1	1	Feeney
IC	07/02/53	1	Cliftonville	A	W	6	2	S.Hughes 2, Williamson, Ewing 2, Deakin
IC	07/03/53	2	Ards	A	W	5	4	Lowry 3, S.Hughes, Feeney
IC	28/03/53	SF	Linfield	Solt	L	1	2	S.Hughes
MC	10/02/53		Crusaders	GP	W	5	1	Neill, Carlyle og, S.Hughes, Ewing, Moore
MC	24/02/53		Distillery	A	W	2	0	Deakin, Ewing
CAS	31/03/53	2	Cliftonville	H	W	3	1	Lowry, Deakin, Ewing
CAS	02/05/53	SF	Distillery	Solt	D	1	1	McFarlane
CAS	05/05/53	SFR	Distillery	Solt	L	0	2	-
GC	27/04/53	1	Glenavon	A	D	3	3	S.Hughes 3
GC	30/04/53	1R	Glenavon	H	D	1	1	Williamson
GC	04/05/53	1R2	Glenavon	A	W	3	1	Cunningham 2, Deakin
GC	12/05/53	2	Cliftonville	A	W	2	1	Ewing 2
GC	16/05/53	SF	Portadown	WP	L	0	1	-
F	12/01/53		Distillery	A	W	4	3	Williamson, Giffen, Smith, Lowry
F	06/05/53		Huddersfield Town	H	D	2	2	Unknown Tommy Hughes Benefit
F	18/05/53		Jack Kyle's XI	H	W	4	1	McFarlane 2, Deakin, Cunningham

* = held over from 1951/2

Meanwhile we got on with the job of winning the City Cup and rounded it off with a 6-1 win at Bangor. The second half of this match and the entire 9-1 drubbing of Derry were exhibitions of football at its finest in the early fifties. Between them Hughes and Lowry had scored 50 goals already and there were many calls for these two to be called into the Irish international squad to line up with ex-Glenmen Blanchflower, Bingham and McIlroy.

The big question was could Glentoran maintain this form throughout the league championship? Early results cast doubt, only one win from the first five matches, but no defeats either. However our opening game of 1953 brought two unwelcome "firsts" – our first league defeat and our first ever reverse against Crusaders. The Crues had been snappier to the ball and for the next game against Portadown Frank Grice brought our terrier Jimmy Ferran back into the side after 14 months on the injured list. In that game's Gazette Grice praised Ferran on his return and thanked Jim McFarlane for filling in at centre-forward at short notice for the injured Hughes. Sammy returned to lead the team to three more league victories in January and by the end of that month we jointly led the table with Glenavon on 16 points. Ballymena were third, two points behind.

In February attention turned to two cup competitions, one familiar and the other an

Programme Cover 1952/3.

innovation to the local game. Distillery had installed floodlights at Grosvenor Park and arranged many lucrative midweek friendlies against the cream of British football. On the local front a Belfast Floodlit league was set up and consisted of one match each week between the Whites, ourselves, Linfield and Crusaders. There was much interest in the games although managers often took the opportunity to rest key players and give run outs to lesser lights. After winning our first two games we looked set to top the final table but a suitable date for the outstanding game with Linfield could not be found prior to the spring and this match was held over until 1953/4.

The first round of the Irish Cup brought success to both the first and second elevens of Glentoran. After a disappointing Intermediate Cup final defeat against Brantwood the Seconds got through against Shorts Brothers thanks to a last minute Hugh Lowry goal in the replay. The senior XI had an easy 6-2 win at Cliftonville. In Round Two we were involved in a thriller at Ards, emerging 5-4 winners, while the Seconds overcame a feeble Bangor side 2-0. We managed to avoid each other in the semi-final draw but the "dream" final was thwarted when on the 28th March both elevens lost their respective ties. We took on Linfield in front of 25,000 at Solitude but their defence had a solid day and we went down 1-2. Over at Windsor Park Coleraine defeated the Seconds 5-0 before the lowest ever crowd at a post-war Irish Cup semi-final. The "Wee Glens" had a fine run and mention of players Bond, O'Neill, Livingstone, Dawson, Corbett, Hugh Lowry, Boyd, Smith, Giffen, Moore and Lavery must be made.

By this time the league race was reaching its final furlong. We had stuttered in February with defeats against Distillery (our first of the season at home) and Portadown on consecutive Saturdays and were faced with difficult games against Linfield and Glenavon. The Blues came to the Oval boasting a fifteen match unbeaten run but time and time again Sammy Lowry opened them up and we won 3-1. This left us two points behind Ballymena and one ahead of Glenavon with seven games remaining.

The goalscoring of Sammy Hughes was the difference between the two Glens at Mourneview Park and his hat-trick there took his season's tally past the 50 mark. The Easter period in early April proved to be vital in deciding the outcome of the league, which by now was down to ourselves or Ballymena. Both teams won convincingly on the Saturday, ourselves 7-1 over Cliftonville and United 4-0 against Distillery. However while we were seeing off Crusaders 2-0 on the Monday the Braidmen were drawing 1-1 at Portadown. Their lead over us had therefore been cut to a single point before the Tuesday clash at the Ballymena Showgrounds.

As could have been expected this game was a dour battle of few chances but the one that did come our way was tucked away by Hughes and so we were top with only three games

Team Group 1952/3 Back Row: J.Clark, N.McCarthy, J.McFarlane, W.Neill, H.Bond, W.King, S.Hughes, T.Lucas, S.Ewing, T.Edgar Front Row: S.Lowry, T.Williamson, T.Hughes, J.Deakin, J.Feeney.

left. Both sides then secured comfortable wins on the 11th April but were then faced with difficult north west away trips the following Saturday – the Glens at Derry and Ballymena at Coleraine. Derry City, fighting to avoid re-election, were in no mood to surrender and actually led 2-1 at half-time through goals by Coyle and McCaffrey. However a tremendous second half display culminated in Sammy Ewing's 87th minute winner and when news came through of Ballymena's 2-1 demise the champagne corks were popped as we became league champions for the second time in three years.

Glentoran were knocked out of both remaining competitions, the County Antrim Shield and the Gold Cup, at the semi-final stage as the season fell a bit flat in May. Sammy Hughes had the personal satisfaction of breaking Jimmy Jones' post-war seasonal scoring record of 62 by netting a hat-trick against Glenavon in the Gold Cup. After we had scored at least one goal in each of our first 54 games the well dried up against Distillery and Portadown. A second minute penalty miss in the latter was the nearest we came to a goal.

Noel McCarthy.

The season was wound up when Ireland's rugby out-half Jack Kyle brought an XI to the Oval for a friendly. As a gesture the first ten minutes of the game were played with a rugby ball, during which time McFarlane managed to score! Reverting to the more traditional football brought little joy for Kyle's XI as it finished 3-1 to the Glens.

In mid-May Billy Neill and Sammy Hughes had set off with the IFA on an eleven match month long tour of Canada. Hughes bloated his scoring tally for the season to 75, scoring eleven of the Irish team's 39 goals.

Appearances and Goals								
	App.	Goals		App.	Goals		App.	Goals
Hughes T.	51		Williamson	41	18	Livingstone	3	
Neill W.	50	2	McCarthy	40		Corbett	3	
Clark	49		Lucas	25	1	Smyth	2	
Lowry S.	48	34	Feeney	23	11	McCaul	1	
Hughes S.	47	64	Ferran	16		Unknown	33	
King	46		Cunningham	13	6	Own Goals		3
McFarlane	45	5	Bond	6		TOTAL	638	183
Ewing	45	24	Dawson	5				
Deakin	42	14	Moore	4	1			

1953/54

So near but yet so far – New grandstand opens –
Cup finals watched by over 93,000

If the previous season had been that of entertainment, success and goals then 1953/4 could be described as "the nearly year". We finished runners-up to Linfield by a single point in the Irish League, lost in the Irish Cup final to Derry City after two replays, came second in the City Cup table and in our Ulster Cup section and were knocked out at the semi-final stage in both the County Antrim Shield and the Gold Cup! Over 150 goals were scored but the season could be summed up in one word - frustration. Some silverware did come our way when we defeated the Blues in the remaining 1952/3 Belfast Floodlight League fixture. The trophy, known as the Mercer Cup, had been donated by the wife of Glentoran chairman Johnny Mercer.

The name of Hughes was missing from early season Glentoran line-ups for the first time in several years. Centre-forward Sammy was injured while centre-half Tommy had moved

Hughes and Feeney await a mistake in the Irish Cup final as Wilson heads clear.

to England for business reasons continuing his footballing career with Nuneaton Borough. Young Jim Clugston stepped successfully into the centre-forward role and at the end of August Bangor's centre-half Jim Murdough was brought to the Oval as Tommy's replacement.

Work on the new grandstand was finally completed and it was formally opened for the Ulster Cup game with Cliftonville. The original seating capacity was 2,600 and the structure of the stand remains much the same today. The City Cup began with a volatile encounter at Coleraine. A poor game was approaching half-time when a punch up flared between Willie "Flash" King and Coleraine's Montgomery - both players were sent off. The second half was also full of nasty incidents but no more dismissals as the home side clawed back from 1-3 to draw 3-3. Jim McFarlane had looked uncomfortable in the centre-half role.

After relying on a last minute equaliser to draw at Derry we went down by the odd goal in seven at Seaview leaving us three points behind section leaders Crusaders. Despite beating "the Hatchetmen" in the Oval return the Crues won the section by two points from us and went on to beat Linfield 2-1 in the final. Jimmy Ferran scored our best goal in the tournament with a 20 yard drive against Derry in the last match, when we again had to come from behind to force a draw with the Derry men.

By this time the City Cup was in full swing but we had started poorly, picking up only two points from the opening three games. Fans were bemoaning the absence of Sammy Hughes as Crusaders overturned us 3-2 after trailing 0-2 at half-time. However there was nothing anyone could do about Wilbur Cush's equaliser against us a week later. Cush picked up the ball around the half-way line and beat three men in a mazy run before shooting home.

Around the start of October the team began to click again as 33 goals were scored in eight

Bangor's McNulty punches clear from Hughes as Truesdale (left) and Cunningham look on.

games as we commenced on an 18 match unbeaten run. Ironically on the day Hughes returned to action with the reserves, Clugston helped himself to a hat-trick in an 8-1 demolishing of Cliftonville. Frank Grice solved the potential dilemma by bringing Sammy Hughes back at inside-right against Portadown, preserving Clugston at centre-forward. The 5-0 win lifted us into joint second place in the City Cup, two points behind Coleraine, after we had been lying seventh just three weeks previously. The Bannsiders dropped a point in their penultimate match (2-2 with Glenavon) but beat Ballymena 4-1 on 14th November meaning our wins over Bangor and Derry City were in vain.

We emerged as the early pacesetters in the league championship after overcoming our Seaview "bogey" in the second match. With five minutes remaining the Crues were holding us 1-1 but Lowry and Hughes popped up with decisive goals much to the relief of Danno Feeney, who had earlier missed many chances. We continued our "floodlit" form with an excellent 4-3 win at Tolka Park over a Drumcondra XI in a benefit match for their players Daly and Robinson.

Things were going well until a visit to Bangor just before Christmas. A shock awaited us as the young Bangor side ran us off our feet and ended our unbeaten run. This was the last thing we wanted going into the Christmas Day encounter with third placed Linfield. The Glens were further hampered due to the absence of the injured Murdough and then Billy Neill sustained a knock during the game. 20,000 saw the Blues win 2-0 and knock us off the top of the table.

The team pulled itself together to win the next four league matches including coming from two down against Glenavon to win 5-3. However the Lurgan men reversed that scoreline at Mourneview Park nineteen days later with an inspired display. After gaining revenge on Bangor the table stood thus with ten games remaining:
1. Ballymena 19 points, 2=. Linfield, Glentoran 18, 4. Glenavon 16.

We then lost vital ground by playing nervously at Windsor Park and going down 2-3 to the Blues. Jackie Scott made his debut in this match and over the next few weeks Scott pulled the forward line together enabling victories over Derry City, Cliftonville (a romp) and Distillery to be recorded. Ballymena, boosted by the signing of McFarlane from us, forced a 2-2 draw with Linfield. We therefore only trailed the Blues by a point with six games to go.

The league paused for the second round Irish Cup ties. We had struggled to overcome B Division Larne in Round One but easily shrugged off Ards to qualify for the semi-final. A week later we were fortunate to come away from Coleraine with a point after having to play most of the game with ten men due to an injury to Tommy Lucas. Ballymena, now out of the title race, gave us no problems and neither did Distillery in the cup semi-final despite a late rally.

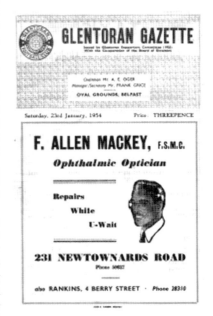

Programme Cover 1953/4.

Results 1953/54

Played 56. Won 35. Drew 12. Lost 9. Goals For 157. Against 74. % 73.2.

Honours: Mercer Cup

UC	15/08/53		Coleraine	A	D	3	3	Feeney 2, Clugston
UC	18/08/53		Ballymena United	H	W	5	1	Feeney 3, Lowry (p), Ewing
UC	20/08/53		Derry City	A	D	2	2	Clugston, Ewing
UC	22/08/53		Cliftonville	H	W	2	0	Lowry 2
UC	25/08/53		Crusaders	A	L	3	4	Cunningham, Clugston, Neill
UC	01/09/53		Ballymena United	A	D	1	1	Cunningham
UC	10/09/53		Cliftonville	A	W	4	2	Ewing, Feeney, Clugston 2
UC	15/09/53		Coleraine	H	W	3	0	Ewing 2, Deakin
UC	17/09/53		Crusaders	H	W	2	1	Clugston, Deakin
UC	21/09/53		Derry City	H	D	3	3	Ferran 2, Feeney
CC	29/08/53		Linfield	H	D	0	0	-
CC	05/09/53		Crusaders	A	L	2	3	Lewis, Ewing
CC	12/09/53		Glenavon	H	D	1	1	King
CC	19/09/53		Ballymena United	A	W	3	0	Ewing 2, Clugston
CC	26/09/53		Ards	H	W	6	0	Cunningham, Feeney 4, Ewing
CC	10/10/53		Coleraine	A	D	2	2	Lowry, Ewing
CC	17/10/53		Distillery	H	D	1	1	Feeney (p)
CC	24/10/53		Cliftonville	A	W	8	1	Feeney 4 (1p), Clugston 3, Ewing
CC	31/10/53		Portadown	H	W	5	0	S.Hughes 2, Clugston, Feeney, Lowry
CC	07/11/53		Bangor	H	W	2	0	S.Hughes 2
CC	14/11/53		Derry City	A	W	3	1	S.Hughes, Lewis, Curran og
MC	02/10/53		Linfield	GP	W	5	1	Lowry, Ewing 3, Clugston
IL	21/11/53		Ballymena United	A	W	4	1	Lowry 2, Cunningham 2
IL	28/11/53		Crusaders	A	W	3	1	Feeney, Lowry, S.Hughes
IL	05/12/53		Portadown	H	W	4	1	S.Hughes 3, Lowry
IL	12/12/53		Ards	A	W	4	0	S.Hughes, Lowry, Feeney, Clugston
IL	19/12/53		Bangor	A	L	0	2	-
IL	25/12/53		Linfield	H	L	0	2	-
IL	26/12/53		Derry City	A	W	3	2	Feeney, Clugston, S.Hughes
IL	28/12/53		Glenavon	H	W	5	3	Lowry 3, Clugston 2
IL	02/01/54		Distillery	A	W	3	2	Deakin, Cunningham, Lewis
IL	09/01/54		Cliftonville	H	W	5	1	Cunningham, Deakin, Lowry, S.Hughes, Clugston
IL	16/01/54		Glenavon	A	L	3	5	Cunningham, Clugston, Lewis
IL	23/01/54		Bangor	H	W	3	2	Neill, Lewis, S.Hughes
IL	30/01/54		Linfield	A	L	2	3	Deakin, Lowry
IL	13/02/54		Derry City	H	W	1	0	Lowry (p)
IL	20/02/54		Cliftonville	A	W	6	1	Lowry 2 (1p), Scott 2, S.Hughes 2
IL	27/02/54		Distillery	H	W	2	1	S.Hughes, Scott
IL	13/03/54		Coleraine	A	D	1	1	Cunningham
IL	20/03/54		Ballymena United	H	W	4	1	S.Hughes 3, Cunningham
IL	03/04/54		Crusaders	H	W	5	3	King, S.Hughes 2, Lowry (p), Lewis
IL	10/04/54		Portadown	A	W	3	1	S.Hughes 2, Lewis
IL	17/04/54		Ards	H	W	2	0	S.Hughes, Scott
IL	20/04/54		Coleraine	H	W	4	1	Lowry 2(1p), S.Hughes, Cunningham
IC	06/02/54	1	Larne	A	D	2	2	S.Hughes, Lowry

IC	10/02/54	1R	Larne	H	W	2	0	Lowry (p), S.Hughes
IC	06/03/54	2	Ards	A	W	4	0	S.Hughes 2, Lewis, Lowry
IC	27/03/54	SF	Distillery	WP	W	2	1	Feeney, Cunningham
IC	24/04/54	F	Derry City	WP	D	2	2	Cuningham, Feeney
IC	29/04/54	FR	Derry City	WP	D	0	0	-
IC	10/05/54	FR2	Derry City	WP	L	0	1	-
CAS	31/03/54	2	Bangor	H	W	2	0	S.Hughes, Lowry
CAS	01/05/54	SF	Ballymena United	Solt	L	2	3	Lowry 2
GC	14/04/54	1	Glenavon	H	W	3	1	Chapman 2, Murdough
GC	06/05/54	2	Ballymena United	A	W	4	1	Feeney 3, Scott
GC	11/05/54	SF	Distillery	WP	L	1	2	Lowry
F	09/12/53		Drumcondra Select	A	W	4	3	S.Hughes, Ewing, Feeney 2 (1p)
F	27/04/54		Dundela	A	W	2	1	J.Neill, Chapman George Stirling Benefit
F	04/05/54		Blackburn Rovers	H	L	0	2	Jimmy Ferran Benefit
F	19/05/54		Jack Kyle's XI	H	W	3	1	Unknown

The season was boiling up nicely and five wins in the next three weeks kept our hopes very much alive on all four fronts. Bangor did us a big favour by drawing 1-1 with Linfield in the last but one league match cutting the Blues' lead back to a single point again. We duly beat Coleraine on the last week but the Blues won 2-0 at Derry to become champions.

Derry City were our opponents in the Irish Cup final. A record crowd of 35,000 turned up to Windsor Park and what an occasion it was. The game, played against a background

Team Group 1953/4 Back Row: Murdough, Neill, Bond, Hughes, King, Lewis Front Row: Cunningham, Scott, McCarthy, Chapman, Deakin. Insets: Feeney and Lowry.

of noise and colour, justly finished 2-2. Over 30,000 attended the replay the following Thursday when Glentoran had the better of things but neither side could score. Jim Lewis was named man of the match. So a third meeting was required and this time Derry's "smash and grab" tactics won the day - the only goal coming from O'Neill on 43 minutes. The ten-men Glens (Scott sustained an injury after fifteen minutes) threw everything at Derry after the break but goalkeeper Heffron continually denied us. Derry City's victory enabled Jimmy Delaney to complete his set of English, Scottish and Irish FA Cup winner's medals. In all 93,285 attended the three games, producing gate receipts of £12,226.

Defeat the following day against Distillery in the Gold Cup semi-final completed our season. Sammy Lowry scored a grand goal in the closing seconds but must have been ruing an earlier penalty miss when he shot straight at the keeper.

Popular left-half Jimmy Ferran had a well deserved benefit match against Blackburn Rovers, who had just finished third in the English Second Division, a point off promotion. The Lancashire men, managed by Johnny Carey and with ex-Glenman Bobby Langton in their ranks, won 2-0, one of the goals scored directly from a corner kick. Note in competitive football Glentoran had scored 628 goals in the past four seasons, an average of 157 per year!

On the 1st June 1954 the players of Glentoran and Linfield met once more - but this time on a cricket pitch. The match took place at Cliftonville CC and was in aid of the local club's funds. A big crowd watched the Glens bat first and we knocked up 70 runs for 8 wickets in our 20 overs. In reply the Blues scored 71 for 7 (Isaac McDowell 45) getting home comfortably with six overs to spare.

Appearances and Goals

	App.	Goals		App.	Goals		App.	Goals
Bond	56		Hughes S.	37	30	Press	2	
McCarthy	56		King	35	2	McIlroy	2	
Lewis	56	8	Lucas	26		Chapman	2	2
Neill W.	54	2	Scott	19	5	McFarlane	1	
Lowry S.	54	29	Ewing	18	14	Corbett	1	
Cunningham	45	13	Deakin	15	5	Neill B.	1	
Feeney	43	25	Kavanagh	6		Own Goals		1
Murdough	41	1	Shanahan	5		TOTAL	616	157
Clugston	37	18	Ferran	4	2			

1954/55

Injury to Sammy Lowry – Grice departs – McIntosh arrives

One preview of the Irish League season forecast a fight between the two Glens (Glentoran and Glenavon) for the major honours of 1954/5. They got it half-right with Glenavon but for Glentoran one era was about to come to an end and a longer than expected transitional period was about to begin. Followers of the local game welcomed the introduction of Malcolm Brodie's "Soccer Survey" in the Ireland's Saturday Night, the forerunner of "Soccer Page" and "Soccer Scene".

Among the new faces at the Oval were two wingers of the same name - Tom McCabe. The left-wing variety was to establish himself as a regular in the senior side. The Ulster Cup had a sensible change in format. Teams would now only meet each other once in the sectional games and the City Cup would not commence until these games had been completed.

There were signs in our early Ulster Cup performances that the heady days of the early fifties were fading memories. Of the forwards only Sammy Hughes was on form, and his strike against Derry City on 25th August was his 200th goal for the club. Against Coleraine we were torn apart by McKennan and our two wins in the last two games only enabled us to finish third in the section. Glenavon beat Coleraine in the final.

Ards keeper Smyth dives full length to stop the ball reaching Sammy Hughes at Castlereagh Park,

The first meeting of the season with Linfield ended in defeat in the City Cup. Hughes had a great chance to put us ahead in the first minute but missed and within sixty seconds the Blues had gone 1-0 up. The half-back looked weak as we went down 1-3. Billy Neill returned a week later but Sammy Lowry was the star of the show with a hat-trick to sink Crusaders. Unfortunately Lowry also broke an ankle in this game and was out of action for seven months.

Although the team was not performing particularly well as a unit there were some outstanding individual contributions. For example, Cush's great display at left-back against Glenavon, Noel McCarthy's magnificent 35 yard drive against Ballymena and Sammy Chapman's shot from a similar distance versus Coleraine. The Ards game had a remarkable finale. With 80 minutes gone Ards led 1-0 but a flurry of scoring saw it conclude 3-3!

The second half of our City Cup campaign was completely forgettable. Jimmy Murdough was fighting hard to hold the defence together but the team was a shadow of its former self. Only one points was picked up from the last five games, a return that made us slip down to a final position of eighth, eleven points behind winners Glenavon. We even lost at Bangor after Sammy Hughes had given us a lead within ten seconds!

The Lurgan Glens also won the Gold Cup, hammering us 6-2 along the way. At one stage we were six behind and with Murdough off injured a record defeat was on the cards. However a bit of spirit came through, Willie "Flash" King making up for his earlier own goal by scoring one of our consolations.

A rare bright spot arrived when we retained the Mercer Cup. This was now relatively easy to do as the competition had been reduced to a one-off match between ourselves and Distillery under the Grosvenor Park lights. With the score standing at 2-2 ten minutes into

Results 1954/55

Played 48. Won 22. Drew 5. Lost 21. Goals For 108. Against 99. % 51.0
Honours: Mercer Cup

UC	21/08/54		Crusaders	H	W	2	1	S.Hughes 2
UC	25/08/54		Derry City	H	L	1	3	S.Hughes
UC	28/08/54		Coleraine	A	L	2	5	Lowry, S.Hughes
UC	01/09/54		Ballymena United	A	W	3	0	McCabe 2, Ewing
UC	04/09/54		Cliftonville	H	W	5	0	Lowry 2, S.Hughes 2, McCabe
CC	11/09/54		Linfield	A	L	1	3	Ewing
CC	18/09/54		Crusaders	H	W	4	1	Lowry 3, Ewing
CC	25/09/54		Glenavon	A	L	1	2	Neill
CC	09/10/54		Ballymena United	H	W	6	1	S.Hughes 3, Lewis, McCarthy, Cunningham
CC	16/10/54		Ards	A	D	3	3	Scott, Cunningham, S.Hughes
CC	23/10/54		Coleraine	H	W	3	1	Scott, S.Hughes, Chapman
CC	30/10/54		Distillery	A	L	1	3	McCabe (p)
CC	06/11/54		Cliftonville	H	D	1	1	Lewis
CC	13/11/54		Portadown	A	L	1	4	S.Hughes
CC	20/11/54		Bangor	A	L	1	3	S.Hughes
CC	27/11/54		Derry City	H	L	1	2	Neill
GC	21/09/54	1	Cliftonville	H	W	2	1	McCabe (p), Chapman
GC	13/10/54	2	Glenavon	A	L	2	6	King, McCabe (p)
MC	17/11/54		Distillery	A	W	4	2	S.Hughes 2, Chapman, McCabe
IL	04/12/54		Coleraine	H	W	3	1	S.Hughes 2, McCabe
IL	11/12/54		Bangor	A	W	3	2	McCabe 2, McCabe (RW)
IL	18/12/54		Cliftonville	H	L	1	3	Kingsmore
IL	25/12/54		Linfield	A	L	0	3	-
IL	27/12/54		Distillery	H	L	1	4	King
IL	01/01/55		Ballymena United	A	W	4	0	Lewis 2, McCabe, Chapman
IL	08/01/55		Glenavon	H	L	2	5	S.Hughes, Cunningham
IL	15/01/55		Crusaders	A	W	5	1	S.Hughes 3, Chapman, McCarthy (p)
IL	22/01/55		Portadown	A	L	2	3	Chapman, S.Hughes
IL	29/01/55		Ards	H	W	3	2	Chapman, Humphreys, Johnston
IL	12/02/55		Derry City	A	L	1	2	Johnston
IL	19/02/55		Coleraine	A	D	1	1	Humphreys
IL	26/02/55		Bangor	H	W	5	3	Corry, Humphreys 2, Chapman, S.Hughes
IL	12/03/55		Cliftonville	A	W	2	1	Cunningham, Gamble og
IL	19/03/55		Linfield	H	L	1	2	S.Hughes
IL	02/04/55		Distillery	A	W	3	1	McCabe, Scott, McConkey
IL	09/04/55		Ballymena United	H	W	4	1	S.Hughes 2, Murdough 2
IL	11/04/55		Glenavon	A	L	1	3	S.Hughes
IL	12/04/55		Crusaders	H	L	1	2	McCabe
IL	16/04/55		Portadown	H	W	4	2	Scott, Buchanan og, McCabe, Lewis
IL	27/04/55		Derry City	H	W	6	1	Lowry 2, S.Hughes, McCabe, Quee 2
IL	30/04/55		Ards	A	L	1	3	Quee
IC	05/02/55	1	East Belfast	H	W	1	0	McCabe
IC	05/03/55	2	Portadown	H	D	1	1	McCabe
IC	10/03/55	2R	Portadown	A	D	1	1	S.Hughes
IC	14/03/55	2R2	Portadown	Solt	W	2	0	S.Hughes 2

IC	26/03/55	SF	Glenavon	WP	L	0	5	-
CAS	21/03/55	1	Dundela	H	W	4	1	Deakin, S.Hughes, Scott, Johnston
CAS	06/04/55	2	Bangor	A	L	1	3	King
F	06/05/55		Leeds United	H	L	1	2	Lowry
F	09/05/55		Aberdeen	H	W	4	3	McQuade, S.Hughes, Young og, Weatherup Noel McCarthy Benefit

the second half captain Sammy Ewing had to retire. The Whites were now favourites but it was the Glens who came on strongest, scoring twice more and having Gill in goals to thank for preventing Distillery replying.

After we won our opening two league games the press were proclaiming, "Happy Days are Here Again" at the Oval. This was premature talk, however, as manager Frank Grice stated his intention to leave the club and take over the reins at Chelmsford City. Grice left after we had been routed by Glenavon and Jimmy Jones at the Oval in January 1955 - our fourth defeat in five league games. Johnny Geary took temporary charge of the team until a suitable new manager could be found.

Some of the Glens' displays had been listless, dispirited and jointless but not so the performances of right-half Billy Neill, who maintained excellent form throughout. By the half-way stage of the league we had picked up only 10 points from 11 games and it was clear that we would not be serious title contenders. Many new players were tried, Tommy Lowry (brother of Sammy), Bertie Neill, Weatherall, Press, Humphries, Kingsmore, Johnston and Donaghy but results continued to be mediocre.

The Irish Cup campaign began with a narrow win over juniors East Belfast but the second round tie versus Portadown was much more typical of cup football. The first game at the Oval was a fierce encounter with plenty of fisticuffs including at one stage over a dozen players involved in a free for all. The replay at Shamrock Park was disappointing but in the decisive match at neutral Solitude veteran Johnny Deakin made a rare appearance and inspired us to victory.

We entered the semi-final with Glenavon as rank outsiders and so it proved once they went ahead on ten minutes. The through balls of the Glenavon half-back trio were superb and once the fourth goal went in the Glenmen in the 9,000 crowded headed for the exits. The Lurgan men eventually won 5-0 but were shocked in the final by another east Belfast side as Dundela sprang the surprise of the century to become the first junior side to lift the cup. The result, Glenavon 0 Dundela 3, unbelievable after we had easily beaten the Duns in the Shield just a few weeks earlier.

Meanwhile our fortunes had plummeted further with a Shield exit at the hands of Bangor and consecutive Easter defeats against Glenavon and Crusaders. The directors then took the step of appointing 37 year old Jimmy McIntosh as manager. McIntosh, who had been Distillery's player-manager for nearly three years, had played over 125 Football League games for Blackpool and Everton.

The Scot began on the right foot with a win over Portadown and then welcomed Sammy Lowry back from injury for the Derry City game. Lowry was outstanding and netted twice, as did a young

Programme Cover 1954/5.

debutant inside-left Sammy Quee. We wound up the league by losing at Castlereagh Park for the first time in seven years and finished sixth. Glenavon and Linfield shared top spot - the Blues winning the resultant Oval test match 2-0.

For Glentoran though a poor season concluded with two friendlies. Firstly we narrowly lost to a strong Leeds United after holding an interval lead. Harry Bond fumbled a back pass for the first Leeds goal and then Mack got the winner. Leeds won their other two tour games more comfortably - 6-2 over Ballymena and 8-1 over Ards. In Noel McCarthy's benefit game against Aberdeen we were strengthened by four guest players, two of whom (McQuade of Derry City and Syd Weatherup of Distillery) got on the scoresheet. Aberdeen had led 2-0 early on but were pegged back to 3-3 at half-time before the Glens won 4-3.

A nice bonus but Jimmy McIntosh had a huge task on his hands as he attempted to return Glentoran back to the top of the Irish League in 1955/6.

Appearances and Goals

	App.	Goals		App.	Goals		App.	Goals
Lewis	43	5	Johnston	14	3	Quee	2	3
McCarthy	40	2	Humphreys	12	4	Kingsmore	2	1
McCabe (LW)	40	16	Neill B.	11		McCauley	1	
Hughes S.	39	32	Weatherall	10		Lyons	1	
Bond	38		Donaghy	10		Nicholl	1	
King	34	3	Gill	7		Michael	1	
Murdough	33	2	Press	7		Bell	1	
Chapman	30	9	Ewing	6	3	Corry	1	1
Neill W.	24	2	Lowry T.	5		Unknown	33	
Cunningham	20	4	McCabe (RW)	4	1	Own Goals		2
Cush	18		Deakin	4	1			
Scott	17	5	Lucas	2		TOTAL	528	108
Lowry S.	15	8	McConkey	2	1			

1955/56

Another mediocre season – Cup final trilogy again –
New physio Bobby McGregor

Overall season 1955/6 was a slight improvement on 1954/5 but still Glentoran were a long way from being a force to be reckoned with. Once again the Ulster Cup kicked off affairs and we commenced with a useful point at Seaview. However a midweek trip to Derry was less fruitful, Delaney notching a hat-trick for the home side in a 5-1 hammering. In the Coleraine game the referee had to retire after half an hour following an accidental collision with a player. One of the linesmen took over the whistle. After defeating Ballymena we completed our group matches with a return to Celtic Park. Cliftonville were using Celtic's old stadium while Solitude was being returfed. Defeat here left us one from bottom of the final group table, well behind leaders Coleraine, who lost 1-5 to Linfield in the final.

By the commencement of the City Cup the team were starting to blend together and show some fighting spirit. Jimmy McIntosh had introduced many new faces, Eddie Mulvey, Eamon McMahon (ex-Glasgow Celtic) in goals and Southern Irelander Ambrose Fogarty (ex-Bohemians) to go alongside the established players Billy Neill, Noel McCarthy, Tommy Lucas, Jimmy Murdough, Willie "Flash" King, the two Lowrys and Sammy Hughes. This was also Bobby McGregor's first season as physiotherapist. Bobby had replaced Tommy Edgar.

Sandwiched between hard fought draws with Linfield and Glenavon was a win over Crusaders when we laid siege to Walker's goal but had to be content with one goal. Sammy Quee continued to find the net regularly as we gave footballing lessons to Ards and Glenavon and moved into fourth position in the City Cup. Two late goals by Cliftonville killed off our hopes but this did not prevent scouts of many English clubs coming to watch our games. It was reported that Newcastle, Sheffield United and Man. City were all after Fogarty. A deserved win at Derry ensured our fourth place. A play-off was necessary to decide the fate of the City Cup after Glenavon and Coleraine finished level on points. The Lurgan men won this 4-0.

Jimmy McIntosh.

Three days earlier the Blues had knocked us out of the Gold Cup at the semi-final stage. The Glens were down to ten men after only 25 minutes but we still managed to turn round 2-1 up. Linfield gradually took over in the second half and the dismissal of Sammy Lowry and Rice seven minutes from time made no difference to the final outcome.

Early results in the League Championship suggested we might again finish in a mid-table position. We threw away a two goal lead at Bangor (losing 2-4) but again forced draws against the "big guns" of Glenavon and Linfield. The 4-4 game at Mourneview Park was a rough-house both on and off the pitch. Glenavon had another three goals disallowed and many Glentoran fans were arrested. One of the Glentoran goals came from young John Tully. He and Cyril Nolan shared the left wing berth during the season.

Reduced success usually leads to financial trouble and the board of directors were considering asking the IFA for a £5,000 loan to facilitate ground improvements.

January 1956 was a bad month for us as we lost our first three games of the new year. The only home cheer at the Portadown match came when the ball burst following a free-kick.

A youthful Bobby McGregor.

McCarthy had a chance to equalise but missed an 89th minute penalty. The Glens had tried to play it too close on a muddy surface but at least Beggs had a good debut at outside right.

We recorded back to back wins against Ards to move up into fifth. Sammy Lowry got the winner in the second match in the last minute after Harry Bond had saved Hedley's penalty five minutes earlier. Bangor were proving to be the surprise team of the season and confirmed that by coming to the Oval and opening up a 3-0 interval lead. We fought back and only another last minute penalty miss prevented us earning a draw.

Our best league display of the campaign came at home to Glenavon on 3rd March. The whole forward line of Lowry, Fogarty, Hughes, Mulvey and Nolan were excellent and Sammy Hughes crowned the win with a brilliant diving header. The Gazette editor wondered if this display indicated that our former greatness had returned and urged supporters to re-create "the Oval Roar". However it was not to be and two goals in the last eight minutes enabled Cliftonville to defeat us in the very next league match.

After defeats by Distillery in the Mercer Cup and County Antrim Shield we only had the Irish Cup to play for. McIntosh used the remaining league games to try out many reserves including young inside-forwards Walter Bruce and Ned Dubois. Three wins in the last four games enabled us to finish fifth, a long way behind champions Linfield.

The road to the Irish Cup final had begun back in early February at Ballymena Showgrounds. After a scoreless first half we took command after the interval scoring four goals in a 22 minute spell to totally eclipse Ballymena. Drawn away to Linfield Swifts in round two forced a Friday night floodlit game at Grosvenor Park as Linfield were using Windsor Park on the Saturday. Over 12,000 turned up but the Swifts just did not measure up and Nolan was the main destroyer in our 3-0 win. In the semi-final we easily swept away the Ports 4-0 as we maintained our record of not conceding a goal in the Cup.

This set up the final against Jimmy McIntosh's old team Distillery. The tie drew 16,000 to Windsor Park but the game lacked any real zest or enthusiasm. Twice Glentoran were ahead through Fogarty and Nolan but the "never say die" Whites came back to force a replay. That took place the following Thursday but again it was a disappointing encounter and no-one was sorry when the final whistle went. Distillery's ex-Glens keeper Beare was man of the match.

So for the fifth time in our history we went to a third match in the Irish Cup final. This time it was to be Distillery's cup, Currie scoring the only goal as we suffered our fifteenth defeat in 22 Irish Cup finals. The future Irish internationalist, Derek Dougan, was in Distillery's ranks. Glentoran shareholders called for an EGM to discuss the club's future.

Willie King was this season's beneficiary and Bedford Town visited the Oval in early May. Bedford defeated a supposedly strengthened Glens XI 6-1, the goals coming from Staroschik (2), Yates (2), Stobbart and Berry. So another poor season finished with the Glens failing to register 100 goals for the first time since 1948/9.

Eamon McMahon.

Results 1955/56

Played 49. Won 21. Drew 11. Lost 17. Goals For 97. Against 74. % 54.1

UC	20/08/55		Crusaders	A	D	1	1	Quee
UC	24/08/55		Derry City	A	L	1	5	Warren
UC	27/08/55		Coleraine	H	L	2	3	Quee, Warren
UC	31/08/55		Ballymena United	H	W	3	0	Quee, Mulvey, S.Hughes
UC	03/09/55		Cliftonville	CP	L	0	2	-
CC	10/09/55		Linfield	H	D	0	0	-
CC	17/09/55		Crusaders	A	W	1	0	Fogarty
CC	24/09/55		Glenavon	H	D	1	1	Liggett og
CC	01/10/55		Ballymena United	A	L	1	2	King
CC	15/10/55		Ards	H	W	3	0	Quee 2, McConnell
CC	22/10/55		Coleraine	A	D	1	1	Quee
CC	29/10/55		Distillery	H	W	4	0	S.Lowry 3, Quee
CC	05/11/55		Cliftonville	A	L	1	2	McCarthy
CC	12/11/55		Portadown	H	W	6	0	Quee, S.Lowry 2, Fogarty, S.Hughes 2
CC	19/11/55		Bangor	H	D	1	1	S.Lowry
CC	26/11/55		Derry City	A	W	2	1	Fogarty 2
GC	26/09/55	1	Crusaders	H	W	4	1	S.Lowry 2, Neill, Quee
GC	05/10/55	2	Derry City	H	W	5	3	T.Lowry, King, Quee, Curran og, Fogarty
GC	23/11/55	SF	Linfield	Solt	L	2	4	S.Hughes, Fogarty
IL	03/12/55		Derry City	H	W	4	2	Fogarty 2, S.Hughes, Mulvey
IL	10/12/55		Bangor	A	L	2	4	Mulvey, Fogarty
IL	17/12/55		Distillery	H	D	0	0	-
IL	24/12/55		Cliftonville	A	W	1	0	Fogarty
IL	26/12/55		Linfield	H	D	1	1	S.Lowry (p)
IL	27/12/55		Glenavon	A	D	4	4	S.Hughes 2, Tully, S.Lowry
IL	31/12/55		Crusaders	A	W	3	2	King, S.Hughes 2
IL	07/01/56		Coleraine	H	L	0	1	-
IL	14/01/56		Ballymena United	A	L	1	4	S.Hughes
IL	21/01/56		Portadown	H	L	0	1	-
IL	28/01/56		Ards	H	W	2	1	S.Lowry, S.Hughes
IL	11/02/56		Ards	A	W	3	2	S.Lowry 2(1p), S.Hughes
IL	18/02/56		Bangor	H	L	2	3	S.Lowry 2
IL	25/02/56		Derry City	A	W	2	1	Mulvey 2
IL	03/03/56		Glenavon	H	W	4	2	S.Lowry 2, S.Hughes, Armstrong og
IL	17/03/56		Cliftonville	H	L	3	4	S.Hughes 2, Mulvey
IL	31/03/56		Linfield	A	L	0	1	-
IL	03/04/56		Distillery	A	D	0	0	-
IL	07/04/56		Crusaders	H	W	2	1	S.Lowry 2(1p)
IL	14/04/56		Coleraine	A	W	3	2	Mulvey, S.Lowry, Dubois
IL	28/04/56		Ballymena United	H	L	2	3	S.Hughes, S.Lowry
IL	04/05/56		Portadown	A	W	4	1	Cush, Dubois 2, McCauley
IC	04/02/56	1	Ballymena United	A	W	4	0	S.Hughes 2, S.Lowry, Fogarty
IC	09/03/56	2	Linfield Swifts	GP	W	3	0	Nolan, S.Hughes, Fogarty
IC	24/03/56	SF	Portadown	WP	W	4	0	Mulvey 2, Nolan, S.Hughes
IC	21/04/56	F	Distillery	WP	D	2	2	Fogarty, Nolan
IC	26/04/56	FR	Distillery	WP	D	1	1	Nolan
IC	30/04/56	FR2	Distillery	WP	L	0	1	-
MC	22/02/56		Distillery	A	L	1	2	Mulvey
CAS	09/04/56	2	Distillery	A	L	0	1	-
F	07/05/56		Bedford Town	H	L	1	6	McKinstry

Willie King Benefit

Appearances and Goals

	App.	Goals		App.	Goals		App.	Goals
Neill W.	43	1	Tully	16	1	Kearns	1	
Fogarty	43	13	Nolan C.	15	4	Elder	1	
Murdough	42		Bond	11		Potter	1	
Lowry S.	42	22	Dubois	10	3	Gallagher	1	
McCarthy	38	1	McConnell	7	1	Doherty	1	
McMahon	37		Bruce	5		Neill B.	1	
Hughes S.	36	20	Courtney	4		McCauley	1	1
Cush	35	1	Collins	3		Unknown	11	
Mulvey	32	10	Lewis	3		Own Goals		3
Lowry T.	27	1	Cairns	3				
King	24	3	Warren	3	2	TOTAL	539	97
Lucas	19		McCabe (LW)	2				
Quee	19	10	Beggs	2				

1956/57

Two stalwarts honoured – Trevor Thompson debuts -
Silverware finally captured

The format of the season changed again in 1956/7. The Ulster Cup became a carbon copy of the City Cup with all the teams playing each other once. The City Cup itself was moved to the end of the season with the Irish League bisecting these two tournaments, commencing in mid-October. For Glentoran our slow improvement continued but it was not until the latter part of May that a trophy came our way - the first since the 1952/3 League Championship!

The Glens, boosted by the signing of Ballymena's right-winger Frank Haslett, began the season badly, finishing a lowly seventh in the Ulster Cup. On the opening day we had led Coleraine 2-1 when Mulvey missed a penalty and the chance to complete a personal hat-trick. The Bannsiders took their chance to comeback and win 4-2.

Our defence was strengthened for the visit of Distillery on the Wednesday night by the inclusion of the previously unsigned trio of Billy Neill, Jimmy Murdough and Sammy Lowry. We won 3-1 but it was a dreary game, typical of many of our Ulster Cup fixtures. Walter Bruce got his first goal for the club in the 82nd minute to earn a win at Solitude but luck deserted us at Windsor Park four days later. With half an hour remaining we led 2-1 then Billy Neill fractured his ankle in making a dramatic goal-line clearance. The ten man Glens fought hard but eventually Ervine gave the Blues victory with an 85th minute shot.

The fans were becoming impatient as we suffered four 2-3 defeats in five games. Even our first goal against Portadown was a farce - a defender in attempting to clear blasted the ball against Sammy Lowry's back and the ball cannoned into the net. Sammy Hughes marked his comeback against Ards with a brilliant diving header in the 26th minute - his 250th Glens goal. Seventeen year old Jim Weatherup made his debut the following Saturday against Bangor in a match where we only scored one penalty out of three awarded, Lowry and Haslett the two culprits.

Ambrose Fogarty

Flash King had a great game against his old team-mates kicking one off the line. Before the game Mrs. G.B.Hannah had opened the new dressing rooms at the Oval. She paid tribute to he supporters' clubs' financial efforts and IFA secretary Billy Drennan remarked that, "It was an auspicious start to getting back to the pre-war eminence of the old Oval."

Winning the last three Ulster Cup games lifted us away from the bottom of the table. Hughes was showing some old-time sprightliness but our best forward was Haslett who capped his form with a brilliant goal against Crusaders.

The second half of October was a busy time as we played six games of varying nature. The league kicked off with defeat against a more polished Linfield side but we were soon on the winning trail as Fogarty ran into scoring mood. Ambrose netted twice against Cliftonville with stunning shots. Far from full strength Glentoran and Distillery teams contested the Mercer Cup with Trevor Thompson making his debut in the first game. The Whites had the replay sewn up in the first fifteen minutes, going 3-0 up. Our young side gave everything in the second half and only good goalkeeping by Beare contained the score to 2-4.

Sammy Hughes opens the scoring against Derry City.

The Glens came up against Stanley Matthews in a floodlit friendly at Drumcondra. The old maestro, guesting for the Dublin side, had a superb game showing off his shuffling dribbles, body swerves and accurate crossing. Cross netted a hat-trick in the home side's 3-2 win.

Maybe some of Matthews skill rubbed off on our players as we suffered only one defeat in 13 league games. Glenavon were our conquerors but we were handicapped by the loss of McMahon to a thumb injury. Haslett had to don the goalkeeper's jersey in the second half.

A major factor in this satisfying spell was the team spirit emerging from having a settled side. Our half-back line of Billy Truesdale, Murdough and Patton provided the base for many attacking moves while the versatile Ned Dubois was effective at centre-forward in the ever increasing absence of Hughes.

A good example came in the floodlit return fixture with Linfield, re-arranged for New Year's Eve after all the Christmas fixtures had been snowed off. The Blues were 2-0 up in ten minutes but we refused to lie down and two Haslett goals ensured a share of the points. After we beat Bangor the first league table of 1957 read:

Linfield, played 15, points 23, Glenavon 13-21 Glentoran 14-21.
A tight situation.

Our great run came to an end at a muddy Brandywell but a week later Hughes returned to the side for the vital encounter with Glenavon. Sammy gave a heroic performance and scored both our goals as the Lurgan men were outclassed - a rare event. However our League hopes were ruined at Seaview in the next match when once again despite laying siege to the Crues goal we went down 1-3.

Attention turned to the Irish Cup and what looked on paper like a relatively easy tie with Linfield Swifts proved anything but. One of the largest crowds of the season so far turned up and saw the Swifts control most of the game. Twice they led until a late disputed goal from Hughes saw them off.

Following a couple of exciting high scoring league fixtures, including a sensational second half recovery at Portadown after being 1-3 down, Linfield's 1st XI came to the Oval in the second round of the cup. The 30,000 crowd created a wonderful atmosphere as the teams served up 90 minutes of honest endeavour. Sammy Lowry was hailed as "the Monarch of the Glens" as he gave us the lead on nine minutes and then equalised in the 81st after Linfield goals by Tommy Dickson and Matt Nixon. Nearly 30,000 more attended the replay when the Blues won 2-1 with a doubtful goal.

Glentoran played some flowing football in our last few league games although there was nothing at stake. Youngsters John Frazer and Matt Crothers made their debuts. The most notable events of these matches were the goals of 19 year old centre-forward Trevor Thompson. He opened his account with four against Ballymena including a first half hat-trick after we had trailed 0-2 after eleven minutes. The Glens finished fourth in the league behind champions Glenavon. The Lurgan men completed the double as they defeated Derry City 2-0 in the Irish Cup final.

The City Cup opened with another unlucky defeat against Linfield after we ran the game for 75 minutes. Frustration among our fans resulted in many fights breaking out on the terraces. However after this reverse we remained unbeaten in the competition. Manager Jimmy McIntosh was being heavily criticised for the team's off-side tactics and he reacted angrily in the press and club programme,

"I am against any team going out deliberately to lure their opponents into the offside trap. Glentoran don't do that. Irish League forwards are moaning that our defence is frustrating them but a player is not worth his first team place if he is consistently caught off-side. The player blamed most is Jimmy Murdough but though he is an expert in catching forwards on the hop, he does not do it deliberately. Blame our opponents - they are suckers if they are so easily beaten."

At the other end of the pitch Thompson continued his remarkable scoring form throughout the City Cup and the County Antrim Shield. Thompson acknowledged the contribution made by Sammy Hughes, who was now playing at inside-forward but unselfishly passed on positional and scoring advice to the Glengormley youngster. The only points we dropped in these matches came at Portadown (when they equalised in the 86th minute) and at Ards after McCarthy had to take McMahon's place in goals when the latter was hit on the chin by a fierce drive from Langton.

Our game with Distillery was played on a Saturday evening to avoid clashing with the Aston Villa - Man. Utd. FA Cup Final and after Truesdale's outstanding display had inspired us to victory the City Cup table read:

Glentoran played 9, points 14, Linfield 8-13, Distillery 8-12.

Favourites Linfield then drew their next two games and when Distillery beat the Blues 1-0 at Windsor in the last match it meant a play-off was needed between ourselves and the Whites to decide the trophy's destination.

Eddie Mulvey.

Meanwhile we had been surprisingly knocked out of the Gold Cup by Crusaders but had battled through to another meeting with Distillery in the final of the Shield. In our semi-final with Ards one of the Grosvenor Park floodlights was broken by the ball!

The County Antrim Shield final was a tale of missed chances by two evenly matched teams. Before the replay Glentoran had a chance to pay tribute to two great stalwarts of the 1950's Sammy Hughes and Billy Neill. The club had awarded the duo a joint benefit and the numerous fund raising events culminated in a match against Everton. The game itself was not a classic as the Glens fielded eight guest players. Haughey scored the only goal for Everton near the end.

We grasped a trophy at last by beating Distillery 4-0 in the Shield final replay. The Whites defence made one blunder after another and the score could have been much heavier. Two days later the teams were back at Solitude to play off for the City Cup. A much more determined Grosvenor Park outfit took the lead but Thompson equalised on 25 minutes. The Whites lost their centre-half five minutes after the interval and tired towards the end but their was no further scoring until 18 minutes into extra-time when Sammy Hughes notched the decider.

Results 1956/57

Played 55. Won 31. Drew 10. Lost 14. Goals For 126. Against 89 .% 65.5.
Honours: City Cup, County Antrim Shield

UC	18/08/56		Coleraine	A	L	2	4	Mulvey 2
UC	22/08/56		Distillery	H	W	3	1	Haslett, Fogarty, Mulvey
UC	25/08/56		Clftonville	A	W	2	1	C.Nolan, Bruce
UC	29/08/56		Linfield	A	L	2	3	C.Nolan, Haslett
UC	01/09/56		Portadown	H	L	2	3	S.Lowry, Haslett
UC	03/09/56		Ards	H	D	3	3	Feeney og, S.Hughes, Haslett
UC	08/09/56		Bangor	H	L	2	3	Mulvey, Halsett (p)
UC	11/09/56		Ballymena United	A	L	2	3	S.Lowry 2
UC	15/09/56		Derry City	A	W	2	1	S.Hughes, O'Boyle og
UC	22/09/56		Glenavon	H	W	2	1	S.Hughes, Haslett
UC	29/09/56		Crusaders	A	W	3	1	Mulvey, S.Lowry, Haslett
IL	13/10/56		Linfield	H	L	1	3	S.Hughes
IL	20/10/56		Ballymena United	A	W	3	1	Mulvey 2, Fogarty
IL	27/10/56		Cliftonville	H	W	2	1	Fogarty 2
IL	03/11/56		Bangor	A	D	1	1	Haslett
IL	10/11/56		Derry City	H	W	4	0	S.Hughes 2, S.Lowry, Bruce
IL	17/11/56		Glenavon	A	L	1	3	Bruce
IL	24/11/56		Crusaders	H	W	3	1	S.Hughes, Campbell og, S.Lowry
IL	01/12/56		Portadown	A	W	3	2	Dubois 2, Mulvey
IL	08/12/56		Ards	H	W	1	0	Mulvey
IL	15/12/56		Distillery	A	D	2	2	Haslett, Mulvey
IL	22/12/56		Coleraine	H	W	3	2	Montgomery og, S.Lowry, Fogarty
IL	29/12/56		Cliftonville	A	W	4	2	Dubois 2, Mulvey, S.Lowry
IL	31/12/56		Linfield	A	D	2	2	Haslett 2(1p)
IL	05/01/57		Bangor	H	W	3	1	S.Lowry, Dubois, Mulvey
IL	12/01/57		Derry City	A	L	1	2	Mulvey
IL	19/01/57		Glenavon	H	W	2	1	S.Hughes 2
IL	26/01/57		Crusaders	A	L	1	3	Mulvey
IL	09/02/57		Portadown	H	W	5	4	C.Nolan, S.Hughes 2, Truesdale, Fogarty
IL	16/02/57		Ards	A	D	3	3	S.Lowry, Fogarty, S.Hughes
IL	09/03/57		Coleraine	A	L	1	3	S.Lowry
IL	13/03/57		Ballymena United	H	W	7	2	Thompson 4, Lynch og, Neill 2
IL	18/03/57		Distillery	H	W	3	0	Cush (p), Thompson, Frazer
MC	16/10/56		Distillery	A	D	2	2	Haslett 2
MC	29/10/56	R	Distillery	A	L	2	4	Frazer, Weatherup
IC	02/02/57		Linfield Swifts	H	W	3	2	S.Lowry, Haslett, S.Hughes
IC	02/03/57		Linfield	H	D	2	2	S.Lowry 2
IC	06/03/57		Linfield	A	L	1	2	Haslett (p)
CC	16/03/57		Linfield	H	L	1	2	Thompson
CC	23/03/57		Portadown	A	D	2	2	Thompson, Fogarty
CC	30/03/57		Crusaders	H	W	4	0	Thompson 3, S.Hughes
CC	06/04/57		Glenavon	A	W	1	0	S.Lowry
CC	20/04/57		Ballymena United	H	W	4	2	Thompson 3, Mulvey
CC	23/04/57		Ards	A	D	1	1	S.Hughes
CC	30/04/57		Coleraine	H	W	2	1	S.Hughes, Mulvey
CC	02/05/57		Bangor	A	W	2	1	Mulvey, Dubois
CC	04/05/57		Distillery	A	W	2	1	S.Hughes, Fogarty
CC	08/05/57		Derry City	H	W	3	1	Mulvey 2(2p), S.Lowry
CC	11/05/57		Cliftonville	H	W	3	0	Thompson, S.Lowry, Truesdale
CC	20/05/57	TM	Distillery	Solt	W	2	1	aet – Thompson, S.Hughes

CAS	28/03/57	2	Bangor	A	W	1	0	S.Lowry
CAS	29/04/57	SF	Ards	GP	W	2	0	Thompson 2
CAS	13/05/57	F	Distillery	Solt	D	0	0	-
CAS	18/05/57	FR	Distillery	Solt	W	4	0	Thompson 2, Mulvey, S.Hughes
GC	16/04/57	1	Crusaders	A	L	1	2	Mulvey
F	24/10/56		Drumcondra	A	L	2	3	D.Nolan, C.Nolan (p)
F	15/05/57		Everton	H	L	0	1	Billy Neill/Sammy Hughes Benefit

Ironically after these much waited for successes the club and manager parted company - Jimmy McIntosh soon became Greenock Morton's manager. Financially the club announced a profit of £348 for the season, comparing favourably with a deficit of £315 in 1955/6.

Appearances and Goals

	App.	Goals		App.	Goals		App.	Goals
Murdoch	50		Dubois	32	6	Weatherup	3	1
McMahon	48		Patton	23		Bond	3	
Lowry S.	48	18	Neill W.	20	2	Fullerton	2	
Fogarty	46	9	Thompson	18	19	Ferguson	1	
Lucas	43		Nolan C.	17	3	Pinkerton	1	
Truesdale	37	2	Bruce	15	3	Leeman	1	
Mulvey	36	21	Nolan D.	13		Unknown	22	
McCarthy	35		Cush	11	1	Own Goals		5
Haslett	34	15	Frazer	8	2	TOTAL	605	126
Hughes S.	34	19	White	4				

1957/58

Fogarty's transfer – Seconds amazing win - The short reign of Ken Chisholm

The board of directors brought several new faces to the Oval in time for the start of the season. These included Lindsay (ex-Bangor), R.Bennett (ex-Ards) and Desmond McGreevy (ex-Derry City) but the newcomer to have most impact was 18 year old 6'3" goalkeeper George Fullerton. Fullerton was our regular goalie, until he joined Leeds United as a part-time professional in March, as Eamon McMahon was suspended due to breach of contract. He never made the Elland Road first team but later played a dozen league games for Barrow. The format for the season reverted back to that of 1955/6, earning the general approval of players and supporters alike.

Derry, including ex-Glenman Haslett, shocked us in the opening Ulster Cup fixture. This was the first time City had won their opening match in 17 years! However we recovered to

George Fullerton gathers the ball against Bangor in the Irish Cup.

win our remaining four sectional games. "Bimbo" Weatherup was the star against Coleraine, after coming in as a late replacement for Lindsay at outside-left. The Glens won 4-2 but the fans on the terraces had gone wild when the referee disallowed a goal from a 20 yard Sammy Lowry free-kick. Lively wins over Cliftonville and Crusaders enabled us to qualify for the final with Distillery.

Before that match the Gold and City Cups got underway. In the former Coleraine gained revenge for that earlier defeat, the only goal coming from Hubert Barr in the 48th minute. Two days later we visited Windsor Park in the City Cup. After a scoreless first half Hughes headed us ahead then Tommy Dickson equalised. Sammy Lowry then took over, blasting home a 25 yard shot and firing in from nine yards to make it 3-1. Dickson pulled one back from the penalty spot and then, with only eight minutes remaining, Fullerton and Murdough got into a mix-up and new Linfield player-coach Jackie Milburn tapped home the equaliser. After an easy win at Seaview we entertained Glenavon and again Fullerton gave an excellent display. "Jungle Jim" Murdough subdued Jimmy Jones and only an 85th minute goal earned the visitors a point.

Distillery maintained their unbeaten start to the season when they defeated us 4-1 in the replay of the Ulster Cup final. We had come in for criticism for our "off-side" tactics in the first match but the smooth working Whites clicked in the replay, despite missing Derek Dougan who had just been transferred to Portsmouth. Ambrose Fogarty scored for us but also missed a penalty.

The team rolled its sleeves up and recorded four high scoring City Cup wins. We were 3-0 up after 28 minutes at Ballymena and in a similar position against Bangor inside 17 minutes. Fogarty netted one of the goals in that match and later that evening became a Sunderland player as their manager Alan Brown agreed a transfer fee of £3,500 with the directors. The 24 year old Dubliner was delighted at the chance of full-time football and intended to get really fit and make it in England. This he did and Fogarty went on to make nearly 300 Football League appearances for the Black Cats and Hartlepool over nine years and win 11 full caps for the Republic of Ireland.

Going into the City Cup game with Distillery on 2nd November the table read:

1. Linfield 13 points, 2. Glentoran 12, 3. Distillery 11 after seven matches. The Whites had lost 1-7 to Linfield in the Gold Cup but quickly regained their composure to defeat us 3-1 and severely dent our City Cup hopes. A week later though Eddie Mulvey's hat-trick condemned Derry to their first home defeat of the season and on the following Thursday Mulvey was transferred to Stockport County. Ironically Stockport's manager, Willie Moir, had been trying to sign Mulvey's schoolboy friend Fogarty. Mulvey went on to score five times in 26 games for the Edgeley Park men.

Programme Cover 1957/8.

While the firsts were winning at Derry, Glentoran II were involved in a remarkable Intermediate Cup tie with Coleraine Crusaders at the Oval. Trailing 1-3 at the interval, they scored nine in the second half to win 10-5! The team, with scorers in brackets, was: Dunlop; Leeman, Crothers; Patton, White, Keenan; Frazer (3, 1p), Bruce (3), Murphy (2), Pinkerton (2), McGreevy.

When Coleraine beat Linfield in the penultimate City Cup match there was all to play for. The Blues held a single point lead over ourselves and Distillery and they were down to meet the Whites in the last fixture. Our comfortable win at Portadown was deemed irrelevant though as the Blues beat Distillery 2-1 to take the City Cup to Windsor.

A few eyebrows moved upwards when we lost our opening league match to Ards at the Oval and the County Down men would raise a few more before the end of the campaign. George Barr's goal set us on our way to victory at last over Distillery and Trevor Thompson was making himself a real nuisance for defences. Christmas brought mixed fortunes for the club - two league defeats for the 1st XI (including 1-5 at Ballymena after going ahead) but the Seconds captured the Steel and Sons Cup with a 3-0 win over Larne.

Our inconsistent form continued into early 1958 and the directors stepped up their efforts to appoint a manager. We had carefree frolics against the Reds and Derry but had a nightmare second half at Mourneview Park, conceding five after holding an interval lead. At the end of January the directors announced that Ken Chisholm would be the new player-manager at the Oval. Chisholm, a Scot, had played for Partick Thistle, Leeds, Leicester, Coventry, Cardiff, Sunderland and Workington, thus completing his "round Britain" tour by coming to Belfast.

The Glens playing fortunes reached a trough for the season with a first round exit in the Irish Cup at Bangor. The Seconds went out to Ards. Chisholm made his debut against Crusaders and had a great game in our 5-2 victory. Before kick-off a minutes silence was observed for the Manchester United players and officials who had lost their lives in the Munich air disaster. During the game, played on a snowy surface, Sammy Lowry broke his left ankle when colliding with the Crues' keeper Walker, ending his benefit season prematurely.

After a week in charge Chisholm outlined his plans to make Glentoran great again in the Sunday Express. "I want a fitter team, a quicker team, a cleverer team. I have asked the directors to install a lighting system to give enough light to enable training and ball practice to be carried out. They have also agreed to my idea of installing a gymnasium under the stand and buying gymnastic apparatus." As for tactics he went on, "The present defence play square. I want to see them use the diagonal method, adopted by top flight English

263

Results 1957/58

Played 47. Won 27. Drew 5. Lost 15. Goals For 113. Against 75. % 62.8.
Honours: Mercer Cup

UC	17/08/57		Derry City	A	L	1	2	S.Hughes
UC	21/08/57		Ballymena United	H	W	3	2	Lindsay, Thompson, S.Lowry
UC	24/08/57		Coleraine	H	W	4	2	Weatherup 2, F.McIlreavey og, McGreevy (p)
UC	27/08/57		Cliftonville	A	W	5	3	S.Hughes 3, S.Lowry 2
UC	31/08/57		Crusaders	A	W	2	0	Fogarty, Campbell og
UC	17/09/57	F	Distillery	Solt	D	1	1	Fogarty (p)
UC	23/09/57	FR	Distillery	Solt	L	1	4	Fogarty
GC	05/09/57	1	Coleraine	A	L	0	1	-
CC	07/09/57		Linfield	A	D	3	3	S.Hughes, S.Lowry 2
CC	14/09/57		Crusaders	A	W	3	0	Fogarty, McGreevy, S.Lowry
CC	21/09/57		Glenavon	H	D	2	2	Lindsay 2
CC	28/09/57		Ballymena United	A	W	3	2	S.Hughes 2, Weatherup
CC	12/10/57		Ards	H	W	4	2	Thompson 2, S.Hughes, S.Lowry
CC	19/10/57		Coleraine	A	W	4	0	Fogarty, Mulvey, Thompson, S.Lowry
CC	26/10/57		Bangor	H	W	4	0	Thompson 2, Mulvey, Fogarty
CC	02/11/57		Distillery	H	L	1	3	Mulvey
CC	09/11/57		Derry City	A	W	5	3	Mulvey 3(1p), Thompson, S.Lowry
CC	16/11/57		Cliftonville	A	W	3	1	S.Hughes 2(1p), S.Lowry
CC	23/11/57		Portadown	H	W	3	0	Neill, Lindsay, Dubois
IL	30/11/57		Ards	H	L	0	1	-
IL	07/12/57		Crusaders	A	W	1	0	Truesdale
IL	14/12/57		Distillery	A	W	3	1	Barr, S.Hughes, Thompson
IL	21/12/57		Coleraine	H	W	5	1	Thompson 3, S.Hughes 2
IL	25/12/57		Linfield	H	L	0	2	-
IL	26/12/57		Ballymena United	A	L	1	5	S.Lowry
IL	28/12/57		Cliftonville	H	W	7	0	Thompson 2, Frazer 2(1p), S. Lowry, S.Hughes, Bruce
IL	04/01/58		Bangor	A	L	0	2	-
IL	11/01/58		Derry City	H	W	5	1	McGreevy 3, Thompson 2
IL	18/01/58		Glenavon	A	L	1	5	Thompson
IL	08/02/58		Crusaders	H	W	5	2	Bruce, Thompson 2, Frazer, Chisholm
IL	15/02/58		Ards	A	L	1	5	Bruce
IL	22/02/58		Distillery	H	W	3	2	Bruce, Neill, Dubois
IL	08/03/58		Coleraine	A	L	1	2	S.Hughes
IL	15/03/58		Linfield	A	L	1	3	Chisholm
IL	22/03/58		Portadown	A	D	1	1	Barr
IL	29/03/58		Ballymena United	H	W	3	1	Ashe, Barr, White
IL	05/04/58		Cliftonville	A	W	6	2	Bruce 2, Truesdale 2, Chisholm, S.Hughes
IL	08/04/58		Bangor	H	W	3	0	Truesdale, S.Hughes, Barr (p)
IL	12/04/58		Derry City	A	W	1	0	Campbell og
IL	19/04/58		Glenavon	H	L	0	1	-
IL	21/04/58		Portadown	H	W	2	1	Maguire, Murdough
IC	01/02/58	1	Bangor	H	D	1	1	Frazer (p)
IC	05/02/58	1R	Bangor	A	L	1	2	S.Hughes
CAS	01/03/58	1	Larne	H	W	3	0	S.Hughes, Truesdale, Bruce
CAS	16/04/58	2	Cliftonville	A	W	2	0	S.Hughes, Bruce
CAS	02/05/58	SF	Linfield	Solt	L	0	2	-
MC	25/04/58		Distillery	A	W	4	1	Truesdale, Drennan, S.Hughes, Chisholm
F	24/03/58		Stockport County	A	L	0	4	-
F	16/05/58		Linfield	H	L	0	2	Sammy Lowry Benefit

clubs, which means that if an attack threatens on our right, the right-back goes to tackle and the left-back falls in behind the centre-half. This prevents tearaway forwards such as Jackie Milburn taking a quick pass from the left behind the centre-half and racing in on goal." Chisholm rated Irish League football just below English Third Division standard and picked out Tommy Lucas and Walter Bruce as the players who impressed him most.

The plans did not come off as expected though and we only picked up three points from the next five games. Ards, now top of the table, swamped us but we were again unlucky to go down at Windsor Park as we had two goals

Trevor Thompson watches Ards goalkeeper Moffatt push the ball over the bar.

disallowed for minor infringements at vital stages of the game. It was so cold at Shamrock Park on 22nd March 1958 that both linesmen wore tracksuits!

Chisholm had a chance to test his theory when we travelled over to England to play Stockport County as part of the Mulvey transfer deal. Stockport, lying ninth in the Third Division (North) gave us a lesson in finishing after we had been their equal in approach play. County's four goals came from Clempson (2), Kelly and Smyth (in the dying seconds).

We reached the semi-final of the Shield but the Seconds had fallen at the first hurdle to Distillery on 19th March, giving the Whites their first win since Christmas! Our league form improved and five wins from the last six games lifted us from seventh to fourth, eleven points behind champions Ards but one place ahead of Linfield.

At the conclusion of the league campaign there was more disappointment. After we turned on the style in the Mercer Cup, Linfield defeated us 2-0 both in the Shield semi-final and Sammy Lowry's benefit game. Sammy couldn't play but his brother Tommy, now with Ballymena, did and put through his own goal. His Ballymena clubmate Eric Trevorrow (another guest) had done likewise for the first goal!

Ken Chisholm left at the end of the season after a short but controversial spell in charge. The following season a transfer fee of £250 was obtained from Spennymoor United for his services. On the pitch Billy Neill won the inaugural Glentoran player of the season award.

Appearances and Goals								
	App.	Goals		App.	Goals		App.	Goals
Neill W.	46	2	Ashe	13	1	Murphy	4	
Lucas	41		Barr	13	4	Dunlop	3	
Murdough	40	1	McGreevy	10	5	Moore	3	
Hughes S.	39	21	McCarthy	10		Maguire	3	1
Truesdale	36	6	Crothers	10		Pinkerton	2	
Dubois	35	2	Frazer	10	4	Leeman	2	
Fullerton	34		Fogarty	9	6	Bennett (Gk)	1	
Lowry S.	28	12	McMahon	9		Drennan	1	1
Thompson	23	18	Chisholm	8	4	Jennings	1	
Bruce	21	8	Mulvey	7	6	Own goals		3
Lindsay	16	4	Bennett R.	6				
White	14	1	Patton	6		TOTAL	517	113
Weatherup	13	3						

1958/59

Neilson's young side – A bad week in November – More players transferred

The performance of Northern Ireland in reaching the quarter-finals of the 1958 World Cup in Sweden ensured a high level of interest in the resumption of local football in the August. Glentoran had a new player coach, Johnny Neilson, and plenty of young talent too. Ex-Olympic and Seconds players such as Alex Elder, Ernie Ashe, John Frazer, Matt Crothers, Alex Calderwood (ex-Linfield) and George Spiers would emerge as first team regulars. Dubliner Stanislaus (Stan) Pownall also arrived at the Oval.

The season began with an inauspicious Ulster Cup campaign, with only one win recorded in the five sectional games. Crusaders went through our section unbeaten but lost 0-2 to Glenavon in the final.

Neilson dropped himself as centre-forward and brought back Trevor Thompson for the opening City Cup clash with Linfield. He had originally picked Sammy Hughes, now 32,

Tommy Lucas concedes a corner against Crusaders at Seaview. Our goalkeeper is Eamon McMahon.

but Sammy, fearing he was no longer a part of the team plans and not fit enough, handed in a written transfer request, which he later withdrew. George White took over at centre-half from Murdough and was later to assume captaincy of the team.

The game with the Blues finished 2-2 but we should never have had to rely on an 88th minute Thompson goal to share the points. Five times the ball was in the Blues' net but three were disallowed and White also shot wide from the penalty spot. The man of the match though was the cultured Billy Neill. His ball control was masterly as he tackled sharply and effectively, spraying his passes with intelligence and accuracy. Linfield's goals came from Dickson, a penalty, a Milburn drive.

This display seemed to give the team the confidence required for success to go with the existing skill, spirit and enthusiasm. We took away Crusaders' unbeaten record, knocked Glenavon out of the Gold Cup with a fighting display of youth over experience and then showed our mettle in a drawn City Cup tie at Mourneview. Next a win over struggling Ballymena began a run of six successive victories, five in the City Cup including a pulverising seven goal trashing of Coleraine.

However the most significant of these wins came against Linfield in the Gold Cup semi-finals. It was our first victory over the Blues for five years and many of the Glenmen in the 20,000 crowd invaded Grosvenor Park at the finish and chaired off hat-trick hero Trevor "the Terror" Thompson.

Distillery made a bid for Hughes but were brushed off, possibly because on the day we played the Whites in the City Cup scouts of Blackpool and Bolton were spying on Thompson. The Glens forged ahead with a 5-2 win on a porridge like pitch but after dropping a point against Derry a week later the table read:

1. Glentoran 15 points, 2=-. Glenavon, Linfield 14.

All three clubs won their penultimate fixtures but before the last round of games we had to face Coleraine in the Gold Cup Final at Windsor Park. Glentoran went in as clear favourites but retaining the same XI for the thirteenth proved an unlucky omen. We began the game strongly, launching attack after attack on the same beleaguered Coleraine defence that had just conceded seven goals against Linfield at the same venue four days earlier. Thompson was the main culprit, muffing two easy chances and we paid the ultimate price when Johnny Crossan netted the game's only goal in the 17th minute.

Things got worse the following Saturday as defeat at Portadown meant the loss of two trophies in four days! Both Linfield and Glenavon comfortably won their last fixtures and at the end of the season the Blues defeated the Lurgan men 4-0 in the play-off for the City Cup.

Players, officials and supporters were shell-shocked after the promise of the October and early November displays but perhaps the team's lack of experience told when it came to the crunch. Before the

Matt Crothers.

start of the Irish League Blackpool, looking for a right-wing replacement for Stanley Matthews expressed interest in Ernie Ashe. However they were unwilling to meet chairman Jim Morgan's £5,000 valuation of the player.

Few could judge our performance in the opening league game as due to the heavy fog in the second half only the White shirts of Distillery could be seen! The Glens were leading 3-1 when the game was abandoned but we were not to taste victory until the fifth match of the league when John Frazer saw off Ballymena virtually single-handedly. He scored a hat-trick, hit the post and set up the other goal for Derek Woods. This win was straddled by disappointing defeats to Linfield and Glenavon. The Christmas Day fixture with the Blues was attended by over 30,000 and everything pointed to a Glens' victory after we had pulled back from 0-2 to level it. However Linfield applied two more late killer blows. Jimmy Jones was on top form with a hat-trick as Glenavon tore us apart at Mourneview, netting six times in the second half.

The New Year period was much more fruitful as fourteen goals were scored in the meetings with the Whites and the Reds. Walter Bruce was beginning to stand out and make a significant mark with a nap hand against Cliftonville to kick off 1959. However there was frustration on 10th January when the fixture at Derry was called off at 1 p.m. – many fans had already made their way to the Brandywell.

By then Neilson had parted company with the club and soon two younger faces were to leave the Oval for pastures new. Burnley snapped up 17 year old full-back Alex Elder for £3,000 and 20 year old Frazer went to Sunderland for £3,500. Within 24 hours Frazer had made an impressive Football League debut against Huddersfield Town in front of 27,000 and was hailed as the "new Billy Bingham". Elder went on to win 40 caps for Northern Ireland, finishing his English career with Stoke City.

Glenavon proved too strong once again in the Irish Cup. We missed Thompson up front after he had broken his collar bone against Ards the previous Saturday. The club still had an interest in the Cup as the Seconds fought back from 1-3 down to draw with Cliftonville. The "Wee Glens" were enjoying a very successful season built around the strong defensive partnership of David Cloughley and Jimmy Murdough. After a draw at Solitude the Seconds saw off the Reds in the second replay, George Spiers providing the thrust up front with a hat-trick. They went down with honours to eventual cup winners Glenavon in Round Two, Jim Dobbin making two miraculous saves in the process. The Seconds went on to win the B Division by four points from Larne while further down the club Glentoran Olympic defeated Boyland 4-0 (Jim Doherty hat-trick) in the Youth Cup Final, adding this to the already secured Irish League C Division.

Results 1958/59

Played 43. Won 21. Drew 10. Lost 12. Goals For 108. Against 80. % 60.5

UC	16/08/58		Derry City	H	D	2	2	Ashe, Dubois
UC	20/08/58		Ballymena United	A	L	2	3	Ashe, Thompson
UC	23/08/58		Coleraine	A	D	1	1	Pownall
UC	27/08/58		Cliftonville	H	W	2	0	Neill, Spiers
UC	30/08/58		Crusaders	H	L	3	4	Spiers 2, Bruce
CC	06/09/58		Linfield	H	D	2	2	Calderwood, Thompson
CC	13/09/58		Crusaders	H	W	4	1	Thompson, Spiers (p), Ashe 2
CC	20/09/58		Glenavon	A	D	1	1	Thompson
CC	27/09/58		Ballymena United	H	W	4	3	Bruce, Spiers 2(1p), Ashe
CC	11/10/58		Ards	A	W	2	1	Thompson, Calderwood
CC	18/10/58		Coleraine	H	W	7	1	Thompson 4, Bruce, Spiers (p), Calderwood
CC	25/10/58		Bangor	A	W	2	1	Spiers (p), Bruce
CC	01/11/58		Distillery	A	W	5	2	Bruce 2, Spiers, Dubois, Thompson
CC	08/11/58		Derry City	H	D	1	1	Thompson
CC	15/11/58		Cliftonville	H	W	2	1	Spiers (p), Thompson
CC	22/11/58		Portadown	A	L	1	2	Thompson
GC	16/09/58	2	Glenavon	H	W	4	2	Calderwood, Thompson 2, Spiers
GC	01/10/58	SF	Linfield	GP	W	5	2	Calderwood, Spiers, Thompson 3
GC	18/11/58	F	Coleraine	WP	L	0	1	-
IL	06/12/58		Portadown	A	D	1	1	Bruce
IL	13/12/58		Crusaders	H	D	3	3	Bruce, Thompson, Ashe
IL	20/12/58		Coleraine	A	D	1	1	Thompson
IL	25/12/58		Linfield	A	L	2	4	S.Hughes, Thompson
IL	26/12/58		Ballymena United	H	W	4	0	Frazer 3(2p), Woods
IL	27/12/58		Glenavon	A	L	1	7	S.Hughes
IL	30/12/58		Distillery	A	W	6	2	Thompson 3, Frazer 2, S.Hughes
IL	03/01/59		Cliftonville	H	W	8	3	Bruce 5, S.Hughes, Frazer 2(1p)
IL	17/01/59		Bangor	H	W	3	1	S.Hughes, Frazer 2
IL	24/01/59		Ards	A	W	3	2	Bruce, Thompson, Frazer
IL	07/02/59		Ballymena United	A	W	3	2	Frazer 2(1p), Bruce
IL	14/02/59		Derry City	H	W	2	0	Bruce, Spiers
IL	17/02/59		Derry City	GP	W	4	0	Ashe, S.Hughes, Calderwood 2
IL	21/02/59		Bangor	A	L	2	3	Bruce 2(1p)
IL	07/03/59		Ards	H	D	1	1	S.Hughes
IL	14/03/59		Distillery	H	D	3	3	Briggs, Dubois, Woods
IL	28/03/59		Crusaders	A	L	1	2	Spiers
IL	30/03/59		Glenavon	H	L	1	2	Calderwood (p)
IL	31/03/59		Cliftonville	A	W	2	0	Spiers, Calderwood
IL	04/04/59		Portadown	H	L	0	1	-
IL	11/04/59		Linfield	H	W	2	1	Calderwood (p), S.Lowry
IL	25/04/59		Coleraine	H	W	3	2	O'Neill, Briggs, Bruce
IC	31/01/59	1	Glenavon	A	L	2	4	S.Hughes, Ashe
CAS	21/03/59	2	Ards	A	L	0	4	-
F	01/05/59		Motherwell	H	L	1	4	Campbell Tommy Lucas Benefit
F	11/05/59		Newcastle United	H	D	3	3	Calderwood, Keith og, Thompson

However it is in the senior XI that success is really measured and to that end the directors stepped up their search for the right "big name" manager. Don Kichenbrand, the South African who had played for Rangers and was now Sunderland's centre-forward, was mentioned but the man eventually chosen was Tommy Briggs, the ex-Blackburn Rovers, Coventry City, Plymouth Argyle, Birmingham City and Grimsby Town centre-forward. Briggs first game in charge coincided with the return of Trevor Thompson to action, a 3-3 draw with Distillery.

Ernie Ashe was transferred to Leicester City for £3,000 as the Glens stood only three points behind leaders Linfield with six games to go. Performances though went downhill, how could the team cope after the loss of three of its best players? Ards comprehensively dumped us out of the Shield while three league defeats in four games condemned us to third place in the league. The "Dee Street Dynamos" had run down and Linfield became champions, however they had to visit the Oval for their next match. The game stood locked at 1-1 until veteran Sammy Lowry netted the winner with a diving header. The goal marked our first home victory over the Blues in six years and Lowry was chaired off at the finish. Our

Alex Elder.

league programme concluded with victory over Coleraine (3-2) with Briggs hitting the woodwork four times!

Right-back Tommy Lucas' benefit season culminated in a testimonial game with Motherwell in May. The Scottish side triumphed 4-1, two of the goals scored by Ian St. John. Playing matters for the season were wound up ten days later with an exhibition game against Newcastle United. The Glens included ex-keeper Fullerton as a guest but we still found ourselves 1-2 down at half-time, ex-Ardsman George Eastham netting twice for the Geordies. Bruce's shot hit a post and was then helped over the line by Newcastle's Irish International full-back Dick Keith on 58 minutes. White then restored the visitors' lead before Thompson had the last equalising word with five minutes remaining.

Tommy Briggs took stock of the situation in the close season. The Glens had over 90 players on their books and, of the 20 professionals among them, six were made available for transfer – McMahon, Lucas, White, Patton and two famous names from the early fifties Sammy Hughes and Sammy Lowry. Distillery snapped up George White for £200, while Lucas went to Glenavon.

Briggs was confident of success in the near future but stressed that good training facilities for himself, Bobby McGregor and the players were paramount. Billy Neill was also to have a role in the coaching, concentrating on the younger players.

Appearances and Goals

	App.	Goals		App.	Goals		App.	Goals
Neill W.	39	1	Elder	23		Dobbin	5	
Bruce	39	19	Crothers	23		Lowry S.	5	1
McMahon	38		Murdough	17		Neilson	4	
Ashe	33	8	Hughes S.	17	8	Johnston	3	
Lucas	31		Frazer	11	12	Cloughley	2	
Dubois	30	3	Leeman	9		Patton	1	
Spiers	30	15	O'Neill	9	1	McCullough	1	
White	30		Woods	7	2	O'Brien	1	
Thompson	28	25	Pownall	6	1	TOTAL	473	108
Calderwood	25	10	Briggs	6	2			

1959/60

A good pre-Christmas run – The Oval purchased – Glenavon on top

Tommy Briggs began his first full season in charge and strengthened the playing panel with two new signings. Gordon Bradley, who had played in the 1949 FA Cup Final for Leicester City against Wolves and seen service with Notts County and Cambridge City, was to be our new goalkeeper. Bradley had spent the last four summers in Ulster as a tennis professional and had just turned down a tennis coach appointment in Ghana. Ex-Manchester United junior Bertie Campbell returned to Belfast and impressed in the Glens' pre-season trial on 8th August. During the game he figured for both sides and was signed on professional forms immediately after. George Spiers scored a hat-trick in the senior side's 5-2 win.

Bradley had a forgettable debut at Derry in the Ulster Cup as he conceded two goals in the first seven minutes and dislocated a thumb later in the game. Young Bertie McGonigal came into the team for the prestige friendly against Burnley at the Oval on the Monday evening. The game had been arranged as part of the Alex Elder deal and produced gate receipts of around £700. Elder had a good game but the pick of the visitors was ex-Glentoran inside-left Jimmy McIlroy, even though Jim Robson got four of the Burnley goals in an 8-1 rout. At the after match banquet Burnley chairman, Bob Lord, described McIlroy as the best inside-forward in the league and invited the Glens to a return fixture at Turf Moor the following season.

Carlo Fusco heads for goal at Bangor.

Thoughts turned to the "bread and butter" Ulster Cup but our form was indifferent. Briggs was insisting in playing himself at centre-forward to the exclusion of Trevor Thompson but he only yielded one goal in five games. Thompson was brought back for the City Cup with the player-manager moving to inside-forward. Our best Ulster Cup performance came against Coleraine and was a personal triumph for four goal Walter Bruce. The game had begun so drearily that most of the spectators on the unreserved side watched the trains go by to the Bangor seaside. Once again Crusaders qualified for the final from our section but they were beaten by Linfield after a replay.

Despite an outstanding display from Matt Crothers, the Bannsiders gained quick revenge for their Oval hammering by knocking us out of the Gold Cup for the third successive season. The only really bright spot for the Glens early season was the form of 18 year old McGonigal. Cat-like saves endeared him to the fans but meanwhile Bradley was continuing his comeback in an unusual manner. For a B Division game with Queen's University the Seconds found themselves short of strikers and selected the English goalkeeper up front! Bradley played a big part in the 9-0 win, even scoring two of the goal himself.

270

George Spiers runs through the Bangor defence at Clandyboye Park.

The Glens made another "big name" signing on 1st September when Winston Stanley Churchill, a left-winger on National Service at Lisburn, came to the club. Unlike his famous namesake he failed to make his mark in history!

"Lucky Blues Snatch Draw" was the headline following our opening City Cup game. Even though Spike O'Neill was a hobbling passenger on the left-wing we had most of the game but had to settle for a 3-3 scoreline. However this was to be the only point we gained from the first six City Cup fixtures as form plummeted. More young players, including Eric Drennan, Billy McVea and Carlo Fusco, were brought in. The latter had Italian grandparents and formerly played rugby at Blackrock College Dublin before the family moved to Belfast.

Briggs was under immense pressure as the Glens were rooted to the bottom of the City Cup table. Criticism flowed from the supporters, press and television alike, indeed Briggs' only friend appeared to be the editor of the Glentoran Gazette who called for the fans to get behind the team and be patient with the younger players.

Then, for some reason, things began to go right. We luckily beat the Whites to retain the Mercer Cup and then put together a run of nine successive wins, averaging four goals a game, spanning the conclusion of the City Cup and the start of the league. Maybe the secret was in keeping the same team together for these games to see out the 1950's. It read: McGonigal, Leeman, Dubois, Neill, Murdough, McVea, Reynolds, Bruce, Thompson, Spiers, Pownall.

During this run the team had to come from behind three times including at Seaview when Arthur "Mousey" Brady had tortured us in the first half. Dickie Leeman had put through his own goal in this match and did so again versus the Blues on Christmas Day but this was soon forgotten as our forwards put seven past a hapless Irvine at the other end. Stan Pownall even scored one direct from a corner, making it a very Merry Christmas for Glenmen.

Cliftonville's Ghanian goalkeeper, Tommy Wilberforce, had a similar experience to Irvine on Boxing Day despite a below-par Glens' performance. The run came to an end with the first game of the 1960s when Derry City forced a draw at the Oval – both sides missing a penalty. Then, after we had raced into a 3-1 lead within twenty minutes at Ballymena, the Braidmen fought back to win 5-3. However two glorious goals from Briggs enabled a return to winning ways against Ards a week later as we snapped at the heels of table topping Glenavon, who had beaten the Blues 5-2 at Windsor Park.

In January 1960 Glentoran bought the Oval for £4,250 from Dixon Estates, a large

Tommy Briggs.

Jim Weatherup scores against us for Crusaders.

insurance company, and announced an ambitious ten year plan to make it the best ground in Ireland. The phased scheme included increasing the current 40,000 capacity to between 70,000 and 80,000 and the installation of floodlights with the intention of competing with Windsor Park for staging internationals. Chairman Jim Morgan stated that the rent income from staging games such as Ireland v. Wales would help to pay for the improvements, estimated at around £40,000. However the IFA decided to stick with Windsor Park for Northern Ireland games, meaning the Oval was unlikely to add to the Welsh internationals hosted in 1900 and 1920. Meanwhile club secretary Bob Fleming was publicly thanked by the fans for the news service he was providing via the loudspeaker system.

Back to the playing front and after a Thompson hat-trick saw off Portadown we began our assault on the Irish Cup against juniors Ballyclare Comrades. Aston put the B Division side ahead on five minutes, but this time it was Bruce's turn to score three times on a tricky, sticky surface.

The top of the table clash with Glenavon on 6th February was postponed due to heavy fog. Over 60 busloads of Glentoran supporters plus many more by car had travelled to Lurgan but referee Arthur Ellis was unable to see either stand from the half-way line. Meantime the Lurgan Glens got the nod over us to represent the Irish League in a forthcoming club tournament in the United States.

Derry City eliminated us from the Irish Cup after an exciting second round tie. In the drawn game at the Oval City missed a penalty but Thompson blew many chances for us. When Pownall's 25 yard lob put us 2-0 up in he replay we looked to be home and dry but one of the biggest crowds at Brandywell for a long time cheered Derry on to a 3-2 win.

Wins over the Crues and Coleraine kept us going in the league but B Division Larne shocked us in the County Antrim Shield at Inver Park. The Seconds fared much better, defeating first Ards then Ballymena 1-0 at the Oval to reach the semi-final. Linfield proved too strong for the Wee Glens, winning 5-1, while Crusaders overcame their own reserves 3-2 in the other semi-final.

The Shield defeat was poor preparation for our big league match with the Blues at Windsor Park on 19th March. We had two more young debutants in

Cliftonville goalkeeper Tommy Wilberforce punches clear.

Tom Turkington, replacing the injured Murdough at centre-half, and Brian McCaul, a Donegal lad signed from Leeds United. Things looked good when Thompson put us ahead after 78 minutes but the Blues came through in a storming finish to win 3-2. We then had just a week to lift ourselves for the re-arranged meeting with Glenavon. A ding-dong battle

Results 1959/60

Played 44. Won 22. Drew 7. Lost 15. Goals For 103. Against 78. % 58.0.
Honours: Mercer Cup

UC	15/08/59		Derry City	A	L	1	2	Calderwood
UC	19/08/59		Ballymena United	H	D	1	1	Calderwood (p)
UC	22/08/59		Coleraine	H	W	5	2	Bruce 4, Briggs
UC	25/08/59		Cliftonville	A	W	2	0	Calderwood 2(1p)
UC	29/08/59		Crusaders	A	L	0	4	-
GC	03/09/59	1	Coleraine	A	L	2	3	Woods, Briggs
CC	05/09/59		Linfield	A	D	3	3	Briggs, Pownall, Thompson
CC	12/09/59		Crusaders	A	L	2	5	Briggs, Thompson
CC	19/09/59		Glenavon	H	L	1	4	Briggs
CC	26/09/59		Ballymena United	A	L	0	4	-
CC	10/10/59		Ards	H	L	1	2	Drennan (p)
CC	17/10/59		Coleraine	A	L	0	1	-
CC	24/10/59		Bangor	H	W	2	0	Pownall, McVea
CC	31/10/59		Distillery	H	L	2	3	Spiers, Bruce (p)
CC	07/11/59		Derry City	A	W	2	1	Bruce, Thompson
CC	14/11/59		Cliftonville	A	W	5	1	Bruce, Thompson 3, Spiers
CC	21/11/59		Portadown	H	W	5	2	Thompson, Bruce 2, Spiers 2
MC	02/10/59		Distillery	A	W	2	0	Fusco, Pownall
IL	28/11/59		Distillery	A	W	2	1	Thompson, Spiers
IL	05/12/59		Bangor	H	W	3	1	Bruce 2, McVea
IL	12/12/59		Crusaders	A	W	3	1	Bruce, Pownall, Spiers
IL	19/12/59		Coleraine	H	W	4	1	Thompson 2, Bruce, Pownall (p)
IL	25/12/59		Linfield	H	W	7	3	Bruce 2, Thompson, Pownall, Reynolds, Spiers 2
IL	26/12/59		Cliftonville	A	W	5	0	Thompson 2, Spiers 2, Bruce
IL	02/01/60		Derry City	H	D	2	2	Bruce, Pownall
IL	09/01/60		Ballymena United	A	L	3	5	Briggs, Spiers 2
IL	16/01/60		Ards	H	W	5	1	Spiers, Briggs 3, Bruce
IL	23/01/60		Portadown	A	W	3	1	Thompson 3
IL	13/02/60		Distillery	H	L	1	2	Briggs
IL	20/02/60		Bangor	A	D	2	2	Pownall, Fusco
IL	05/03/60		Crusaders	H	W	3	0	Thompson, Bruce 2
IL	12/03/60		Coleraine	A	W	2	1	Thompson 2
IL	19/03/60		Linfield	A	L	2	3	Thompson, Pownall (p)
IL	26/03/60		Glenavon	A	D	0	0	-
IL	02/04/60		Ballymena United	H	W	2	0	Calderwood 2
IL	09/04/60		Ards	A	W	2	1	Calderwood, Spiers
IL	16/04/60		Glenavon	H	L	3	4	Thompson, Spiers, Trainor
IL	18/04/60		Cliftonville	H	W	3	1	Trainor, Campbell, Thompson
IL	19/04/60		Derry City	A	W	2	0	Spiers 2
IL	23/04/60		Portadown	H	D	1	1	Thompson
IC	30/01/60	1	Ballyclare Comrades	H	W	3	1	Bruce 3
IC	27/02/60	2	Derry City	H	D	1	1	Bruce
IC	03/03/60	2R	Derry City	A	L	2	3	Bruce, Pownall
CAS	16/03/60	1	Larne	A	L	1	4	Thompson
F	17/08/59		Burnley	H	L	1	8	Calderwood (p)
F	13/05/60		Third Lanark	H	D	0	0	Jim Murdough Benefit

Gordon Bradley.

finished scoreless, leaving Glenavon holding a four point lead over ourselves and Linfield with six games remaining.

We stayed in the championship race until the return clash with the Lurgan side three weeks later. Glenavon had ended Linfield's challenge with a 2-1 win the week before and repeated the dose to us at the Oval when Jimmy Jones hit a last minute winner. They now just required one point from their last three games to secure the championship. A Glentoran marksman in that game was Robin Trainor, whom Briggs had just signed from Corby Town from under the noses of Trainor's old club, Coleraine.

While we were recording haphazard wins over Cliftonville and Derry on Easter Monday and Tuesday, Glenavon were beaten by both Ards and Distillery, keeping alive our feint hopes of a play-off. These were dispelled the following Saturday as we could only manage a draw with the Ports and Glenavon defeated Bangor 5-2 to clinch the title. We had some personal consolation though when Billy Neill was voted the Ulster Footballer of the Year.

Jimmy Murdough completed a successful benefit year by being named Glentoran player of the season. Walter Bruce returned to action after eight weeks out with a mystery illness in Murdough's benefit match with Third Lanark. Who would have thought that the Scottish team would finish third in their league the following season but go out of existence within seven years.

So another unsuccessful season came to an end, again much promise but no major trophy to show for it. Six players were released including McVea and Eddie Dubois who signed for Ards and Exeter City respectively. For 24 year old Dubois it was a surprise fulfilment of his ambition after he had almost given up football when the Glens sacked him despite being the regular left-back all season.

Appearances and Goals

	App.	Goals		App.	Goals		App.	Goals
Neill W.	40		Crothers	24		Turkington	8	
Murdough	37		Leeman	23		Woods	6	1
Bruce	37	25	O'Neill	23		Cloughley	4	
Spiers	34	17	Briggs	20	10	Fusco	4	2
Thompson	32	24	Reynolds	19	1	Trainor	4	2
Pownall	32	10	Bradley	15		McCaul	3	
Dubois	30		Calderwood	14	7			
McGonigal	29		Drennan	11	1	TOTAL	484	103
McVea	26	2	Campbell	9	1			

1960/61

Three managers – Visitors from Israel - Gold Cup success

Bobby Ervine, released by Linfield, was the only new signing on view when the Seniors defeated the Reserves 3-1 in a dull trial match on 13th August. Trevor Thompson netted a hat-trick with Furlonger replying for the 2nd XI. The season ahead was to be a calamitous one in terms of managers with three different men holding the post during the term. Tommy Briggs started in charge but lasted only until November when Len Kane had a brief five months reign. Ex-Belfast Celtic centre-half and former Portadown and Glenavon manager Harry Walker was appointed in March 1961 and he was to lead the team to its first trophy in four years, the Gold Cup.

But back to the early months of the season. Derry City, to whom we had donated our old unreserved stand, showed no favours as they came from two behind for the second time in five months to beat us 3-2 in our opening Ulster Cup fixture. Gordon Bradley was at fault for their long range goals and was immediately replaced by Bertie McGonigal. Bradley regained his place after McGonigal was beaten five times at Coleraine as once again we failed to mount a serious challenge for the Ulster Cup. Even the wins

Gordon Bradley makes a save from Linfield's Jimmy Walker.

over Cliftonville and Crusaders were dreary affairs although in the latter 17 year old centre-forward Robert McDowell looked to be a good prospect. Pownall put a penalty wide against the Crues. Ballymena won the competition defeating Glenavon 3-1 in the final.

For the first City Cup fixture it was Linfield's turn to have 75% of the play but miss chances and have to settle for a draw. In mid-September we entertained Israeli visitors in the shape of Petach Tikva. Stellmach put Tikva ahead but an own goal put us level on 24 minutes. After the interval the game developed into a "roughhouse" before Robin Trainor netted a last minute winner. Attendances at games were starting to fall and the Glenmen who stayed away from Mourneview Park on September 24th must have been relieved when they heard the result. Two soft goals midway through the second half helped Glenavon to a 5-2 win. Felix Reynolds had been our best player.

This result seemed to be the stimulus for more workmanlike displays as we managed to win our next six games against Northern Irish opposition. Ballymena were twice our victims, in both Gold and City Cup. Scotsman Billy Japp had an excellent debut in the latter. Our only defeat in October came at Burnley in the return friendly with the English League Champions. Although fielding a reserve XI before 7,912 spectators the Lancashire team demolished us 9-1 after holding a 5-0 half-time lead. It is interesting to note that only two of the Glens players (Neill and Murdough) were over 23. Left-half H.Best scored an unusual "hat-trick", one for us but two own goals in favour of Burnley.

Official Programme — Price One Penny

Burnley Football and Athletic Co., Ltd.

Season 1960-61

OFFICIALS

President: J. N. GRIMSHAW, Esq.

Directors:

R. W. LORD, Esq. (Chairman); R. COOK, Esq., J.P. (Vice-Chairman);
W. HOPKINSON, Esq.; W. PICKARD, Esq.; F. R. KAY, Esq.; F. HARTLEY, Esq.

Medical Officers:

Dr. D. A. KER, J.P.
Dr. R. D. IVEN

Manager: HARRY POTTS   Secretary: HENRY SMITH.

Ground & Registered Office: Turf Moor, Burnley.

No. 6   **TUESDAY, 4th OCTOBER, 1960**

BURNLEY

Colours : Claret and Blue

McDONALD   Thomson

ANGUS   MARSHALL

JOYCE   CUMMINGS   SCOTT

ROBSON   HARRIS

MEREDITH   LOCHHEAD   PILKINGTON

Referee :

Mr. K. Hiley   Linesmen :
(Football League)   Mr. F. Carter (Red Flag)
                      Mr. H. Hadsum (Yellow Flag)

SPIERS   McDOWELL   REYNOLDS

ERVINE   BRUCE

BEST   MURDOUGH   NIELL

CROTHERS   O'NEILL   GEOGHEGAN

McGONIGAL

GLENTORAN

Colours : Green jerseys, red shorts

HAMILTON PUBLICATIONS (BURNLEY) LTD

Team-sheet for our friendly fixture at Burnley.

Our good run had taken us to joint top of the City Cup, along with Glenavon after eight games. However two defeats in the last three matches forced us down to third and paved the way for the departure of Briggs.

Len Kane took over as manager in time for the start of the League and in his first game in charge the Glens played like men inspired to defeat Glenavon 2-0. It was described as "the type of football to bring the crowds back". Only the keeping of Roy Rea saved Glenavon from a heavy defeat.

We were involved in two thrillers just before Christmas against Ballymena and Linfield but lost on both occasions. However we then toyed with the Whites and the Reds and concluded 1960 with a polished win at Seaview to leave us third in the table, three points behind leaders Linfield. To offset the loss of Stan Pownall to Drumcondra, Matt Doherty was signed from Derry City for £2,000 and he helped himself to five goals in those two Christmas games. Doherty would later gain an Ireland 'B' cap, playing against the Army.

We suffered only one defeat in January - a scrappy affair at Ards. Kane bemoaned the fact that we had held 90% of the possession but allowed Ards two breakaway goals. Our next game against Derry was thrill-packed, indeed the game stood at 3-3 after only 32 minutes. Murdough then missed a penalty before second-half strikes from Bruce and Keenan gave us victory.

The game against the Blues at Windsor Park on 4th February was vital for both teams and was confirmed by that morning's half-way stage league table:

1. Linfield and Ards 18 points, 3. Portadown 16, 4. Glentoran 15.

In that game we led 1-0 until the Blues struck in the 86th, 87th and 89th minutes! Doherty scored again in injury time to complete a dramatic finish and a 3-2 Linfield win.

A dismal defeat against Distillery the following Saturday ended our title hopes and when this was followed by a first round Irish Cup defeat by the same opposition a fortnight later the writing was on the wall for Kane's brief tenure in charge.

The incoming Harry Walker was left under no illusions as to the extent of his task as we spluttered to an unconvincing win over Crusaders in his first game in charge. A win over Ards brought us back to within two points of the leaders but while Linfield were going down 4-5 to Distillery we blew our chances thanks to an awful display at Derry.

Under Walker the team's play had become more rugged and our fighting qualities were demonstrated at Glenavon in April. Two goals down in 18 minutes we fought back to 2-2 before Jimmy Jones' late winner condemned us to defeat. Fittingly a play-off was necessary to decide the outcome of the championship after an exciting conclusion. Linfield beat Portadown 3-2 at the Oval in that after the two teams had drawn 1-1 with each other in their final game. Ards finished third and the Glens fourth.

There was still plenty to keep Glentoran's interest in May as we were doing battle on three cup fronts. Firstly was the resumption of an all-Ireland competition, reviving memories of the Inter-City Cup, abandoned in 1949. St. Patrick's Athletic became the first Eire team to play in Northern Ireland since that date when they took us on at Windsor Park in the first leg of the quarter-final. A poor attendance witnessed the Glens build up a two goal lead for the Dublin return.

The date of that match was put back to allow for live television coverage of the Burnley - SV Hamburg European Cup quarter-final. However the IFA pulled the plug on the transmission, angering many fans including the Albertbridge Glentoran Supporters' Club who poignantly stated;

"Television is here to stay, and people who pay for entertainment should be allowed to see any programme which has been given the right to be shown. Further many people in

Results 1960/61

Played 49. Won 30. Drew 4. Lost 15. Goals For 126. Against 66. % 65.3.
Honours: Gold Cup

UC	20/08/60		Derry City	H	L	2	3	Ervine, Bruce
UC	24/08/60		Ballymena United	A	D	1	1	Pownall (p)
UC	27/08/60		Coleraine	A	L	3	5	Bruce 2, Lawther og
UC	31/08/60		Cliftonville	H	W	3	0	McDowell 2, Bruce
UC	03/09/60		Crusaders	H	W	3	0	McDowell, Trainor, Bruce
CC	10/09/60		Linfield	A	D	2	2	Thompson 2
CC	17/09/60		Cliftonville	H	W	2	0	McDowell, Trainor
CC	24/09/60		Glenavon	A	L	2	5	Pownall, Trainor
CC	01/10/60		Derry City	H	W	3	0	Bruce, Thompson, Spiers
CC	15/10/60		Bangor	A	W	3	0	McDowell, Spiers 2
CC	22/10/60		Ballymena United	H	W	3	0	McDowell, Thompson 2
CC	29/10/60		Distillery	A	W	4	1	Thompson 2, McDowell, Bruce
CC	05/11/60		Crusaders	H	W	6	1	Thompson 3, McDowell, Bruce, Ervine
CC	12/11/60		Portadown	A	L	0	1	-
CC	19/11/60		Coleraine	H	W	3	0	Thompson 2, McDowell
CC	26/11/60		Ards	A	L	0	3	-
GC	28/09/60	2	Ballymena United	H	W	3	1	Thompson, Reynolds, Bruce
GC	02/05/61	SF	Glenavon	WP	W	2	0	McDowell, Thompson
GC	09/05/61	F	Linfield	Solt	W	4	2	Thompson 2, Drennan, O'Neill
IL	03/12/60		Glenavon	H	W	2	0	O'Neill, Murdough
IL	10/12/60		Portadown	H	W	1	0	Thompson
IL	17/12/60		Ballymena United	A	L	1	2	Thompson
IL	24/12/60		Linfield	H	L	0	1	-
IL	26/12/60		Distillery	A	W	7	1	Thompson 4, Doherty 3
IL	27/12/60		Cliftonville	H	W	7	0	Bruce 4, Doherty 2, Neill
IL	31/12/60		Crusaders	A	W	2	1	Bruce, Thompson
IL	07/01/61		Bangor	H	W	3	0	Thompson 2, Mitchell
IL	14/01/61		Ards	A	L	1	2	Doherty
IL	21/01/61		Derry City	H	W	5	3	Thompson 2, Bruce 2, Keenan
IL	28/01/61		Coleraine	A	D	1	1	Thompson
IL	04/02/61		Linfield	A	L	2	3	Doherty 2
IL	11/02/61		Distillery	H	L	1	3	Thompson
IL	18/02/61		Cliftonville	A	W	3	0	McDowell, Mitchell, Doherty (p)
IL	04/03/61		Crusaders	H	W	3	0	Doherty, Thompson 2
IL	11/03/61		Portadown	A	D	2	2	Bruce, Thompson
IL	18/03/61		Bangor	A	W	4	1	Thompson 2, Bruce, McDowell
IL	01/04/61		Ards	H	W	2	0	Thompson, Murdough
IL	04/04/61		Derry City	A	L	1	2	Doherty (p)
IL	08/04/61		Coleraine	H	W	4	1	Bruce 3, Thompson
IL	15/04/61		Glenavon	A	L	2	3	Doherty, Thompson
IL	21/04/61		Ballymena United	H	W	4	0	Thompson 2, Doherty, Bruce
IC	25/02/61	1	Distillery	H	L	3	4	Doherty 2, McDowell
NSC	21/03/61	1.1	St. Patrick's Athletic	WP	W	3	1	Doherty 2, Thompson
NSC	17/04/61	1.2	St. Patrick's Athletic	A	W	3	2	Doherty, Thompson 2
NSC	28/04/61	SF.1	Drumcondra	WP	W	5	2	Thompson 3, Doherty, Smyth
NSC	16/05/61	SF.2	Drumcondra	A	L	0	2	-
CAS	11/04/61	2	Ballyclare Comrades	A	W	3	2	Thompson, McDowell, Doherty
CAS	05/05/61	SF	Ballymena United	Solt	W	1	0	Thompson
CAS	13/05/61	F	Linfield	Solt	L	1	2	Thompson
F	14/09/60		Petach Tikva	H	W	2	1	Redler og, Trainor
F	04/10/60		Burnley	A	L	1	9	Best

Walter Bruce

hospital were looking forward to an evening's entertainment. Let us be realistic and live in the future. Games like this cannot be seen every week." For the record Burnley won 3-1 but went down 1-4 in Germany.

In our second leg at Tolka Park St Pat's were booed off at half-time as the Glens had built up a 3-0 lead, setting up a 6-3 aggregate success. Within the space of seven days we had recorded three semi-final wins in outplaying Drumcondra in the North-South Cup, surprising Glenavon in the Gold Cup and grinding down Ballymena in the County Antrim Shield.

For the Gold Cup final Walker signed Roy Borne from Sunderland and threw the 18 year old into a Solitude cauldron for his debut, allocating him the job of marking Bobby Braithwaite. The plan worked and at the other end Trevor Thompson gave a five star performance in our 4-2 win. Spike O'Neill was a tireless worker but it was Thompson whom the celebrating supporters chaired off at the finish. Borne was ineligible for the Shield final four days later when the Blues took revenge by 2-1. Although losing 0-2 to Drumcondra in Dublin we still qualified for the North-South final, potentially setting up a third showdown with Linfield. However it was decided to hold that one over until 1961/2. Incidentally, Drumcondra's first goal at Tolka Park came from ex-Glenman Pownall with the second a Billy Neill own goal.

Appearances and Goals

	App.	Goals		App.	Goals		App.	Goals
Bruce	49	22	McDowell J.	19	14	Borne	2	
Murdough	48	2	Spiers	12	3	Matier	2	
Neill W.	47	1	Japp	12		Dowd	2	
Crothers	46		Mitchell	12	2	Shields	2	
Thompson	43	48	Trainor	8	3	Lawther	1	
McGonigal	42		Bradley	7		Logue	1	
Ervine	33	2	Best	7		Moore	1	
O'Neill	28	2	Smyth	7	1	Own Goals		1
Doherty M.	26	20	Pownall	6	2			
Drennan	22	1	Harvey	6		TOTAL	539	126
Reynolds	22	1	Watt	3				
Geoghegan	20		Keenan	3	1			

1961/62

Linfield's seven trophies – Thompson's inconsistency – A vital penalty save

The season 1961/2 will always be remembered for Linfield's feat of lifting no less than seven of the eight trophies on offer, one of those being the North-South Cup held over from 1960/1. The Glens and Portadown were the main challengers to the Blues, indeed we lost in four finals to them while the Ports were runners-up in the League, City Cup and Irish Cup. One remarkable, but not widely recalled, fact is that Portadown only wanted one point from their final league game to become champions but lost at home by 2-3 to .... seventh placed Glentoran!

There were few early season indicators to the forthcoming Blues dominance especially as we beat them 3-1 at Windsor in a pre-season practice. Following our internal club practice the previous Saturday we included five new faces; John Kennedy, Arthur Stewart, Hugh Forde, Billy McCullough and Tom Doherty, brother of Matt. The first game of the season at the Oval had been on the 4th August when an ex-Glentoran XI went down 1-4 to an ex-International team in front of a fair crowd. Sammy Nimmick scored for the Old Glens. Our now familiar slaughtering at the hands of Burnley, this time their first team, brought the warm-up games to an end.

Jungle Jim Murdough heads away from Keenan of Distillery.

For once our Ulster Cup sectional results were good, with plenty of excellent football to boot. We held a two point lead over Crusaders going into the last match with the Crues at Seaview. A hard and keenly fought game finished in favour of "the Hatchetmen" to set up a play-off. This took place ten days later at Solitude when Trevor Thompson was the difference between the two sides as Crusaders lost their unbeaten record.

That came just after our best early season display against Ballymena in the Gold Cup and the first competitive match of 61/2 with Linfield in the City Cup. We roasted the Blues defence in the first half and went ahead, however the turning point came on the hour when Jimmy Murdough put through his own goal. The Blues then took control, Barr netting their winner. Results for the rest of September and most of October were satisfactory but the form of "Sadie" Thompson was totally inconsistent. Against Ards in the Gold Cup he scored a supreme a hat-trick but then only five days later he could do nothing right against Glenavon. These erratic displays prompted one local journalist to describe Thompson as "both a world beater and an egg beater!" Another man to impress against Ards was young debutant Richie Warburton on the right wing.

The first half of the Bangor game on 14th October produced nine goals, six to the Glens. The Seasiders new manager, Clancy McDermott, predicted that better times were ahead for Glentoran. A win at Ballymena took us to fourth in the City Cup and we qualified for the Gold Cup Final thanks to a dramatic comeback, Matt Doherty leading the fight with the winner in the closing seconds after Coleraine had led 3-1.

279

Results 1961/62

Played 54. Won 27. Drew 9. Lost 18. Goals For 121. Against 109. % 58.3

UC	19/08/61		Derry City	A	W	2	1	M.Doherty, Thompson
UC	22/08/61		Ballymena United	H	W	3	2	Bruce, M.Doherty, Thompson
UC	26/08/61		Coleraine	H	W	4	0	M.Doherty (p), Stewart, T.Doherty, Thompson
UC	29/08/61		Cliftonville	A	W	2	0	T.Doherty, Thompson
UC	02/09/61		Crusaders	A	L	1	2	Bruce
UC	12/09/61	PO	Crusaders	Solt	W	2	1	Thompson 2
UC	14/11/61	F	Linfield	A	L	0	2	-
GC	05/09/61	1	Ballymena United	H	W	4	1	Thompson 2, M.Doherty 2 (1p)
GC	18/09/61	2	Ards	H	W	6	1	Harvey, Thompson 3, M.Doherty, Bruce
GC	25/10/61	SF	Coleraine	WP	W	4	3	T.Doherty, Smyth, Stewart, M.Doherty
GC	05/12/61	F	Linfield	GP	L	0	4	-
CC	09/09/61		Linfield	H	L	1	2	Thompson
CC	16/09/61		Cliftonville	A	W	2	1	Thompson 2
CC	23/09/61		Glenavon	H	D	2	2	M.Doherty 2
CC	30/09/61		Derry City	A	D	2	2	Bruce 2
CC	14/10/61		Bangor	H	W	6	4	M.Doherty 2, Thompson 2, Stewart (p), Bruce
CC	21/10/61		Ballymena United	A	W	3	1	Thompson, Bruce, Ervine
CC	28/10/61		Distillery	H	L	1	3	Thompson
CC	04/11/61		Crusaders	A	L	2	3	Shields, Thompson
CC	11/11/61		Portadown	H	D	4	4	Bruce, Thompson 2, M.Doherty
CC	18/11/61		Coleraine	A	L	1	2	Thompson
CC	25/11/61		Ards	H	L	1	9	Thompson
IL	02/12/61		Ballymena United	H	L	1	2	Thompson
IL	09/12/61		Bangor	A	L	1	4	M.Doherty
IL	16/12/61		Derry City	H	W	5	1	Hale. McGrath 2, Thompson 2
IL	23/12/61		Glenavon	A	W	3	2	Thompson, Hale, McGrath
IL	25/12/61		Distillery	H	W	3	0	Smyth, Thompson, Hale
IL	26/12/61		Ards	A	L	2	4	Smyth, M.Doherty
IL	30/12/61		Portadown	H	D	2	2	Smyth, M.Doherty (p)
IL	06/01/62		Coleraine	A	D	1	1	M.Doherty
IL	13/01/62		Crusaders	H	L	0	1	-
IL	20/01/62		Linfield	A	L	1	3	Bruce
IL	27/01/62		Cliftonville	A	W	2	1	Thompson 2
IL	03/02/62		Coleraine	H	W	2	1	M.Doherty (p), Hume
IL	10/02/62		Crusaders	A	L	0	1	-
IL	17/02/62		Linfield	H	D	1	1	Hume
IL	03/03/62		Cliftonville	H	W	6	0	Thompson 3, Bruce, Callendar, Hume
IL	17/03/62		Ballymena United	A	D	1	1	Stewart
IL	31/03/62		Bangor	H	W	2	0	Thompson 2
IL	07/04/62		Derry City	A	W	1	0	Stewart
IL	21/04/62		Ards	H	W	1	0	Thompson
IL	23/04/62		Distillery	A	L	3	4	Thompson 2, Bruce
IL	28/04/62		Glenavon	H	D	4	4	Todd, Thompson 2, M.Doherty
IL	01/05/62		Portadown	A	W	3	2	Todd 2, Thompson
NSC*	30/01/62	F.1	Linfield	A	D	0	0	-
NSC*	05/02/62	F.2	Linfield	GP	L	1	7	M.Doherty
NSC	28/02/62	1.1	St. Patrick's Athletic	GP	W	3	1	Hale, Bruce, Thompson
NSC	21/03/62	1.2	St. Patrick's Athletic	A	W	4	2	Murdough, Hume 2 (1p), Clarke og

IC	24/02/62	1	Distillery	A	W	4	2	Thompson, Creighton og, Hale 2
IC	10/03/62	2	Bangor	A	L	0	1	-
CAS	05/03/62	1	Dundela	H	W	3	2	Hamilton, Thompson, Stewart
CAS	09/04/62	2	Ards	H	W	6	3	Hume 2, Thompson 2, M.Doherty, Stewart
CAS	04/05/62	SF	Crusaders	Solt	W	2	1	Hume, Bruce
CAS	12/05/62	F	Linfield	Solt	L	0	5	-
F	09/08/61		Linfield	A	W	3	1	Stewart (p), Thompson, O'Neill
F	12/08/61		Burnley	H	L	1	7	McCullough

* = held over from 1960/1

Then, inexplicably, events took a dramatic downhill slide. From our next nine fixtures we recorded one draw and eight defeats. This "run" included two cup final reverses and our worst ever defeat at the Oval! It was a mysterious turnaround, even in the game we drew a three goal lead was thrown away as our defence presented the Ports with gift goals.

The Blues lifted the Ulster Cup as we failed to score in a match for the first time this season. Our best chance had fallen to Shields but he fluffed. Then in the Gold Cup Final Tommy Dickson inspired Linfield to a comfortable win on a snow covered Grosvenor Park surface.

However our biggest humiliation came in last City Cup game when Ards visited east Belfast. After eight minutes the score stood 1-1 but then Ards ran riot, Mick Lynch scoring five and Billy Humphries three in their 9-1 win. It was hard to believe that only a missed penalty from Matt Doherty had prevented us running up a score of 7-1 against the same opposition at the same venue just two months previously!

The poor form continued as the league commenced, we lost 1-4 at Bangor after being ahead. A win was eventually recorded, over Derry, debutant Danny Hale getting on the scoresheet. Hale was again on target in the next match against Glenavon, another dramatic comeback as we had trailed 0-2 before netting in the 70th, 71st and 72nd minutes! On the terraces the fans went wild with delight.

Right-winger John Smyth scored in all three of our Christmas fixtures but as 1962 dawned we found ourselves well down the league table, behind joint leaders Ards, Portadown, Ballymena and Linfield. The Seconds won the Intermediate Cup with a 2-0 defeat of Ballyclare Comrades, Rob McDowell and Warburton on target.

January was a disappointing month with only one win in five matches. The team had all the talent and experience but just couldn't produce the goods. We gained a draw with the Blues under the Windsor Park lights in the first leg of the 1960/1 North-South Cup Final but came a total cropper in the return "home" leg under Distillery's lights. The Glens were torn apart 7-1 by a devastating Linfield display with Dickson netting twice. What a send off for keeper Bertie McGonigal in his last appearance before his transfer to Brighton, where he would play 57 league games. Linfield fans herded around his goal in the second half, invading the pitch each time the Blues scored.

Ken Savage came into the side as McGonigal's replacement and Roy Borne was recalled at right-back. We gave a pathetic display at Seaview, losing 0-1 to the Crues for the second time in a month but a week later all eleven players gave 90 minutes of effort to hold Linfield 1-1 at the Oval in the league.

Billy Neill and Walter Bruce came back to their best form as we knocked Distillery out of the cup and walloped Cliftonville in the league after the Reds had beaten our Seconds in the Irish Cup. Billy Hume, a Scot signed from Bangor, was settling in well. After progressing to the second round of the Shield, luckily

Programme Cover 1961/2.

overcoming Dundela, we visited Bangor in the Irish Cup. Harry Walker decided to field battling centre-half Jim Murdough at outside-left for this game, the thinking being that the mud on the periphery of the Clandeboye pitch would suit him. It was a tactic that failed miserably and a jittery Glens were cut and blown from the competition by a 72nd minute goal from Greenfield, a hairdresser by profession! Enough was enough and at an emergency board meeting on the Monday night Walker was sacked from his position.

Ironically results immediately improved and Bangor were beaten in the league, the game kicking-off late to avoid a clash with the Grand National commentary. Ballymena and Ards were the likely lads as the league race entered its final furlong but we showed our potential with two wins over Ards in April. In the County Antrim Shield we romped home 6-3 after trailing 1-3 and fearing a repeat of the City Cup result. Next we put a big dent into the County Down men's league hopes with a 77th minute Thompson winner.

Although we were completely out of the league race our last three fixtures were action packed. Against Distillery we had an 86th minute equaliser disallowed for off-side. Supporters staged a demonstration, the referee was jostled and the linesman hit with a stone before police stepped in to quell the situation. The game against Glenavon finished 4-4 with a 19 year old Billy Johnston scoring all four for the Lurgan Glens.

By beating Ballymena 3-1 the same day Portadown narrowed the title race down to between themselves and Linfield. On Monday 30th April the Blues drew 0-0 with Derry City at Windsor in their last league game, bringing them level on points with the Ports who were down to face us at Shamrock Park on the following evening. This game was to produce a fascinating sequence of events as the climax to the league unfolded. The ground was packed and in the first half Portadown were well in control going ahead through a Murdough own goal. However after the break the home side fell to pieces as the Glens, with Neill immaculate, moved into a 2-1 lead. The Ports fans fell silent but on 73 minutes Gorman equalised, a goal which led to joyous scenes, a pitch invasion, and possibly a lack of concentration as within a minute of the restart Todd had scored his second to restore the Glens' lead! As time ticked away the real drama came. Three minutes remained when Portadown were awarded a penalty, and the man with the responsibility of taking the kick was Albert Mitchell, who had been released by the Glens the previous season. History shows that Savage saved the penalty, Glentoran won the game, and the Ports lost the resultant title play-off to Linfield 1-3 at Solitude.

This win completed "the seven" for Linfield five days after their sixth trophy success when they had ripped us apart in the Shield final. The only blot on their season came in the North-South Cup. We reached the second round after beating St. Patrick's Athletic 7-3 on aggregate but the conclusion of the tournament was held over until 1962/3.

On 2nd July 1962 Isaac McDowell was appointed Glentoran manager. McDowell, a scourge of the Glens in his playing and coaching days with Linfield and Ards, now had his chance to take the club back to former heights.

Appearances and Goals

	App.	Goals		App.	Goals		App.	Goals
Crothers	53		Savage	18		Shirlow	3	
Thompson	53	46	Hume	17	8	Harvey	2	1
Stewart A.	52	7	Hale	12	6	Bradley	2	
McCullough	52		Geoghegan	8		McDowell R.	2	
Bruce	45	13	McGrath	7	3	Hamilton	2	1
Doherty M.	45	20	Forde	6		McIntyre	2	
Murdough	34	1	Callender	6	1	Warburton	1	
Kennedy	32		Shields	5	1	Doherty R.	1	
McGonigal	31		Reynolds	5		Spicer	1	
Borne	23		Todd	5	3	Own Goals		2
Neill W.	21		Ervine	4	1	TOTAL	594	121
Smyth	19	4	McDowell J.	3				
Doherty T.	19	3	O'Neill	3				

1962/63

New manager Isaac McDowell – Entry into Europe –
Pavis earns Gold Cup win

Isaac McDowell's first game in charge was a "challenge match" against the seven-trophy Blues on 10th August. The Glens, 3-2 up going into injury time, were robbed of a win when Linfield substitute Bobby Stewart scored long after many thought that the final whistle should have been blown. It was an encouraging start for the big Scot as challenging times lay ahead. Roy Rea, the goalkeeper formerly of Banbridge, Glenavon, Amateur Ireland and the Irish League, made his debut in the friendly versus Drumcondra. Other new players to figure early on this season were Conway (centre-half), Davidson (outside-left), Victor Wilson (left-back) and the bespectacled Eric Ross. Richie Warburton established himself at outside-right and was to gain an Irish Amateur cap.

The competitive season opened with an Ulster Cup visit from Derry City. Twice Glentoran were ahead but brilliant play by the Derry forwards forced a draw and indeed only spectacular saves by Ken Savage kept us level. The referee, Mr. J. Kelly of Chorley, was knocked out when a goalbound shot hit him directly in the stomach. It took the attentions of both trainers and linesmen to enable him to resume. After an easy win over Ballymena United we travelled North to face Coleraine. Scouts from Newcastle United attended to run their eye over home goalkeeper Iam McFaul, but he had virtually nothing to do as Coleraine's outfield players were on top form and efficiently beat us 4-0.

By winning our last two games we finished a point behind the Bannsiders in Section B, but they lost 0-1 to Glenavon in the final. Walter Bruce was the Glens best player of the tournament, and in an explosive finish in the Crusaders game he scored twice to complete a hat-trick.

Linfield, stung by the loss of the first trophy, now faced up to us twice in four days in the City and Gold Cups. In the first meeting at Windsor Park Glentoran were a shambles. We showed no life or punch and deservedly went down by three goals. However it was a different story at the Oval on the Tuesday

Trevor Thompson heads for goal against Glenavon at the Oval.

night. The game stood scoreless with a minute to go when Trevor Thompson, who had been written off as "done" after the City Cup game, fired home the winner. The ground erupted and the many fans who had been heading for the exits rushed back to join in the singing and cheering which went on long after the game had ended. However one swallow does not make a summer and we were brought back to earth with a City Cup defeat at Glenavon just before we took our first steps into the new horizons of European club football.

Irish League clubs had been competing in the European Cup and Cup Winners Cup since 1957 with Glenavon, Ards and Linfield the early representatives. A third competition, the Inter City Fairs Cup, had been running on an erratic basis from 1955 but had now taken on a similar look to the other two cups with club sides taking part rather than representative XIs from those cities which staged European Trade Fairs. The Irish League selected Glentoran to be Ulster's first competitors in the Fairs Cup and we were drawn against Real Zaragosa of Spain.

In the first leg at the Oval the Glens were in hospitable mood both on and off the pitch. The Glentoran officials made sure the Zaragosa enjoyed their Ulster trip while Roy Borne put through his own goal to open the Spaniards account! A back-pass from Billy

Results 1962/63

Played 53. Won 24. Drew 13. Lost 16. Goals For 107. Against 86. % 57.5.
Honours: Gold Cup

UC	18/08/62		Derry City	H	D	2	2	Warburton, Hume
UC	22/08/62		Ballymena United	A	W	4	1	Bruce 2, Stewart, Thompson
UC	25/08/62		Coleraine	A	L	0	4	-
UC	29/08/62		Cliftonville	H	W	4	3	Stewart, Thompson, Davidson 2
UC	01/09/62		Crusaders	H	W	4	2	Hume (p), Bruce 3
CC	08/09/62		Linfield	A	L	0	3	-
CC	15/09/62		Cliftonville	H	W	2	0	Thompson, Bruce
CC	22/09/62		Glenavon	A	L	1	2	Ross
CC	28/09/62		Derry City	H	W	1	0	McKenna
CC	06/10/62		Bangor	A	W	2	0	Hume 2 (2p)
CC	13/10/62		Ballymena United	H	D	1	1	Bruce
CC	27/10/62		Distillery	A	L	2	4	Thompson, Hume
CC	03/11/62		Crusaders	H	L	0	1	-
CC	10/11/62		Portadown	A	D	1	1	Thompson
CC	17/11/62		Coleraine	H	W	2	0	Thompson, Mitchell
CC	24/11/62		Ards	A	W	7	3	M.Doherty 2, Mitchell 2(1p), Thompson 3
GC	11/09/62	1	Linfield	H	W	1	0	Thompson
GC	19/10/62	2	Glenavon	H	D	1	1	Stewart
GC	14/11/62	2R	Glenavon	A	D	2	2	Thompson 2
GC	27/11/62	2R2	Glenavon	GP	W	2	1	Davidson, Thompson
GC	11/12/62	SF	Distillery	WP	W	2	1	Stewart 2
GC	14/03/63	F	Derry City	WP	W	3	1	Pavis 2, Hume
FC	26/09/62	1.1	Real Zaragoza	H	L	0	2	-
FC	10/10/62	1.2	Real Zaragoza	A	L	2	6	M.Doherty 2
NSC*	23/10/62	2.1	Shelbourne	GP	D	1	1	Pavis
NSC*	30/10/62	2.2	Shelbourne	A	L	2	7	Thompson 2
IL	01/12/62		Cliftonville	H	D	1	1	M.Doherty
IL	08/12/62		Ards	A	W	6	1	Stewart, Thompson, Mitchell 2(1p), Warburton 2
IL	15/12/62		Portadown	H	L	1	3	Bruce
IL	22/12/62		Distillery	A	D	1	1	McDowell
IL	25/12/62		Coleraine	H	L	2	3	Mitchell (p), Pavis
IL	26/12/62		Ballymena United	A	L	3	4	Warburton, M.Doherty, Pavis
IL	29/12/62		Bangor	H	D	2	2	Pavis, M.Doherty (p)
IL	05/01/63		Glenavon	A	W	1	0	Warburton
IL	12/01/63		Linfield	H	D	1	1	Thompson
IL	19/01/63		Derry City	A	W	1	0	Mitchell
IL	26/01/63		Crusaders	H	D	1	1	Thompson
IL	02/02/63		Ards	H	W	2	1	Hume, M.Doherty
IL	09/02/63		Portadown	A	W	1	0	Stewart
IL	16/02/63		Distillery	H	W	5	1	Warburton, Bruce, Hume, Thompson 2
IL	02/03/63		Coleraine	A	L	1	2	Mitchell
IL	16/03/63		Ballymena United	H	W	5	1	Hume 2, McDowell, Thompson 2
IL	30/03/63		Bangor	A	W	5	0	Pavis 3, Mitchell, Thompson
IL	06/04/63		Glenavon	H	W	2	1	M.Doherty, Mitchell
IL	13/04/63		Linfield	A	D	1	1	Mitchell
IL	16/04/63		Derry City	H	L	0	2	-
IL	19/04/63		Cliftonville	A	W	3	0	Thompson, M.Doherty, Mitchell
IL	27/04/63		Crusaders	A	W	4	1	Hume, Mitchell 2, Pavis
IC	23/02/63	1	Ballyclare Comrades	H	W	4	1	Mitchell 2, Warburton, Hume
IC	09/03/63	2	Ballymena United	A	L	1	3	Thompson
CAS	09/04/63	2	Linfield	A	D	2	2	Mitchell, Pavis
CAS	23/04/63	2R	Linfield	H	D	1	1	Thompson

CAS	01/05/63	2R2	Linfield	Solt	L	1	3	Hume
F	10/08/62		Linfield	H	D	3	3	Thompson 2, Warburton
F	14/08/62		Drumcondra	H	W	3	2	Davidson, Thompson, M.Doherty
F	28/02/63		Glasgow Celtic	H	L	4	5	Thompson 2, Pavis 2
F	17/05/63		Dublin Selection	H	W	4	2	Stewart, Jones, Weatherup McCullough Walter Bruce Benefit

* = held over from 1961/2

McCullough was intercepted by Duca who strode through to make it 2-0. The uphill task for the second leg was compounded by a six-hour flight and a mix-up over Matt Doherty's passport. Doherty actually put us ahead after ten minutes but by half-time we trailed 1-2. Our overworked defence conceded four more after the break before Doherty gained a late consolation in the 80th minute. The 25,000 gave Zaragosa a standing ovation as we sharply learnt about the difference between part-time and full-time football.

Generally October was a poor month. Sammy Pavis made his debut versus Ballymena and "scored" a hat-trick of offside goals. The offending linesman was slow handclapped. Defeat at Grosvenor Park ended our interest in the City Cup but worse was to follow in midweek when we visited Tolka Park, Dublin for the second round second leg 1961/2 North-South Cup clash with Shelbourne. After the drawn first leg in Belfast people were asking, "Just how bad can the Glens get?", and this question was emphatically answered. Thompson actually put us ahead but we were outplayed and our understrength team could not cope with the force of the Shelbourne side. The Dubliners won 7-2! Amongst the crowd that night was our latest signing, defender Eamon Byrne who cost £500 from Drumcondra.

Byrne had a busy debut on the Saturday as Crusaders won 1-0 at the Oval in a tedious game. Results and displays could only improve and they did. Our draw at Portadown was described as "a hacking war, a robust and uncouth encounter with scant attention paid to the niceties of the game." Albert Mitchell rejoined the Glens from the Ports and was on target in the last two City Cup games – both resounding wins but only enough to lift us to eighth place in that competition.

The Gold Cup second round tie with Glenavon became something of a saga and it needed a third match at neutral Grosvenor Pak to separate the teams. In a "rip-roaring" affair Thompson netted a deflected winner in 78 minutes and it was reported that the watching Billy Bingham jumped with joy when the goal went in.

Glentoran supporters were calling for the installation of floodlights at the Oval and to address this and other issues the Glentoran Improvements Committee was formed on 12th November. The body consisted of both supporters and officials and was presided over by club director Adam Gilmour. The cost of the floodlight project was estimated at between £13,000 and £17,000.

The league began in December and we promised much by thrashing Ards for the second time in a fortnight. We only flattered to deceive, however, and by the end of the year we had gained just five points from seven games. Weatherwise, the winter of 1962/3 was one of the worst although Northern Ireland did not suffer quite as badly as mainland Britain. Many games were played in three or four inches of snow or on mudheaps of pitches. Meanwhile we reached the final of the Gold Cup for the third time on the trot with a deserved win over Distillery, thanks to two grand goals from Arthur Stewart.

The team adapted well to the trying conditions in early 1963, relying on a power based game. Roy Rea in goals was brilliant as we ended Glenavon's unbeaten home record and held Linfield at the Oval. Our Gold Cup rehearsal with Derry was the only game to survive the weather a week later so Mitchell's freak goal was the only recorded senior one in the country that day. The bad weather caused the postponement of the Gold Cup Final but three league wins in February took us to the top of the table. Linfield, a point behind, had two games in hand. The only blot came when Bruce was sent off at Portadown by Mr. Duxbury of Preston, a decision that mystified the crowd. However Bruce's wizardry was soon back in evidence against Ballyclare in the Irish Cup.

Glasgow Celtic travelled to Belfast in order to give their players some match practice. Although the 5-4 scoreline implied a close game it was anything but as Celtic were a class apart. Their sojourn did not help them much, though, as Rangers went on to complete the double in Scotland.

Although Coleraine scored twice in the last seven minutes to defeat us at the Showgrounds we remained top of the league as the Blues went down 2-3 to Glenavon. A busy week in March began with a trip to Ballymena in the Irish Cup. Thompson put us ahead but careless defensive covering allowed Ballymena to come back and win 3-1 in a pulsating last twenty minutes. On the Thursday night 6,000 ventured to Windsor Park for the Gold Cup Final with Derry City. It turned out to be a poor game but two late goals from the lurking "poacher" Pavis ensured we were back among the silverware again. Just two days later we gained revenge on Ballymena in the league. Trevor Thompson scored two to bring up his 200th goal for the club as United were reduced to nine men in the second half due to an injury and a sending-off. We put another five past Bangor and at the end of March the league table read:

Linfield played 17 points 23, 2. Glentoran 17-21, 3. Distillery 15-20, 4. Portadown 16-20.

After another rugged win over Glenavon we made two trips to Windsor Park to face Linfield in the Shield and league. Both matches finished all square meaning we still had not beaten the Blues in a competitive match on their own ground for sixteen years. Mitchell scored in both games, giving us the lead in the Shield meting and then equalising Braithwaite's goal in the league. Linfield keeper Irvine protested that he had not carried the ball over the line in the latter. Meantime Portadown, inspired by Jimmy Jones, moved up into second place in the league.

Our title hopes vanished on Easter Tuesday when Derry came and beat us 2-0 but we only had ourselves to blame as the forward line contrived to miss five open goals between them. The crowd just could not believe it and did not know whether to boo, slow handclap or cry! Chances again went a-begging in the Shield replay with Linfield as the clubs shared honours for the third time in a fortnight. Rea, named Ulster Footballer of the Year, made a magnificent save in what was his final game for the Glens before he moved to Canada to play for Toronto Italians. Rea was soon followed by full-back Roy Borne who joined Toronto City and actually played against Rea once as an emergency centre-forward.

We signed off league business with a terrific display against the Crues to earn joint third spot with Portadown. Linfield eventually beat us in the Shield, mainly thanks to the efforts of Tommy Dickson. The Blues saw off Bangor in the final before having a showdown with Distillery for the championship. Both teams were on 29 points and met in the last fixture. The Whites came out on top by 4-2 to win the league outright for the first time since 1903 and gain revenge for their 1-2 Irish Cup final defeat at the hands of Linfield.

Overall for Glentoran it was a strange season as the players adjusted to the new training methods employed by Isaac McDowell. Billy Neill formally retired and was appointed assistant manager for 1963/4. The season culminated with Walter Bruce's benefit game when a Glentoran Selection took on a Dublin Selection in a match billed as "North v South". The Glens XI won 4-2 with goals from Stewart, Jones, Weatherup and McCullough but generally it was a light-hearted game. Evidence of this came when Lynch missed two penalties for the Dublin side and claimed that "it was not right to score penalties in benefit games". The man facing those spot-kicks was our new goalkeeper Albert Finlay.

Appearances and Goals

	App.	Goals		App.	Goals		App.	Goals
Borne	48		McCullough	33		Murdough	7	
Wilson	47		Neill W.	31		Kennedy	5	
Stewart A.	46	7	Byrne	30		McKenna	5	1
Thompson	46	26	Hume	27	13	McDowell R.	4	2
Rea	46		Davidson J.	17	3	Conway	2	
Doherty M.	40	10	Pavis	16	11	Davidson D.	2	
Bruce	38	9	Savage	7		McAuley	1	
Warburton	36	7	Crothers	7		Callender	1	
Mitchell	34	17	Ross	7	1	TOTAL	583	107

1963/64

Windsor Hoodoo ended in style – League success – Cup final loss to Derry

By now the pre-season friendly or "challenge" game had replaced the internal public practice match as the traditional method of opening up a season. Glentoran had three such games against Larne, Linfield and Drumcondra and all were high scoring affairs as around twenty players were tried out. These included two ex-Distillery men, Harry Creighton and Tony Curley, and Gerry Green, formerly of Crusaders. Jim Murdough had left to manage the Crues and Matt Doherty returned to Derry City.

This was to be the season when Isaac McDowell led the club in from the wilderness as we became league champions for the first time in eleven years and ended our barren seventeen year spell without a competitive win over the Blues at Windsor Park – and in some style too! It was not all harmonious though as there were many disappointments along the way and on more than one occasion McDowell was before the board to explain his actions and methods.

To add variation to the Ulster Cup we swapped qualifying sections with Linfield and took on Distillery in the opening game of the season, our 800th post-war fixture. The match was close throughout and we held a

Team Group 1963/4 Back Row: Gerry Green, Sammy Pavis, Albert Finlay, Roy Borne, Tommy Brannigan Front Row: Harry Creighton, Trevor Thompson, Eamon Byrne, Walter Bruce, Tony Curley, Billy McCullough.

2-1 lead going into the last ten minutes, but an inspired Whites forward line netted three time to emerge 4-2 winners. The result set the pattern for a poor Ulster Cup campaign, and a final position of fourth out of six. Our worst display came at Glenavon (1-5), Billy Hume missing a penalty while against Ards the biggest round of applause was reserved for the band! On the bright side Eric Ross confirmed his promise with a 20 yard drive against Bangor and in the same match Walter Bruce completed a century of goals for the Glens.

Matters reached crisis proportions following three home defeats in September at the hands of Linfield and Glenavon (City Cup) and Partick Thistle (Fairs Cup). Yawns, slow handclaps and hoots of derision had become the norm for disgruntled supporters. At least the team went down fighting against Partick in the second leg, all the Scottish club's goals coming in the last half-hour.

It was generally accepted that our playing panel had the necessary skill and ability, but some of the displays had to be seen to be believed. McDowell wondered if the problems were psychological and for the Bangor game on 5th October he invited well known hypnotist Edwin Heath into the dressing room before kick-off. Maybe it worked as we won this game 2-1, coming from behind. Norman Gaunt, a soldier stationed at Palace Barracks, had a fine debut and scored the winner. Then, in a trend reminiscent of the 1950's, the confidence returned and the team put together an unbeaten run of thirteen games, including ten victories. Smiles returned to faces during this revival with the outstanding players being Pavis, Bruce and Ross.

Fionbarr Flood, vying with Albert Finlay for the goalkeeping berth, saved a crucial penalty at Ballymena but Finlay played well too when he got the chance and attracted the attention of Hull City. Linfield won the City Cup with a match to spare but our late challenge ensured second place, just two points behind. Before the last match at home to Ards a minutes silence was observed for President John F. Kennedy, who had been assassinated the day before.

Meantime we had progressed to the Gold Cup final, after requiring five matches to see off Ballymena and Derry. Only a late penalty earned a draw in the first game with Ballymena and

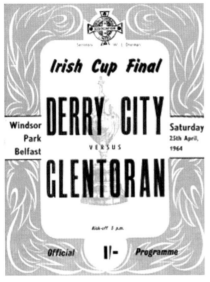

it took a Sammy Pavis hat-trick to eliminate the Braidmen at the third time of asking. The press were comparing Sammy's goal snatching ability to that of Jimmy Greaves. Pavis was again prominent in the semi-final with Derry City. We trailed 0-2 after only seven minutes, but then mounted a tremendous barrage to go 3-2 up before Pavis missed a 65th minute penalty. McGeough then levelled for Derry in the final minute. The Glens won the replay 2-0 but just two days later Derry gained comprehensive revenge by annihilating us 5-0 in the league at Brandywell, ending our unbeaten run in the process. Four of those goals came in the first half-hour.

The players appeared to be tired and purposeless but recovered to draw at Coleraine before the taxing Christmas period. There was jubilation at the Oval when Linfield were defeated 3-2 in front of 10,000, Pavis netting the winner after 82 minutes, but this turned to despair as we lost to the unfancied Crusaders on Christmas Day. The year ended with two wins but we still trailed leaders Coleraine by four points.

Irish Cup Final 1964 Programme Cover.

The months of January and February 1964 were extremely busy, even given the fact that we, along with Linfield pulled out of the North-South Cup on financial grounds. The year opened with a "crackerjack" 3-3 draw against Distillery at Grosvenor Park and then a week later Eamon Byrne became the seventh player (and the sixth Glenman) in a row to miss a penalty at the Oval when Kydd saved his attempt. A comfortable win over Bangor took us to within three points of Coleraine and Portadown as the former lost 0-3 to Linfield. The Ports, with Brian Jennings, brother of Pat, starring, dealt us a severe blow a week later when Finlay fumbled in a Newell shot for the only goal of the game.

Glentoran's board decided to forego the neutral venue of Grosvenor Park for the Gold Cup final in favour of a cash generating floodlight clash at Windsor Park. In that match Pavis put us ahead but Craig netted twice for the Blues and they led until Byrne's last gasp equaliser. The board then wanted to play the replay at Grosvenor Park but the floodlights there were broken and the League Management Committee ordered a return at Windsor Park. The fans were furious at this but still turned up in their thousands to watch Linfield win a pulsating game by the odd goal in five. Phil Scott netted a hotly disputed penalty and the Glens had an apparently good goal disallowed. Sometimes it's just not your night!

Ards were familiar opponents around this time, the sides meeting on five occasions within seven weeks. It took three games to dismiss them from the Irish Cup after Curley had missed a penalty in the first game and Billy McCullough scored an 87th minute own goal in the second. We strolled through in the second replay at Cliftonville with both Arthur Stewart, who was struggling to command a regular first team place and recent signing from Distillery Tommy Brannigan on the scoresheet.

Roy Borne returned from Canada and wore the left-back shirt for the league game against leaders Portadown at the end of February. This game indicated the seriousness of our championship hopes as we restricted the Ports to only one shot on target and netted four times ourselves. That night, with seven games remaining, the league table read as follows:

Coleraine 23 points, 2. Portadown 22, 3. Linfield 21, 4. Glentoran 20.

We knocked a dogged Crusaders side out of the Irish Cup at the second attempt and recorded narrow, hard-earned wins over Glenavon and Derry City as the excitement mounted. Pavis returned to the side, after transfer speculation, for the Cup semi-final and became an instant hero by scoring the first goal in our 2-0 victory. Every match had now assumed vital importance as the double became a distinct possibility.

Goalkeepers and defences were on top when Coleraine visited the Oval on Easter Monday but the scoreless draw kept both sides in contention, unlike the Ports whose title challenge faded with defeats to Distillery and Ballymena. The scene was now set for a potentially monumental encounter against Linfield at Windsor Park on Saturday 4th April. That day will go down as one of the greatest in Glentoran history as we thrashed the Blues 8-1 and in so doing knocked them off the top of the league and recorded our first victory over them there since March 1947! Walter Bruce was the architect of victory and Trevor Thompson the executor with four of the goals. However there were eleven Glentoran heroes that day and the teams were:

GLENTORAN: Finlay, Creighton, Borne, Byrne, McCullough, Bruce, Pavis, Curley, Thompson, Brannigan, Green.

LINIELD: McFaul, Gilliland, Graham. Andrews, Hatton, Wilson, Stewart, Scott, Craig, Nixon, Ferguson.

The headline in the Ulster said it all – "Glens ate the Blues." Incredibly many Glenmen missed the game as they had gone on an organised Supporters' Club trip to watch Liverpool v. Man. Utd. at Anfield! One can only imagine their mixed emotions on hearing the result.

Linfield went to pieces totally after this and lost their last two home league games to Ballymena and Derry, losing their title chances in the process. Coleraine also lost at home to Derry City and we leapfrogged them by defeating Crusaders the same day. A difficult trip to Ballymena was our next hurdle but goals in the 25th, 35th and 54th minutes set up a decisive as chants of "Here, here, the Glens are here" rang out from the terraces.

The small matter of the Irish Cup final took place the following Saturday with Derry City Our opponents. We gave a spluttering, unimpressive display and with only three minutes left the game was heading for a scoreless stalemate. Then Wilson, looking offside, scored for Derry and pandemonium broke out. Celebrating Derry fans invaded the pitch and within two minutes of them being cleared off Doherty made it 2-0 and so the cup went North West.

Albert Finlay

Could the team recompose itself to beat Cliftonville at Solitude and win the league? The answer was yes, Brannigan getting both the goals in our 2-0 victory as the Gibson Cup came to the Oval for the eleventh time. A key factor in this was that only sixteen players were required to play in the 22 games. This was the lowest number since the previous championship success in 1952/3 and compared with the seventeen players during the successful 1950/1 campaign.

Results 1963/64

Played 58. Won 32. Drew 13. Lost 13. Goals For 144. Against 91. % 66.4.
Honours: Irish League

UC	17/08/63		Distillery	A	L	2	4	White og, Mitchell
UC	20/08/63		Portadown	H	D	2	2	Thompson, Pavis
UC	24/08/63		Glenavon	A	L	1	5	Curley
UC	27/08/63		Bangor	H	W	2	0	Ross, Bruce
UC	31/08/63		Ards	H	W	3	1	Curley, McCullough, Hume
CC	07/09/63		Linfield	H	L	1	5	Thompson
CC	14/09/63		Cliftonville	A	W	6	0	Curley, Thompson, Walker og, McDowell 3
CC	21/09/63		Glenavon	H	L	0	2	-
CC	28/09/63		Derry City	A	L	1	2	McDowell
CC	05/10/63		Bangor	H	W	2	1	Mitchell, Gaunt
CC	19/10/63		Ballymena United	A	W	2	0	Thompson, Bruce
CC	26/10/63		Distillery	H	W	3	2	Pavis, Curley 2
CC	02/11/63		Crusaders	A	W	3	2	Curley, Warburton, Thompson
CC	09/11/63		Portadown	H	W	5	1	Thompson 2, Pavis 2, Creighton
CC	16/11/63		Coleraine	A	W	4	1	Ross, Thompson, Pavis 2
CC	23/11/63		Ards	H	W	4	2	Thompson 3, Curley
FC	16/09/63	1.1	Partick Thistle	H	L	1	4	Thompson
FC	30/09/63	1.2	Partick Thistle	A	L	0	3	-
GC	09/10/63	2	Ballymena United	A	D	3	3	Hume 2(1p), Pavis
GC	16/10/63	2R	Ballymena United	H	D	2	2	Thompson, Ross
GC	23/10/63	2R2	Ballymena United	A	W	4	1	Pavis 3, Warburton
GC	14/11/63	SF	Derry City	WP	D	3	3	Pavis, Crossan og, Thompson
GC	05/12/63	SFR	Derry City	WP	W	2	0	Pavis, Curley
GC	15/01/64	F	Linfield	A	D	2	2	Pavis, Byrne
GC	12/02/64	FR	Linfield	A	L	2	3	Thompson, Pavis
IL	30/11/63		Glenavon	H	D	1	1	Pavis
IL	07/12/63		Derry City	A	L	0	5	-
IL	14/12/63		Coleraine	A	D	2	2	Warburton, Pavis
IL	21/12/63		Linfield	H	W	3	2	Ross, Pavis 2
IL	25/12/63		Crusaders	A	L	1	3	Thompson
IL	26/12/63		Ballymena United	H	W	3	2	Thompson 2, Pavis
IL	28/12/63		Cliftonville	H	W	5	0	Pavis, Curley, G.Stewart og, Thompson, Stewart
IL	04/01/64		Distillery	A	D	3	3	Thompson, Curley, Pavis
IL	11/01/64		Ards	H	W	2	0	Thompson 2
IL	18/01/64		Bangor	H	W	4	0	Warburton 2, Thompson 2
IL	25/01/64		Portadown	A	L	0	1	-
IL	01/02/64		Distillery	H	W	3	1	Pavis, Curley 2(1p)
IL	08/02/64		Ards	A	D	2	2	Byrne, Curley
IL	15/02/64		Bangor	A	W	5	1	Curley 2, Thompson, Byrne, Brannigan
IL	29/02/64		Portadown	H	W	4	0	Thompson 3, Curley
IL	14/03/64		Glenavon	A	W	1	0	Green
IL	28/03/64		Derry City	H	W	4	3	Brannigan, Pavis, Thompson 2
IL	30/03/64		Coleraine	H	D	0	0	-
IL	04/04/64		Linfield	A	W	8	1	Thompson 4, Hatton og, Pavis, Brannigan, Green
IL	11/04/64		Crusaders	H	W	3	2	Thompson, Curley, Pavis
IL	18/04/64		Ballymena United	A	W	3	0	Brannigan, Pavis, Thompson
IL	30/05/64		Cliftonville	A	W	2	0	Brannigan 2
IC	22/02/64	1	Ards	A	D	1	1	Pavis

IC	26/02/64	1R	Ards	H	D	2	2	Thompson, Curley
IC	02/03/64	1R2	Ards	Solt	W	4	0	Stewart 2, Brannigan, Thompson
IC	07/03/64	2	Crusaders	A	D	2	2	Pavis, Thompson
IC	11/03/64	2R	Crusaders	H	W	2	0	Thompson, Curley
IC	21/03/64	SF	Coleraine	WP	W	2	0	Pavis, Thompson (p)
IC	25/04/64	F	Derry City	WP	L	0	2	-
CAS	07/04/64	1	Dundela	H	W	3	0	Pavis 2, Thompson
CAS	20/04/64	2	Ards	H	W	3	1	Thompson 2 (1p), Brannigan
CAS	02/05/64	SF	Linfield	Solt	W	5	1	Thompson 2, Brannigan, Pavis 2
CAS	09/05/64	F	Distillery	Solt	L	1	2	Bruce
F	06/08/63		Larne	A	W	5	2	Thompson, Ross, Curley 3
F	10/08/63		Linfield	A	W	4	3	McCullough, Mitchell, Bruce, Ross
F	13/08/63		Drumcondra	H	L	4	6	Thompson 3, Warburton
F	13/05/64		Carrick Rangers	A	Unknown			
F	18/05/64		Partick Thistle	H	D	1	1	Thompson Trevor Thompson Benefit

There was still time to humiliate Linfield again, this time to the tune of 5-1 in the County Antrim Shield semi-final. Thompson, who had recorded his 250th goal for the club in the pervious round against Ards, netted twice. The joke around the east of the city was that Linfield's new telephone number was Belfast 8151 in memory of the two defeats. We lost to Distillery in the final but few seemed to care.

A momentous season was wound up with a couple of friendlies. We took a side to play Carrick Rangers, now managed by our ex-centre-forward Sammy Hughes, and Partick Thistle visited the Oval again – this time for Trevor Thompson's benefit. Heroics from Albert Finlay in the latter earned the Glens a draw in front of 6,000.

Finally, Isaac McDowell informed the board that he was quitting the pressures of the managerial role and having a break from football.

Appearances and Goals

	App.	Goals		App.	Goals		App.	Goals
Bruce	56	3	Warburton	42	5	Mitchell	7	2
Byrne	55	3	Wilson	37		Kennedy	6	
Creighton	52	1	Ross	27	4	Hume	6	3
McCullough	50	1	Green	27	2	McDowell R.	6	4
Curley	50	19	Brannigan	27	9	Gaunt	2	1
Finlay	49		Stewart A.	22	3	Own Goals		5
Thompson	49	46	Borne	17		TOTAL	638	144
Pavis	42	33	Flood	9				

1964/65

Another new manager – City Cup success – Greeks under the Oval lights

Glentoran made two important announcements in the summer of 1964. Firstly Paddy Hunt was elected to the board and then Gibby McKenzie was appointed manager after he had been coaching in South Africa. McKenzie, a Scot like his predecessor, brought Irish League player-coaching experience at Bangor, Linfield and Portadown. Chairman John Sholdis, Vere Law and Hunt were to oversee the installation of floodlights in the early part of the season and they were officially switched on in December for a friendly with St. Mirren. The Glens lost this game 2-3 after being ahead but it was notable for the first team debut of Tommy Jackson. The lights had been used for earlier games including our first ever European Cup fixture. Another ground improvement was the completion of the pitch perimeter wall.

The only additional senior player to the league winning 1st team squad of 1963/4 was Eire international Paddy Turner, an inside-forward signed from Glasgow Celtic. Tony Curley, deemed surplus to requirements, moved to Coleraine. The 2nd XI welcomed back Jackie Fullerton, then aged 20 later of television fame, after he had given up football for four months due to a Saturday job.

Although we lost our two pre-season friendlies against Stoke City and Drumcondra plenty

Thompson helps Ross off the field at Windsor Park.

of good football was played. John Ritchie scored both of Stoke's goals in the first game but Jimmy McIlroy had to go off injured. Against Drumcondra Muir missed a penalty but scored later. Victor Wilson and the visitors' Dixon were sent off in the second half for indulging in "fisticuffs".

With a return to our more traditional Ulster Cup section Glentoran made an impressive start to the season. We came from behind to beat the Crues, afforded the luxury of a Thompson penalty miss versus the Reds and were inspired by Turner to overcome Coleraine. Sammy Pavis returned against Ballymena and was immediately in the goals but the game will possibly be remembered for probably the best goal of Trevor Thompson's career. He controlled a cross with his chest, then knee before turning and volleying into the net!

Both ourselves and Derry City returned 100% records from the first four games so the match at the Oval with the Derrymen became more or less an Ulster Cup semi-final. In an absorbing encounter Derry were twice ahead but we pulled back to force a play-off. Unfortunately Eamon Byrne sustained a knee injury which kept him on the sidelines for the rest of the season.

Prior to the play-off we had battle to do on three fronts. It took a replay to see off Distillery in the first round of the Gold Cup but Derry City, the eventual competition winners, accounted for us in Round Two, thus handing us our first domestic defeat of the season. There were no such problems in the City Cup. Richie Warburton, one of our most improved players, was on scoring form netting twice versus Linfield and following that with a hat-trick against a feeble Cliftonville outfit. Paddy Turner was looking a yard faster than the rest of the players.

Floodlights were used at the Oval for the first time on 16th September 1964 for the visit of Greek champions Panathanaikos. Admission to the game ranged from 3/6 for the unreserved terracing to 12/6 for a grandstand tip up seat or £1 for a seat in the directors' box. The 30,000 who paid in witnessed a courageous display from Glentoran against the more skilful Greeks but a 2-2 scoreline, after being 0-2 down suggested a difficult second leg in the "Bear Pit" in Athens.

In between the two European ties domestic form was brilliant as the free-scoring forward line put five past both Glenavon and Derry. Peter Gillespie was named "man of the match" in the latter. The City Cup was proving to be an entertaining tournament as 38 goals were scored in the six games played on 19th September.

A gallant display in Athens was not enough and we lost narrowly on aggregate to Panathanaikos by 4-5. Every player rose magnificently to the occasion with Billy McCullough particularly outstanding. The Greeks had gone ahead thanks to a dubious penalty award, when the ball appeared to strike Harry Creighton's thigh not arm. At one stage it stood 2-2 before Papoutsakis got the vital winner for the home side.

Programme Cover 1964/5.

After the Gold Cup exit, when we were denied three of our players due to work commitments, we returned to winning ways and sauntered through the remainder of the City Cup programme, dropping just one point out of a possible 22 overall, and averaging four goals per game. Distillery were the only XI to prevent us from winning, indeed we had to come from behind twice to obtain a draw. The cup was won with a game to spare. Our best performers during the competition were Turner, Thompson and goalkeeper Albert Finlay.

Big Trevor was the terror of many defences and Derry City felt his goalscoring ability in the Ulster Cup Section B play-off when he put away four of the six chances that came his way. The following Saturday we opened our defence of the league against Ballymena, who included four Englishmen, in atrocious conditions. Sleet and thick snow fell throughout the match but a good all round display engineered a 3-2 win.

We entered the Ulster Cup final as 4/5 favourites with Linfield listed at 3/1. The bookmakers were proved wrong as the Blues roasted our defence and the 0-1 loss was no more than we deserved. It is interesting to note the respective fortunes of the two finalists in their next league games. Linfield won 8-2 (Phil Scott 5) at Seaview while the Glens went down 0-5 (0-4 at half-time) to Portadown at Shamrock Park!

December was a demoralising month as we tasted defeat in five of our seven fixtures and had our Boxing Day clash with Distillery frozen off. Mid-Ulster was not our favourite part of the country as Glenavon, inspired by Billy Johnston, went one better than the Ports and knocked us for six! What had happened? Where had the dazzling early season form gone? Too many games on heavy pitches was one possible reason.

Pavis, leading scorer with the Seconds, was recalled but had little impact. McKenzie secured the services of John Hall, an RAF man home on a month's Christmas leave. Hall had a good debut, scoring both goals and having a third disallowed in a Monday night game against Ards. In a further attempt to arrest the slide Harry Millar was brought in as centre-half with McCullough switching to left-half and Walter Bruce moving up to inside-forward.

January 1965 brought little improvement in results however, only five points were picked up from the same number of league games. Sammy Pavis was transferred to Linfield and immediately made us pay by scoring the Blues' fourth goal against us just two days later! Graham Williams was signed from Wrexham but by the end of the month our title hopes had all but gone when Derry recorded their third win of the season over us. The gloom was

Results 1964/65

Played 50. Won 28. Drew 10. Lost 12. Goals for 114. Against 72. % 66.0.
Honours: City Cup

UC	15/08/64		Crusaders	H	W	2	1	Byrne, Ross
UC	18/08/64		Cliftonville	H	W	4	0	Warburton, Turner (p), Brannigan, Thompson
UC	22/08/64		Coleraine	A	W	2	0	Turner (p), Thompson
UC	26/08/64		Ballymena United	A	W	4	3	Pavis 2, Thompson, Warburton
UC	29/08/64		Derry City	H	D	2	2	Pavis, Warburton
UC	18/11/64	PO	Derry City	WP	W	4	2	Thompson 4
UC	02/12/64	F	Linfield	WP	L	0	1	-
GC	02/09/64	1	Distillery	A	D	1	1	Pavis
GC	09/09/64	1R	Distillery	H	W	2	1	Turner (p), Thompson
GC	08/10/64	2	Derry City	A	L	0	1	-
CC	05/09/64		Linfield	A	W	2	1	Warburton 2
CC	12/09/64		Cliftonville	H	W	6	0	Warburton 3, Thompson, Pavis 2
CC	19/09/64		Glenavon	A	W	5	4	Thompson, Brannigan, Stewart (p), Pavis, Murphy og
CC	26/09/64		Derry City	H	W	5	1	Thompson 3, Gillespie, Bruce
CC	10/10/64		Bangor	A	W	4	0	Thompson, Pavis 2, Turner
CC	17/10/64		Ballymena United	H	W	3	1	Warburton 2, Thompson
CC	24/10/64		Distillery	A	D	2	2	Thompson, Turner (p)
CC	31/10/64		Crusaders	H	W	4	0	Turner, Thompson 2, Creighton
CC	07/11/64		Portadown	A	W	4	1	Thompson, Turner 2, Warburton
CC	14/11/64		Coleraine	H	W	3	1	Gillespie, Bruce, Thompson
CC	21/11/64		Ards	A	W	5	0	Warburton, Thompson, Gillespie, Brannigan, Turner
EC	16/09/64	P.1	Panathanaikos	H	D	2	2	Turner, Thompson
EC	30/09/64	P.2	Panathanaikos	A	L	2	3	Turner, Pavis
IL	28/11/64		Ballymena United	H	W	3	2	Warburton, Bruce, Brannigan
IL	05/12/64		Portadown	A	L	0	5	-
IL	12/12/64		Coleraine	H	W	3	2	Thompson 2, Warburton
IL	19/12/64		Glenavon	A	L	0	6	-
IL	25/12/64		Derry City	H	L	0	1	-
IL	28/12/64		Ards	H	D	2	2	Hall 2
IL	02/01/65		Crusaders	H	W	2	1	Warburton, Thompson
IL	09/01/65		Linfield	A	L	1	4	Potter og
IL	16/01/65		Bangor	H	D	1	1	Turner
IL	23/01/65		Cliftonville	A	W	4	0	Stewart (p), Ross, Warburton, Williams (p)
IL	30/01/65		Derry City	A	L	0	2	-
IL	06/02/65		Distillery	H	W	2	0	Lunn 2
IL	13/02/65		Ards	A	W	4	1	Ross, Warburton, Houston og, Williams
IL	27/02/65		Crusaders	A	L	0	1	-
IL	13/03/65		Linfield	H	D	1	1	Warburton
IL	20/03/65		Bangor	A	D	2	2	Warburton, Lunn
IL	03/04/65		Cliftonville	H	L	0	3	-
IL	10/04/65		Ballymena United	A	W	2	0	Lunn 2
IL	13/04/65		Glenavon	H	W	3	2	Thompson 2, Turner
IL	17/04/65		Portadown	H	D	1	1	Lunn
IL	19/04/65		Coleraine	A	D	0	0	-
IL	23/04/65		Distillery	A	W	2	1	Thompson 2
IC	20/02/65	1	Ballyclare Comrades	A	W	5	0	Warburton 3, Ross, Molyneaux og
IC	06/03/65	2	Portadown	H	W	4	0	Lunn, Thompson, Turner, Bruce
IC	27/03/65	SF	Coleraine	WP	L	0	1	-
CAS	30/03/65	1	R.U.C.	H	W	3	1	Newell 2, Jackson
CAS	05/04/65	2	Larne	A	L	1	4	Stewart (p)

F	06/08/64	Stoke City	H	L	1	2	Warburton
F	08/08/64	Drumcondra	H	L	2	4	Turner, Muir
F	07/12/64	St. Mirren	H	L	2	3	Thompson 2
							Opening of Oval Lights
F	14/05/65	Rathfriland Swifts	A	W	5	2	Warburton 2, Newell, Lunn, Thompson
							Opening of New Ground

lifted slightly as a result of wins over Distillery and Ards but with only nine games remaining we trailed runaway leaders Derry by ten points.

Thompson and Bruce were dropped as McKenzie gave chances to Eric Ross, Sammy Lunn (a graduate of Parkgate Olympic), Cecil Newell and a promising full-back Billy McKeag. However the resultant experienced 2nd XI including Thompson, Bruce, Borne and Brannigan went down 0-2 to Dundela in the George Wilson Cup.

The Irish Cup came as a welcome break from the league struggle and B Division Ballyclare Comrades were easy meat in Round One. We had little difficulty in the second round against a struggling Portadown side, player managed by Wilbur Cush. Thompson was recalled for this tie but could only net once from a hatful of chances.

Sammy Pavis haunted us once more on 13th March, scoring for the Blues after fourteen minutes on his return to the Oval. Warburton equalised and only the brilliance of Linfield keeper Cowan prevented us winning. Then a week later an 88th minute header from Dennis Light denied us a win at Bangor. Thompson was again dropped for the Irish Cup semi-final and hard though his inexperienced replacement Lunn tried we could not find a way past the Coleraine defence. The game was in its last minute when Coleraine centre-half Allan Hunter, later to play for Ipswich Town and Northern Ireland, went forward to grab the only goal of the match. The Bannsiders duly lifted the Cup thanks to a 2-1 final success over Glenavon.

More disappointment followed in early April. Firstly bottom of the league Cliftonville, having lost all their previous seventeen games, came to the Oval and trounced us 3-0. It was described as the shock of the year and for the Reds, who used 105 players during the season, it was their only points of the league campaign. They would have otherwise emulated Milford (14 games in 1890/1) and the North Staffordshire Regiment (ten games in 1898/9) as the only teams to lose all their league games. We sank to further depths on the Monday night at Larne in the County Antrim Shield. Larne looked more like the senior team as they rubbed our noses in the dust.

When Tommy Brannigan was transferred to Ballymena only Thompson remained from the forward line which had put eight goals past Linfield exactly a year previously.

At least we restored some pride by finishing the league with a five match unbeaten run but there were very few present to witness this. Albert Finlay was named Glentoran player of the year, polling around 400 of the 900 votes cast. The players had two relaxing events to look forward to at the end of a topsy-turvy season. Firstly we opened Rathfrailand Swifts' new Iveagh Park grounds in May. Gibby McKenzie actually made an appearance as a player in that one. Then on the weekend of 4th/5th June the first team enjoyed an outing to Butlin's at Mosney. No doubt they were informed that better things were expected in 1965/6.

Appearances and Goals

	App.	Goals		App.	Goals		App.	Goals
Finlay	50		Millar	22		Curley	2	
Warburton	47	22	Ross	21	4	Hall	2	2
Turner	46	15	McKeag	18		Archdeacon	1	
Bruce	45	4	Pavis	16	10	Wilson	1	
Borne	44		Gillespie	13	3	Mitchell	1	
Stewart A.	43	3	Lunn	11	7	Gorman	1	
Thompson	41	29	Newell	8	2	Own Goals		4
McCullough	41		Williams	6	2	TOTAL	550	114
Creighton	35	1	Byrne	5	1			
Brannigan	25	4	Jackson	5	1			

1965/66

Boardroom battles – "Duke of Windsor" signs - Conroy's Cup

There was hectic activity on the both transfer front and in the Glentoran boardroom in late summer 1965. While the players were training at both Celtic Park and the RUC grounds Gibby McKenzie was in Scotland looking for forwards. He signed 33 year old ex-Scottish international centre forward "Handy" Andy Kerr from Aberdeen on a free transfer but he departed after just one poor performance. Attempts to obtain Turlough O'Connor from Bohemians failed but McKenzie made sure he got his man when it came to Bangor's 19 year old Scottish winger Steve Gnaulati. The player was holidaying in Genoa at the time he signed his contract! Another Scot, Ken Hamilton, joined from Distillery. Eamon Byrne resumed training after his long term leg injury.

Meanwhile three directors, Sandy Chambers, Jim Morgan and Paddy Hunt along with club patron Adam Gilmoure, resigned from the board over the way the club's affairs were

Andy Kerr.

being run. Billy Pollock, Al Gregg and Joseph Kitzler were co-opted to the board but Kitzler had to resign for health reasons and following an Extraordinary General Meeting, demanded by the shareholders, Hunt and Morgan were re-elected.

It was a relief to return to "on the field" matters. The season opened a week earlier because of the extra fixtures created by changing the Ulster Cup format to a single section. The League Championship was brought forward to run from September to February with the City Cup to be played for at the back end of the season.

Glentoran began badly, losing our first three Ulster Cup games as our weakness up front was exposed. McKenzie described the performance against the Blues as "simply terrible" as Pavis netted a hat-trick in our 1-4 defeat. Surprisingly we beat Second Division Huddersfield Town, who included Bob McNab and Northern Ireland international Jimmy Nicholson in their ranks, in a friendly. Our first domestic win arrived on 18th August when we came from behind to beat Glenavon, Thompson netting the winner in his first game of the season. After a lack-lustre display against Bangor McKenzie announced a coup when he revealed

that Tommy Dickson, the "Duke of Windsor", had signed for the Glens after his sacking by Linfield. Would he now become "Lord Glentoran"? Meanwhile the real Duke of Windsor was released from hospital in New York after having trouble with his right eye!

With Dickson watching from the sidelines performances improved slightly and we finished the Ulster Cup in third position behind Linfield and Coleraine. The team's strength was in the middle line of Stewart, Millar and Bruce but not enough chances were being put away. Junior teams at the Oval did not have that problem – the Seconds beat Bangor Reserves 11-2 on the same day that the Olympic defeated the 15th Scouts by 9-2!

Albert Finlay was in good form at the other end, saving a penalty at Portadown, but we lost that match handicapped by an injury to PaddyTurner. This brought calls for the introduction of substitutes into Irish League soccer, as had been allowed for the Football League in England. It was noticeable that attendances at away games had dropped. Glentoran fans blamed the fact that the Ulsterbus fares had been maintained at their higher summer prices. Those attending games could view our new strip, red jerseys with a green "V" and numbers on the players' shorts.

Tommy Dickson made his debut in a Friday night league game versus Ballymena. The game finished scoreless and the best chance had fallen to Dickson but he pulled his shot wide with only keeper Walsh to beat. Once again we were Northern Ireland's Fairs Cup representatives and were drawn against Royal Antwerp of Belgium. The first leg was away and we returned thankful to be only 0-1 down. Throughout the game the Glens had been cheered on by a group of around 75 Belfast soldiers on an evening's leave from their military manœuvres. The return leg at the Oval was a farcical fog-bound game and was described in one quarter as "the best match that was never seen". Spectators could see virtually nothing but the referee, E. Syme of Glasgow, insisted that conditions were fit for play. With one minute left the Glens led 3-2 on the night but the Belgians scored (we think!) to go through saving the expense of a play-off at a neutral venue in those pre "away goals count double" days.

We were also finding the going tough domestically. Glenavon knocked us out of the Gold Cup after a controversial display by the referee in the first game at the Oval. Once again we were cursed by an injury, this time to full-back Creighton who became a passenger on the left wing in the second half of the replay. In the league a two goal lead was thrown away at Derry City despite the battling of McCullough. McKenzie had been hit by a stone at the Brandywell and, after midweek home draws with Home Farm (friendly) and Glenavon completed a nine match winless sequence, he tendered his resignation to the board. This was accepted and Billy Neill stepped up from the assistant's role to take over the reigns of the first team.

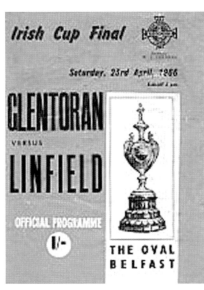

Irish Cup Final 1966 Programme Cover.

Our bad form threatened to continue at Cliftonville as we trailed 1-3 with fifteen minutes to go. Then a blitz was launched on the Reds and we rattled in four goals in ten minutes to win 5-3. The fans who had been disgruntled all through the game suddenly began chanting "We want six!" This match was the catalyst for seven league wins in a row including a famous one over Linfield. Tommy Dickson ran the show against his former colleagues while Eric Ross added the finishing touch with a 25 yard shot past McFaul in the 86th minute.

Ross and Walter Bruce inspired the "new" Glens during this run, although the former encountered an unusual difficulty against Crusaders at Seaview. A thick mist enveloped the ground during the last twenty minutes forcing Ross to remove his glasses and play virtually "blind". The defence too was solid with Billy McCullough energetic in his tackling and Billy McKeag competent in his covering. Grimsby Town, Man. Utd. and Rangers were all rumoured to be interested in McKeag but no transfer ever materialised. At the half-way stage in the league Linfield led us by two points.

This fine spell culminated with a "five-star show" in the second half against Distillery at the Oval. The game stood 2-2 at the interval but we netted five more, Thompson turning provider for Turner. Big Trevor's goal in the seventh minute took him past Sammy Hughes in the all-time Glentoran scoring chart and against Ards later in the month he brought up his 300th goal. In the same match a 19 year old Dubliner, Terry Conroy, made an impressive senior debut. Conroy, signed from Home Farm, had taken part in the Steel and Sons Cup final just three days earlier when Glentoran II defeated Larne 1-0.

The Oval had hosted more European visitors in December in the shape of Czech army outfit Dukla Prague. The Glens, strengthened by the inclusion of Terry Neill (Arsenal), Jimmy McIlroy (Stoke), Steve Chalmers (Celtic) and George Armstrong (Arsenal) went

Richie Warburton celebrates a goal versus Linfield.

down 0-2 to goals from Strunc (26 minutes) and Roeder (73 minutes), but it was Ross who displayed most skill. Neill kindly donated his match fee to a leukemia fund. Also in December Vere Law was elected club president and Gibby McKenzie became manager of Shelbourne.

Emigration to South Africa was becoming a popular attraction for local footballers past and present. Ex-manager Isaac McDowell and ex-Glens players Vic Wilson, Dickie Leeman and Jackie Fullerton all moved there, McDowell to coach at Bloemfontein.

The year of 1966 began with a horrendous defeat at Mourneview Park. Glenavon raced into a 5-0 half-time lead, and our only consolations in an 8-2 defeat were Dickson's two goals, one of them a superb right-foot volley. Dennis Guy netted five for the home side. Linfield pulled away at the top with a 10-0 win at Solitude but just a fortnight later we went to Windsor Park and won 2-1 to leave the league table as follows after 18 games:

1. Linfield 28 points, 2. Derry City 25, 3. Glentoran 24.

We won our next three games in leisurely style introducing many new faces in the process – Tommy Jackson and Tommy Craig from the Seconds, Tony Nelson, Charlie McDonnell (ex-Southport) and Bobby McAlinden (from Port Vale). Paddy Turner went in the opposite direction, joining Dundalk, while we failed in an attempt to sign Bobby Braithwaite from Linfield. Port Vale, being managed by Sir Stanley Matthews, agreed to come to Belfast for a friendly, but this, along with proposed meetings with Shamrock Rovers and Torino of Italy, were cancelled due to the already overcrowded fixture list. This was compounded by the decision to inaugurate a "Top Four" competition involving, as the name suggests, a play-off series between the sides finishing first to fourth in the league.

We were assured of a place in this despite having our last fixture against Crusaders put back two months. Derry's lingering championship hopes faded when they could only draw 0-0 with Linfield at Brandywell, and they eventually shared second spot with us. The Top Four and a play-off therefore gave us two cracks at avenging our two league defeats at the hands of the Derrymen. They held the upper hand in the former, winning 3-1, but we became league runners-up outright on a ridiculously late 28th May with a convincing 6-1 in after a 2-2 draw at the Brandywell. We had led 2-0 in the first game whereas Derry took the lead in the replay.

Both the Irish Cup and City Cup had commenced in February. "Champagne" Charlie McDonnell's hat-trick was the only bright spot in a dull Irish Cup 1st round tie with Banbridge Town. Distillery were tough opponents in Round Two and it took three matches before we saw them off. Finlay saved a penalty in the first match while Bryan Hamilton was the Whites' best player over the three games. The semi-final meeting with Coleraine was spoilt by a strong wind and driving rain. It finished 1-1 but both Des Dickson and Terry Conroy had simple chances to win it for either side. Glentoran had a surprisingly easy victory, 5-0, in the replay three days later.

This result set up an exciting finale with Linfield, 2-0 conquerors of Crusaders in the other semi-final. Glentoran won the toss for venue and a huge crowd packed out the Oval on 23rd April. Both sides sported new strips, Linfield in all-blue, the Glens in white with a red, green and black horizontal band. The drama began during the pre-match warm up when Finlay was hit in the groin by a stone thrown from a group of Linfield supporters. He was helped off by Thompson and Creighton but was able to play after treatment from Bobby McGregor.

This event steeled the Glens' resolve even more and we ran out 2-0 winners with Terry Conroy the two-goal hero, his strikes coming in the 32nd and 88th minutes. It was a great day for Glentoran but was slightly marred by incidents of bottle throwing – indeed at one stage referee Jack Adair had threatened to abandon the game. The day also marked the opening of the lower stand, adding 1,100 more seats to the existing 2,500 in the upper section.

Linfield gained a measure of revenge by eliminating us from the County Antrim Shield nine days later. Our Seconds had been beaten 1-0 by Distillery in the first round.

The City Cup had begun well but was suffering from a general end of season apathy as it reached the half-way stage. Our most dramatic match was against Distillery. After 50 minutes we led 3-1, twenty minutes later it was 4-2 then the Whites brought it back to 4-4 with five minutes to go, before Conroy's late winner. Ken Hamilton had an excellent game against his former team. Glenavon beat us 3-0 and went on to lift the City Cup with two games to spare.

Before the game with Bangor on 30th April Albert Finlay found out that he had retained his Glentoran Player of the Year award and received the J.L.Morgan trophy. As a curtain raiser to that game the final of the Belfast Schools seven-a-side tournament took place with Grove meeting Orangefield. Two ten year olds in opposition that day were Billy Murray (Orangefield's leading scorer with 48 goals and later to star for Linfield) and Billy Hamilton whose future achievements would include 42 Northern Ireland caps and World Cup finals fame.

There was still plenty of football to play in May. Only a last minute equaliser prevented us from beating Linfield in the City Cup as for the first time in the club's history we completed 60 competitive games in a season. There were trips to Downpatrick, for a Civic Week game with Glenavon, and Ballyclare, a friendly as part of the deal which saw Tommy Morrow transferred to us. The club also took part in a five-a-side competition at Dixon Park when manager Billy Neill turned out again.

Team Group 1965/6 under Gibby McKenzie

Results 1965/66

Played 60. Won 32. Drew 13. Lost 15. Goals For 134. Against 89. % 64.2.
Honours: Irish Cup

UC	07/08/65		Crusaders	A	L	1	4	Gnaulati
UC	11/08/65		Derry City	H	L	1	2	Ross
UC	14/08/65		Linfield	A	L	1	4	Gnaulati
UC	18/08/65		Glenavon	H	W	2	1	Lunn, Thompson
UC	21/08/65		Bangor	A	W	2	1	Gnaulati, Stewart
UC	25/08/65		Ballymena United	H	W	4	1	Thompson 2, Lunn, Stewart (p)
UC	28/08/65		Coleraine	A	D	1	1	Thompson
UC	31/08/65		Distillery	H	W	2	1	Ross, Bruce
UC	04/09/65		Portadown	A	L	0	1	-
UC	07/09/65		Ards	H	W	3	2	Hamilton, Thompson, Stewart (p)
UC	11/09/65		Cliftonville	A	W	3	1	Warburton, Stewart (p), Thompson
IL	18/09/65		Distillery	A	W	4	0	Thompson 2, Ross, Hamilton
IL	24/09/65		Ballymena United	H	D	0	0	-
IL	09/10/65		Ards	H	L	2	3	Thompson, Stewart
IL	16/10/65		Derry City	A	L	2	3	Stewart (p), Thompson
IL	22/10/65		Glenavon	H	D	0	0	-
IL	30/10/65		Cliftonville	A	W	5	3	Thompson 2, McCullough, Warburton, Dickson
IL	06/11/65		Linfield	H	W	2	0	Warburton, Ross
IL	13/11/65		Coleraine	H	W	2	0	Ross, Hamilton
IL	20/11/65		Bangor	A	W	4	0	Bruce, Thompson, Warburton, Gnaulati
IL	27/11/65		Portadown	H	W	2	0	Bruce, Gnaulati
IL	04/12/65		Crusaders	A	W	1	0	Thompson
IL	11/12/65		Distillery	H	W	7	3	Thompson, Turner 4, Bruce 2
IL	18/12/65		Ballymena United	A	L	1	2	Thompson
IL	25/12/65		Derry City	H	L	0	1	-
IL	28/12/65		Ards	A	W	3	2	Gnaulati, Thompson, Conroy
IL	01/01/66		Glenavon	A	L	2	8	Dickson 2
IL	08/01/66		Cliftonville	H	W	2	0	McGucken og, Turner
IL	15/01/66		Linfield	A	W	2	1	Thompson 2
IL	22/01/66		Coleraine	A	W	1	0	Ross
IL	28/01/66		Bangor	H	W	3	1	Thompson 2, Stewart
IL	05/02/66		Portadown	A	W	3	1	Thompson 2, Ross
IL	11/04/66		Crusaders	H	W	2	1	McAlinden, Thompson
IL	21/05/66	TM	Derry City	A	D	2	2	Stewart, Nelson
IL	28/05/66	TMR	Derry City	H	W	6	1	Warburton 2, Thompson 3, Conroy
FC	28/09/65	1.1	Royal Antwerp	A	L	0	1	-
FC	06/10/65	1.2	Royal Antwerp	H	D	3	3	Hamilton, Thompson 2
GC	01/10/65	1	Glenavon	H	D	2	2	Stewart, Thompson
GC	13/10/65	1R	Glenavon	A	L	1	2	Thompson
IC	11/02/66	1	Banbridge Town	H	W	4	2	McDonnell 3, Thompson
IC	05/03/66	2	Distillery	A	D	1	1	Nixon og
IC	09/03/66	2R	Distillery	H	D	1	1	McDonnell
IC	14/03/66	2R2	Distillery	WP	W	2	1	McDonnell, Stewart (p)
IC	26/03/66	SF	Coleraine	WP	D	1	1	McDonnell
IC	29/03/66	SFR	Coleraine	WP	W	5	0	Thompson 2, McAlinden, Stewart (p), McDonnell
IC	23/04/66	F	Linfield	H	W	2	0	Conroy 2
CC	25/02/66		Cliftonville	H	W	7	2	Nelson 3, Thompson, McDonnell 3
CC	12/03/66		Ards	A	D	1	1	Thompson

CC	19/03/66		Portadown	H	D	1	1	McDonnell
CC	02/04/66		Distillery	A	W	5	4	Conroy 2, Thompson, Hamilton 2
CC	07/04/66		Coleraine	H	W	3	2	Stewart, Ross, Thompson
CC	09/04/66		Ballymena United	A	D	1	1	Stewart
CC	16/04/66		Glenavon	A	L	0	3	-
CC	26/04/66		Derry City	A	W	1	0	Stewart
CC	30/04/66		Bangor	H	W	3	0	Thompson, Conroy, McDonnell
CC	13/05/66		Crusaders	H	L	0	3	-
CC	17/05/66		Linfield	H	D	1	1	Jackson
CAS	04/04/66	1	Chimney Corner	H	W	8	0	Thompson 5, Nelson 2, McDonnell
CAS	02/05/66	2	Linfield	A	L	2	3	Thompson 2
T4C	14/04/66	SF	Derry City	WP	L	1	3	Conroy
F	09/08/65		Huddersfield Town	H	W	2	1	Warburton, Lunn
F	19/10/65		Home Farm	H	D	1	1	Thompson
F	06/12/65		Dukla Prague	H	L	0	2	-
F	03/05/66		Glenavon	*	L	1	3	Thompson Downpatrick Civic Week

* played at Downpatrick

At the start of June the club announced a profit of £2684 – gate receipts for the season had been £14,647, transfer fee surplus £600, Improvement Committee £3513, donation £1000 and social club £2000. On 18th June Billy Sinclair was signed from Chelsea but ten days later Billy Neill decided to stand down from his duties and so the search for a manager was on again.

Appearances and Goals

	App.	Goals		App.	Goals		App.	Goals
Finlay	59		Turner	21	5	Craig	6	
Creighton	56		Gnaulati	18	6	Wright	3	
Stewart A.	56	14	McDonnell	18	13	Kerr	1	
Thompson	56	46	McAlinden	18	2	Fletcher	1	
Bruce	47	5	Borne	17		Newell	1	
McKeag	44		Warburton	17	6	Rainey	1	
Ross	43	8	Hamilton	16	6	Own Goals		2
Millar	35		Nelson	15	6	TOTAL	660	134
McCullough	35	1	Jackson	11	1			
Byrne	25		Lunn	9	2			
Conroy T.	22	8	Dickson	9	3			

1966/67

Encounters with Rangers - A four-trophy season - The Detroit Cougars

The appointment of John Colrain, the ex-Glasgow Celtic and Ipswich Town forward, as the new Glentoran player-coach-manager in July 1966 was to herald probably the most successful mini-era in the club's history and arguably produce the greatest ever team to play in the Irish League. Colrain, a tall Scot, soon picked up the nickname "Big John" and became a real players' manager during his two year spell. He was also to lead the club on an historic tour of North America when Glentoran played as the Detroit Cougars in a twelve team tournament involving clubs from Italy, Brazil, England, Scotland, Holland and the Republic of Ireland.

But first back to the domestic season of 1966/7. The Glens kicked off with a pre-season friendly against Southport just four days after England's 4-2 defeat of West Germany in the Wembley World Cup final. We won an entertaining game by 2-0, Billy Bingham turning out for both sides. In the first match programme Colrain thanked everyone for the warm welcome to the Oval and stated his intention "to do the utmost on and off the field to put Glentoran where they belong – top in Irish League football." The Gazette also welcomed new coach Norman Kernaghan and players Tom Lyons from Dundalk (who was to play

Terry Conroy in his Stoke City days.

mostly in the Seconds) and Jim "Bimbo" Weatherup, returning to the club after a spell with Crusaders.

Colrain introduced a 4-2-4 playing system but early Ulster Cup performances were unremarkable even though we were getting the wins, including coming from behind against Crusaders and Derry. The only early defeat suffered was to Harry Catterick's Everton in a friendly, when our lack of full-time training took its toll as two of the visitors' three goals came late on. Despite the retirement of Eamon Byrne due to a recurring leg injury Glentoran had a large first team panel and this was amply illustrated when the Seconds beat Linfield Swifts 7-0.

Trevor Thompson was a major figure in the defeat of Linfield and Billy Sinclair won his way into fans' favours by scoring both goals in a win at Glenavon. Our next away win at Ballymena was made easier by the Braidmen having to start with ten players, as one of their Scottish imports had a flight delay! Their keeper did not help by putting through his own goal.

We met Coleraine at the end of August with both sides defending a 100% record. It was a dreary and tension filled match, only left-back McKeag impressed, but still the right result came our way (1-0). The following Monday we played a friendly against the Blues at Seaview in order to raise money for Crusaders' fire damaged dressing rooms. The match was significant not only for our winning of the replica World Cup at stake but also it was the first time the team had really jelled together stylishly. There were no weak links in our side and we went on to win the Ulster Cup for the first time since 1953 dropping only one point, to Ards, in the process. Our final game with Distillery became an exhibition match as flag-waving fans celebrated each of our six spectacular goals with pitch invasions. The fifth of these was a special landmark for Thompson as it took him past Freddie Roberts' all-time club scoring record of 332 goals.

After winning our two opening games in the Irish League, in which substitutes were allowed for the first time for injured players, attention turned to our eagerly awaited European Cup Winners Cup clash with Glasgow Rangers. The first leg at the Oval drew a 35,000 crowd and the Glentoran XI put on a glorious fighting and skilful display. It looked like we would have to settle for a 0-1 defeat until Sinclair, a Rangers fan during his youth in Glasgow, drove home a shot via a post past Ritchie in the 89th minute. Not surprisingly the Oval erupted. The return leg was disappointing from our viewpoint as mistakes and missed chances helped Rangers to a flattering 4-0 win in front of 33,000. The Glasgow – Belfast steamer was delayed until 10 p.m. that night to accommodate returning Glentoran fans. Many described the Rangers team as one of their poorest ever but credit

Programme Cover 1966/7 .

must be given to Colrain for his shackling tactics, born from his spying missions to Ibrox early season. He rated the draw at the Oval as the proudest moment of his career.

In between the two Rangers games there was an amazing encounter with Derry City at the Oval. We blazed into a 4-0 half-time lead playing what was described as "milk and honey" football but Derry drew level to 4-4 after the break with some brilliant football of their own.

Harry McNeely became club chairman when John Sholdis resigned due to business commitments with Jack Dornan assuming the role of vice-chairman and treasurer. The out of favour Walter Bruce resumed training with the 2nd XI as the firsts carried on their winning ways during October. We recorded five wins in the League and Gold Cup although it needed last minute goals to defeat Glenavon (John Colrain 25 yard shot) and Distillery (Eric Ross angled drive) for the third time in four weeks. We reached the Gold Cup semi-final after a thrilling last eighteen minutes against Ballymena when we came from 2-3 down to win 7-3! Remarkably we had been 2-0 ahead earlier in the second half.

More foreign visitors frequented the Oval when a Sofia Select XI (in reality the Bulgarian Olympic team preparing for Mexico '68) played their part in an exhilarating friendly. Debut boy Jim Smart scored our goal in a 1-2 defeat. That word, however, was not in our domestic vocabulary although we had to come from behind twice to force a draw with Ards before paying a visit to Windsor Park.

Linfield and ourselves shared league leadership with 16 points each from nine games and it turned out to be a bruising encounter before 20,000. Ross had his nose broken in the first half and Weatherup finished with bruised ribs. "Bimbo" had earlier given us the lead but the Blues equalised with six minutes remaining after constant pressure.

Our unbeaten 25 match domestic run ended in the Brandywell mud when a 38th minute penalty from Wood was enough to give Derry City a 1-0 win. The league table, with ten matches to go, that night read: 1. Linfield 20 points, 2=. Glentoran, Derry City 18.

The team bounced back from this reverse to record five successive league wins, scoring 20 goals in the process. Meantime the Seconds retained the Steel and Sons Cup. Terry Conroy was in a rich vein of form earning many "man of the match" awards from his free role behind the forward line. Tommy Morrow forced his way into the side after scoring six goals for the Seconds in an 11-1 defeat of Killyleagh YC.

303

Coleraine gave us a jolt in January as they gained revenge for their Gold Cup semi-final defeat but we still led Linfield by a point as they had only managed to draw 4-4 with Crusaders the same day. The Hatchetmen the provided our opposition in the Gold Cup final the following Wednesday night at a sodden Windsor Park. It was a game of action, the excitement never dropping, and we picked up our second trophy of the season with a 5-2 win. Colrain was outstanding in his roaming role.

We endured a couple of frights as the championship race reached a climax. Arthur Stewart missed two penalties against Bangor and it needed two goals in the final thirteen minutes to gain a win. Then Glenavon's Peter Watson scored a last minute equaliser at the Oval allowing Linfield to draw level with us with only two games left. A deciding test match was on the cards when we drew 2-2 with a Blues a week later. Glentoran were sickened by a Sammy Pavis goal five minutes into injury time after we had been the more accomplished side throughout.

So on decision day we travelled to Shamrock Park to face Portadown. Things began badly as the Ports scored twice in the first eleven minutes but we staged a majestic comeback to go 4-2 up by half-time. A fifth was added after the interval and when news filtered through that Linfield had been booed off after a 2-2 home draw with Bangor the Gibson Cup was ours. The players from Finlay through to Weatherup were hailed as heroes.

However there was no time for prolonged celebration as the Irish Cup began seven days later. The Glens were opposed to Derry City, whom we had never beaten in the Cup. The first game ended all square (1-1) at a rain drenched Oval, an 82nd minute penalty from Wood earning Derry a replay. The continuing rain caused the postponement of the replay and when it eventually took place in early March the sticky surface rendered good football impossible. It required a third game and a piece of magic to separate the teams. In the 23rd minute, and from all of 25 yards, John Colrain lobbed the only goal but much credit must also be given to Roy Borne, who had been recalled from the Seconds to mark Derry's dangerman Roy Seddon. Tommy Jackson and 19 year old Johnny Johnston, who had only made his debut two days earlier, also battled hard. Johnston came into the side as a replacement for Conroy who had been transferred to Stoke City for £15,000.

This season had seen a change in the regular club playing strip with white becoming the major colour. Many variations of red, green and black stripes were to appear over the next sixteen years before green became predominant once more. The Gazette too changed from a green cover to a white one for the City Cup onwards. This was a competition in which the Glens began with style and confidence and grew stronger! Nine straight wins brought this trophy to the Oval and only a last game defeat by Linfield (courtesy of that man Pavis again!) spoilt our 100% record. This was one of only four goals conceded in the eleven games.

Back to the Irish Cup and Walter Bruce was the architect of victory against Distillery in Round Two. His hat-trick and all-round form earned him a recall to the Northern Ireland international team. Bruce was again on target in the semi-final with Linfield, played on a mudbath at Solitude. The Glens even had to change jerseys at half-time, reverting back to the traditional green. That one goal was enough to see us through.

Crusaders had qualified for their first ever Irish Cup final by beating Bangor 3-2 in the other semi-final and proved it was their year for the cup by overcoming us 3-1 in the final. We faced an uphill battle from the moment Danny Trainor put them ahead in the fourth minute.

Before jetting out to the U.S.A. there was still the

Programme Cover 1966/7 .

Top Four and the County Antrim Shield to contest but both these tournaments were to end acrimoniously. We met Linfield (who had eliminated our Seconds by 3-2 in Round One after twice coming from behind) in the Shield semi-final at Solitude and were due to meet them there again in the Top Four. However unsavoury events at the Shield semi-final caused us to refuse to play the Top Four game at Solitude. We claimed that there was inadequate protection for goalkeeper Albert Finlay who had been stoned during the Shield game. The Irish League were unimpressed however and kicked us out of the Top Four competition. Two second half goals from Sammy Pavis had enabled the Blues to triumph in the Shield, after Bruce had given us the lead on 22 minutes.

The domestic season concluded with Eamon Byrne's benefit against Eire league champions Dundalk. We won a low key affair 2-1.

Richie Warburton.

THE DETROIT COUGARS 1967

The U.S.A. and Canada were the two big untapped areas in the western world for association football. Over the years there have been many attempts to introduce soccer to the Americans and the tournament arranged for the summer of 1967 was one such venture. Planning had commenced towards the end of 1966 and the organisers decided to invite two Irish teams to compete due to the large "Irish" population in the states. Initially it was to be Shamrock Rovers and Linfield but the Blues pulled out due to the possibility of having to play on Sundays. Glentoran were asked to step into the breech and immediately agreed, although the I.F.A. required all players to re-register on their return. Glentoran were allocated to the city of Detroit, adopting the name of Detroit Cougars and would play in all black shirts with a change strip of all white.

The Cougars story has been adequately documented in other Glentoran publications but a summary of the tournament and our performances in it is well worth repeating here. Glentoran left Belfast on 23rd May 1967 with the following "roster" of players:

No.	Name	Height	Weight	Age	No.	Name	Height	Weight	Age
1	John Kennedy	5'11"	11st 4	27	15	Billy Sinclair	5'7"	10st 10	20
1	Sam Kydd	5'11"	12st 7	26	20	Trevor Thompson	6'	12st	31
2	Harry Creighton	5'11"	11st 6	27	21	Jim Weatherup	5'6"	10st 7	21
3	Billy McKeag	5'8"	10st 5	21	22	John Colrain	6'	12st 12	30
4	Roy Borne	5'8"	10st 11	26	23	Alan McNeill	6'	11st 1	21
10	Tommy Jackson	5'8"	11st	20	24	Eric Ross	5'11"	10st	22
11	Billy McCullough	5'10"	12st	27	25	Danny Trainor	5'11"	11st	28
12	Walter Bruce	5'9"	11st 7	29	30	Johnny Johnston	5'8"	11st 6	19
14	Arthur Stewart	5'9"	11st	25	32	Tommy Morrow	5'10"	11st 11	20

Note the numbering system, 1 for goalkeepers, under 10 for defenders, 10-19 for half-backs, 20-29 for attackers and 30+ for "fringe" players. There were four guests in the roster namely Kennedy (Glasgow Celtic), Kydd (Ards) and Trainor and McNeill (both Crusaders).

The official Glentoran party was completed by: President: Vere Law, Chairman: Harry McNeely, Vice-Chairman: Jack Dornan, Secretary: Billy Ferguson, Directors: Billy Pollock, Paddy Hunt, Andrew Patterson, Jim Morgan, John Ewart, Life Member: Ernie Stewart, Vice-Presidents: Billy Clark, Johnston Nelson, Trainer: Bobby McGregor, Journalist: Malcolm Brodie.

The tournament was organised on a two groups of six basis, one known as the Eastern Division and the other as the Western. The top two from each group would play-off in the semi-finals and final. Each team would play all other teams once plus an extra match

Results 1966/67

Played 58. Won 42. Drew 10. Lost 6. Goals For 158. Against 67. % 81.0.
Honours: Irish League, Ulster Cup, Gold Cup, City Cup

UC	06/08/66		Crusaders	H	W	4	2	Sinclair, Ross, Conroy (p), Colrain
UC	11/08/66		Derry City	A	W	3	1	Colrain, Conroy, Thompson
UC	13/08/66		Linfield	H	W	2	1	Colrain, Thompson
UC	17/08/66		Glenavon	A	W	2	1	Sinclair 2
UC	20/08/66		Bangor	H	W	4	0	Conroy, Ross, Colrain, Thompson
UC	24/08/66		Ballymena United	A	W	2	1	Dobbin og, Ross
UC	27/08/66		Coleraine	H	W	1	0	Thompson
UC	03/09/66		Portadown	H	W	3	0	Conroy, Thompson, Colrain
UC	08/09/66		Ards	A	D	1	1	Ross
UC	10/09/66		Cliftonville	H	W	3	1	Conroy 2, Ross
UC	13/09/66		Distillery	A	W	6	0	Colrain, Ross, Creighton, Warburton, Thompson 2
IL	17/09/66		Distillery	H	W	2	0	Bruce, Thompson
IL	24/09/66		Ballymena United	A	W	3	2	Ross, Thompson, Colrain
IL	01/10/66		Derry City	H	D	4	4	Conroy 2, Thompson 2
IL	08/10/66		Bangor	H	W	6	0	Thompson 3, Colrain, Conroy 2 (1p)
IL	15/10/66		Glenavon	A	W	2	1	Sinclair, Colrain
IL	29/10/66		Coleraine	A	W	2	1	Thompson, Conroy
IL	05/11/66		Cliftonville	H	W	5	0	Conroy, Stewart, Thompson, Bruce, Smart
IL	12/11/66		Ards	H	D	2	2	Ross, Thompson
IL	19/11/66		Crusaders	A	W	3	1	Weatherup 2, Thompson
IL	26/11/66		Linfield	A	D	1	1	Weatherup
IL	03/12/66		Portadown	H	D	2	2	Lunn, Conroy (p)
IL	10/12/66		Derry City	A	L	0	1	-
IL	17/12/66		Ballymena United	H	W	5	2	Thompson 2, Morrow, Bruce 2
IL	24/12/66		Distillery	A	W	4	2	Conroy 3 (1p), Bruce
IL	27/12/66		Crusaders	H	W	3	2	Sinclair, Conroy, Thompson
IL	31/12/66		Ards	A	W	3	1	Thompson, Morrow, Ross
IL	07/01/67		Cliftonville	A	W	5	2	Stewart, Morrow, Conroy 2, Ross
IL	14/01/67		Coleraine	H	L	2	3	Ross, Stewart (p)
IL	21/01/67		Bangor	A	W	4	2	Thompson 3, Conroy
IL	28/01/67		Glenavon	H	D	2	2	Ross, Lowry og
IL	04/02/67		Linfield	H	D	2	2	Sinclair, Ross
IL	11/02/67		Portadown	A	W	5	2	Thompson, Weatherup 2, Creighton, Conroy
ECW	27/09/66	1.1	Glasgow Rangers	H	D	1	1	Sinclair
ECW	05/10/66	1.2	Glasgow Rangers	A	L	0	4	-
GC	11/10/66	1	Distillery	H	W	3	2	Colrain, Thompson, Ross
GC	21/10/66	2	Ballymena United	H	W	7	3	Weatherup 2, Thompson 2, Conroy 2, Jackson
GC	23/11/66	SF	Coleraine	WP	W	4	0	McKeag, Thompson, Conroy (p), Sinclair
GC	18/01/67	F	Crusaders	WP	W	5	2	Thompson 2, Bruce, Colrain, Stewart (p)
IC	18/02/67	1	Derry City	H	D	1	1	Thompson
IC	02/03/67	1R	Derry City	A	D	0	0	-
IC	06/03/67	1R2	Derry City	BS	W	1	0	Colrain

IC	11/03/67	2	Distillery	H	W	3	1	Bruce 3
IC	01/04/67	SF	Linfield	Solt	W	1	0	Bruce
IC	22/04/67	F	Crusaders	WP	L	1	3	Thompson
CC	25/02/67		Cliftonville	A	W	2	0	Conroy, Thompson
CC	04/03/67		Ards	H	W	5	0	Weatherup, Colrain 2, Johnston, W.Stewart og
CC	18/03/67		Portadown	A	W	2	0	Weatherup, Bruce
CC	25/03/67		Distillery	H	W	4	0	Thompson, Stewart, Johnston, Weatherup
CC	27/03/67		Coleraine	A	W	4	1	Thompson, Weatherup, Johnston, McKeag
CC	08/04/67		Ballymena United	H	W	1	0	Morrow
CC	11/04/67		Bangor	A	W	1	0	Morrow
CC	15/04/67		Glenavon	H	W	3	1	Morrow 2, Thompson
CC	27/04/67		Derry City	H	W	3	0	Morrow 2, McCullough
CC	29/04/67		Crusaders	A	W	2	1	Ross, McCullough
CC	02/05/67		Linfield	A	L	0	1	-
CAS	24/04/67	2	Ards	A	W	2	1	Stewart, Thompson
CAS	06/05/67	SF	Linfield	Solt	L	1	2	Bruce
F	03/08/66		Southport	H	W	2	0	Warburton, Thompson
F	08/08/66		Everton	H	L	0	3	-
F	29/08/66		Linfield	Sv	W	6	3	Weatherup 3, Thompson, Colrain, Craig
F	03/11/66		Sofia Select XI	H	L	1	2	Smart
F	13/04/67		British Police	H	D	2	2	Thompson 2
F	10/05/67		Dundalk	H	W	2	1	Johnston 2 Eamon Byrne Benefit

against one other team to make up 12 fixtures! Detroit Cougars were part of the Eastern Division and the other competing teams were:

Eastern Division	Western Division
Shamrock Rovers representing Boston	Sunderland representing Vancouver
Aberdeen representing Washington DC	Bangu (Brazil) representing Houston
Cerro (Uruguay) representing New York	Wolves representing Los Angeles
Stoke City representing Cleveland	ADO Hague representing San Francisco
Hibernian representing Toronto	Dundee United representing Dallas
	Cagliari (Italy) representing Chicago

Glentoran's match playing record during the tour read:

	Date	Opponents			Result	Scorers	Attendance
1	28 May	Shamrock Rovers	A	D	1-1	Colrain	7,000
2	4 June	Sunderland	H	D	1-1	Trainor	11,629
3	7 June	Shamrock Rovers	H	W	1-0	Stewart (p)	648
4	11 June	Aberdeen	H	D	2-2	Thompson 2	5,134
5	14 June	Bangu	H	L	0-2*	-	7,196
6	18 June	Wolves	A	L	1-4	Thompson	5,381
7	21 June	ADO Hague	A	L	1-6	Trainor	4,729
8	25 June	Dundee United	H	W	1-0	Morrow	5,000
9	28 June	Cagliari	A	D	1-1	Stewart (p)	2,013
10	2 July	Cerro, Montevideo	A	W	1-0	Weatherup	3,517
11	5 July	Stoke City	A	D	0-0	-	4,729
12	9 July	Hibernian	A	D	1-1	Weatherup	3,000

* Abandoned after 73 minutes due to riot – result stood.

Only one game was played on a Sunday, the last against Hibs. Home matches were played in the University Stadium in Detroit.

Players' Statistics

	Apps	Sub	Goals		Apps	Sub	Goals
McCullough	12	-	-	Trainor	7	-	2
Stewart	12	-	2	Morrow	6	2	1
Creighton	12	-	-	Ross	5	-	-
Jackson	12	-	-	Thompson	5	-	3
Kennedy	11	1	-	Johnston	4	2	-
Bruce	10	1	-	Colrain	3	-	1
McKeag	10	-	-	McNeill	2	1	-
Sinclair	9	1	-	Borne	2	-	-
Weatherup	9	-	2	Kydd	1	-	-

The final group tables read:

Eastern	P	W-D-L	Pts	Western	P	W-D-L	Pts
Aberdeen	12	4-6-2	14	Wolves	12	5-6-1	16
Stoke City	12	5-4-3	14	Cagliari	12	3-7-2	13
Hibernian	12	4-5-3	13	ADO Hague	12	5-3-4	13
Glentoran	12	3-6-3	12	Bangu	12	4-4-4	12
Cerro	12	2-6-4	10	Sunderland	12	3-5-4	11
Shamrock Rvs	12	2-3-7	7	Dundee Utd	12	3-3-6	9

Although only finishing two points behind the leaders we were actually the tournaments' lowest goalscorers, averaging less than one per game. Aberdeen and Wolves battled their way through to the final where the English team emerged 6-5 victors after extra time (90 minute score 5-5). A crowd of 17,824 attended the Los Angeles final and the 75 games throughout the tournament drew an average attendance of 7,728. John Kennedy made 105 saves in his 12 appearances, the only goalkeeper to break the 100 mark.

Considering Glentoran were a part-time outfit the achievements on this tour were nothing shot of magnificent. From all accounts the party was one big happy family of characters and we left an extremely favourable impression on the Detroit public. There were many incidents of note during the tour:

- the suspension of John Colrain for allegedly striking a linesman when a goal was disallowed in the first Shamrock Rovers game. Colrain pleaded innocence and later dropped himself from the team believing he had become a marked man. At least he got to meet his hero, Frank Sinatra, on the trip, in a New York bar.
- the flying of the Irish tricolour at the Wolves and Cerro games. Jack Dornan ensured the error was quickly corrected and the offending item was replaced with a union flag in the former.
- the quelling of stars such as Jim Baxter (Sunderland), Roberto Boninsegna (Cagliari), leading scorer with 10 goals, and ex-Glenman Terry Conroy (Stoke).
- the riot against Bangu involving over 200 people. The Brazilian players went berserk using corner flags as spears! The riot made the national U.S. television news programmes.
- the stifling humidity in Detroit and the demanding six week itinerary.
- the return to form, after a humiliating defeat by Dutch amateurs ADO Hague, with a win over Dundee United - the only team to defeat Celtic during the 1966/7 Scottish season.
- the marvellous ten minute kaleidoscope of fireworks after the Cagliari game.
- celebrations in the Red Hand of Ulster pub after victory over Cerro.
- the 38 shots against Gordon Banks and Paul Shardlow in Stoke's goal , to 18 by Stoke
- being robbed of finishing the tour in Canada on a winning note when McCullough's back deflected in Jim Scott's effort for Hibernian in the 89th minute.

Throughout the tournament Glentoran fell victim to many strange refereeing decisions. Indeed John Colrain claimed that these had made us miss out on qualifying for the semi-finals.

The morale of the party was lifted on 4th July when news filtered through that we had been drawn against the illustrious Portuguese champions Benfica in the European Cup.

Eight days later the party returned home to Belfast for a heroes welcome and a civic reception. The players were told to forget about football until the new season, only four weeks away.

A supporters' club was formed to mark the tour. The first chairman of the Cougars Glentoran Supporters' Club was Davy McKeown, one of the most popular people ever to follow the Glens.

Appearances and Goals

	App.	Subs.	Goals		App.	Subs.	Goals
Finlay	57			Morrow	14	2	9
Creighton	55		2	Borne	10	1	
Ross	55		15	Warburton	7		1
Stewart A.	54		6	Wright	3		
Thompson	53		40	Johnston J.	3		2
McKeag	51		2	Lunn	2		1
Bruce	45		12	Smart	2		1
McCullough	45	1	2	Craig	1		
Sinclair	43		8	Peden	1		
Weatherup	38		12	Own goals			3
Conroy T.	37		25				
Colrain	36	3	14	TOTAL	638	7	158
Jackson	26		3				

Billy Sinclair (Number 15) in action for the Detroit Cougars against Sunderland.

1967/68

Colrain's success continues – Benfica held – League retained

The events of the previous twelve months were certainly a hard act to follow for the Glentoran squad when the Ulster Cup kicked off in early August 1967. Eric Ross had been transferred to Newcastle United for £4,750 and was replaced by Willie Hunter from the newly formed Detroit Cougars. Hunter had gained three full Scottish international caps while with Motherwell in the early 1960s.

The season began up at Coleraine and after 76 minutes we found ourselves trailing to a Des Dickson goal. Then in a spell of sheer brilliance we quickly scored three goals to ensure a winning start. Despite remaining unbeaten for the next three weeks all our early games were hard fought affairs. Tommy Morrow was establishing himself as the natural successor to Trevor Thompson.

At the end of August we stood joint second in the Ulster Cup with Linfield, just a point behind leaders Glenavon. Then three results in a week enabled the Blues to take the trophy. Firstly a Bryan Hamilton goal seven minutes from time settled a thrilling derby clash at Windsor Park, then three days later we beat Glenavon at the Oval. John Colrain scored the decisive goal in his comeback match after injury. Finally on the following Saturday a rampant Bangor side hammered us at Clandeboye and in so doing condemned us to joint second in the table along with the Lurgan Glens.

Mick Conroy challenges Linfield goalkeeper Bertie McGonigal in the City Cup tie at the Oval.

Just prior to that Ards ended our Gold Cup hopes and our 14 match unbeaten home run. Hardly ideal preparation for our big European Cup tie with Portugal's finest – Benfica. However the players lifted themselves to produce arguably the greatest two scorelines in our history. In the first leg at the Oval, before close on 40,000 spectators, Colrain fired us ahead with a ninth minute penalty after Morrow had been brought down. The Glens' players, on £6 a week, fought hard and skillfully against European superstars to retain that lead. Tommy Jackson marked Eusebio tightly receiving great support from fellow half-backs McCullough and Sinclair. Then on the hour Benfica were awarded a penalty after a collision between McCullough and Eusebio. Up stepped Graca to shoot but Albert Finlay produced a magnificent save to keep us ahead. Time marched on, there were further efforts from Torres and Coluna but still the Glens held on. Then, with only five minutes left, Eusebio lived up to his "Black Panther" nickname as he pounced to snatch an equaliser. It was disappointing not to win but we could hold our heads high for the second leg in Lisbon.

The Glens were based at Estoril and trained on the famous beach there before venturing into the famous "Stadium of Light" were many of the 50,000 crowd fully expected them to be the proverbial lambs to the slaughter. But far from it as another glorious display prevented Benfica from scoring. It took the away goals rule to eliminate Glentoran. Again Jackson shackled Eusebio and Finlay stopped all of the shots on his goal. It was an exit covered in glory and probably the peak of Colrain's managerial reign. As for Benfica they went on to reach the final defeating St. Etienne, Vasas Budapest and Juventus before losing 1-4 at Wembley to a George Best inspired Manchester United – maybe some measure of revenge for East Belfast!

After the European glamour the Glens got down to the business of defending the Irish League championship. It began with a home draw with Linfield, another late goal from Hamilton thwarting us, in a game marred by hooliganism as the rival supporters changed ends at half-time. Celebration and over exuberance when your team scored was one thing but an unwelcome violent element had crept in.

As autumn turned to winter the team put together a string of victories with many stylish performances. The goals came thick and fast, even full-back Harry Creighton got onto the scoresheet against Cliftonville following a run which took him two thirds of the length of the pitch!

Ironically we became victims of our own success as many players were transferred cross-channel to full-time football. Billy Sinclair went to Kilmarnock for £8,000 and Arthur Stewart, our best performer of the season so far, joined Derby County for £10,000 making an immediate first team debut against Middlesbrough. Both would return to the Oval in different capacities later in their careers. Replacements were found – Roy Welsh came from Distillery for £2,000 only a month after being sent off against us in the league. Nigel McGucken and Eamon Gorman arrived from Portadown and Cliftonville respectively and a young Tommy Cassidy began to figure in the seconds line up.

International honours came the way of many of our players. Billy McKeag was at right-back when Northern Ireland beat Scotland 1-0 at Windsor Park in "Best's Match". Arthur Stewart played right-half in both this match and against England at Wembley a month later. Jackson and Johnny Johnston were picked for Amateur Ireland.

Notable victories were recorded over Newcastle United and Dundalk, the latter a fixture dubbed the Unofficial All-Ireland championship for the Harp Lager Trophy. This great run of form culminated in a 10-1 thrashing of hapless Bangor at the Oval in early December. Amazingly the first goal did not arrive until the 27th minute but then the floodgates opened. Despite conceding ten, Billy Irwin in the visitors' goal put in a courageous display. The team confirmed it would still function smoothly despite the loss of star players when Glenavon were comfortably beaten in the Ulster Cup runners-up play-off match.

A fall of snow caused the postponement of our big game at Coleraine on 9th December, giving us an extra week to prepare for the vital clash with Linfield at Windsor Park. It was to be a day of frustration for the Glens as our ex-keeper Bertie McGonigal was in top form and our ex-forward Sammy Pavis netted a hat-trick for the Blues before 16,000 fans. So, at the half-way stage the league table read as

John Colrain scores from the spot against Benfica.

follows: 1. Glentoran 19 points, 2. Coleraine 18, 3=. Ards, Linfield 16.

Derry City were easily beaten at the Oval the following Friday night and we completed a happy Christmas with wins over Crusaders and Distillery. After the decisive fourth goal against the Whites we tore their defence to shreds at will. Jackie Hutton's 18 yard volley

Finlay saves Benfica's Graca's penalty.

had been the best moment of the match. Coleraine's surprise home defeat to Bangor meant we began 1968 with a three point lead over the Blues with seven games remaining.

We strolled to victory in our first three games of the year, netting 15 times in the process. Walter Bruce played his last game against Portadown before jetting out to America to play for Detroit Cougars in the new USA league. Alan Bell arrived from Crusaders to take his place and the panel was further strengthened by the signing of Distillery full-back John Hill.

Linfield proved their championship challenge was still serious by hammering Bangor 11-1 after they drew 5-5 with Coleraine at the Showgrounds.

Against Ballymena we had to come from behind to draw and this allowed the Blues to close the gap back to three points with three games left. However we found no problems against Bangor a week later and went into our last home game with Coleraine knowing a win would give us the Gibson Cup. The Bannsiders had other ideas and within 26 minutes they had gone 2-0 up. We could not really get going but Jim Weatherup pulled one back and then with ten minutes to go we were awarded a dubious penalty. Tommy Jackson put it away and shortly afterwards the celebrations began when news came through that Linfield had only drawn at home to Glenavon. So we had retained the league title and even defeat at Coleraine for the first time in five years in our last fixture could not dampen the achievement. Jackson, scorer of that vital penalty, looked forward to a career in English football, as he was transferred to Everton for £15,000.

The season was far from over, however, as there was still a further four trophies to play for. Our Irish Cup hopes were dashed by Derry City as for the second successive season it took three meetings to decide the outcome of the tie. The first match at the Oval was a story of continual Glens' attacks until Derry broke away to score twice. Only 60 seconds remained when Bimbo Weatherup, down on his knees, headed the equaliser. Again we had to come from behind in the Brandywell replay, player-manager John Colrain, on as sub, saving the bacon in the 78th minute. A grim second replay at Ballymena was locked scoreless until five minutes from time when a Billy McCullough slip allowed Jim Doherty in to snatch the decisive goal.

We had begun sluggishly in defence of the City Cup losing at home to the Ports before

Programme Cover 1967/8.

seeing off Ards, who included a youthful Warren Feeney in their ranks. The heavy rain which caused the postponement of the Cliftonville fixture forced us into a ridiculous period of seven games in 20 days covering three tournaments. The most exciting of these was our 4-3 "revenge" win at Derry in the City Cup when Morrow scored the winner in the 87th minute. Linfield continued to be a hoodoo team when they beat us in the Top Four Competition and the City Cup, both at the Oval. Most of the action in the latter fixture came in a frenetic last two minutes. Trevor Thompson, back in the side for the first time in seven months, was pulled down for an obvious penalty that was not given. Then 30 seconds later the Blues were awarded a penalty but Finlay was equal to the task.

Although we were well out of contention for the City Cup our last two matches were thrillers. At Glenavon the home side raced into a 3-1 lead but we pulled back to 4-4, our fourth a penalty from Roy Borne. For Borne, in his benefit season and now captain of the Seconds, this was his only senior goal for the club in 175 appearances. Glenavon spoiled the occasion with a last minute winner. Our final game against Crusaders was full of fine football, near misses and good goals. Mick Conroy's 81st minute winner sent the City Cup to Windsor Park, disappointing all Cruemen including their star player Johnny Jamison.

April's fixture congestion had forced us to turn down opportunities to play in Majorca and a friendly against Cleveland, but in May there was still the County Antrim Shield to play for. Again heavy rain cancelled our semi-final with Bangor but it did relent to enable the match to be played four days later. The Glens were strengthened by Tony Macken, a recent opponent in a friendly versus Home Farm. We had most of the play but had to rely on a 77th minute Weatherup goal to get through. Linfield beat Larne 3-0 to set up an excellent finale to the season.

The Blues had completed a 34 match unbeaten run before losing to Crusaders in the Irish Cup final and had not lost to us in the previous eight meetings. The final at Solitude was spoiled by the wind and this, coupled with poor defensive play, saw the game finish 3-3. The replay was a blood tingling battle and we beat Linfield at last with Trevor Thompson netting once

Billy McKeag tackles Eusebio.

more to complete his all-time record tally of 375 goals for the Glens in competitive games. Determination was the key as we gradually wore our rivals down. This win gave John Colrain his sixth trophy success in two seasons.

There was time for a Thompson swansong in an end of season friendly against the 1st Battalion King's Regiment at Ballykinlar. The regiment were bidding farewell to Northern Ireland and Big Trevor sent them packing with a hat-trick. These goals brought his grand total for the 1st team to exactly 400 including friendlies and benefit games. One other more obscure honour that came Trevor's way had come earlier in the season when he became Glentoran's first ever tactical substitute in a league game.

Despite all the trophies and playing success over the past two seasons the board and manager were frequently at loggerheads. Colrain was aggrieved that he would not receive a salary increase despite his achievements and with neither party inclined to give way the board sacked him in July 1968. This decision caused a split within the board itself and both Vere Law (President) and Paddy Hunt resigned. Johnston Nelson took over the President's role but no successor to the "Jock Stein of Irish football" was found during the close season Billy Neill was appointed caretaker manager until such a person could be identified.

Results 1967/68

Played 58. Won 34. Drew 13. Lost 11. Goals For 157. Against 72. % 69.8
Honours: Irish League, County Antrim Shield

UC	05/08/67		Coleraine	A	W	3	1	Morrow 2, Thompso
UC	09/08/67		Distillery	H	W	2	0	Johnston, Thompson
UC	12/08/67		Portadown	A	W	3	0	Hunter, Thompson, Weatherup
UC	16/08/67		Ards	H	D	1	1	Hunter
UC	19/08/67		Cliftonville	A	W	3	0	Hunter, Morrow 2
UC	23/08/67		Crusaders	A	D	0	0	-
UC	26/08/67		Derry City	H	W	2	1	Weatherup 2
UC	30/08/67		Linfield	A	L	2	3	Hutton, Weatherup
UC	02/09/67		Glenavon	H	W	2	0	Johnston, Colrain
UC	09/09/67		Bangor	A	L	1	4	Morrow
UC	16/09/67		Ballymena United	H	W	6	1	Weatherup 2, Bruce, Morrow 2, Thompson
UC	05/12/67	RUPO	Glenavon	H	W	3	1	Welsh, Morrow, Gorman
GC	04/09/67	1	Ards	H	L	0	1	-
EC	13/09/67	1.1	Benfica	H	D	1	1	Colrain (p)
EC	04/10/67	1.2	Benfica	A	D	0	0	-
IL	23/09/67		Linfield	H	D	2	2	Morrow 2
IL	30/09/67		Derry City	A	W	4	1	Morrow 2, Weatherup 2
IL	07/10/67		Crusaders	H	W	2	1	Jackson, Morrow
IL	14/10/67		Distillery	A	W	3	1	Morrow 2, McGucken
IL	28/10/67		Glenavon	H	W	4	2	Bruce, Weatherup, Morrow, Stewart (p)
IL	04/11/67		Cliftonville	H	W	5	0	Morrow, McGucken 2, Weatherup, Creighton
IL	11/11/67		Portadown	A	W	4	1	Morrow, McGucken 2, Bruce
IL	18/11/67		Ards	H	W	3	0	W.Stewart og, McGucken 2
IL	25/11/67		Ballymena United	A	W	5	2	Morrow, Bruce 2, McGucken 2
IL	02/12/67		Bangor	H	W	10	1	Morrow 3, McGucken 4, Hutton 2, Bruce
IL	16/12/67		Linfield	A	L	1	3	McGucken
IL	22/12/67		Derry City	H	W	4	2	Morrow 2, Creighton, Hutton
IL	25/12/67		Crusaders	A	W	2	0	McGucken 2
IL	26/12/67		Distillery	H	W	4	1	Hutton, Morrow, Bruce (p) Welsh
IL	30/12/67		Glenavon	A	W	2	0	McGucken 2
IL	06/01/68		Cliftonville	A	W	5	0	Morrow 3, Wright (p), Weatherup
IL	13/01/68		Portadown	H	W	4	1	Morrow 3, Weatherup
IL	20/01/68		Ards	A	W	6	1	Hutton, McGucken 3, Jackson, Morrow
IL	27/01/68		Ballymena United	H	D	2	2	McGucken, Weatherup
IL	03/02/68		Bangor	A	W	5	0	Morrow 2, McGucken 2, Weatherup
IL	10/02/68		Coleraine	H	D	2	2	Weatherup, Jackson (p)
IL	24/02/68		Coleraine	A	L	0	1	-
IC	17/02/68	1	Glenavon	H	W	3	1	Morrow 2, Welsh
IC	09/03/68	2	Derry City	H	D	2	2	Johnston, Weatherup
IC	14/03/68	2R	Derry City	A	D	2	2	Welsh, Colrain
IC	18/03/68	2R2	Derry City	BS	L	0	1	-
CC	02/03/68		Portadown	H	L	2	3	Johnston 2
CC	16/03/68		Ards	A	W	2	0	Gorman 2
CC	04/04/68		Cliftonville	H	W	4	0	Weatherup, Hill, Welsh 2
CC	06/04/68		Derry City	A	W	4	3	Gorman, Morrow 2, Johnston
CC	11/04/68		Bangor	H	D	3	3	Gorman 2, Welsh
CC	13/04/68		Ballymena United	A	D	1	1	Johnston

CC	15/04/68		Distillery	A	L	0	1	-
CC	16/04/68		Coleraine	H	W	2	1	Conroy, Hill (p)
CC	20/04/68		Linfield	H	L	0	1	-
CC	24/04/68		Glenavon	A	L	4	5	Thompson, Creighton, Morrow, Borne (p)
CC	29/04/68		Crusaders	H	W	3	2	Anderson og, Johnston (p), Conroy
CAS	29/03/68	2	Distillery	A	W	6	0	Gorman 3, Bell, Weatherup, Conlon og
CAS	08/05/68	SF	Bangor	GP	W	2	1	Weatherup 2
CAS	11/05/68	F	Linfield	Solt	D	3	3	Thompson 2, Gregg og
CAS	13/05/68	FR	Linfield	Solt	W	3	0	Weatherup, Thompson, Morrow
T4C	01/04/68	SF	Linfield	A	D	2	2	Morrow, Weatherup
T4C	09/04/68	SFR	Linfield	H	L	1	2	Johnston
F	20/10/67		Newcastle United	H	W	2	1	Weatherup, Jackson
F	28/11/67		Dundalk	A	W	2	1	McGucken 2 Harp Lager Trophy
F	22/04/68		Home Farm	H	W	4	1	Hutton, Welsh, Thompson, McGucken
F	17/05/68		Dundalk	N*	L	1	2	Unknown – Civic Week
F	20/05/68		1st Batt King's Reg.	A	W	3	0	Thompson 3

* played at Rathfriland

Appearances and Goals

	App.	Subs.	Goals		App.	Subs.	Goals
Creighton	58		3	Hunter	11		3
Weatherup	55	1	22	Borne	8		1
McCullough	53			Colrain	8	3	3
Finlay	51			Gorman E.	8	1	9
Morrow	51		41	Cassidy J.	7		
McKeag	46			Conroy M.	7		2
Jackson	35		3	Wright	6		1
Johnston J.	32	1	9	Lyons	3		
Welsh R.	32		7	Bamford	2		
Hutton	31	1	6	Stewart R.	2		
McGucken	23	1	24	Welsh A.	2		
Bell	22		1	McKay	1		
Hill	19		2	Lunn	1		
Bruce	19		7	Own Goals			4
Sinclair	17	1					
Stewart A.	14		1	TOTAL	638	12	157
Thompson	14	3	8				

Player-manager John Colrain.

1968/69

Short-lived Golden Vision – No trophies in nine attempts -
McParland appointed

With Billy Neill in temporary charge Glentoran began the season with a couple of friendlies. We gained a draw with Kilmarnock in front of 8,000 thanks to an 85th minute penalty from Johnny Johnston. Two Scottish trialists, F.Thornton and Ian Anderson, played for the Glens in a match marred by an incident in the second half when boots and fists flew freely. Three days later First Division Sheffield Wednesday gave us the runaround in winning 3-0, the highlight being a brilliant 25 yard shot from Johnny Fantham for their third goal. The same day Kilmarnock put our result into perspective when they beat Glenavon 7-2.

The Glentoran 3rd XI, known as the Olympic, were reformed under the guidance of Hugh "Bud" McFarland. Their first game was a friendly against a team from Toronto (lost 1-2) when a band played before the game and at the interval. The retired Trevor Thompson was looking after the 2nd XI, though he did put in an Ulster Cup appearance against the Blues.

Alex Young.

Early results under Neill were disappointing – a two goal lead against Derry was thrown away and then we lost at home to Bangor. After this game the Seasiders' forward Jim Heron was signed and four days later the directors finally announced the "big name" player-manager to replace John Colrain. It was Alex Young, known as the "Golden Vision" because of his blond hair and the foresight in his midfield play. The 28 year old Young could boast a successful playing career with Hearts and Everton, winning the league with Everton in 1963 and the FA Cup in 1966, in addition to his eight full Scottish caps. He was hailed as the most exciting newcomer to the Irish League since Jackie Milburn. Young's vision of improvement at the Oval included bringing in an extra training night and placing a greater emphasis on younger players. His signing cost the Glens £10,000.

The same number of people came to the Oval for Young's debut against Coleraine. He had a quiet game alongside the hardworking Roy Welsh as defeat in this game ended our interest in the Ulster Cup. But over the next week we recorded encouraging wins over Distillery and Portadown with Young getting on the scoresheet after twelve minutes in the latter. A tepid defeat at Ards however meant the best we could do was to finish fourth, seven points behind Coleraine. It is interesting to note the average attendance for the 66 Ulster Cup games was given at 2,779, an increase of 12% on the corresponding games played two season's previously when the average was 2,470.

Our efforts for a hat-trick of league titles began with an ordinary win at Solitude – indeed the team was slow-handclapped in the first half. Maybe too many minds were on the European Cup tie with Anderlecht in Brussels the following Wednesday. The Glens went into this games as 10/1 outsiders and were totally outclassed by the Belgians in the first half, finding ourselves two down within 22 minutes. We improved our work rate after the interval and only a sloppy third goal in the 87th minute spoilt our display. At least the trip was memorable for Glentoran supporter Billy Richie as it gave him an opportunity to stage a re-union in Arnhem with a Dutch family who had looked after him for a week after he had parachuted down during a war mission in 1944.

Before the return leg we managed two league wins including a devastating last 30 minutes against Glenavon when we rattled in six goals! Earlier Roy Welsh and the visitors' Jackie Hughes were sent off after a scuffle. This was the second such incident of the season , Harry Creighton and Coleraine's McCurdy having similarly been dismissed in the Ulster Cup. Welsh received a six week suspension.

Admission prices for the home match with Anderlecht ranged from 5/- to £1 – compare this with the all-in day return flight fare of £22 for the game in Brussels. The Glens added to their growing reputation with a 2-2 draw before 20,000 fans. After falling

Finlay and his defence can only watch as Coleraine take the lead from a deflected shot by Ken Halliday.

behind we held the lead in the second half for nearly a quarter of an hour but a goal from Bergholtz on 68 minutes finally killed off our hopes. Young had his best game for the Glens in this match.

Our October league form was abysmal as we captured only two points from four games. The only real bright spot was a 5-0 hammering of Coleraine in the Gold Cup when Johnny Johnston's dazzling display and hat-trick went a long way towards securing his eventual transfer to Blackpool in November for £15,500. Johnston would make over 225 league appearances for the Tangerines, Halifax Town (two spells), Bradford City and Southport before returning to the Irish League with Portadown in the early 1980s.

In early November the club announced that they and Alex Young would be parting company. Young felt he could not settle with his family in Belfast and found the alternative of commuting from Liverpool too much. Young resumed his Football League career with Stockport County as once more Billy Neill stepped in as caretaker manager.

Results improved but displays remained inconsistent. On 9th November we inflicted Linfield's first local defeat of the season (3-1), two goals from Weatherup setting up the win. However a week later we lost at home to Coleraine, putting in a lifeless performance. A scrappy win over Portadown lifted us to joint third in the league at the half-way stage, six points behind leaders Linfield. Two new players, Syd Patterson and Peter Watson, came to the Oval from Glenavon and this coincided with a good league run during December.

We clashed with the Blues in the Gold Cup semi-final at Windsor Park. Linfield had more of the play but failed to penetrate our defence in which McCullough, recent recipient of Inter League and Irish Amateur recognition, and Hill were outstanding. A fortnight later 20,000 attended the Oval replay when Bryan Hamilton inspired the Blues to a 2-1 win. Morrow and Heron worked hard up front to no avail as we failed to snatch an equaliser in a desperate last five minutes.

Just before Christmas the board announced the latest famous player-manager for the Glens, this time going for a Ulsterman in the form of Peter McParland. Newry born McParland, winner of 34 Irish international caps, also had an excellent playing career in England behind him mainly at Aston Villa but also briefly with Wolves, Plymouth and non-league Worcester City. He won an FA Cup winners medal in 1957 scoring the two goals which beat Man. Utd from the left wing. Some may remember him for his clash with United keeper Ray Wood in that match or maybe his five goals for Northern Ireland in the 1958 World Cup finals in Sweden.

Results 1968/69

Played 60. Won 31. Drew 10. Lost 19. Goals For 116. Against 75. % 60.0

UC	03/08/68		Derry City	A	L	2	3	Morrow 2
UC	05/08/68		Linfield	H	D	1	1	Creighton
UC	10/08/68		Glenavon	A	W	2	1	Weatherup, Morrow
UC	13/08/68		Bangor	H	L	0	1	-
UC	17/08/68		Ballymena United	A	W	2	0	Anderson 2
UC	22/08/68		Coleraine	H	L	1	2	J.Johnston (p)
UC	24/08/68		Distillery	A	W	4	0	A.Welsh, Heron 2, Bell
UC	28/08/68		Portadown	H	W	4	0	Young, Heron 2, Morrow
UC	31/08/68		Ards	A	L	2	3	Conroy, Heron
UC	05/09/68		Cliftonville	H	W	4	1	Young, Morrow, Heron, Weatherup
UC	07/09/68		Crusaders	H	W	4	1	R.Welsh, Heron 2, Weatherup
IL	14/09/68		Cliftonville	A	W	3	1	Hill, R.Welsh, Young
IL	21/09/68		Glenavon	H	W	7	1	Heron 2, J.Johnston 2(1p), Morrow 2, Hill
IL	28/09/68		Distillery	A	W	2	1	Barclay og, R.Welsh
IL	05/10/68		Bangor	H	L	1	2	R.Welsh
IL	12/10/68		Crusaders	A	D	1	1	McCullough
IL	19/10/68		Ards	H	D	1	1	Morrow
IL	26/10/68		Derry City	A	L	1	2	D.Johnston
IL	09/11/68		Linfield	A	W	3	1	Weatherup 2, Heron
IL	14/11/68		Ballymena United	H	W	2	1	Weatherup, Torrens og
IL	16/11/68		Coleraine	H	L	0	1	-
IL	23/11/68		Portadown	H	W	2	0	R.Welsh, Toland og
IL	30/11/68		Glenavon	A	W	2	1	Heron, Watson
IL	07/12/68		Distillery	H	W	1	0	Heron
IL	14/12/68		Cliftonville	H	W	4	0	Heron, Macken, Watson, Patterson
IL	21/12/68		Bangor	A	W	2	0	Heron, Stewart
IL	25/12/68		Crusaders	H	L	0	2	-
IL	26/12/68		Ards	A	W	2	1	McParland, Macken
IL	28/12/68		Derry City	H	D	1	1	McParland
IL	04/01/69		Ballymena United	A	D	2	2	Weatherup, Watson
IL	11/01/69		Linfield	H	W	2	1	McParland, Hutton
IL	18/01/69		Coleraine	A	L	1	2	Weatherup
IL	25/01/69		Portadown	A	W	2	0	Creighton, Stewart
EC	18/09/68	1.1	Anderlecht	A	L	0	3	-
EC	02/10/68	1.2	Anderlecht	H	D	2	2	Morrow, J.Johnston
GC	15/10/68	2	Coleraine	H	W	5	0	J.Johnston 3, Morrow, Heron
GC	06/11/68	SF	Derry City	WP	W	2	1	Heron 2
GC	20/11/68	F	Linfield	A	D	0	0	-
GC	14/12/68	FR	Linfield	H	L	1	2	Weatherup
CC	01/02/69		Ballymena United	H	W	3	1	McParland 2, Morrow
CC	22/02/69		Linfield	A	L	0	2	-
CC	01/03/69		Glenavon	H	L	1	3	Patterson
CC	15/03/69		Bangor	A	W	4	3	R.Welsh, Morrow, Bruce, Weatherup
CC	22/03/69		Derry City	H	W	7	3	McParland 3, Bruce 2, Weatherup 2
CC	05/04/69		Crusaders	A	L	1	2	Morrow
CC	07/04/69		Cliftonville	A	W	2	0	Hutton (p), Heron
CC	12/04/69		Ards	H	W	2	1	Patterson 2
CC	19/04/69		Coleraine	A	L	0	2	-
CC	24/04/69		Portadown	A	W	3	2	Weatherup 2, R.Welsh

CC	13/05/69		Distillery	H	W	3	0	Lavery, Cassidy, Henderson
T4C	18/03/69	SF	Linfield	A	L	0	1	-
IC	26/02/69	1	Linfield	A	D	2	2	Weatherup, Stewart
IC	03/03/69	1R	Linfield	H	W	2	0	Patterson, Morrow
IC	08/03/69	2	Derry City	H	W	3	2	Morrow, McParland 2
IC	29/03/69	SF	Distillery	WP	D	1	1	R.Welsh
IC	02/04/69	SFR	Distillery	WP	D	0	0	-
IC	10/04/69	SFR2	Distillery	WP	L	1	2	Morrow
BxC	29/04/69	1	Shamrock Rovers	H	L	0	2	-
CAS	02/05/69	2	Ards	H	W	3	1	Morrow 2, Heron
CAS	09/05/69	SF	Crusaders	Solt	L	0	2	-
F	29/07/68		Kilmarnock	H	D	2	2	Anderson, J.Johnston (p)
F	01/08/68		Sheffield Wednesday	H	L	0	3	-
F	28/01/69		Drogheda	H	W	7	1	Stewart 2, R.Welsh, Heron 3, Morrow

There was little festive cheer on Christmas day as Crusaders deservedly beat us as the Oval in the league and our Seconds went down 1-3 to Larne in the Steel and Sons Cup final. McParland marked his Boxing Day debut with a goal and was again on target against second placed Derry two days later. Our lingering league chances seemed to have gone when we threw away a 2-0 interval lead at Ballymena, including an own goal from Jackie Hutton, but a battling win over Linfield kept the race wide open. The manager himself opened up the scoring on seven minutes before Scott equalised on the half-hour. Twenty minutes into the second half Hutton fired home the winner and with Derry beating third placed Ards 3-0 the table that night read:

1. Linfield played 19 points 31, 2. Derry City 20-30, 3. Glentoran 20-28, 4. Ards 20-26.

A week later Linfield wrapped things up with an 8-1 hammering of Portadown while Derry lost 1-4 at Seaview. Ironically Derry then beat the Blues 2-1 in their last match. For us, a win at Shamrock Park ensured third place, Harry Creighton celebrating the start of his benefit year by scoring the first goal.

So from February onwards it was into the City Cup and the various knock-out tournaments. In fact there were a total of five different cups to play for inside three months, too many for most critics, fans and players alike! February 1969 was, weatherwise, one of the worst months. Three of our games were snowed off, versus Coleraine City Cup and Linfield Top Four and Irish Cup, and those games that were played saw groups of fans huddling together to keep warm.

We faced two trips to Windsor within the space of four days at the end of the month. The Blues had just been beaten by Cliftonville for the first time in twenty years but were in a less charitable mood against us in the City Cup. Warren Feeney scored the first of their goals in our 0-2 defeat. In the Irish Cup meeting the Glens, bolstered by the return of Walter Bruce from US soccer, went 2-0 up before the Windsor men fought back to draw. However we made no mistake in the replay, Syd Patterson netting one of the goals before being sent off along with Isaac Andrews in the 71st minute.

More inconsistent displays in the City Cup ended our interest in that competition. High points were a six-goal 39 minute spell against Derry City (McParland hat-trick) and two goals in the last five

Programme Cover 1968/9,

minutes to overcome Bangor. This was off-set when Crusaders scored in the 83rd and 89th minutes to beat us at Seaview. Ards' chairman Harry Cavan stated that low attendances at the City Cup games could force some clubs to drop out of the league. For example Portadown, having their worst ever season in senior circles, were a candidate for this as only 250 people attended when we beat them 3-2 in April at Shamrock Park.

We progressed to the Irish Cup semi-final following a "rip roaring all-action" tie with Derry City – the first time we had beaten the North West men at the Oval in the cup. Our hate-hate relationship with the Top Four competition ended in a 0-1 defeat by Linfield, meaning that we failed to register a single victory in the four year history of this contrived tournament. Distillery were our cup semi-final opponents and the tie meant three more trips to Windsor Park. The Whites had the best of the first two draws yet were amazingly made 7/2 outsiders for the third meeting. Goals from Peter Rafferty and Gerry McCaffrey made a nonsense of this – in return we could only manage a 63rd minute consolation goal from Tommy Morrow.

Qualification for the cup semi-final earned us a place in the All Ireland Blaxnit Cup. We were paired with Shamrock Rovers whose recent cup pedigree was reflected in the fact that they were about to lift the FAI Cup for the sixth year in a row. The Dublin side easily progressed with a slick 2-0 win, both goals coming from Mick Leach.

Tommy Morrow.

The last hope for some silverware was the County Antrim Shield. Ards beat our Seconds 5-0 in Round One but came unstuck against the Glens' 1st XI in the quarter-finals. However we then hit rock bottom against the Crues in the semis, despite dominating the midfield, and lost 0-2. Before the game we had been given the nod over Coleraine to be Ulster's Fairs Cup representatives in 1969/70. Many at the club felt slightly embarrassed at the decision.

So Peter McParland knew that he had his work cut out but at least he could have been satisfied with the displays of youngsters Tommy Cassidy, Jim Lemon, Jim Lavery and Scottish trialist Ian Henderson in the concluding games of a testing trophy-less transitional season.

Appearances and Goals

	App.	Subs.	Goals		App.	Subs.	Goals
Finlay	53			Conroy M.	6		1
Hill	51		2	Wright	4	1	
McCullough	51		1	Anderson	4		2
Stewart R.	48	1	3	Johnston D.	4		1
Weatherup	48	1	15	Cassidy J.	3		
McKeag	46			Welsh A.	3	1	1
Morrow	42	1	18	Cassidy T.	3	1	1
Creighton	33		2	Lavery	2		1
Welsh R.	27	7	8	Lilley	1		
Macken	26		2	Brown	1		
Hutton	26	2	2	Thompson	1		
Heron	26	1	20	Bamford	1		
Johnston J.	24		7	Henderson	1		1
Watson	19		3	Lemon	1		
McParland	17	1	10	Unknown	44		
Patterson	13	2	5	Own Goals			3
Bruce	13		3				
Young	12		3	TOTAL	660	19	116
Bell	6		1				

1969/70

Gibson Cup regained – A hammering for Bangor – Local "Match of the Day"

The format of the Irish League season was reorganised as a result of the end of season congestion in 1968/9 and also partly to cater for a "break" before the 1970 World Cup finals in Mexico. The season would conclude in early April with the Irish Cup final, with the final league games to be played by the end of March. The City Cup was brought forward to September / October and reverted to a "two groups of six" format.

Peter McParland, in his first full season in charge, welcomed back Billy Sinclair from Scotland to strengthen the squad and offloaded Jim Heron to Ballymena. We warmed up with pre-season friendlies against Stoke City, Partick Thistle and Lincoln City. Terry Conroy returned to the Oval in the Stoke game but it was a poor match. The Partick fixture was actually Harry Creighton's benefit game and Creighton, now with Bangor, guested for the Glens in the second half. Lincoln beat us 2-1 and had a certain Graham Taylor to thank as the future England manager hooked a shot off the line in the last minute. This match saw an unusual mix-up as two referees turned up to officiate. As a compromise Jack Adair blew the whistle in the first half with Billy Smith taking over for the second.

The start of the competitive season coincided with the commencement of "The Troubles" in Northern Ireland. British troops were drafted in as many areas in Belfast became "no-go zones". Each football match

Despite the attentions of John Hill and Roy Coyle Arsenal's Bobby Gould flicks on during our Fairs Cup tie at Highbury.

was vetted with respect to potential security problems with Derry City and Distillery suffering particularly as their grounds were in close proximity to flashpoint areas.

Against this unwanted background we began tamely against Crusaders at Seaview. The game finished 1-1, John McPolin scoring for both sides, but two of our more experienced players were on the receiving end from the press. "Bruce and Weatherup could be classed as stars of yesteryear", was one of the kinder comments. Tommy Morrow silenced his critics with a hat-trick against Derry but unfortunately our eagerly awaited clash with the Blues at Windsor the following Saturday was postponed due to the civil unrest.

On the bright side the club acquired new training facilities when we took over the Sirocco Works ground at Donovan Parade. This became known as Glen Park and hosted many 2nd XI and Olympic games.

After two impressive wins we visited the Coleraine Showgrounds for a top of the table clash on 27th August. It turned out to be a tremendous game, the feature of which was the battle between Glens' half-backs Roy Coyle and Billy McCullough and the ever-dangerous Des Dickson. The game stood at 1-1 until two late goals sealed the match in Coleraine's favour. We bounced back with a last gasp win over Ballymena despite Jim Platt's efforts in goal and then recorded convincing wins over the Whites and Portadown with Scottish trialist Ian Henderson playing a starring role. Walter Bruce had also returned to form as we looked forward to our Fairs Cup tie against Arsenal in September.

The first half of the first leg at Highbury was a disaster as we conceded three goals without reply against a much below strength Gunners team. George Graham (2) and Bobby Gould were the scorers. After the interval we demonstrated to the 24,000 present that we could fight and defend, and with John Hill playing particularly well no further goals were conceded.

Before playing Ards the following Saturday our new £20,000 dressing rooms were opened by visiting chairman Harold Black. We won 3-1 that day but with Coleraine registering a 3-2 success at Windsor Park the Bannsiders remained favourites to lift the

McCullough and Finlay in a snowy goalmouth scramble at Derry during our first game of the 1970s.

Ulster Cup. Linfield, however, won their four games in hand later in the year and, when the tournament came round for completion in January the leading positions were as follows (ten games played):

1. Coleraine 19 points, 2. Glentoran 17, 3. Linfield 16.

We needed to beat Linfield and then hope Coleraine would lose out to Distillery the following night. It failed to work out for us as we could only manage a scoreless draw with the Blues, thanks to Albert Finlay saving a Billy Millen penalty, and then Coleraine, with the pressure off, came from two down to beat the Whites 4-2.

The City Cup, however, was the competition where the team really began to click. We opened up with a hard earned point at Coleraine and then rammed in the goals against Distillery (Gold Cup) and a hapless Cliftonville. Seven came in the first 52 minutes, even full-back Billy McKeag

getting amongst the scorers. This set us up nicely for the return fixture with the Arsenal, over 13,000 coming to the Oval despite our slim chances of progressing. Spurred on by an early goal, a penalty by Henderson awarded for hand ball against Terry Neill, we gave the Gunners a roasting. Arsenal were rattled and matters were made worse for them when in the 67th minute Charlie George was sent off for swearing. We were unable to take advantage but all at the club were well satisfied with a 1-0 win, Arsenal's first ever defeat in European competition.

Confidence now flowed through the team and two further wins brought us to a showdown with Crusaders to determine the City Cup Group B winners. The Crues had home advantage but we took the lead through Morrow and held it until half-time. Crusaders equalised and, just when a play-off looked probable Bruce, who had a terrific battle with Johnny Jamison throughout, netted the winner in the 89th minute.

Bangor, surprise winners of Section A, were our final opponents. The final turned out to be one of the most one-sided in the history of Irish football and a particularly memorable one for two of our players. In our 7-1 win Syd Patterson scored four goals and young Tommy Cassidy a hat-trick in his first City Cup game.

The commencement of the league championship gave local players a chance to display their skills to a much wider audience than before. BBC Northern Ireland launched their own "Match of the Day" programme, broadcast immediately after the Football League version on Saturday nights. The programme was not only a hit in the province but also in western Scotland for those who could tune in.

After a poor opening league win over Derry the Glens stated their intentions with a superb 2-0 defeat of the Blues on their home soil. Linfield were completely outplayed and we should have had more than the two goals. Indeed goalscoring had become a bit of a problem and after draws with Ards and Derry (Gold Cup) we failed to score when beaten at Seaview. McParland recognised the deficiency and again made a bid for Distillery's centre-forward Gerry McCaffrey, but the Whites refused to sell.

Then the goals started to flow for Tommy Morrow, as he scored two in each of our next three games, including the decisive strikes in the Gold Cup replay at Derry, the fourth time we had beaten the men from the Maiden City inside three months.

Violence was connected with football again when Glentoran supporters leaving Grosvenor Park were stoned by a crowd of youths. Many arrests were made on the Grosvenor Road but hooliganism was by no means confined to the Irish League. Over in Manchester police made 30 Man. Utd. fans watch the derby match in their bare feet, having confiscated their boots on the grounds that they were offensive weapons!

After one third of the league games we stood in second place, just a point behind leaders Ards. Fans inevitably discussed the improvements since the previous season and a popular opinion was that Roy Coyle's ferocious tackling in defence was one of the main factors in this. Also, down the club, Glentoran Olympic showed their form with a 10-0 win over Hillock United in the first round of the Irish Youth Cup. First teamers of the future, Paul Kirk and Peter Dickinson, were responsible for five of the goals.

However hopes of a second trophy were dashed when we went down to Coleraine in the Gold Cup Final. Brian Jennings got the only goal on 55 minutes but it could have been worse as the Bannsiders had three other "goals" disallowed for offside.

Eventually McParland obtained the signature of McCaffrey and he made a scoring debut on Boxing Day at Ballymena. He did not come cheap and in fact became our most expensive signing, costing £3,000 plus players Peter Watson and Jim Lemon in exchange. McCaffrey netted both goals on his home debut versus Glenavon a day later and with Ards only drawing at Portadown we shared top spot in the last Irish League table of the 1960s (eleven games played, Derry City had a game in hand):

1=. Ards, Glentoran 18 points, 3= Derry, Portadown, Coleraine 13, 6. Linfield 12

Glentoran began the seventies in two inches of snow at Brandywell. It was a surprise that referee Ron Challis allowed the game to go ahead, indeed the Glentoran party had been informed that the game was off when they reached Ballymena and were considering turning around and going home. Thankfully they did not but the resultant game failed to produce a goal.

The following Saturday saw a vital visit from Linfield and calls from the Glentoran Gazette to abandon Amateur Internationals. The reason – two of our players, Coyle and Morrow, had been selected to play for Amateur Ireland versus Wales against their own wishes. Still we managed a draw from a typically uncompromising battle but fell a point behind Ards in the title race. This was rectified a week later when McCaffrey notched a dramatic 86th minute winner at Castlereagh Park. Gerry was "helped" to score by trainer Bobby McGregor as minutes earlier Bobby had fixed the striker's contact lenses back in place! We strengthened our position further, easily gaining revenge over the Crues for that earlier defeat while Ards went down 1-2 at Coleraine.

January 1970 ended on a poor note when 7/1 outsiders Ballymena United came to the Oval and dumped us out of the Irish Cup. Jimmy Martin did the damage with goals in the 61st and 80th minutes.

Joe Cassidy makes a flying save from Linfield's Billy Millen in the 1969 County Antrim Shield final.

The countdown to the title began with a win at Portadown but then defeat at Coleraine when McKeag put through his own goal. Ards failed to take full advantage though, their 0-0 draw with Distillery reducing our lead to two points with five games remaining. Then things turned our way and while we recorded comfortable wins over the Whites and the Reds, Ards only picked up one point

Results 1969/70

Played 48. Won 31. Drew 10. Lost 7. Goals For 115. Against 44. % 75.0.
Honours: Irish League, City Cup

UC	09/08/69		Crusaders	A	D	1	1	McPolin og
UC	14/08/69		Derry City	H	W	4	2	Morrow 3, Patterson
UC	20/08/69		Glenavon	H	W	3	1	Morrow, Lavery, Bruce
UC	23/08/69		Bangor	A	W	6	0	McCullough, McAllister og, Morrow 2, Macken, Patterson
UC	27/08/69		Coleraine	A	L	1	3	Patterson (p)
UC	30/08/69		Ballymena United	H	W	3	2	Lavery 2, Morrow
UC	02/09/69		Distillery	H	W	6	0	Morrow, Henderson 2, Lavery 2, Bruce
UC	06/09/69		Portadown	A	W	2	0	Weatherup, Henderson
UC	13/09/69		Ards	H	W	3	1	Weatherup, Henderson 2
UC	16/09/69		Cliftonville	A	W	3	0	Kirk 2, Weatherup
UC	20/01/70		Linfield	A	D	0	0	-
FC	09/09/69	1.1	Arsenal	A	L	0	3	-
FC	29/09/69	1.2	Arsenal	H	W	1	0	Henderson (p)
CC	20/09/69		Coleraine	A	D	0	0	-
CC	27/09/69		Cliftonville	H	W	8	2	Kearney og, Bruce 2, Henderson, Patterson, McKeag, Morrow, Weatherup
CC	04/10/69		Ballymena United	A	W	3	0	Henderson, Morrow 2
CC	11/10/69		Derry City	H	W	3	2	Weatherup, Henderson, Bruce
CC	18/10/69		Crusaders	A	W	2	1	Morrow, Bruce
CC	28/10/69	F	Bangor	WP	W	7	1	Patterson 4, Cassidy 3
GC	23/09/69	1	Distillery	A	W	5	1	Patterson 3, Macken 2
GC	05/11/69	2	Derry City	H	D	1	1	Morrow
GC	13/11/69	2R	Derry City	A	W	3	1	Patterson, Morrow 2
GC	03/12/69	SF	Crusaders	WP	W	4	1	Henderson 3, Macken
GC	09/12/69	F	Coleraine	WP	L	0	1	-
IL	25/10/69		Derry City	H	W	1	0	Patterson
IL	01/11/69		Linfield	A	W	2	0	Hutton, Patterson
IL	08/11/69		Ards	H	D	1	1	Henderson
IL	15/11/69		Crusaders	A	L	0	2	-
IL	22/11/69		Portadown	H	W	2	1	Morrow 2
IL	29/11/69		Coleraine	H	W	2	1	Morrow 2
IL	06/12/69		Distillery	A	W	5	0	Hutton 2, Weatherup 2, Macken
IL	13/12/69		Cliftonville	H	W	2	0	Morrow, Henderson
IL	20/12/69		Bangor	A	D	1	1	Hutton (p)
IL	26/12/69		Ballymena United	A	W	3	0	Sinclair, McCaffrey, Morrow
IL	27/12/69		Glenavon	H	W	2	0	McCaffrey 2
IL	03/01/70		Derry City	A	D	0	0	-
IL	10/01/70		Linfield	H	D	2	2	Hutton, McCullough
IL	17/01/70		Ards	A	W	3	2	McCullough, Weatherup, McCaffrey
IL	24/01/70		Crusaders	H	W	7	2	Hutton 3, Morrow 2, Weatherup, McCaffrey
IL	07/02/70		Portadown	A	W	3	1	McCaffrey 2, Hutton
IL	14/02/70		Coleraine	A	L	0	2	-
IL	28/02/70		Distillery	H	W	3	0	Morrow, McCaffrey (p), Weatherup
IL	07/03/70		Cliftonville	A	W	3	0	Macken 2, Weatherup
IL	21/03/70		Bangor	H	W	2	0	Morrow, Bruce
IL	28/03/70		Ballymena United	H	D	0	0	-
IL	31/03/70		Glenavon	A	D	2	2	Morrow, McCaffrey

IC	31/01/70	1	Ballymena United	H	L	0	2	-
CAS	14/03/70	1	Larne	A	L	0	1	-
F	28/07/69		Stoke City	H	L	0	2	-
F	30/07/69		Partick Thistle	H	W	3	2	Henderson 2, Bruce (p) Harry Creighton Benefit
F	01/08/69		Lincoln City	H	L	1	2	Coyle
F	06/04/70		Waterford	A	W	8	1	Cassidy 4, Bruce, McParland, McCullough, Hutton Jimmy McGeough Benefit
F	30/04/70		Linfield	A	W	2	0	McParland, Lavery Isaac Andrews / Sammy Hatton Benefit
F	05/05/70		Newry Town	A	W	2	0	Morrow, McParland
F	15/05/70		Dundalk XI	A	D	2	2	Morrow, Lavery Patsy McKeown Benefit

from their two games. Thus we stretched our lead to five points meaning a win over Bangor would give us our third title in four years.

Before that we ventured to Larne for a County Antrim Shield tie. The B Division side, offered at 6/1, caused a mild sensation by knocking us out 1-0, maintaining the pattern of doing so every five years, following similar results in 1960 and 1965! It would have been worse had Finlay not saved a penalty on the half hour.

Despite this setback the team bounced back to become champions a week later with a 2-0 win over Bangor. Two goals in the first twenty minutes did the trick and nobody really cared about the string of missed chances later. The celebrations began at the Oval at 4.45 p.m. as the players reaped the reward for some magnificent displays during the season. So by the end of March we had completed our competitive fixtures for the season and retained the following list of players for 1970/1: Finlay, Hill, McKeag, Patterson, Coyle, Macken, Bruce, Weatherup, Morrow, Hutton, McCaffrey, Sinclair, McParland, Cassidy.

April and May were given over to friendlies and the first of these was a benefit match against League of Ireland champions Waterford. The game proved all too easy for the Glens and we ran up an 8-1 scoreline, Tommy Cassidy getting four. Intriguingly the draw for the following season's European Cup paired the sides together, giving us cause for optimism.

The joint benefit for Linfield players Sammy Hatton and Isaac Andrews turned into a financial flop as only 1000 spectators, paying £140, turned up. The Glens rubbed further salt into the wounds with a 2-0 win and Phil Scott even missed a penalty for the Blues. Two more friendlies followed to complete another successful season.

Appearances and Goals

	App.	Subs.	Goals		App.	Subs.	Goals
Finlay	47			Stewart R.	16	1	
McKeag	47		1	McCaffrey	16		9
Weatherup	47		11	Patterson	15	3	14
McCullough	46		3	Sinclair	9		1
Hill	45			Cassidy T.	4		3
Coyle	43			Kirk	1		2
Morrow	39	1	26	Lemon		2	
Lavery	39		5	Unknown	11		
Macken	37		7	Own goals			3
Bruce	25		7				
Henderson	24	2	14	TOTAL	528	11	115
Hutton	17	2	9				

1970/71

A surprise European exit - League showdown lost – Leeds United defeated

Despite the continued Civil Unrest four cross-channel teams came to Belfast to play the Glens in pre-season warm-up matches. McParland used the games to experiment with some younger players and one, Jim Hall signed from Manchester United, had the privilege of scoring past Gordon Banks in the Stoke game. Ex-Glenman Terry Conroy replied for the visitors. Our only defeat in these fixtures came at the hands of Greenock Morton, their goal a penalty awarded against young defender Bill Brown. Against Reading Tommy Cassidy was our star man, constantly probing the visitors' defence as we recovered from two goals down to draw.

Peter McParland in his Aston Villa days.

One loss to the playing panel was Billy Sinclair. The Scot had picked up a knee injury against Cliftonville in 1969/70 and had undergone an operation. The Glens wanted to retain his registration but not pay any wages until he was fully fit again. The naturally aggrieved Sinclair obtained freedom from his contract and quickly joined cross-town rivals Linfield. Off the field of play there were changes too as Paddy Hunt and Vere Law returned as Patron and President respectively while Billy Ferguson was appointed full-time secretary. An amalgamation of Glentoran Supporters' Clubs was formed with John Chapman as its first secretary.

In early August League officials met with the Security Forces and decided that games containing a security risk would be played at neutral or "switched" venues rather than be postponed. By changing the City Cup back to a mini-league the season itself would be extended by a month.

For the first few weeks of the season we played like anything but reigning champions. We achieved only one win in the first six Ulster Cup games and that was in the Derry City fixture switched to the Oval. Linfield, under Billy Bingham, won in east Belfast despite having Sinclair sent off for a foul on Roy Coyle twenty minutes into the game. Substitute Jackie Hutton missed a 76th minute penalty, his shot saved by Humphries. Against Glenavon referee Hugh Wilson sent off Billy McKeag. Our full-back was so incensed by the decision that he had to be virtually dragged to the dressing room.

Five players were dropped for the visit of Coleraine in early September but even a resounding 4-1 win could not lift us above tenth in the table. There were many more calls for changes in personnel, with particular emphasis on the need to introduce more skilful players. Results went from bad to worse and McParland's shoulders noticeably drooped at the conclusion of a 4-1 hammering by Distillery, now playing at Windsor Park.

Unfortunately our European Cup tie with Waterford came in the middle of this rut and we suffered our first home defeat in this competition (1-3) against a side we had put eight past in a friendly just eight months previously. The board reacted by taking matters into their own hands and signing two players from Dublin, Mick Millington and Kevin Murray, over the manager's head. McParland was none too pleased and informed the board that the playing side was his responsibility.

Tommy Cassidy was at the peak of his form scoring four times as we concluded the Ulster Cup with two solid wins. Linfield won the trophy despite a 5-0 home defeat to Ballymena. The cruel reality of our situation was revealed when Cassidy was sold to First Division Newcastle United for £15,000. How could we improve by selling our best players? The Newcastle chairman believed he had picked up a real bargain and so it proved as Cassidy went on to play 250 plus games for the Geordies, scoring 28 goals, and making 24 full international appearances in the process before moving into management with Gateshead United and later Glentoran and Ards.

McParland played himself at inside-left in the return leg at Waterford but, despite a fighting display in front of a capacity crowd swelled by many Glenmen, we lost 0-1. Albert Finlay made his 400th appearance in goal in this game but our European reputation had been dinted especially as Linfield beat Man. City 2-1 (only to lose on away goals) and Coleraine knocked out Kilmarnock, wining 3-2 at Rugby Park courtesy of a Des Dickson hat-trick. Insult was added to injury when Waterford landed a plum draw against Glasgow Celtic in Round Two.

One bright spot at the club was the form of young Peter Dickinson. When the Olympic defeated Belmont Star 17-0 in the first round of the IFA Youth Cup, he helped himself to a personal tally of ten goals!

As the City and Gold Cups progressed and winter approached our form and results markedly improved. Jim Magill came into the team and, along with Tommy Morrow, found the net regularly. The City Cup game at the Oval with Derry City kicked off fifteen minutes late due to a combination of flooded roads and an Army checkpoint. The match more resembled water polo as the players splashed around in the mud but the win enabled us to stay joint top of the table with Bangor.

In early November we signed Crusaders inside-forward Johnny Jamison for £2,000. Jamison was initially earmarked as "Cassidy's replacement" but immediately made his own mark with a dazzling display against the Blues. An Eric Bowyer own goal gave us victory in this match and the favourites tag for the City Cup. However we blew it at home to Glenavon a week later, going down 0-3, and then could only draw at Bangor, a result which virtually ensured the Cup would end up at Clandyboye. A win at Coleraine in the last match ensured us of third place but not without a scare. After an hour we were 4-0 up but the home side pulled it back to 3-4 with the help of two penalties. Referee Lawther needed a police escort at the end!

Jim Magill was in great form in the Gold Cup, scoring in all four of our games leading up to the final. The most of these was a stunning header against Portadown in the semi-final past a flat-footed Bobby Carlisle.

Tommy Cassidy in his Newcastle United days.

The final with Linfield was twice postponed due to electricity power cuts and was moved forward to the spring of 1971. The biggest crowd of the season (approximately 15,000) saw Tony Macken put the Glens 1-0 up on ten minutes but the Blues fought back to win 2-1.

Albert Finlay was in great form in his benefit season (the event renamed from benefit year) and his committee arranged a match with a difference for him on a Monday night at the Oval. It was billed as a "Glens XI versus a Showbiz XI" game but was generally a slap-stick comedy due to the non-stop antics of the comedians. Many ex-players of the previous 30 years turned out and were part of a farcical game which saw at one stage 16 players on one side and then the referee "scalped" by a man dressed as a Red Indian. Various sources

Results 1970/71

Played 56. Won 34. Drew 8. Lost 14. Goals For 115. Against 60. % 67.9.
Honours: County Antrim Shield

UC	15/08/70		Crusaders	H	L	0	1	-
UC	20/08/70		Derry City	H	W	4	1	Weatherup 2, Morrow, McKeag
UC	22/08/70		Linfield	H	L	1	2	Morrow
UC	27/08/70		Bangor	H	L	0	1	-
UC	29/08/70		Glenavon	A	D	1	1	Hall
UC	02/09/70		Ballymena United	A	L	1	2	Morrow
UC	05/09/70		Coleraine	H	W	4	1	Stewart, Hall 2, Hutton
UC	10/09/70		Distillery	WPL		1	4	Kirk
UC	12/09/70		Portadown	H	D	1	1	Hall
UC	19/09/70		Cliftonville	H	W	4	1	Cassidy 3(1p), W.McCullough
UC	21/09/70		Ards	A	W	3	0	Cassidy, Morrow 2
EC	16/09/70	1.1	Waterford	H	L	1	3	Hall
EC	30/09/70	1.2	Waterford	A	L	0	1	-
CC	26/09/70		Distillery	H	W	2	0	Hall, Morrow
CC	03/10/70		Portadown	A	W	3	2	Murray, Coyle (p), Hall
CC	10/10/70		Ards	H	L	0	2	-
CC	17/10/70		Cliftonville	A	W	2	0	Morrow, Magill
CC	24/10/70		Crusaders	A	D	1	1	Morrow
CC	31/10/70		Derry City	H	W	3	1	Morrow, Magill, McCaffrey (p)
CC	07/11/70		Linfield	A	W	2	1	Magill, Bowyer og
CC	14/11/70		Glenavon	H	L	0	3	-
CC	21/11/70		Bangor	A	D	1	1	Magill
CC	28/11/70		Ballymena United	H	W	2	0	Kirk 2
CC	05/12/70		Coleraine	A	W	4	3	Magill 2, Murray 2
GC	07/10/70	1	Glenavon	H	D	3	3	Hall, Magill, Coyle (p)
GC	14/10/70	1R	Glenavon	A	W	3	0	Lavery, Morrow, Magill
GC	28/10/70	2	Ards	H	W	2	1	Magill 2
GC	25/11/70	SF	Portadown	WPW		2	1	Morrow, Magill
GC	17/03/71	F	Linfield	H	L	1	2	Macken
IL	12/12/70		Coleraine	H	D	1	1	Hall
IL	19/12/70		Ards	A	D	2	2	Jamison, McCaffrey
IL	26/12/70		Distillery	H	W	4	1	Morrow, Rafferty og, McCaffrey, Kirk
IL	28/12/70		Derry City	A	W	3	0	Magill 2, McCaffrey (p)
IL	02/01/71		Ballymena United	H	L	0	2	-
IL	09/01/71		Glenavon	A	W	2	1	Morrow, McCaffrey
IL	16/01/71		Crusaders	H	W	1	0	Magill
IL	23/01/71		Bangor	H	W	1	0	Magill
IL	06/02/71		Cliftonville	H	W	5	0	W.McCullough, Magill 3, Jamison
IL	20/02/71		Linfield	A	D	1	1	Magill
IL	06/03/71		Coleraine	A	L	1	3	Jamison
IL	13/03/71		Portadown	A	W	2	0	Macken, Morrow
IL	20/03/71		Ards	H	W	4	0	Morrow 2, Kirk, Weatherup
IL	27/03/71		Distillery	WPW		2	1	McCaffrey (p), Coyle
IL	07/04/71		Derry City	H	W	2	0	Hall 2
IL	10/04/71		Ballymena United	A	W	2	0	Morrow, Hall
IL	12/04/71		Glenavon	H	W	4	1	Hall 2, Morrow, Magill
IL	17/04/71		Crusaders	A	W	4	0	Jamison, Morrow, Magill, Hall
IL	20/04/71		Bangor	A	W	3	0	Stewart 2, Morrow
IL	24/04/71		Portadown	H	W	3	0	Macken, Jamison, Conlon og
IL	27/04/71		Cliftonville	A	W	5	1	Coyle, Morrow 2, McCaffrey (p), Hall

IL	01/05/71		Linfield	H	L	0	3	-
IC	13/02/71	1	Ballymena United	H	L	0	1	-
CAS	24/03/71	1	Dundonald	H	W	5	0	Morrow 2, Magill 2, McCaffrey
CAS	03/04/71	2	Ards	A	W	2	1	Macken, Magill
CAS	10/05/71	SF	Distillery	Sol	W	2	0	Jamison, Meldrum og
CAS	17/05/71	F	Crusaders	Sol	W	2	1	Magill, Morrow
F	29/07/70		Aston Villa	H	D	0	0	-
F	31/07/70		Stoke City	H	D	1	1	Hall
F	03/08/70		Morton	A	L	0	1	-
F	05/08/70		Reading	H	D	2	2	Bruce, Cassidy
F	30/11/70		Showbiz XI	H	Unknown		Unknown	
								Albert Finlay Benefit
F	05/05/71		Leeds United	H	W	3	1	Jamison, Morrow 2
								Esso Cup (Ulster '71)
F	11/05/71		Ballynahinch United	A	W	2	0	Bell 2
F	24/08/70		Crusaders	A	W	2	0	Lavery, Magee
								Glentoran / Linfield XI

put the score at 4-3, 4-4, 5-5 or even 9-3 to the Glens XI but it didn't really matter as a much needed night of fun was had by all.

In mid-December we began our defence of the league title and opened up with two draws, coming from behind in both games. Walter Bruce made a welcome return to the side on Boxing Day and linked up well with Jamison as we destroyed Distillery. The Whites' centre-half Peter Rafferty had a nightmare, scoring an own goal and giving another goal away because of an intercepted back pass. Paul Kirk though scored the goal of the match with an overhead kick.

We opened 1971 with a defensive muddle against Ballymena and Jim Martin took advantage after only 90 seconds to send the Braidmen on their way to a 2-0 win. Bimbo Weatherup returned to the side after an absence of two months and set up the only goal of the game for Magill (49 minutes) against Crusaders. This win kept us tucked nicely in third place after seven games, two points behind leaders Linfield and just one behind Coleraine. Magill was again on target with the only goal versus Bangor and then helped himself to a hat-trick against Cliftonville as we cracked open the Reds' defence in the second half.

Glenmen held their heads in horror when they discovered the first round draw for the Irish Cup. Yes, we were given a home tie against our "hoodoo" team Ballymena United and the seemingly inevitable defeat followed. Despite having 80% of the play we were unable to equalise Jim Martin's 12th minute goal and crashed out.

A week later it was Linfield who had all the play against us in a vital league fixture at Windsor Park. Magill had given us the lead eight minutes before the break and the second half was a catalogue of Linfield misses and Finlay saves until Bryan Hamilton maintained his habit of late, crucial goals with an 81st minute strike to equalise.

The Gazette, now sporting a bright spot colour cover surrounding an Albert Finlay save, added its opinion to the ever increasing debate concerning the future structure of Irish League soccer. There were two schools of thought; one promoting the extension of the league to 14 or 16 clubs with the addition of Larne, Newry, Ballyclare and Carrick and the other advocating two divisions with promotion and relegation. In addition it was felt that tournaments sponsorship would generate much needed funds.

The club acquired a new 41-seater coach, painted in red, green and black. Two supporters volunteered to drive the team to away matches, refusing to accept any payment for their services.

Back to playing matters and after defeat at Coleraine the team pieced together a run which yielded 12 successive victories in League and Shield. A convincing win was gained over Distillery at Windsor Park, notable for the fighting spirit shown when coming from behind and also for being the first football game this author ever attended at the ripe old age of six! Distillery's best player was Martin O'Neill, a target for many English clubs.

In early April and over Easter the team looked sharp and dangerous. Jim Hall returned from injury to score both goals against Derry City and four more in the next three games. With four league games to go we stood a point behind Linfield and had qualified for the Shield semi-finals with wins over Dundonald (Amateur League) and Ards (last minute winner from Magill). Billy McKeag's form was rewarded with a recall into the Northern Ireland squad for the game against Cyprus.

There was no stopping ourselves and Linfield as both sides won their next two games comfortably. Our penultimate match was at Solitude on a Tuesday night and an early goal from Coyle sent us on the way to a 5-1 win. The Blues visited Bangor the next night and, under pressure, came away with a 1-0 win meaning they only required a point from the title decider at the Oval on the following Saturday.

The match was played in glorious sunshine before a packed crowd including the local Match of the Day cameras. The Glens had to win to retain the championship but right from the kick-off the Linfield defence was tight and when the Blues went ahead on four minutes it gave them the confidence they needed. Two more goals after the break wrapped up the title for the Windsor men, condemning us to the runners-up spot. There was scant consolation in the fact that we would be Ulster's first representatives in the new UEFA Cup in 1971/2.

As part of the Ulster '71 festivities Glentoran met Leeds United in a prestige friendly for the Esso Cup. Like the Glens, Leeds had just been pipped for the title (by double winning Arsenal). Glentoran, bolstered by ex-stars Johnny Johnston and Tommy Cassidy proceeded to take Leeds apart and we eventually ran out 3-1 winners. It was certainly no fluke result as only Johnny Giles played well for the well-beaten visitors. Teams:

Glentoran: Finlay, Hill, McKeag, Coyle, McCullough, Macken, McCaffrey, Johnston, Cassidy, Morrow, Jamison.

Leeds: Sprake (sub. Harvey), Reaney, Davey, Bates, Madeley, Hunter, Lorimer, Belfitt (sub. Galvin), Jones, Giles, Gray.

From here we went to Ballynahinch for a game as part of the Civic Week and then on to lift our first trophy of the season by defeating Crusaders 2-1 in the County Antrim Shield at Solitude. The Crues' late onslaught was in vain.

In financial terms the club announced a profit of £739 for the season. Attendances and gate receipts at the Oval had dropped from 1969/70, down from 220,334 (£12,632) to 187,014 (£11,638). Despite this season ticket prices had risen from £1,424 to £1,827 in the same period while players' wages were fixed at £6 a week basic. Generally the early seventies saw attendances at local games drop well below the halcyon days of the fifties and sixties. There had been a dramatic dip of some 42% at all games from 1968/9 to 1970/1. At the end of the season Walter Bruce retired from football, thus ending an 18 year playing association with the Glens. Walter later ran the Boulevard newsagency on the Holywood Road.

Appearances and Goals

	App.	Subs.	Goals		App.	Subs.	Goals
Coyle	55		4	Millington	16	2	
Finlay	52			Kirk	12	3	5
McKeag	51		1	Lavery	10		1
Hill	50			Brown	7	2	
Morrow	49	3	25	Cassidy T.	6		4
Macken	38	1	4	Hutton	5	3	1
McCaffrey	36	1	8	McCullough T.	3		
Magill	34	5	25	Roy	3		
Weatherup	33	3	3	Black	2		
Jamison	28	1	6	Gorman G.	2		
McCullough W.	27	1	2	McParland	1		
Stewart R.	23	1	3	Unknown	11		
Hall	22	2	16	Own Goals			4
Bruce	20	1					
Murray K.	20		3	TOTAL	616	29	115

1971/72

The "Troubles" take effect – League Champions but no Europe –
Interesting tour declined

After concluding our pre-season friendlies with a win over the Israelis, Beitar, the heightening of the Troubles caused the postponement of the early Ulster Cup games. Indeed it was not until the 25th August that Glentoran first took the field for a competitive game with a visit to Bangor. New signing Tony Cavanagh put us ahead after only six minutes but a late equaliser from Tommy Craig frustrated us. Season ticket prices were set at post decimal prices of £5 (patrons), £4 (members) and £2 (boys and ladies). The Gazette, priced at 4p, featured an action picture of Roy Coyle on the cover.

Our first home game of the season ended in defeat against Glenavon, 1-2, but the goal we did score was a crazy one. Visiting centre-half Jackie Hughes seemed to foul Tommy Morrow and casually played the ball back to his keeper, Errol McNally. McNally, assuming a free-kick had been given, did not bother to save the ball as it rolled past and stood in disbelief when the referee awarded a goal. This defeat led to the resignation of manager Peter McParland. Kieran Dowd, who had only been appointed as first team coach a fortnight previously, stepped into the caretaker-manager role.

The effect of the civil unrest on football was plain to see as some matches were attended by only handfuls of spectators. In addition there were many indirect sectarian attacks on players. It looked like Gerry McCaffrey would have to leave the Oval because of the constant bombing of his firm. Many of our Ulster Cup games were boring affairs, the lack of direction in the team was clear to all.

Billy McKeag.

Eintract Brunswick decided to travel to Belfast after threatening not to because of the bombs. Before kick-off the Brunswick players presented each of their opposite numbers with a pennant. We were unlucky to lose the game itself to a single goal, as visiting German keeper Horst Wolter had to make many fine saves.

Paul Kirk returned to the side against Ards and scored the only goal with his first touch after only 30 seconds. Incidentally this was our 3,000th post-war competitive goal. A week later at Solitude we at long last gave the fans some entertainment as we went on a second half scoring spree.

Despite a brave display in the return leg of the UEFA Cup we took a 6-1 pounding but certainly were not disgraced. Our chief tormentor was Ludwig Brundl, score of five of the East Germans' goals. Many Glens' fans were calling for the return of John Colrain but nothing materialised.

The City Cup (switched again to a "two groups of six" format") commenced on schedule on 2nd October leaving our remaining three Ulster Cup fixtures to be played on midweek dates. To accommodate this the Gold Cup was moved back to the spring. Our opening City Cup game was a cracking 3-3 draw at Coleraine. All six goals were superb and one reporter noted, "What a change to hear the fans applauding first class football again."

From there we recorded encouraging wins over Derry (Ulster Cup) and Cliftonville by the tune of 7-1. On the evening of that latter match Alex McCrae was appointed manager, vacating a similar post at Ballymena. McCrae was to suffer defeat in four of his first five games, the only bright spot being a 6-0 hammering of Derry City. Tommy Morrow scored four in that match after having netted against the Blues the previous Wednesday night with a 20 yard free-kick. Also in October Northern Ireland played their last match in Belfast for three and a half years, a 1-1 draw with USSR on a dank Tuesday afternoon.

McCrae was therefore left under no illusions as to the magnitude of his task and many wisened observers felt that the league was as wide open as it was for many years. We

Albert Finlay.

signalled our intentions with a slick opening 4-0 win over Bangor, Johnny Jamison pulling the strings in midfield. We were then faced with a stern task in the form of Linfield at Windsor Park. It proved to be a see saw ninety minutes with the goals shared equally – Morrow's two cancelled out by a brace from 19 year old Paul Malone.

Atrocious weather conditions caused referee Malcolm Wright to abandon the game against Coleraine at half-time on 20th November. Players were suffering from exposure and goalkeeper Albert Finlay was on the point of collapse due to the freezing rain and biting winds. "It was just awful", summed up Albert.

Our first league defeat came in bad circumstances against Portadown. The army checkpoints, out because of bomb scares in the town, held the team up and the kick-off was delayed by ten minutes. In addition Tony Macken, travelling north from Newry, could not get through to the ground so we were afforded the luxury of a substitute. Within 16 minutes the Ports had gone 3-0 up and, despite a plucky attempt in the second half we were never really able to get back into it. This defeat dropped us to sixth in the table but the remainder of December was a much happier time as we recorded four straight wins including a Christmas feast of eleven goals on 25th and 27th December. Finlay was a mere spectator and he saw Morrow knock in four against the Whites and Weatherup grab a hat-trick versus Glenavon. At the end of 1971 Tommy Morrow's 21 goals left him third in the country behind Jim Martin (Ballymena) and Des Dickson (Coleraine). Down the club Glentoran Olympic completed the year on a high note by seeing off Linfield Rangers 2-0 in the IFA Youth Cup final at Seaview. The goals came from Dickinson and Kennedy whilst Alan Paterson kept a clean sheet at the other end. Off the field the bingo section of the Oval Sports club paid for new training kit and substitutes benches.

We began 1972 as league leaders and strengthened our position with a narrow win over Derry before travelling to Coleraine. That turned out to be a dramatic and controversial match and our 1-2 defeat brought inevitable cries of "We were robbed". The complaints surrounded Coleraine's winning goal. Current beneficiary Billy McKeag while attempting to clear his lines was virtually strangled by Sean Dunlop right in front of a linesman but play was waved on for Barney Mullan to score! Linfield won 2-0 at Glenavon that day to leave the leading league positions as follows:

1. Glentoran played 11 points 16, 2. Linfield 12-16, 3. Portadown 11-15.

The Blues then drew their next two games as we easily beat Cliftonville and fought out a tight scoreless draw with the third placed Ports.The Irish Cup was a welcome break from the league pressures especially as we had a relatively easy first round draw against amateurs Ards Rangers. Despite the heroics of Alfie Wright in the juniors goal we scored five times, the best a 30 yard drive from Billy McCullough. Paul Kirk netted for the first time since signing professional forms. The second round tie with Coleraine was just as explosive as the league meeting six weeks earlier. With 14 minutes remaining we led 1-0 whereupon Dickson equalised. Jamison immediately restored our lead but goals from Curley (83) and Dunlop (89) earned the visitors the win. At the final whistle some players exchanged punches and the Coleraine party later had to be smuggled out of the Oval. The league race remained wide open during February. In a game played at the Coleraine Showgrounds for security reasons we dropped a point to Derry after leading 2-0 with only eight minutes to go. Then, as Linfield and Portadown drew 2-2 with each other, a chested Jim Weatherup goal was enough to defeat Ballymena. However we lost the services of Jim Magill, who emigrated to Australia and got fixed up with the Hakoah club. Glentoran were invited to tour Israel (three matches), Turkey and Italy (one match each) at the end of the season. A guarantee was put up by the Beitar club of Tel Aviv but the directors felt that it was not sufficient to cover the players' lost work wages and the invitation was reluctantly declined. Defeat at Ards knocked us off top spot and then we failed to beat Distillery at Seaview. The saviour for the Whites that day was their diminutive keeper Charlie McGuile. Now there were four teams in with a shout for the league and when a break was taken on Irish Cup semi-final day the table read:

1. Linfield played 18 points 25, 2. Portadown 17-24, 3=. Glentoran and Ards 17-23.

In such a tight race the title would probably go to the hungriest team in the run in. We certainly started in determined mood at Glenavon when Tony Macken, playing the best football of his career to date, scored in the first minute and then Jamison hit the bar two minutes later. One goal was enough however and the pendulum swung our way again as Ards beat Portadown (4-3) and Linfield went down at Ballymena. However it was the results of 1st April that really saw us installed as favourites. While we held out for a 2-1 win at Bangor (coasting 2-0 at one stage) the news came through of the challengers; Crusaders 4 Ards 0 ... Ballymena 1 Portadown 6 ... Linfield 0 Derry 2! The bad news of the day was that Alex McCrae felt that he had to quit his managerial post due to a family illness and return to Scotland. Another big game followed on Easter Monday when Linfield visited the Oval, bringing back vivid memories of their clinching win at the same venue eleven months previously. This was to be the Glens' turn however as time and time again Jamison's through balls tore the Blues to ribbons. The goals came fast and frequently, Gerry Brammeld getting the first on 34 minutes with a magnificent header. Two minutes into the second half "Stumpy" himself made it 2-0 and further goals from Morrow and Jamison again wrapped it up before the hour. It was a complete rout, Linfield were paralysed and humiliated as they were beaten by a bigger margin that their Swifts in the County Antrim Shield just twelve days before! We now just needed to beat Crusaders to become champions for the fifth time in eight years but before that we stuttered to defeat at Ards in the Shield, albeit to a last minute goal. Questions were asked, could a managerless team win the Gibson Cup? We duly did with a comfortable 2-0 win over the Crues, the goals coming from Cavanagh (2 minutes) and Morrow (26). Consistency was sited as the key reason for

our success but one player for whom that description was most apt had left for pastures new. Sheffield Wednesday had signed Roy Coyle for a ridiculously low fee. Coyle became the latest Glentoran product to appear in the Football League. After Wednesday he went on to a spell at Grimsby Town and gained five Northern Ireland caps in 1973/4. He subsequently moved into management and became the most successful manager in Irish

Jim Weatherup takes on Crusaders' McFarland and Nicholson at Seaview.

Results 1971/72

Played 47. Won 24. Drew 9. Lost 14. Goals For 98. Against 51. % 60.6.
Honours: Irish League

UC	25/08/71		Bangor	A	D	1	1	Cavanagh
UC	28/08/71		Glenavon	H	L	1	2	Hughes og
UC	31/08/71		Crusaders	A	W	2	0	Jamison, Magill
UC	04/09/71		Ballymena United	H	D	0	0	-
UC	07/09/71		Coleraine	A	L	2	3	Magill, Jamison
UC	11/09/71		Distillery	H	W	1	0	Macken
UC	18/09/71		Ards	H	W	1	0	Kirk
UC	25/09/71		Cliftonville	A	W	4	2	Coyle, Kirk 2, McCaffrey (p)
UC	07/10/71		Derry City	H	W	4	1	Cavanagh 2, Kirk, Morrow
UC	14/10/71		Portadown	A	L	0	2	-
UC	20/10/71		Linfield	A	L	1	2	Morrow
UEFA	14/09/71	1.1	Eintract Brunswick	H	L	0	1	-
UEFA	28/09/71	1.2	Eintract Brunswick	A	L	1	6	McCaffrey
CC	02/10/71		Coleraine	A	D	3	3	Kirk, Morrow, McCaffrey
CC	09/10/71		Cliftonville	H	W	7	1	Jamison 2, McCaffrey, McKeag, Kirk 2, Morrow
CC	16/10/71		Ballymena United	A	L	1	3	Macken
CC	23/10/71		Derry City	H	W	6	0	Morrow 4, Weatherup, Jamison
CC	30/10/71		Crusaders	A	L	0	1	-
IL	06/11/71		Bangor	H	W	4	0	Morrow, Hall 2, McKeag
IL	13/11/71		Linfield	A	D	2	2	Morrow 2
IL	20/11/71		Coleraine	H	A	1	2	Jamison (p) Abandoned at half-time
IL	27/11/71		Cliftonville	A	W	6	0	McAleavey, Jamison 2, Morrow, Macken, Hall
IL	04/12/71		Portadown	A	L	2	4	Coyle, Morrow
IL	11/12/71		Ards	H	W	2	1	Weatherup 2
IL	18/12/71		Ballymena United	A	W	2	1	Morrow, Magill
IL	25/12/71		Distillery	H	W	6	0	Morrow 4, Magill, Jamison
IL	27/12/71		Glenavon	H	W	5	0	Weatherup 3, Magill, Morrow
IL	01/01/72		Crusaders	A	D	0	0	-
IL	08/01/72		Derry City	H	W	1	0	Weatherup
IL	15/01/72		Coleraine	A	L	1	2	Morrow
IL	22/01/72		Cliftonville	H	W	4	0	Weatherup, Morrow, Magill 2
IL	29/01/72		Portadown	H	D	0	0	-
IL	12/02/72		Derry City	A	D	2	2	Kirk, Morrow
IL	19/02/72		Ballymena United	H	W	1	0	Weatherup
IL	04/03/72		Ards	A	L	0	2	-
IL	11/03/72		Distillery	A	D	2	2	Morrow, Weatherup
IL	25/03/72		Glenavon	A	W	1	0	Macken
IL	01/04/72		Bangor	A	W	2	1	Jamison, Morrow
IL	03/04/72		Linfield	H	W	4	0	Brammeld, Jamison 2, Morrow
IL	15/04/72		Crusaders	H	W	2	0	Cavanagh, Morrow
IL	29/04/72		Coleraine	H	W	1	0	Morrow
IC	05/02/72	1	Ards Rangers	H	W	5	1	Morrow, McCullough 2, Weatherup, Kirk
IC	26/02/72	2	Coleraine	H	L	2	3	Morrow, Jamison
CAS	22/03/72	1	Linfield Swifts	H	W	3	0	Morrow, Jamison 2
CAS	12/04/72	2	Ards	A	L	0	1	-
GC	18/04/72	2	Linfield	A	D	0	0	-
GC	25/04/72	2R	Linfield	H	W	3	0	Morrow, Kirk, Weatherup
GC	10/05/72	SF	Portadown	WPL		0	1	-
F	31/07/71		Morton	H	L	0	4	-
F	02/08/71		Sheffield Wednesday	H	D	1	1	McCaffrey
F	05/08/71		Beitar	H	W	1	0	Cavanagh

history while at Linfield. He later took over the reigns at Ards (twice) and Derry City in the League of Ireland before returning to the Oval as manager in 1997. Before the curtain came down on the season there was still the Gold Cup to play for. Round Two gave Linfield a chance for a quick revenge over us and we had Finlay to thank for scoreless draw at Windsor, one save from a Gary Prenter six yard volley particularly memorable. We gave the Blues another hiding in the second half of the replay, all three goals condensed into a 19 minute spell. The season ended on a low note when an 86th minute penalty gave Portadown a semi-final success over us. Further disappointment followed when the Irish League decided that no entry would be made into European competition the next season due to the civil unrest, thus denying us of another European Cup appearance.

Appearances and Goals

	App.	Subs.	Goals		App.	Subs.	Goals
Hill	46			McAleavey	17		1
McKeag	46		2	Kirk	15	9	10
McCullough W.	45		2	Dickson	13		
Jamison	45		15	Stewart R.	12		
Morrow	45		31	Gorman G.	11	1	
Macken	38		4	McCaffrey	11	2	4
Coyle	36		2	Brammeld	8		
Weatherup	32	2	12	Hall	6		3
Finlay	29			Dickinson	1		
Cavanagh	24		4	Own Goals			1
Magill	19	1	7	TOTAL	517	15	98
McCullough T.	18						

Team Group 1971/2 Back Row: John Hill, Tommy Morrow, Trevor McCullough, Paul Kirk, Gerry McCaffrey, Jim Magill, Geoff Gorman. Front Row: Alan Dickson, Tony Macken, Billy McCullough, Billy McKeag, Roy Coyle.

335

1972/73

Farewell to Derry, hello Larne – George Eastham appointed –
Three cup final wins

One of the side effects of the Troubles was that general public interest in Irish League football continued to wane in the mid-seventies. The directors made the gesture of not increasing season ticket prices despite growing inflation. From the playing panel we lost our Southern personnel, Macken and Cavanagh, plus steeplejack Albert Finlay due to a recurring work related injury. These were offset slightly by the signing of Billy Murray from Preston. It was agreed that no floodlit would be played in Belfast early season in order to avoid potential further trouble after dark. Cliftonville finally decided to drop their amateur status after 93 years.

The season began with the new Carlsberg Cup, a tournament which attempted to give players some match practice in lieu of pre-season friendlies but also marked the first flirting signs of sponsorship in local football. The managerless Glens, turning out in a new strip with diagonal stripes, black shorts with a white stripe and white socks with a thick green top, continued our dismal record in short-lived minor competitions by losing at home to Bangor.

Billy McCullough holds aloft the City Cup watched by Weatherup and Rab McCreery.

This poor form was carried into the Ulster Cup as we suffered further home defeats to Crusaders (Jackie Fullerton hat-trick) and Linfield (two from Billy Millen) before very small crowds. In between we beat Derry City 2-0 at Coleraine Showgrounds, only goal-scorer Kirk and stocky winger Harry Connor playing well. Glentoran had refused to go to the Brandywell following the hijacking and burning of the Ballymena United bus earlier in the year. The match, played in a ghostly atmosphere in front of barely 150 spectators, was our last match against Derry under Irish League jurisdiction as six weeks later they withdrew from the league when the Management Committee turned down their application to play at Brandywell.

Meanwhile we struggled on, picking up three points from our next four fixtures. In the game at Ballymena three men were sent off, Gowdy and Scott for the home side and Johnny Jamison. We had slipped to ninth in the table but thinks looked brighter when we came from behind to beat joint leaders Distillery. Further good news was the return of trainer Bobby McGregor after illness and the appointment of a new full-time manager in George Eastham, Senior. Eastham, who was then managing in South Africa, had built excellent footballing sides while at Ards and Distillery in the 1950s and would commence his Oval post in mid-October. From his playing career he could boast an England cap, won against Holland in 1935.

The first game under floodlights was against Portadown but after we had been pulled back from two up to 2-2 the match developed into a vicious farce. Punches and boots flew as referee McFadden totally lost control. The great shame of it was that the first half had been full of good football and included a rare goal from 30 yards by full-back Billy McKeag. We rounded off the Ulster Cup with a high scoring win over the Reds but our final position of 9th left one scribe pointing out, "There is still a lot of work to be done before the Glens can woo back the missing fans."

Glentoran and Linfield swapped groups in the City Cup – the Blues' Section B was played out with five teams in the absence of Derry City. In our opening game Bangor looked like they wanted to wipe the floor with us but somehow we contrived a 2-0 win. For the next match with Glenavon two players linked up for the first of many successful times. Jamison returned after his month long suspension to play alongside Eastham's first signing, from Stoke City, left-winger Warren Feeney, and lead the team to a 3-0 win.

We entertained Portadown on 11th November in a vital top of the section clash. Feeney got his first goal for us in a 1-1 draw but we had Alan Paterson to thank for a late save from Ward to keep us top on goal average. In the last match at Seaview versus Distillery we led 2-0 with four minutes to go when

CORK HIBS.
v GLENTORAN

Blaxnit Cup final Programme Cover.

referee Malcolm Moffatt decided to abandon the match due to bad light. Moffatt claimed that he could not see his linesmen but Eastham was furious at the possibility of a re-match (Portadown had beaten Glenavon 2-0) countering that he and supporters around him could see perfectly adequately. In any event the result was allowed to stand and thus we qualified to meet Coleraine in the final at Ballymena Showgrounds a fortnight hence.

In that match Coleraine were the masters in the first half but we came back into it after the break. After 72 minutes of deadlock Feeney tried a long range shot which was fumbled by keeper Eddie Crossan and Tommy Morrow nipped in to slip the rebound into the net. Then seven minutes later Alan Dickson, the son of Tommy "the Duke of Windsor", and recently signed from Cliftonville, sealed the win when Crossan misjudged his speculative effort from all of 30 yards. So Eastham recorded an early trophy success, part of which was due to the emergence in the first team of youngsters Paterson, Rab McCreery and Peter Dickinson. Hugh "Bud" McFarland was praised for his efforts in maturing these players through the Olympic and 2nd XI. Eighteen year old Paterson was strongly tipped for the "big time".

The league had begun in late November 1972 with Larne taking the place of Derry City. The East Antrim side had last held senior status in 1939/40 and returned after dominating the B Division, boasting eight title successes in the preceding nine years. The bookmakers had Linfield and Glentoran joint championship favourites at 7/2 but the Blues made a mockery of those odds by cruising to a 2-0 win over us in the opening fixture at the Oval. A further shock awaited at Seaview a couple of weeks later, after Jamison had put us ahead against the Whites. A one-man show from Martin Malone earned him a personal tally of four goals and only Distillery's third win over us in eight years. We went down again at the same venue the following Saturday to the Crues but then went on a post-Christmas scoring spree against Cliftonville and at Larne, where Jamison and Paterson were magnificent. Crusaders stated their league intentions with an 8-0 win over the Whites on Boxing Day.

At the turn of the year we languished in eleventh place and not many people turned up to watch us whip a poor Glenavon outfit 4-0. Two further wins lifted us up to sixth but our inconsistency was highlighted on 3rd February when Glenavon turned the tables and beat us 4-0 at Mourneview Park! The previous result was hard to believe as the Lurgan men toyed with us in the second half. Paul Kirk, frustrated by his lack of a regular first team place, was transferred to Ballymena while John Anderson came into the side.

Linfield had now dropped to tenth in the league but that was the last thing on our mind as we ventured north for a first round Irish Cup tie with Limavady United. There was doubt over the suitability of the Lims' ground but a hastily erected fence solved the problem. Limavady issued their first ever match programme but Jim Hall ended their dreams with a hat-trick in our 3-1 on a proverbial gluepot of a pitch.

Form was maintained with wins over the bottom two, Larne (in Arctic conditions) and Cliftonville, who were tortured by four-goal Jamison. We then faced two double headers in succession with table toppers Crusaders and Distillery. The Irish Cup tie with the Crues was an emotional affair as it was Tommy Morrow's last game before he too emigrated to Australia to play for Hakoah. Morrow received a "guard of honour" from the other Glens' players as he ran out but he failed to score in our solid 2-1 win. (He did find the net on his

George Eastham senior directs a training session.

debut for Hakoah.) Alan Paterson provided the most memorable moment of the match when producing a magnificent reflex save, similar to the one that Jim Montgomery was to pull-off in the FA Cup Final a few months later. Next we dented Crusaders league hopes when the tall ginger haired substitute Rob Saunders scored a 76th minute equaliser at the Oval.

Colin Morgan had an exciting scoring debut against Distillery in the Shield as we raced into a 3-0 interval lead. The Whites could only pull one back but were in more determined mood in the league encounter and two opportunist goals from their substitute Cyril Hewitt put them 3-2 ahead before Feeney squared matters from the penalty spot.

Feeney was again on target from a spot-kick in the Irish Cup semi-final against Glenavon, this goal in the 57th minute enough to see us through. Old hand McKeag and new boy Billy Walker were sound in defence. Despite this George Eastham was still unhappy and openly criticised the structure of the league and the standard of refereeing. He put forward that from his experience in South Africa that there should be no more than four competitions topped up by a "Champion of Champions" tournament amongst the four winners.

Our league results in April were largely academic but we had the satisfaction of beating Linfield 1-0 at Windsor Park and in so doing sent a message to those critics prophesying a one-sided cup final. We blooded more promising new players, such as Roy Walsh (returning to Belfast after a spell at Man. Utd.) and Billy McAllister.

By far the most exciting match of the month was the second round Shield tie with Ballymena. It was a game of goals and drama, as the pendulum of advantage swung one way then the other. Ballymena led 3-2 at half-time then scores from Anderson (76 minutes) and Weatherup (82) put us ahead only for the Braidmen to equalise on the stroke of time. Six minutes into extra time Feeney made it 5-4 but within three minutes it was all square again and so it remained meaning that for the first time in our history a match would be settled via a penalty shoot out. We returned a 100% record through Feeney, Jamison, Walker, McKeag and Anderson but for Ballymena Gowdy (saved by Paterson) and Scott (over the bar) were the culprits again, following their sendings-off earlier in the season.

That win set up a two legged semi-final with the Blues but before that there was the little matter of the Irish Cup final to settle. On

Warren Feeney scores against Crusaders in the Irish Cup.

home territory Linfield began as firm favourites but we were ahead by half-time, a goal from Feeney just before the break. Alan Paterson had been injured in a clash with Millen and was unable to resume, forcing Roy Stewart to take over the Number One jersey. Stewart performed admirably but could not prevent two Linfield goals from Millen and Magee. Jamison had scored for us and with three minutes left it still stood at 2-2. Then as Feeney ran through on goal referee Malcolm Wright adjudged him to have been unfairly challenged by Billy Sinclair and awarded a penalty. Warren himself stepped up to convert and thus sent the Cup to East Belfast for the first time in seven years. Amazingly we had therefore qualified for Europe despite finishing eighth in the league.

For our final league fixture Eastham decided to field a virtual 2nd XI as the game fell between the Cup Final and the Shield semi-final with the Blues. So, unfamiliar names such as Trevor McCullough, Gordon Govan and Andy Dougan took the field for the Glens on a Tuesday afternoon at Coleraine. In addition centre-half Billy McCullough was playing his first game for three months. In front of a meagre 300 crowd Coleraine unsurprisingly won 4-1 and in doing so leapt-frogged above Linfield into fourth position to earn a place in the potentially money spinning Texaco Cup of 1973/4.

Linfield came all out at us in the Shield semi-final and after a drawn first game a late winner from Eric Magee gave them a 4-3 aggregate win. In between the ties Portadown

Alan Paterson and Roy Stewart after the Irish Cup final.

ended our Gold Cup hopes as we seemed content to go through the motions.

By winning the Irish Cup we qualified for a two-legged meeting with the FAI Cup winners Cork Hibs for the Blaxnit Cup. It initially appeared that these games would be held over due to fixture congestion but they were slotted in at the end of May. The directors decided to fly the team to the first leg in Cork but that idea almost met with disaster. On the way to Aldergrove the team coach caught fire but luckily the team was able to catch a service bus coming just behind. In the game itself we were forced into a "backs to the wall" effort and were eternally grateful when Cork's Sheehan lobbed the ball over his own keeper to give us the lead. The home sides pressure finally paid off with an equaliser in the 72nd minute.

The second leg was played at Castlereagh Park as a gesture to the Newtownards based

339

Results 1972/73

Played 51. Won 24. Drew 9. Lost 18. Goals For 106. Against 81. % 55.9.
Honours: Irish Cup, City Cup, Blaxnit Cup

CbC	08/08/72	2	Bangor	H	L	0	1	-
UC	19/08/72		Crusaders	H	L	1	4	Jamison
UC	24/08/72		Derry City	CS	W	2	0	Kirk 2
UC	26/08/72		Linfield	H	L	1	2	Jamison
UC	31/08/72		Bangor	H	D	2	2	Kirk, Jamison
UC	02/09/72		Glenavon	A	W	2	1	Jamison, Dickinson
UC	09/09/72		Ballymena United	A	L	1	2	Stewart
UC	16/09/72		Coleraine	H	L	0	2	-
UC	23/09/72		Distillery	A	W	3	1	Jamison, Kirk, Morrow
UC	29/09/72		Portadown	H	D	2	2	McKeag, Kirk
UC	07/10/72		Ards	A	L	1	2	Hall
UC	14/10/72		Cliftonville	H	W	5	3	Hill, Morrow 2, Hall 2
CC	21/10/72		Bangor	H	W	2	0	Stewart, Hall
CC	28/10/72		Glenavon	A	W	3	0	Jamison 2, Dickinson
CC	04/11/72		Ards	A	W	2	0	Kirk, Dickinson
CC	11/11/72		Portadown	H	D	1	1	Feeney
CC	18/11/72		Distillery	A	W	2	0	Jamison, Morrow
CC	02/12/72	F	Coleraine	BS	W	2	0	Morrow, Dickson
IL	25/11/72		Linfield	H	L	0	2	-
IL	09/12/72		Portadown	H	D	1	1	Feeney
IL	16/12/72		Distillery	A	L	2	4	Jamison, Feeney
IL	23/12/72		Crusaders	A	L	0	2	-
IL	26/12/72		Cliftonville	H	W	9	0	Morrow 3, Jamison 2, Dillon og, Sands og, McKeag, Dickinson
IL	30/12/72		Larne	A	W	5	1	Hall 2, Jamison 2, Morrow
IL	06/01/73		Glenavon	H	W	4	0	Stewart, Hall 2, Hill
IL	13/01/73		Ards	A	W	3	2	Anderson, Hall, Feeney (p)
IL	24/01/73		Ballymena United	H	L	0	1	-
IL	27/01/73		Bangor	H	W	3	0	Jamison, Dickson, Hall
IL	03/02/73		Glenavon	A	L	0	4	-
IL	17/02/73		Larne	H	W	3	2	Hall, Feeney, Anderson
IL	24/02/73		Cliftonville	A	W	5	0	Jamison 4, Hall
IL	10/03/73		Crusaders	H	D	2	2	Stewart, Saunders
IL	17/03/73		Distillery	H	D	3	3	Feeney 2(1p), Weatherup
IL	31/03/73		Portadown	A	L	1	2	Feeney
IL	07/04/73		Coleraine	H	L	1	3	Dickinson
IL	11/04/73		Linfield	A	W	1	0	Feeney
IL	14/04/73		Ards	H	L	0	1	-
IL	18/04/73		Ballymena United	A	L	1	4	Brown og
IL	21/04/73		Bangor	A	W	3	2	Anderson, McCreery, Dickinson
IL	01/05/73		Coleraine	A	L	1	4	McCreery
IC	10/02/73	1	Limavady United	A	W	3	1	Hall 3
IC	03/03/73	2	Crusaders	A	W	2	1	Hall, Feeney
IC	24/03/73	SF	Glenavon	CrP	W	1	0	Feeney (p)
IC	28/04/73	F	Linfield	A	W	3	2	Feeney 2(1p), Jamison
CAS	14/03/73	1	Distillery	H	W	3	1	Morgan, Jamison, Feeney
CAS	04/04/73	2	Ballymena United	H	D	5	5	aet – Jamison 2, Anderson, Weatherup, Feeney (Won 5-3 on penalties)
CAS	03/05/73	SF.1	Linfield	A	D	1	1	Feeney
CAS	12/05/73	SF.2	Linfield	H	L	2	3	Jamison, Walsh
GC	09/05/73	1	Portadown	H	L	0	2	-
BxC	23/05/73	F.1	Cork Hibs	A	D	1	1	Sheehan og
BxC	25/05/73	F.2	Cork Hibs	CrP	W	5	1	Jamison, Anderson, Feeney, Weatherup 2

sponsors. The game was very tight (half-time 1-1) up until the last twenty minutes when, despite being reduced to ten men, we tore open the Cork defence to score four times. There were scenes of pandemonium both on and off the terraces as Cork "folded like a pack of cards!" The hard-working Jim Weatherup was named man of the match as we collected the trophy and the £800, with half that sum going to the runners up.

That concluded what could only be described as a mixed season, three trophies but many poor displays and defeats to go with them.

Appearances and Goals

	App.	Subs.	Goals		App.	Subs.	Goals
Stewart R.	49		4	Walker	10	2	
Weatherup	45		4	McCullough T.	6		
McKeag	43		2	Walsh	6		1
Jamison	40	1	24	Finlay	5		
Paterson	38			Craig	5	1	
Hill	38		2	McAllister	4		
Feeney	33	1	17	Connor	3		
McCreery Rab	30	4	2	Morgan	2		1
McCullough W.	29			Brammeld	2		
Morrow	28	3	9	Gorman G.	1		
Hall	26	1	16	Govan	1		
Anderson	23		5	Kennedy	1		
Dickinson	18	4	6	Unknown	22		
Murray W.	15	1		Own Goals			4
Saunders	14	1	1				
Dickson	12	1	2	TOTAL	561	24	106
Kirk	12	4	6				

Team Group 1972/3 Back Row: Billy McKeag, Roy Stewart, Billy Walker, Alan Paterson, Peter Dickinson, Roy Walsh, Tommy Craig Front Row: Johnny Jamison, John Hill, Jim Weatherup, John Anderson, Warren Feeney.

1973/74

Quarter-finals in Europe – Broken legs jinx – Roy Stewart mourned

Manager George Eastham's problems mounted as the new season rolled in at the start of August 1973. Many of the Glens' first team panel, including Billy McKeag, Johnny Jamison and Peter Dickinson refused to re-sign and did not turn up for pre-season training. Jamison eventually put pen to paper just twenty minutes before our first round Carlsberg Cup match with Brantwood and celebrated by scoring the only goal against a stout defence. However the following Wednesday we ominously went down 2-4 at Ards in Round Two, Billy McAvoy claiming a hat-trick.

Ards went on to lose to Crusaders in the final (0-3) but we inflicted the Crues' first defeat of the season in the opening Ulster Cup fixtures. This was despite young left back Gordon

Billy Walker is carried off with a broken leg sustained during the match against Borussia.

Govan being hit on the head by a missile thrown from the terracing. However our shortcomings were amply illustrated over the next week as Jim Lemon tore us apart at Larne (his only blot a missed penalty) and then Linfield walloped us 6-0 at Windsor! It was so easy for the Blues that while their forwards scored four goals in a 19 minute spell centre-half Ivan McAllister was able to sit on his backside and watch from the half-way line.

Further catastrophe followed when Billy Murray broke a leg at Bangor and put himself out for the season. On the bright side Warren Feeney began to run into scoring form. Indeed his eight goals in the next five games coupled with Jamison's return from suspension took pressure of young players such as Andy Dougan, Victor Hooks and Geoff Gorman who had been thrown into first team action. This run lifted us to mid-table in the Ulster Cup and importantly installed much needed confidence before our European tie.

In the first round of the Cup Winners Cup we had been drawn to face Chimia Ramnicu Vilcea who stood top of Division Two in Romania going into the away leg in mid-September. The Glens party had to undergo three days of haphazard travel to get to their stadium but despite this we came away with a 2-2 draw. Rab McCreery worked beaverishly but the result was earned by the guts and tenacity of the entire XI. One embarrassing incident occurred during the second half when the Cypriot referee refused to let Jim Weatherup come on as substitute as his jersey had no number. Jim Hall had to remain on for the last twenty minutes!

Before the return leg we qualified for the semi-final of the newly sponsored Hennessy Gold Cup but went down to Portadown in the Ulster Cup. Jim McIlwaine made his debut in the latter and was one of three teenagers in our back four.

342

The second game with Chimia was more notable for the visitor's rough tactics, especially those of Donose who was sent off in the 38th minute, than for any creative football. We won 2-0 in front of 6,000 (who paid between 30p and £1 to watch) and in doing so restored the pride of the Irish League in the eyes of Rumanians as earlier that day Dinamo Bucharest had thrashed Crusaders 11-0. Dutch referee H. Pijer took a lot of credit for his handling of this tie as we became the first Ulster side to qualify for the second round of this competition.

After this success, though, it was back to local matters and in the space of four days we suffered back-to-back defeats against Ards at the Oval. In the second match, the Gold Cup semi-final, Alan Paterson was given the captain's armband to mark his last appearance before a £20,000 move to Sheffield Wednesday. Paterson played well but was unable to save any shots in the resultant penalty shoot out. Ards won 5-4, Gorman missing for us, meaning the spot-kicks put away by Jamison, Anderson, beneficiary Weatherup and Andy Dougan were in vain. Ards went on to add the Gold Cup to the already captured Ulster Cup.

Our City Cup hopes were dented early by

COUNTY ANTRIM AND DISTRICT FOOTBALL ASSOCIATION
Secretary—W. F. BROOKS

STEEL AND SONS CUP FINAL

Ballyclare Comrades
v.
Glentoran Seconds

At SEAVIEW, BELFAST
on
WEDNESDAY, 25th DEC., 1974
Kick-off at 11 a.m.

Souvenir Programme   10p

Steel and Sons Cup final programme 1974.

a heavy defeat at Coleraine but four days later we redeemed ourselves after a much longer trip North! It was to Bergen in Norway we had ventured to take on the local Brann team, 9-0 winners over Gzira in Round One. Heavy rain preceded kick-off, turning the pitch into a lake and it was a surprise to all, including the 70 Glenmen who had made the trip, when the referee declared the game on. As the rain sheeted down and made play resemble a "water ballet" Brann took the lead on 11 minutes. However we battled on bravely until receiving a sickening blow in the 73rd minute. Rab McCreery broke his leg in two places going into a tackle and had to be stretchered off. Despite this body blow Billy Walker equalised seven minutes later to leave us favourites for the second leg.

That return took place at the Oval on 7th November before only 5,200. A UEFA ruling forced an afternoon kick-off as our floodlights did not meet their required standards. However that had little effect on our players and with Weatherup and Feeney starring we won 3-1 to repeat our first round 4-2 aggregate success. Amazingly we found ourselves in the last eight of a European competition and, with Rangers, Cardiff City and Sunderland knocked out, the only remaining British representatives.

Overall our season had become enigmatic as we were totally unable to reproduce our European form in domestic soccer. We drew our final three City Cup games and finished fourth out of six in Section B. Jim Hall left the club to join Glenavon while another teenager, Victor Moreland, forced his way into the side and made his debut at Seaview amongst "a parade of young ones".

Maybe the league would bring a change of fortunes but hopes were dashed quickly as we failed to win any of our opening five games. Youth again blossomed when 16 year-old Robin Clarke scored after only two minutes of his debut at Bangor. We lost to Larne (Harry Rainey) hat-trick and had Feeney sent off in the process. Then against Glenavon Hall sunk us with an 85th minute winner! Eastham reacted by signing ex-Ards and Larne centre-half Billy Stewart to tighten the defence but he had a forgettable debut, putting through his own goal after four minutes as we went down against at Coleraine Showgrounds. Transfer

343

requests came in from John Hill and Johnny Jamison and further bad news arrived with the death of Davy Lyner, a member of the 1914 Vienna Cup winning team.

Billy McKeag settled his differences and returned at left-back for the Christmas Day encounter with Linfield at the Oval. The team battled to a 3-2 win, Jamison netting the winner, to lift us out of the bottom two. It was not all joy however as in the morning the Seconds, coached by Walter Bruce and Bud McFarland, had lost 0-2 to Chimney Corner in the Steel and Sons Cup final. Tommy Craig gained the consolation of the man of the match award.

We received a shock in our first match of 1974, losing 1-2 to Cliftonville at Solitude. This was the Reds' first home victory over us in nearly 19 years and also marked the end of our run stretching back to 1965 of 33 consecutive victories over the North Belfast men. Cairns was the Cliftonville hero with both goals.

Jim Weatherup on the attack against Brann Bergen.

George Eastham stated that he could hardly blame people for not coming to games as he felt the standard of both playing and refereeing was poor. Low crowds were not only a feature of Irish League games as over in England the drop in attendances was blamed on increased TV coverage. Bobby Charlton was advocating a blanket ban on televised football for 1974/5 while ex-Glenman Danny Blanchflower put forward the theory of covering one big game on a Monday night. Nearly twenty tears later Sky TV put this idea to the test!

During January there were plenty of scrappy, disappointing matches as we hovered in ninth and tenth place in the league. The weather matched our form and the game at Larne was abandoned at half-time and those versus Glenavon and Linfield postponed. We suffered an early Irish Cup exit too but at least there was the ECWC quarter final to look forward to. However preparations for that were dashed when Jamison was carried off on a stretcher against Coleraine with a two inch gash on his leg. Maybe our change of socks colour to red for this season was a bad move!

For the European match we had landed the "plum" draw in the shape of West Germans Borussia Moenchengladbach. Borussia had finished runners-up to Liverpool in the 1973 UEFA Cup and included many members of the West German squad who would go on to win the 1974 World Cup. They oozed class from goalkeeper Wolfgang Kleff to outfield players Bertie Vogts, Rainher Bonhoff, Ule Stielike, Jupp Heynckes and the Dane, Henning Jensen.

The first leg was switched to the Oval and a 12,000 crowd turned up on a Tuesday afternoon for the 4.15 pm kick-off. The Glens fielded five teenagers and were never in the game, eventually going down 0-2 to goals from Heynckes and Koppel. Trevor McCullough made many saves but generally it was too comfortable for Borussia. There were two tragic events associated with the game – centre-half Billy Walker became the third Glenman to break a leg this season, after a collision with Bonhoff but worse still was the untimely death of Roy Stewart, just hours after the final whistle. The entire local soccer scene was shocked at the loss of one of its most sporting and popular figures. Stewart's consistency had been rewarded by the 1972/3 Glentoran player of the year award and his passing away left a huge void at the Oval.

As a mark of respect play was halted in the second leg by the referee and a minute's silence was held in Roy Stewart's memory. That game was a "backs to the wall " damage

Results 1973/74

Played 51. Won 20. Drew 8. Lost 23. Goals For 71. Against 89. % 47.1

CbC	03/08/73	1	Brantwood	H	W	1	0	Jamison
CbC	08/08/73	QF	Ards	A	L	2	4	Feeney 2(1p)
UC	18/08/73		Crusaders	A	W	2	1	Jamison 2
UC	22/08/73		Larne	H	L	0	1	-
UC	25/08/73		Linfield	A	L	0	6	-
UC	29/08/73		Bangor	A	W	3	1	Feeney 2(1p), Hall
UC	01/09/73		Glenavon	H	W	5	2	Craig 2, Feeney 3
UC	08/09/73		Ballymena United	H	L	1	2	Feeney
UC	15/09/73		Coleraine	A	W	3	1	Jamison 2, Feeney
UC	22/09/73		Distillery	H	W	1	0	Jamison
UC	29/09/73		Portadown	A	L	1	3	Hall
UC	06/10/73		Ards	H	L	0	2	-
UC	13/10/73		Cliftonville	A	W	1	0	Hooks
GC	11/09/73	1	Distillery	H	W	1	0	Feeney
GC	26/09/73	2	Crusaders	H	W	3	1	Jamison 3
GC	09/10/73	SF	Ards	H	D	1	1	aet – R.Stewart (lost 4-5 on penalties)
ECW	19/09/73	1.1	Chimia Ramnicu Vilcea	A	D	2	2	McCreery, Jamison
ECW	03/10/73	1.2	Chimia Ramnicu Vilcea	H	W	2	0	Jamison, Craig
ECW	24/10/73	2.1	Brann Bergen	A	D	1	1	Walker
ECW	07/11/73	2.2	Brann Bergen	H	W	3	1	Jamison 2, Feeney
ECW	05/03/74	QF.1	B. Moenchengladbach	H	L	0	2	-
ECW	20/03/74	QF.2	B. Moenchengladbach	A	L	0	5	-
CC	20/10/73		Coleraine	A	L	0	3	-
CC	27/10/73		Cliftonville	H	W	4	1	Dougan, Weatherup, Hooks, Craig
CC	03/11/73		Ballymena United	A	D	2	2	Feeney 2
CC	10/11/73		Larne	H	D	2	2	Feeney (p), Walker
CC	17/11/73		Crusaders	A	D	1	1	Dougan
IL	24/11/73		Ballymena United	H	L	0	2	-
IL	01/12/73		Bangor	A	D	1	1	Clarke
IL	08/12/73		Larne	H	L	2	3	Feeney, Jamison
IL	15/12/73		Glenavon	A	L	1	2	Feeney (p)
IL	22/12/73		Coleraine	A	L	2	3	Feeney, Jamison
IL	25/12/73		Linfield	H	W	3	2	Walker, Feeney, Jamison
IL	26/12/73		Portadown	A	L	0	2	-
IL	29/12/73		Distillery	H	W	4	2	McKeag, Walsh, Jamison, R.Stewart
IL	05/01/74		Cliftonville	A	L	1	2	W.Stewart
IL	12/01/74		Crusaders	A	D	1	1	Jamison
IL	19/01/74		Ards	H	W	1	0	Feeney
IL	26/01/74		Bangor	H	L	0	1	-
IL	02/02/74		Larne	A	A	1	0	Jamison (p) abandoned at half-time
IL	23/02/74		Coleraine	H	L	0	2	-
IL	16/03/74		Portadown	H	W	1	0	Clarke
IL	30/03/74		Distillery	A	L	0	3	-
IL	04/04/74		Linfield	A	L	1	5	Feeney
IL	06/04/74		Cliftonville	H	W	1	0	Feeney
IL	13/04/74		Crusaders	H	L	0	3	-
IL	15/04/74		Ards	A	L	0	3	-
IL	20/04/74		Ballymena United	A	W	2	1	Craig, Gowdy og
IL	23/04/74		Larne	A	W	3	1	Feeney (p), Craig, Walsh
IL	25/04/74		Glenavon	H	W	4	0	Dougan, Dickinson, Hill, McIlwaine
IC	09/02/74	1	Crusaders	H	L	1	4	R.Stewart
CAS	26/04/74	1	Bangor Reserves	H	L	0	1	-

limitation exercise and we kept the margin of defeat down to 0-5. Roy Walsh was our coolest player.

The remainder of the season fizzled out in disappointing fashion and only winning our last three league games saved us from the ignominy of having to apply for re-election to the league. The only other bright note was our first win over Portadown in three years but there were plenty of low moments including another drubbing at Windsor Park. A brilliant solo goal from Feeney put us ahead on the hour but Linfield found the net five times in a disastrous last seventeen minutes. John Hill was sent off during the defeat at Ards and we handed Distillery their first win of any sort in seven months! However the worst form of humiliation came in the County Antrim Shield against Bangor Reserves at the Oval. The juniors beat us 1-0 – the goal scored by Jackie Reid after good work by a young Gerry Armstrong. This result can be put into perspective by the fact that our Seconds had beaten the same opposition 5-1 just a month previously. Glentoran Seconds never got a chance in the Shield as they had to withdraw from their first round tie with Ards due to heavy end of season fixture congestion.

The Oval hosted the Club Orange five-a-side tournament on May 1st/2nd. Fourteen teams entered with Crusaders defeating Cliftonville 2-1 in the final. We lost 0-3 to Linfield in the first round. The Crues ladies won the female match, 3-1 against Comber.

The calls on Eastham to resign intensified and in May his contract was terminated by mutual consent. Despite bringing the Irish Cup to the club in 1973 the record of 41 defeats in two seasons was totally unacceptable. We could only look to the future and hope the promise of youngsters such as McIlwaine, McCullough, Moreland, Dunlop, Dougan and Walsh would come to fruition.

The season was finally wound up with Jim Weatherup's benefit match when an ex-Glens XI took on a "Personality" XI including international footballers and rugby players, the game finishing 3-3.

Appearances and Goals

	App.	Subs.	Goals		App.	Subs.	Goals
Feeney	40	1	22	Paterson	15		
Dougan	35	2	3	Craig	12	4	6
Jamison	35	1	18	Moreland	10		
Stewart R.	34		3	Dickinson	10	1	1
Hill	32		1	Dunlop	8		
McCullough W.	32	3		Govan	7		
Weatherup	29	7	1	Hall	5	2	2
McCullough T.	25			Murray W.	4		
McIlwaine	24		1	Dickson	2	1	
Anderson	24	2		Saunders	1		
Walker W.	23		3	Walker R.	1		
Gorman G.	18			Lunn	1		
Hooks	18	1	2	McAllister	1		
McKeag	17		1	Unknown	33		
Stewart W.	17		1	Own goals			1
Clarke R.	17		2				
Walsh	16	5	2	TOTAL	561	32	71
McCreery Rab	16	1	1				

1974/75

McGregor takes the reins – Plenty of promise – An all-Glentoran semi

Glentoran trainer and physiotherapist Bobby McGregor took on a third role when he was appointed manager for the 1974/5 season. It put Bobby into an extremely demanding position but at least he had the experience of "Bimbo" Weatherup as his assistant. Supporters were expecting big improvements on 1973/4 (when attendances had sunk to an all-time low) but with broken leg victims Walker, Murray, McCreery and Hooks still on the treatment table patience had to be the watchword.

As the Carlsberg Cup had been scrapped and the continuing troubles prevented friendlies the Glens did not take the field until mid-August with the commencement of the Ulster Cup. We made good progress in the first month of the season, beginning with an unbeaten seven match run. This involved coming from 0-3 down at half-time to draw 4-4 at Larne and a confidence boosting win over the Blues. There was much interest in the top of the table clash with champions Coleraine in mid-September. A very hard fought game finished 2-2, all the goals coming in the first 26 minutes, and that result left ourselves, Coleraine and Linfield level on eleven points with four games to go.

Then we unfortunately lost our way, losing to Distillery at the claustrophobic Seaview and failing to convert any of numerous chances at home to Portadown. On the first Saturday in October Linfield won decisively at Coleraine (4-2) while we needed a brilliant flicked goal from Johnny Jamison to earn victory at Ards. In the second half of this match McGregor introduced his latest signing, Billy Caskey. Therefore going into the last round of matches we trailed the Blues by two points and we went at Cliftonville from the outset. Just two of our 14 first-half goal attempts found the net but the win was made futile anyway as Linfield beat Distillery to lift the Ulster Cup.

By this stage we had qualified for the Hennessey Gold Cup final and a meeting with Ballymena United, who were managed by our ex-player Arthur Stewart. Our progress to that game began with Tommy Craig's decisive strike against Crusaders and then Feeney, Caskey and McCullough were the architects of victory in the semi-final versus Bangor. Only 2,000 fans braved the elements for the final at Windsor Park but those present witnessed a classic match. The game stood 2-2 until Quinton McFall fired home the winner for the Braidmen, condemning us to another runners-up position.

Johnny Jamison signed this photograph for the taker Gil Irvine.

For the City Cup we again swapped sections with Linfield. Despite missing the injured McKeag and Feeney, we strolled through our first three matches to head up the group. Teamwork and spirit were the order of the day and the improvement in morale since McGregor had taken charge was clearly evident. We put four past Glenavon's Welsh international keeper Tony Millington and drew with Portadown to stay a point ahead of the Ports with one game remaining. Warren Feeney opened the scoring in the latter match when his in-swinging corner flew directly past Bobby Carlisle!

We put in a poor display against Distillery but did enough to win 2-1 and qualify for the final play-off. Feeney again sent us on our way with a brilliant free-kick from 25 yards past Bertie McGonigal. The final against Linfield was arranged for Wednesday 22nd January 1975 but when heavy rain forced a postponement it was decided, somewhat strangely, to hold the match over until the following season.

Torrential rain had also fallen on the opening day of the League Championship. We met Ballymena at the Oval and groundsman Billy Crawford was unanimously praised for his efforts in making the pitch playable. Caskey gave us an early lead but United equalised seven minutes from time. After a last gasp winner from Victor Moreland gave us victory at Larne we conceded four goals against both Crusaders and Portadown as our defence caved in. We were missing the solid Billy Stewart in these games, his absence caused by an accident at work.

The rut continued over Christmas. Caskey was sent off in a scoreless draw at Bangor and Linfield humiliated us 4-1 after we had taken the lead. Even the Seconds failed to lift the gloom as they were beaten 1-0 by Ballyclare Comrades in the Steel and Sons Cup final. McGregor signed Portadown defender Barry Gorman to cover for Stewart but even a win over Glenavon in the last match of 1974 still left us in ninth place at the turn of the year.

All the critics said the team needed strengthening but in early 1975 we put together a remarkable run of form as we reeled off nine wins in a row, scoring 36 goals in the process. Alec Robson, signed from Larne, was on target in most of these games as he filled the problematical centre-forward spot and Stewart returned to steady the defence. The run of success was filled with blistering displays and spectacular goals and even a battling win at Seaview thanks to a late drive from Andy Dougan which almost pierced the net.

Feeney and Jamison were the real cogs in the well-oiled machine, possibly reaching their peak during the second half of the first round Irish Cup tie versus Ballymena when a 1-2 interval deficit was turned into an excellent 6-3 triumph. Suddenly we were back in contention for the league, and at the end of February Linfield, having played a game more, only led us by five points.

Everyone expected our success to continue when we met B-Division Brantwood at Skegoniel Avenue in the second round of the cup. The bookies made us 2/5 favourites with the juniors listed at 5/1. All looked well as Feeney gave us the lead after ten minutes but the "Brants", cajoled by ex-Blueman Phil Scott, fought back to level it and then snatch a dramatic 84th minute winner from Harry Sparrow. Fans screamed hysterically for the Glens to find an equaliser but none came. It was the shock result of the season but Brantwood were put in their place by Coleraine in the semi-final to the tune of 6-0. Furthermore our Seconds placed the cup result into perspective when they easily beat Brantwood 3-0 in the B-Division a couple of months later.

The team was again knocked out of its stride by a 1-3 defeat at Bangor the following Saturday. The Seasiders were three up inside half an hour before Jamison came on as sub to pull one back. McGregor offered his resignation as manager but was talked out of quitting by players and spectators alike. The directors agreed to make funds available should he have wished to strengthen the playing panel.

Our title challenge got back on course when we defeated leaders Linfield 1-0 at the Oval on 15th March. Billy Caskey got the only goal of the game in the 63rd minute but we had created enough chances to win by more. It was the Blues' first defeat in over three months and left the league table as follows that evening:

1. Linfield played 17 points 27, 2. Crusaders 17-24, 3. Glentoran 16-22.

We revealed a brand new all white strip against Glenavon. A vertical red, green and black band replaced the diagonal stripes as well but on the day we could not find a way past the visiting defence and slipped further behind in the title race. McGregor introduced red haired Brian Large for the Easter Monday fixture at Ards and he had a fine debut, setting up one of Feeney's two decisive goals. Our slim league chances were finally buried at Coleraine in early April. Des Dickson did the damage by scoring a hat-trick in the first 33 minutes to send the title to Windsor Park. However two comfortable wins in our last two games ensured UEFA qualification despite finishing third to Coleraine as the Bannsiders went on to defeat Linfield in the Irish Cup final at Ballymena.

The Distillery game was played at the Whites' latest temporary home at Skegoniel

Results 1974/75

Played 47. Won 31. Drew 7. Lost 9. Goals For 108. Against 57. % 73.4.
Honours: City Cup (Final played in 1975/6)

UC	17/08/74		Crusaders	H	W	1	0	Feeney
UC	20/08/74		Larne	A	D	4	4	Robson, Moreland 2, Feeney
UC	24/08/74		Linfield	H	W	2	1	Robson, Moreland
UC	28/08/74		Bangor	H	W	2	1	Dougan, Lyttle
UC	31/08/74		Glenavon	A	D	1	1	Dougan (p)
UC	07/09/74		Ballymena United	A	W	1	0	Clarke
UC	14/09/74		Coleraine	H	D	2	2	Dickinson, Craig
UC	21/09/74		Distillery	A	L	0	1	-
UC	28/09/74		Portadown	H	D	0	0	-
UC	05/10/74		Ards	A	W	1	0	Jamison
UC	12/10/74		Cliftonville	H	W	2	0	Jamison 2
GC	25/09/74	2	Crusaders	H	W	2	1	Dougan, Craig
GC	09/10/74	SF	Bangor	A	W	3	1	Dougan, Feeney 2(1p)
GC	13/11/74	F	Ballymena United	WPL		2	3	Feeney, Caskey
CC	19/10/74		Bangor	H	W	3	1	Robson 2, Jamison
CC	26/10/74		Glenavon	A	W	4	1	Jamison 2, Robson 2
CC	02/11/74		Ards	A	W	2	0	Robson 2
CC	09/11/74		Portadown	H	D	2	2	Feeney, Dougan
CC	16/11/74		Distillery	A	W	2	1	Feeney 2(1p)
IL	23/11/74		Ballymena United	H	D	1	1	Caskey
IL	30/11/74		Larne	A	W	3	2	Feeney 2, Moreland
IL	07/12/74		Crusaders	H	L	1	4	Robson
IL	14/12/74		Portadown	A	L	2	4	Jamison, Caskey
IL	21/12/74		Bangor	H	D	0	0	-
IL	26/12/74		Linfield	A	L	1	4	Feeney
IL	28/12/74		Glenavon	A	W	4	2	Robson, Feeney, Clarke, Caskey
IL	01/01/75		Ards	H	W	4	0	Robson, Feeney 3
IL	04/01/75		Coleraine	H	W	3	1	Stewart, Clarke 2
IL	11/01/75		Cliftonville	A	W	4	0	Robson, Clarke, Feeney 2(1p)
IL	18/01/75		Distillery	H	W	5	1	Robson 2, Caskey 2, Feeney (p)
IL	01/02/75		Larne	H	W	5	1	Clarke 2, Robson, Jamison, Stewart
IL	15/02/75		Crusaders	A	W	3	2	Feeney 2, Dougan
IL	22/02/75		Portadown	H	W	2	0	Clarke, Feeney
IL	08/03/75		Bangor	A	L	1	3	Jamison
IL	15/03/75		Linfield	H	W	1	0	Caskey
IL	29/03/75		Glenavon	H	D	0	0	-
IL	31/03/75		Ards	A	W	2	1	Feeney 2
IL	02/04/75		Ballymena United	A	W	2	1	Moreland, Caskey
IL	05/04/75		Coleraine	A	L	1	3	Jamison
IL	12/04/75		Cliftonville	H	W	4	0	Caskey 3, Clarke
IL	26/04/75		Distillery	A	W	3	0	Robson, Jamison 2
IC	08/02/75	1	Ballymena United	H	W	6	3	Jamison 2, Feeney 3, Robson
IC	01/03/75	2	Brantwood	A	L	1	2	Feeney
CAS	08/04/75	1	Dundela	H	W	2	0	Jamison, Moreland
CAS	22/04/75	2	Cliftonville	H	W	5	0	Feeney, Caskey, Moreland, Jamison, Hill
CAS	09/05/75	SF	Glentoran II	H	W	5	0	Campbell 3, Clarke, Stewart
CAS	13/05/75	F	Bangor	H	L	1	2	Feeney
F	***/05/75		RUC	H	W	2	1	Unknown

*** = exact date not known

Avenue. There was some talk of them using Glen Park as their base but their directors felt that the North Belfast venue was more suitable.

In April international football returned to Belfast after an absence of some three and a half years when Yugoslavia came to play Northern Ireland in a European Championship Qualifying match. Bryan Hamilton scored the game's only goal and the lack of disturbances encouraged the previously reluctant Welsh and English F.A.s to follow suit for the British Championship games in May.

The last tournament on the local scene was the County Antrim Shield. The Glens progressed easily to the semi-finals with one sided wins over Dundela and Cliftonville (the best goal a John Hill volley) but the Seconds were making more unexpected headway. They were playing some excellent football in securing B-Division wins over Limavady United (1-0), Crusaders Reserves (5-0) and Ballymena Reserves (4-2) but were drawn away to the senior Ballymena United side in the first round of the Shield.

Things looked bad when they went a goal down but the youngsters refused to be ruffled and continued to play sweet moving football. This was rewarded with goals by John Caskey (younger brother of Billy), Perry Galbraith and Billy Kennedy in a memorable 3-1 win. Larne were the next opponents at the Oval and the Seconds time and time again had to thank eighteen year old goalkeeper George Dunlop for keeping the game scoreless. Twenty further minutes of extra time failed to break the deadlock and so it went to penalties. Again Dunlop was the hero, saving two of Larne's spot kicks, while McCabe, Nixon and Large converted to give us a 3-1 winning tally.

The semi-final draw paired our 1st and 2nd XIs in a repeat of the famous 1909 match. This time, on a wet Friday evening, the senior side made no mistake and easily won 5-0. The irony of the situation was that the Seconds' centre-forward Jim Campbell, who had started the season in the Olympic side, was promoted to the first team and proceeded to score a hat-trick. Not surprisingly Campbell was in tears at the final whistle as he felt that he had knocked out his own mates.

A large crowd assembled at the Oval for the final against Bangor four days later. It was to be a disappointing night as the Glens put in a ragged performance and lost 1-2. Further the Bangor centre-half Ian Jaffrey was sent off in the 81st minute and hit by a flagpole when leaving the field.

Overall the season flattered to deceive and playing matters were wound up with a friendly against the RUC at the Oval. As a curtain raiser to this game a charity match involving a "Showbiz XI" was played with the magic sponge much in evidence!

At the conclusion of the season Billy Caskey was voted the inaugural "Most Promising Newcomer" by the N.I.P.F.A. He deserved the award for his versatility at least, for as well as fulfilling his own midfield role he had stood in at centre-half and then scored a hat-trick against Cliftonville when asked to wear the No. 9 shirt.

Appearances and Goals

	App.	Subs.	Goals		App.	Subs.	Goals
Walsh	43			McCreery Rab	8		
Stewart W.	41		3	Dickinson	7	1	1
McCullough T.	40			McCullough W.	4		
Moreland	39	1	7	Dunlop	3		
Jamison	39	3	16	Large	3	1	
Robson	36	1	17	Govan	1		
Hill	35		1	Lyttle	1	3	1
Dougan	35	3	6	Gorman G.	1		
Feeney	32	2	29	McAllister	1		
Craig	28	1	2	Campbell		2	3
Clarke R.	27	1	10	Kennedy		1	
Caskey W.	25	1	12	Unknown	44		
McKeag	14	3		TOTAL	517	29	108
McIlwaine	10	5					

1975/76

Dutch masters - Jamison's virtuoso display – League given away

Manager Bobby McGregor had to contend with the loss of two full-backs before the season opened. John Hill had decided to emigrate to New Zealand while Billy McKeag, prematurely in many people's eyes, announced his retirement. On the coaching side Bimbo Weatherup resigned his second team post but Billy McCullough was appointed assistant coach to the first team on his return from a spell in the north-east of England.

We began the Ulster Cup in now traditional fashion by meeting Crusaders. The game was switched to the Oval as the pitch at Seaview was being returfed. The Crues began lethargically and we went into a 2-0 lead through Warren Feeney but two second half goals from Robert Gillespie forced a draw. Feeney went one better in mid-week by scoring a hat trick versus Larne, the first a speculative chip from all of 45 yards!

However any delusions of grandeur we had were completely eradicated at Windsor Park the following Saturday when Linfield hammered us 5-0. In the aftermath of this defeat the press had a field day on the Glens, saying amongst

Walsh and Robson in action against Crusaders.

other things that the players were not good enough, there was no money to buy replacements anyway and that the club itself was heading towards bankruptcy. Chairman John Dornan rebutted all such allegations and stated that any reasonable offer for a player would be met. Derek McKeague was appointed as Public Relations Officer to liase between the board and the supporters.

The team got back on the rails with three successive wins, including coming from behind to beat Glenavon, to lift us into third spot in the Ulster Cup. We lost a vital game to Coleraine, 0-2 both goals from Terry Cochrane, but thoughts then turned to our return to European competition and the UEFA Cup tie with Ajax Amsterdam. The Dutch side, winners of the European Cup in 1971, 72 and 73 were on paper a lesser side than that of the early seventies but still boasted players of the quality of Wim Suurbier, Ruud Krol, Johnny Dusbaba, Ruud Geels and Arnold Muhren. In the game itself Ajax put on a masterly show of brilliant football in front of an appreciative crowd and ran out 6-1 winners, Geels notching four goals. Johnny Jamison scored a late consolation for us. Only a masochist would have looked forward to the second leg and we went down by 0-8, Geels only managing a hat-trick this time. PSV Eindhoven emphasised the strength of Dutch football of this era by beating Linfield by the same score in the European Cup.

We defeated Bangor in the Gold Cup on "sudden death" penalties but our outside chance in the Ulster Cup almost foundered due to a mini injury crisis at Portadown. Alec Robson was standing in for the injured Billy Stewart at centre-half and then Andy Dougan had to act as an emergency goalkeeper when Trevor McCullough became the latest casualty.

351

Somehow we won 3-0, our latest signing Derek Clarke from Manchester City getting on the scoresheet. Coleraine, however, wrapped up the Ulster Cup by beating Linfield 1-0 at Windsor Park the following Saturday.

The Bannsiders were our next obstacle in the Gold Cup and we gave probably our best display of the season at the Coleraine Showgrounds only to lose 0-2! There were cries of "robbery" as we had two "goals" disallowed. Feeney was called up for "speech play" in one (Warren later protested that he called out a team mate's name) and then the referee ruled that Billy Caskey's header had not crossed the line when even the Coleraine defenders thought it was a goal!

Before commencing the City Cup there was still the small matter of playing off the 1974/5 final with Linfield. Ludicrously, this took place at Windsor Park just three days before the start of the 1975/6 competition! The match itself will go down as possibly the greatest ever display by Johnny Jamison. Not only did he score a personal hat-trick in our 3-1 win but he constantly tormented the Linfield defence and brought many saves out of Ken Barclay. So Bobby McGregor gained his first trophy as manager.

Denis Guy heads for goal against Distillery (white shirts).

We only held the trophy for two months however as our attempts to retain it were feeble by comparison. We finished joint bottom of our section with only one win and were again involved in controversy at Coleraine. We led 2-0 after 53 minutes but the home side pulled back to 2-2 only for Feeney to appear to score a third. The referee gave it but, after a linesman flagged, he ruled it offside. Coleraine took their 35 match unbeaten run into the final but that, and their hopes of a domestic clean sweep, were ended by Bangor. The Seasiders won 3-1 on penalties after a 0-0 draw and in so doing became the last ever winners of the City Cup as the old competition was scrapped to ease early season fixture congestion. Glentoran won it 16 times in its 80-year existence.

Jamison's form in his benefit year earned him an International cap against Norway in October. Northern Ireland won the game 3-0 at Windsor Park.

The league programme commenced at Ballymena and we recorded our first win for a month, indeed since our previous visit to the Showgrounds. Our ex-keeper Dunlop was to blame for one of the goals. However on our next away trip to Bangor we succumbed to defeat when conceding two late goals. McGregor reacted by signing Portadown full-back Ronnie McFall, a nephew of Tommy Hughes, our centre-half of post war days. Billy Caskey was rested as he appeared to be suffering the affects of playing summer football in the close season.

McFall settled in well as the team began to build an unbeaten fourteen match run in the league. The best win of December was an "all-action" Boxing Day clash with Linfield at the Oval. The biggest crowd of the season witnessed a terrific battle, settled by a bullet-like Feeney header in the 85th minute.

Our second game of 1976 was equally incident packed. We visited Seaview, with new centre-forward Denis Guy on and Alec Robson now a fixture at centre-half. The controversy really started when Rab McCreery was sent off for aiming a punch at Paul Kirk and then Feeney had a goal disallowed for an alleged handball. Warren protested vehemently that he had chested down before firing home. Our misery was completed when the Crues

352

snatched an equaliser five minutes from time. That result meant only two points divided the top five teams after nine matches.

However by the end of January we had emerged as clear leaders, three points ahead of Crusaders and four of Coleraine. Guy was an instant hit with the fans, scoring twice on his home debut and then Johnny Jamison's tenth minute goal was enough to ensure victory at the Coleraine Showgrounds. We scored ten goals in our next two matches but still the press were reluctant to praise our efforts – it seemed we only got newspaper inches when things were going badly!

We rolled on with five more victories during February but early March brought mixed fortunes for two of our players. Warren Feeney's excellent form was rewarded with an international cap against Israel in Tel Aviv. It was Feeney's first personal honour of the season but soon he was to be the recipient of a unique hat-trick when he was named the footballer of the year by the NIPFA, the NI football writers and also the Ulster award, organised by the Castlereagh Glentoran Supporters Club. Our talented right-back Jim McIlwaine, though, tasted life at the other end of the spectrum as he suffered a leg break against Cliftonville on 6th March. Two operations the following January proved unsuccessful and McIlwaine had to retire prematurely from the game. Rab McCreery moved back into the number two shirt.

The Irish Cup semi-final at the Oval featured Belfast's big two as the season boiled up to an exciting climax. The match became known as "the battle of the Oval" for all the wrong reasons. Early in the second half Ronnie Bell scored his second to put the Blues 2-0 up and in doing so collided with Glens' keeper Trevor McCullough. McCullough appeared to kick Bell on the head and the ground erupted. Linfield player-manager Roy Coyle's early challenges on Billy Caskey seemed nothing by comparison as tacklers flew into almost every situation. The violence spread to the terraces and a posse of Glentoran players were showered with bottles and stones while waiting to take a free-kick. One of them reacted by

throwing a bottle back into the crowd! It was certainly a black day in the history of the club and defeat made it even worse.

Tantalisingly the two teams were due to meet at Windsor Park in the league just seven days later. Thankfully there was no repeat of the previous Saturday's scenes, either on or off the pitch, as a skilful display earned us a 2-1 win. We thus retained our five point lead over Crusaders with five league games to go.

Then, inexplicably, the jitters set in. We went down to Larne at a bumpy Inver Park at the end of March and then lost at home to Ards despite controlling he game. Ards' winning goal summed up the afternoon. It stood 2-2 when we were awarded an indirect free-kick about eight yards from goal. The visitors lined up on the goal line, managed to charge down the kick and then, in the same movement, broke away upfield to score the winner. This allowed the Crues to draw level at the top following their scoreless draw with Coleraine.

The Oval hosted the Irish Cup final on 10th April when juniors Carrick Rangers beat Linfield 2-1, and seven days later it became the venue for the Irish League decider when we took on Crusaders. Again it was a match to leave a sour taste in

Billy Caskey.

Results 1975/76

Played 47. Won 25. Drew 9. Lost 13. Goals For 94. Against 71. % 62.8

UC	16/08/75		Crusaders	H	D	2	2	Feeney 2(1p)
UC	20/08/75		Larne	H	W	4	0	Feeney 3, Robson
UC	23/08/75		Linfield	A	L	0	5	-
UC	27/08/75		Bangor	A	W	2	0	Moreland, Kennedy
UC	30/08/75		Glenavon	H	W	4	1	W.Caskey, Robson, Feeney 2(1p)
UC	06/09/75		Ballymena United	H	W	3	1	Jamison, Robson, Feeney
UC	13/09/75		Coleraine	A	L	0	2	-
UC	20/09/75		Distillery	H	W	3	0	Feeney, Dickinson, W.Caskey
UC	27/09/75		Portadown	A	W	3	0	Clarke, Jamison, W.Caskey
UC	04/10/75		Ards	H	D	2	2	Moreland, Dickinson
UC	11/10/75		Cliftonville	A	W	2	0	McCreery, W.Caskey
UEFA	16/09/75	1.1	Ajax Amsterdam	H	L	1	6	Jamison
UEFA	01/10/75	1.2	Ajax Amsterdam	A	L	0	8	-
GC	23/09/75	2	Bangor	H	D	0	0	(won 5-4 on penalties)
GC	07/10/75	SF	Coleraine	A	L	0	2	-
CC*	15/10/75	F	Linfield	A	W	3	1	Jamison 3
CC	18/10/75		Ballymena United	A	W	2	1	Feeney 2
CC	25/10/75		Cliftonville	H	D	4	4	Feeney 2, Moreland, Large
CC	01/11/75		Coleraine	A	D	2	2	Dickinson, Feeney (p)
CC	08/11/75		Crusaders	A	L	1	3	Feeney
CC	15/11/75		Larne	H	L	2	3	Feeney 2
IL	22/11/75		Ballymena United	A	W	2	1	W.Caskey, Jamison
IL	29/11/75		Distillery	H	W	3	0	Feeney 2, Jamison
IL	06/12/75		Bangor	A	L	0	2	-
IL	13/12/75		Portadown	H	W	1	0	Feeney
IL	20/12/75		Cliftonville	A	W	4	2	Feeney 2, J.Caskey, W.Caskey
IL	26/12/75		Linfield	H	W	2	1	Feeney 2(1p)
IL	27/12/75		Larne	H	D	1	1	J.Caskey
IL	01/01/76		Ards	A	W	3	0	Feeney (p), Craig, W.Caskey
IL	03/01/76		Crusaders	A	D	2	2	W.Caskey, Feeney
IL	10/01/76		Glenavon	H	W	2	0	Guy 2
IL	17/01/76		Coleraine	A	W	1	0	Jamison
IL	24/01/76		Ballymena United	H	W	5	2	Feeney 3 (1p), W.Caskey, Jamison
IL	07/02/76		Distillery	A	W	5	0	Guy, Feeney 2(1p), Jamison, J.Caskey
IL	14/02/76		Bangor	H	W	3	0	Jamison 2, W.Caskey
IL	28/02/76		Portadown	A	W	2	0	Feeney, Guy
IL	06/03/76		Cliftonville	H	W	4	1	Feeney, Walsh, McGuicken og, Guy
IL	20/03/76		Linfield	A	W	2	1	Feeney, Moreland
IL	27/03/76		Larne	A	L	1	2	Feeney (p)
IL	03/04/76		Ards	H	L	2	3	W.Caskey, Moreland
IL	17/04/76		Crusaders	H	L	0	1	-
IL	19/04/76		Glenavon	A	D	1	1	Feeney (p)
IL	24/04/76		Coleraine	H	D	2	2	Dickinson, Robson
IC	31/01/76	1	Distillery	A	W	2	0	Guy, Jamison
IC	21/02/76	2	Cliftonville	H	W	3	1	Guy, Feeney, Jamison
IC	13/03/76	SF	Linfield	H	L	0	2	-
CAS	27/04/76	1	Carrick Rangers	A	L	1	3	Moreland

* = held over from 1974/5

Glentoran mouths. The Crues' defence was magnificent in subduing Feeney and Jamison, with Roy McDonald and Robert Strain particularly outstanding. At the other end Ronnie McAteer scored the only goal of the game thirty seconds into the second half with a near post header. Crusaders manager Billy Johnston stated that the league was over and Glens' fans could not believe how we had thrown away the title after so much good work. "This match should never have mattered!" was one poignant comment as the terraces emptied. Near the end Alec Robson was sent off for aiming a kick at Paul Kirk. Kirk lay writhing in mock agony but by then the damage had been done.

The Crues duly became champions on Easter Monday when winning 2-0 at Larne while we were held to a draw at Glenavon. Coleraine then came to the Oval on the Saturday knowing a win would gain them a UEFA Cup spot at our expense. Des Dickson put the visitors 2-0 up and our fourth consecutive home defeat was on he cards. However Peter Dickinson pulled a goal back before half-time and then, with only thirteen minutes left, Robson equalised in a scramble and ensured the runners-up spot and European qualification to everyone's relief.

There was still time for one last defeat in the County Antrim Shield at Taylor's Avenue. Carrick, still buoyant after their Irish Cup success, led us 2-1 at the interval. The second half brought constant pressure from the Glens but only produced a parade of incredible near misses and bad luck. Gary Reid sealed Carrick's win in the last minute to bring a calamitous season to an end. Bobby McGregor released Billy Stewart and Denis Guy as part of a clear out.

More bad news came in June with the death of chairman John Dornan, a figure who would be sadly missed at the club.

Appearances and Goals

	App.	Subs.	Goals		App.	Subs.	Goals
McCullough T.	46			Dickinson	9	3	4
Walsh	46		1	McIlwaine	8		
Feeney	45		37	Kennedy	7	5	1
Robson	44		4	Caskey J.	6	7	3
Jamison	43	1	15	Clarke D.	5	3	1
Caskey W.	41	1	11	Dalzell	1		
Craig	40		1	Allely	1		
Dougan	39	3		Large	1	1	1
McCreery Rab	36		1	Unknown	11		
Moreland	30	2	6	Own Goals			1
McFall R.	26						
Stewart W.	17			TOTAL	517	26	94
Guy	15		7				

Footnote:
Two unconfirmed friendlies from the mid-1970s have also been traced. They are:
1972/3 Northern Ireland Youth XI 2, Glentoran 7
1974/5 Dundela 4, Glentoran 1

1976/77

Undefeated at home – Linfield thrashed twice - No mistakes in League race

For the first time in five years we played a pre-season friendly and probably wished we hadn't! Our opponents were Rolls Royce from the Amateur League and in a match to open their new grounds at Dundonald we incredibly lost 0-1. All credit went to the juniors goalkeeper, J. Wallace, for a brilliant display. Worse still Johnny Jamison received an injury during the game and missed the early part of the season.

Manager Bobby McGregor used the opportunity to assess all players including some of our new signings. These were midfielder / defender Tom McVeigh (ex-Linfield), goalkeeper Denis Matthews (ex-Ards) and centre-forwards Alan Hay (ex-Crusaders) and shipyard worker Freddie Devine. Off the field there were changes too, Tom McNeice was installed as the new chairman with Walter McFarland as his second in command, while John Crossan and Raymond Hall joined the board. Sandy Chambers was appointed as club treasurer.

As the long hot summer of 1976 reached its twilight the Glens commenced the Ulster Cup in spectacular form. Despite missing the suspended Robson we triumphed 2-0 at Coleraine and four nights later completely hammered the Blues 6-2 at the Oval. For Warren Feeney it was a personal triumph, four goals and a fifth deflected in by Frankie Parkes. The only solace for a demoralised Linfield camp was an excellent free-kick strike by Davy Graham in the last minute.

From these heady heights we plummeted dramatically to single goal defeats at Ards and Glenavon in the next week before re-discovering our scoring form against Distillery. Again Feeney was the main man with another four goal blitz which prompted some sections of the press to label us a "one man band". To offset this Alan Hay made his debut against the Whites but the big striker's spell at the Oval was to be marred by a lack of interest in training and things never worked out. Indeed at one stage the club suspended Hay.

That man Feeney was at it again on the Wednesday putting us 2-0 up over Crusaders before they fought back to draw. Then goalscorer Billy Caskey earned the man of the match award in a narrow win at Solitude to leave the Ulster Cup table as follows after seven of the eleven games:

1. Portadown 11 points, 2=. Larne and Glenavon 10, 3=. Glentoran and Linfield 9.

The next visitors to the Oval were F.C. Basle of Switzerland in the UEFA Cup. It was a game we should have won handsomely but two unfortunate blunders by keeper Trevor McCullough allowed the Swiss to contain our victory margin to 3-2. McCullough's display lost him his place to Matthews and a spell away from football to "think things over". Happily he returned later in the season to fight for the jersey.

Two convincing domestic wins, including an amazing second half scoring spree of seven goals at Bangor, set us up for the return leg in Basle at the end of September. The Swiss were a completely different outfit on their own patch compared to that seen at the Oval and for long spells they played us off the park with neat, intricate football. Two goals in two minutes just before half-time swung the tie their way and Basle eventually progressed to round two on a 5-3 aggregate. There they lost 2-4 to Athletic Bilbao.

The Glens suffered travel delays on the return journey, indeed the club tried to have our Saturday fixture postponed. However the official party's problems would have meant little to the band of twelve supporters from the Ballymacarrett Supporters Club who undertook the 3,000 mile round trip to see the game via boat and mini-bus!

Remarkably we showed no sign of weariness in overcoming Larne at Inver Park and this result set up an intriguing final Saturday in the Ulster Cup. The equation was simple – we had to beat Portadown at home to win the cup – any other result would allow the Ports to take the trophy. A large crowd turned up to create the requisite atmosphere and Billy Neill made an interesting prophecy in the Gazette when stating, "Portadown's Cleary, Murray and Blackledge have a bright future in the game."

The match itself was fast and furious, cut and thrust, but we emerged to be interval leaders with goals from Dickinson and Feeney. Portadown fought back to level it at 2-2 through Blackledge and Cleary but with only nine minutes remaining the defining moment occurred. Caskey fired in a shot for which the referee gave a goal but the Ports defence claimed the ball never fully crossed the line. However the score stood and so we clinched the Ulster Cup on goal difference from both Portadown and Linfield.

Five weeks later Glentoran could also place the Gold Cup on the Oval sideboard. The competition kicked-off in mid-October using the old City Cup groups format. We strolled through our Section A games in masterly form, scoring sixteen times in the process as Feeney took his personal tally for the season to 26 by the first week of November. The game with Bangor was notable for two players of the same name appearing on either side – Johnny Jamison for us and Johnny Jameson for the Seasiders. Although finishing on the losing side the younger Jameson had the pleasure of scoring with his first touch after coming on as a substitute.

During the Gold Cup Caskey was our best player as he covered every blade of the proverbial grass. Victor Moreland was not far behind as he settled beautifully into his new "sweeper" role, attracting an alleged offer of £16,000 from Sheffield United. The displays must have been pleasing for new first team assistant manager Bimbo Weatherup, but not so for Tommy Craig who could not get into the team and was transferred to Cliftonville.

Linfield were our Gold Cup final opponents at Windsor Park and we were to hand out another hiding to the Blues in this match! With our midfield and forward line on the rampage we raced into a 4-0 half-time lead and at the conclusion ran out 5-1 winners. For Linfield it was a case of total humiliation and despair, compounded when their player-manager Roy Coyle was rushed to hospital with a suspected broken arm.

Our excellent form continued in the early Irish League fixtures and five straight victories extended our consecutive winning sequence to 16 games. Cliftonville were the last victims as our unrelenting pressure football broke their defence in the first half hour despite the heroics of visiting keeper Brian Johnston. The run came to an end at Windsor Park on Christmas Day when a much-improved Linfield gained some revenge with a 3-0 win. Again Alec Robson was sent off, this time for kicking the ball away after being booked.

Glenavon emerged as our nearest challengers for top spot in early 1977 and after pulsating wins over Ards and Crusaders we travelled to meet the Lurgan Glens on 15th January. During the game we held 75% of the play but he issue was settled by a controversial decision in our penalty box. Ronnie McFall tangled with Paul Malone and the Glenavon man appeared to take a dive. "I never touched him", protested McFall afterwards but referee Jack Lorimer had thought otherwise. The resultant spot kick enabled the home side to win and go two points clear at the top of the table. This was increased to four a week later as we were frozen off at Ballymena (the decision to postpone made only forty minutes before kick-off) and Glenavon won 2-0 at Bangor.

The team's thoughts turned temporarily to the Irish Cup and our big first round home tie with Linfield, a repeat of the previous season's semi-final. McGregor's plans were almost wrecked by injury and suspension as he drafted youngsters Steven O'Neill and Paul McCreery (brother of Rab) into mid-field and moved Billy Caskey to centre-half. Predictably the tie was fiercely contested but the Blues looked to have edged it 1-0 until Caskey, thrown forward in the dying minutes, snatched an injury time equaliser. The Oval erupted but Linfield made no mistake in the replay when a Peter Rafferty header sent them on the way to another 3-0 win.

Back to the league and Glenavon conveniently lost their next two games while we won our three (including the re-arranged fixture at Ballymena) to move two points clear with eight games left. Before that game at the Showgrounds the large crowd observed a two minutes silence in memory of Glentoran assistant trainer and kit-man, Frankie Roberts, who had died earlier in the week after 35 years of service.

Results 1976/77

Played 46. Won 34. Drew 4. Lost 8. Goals For 117. Against 53. % 78.3.
Honours: Irish League, Ulster Cup, Gold Cup

UC	21/08/76		Coleraine	A	W	2	0	Feeney 2(1p)
UC	25/08/76		Linfield	H	W	6	2	Feeney 4, Moreland, Parkes og
UC	28/08/76		Glenavon	A	L	1	2	Campbell
UC	01/09/76		Ards	A	L	0	1	-
UC	04/09/76		Distillery	H	W	5	2	Dickinson, Feeney 4(2p)
UC	08/09/76		Crusaders	H	D	2	2	Feeney 2
UC	11/09/76		Cliftonville	A	W	1	0	W.Caskey
UC	18/09/76		Ballymena United	H	W	4	1	Dougan, Hay, Jamison, Feeney
UC	25/09/76		Bangor	A	W	9	1	Feeney 2(1p), Dickinson 3(1p), Jamison, W.Caskey, Devine 2
UC	02/10/76		Larne	A	W	3	1	Dickinson, Feeney (p), W.Caskey
UC	09/10/76		Portadown	H	W	3	2	Dickinson, Feeney, W.Caskey
UEFA	14/09/76	1.1	F.C. Basle	H	W	3	2	Feeney 2, Dickinson
UEFA	29/09/76	1.2	F.C. Basle	A	L	0	3	-
GC	16/10/76		Ards	A	W	3	1	Robson, Feeney (p), W.Caskey
GC	23/10/76		Glenavon	A	W	5	2	Feeney 3(1p), Dickinson, Jamison
GC	30/10/76		Bangor	H	W	3	1	Dickinson, Feeney 2
GC	06/11/76		Distillery	A	W	3	1	Jamison, Feeney, Dickinson
GC	13/11/76		Portadown	H	W	2	0	Keatley og, Willis og
GC	23/11/76	F	Linfield	A	W	5	1	Jamison, Feeney 2(1p), Dickinson, W.Caskey
IL	20/11/76		Ballymena United	H	W	3	1	Dickinson, Walsh, Moreland
IL	27/11/76		Distillery	A	W	4	2	Feeney 2, Dickinson, Jamison
IL	04/12/76		Bangor	H	W	1	0	Jamison
IL	11/12/76		Portadown	A	W	2	0	W.Caskey 2
IL	18/12/76		Cliftonville	H	W	5	0	Dickinson 2, Robson, W.Caskey, Feeney
IL	25/12/76		Linfield	A	L	0	3	-
IL	28/12/76		Coleraine	A	D	0	0	-
IL	01/01/77		Ards	H	W	3	0	Jamison, Dickinson, W.Caskey
IL	08/01/77		Crusaders	H	W	2	1	Feeney 2(1p)
IL	15/01/77		Glenavon	A	L	0	1	-
IL	22/01/77		Larne	H	W	3	1	Feeney 2, Robson
IL	12/02/77		Distillery	H	W	3	0	Feeney (p), Walsh, W.Caskey
IL	19/02/77		Bangor	A	W	4	1	Feeney 2(1p), Jamison, McVeigh
IL	26/02/77		Ballymena United	A	W	4	0	Feeney 2(1p), Jamison, McCreery
IL	05/03/77		Portadown	H	W	3	1	W.Caskey, McCreery, Dickinson
IL	12/03/77		Cliftonville	A	W	3	1	Jamison, Feeney, Dickinson
IL	26/03/77		Linfield	H	W	2	0	Feeney 2(1p)
IL	02/04/77		Coleraine	H	W	4	2	W.Caskey 2, Jamison, Dickinson
IL	09/04/77		Ards	A	W	1	0	McVeigh
IL	11/04/77		Crusaders	A	L	0	2	-
IL	16/04/77		Glenavon	H	W	1	0	Feeney
IL	30/04/77		Larne	A	D	2	2	O'Neill, Feeney (p)
IC	05/02/77	1	Linfield	H	D	1	1	W.Caskey
IC	08/02/77	1R	Linfield	A	L	0	3	-
CAS	06/05/77	2	Cliftonville	A	W	2	1	Feeney (p), Robson
CAS	09/05/77	SF	Bangor	H	W	3	1	Feeney, O'Neill, Jamison
CAS	14/05/77	F	Linfield	A	L	1	3	McCreery
F	14/08/76		Rolls Royce	A	L	0	1	-
F	23/05/77		Northern Ireland XI	H	D	1	1	Feeney (p) Bobby McGregor Testimonial

During March the team went from strength to strength with Tom McVeigh in particular dominating matters from midfield. The month culminated with an excellent 2-0 win over Linfield at a sodden Oval – incidentally on the same day that an official souvenir shop was opened at the ground. Sheffield United now expressed an interest in both Moreland and Caskey, upping their offer to £50,000, but the club did not want to lose any players at such a key stage of the season.

Glenavon's challenge faded in early April and when a brilliant McVeigh volley gave us victory at Ards we required only two points from our last three games to become champions. On Easter Monday however, Crusaders ensured that the champagne stayed on ice by beating us 2-0. We even failed to convert a penalty, McDonald saving Jamison's effort. Five days later that was all forgotten when a Warren Feeney goal in the 67th minute at the Oval was enough to defeat Glenavon and bring the title back to the club after all the disappointment of twelve months earlier. At the final whistle hundreds of fans invaded the pitch and smothered both the players and Bobby McGregor – what a way for the popular physiotherapist to complete his spell as manager and seventeen years at the club.

With the league won NIPFA player of the year Caskey went on trial to Tottenham and we fielded an experimental team in the final game at Larne. Feeney had to come off the bench to score our equaliser in the second half after we had trailed to two Colin McCurdy goals.

The competitive season concluded with the County Antrim Shield. We came through a bruising first round encounter at Solitude and overcame a youthful Bangor side to earn a final place against Linfield. In the final Rab McCreery opened the scoring, a dramatic 70 yard solo effort from the full-back, but the Blues, with Billy Hamilton on top form, came back to win. This victory for them enabled Coyle to claim his first trophy as a manager.

There was one last big night of the season at the Oval when Bobby McGregor's testimonial match against the Northern Ireland Home Championship squad took place on 23rd May. The choice of opposition was highly appropriate as McGregor had also served the national team as physio for many years. Over 8,000 were present to witness McVeigh turn a Sammy McIlroy corner into his own net to give Northern Ireland an early lead but just before half-time Feeney was brought down by Jim Platt and from the resultant penalty Warren equalised. There was no further scoring after the break and so we maintained our unbeaten home record against all teams for the entire season.

The day before the McGregor match the board announced the appointment of ex-player Arthur Stewart at the new manager for season 1977/8. The past had not been forgotten either as a dinner was organised to mark the ten year anniversary of the Detroit Cougars.

Appearances and Goals

	App.	Subs.	Goals		App.	Subs.	Goals
McCreery Rab	45		3	Devine	9	4	2
McFall R.	45			McCullough T.	8		
McVeigh	41	1	2	O'Neill	8	1	2
Feeney	41	2	47	Hay	5	1	1
Robson	39		4	Campbell	2	3	1
Moreland	38	2	2	McCreery P.	2		
Caskey W.	38	2	15	Ritchie		1	
Jamison	38	2	13	Unknown	11		
Matthews D.	37			Own Goals			3
Walsh	36		2				
Dickinson	34	3	19	TOTAL	506	27	117
Dougan	29	5	1				

1977/78

Hopes for further success at the Oval were high in August 1977. We were defending league champions and had appointed tactician Arthur Stewart as player-manager. Since returning to the province from Derby County Stewart boasted managerial experience at Bangor, Cliftonville, Distillery and latterly Ballymena, as well as a spell in America. In addition our new UEFA standard floodlights had been installed, at a cost of around £12,000, to enable the Oval to create once again the special atmosphere of evening games.

There was a slight change to the team's playing kit, green socks replacing the previous white. In terms of playing personnel Stewart's only major signing was midfielder Quinton McFall from Ballymena. Paul McCreery left to join Crusaders. The Seconds would be missing a couple of familiar faces as their captain Perry Galbraith emigrated to Canada but

Jamison shoots against Juventus.

more sadly their former coach, Hugh "Bud" McFarland had passed away in the summer.

In preparation for the competitive season we completed an unbeaten series of friendly matches stretching from Sligo to Moyola. Stewart was pleased with the performances of all the players in these games.

Steve O'Neill got the season off to a great start by netting only 36 seconds into our opening fixture with Glenavon. Despite achieving success in this fixture we only recorded one more win in the next five games. Injuries to Feeney, Dickinson, Moreland, McVeigh and Rab McCreery were cited but ominous signs were emerging.

The floodlights were switched on for the first time for the second half of the Friday night Linfield game but this only enabled the Blues to inflict on us our first home defeat since April 1976, ending a 25 match unbeaten Oval run. Director John Crossan was praised for his efforts in installing the lights and there were some calls for full international games to be played in East Belfast, something that had not been done since 1920 against Wales, instead of the late afternoon kick-offs at Windsor Park!

Centre-half Alex Robson returned from suspension at Coleraine but was unable to prevent Des Dickson making it a happy night for the Bannsiders to the tune of 4-1. With this indifferent domestic form behind us it was with some trepidation that we undertook the journey to Iceland for our first round European Cup tie with Valur. Our opponents had supplied six players to their national team who had beaten Northern Ireland 1-0 in June so they were no mugs. Thus it proved as, in front of 3,000, we also went down 0-1. Stewart, however, was confident of progress as the goals scored by Magnus Bergs only came about as a result of a defensive mix-up.

Before the return leg we gained Ulster Cup wins over Cliftonville and Distillery. This encouraged a crowd of over 7,000 to come to the Oval on a damp Thursday night to watch the Glens, in green, take on the Icelanders. Under the spectacular lights we dominated from start to finish and only the efforts of Siggi Dagsson in the Valur goal kept the score down.

The two goals required came courtesy of Robson and Dagsson himself, when he mispunched an in-swinging Johnny Jamison corner. It was an excellent result against a tall physical side and we were rewarded with a plum second round tie against the giants of the Italian league, Juventus.

This news inspired our players as we played flowing inventive football to overcome Ballymena 4-1, but defeat at Ards to an 88th minute penalty meant we only finished fifth in the Ulster Cup, five points off the pace. Billy Caskey rued hitting the post when faced with an open goal in that Ards game, but this did not prevent him being picked in the Northern Ireland squad for the return World Cup qualifier with Iceland.

The Oval was packed to the rafters, different sources give the attendance anywhere between 25,000 and 40,000, for the visit of Juventus on 19th October 1977. Their line-up read like a Who's Who of Italian football with stars such as Dino Zoff, Cuccuredu, Antonio Cabrini, Claudio Gentile, Romeo Benetti, Marco Tardelli, Scirea, Franco Causio, Roberta Boninsegna and the grey haired Roberto Bettega. Even their substitute Pietra Virdis cost over £1 million. The Glens players gave their all in the face of such odds and only conceded one goal, a rasping drive from Causio in the 38th minute following a misplaced header by Ronnie McFall. Then, with barely five minutes remaining, the crowd erupted when Stewart was brought down and the referee awarded a penalty. Up stepped Warren Feeney, in his testimonial season, but his uncharacteristically weak effort was comfortably saved by Zoff and so we were denied a draw.

The return leg in Turin was mainly a case of shooting-in practice for the Italians as they recorded an easy 5-0 win in the Stadio Communale. Denis Matthews had 34 shots to deal with but gained his reward at the finish when he swapped jerseys with his opposite number Zoff. Indeed for the rest of the season Matthews appeared in the grey jersey, earning the obvious nickname of "Dino" in the process.

Our poor disciplinary record worsened in the Gold Cup as Rab McCreery was sent off as we crashed to defeat at Ballymena. Displays then immediately improved and we rattled off four consecutive wins to top our Section. Victor Moreland's impressive form persuaded QPR to take him on trial for a week but no offer ever materialised. Feeney rediscovered his shooting boots against Larne, scoring all our four goals, but that day marked the end of the Glentoran career of Alec Robson. Robson had been involved in an off the ball incident with Gerry O'Kane, which left the Larne player with a broken nose. Given Robson's previously poor record of offences the directors placed him on the transfer list. Initially there was a mixed reaction to this among Glentoran supporters but when Robson played in the Glenavon team who beat us 2-1 in the league his antics of giving "the fingers" to the directors' box and to fans behind the net united all in the belief that this decision was best for the club.

Glentoran easily won the Gold Cup final over Glenavon (3-1) without Robson and the suspended McCreery. However the night was marred by the actions of some hooligans who invaded the main

The Glentoran squad at the Juventus training camp.

stand and proceeded to wreck the stadium. Seats, wire netting and panels were all destroyed as the name of the club was dragged through the mire.

In the first half of this season the club was vigourously pursuing a youth policy. Scouts Jim Rodgers and Billy Spence recruited many players in the 14 to 17 age group including Ron Manley, Ricky Adair, Alan McFall, David Jeffrey and a fourth footballing McCreery brother, Ron. George Magill's Olympic side went to town scoring 15 goals in one Barry Cup match and recording other big victories over Crusaders Thirds (11-1) and Jordanstown Youth Club (10-5). Unsurprisingly our attempts to re-establish the old Irish League C Division met with resistance from other clubs!

For the first time ever the Irish League became a sponsored competition, backed by the Fiat Motor Group. They generously set up a £10,000 prize fund with £2,500 to go to the champions and other awards including a £250 cheque for the highest scoring team each month. Furthermore, every player scoring a hat-trick in a league game would receive a case of whisky. All this coincided with the first reported increase in attendances at local games for six seasons.

We began the league campaign well with five straight wins and twenty goals. Peter Dickinson replaced the injured Feeney for the Cliftonville game and put away a nap-hand of five goals. Dickinson signalled his intentions to the crowd bearing that whisky prize in mind on completion of his hat-trick! Linfield also won their opening five fixtures and this set up an eagerly awaited Big Two Boxing Day clash at the Oval. The Glens wrested the early initiative, Caskey opening the scoring while many fans were still queuing at the turnstiles. Dickinson made it 2-0 just before the break but in the second half the Blues turned it round and a famous hat-trick of goals in the 54th, 66th and 89th minutes by Jim Martin gave them a 3-2 victory.

We recovered from this set back to pick up five more points from the three games at the turn of the year before suffering defeat at Glenavon. The game was soured even more for us as Feeney missed another penalty and there was an offside doubt over the home side's winner. Linfield failed to take full advantage but their 2-2 draw with Portadown stretched their lead to three points at the half-way mark. At the end of January Feeney became the third Glenman to receive a case of Scotch when he put four past Coulter of Bangor.

The first round of the Irish Cup gave us an interesting tie with the RUC. The police were the B Division's leading scorers but were no match for us, Dickinson another hat-trick in our 5-1 win. The same day gave a poignant reminder of the troubles in Ulster as a woman was killed and a policeman injured as a result of a shooting incident outside Seaview after the Crusaders-Ballymena tie.

The remainder of February was equally depressing for us as our league hopes nose-dived with defeat at Solitude (Dickinson sent off for arguing with Malcolm Moffatt over the

Team Group 1977/8 Back Row: Arthur Stewart, Andy Dougan, Victor Moreland, Ronnie McFall, Denis Matthews, Peter Dickinson, Rab McCreery, Bobby McGregor Front Row: Warren Feeney, Johnny Jamison, Billy Caskey, Alec Robson, Quinton McFall, Roy Walsh.

non-award of a penalty) and a loss to Linfield in the Irish Cup for the third year running. That tie was a real thriller, scant consolation for Glenmen though as we went down by the odd goal in seven.

Many agreed that the team's problems were due to the lack of a rugged centre-half to replace Robson. Even Arthur Stewart filled in at the back but supporters were becoming increasingly

Valur's Siggi Dagsson foils Dickinson.

agitated by some of the goals conceded. One welcome returning face at the club was Billy McKeag who began turning out at full-back for the Seconds.

Realistically, all we could play for was UEFA Cup qualification and, helped by the consistent displays of our "unsung" defenders Ronnie McFall and Roy Walsh, this target became likely as the league went into its home straight. We eventually completed the signing of Bangor centre-half Sammy Cranston and the 6'2" man had a scoring debut at Portadown. Our title hopes were briefly rekindled when a commanding midfield performance enabled us to beat the Blues 2-1 at Windsor but the league was conceded two weeks later at Ards when we could only manage a 1-1 draw. Rab McCreery was sent off again (along with Tom Armstrong) in this match just eleven days after being dismissed at Larne for kicking ex-Glenman Fred Devine.

At the end of March Billy Caskey went to America in time for the start of the NASL season with Tulsa Roughnecks. A fortnight later Victor Moreland joined him. These moves gave young Eddie Houston a first team run and he celebrated with a scoring debut against Coleraine. His marker in this game was none other than Alec Robson, then with his third club of the season. Sammy Beattie made his first appearance against Glenavon and our league campaign concluded with an entertaining 3-3 draw with the Crues at Seaview. Feeney again failed from the spot, Roy McDonald making a good save with twelve minutes to go.

Turning to the County Antrim Shield we had an easy first round passage over Steel and Sons Cup winners Downpatrick Rec., to set up a quarter-final meeting with Cliftonville at Solitude. In the late 1970s the success created by manager Jackie Hutton attracted to the Reds the dormant Belfast catholic support, soon to become known as the "Red Army". This Shield tie was the first occasion that nastiness crept in from the terraces. Although we had controlled the first half Cliftonville went in 1-0 up. During the break sets of rival supporters began singing party songs and when the teams returned Denis Matthews was struck by a stone. The Glentoran players came off the field and our officials refused to complete the tie, threatening never to play at Solitude again. The game was abandoned but Glentoran supporters were stoned when leaving the ground and many letters of complaint appeared in the "Ulster" regarding the inadequate protection. The County Antrim F.A. ruled that the game must be replayed at Ards' Castlereagh Park but the Cliftonville board decided to withdraw from the competition.

Before the Shield resumed in mid-May the latest All-Ireland competition got underway. Sponsored by shoe company Tylers, it was the brainchild of Finn Harps' chairman Fran Fields and was open to teams finishing in the top four in the Irish League and League of Ireland. We received a first round home draw to Bohemians. On May Day afternoon the Bohs were delayed on their way to the ground and maybe this could partially explain their poor performance as a Feeney hat-trick saw them off 4-1. It was a different story against Finn Harps in the semis when we pressurised their defence constantly but could not find a way of beating their inspired keeper Mahon. The Donegal side, conquerors of Linfield in Round One, scored the game's only goal in a rare breakaway.

Results 1977/78

Played 50. Won 32. Drew 5. Lost 13. Goals For 121. Against 63. % 69.0.
Honours: Gold Cup, County Antrim Shield

UC	20/08/77		Glenavon	H	W	3	1	O'Neill, R.McFall, Jamison
UC	23/08/77		Larne	A	D	1	1	W.Caskey
UC	26/08/77		Linfield	H	L	1	2	Jamison
UC	30/08/77		Coleraine	A	L	1	4	Dougan
UC	03/09/77		Bangor	H	W	2	1	W.Caskey, Feeney
UC	10/09/77		Portadown	A	L	3	4	Robson, Feeney 2(1p)
UC	17/09/77		Cliftonville	H	W	2	0	Feeney (p), W.Caskey
UC	24/09/77		Distillery	A	W	4	1	Robson, Moreland, W.Caskey, Dickinson
UC	01/10/77		Crusaders	A	W	2	1	Jamison, Feeney (p)
UC	08/10/77		Ballymena United	H	W	4	1	Jamison 2, Feeney 2(1p)
UC	15/10/77		Ards	A	L	0	1	-
EC	15/09/77	1.1	Valur	A	L	0	1	-
EC	29/09/77	1.2	Valur	H	W	2	0	Robson, Daggson og
EC	19/10/77	2.1	Juventus	H	L	0	1	-
EC	02/11/77	2.2	Juventus	A	L	0	5	-
GC	22/10/77		Ballymena United	A	L	1	2	W.Caskey
GC	29/10/77		Cliftonville	H	W	4	1	W.Caskey, Moreland, Q.McFall, Walsh
GC	05/11/77		Coleraine	A	W	2	0	Feeney 2(1p)
GC	12/11/77		Crusaders	A	W	4	0	Dickinson, Moreland, W.Caskey, Robson
GC	19/11/77		Larne	H	W	4	2	Feeney 4
GC	23/11/77	F	Glenavon	WPW		3	1	Feeney, Jamison, Dickinson
IL	26/11/77		Bangor	A	W	4	0	Moreland, Feeney 2, W.Caskey
IL	03/12/77		Cliftonville	H	W	5	0	Dickinson 5
IL	10/12/77		Ballymena United	A	W	2	0	O'Neill, Dickinson
IL	17/12/77		Portadown	H	W	2	1	W.Caskey 2
IL	24/12/77		Distillery	A	W	5	0	W.Caskey 3, Moreland, Dickinson
IL	26/12/77		Linfield	H	L	2	3	W.Caskey, Dickinson
IL	31/12/77		Larne	H	W	1	0	Feeney (p)
IL	02/01/78		Coleraine	A	D	1	1	W.Caskey
IL	07/01/78		Ards	H	W	4	2	Feeney 2, Walsh, Moreland
IL	14/01/78		Glenavon	A	L	1	2	Dickinson
IL	21/01/78		Crusaders	H	W	4	1	Dickinson 2, Jamison, Walsh
IL	28/01/78		Bangor	H	W	6	1	Feeney 4, Jamison, W.Caskey
IL	11/02/78		Cliftonville	A	L	1	3	Dougan
IL	04/03/78		Portadown	A	W	4	1	Cranston, Q.McFall, Jamison, W.Caskey
IL	07/03/78		Ballymena United	H	W	2	0	Dickinson, Jamison
IL	11/03/78		Distillery	H	D	2	2	Feeney, Moreland
IL	25/03/78		Linfield	A	W	2	1	Feeney (p), Moreland
IL	28/03/78		Larne	A	W	1	0	W.Caskey
IL	01/04/78		Coleraine	H	W	4	1	Jamison, Moreland, Feeney (p), Houston
IL	08/04/78		Ards	A	D	1	1	Feeney
IL	15/04/78		Glenavon	H	W	2	0	Jamison, Feeney (p)
IL	22/04/78		Crusaders	A	D	3	3	Feeney, Strain og, Cranston
IC	04/02/78	1	R.U.C.	H	W	5	1	Dickinson 3, W.Caskey, J.Caskey
IC	25/02/78	2	Linfield	A	L	3	4	Feeney 2(1p), Jamison

CAS	20/04/78	1	Downpatrick Rec.	H	W	3	0	Feeney 2, Walsh
CAS	26/04/78	2	Cliftonville	A	A	0	1	Abandoned at half time. Cliftonville withdrew.
CAS	13/05/78	SF	Distillery	H	W	3	2	Feeney 3
CAS	16/05/78	F	Crusaders	WPW		1	0	Feeney
TC	01/05/78	1	Bohemians	H	W	4	1	Feeney 3, Cranston
TC	01/05/78	SF	Finn Harps	H	L	0	1	-
F	06/08/77		Sligo Rovers	A	D	2	2	Dickinson, Jamison (won 5-4 on penalties)
F	09/08/77		Chimney Corner	A	W	3	1	Hay, W.Caskey, O'Neill
F	11/08/77		Annalong Rangers	A	W	4	1	Unknown
F	16/08/77		Dundela	H	W	3	0	Moreland, W.Caskey, Dougan (p)

The season did end on a high note however as we lifted the County Antrim Shield beating Crusaders in the final after an exciting semi-final win over Distillery. Feeney's four goals in these games took him to 40 for the season and made him the league's highest overall scorer for 1977/8.

Appearances and Goals

	App.	Subs.	Goals		App.	Subs.	Goals
McFall R.	47		1	Cranston	12		3
Walsh	47		4	Houston	6		1
Matthews D.	46			Hay	4		
Jamison	44	1	13	Beattie	3		
McFall Q.	42	1	2	Matthews A.	2	2	
Moreland	39		9	McVeigh	2	1	
Caskey W.	37		19	Caskey J.	2	4	1
Feeney	37		40	McCullough T.	1		
Dougan	35	2	2	Devine		6	
McCreery Rab	33	2		Unknown	33		
Dickinson	27	1	18	Own Goals			2
Stewart A.	17	2		TOTAL	550	28	121
Robson	17		4				
O'Neill	17	6	2				

1978/79

Commercial sponsorship – Team rebuilding – USA visitors

Two landmarks were to have a significant effect on Glentoran in the early part of the 1978/9 season. Firstly the club obtained its first official sponsors – the Wilson Motor Group. This enabled a cash injection to the club and in return the team strip was emblazoned with the sponsor's name and there were frequent displays of Mitsubishi Colt and Lancer cars at the Oval. David Chick, elected to the board to replace the late Billy Spence, was instrumental in setting up the deal.

On the negative side the successful playing team of the mid-seventies dramatically dissipated! Peter Dickinson and Trevor McCullough left to join Bangor and Glenavon respectively and there were strong rumours that Warren Feeney was unhappy with his contract terms and was threatening to either join Linfield or retire from the game. Caskey and Moreland were still in America with transfers to England imminent while Tom McVeigh was a long-term injury casualty and to cap it all Rab McCreery had received a severe 18-week suspension as a result of his three dismissals the previous season.

Arthur Stewart had no option but to introduce more youngsters such as Tom Stewart (signed from Luton Town Reserves and a brother of international David), Tom Dickey (signed from Sheffield United), Sammy Beattie, Tom Pearson, Norman Porter, Ronnie Carleton, David Anderson, Albert Matthews (brother of Denis) and John Caskey (brother of Billy).

Despite these obvious difficulties we remained unbeaten throughout a testing set of pre-season friendlies. This included a creditable 2-2 draw with Fulham, our first English visitors in over seven years. Feeney opened the scoring with a tremendous free-kick, his last goal for the Glens, and the Londoners had to equalise twice, the second a John Margerisson penalty.

We also drew our opening three Ulster Cup fixtures including a rare scoreless encounter with Linfield at Windsor Park. Before this game the players had threatened to go on strike over the with-holding of Feeney's benefit cheque. We finally achieved victory on 29th August against Coleraine – the goals coming from Eddie Houston on his 18th birthday, 16-year-old debutant Carleton and a disputed Vic Moreland effort two minutes from time. However just four days later we crashed at Bangor, where Terry Nicholson saved an Andy Dougan penalty, before setting off on our latest European adventure.

Our UEFA Cup opponents were IBV of Iceland, a team from the Vestmann islands off the coast of Reykjavik. We were fortunate to come away from the frozen North with a scoreless draw in the first leg having Matthews to thank for keeping the scoresheet blank. However the return home match evolved into a night to forget. We had comfortably controlled the game and as full-time approached led 1-0 thanks to a John Caskey goal just before the interval. Then, in a rare IBV breakaway, the ball was flashed across our goalmouth and the diving Oskarsson appeared to fist the ball into the net. The referee, Mr. Mulder, awarded a goal and so went out on the away goals rule! As the Icelanders were leaving the field one of their players, Frif Finnbogsson, was struck by a flag pole and needed several stitches in a head wound. UEFA subsequently fined the club £1,000 for the incident, a penalty many thought lenient.

In between those two matches we entertained visitors from further afield in the form of NASL side Tulsa Roughnecks, as part of their Ulster tour. Tulsa looked a poor side at the Oval and we tore them apart in the second half with Moreland and substitute Carleton outstanding. Surprisingly the Roughnecks, for whom Moreland and Caskey had played for the previous summer, were unbeaten in their other tour games.

Defeat at home to the Crues, even after Quentin McFall had opened the scoring in 35 seconds, condemned us to a mid-table position in the Ulster Cup. Around this time there was hectic Glentoran activity in the transfer market. Tommy Docherty signed Moreland and Caskey for Derby County in a joint deal valued at around £90,000. Feeney joined Linfield with lay-preacher Jim Martin coming to the Oval in part-exchange and we signed Barry Brown from Coleraine in a further attempt to improve our strike force. Billy McKeag came back into the first team, bringing with him much needed experience.

In the opening Gold Cup fixture we were completely demolished by Cliftonville at Solitude, in particular by the Reds teenage sensation Barney Bowers. Soon Bowers too was on his way to Derby were our dynamic duo had quickly broken into the first team, appeared on Match of the Day, and made their international debuts. We recovered from this initial defeat and there were signs that Martin and Brown were recreating their Ballymena scoring partnership of old. Unfortunately we lost out in the final table to Cliftonville on goal difference.

Arthur Stewart was appointed manager of the Irish League team for the one-off fixture against the Scottish League in Motherwell. Despite the heavy press criticism over his team selection, the side earned a creditable 1-1 draw. Roy Walsh, the season's beneficiary, was the only Glentoran player in Stewart's XI.

The Fiat Irish League opened with a scoring bonanza at Castlereagh Park. Ards were 2-0 up within ten minutes but we fought back to lead 4-3 before a late home equaliser. Our mini run of form was abruptly halted at Ballymena Showgrounds when, after taking the lead, we were thrashed 5-1. The team was clearly not good enough but at least Jim Martin was finding the net regularly (including a brilliant hat-trick against Crusaders) and McCreery returned after his 20 game suspension. Just before Christmas Arthur Stewart announced that he would be leaving the club to take up a coaching post in the USA with New Jersey Americans.

In early 1979 many games were postponed due to the inclement weather and the manager-less Glens first ran out for a fixture at Windsor Park on a Tuesday evening. It was to be a night of drama which kept the fans on tenterhooks throughout. Norman Porter put us ahead but from then on it was frustration for Norman as he had the ball in the net three more times only for them all to be disallowed for minor infringements by referee Jack

Team Group 1978/9 Back Row: David Chick, Cecil Leacock, Johnston Nelson, John Crossen, Jack Atkinson Middle Row: Stephen O'Neill, Sammy Cranston, Ronnie McFall, Denis Matthews, Barry Brown, Quinton McFall, Tom Stewart Front Row: Arthur Stewart, Ronnie Carleton, Andy Dougan, Johnny Jamison, Tom McNeice, Rab McCreery, Roy Walsh, Jimmy Martin, Bobby McGregor

Results 1978/79

Played 42. Won 16. Drew 15. Lost 11. Goals For 63. Against 60. % 56.0

UC	19/08/78		Glenavon	A	D	1	1	Moreland
UC	22/08/78		Larne	H	D	1	1	J.Caskey
UC	26/08/78		Linfield	A	D	0	0	-
UC	29/08/78		Coleraine	H	W	3	1	Houston, Carleton, Moreland
UC	02/09/78		Bangor	A	L	1	3	W.Caskey
UC	09/09/78		Portadown	H	W	2	0	Moreland, O'Neill
UC	16/09/78		Cliftonville	A	L	0	1	-
UC	23/09/78		Distillery	H	W	3	1	Houston, R.McFall, Jamison
UC	30/09/78		Crusaders	H	L	1	2	Q.McFall
UC	07/10/78		Ballymena United	A	W	2	1	Houston 2
UC	14/10/78		Ards	H	D	1	1	Martin
UEFA	05/09/78	1.1	I.B.V.	A	D	0	0	-
UEFA	14/09/78	1.2	I.B.V.	H	D	1	1	J.Caskey
GC	21/10/78		Cliftonville	A	L	1	4	Q.McFall
GC	28/10/78		Ballymena United	H	W	3	0	Brown, Martin 2
GC	04/11/78		Crusaders	H	W	2	1	Q.McFall, Martin (p)
GC	11/11/78		Larne	A	D	1	1	Brown
GC	18/11/78		Coleraine	H	W	2	1	Martin, Brown
IL	25/11/78		Ards	A	D	4	4	Cranston, Martin 2, Beattie
IL	09/12/78		Ballymena United	A	L	1	5	Martin
IL	16/12/78		Glenavon	H	D	2	2	O'Neill, Martin
IL	20/12/78		Crusaders	H	W	3	2	Martin 3(1p)
IL	23/12/78		Distillery	A	W	3	1	Martin, Q.McFall, Pearson
IL	26/12/78		Coleraine	H	W	2	1	Martin, Jamison
IL	30/12/78		Larne	H	L	0	2	-
IL	16/01/79		Linfield	A	L	1	2	Porter
IL	23/01/79		Bangor	H	W	3	2	Martin 2, T.Stewart
IL	10/02/79		Ards	H	W	1	0	Porter
IL	13/02/79		Portadown	H	W	1	0	Martin
IL	17/02/79		Crusaders	A	W	2	0	Porter, Martin
IL	20/02/79		Cliftonville	H	D	1	1	Blackledge
IL	27/02/79		Cliftonville	A	W	4	2	Porter, Martin, Blackledge, Dougan
IL	03/03/79		Ballymena United	H	W	2	0	Jamison, Blackledge
IL	10/03/79		Glenavon	A	L	2	3	Walsh, Houston
IL	24/03/79		Distillery	H	D	2	2	Jamison, Martin
IL	31/03/79		Coleraine	A	D	0	0	-
IL	07/04/79		Larne	A	D	1	1	Martin
IL	14/04/79		Linfield	H	D	1	1	Martin
IL	17/04/79		Bangor	A	D	0	0	-
IL	21/04/79		Portadown	A	L	0	2	-
IC	03/02/79	1	Larne	A	L	2	3	Porter, R.McFall
CAS	26/04/79	1	Ards	H	L	0	4	-
F	02/08/78		Fulham	H	D	2	2	Feeney, Houston
F	05/08/78		Bohemians	A	D	1	1	Burke og
F	12/08/78		Finn Harps	A	D	2	2	T.Stewart, Dougan (p)
F	07/09/78		Tulsa Roughnecks	H	W	5	1	Moreland 2, W.Caskey, J.Caskey, Beattie
F	17/03/79		Bangor	A	L	2	3	Moore, Houston

Roy Walsh / Stephen Feeney Benefit

Lorimer. At the other end Feeney, in his first match against us, equalised for the Blues and then in the dying seconds fired home the winner.

The board decided to "promote from within" as 30 year old left-back Ronnie McFall was appointed as the new manager on 22nd January with an 18 month contract. McFall began his reign with a win over Bangor thanks to a last minute Tom Stewart goal. Within a few days McFall had signed Portadown's 20 year-old centre-forward Gary Blackledge and there was even talk of Alec Robson returning to the Oval. The directors stuck to their guns on the previous decision despite Robson's willingness to play for the Glens again.

After a disappointing Irish Cup defeat at Larne (where Walsh obtained a broken nose and cheekbone) the remainder of February was a happy time. We picked up nine points from five league games including an excellent win at Solitude to move into second place in the table, just two points behind Linfield with eight games remaining. For his promising start McFall was named Fiat Manager of the Month. Glentoran Olympic kept up the good work as they beat Cregagh Swifts 6-3 in the re-arranged Youth Cup final at Wilgar Park (admission 25p). Dean Irvine and Ron McCreery were among the scorers in front of a four-figure crowd.

The Glens title hopes nose-dived at Glenavon on 10th March. Officials and supporters alike were seething at the performance of referee Malcolm Moffatt in this game as many blatant penalty appeals were turned down and Johnny Jamison was sent off. There were calls from all quarters for the IFA to do something about the standard of match officials.

Linfield lost their next match but we failed to take advantage and indeed did not record a win in any of our last seven league games. We dropped to a final placing of fourth in the table, having to settle for Fiat prize money of £750. Highlights for the Glens were few and far between in this dismal run, Jamison's 20 yard lob against Distillery and Terry Moore's midfield battling in the Linfield game two notable exceptions.

In mid-April the cool, skilful defender Roy Walsh became our latest export when he too went west and joined New Jersey in the NASL. Walsh could look back upon the season with personal satisfaction as he collected both the Ulster Footballer of the Year honour and also the NIPFA award. In addition he had a joint benefit match with Bangor full-back Stephen Feeney (Warren's brother) when we lost after holding a 2-0 interval lead. Walsh took the consolation of winning the half-time penalty shoot-out with Feeney by 4-3.

Our season finished with a heavy home defeat by Ards in the County Antrim Shield on an occasion when we fielded possibly the most youthful and inexperienced line-up in our history. A proposed friendly with Football League champions Nottingham Forest had to be cancelled due to their cup commitments and the Tylers All-Ireland Cup was held over to August due to similar pressure on dates.

Appearances and Goals

	App.	Subs.	Goals		App.	Subs.	Goals
Matthews D.	34			Brown	9		3
Cranston	32		1	Moreland	8		3
Dougan	30		1	Moore	8		
McFall R.	30		2	McCreery Ron	5	1	
Jamison	28		4	Caskey W.	5		1
Walsh	26		1	Carleton	3	2	1
Martin	22		22	Leslie	2	2	
McFall Q.	18	2	4	Beattie	2		1
Porter	17	1	5	Feeney	2		
O'Neill	15	3	2	Irvine	1		
McKeag	14			Dickey	1	1	
McCreery Rab	14	1		Pearson	1		1
Houston	13	1	5	Unknown	88		
Blackledge	13		3				
Stewart T.	12		1	TOTAL	162	14	63
Caskey J.	9		2				

1979/80

Hooliganism in Donegal – Young side struggles - Embarrassing Shield defeat

R onnie McFall set up his coaching regime for his first full season in charge. Davy Roberts was promoted to help Bobby McGregor with the 1st XI while Jim Weatherup would continue to look after the Seconds. The 3rd XI changed name to Glentoran Colts with Walter Bruce and George Magill at the helm. The Colts would also take part in the Dundonald Floodlit League. Club coach Bob Nesbitt was given the roving role of coaching responsibility for all three teams plus spying missions on forthcoming opponents.

McFall's attempts to strengthen the playing panel was hampered as targets such as Stephen McKee, Lindsay McKeown, Paul Malone, Trevor Anderson and Kevin Mahon were all either too expensive or wanted a high signing-on fee. The only addition to the senior panel was Glenavon's 23 year-old coloured midfielder Alan Gracey. Roy Walsh was appointed captain with Rab McCreery as vice and it was Andy Dougan's benefit season.

Season Tickets were priced at £14 (patron), £12 (member) and £7 ladies and boys. Those attending the Oval would have noticed a ten foot high fence, erected to hopefully prevent incidents like the one at the IBV game the previous season. The old spiked railings were purchased by Glenavon for use at Mourneview Park.

Bearded midfielder Tom McVeigh finally conceded his battle against injury and retired in October. Ironically he had picked up the knock in Bobby McGregor's testimonial game. McVeigh was presented with a cheque by a supporters' club and the ex-plumber looked forward to a new career in preparing dogs for shows.

We had a busy pre-season mix of friendlies, testimonials and the Tyler All-Ireland Cup. After opening Cookstown's new Sports Centre we travelled to Ballybofey in Donegal to meet Finn Harps in the first round of the Tyler's. Jamison inspired us to a 3-2 victory but the evening unfortunately will be remembered for the unsavoury incidents perpetrated by the hooligan element of the Glentoran following. Dundalk proved to be a much superior side to us in Round Two.

We finished the warm up games with a testimonial game for Dundela's long serving trainer Arthur Douglas. Douglas, a Scot had played for the Glens from 1938 to 1943 and was a popular figure locally. Dundela's Invitation XI easily won 4-1, the goals coming from Lennon, Adair, Platt and Bowden with guest Billy Millen netting for us.

Glentoran stuttered in the early Moran's Ulster Cup games, picking up a solitary point from the opening three Oval fixtures. The Ballymena game was switched as the Showgrounds pitch was being re-laid. Gracey was our best performer early season and he gave us the lead against Bangor after only 15 seconds. However we sat back and two late penalties by Billy McCoubrey gave the Seasiders a surprise win.

In early September the team started to click as Blackledge and Martin developed a useful striking partnership. Blackledge scored a brilliant overhead kick winner at Larne but the best match came at Solitude in a pulsating encounter which finished 1-1. The atmosphere was electric as the game was played just before the Reds' European debut, and we had Denis Matthews to thank for the point when he saved a John Platt penalty.

Youngsters Don Leslie and Dean Irvine were now regulars in the team and Irvine scored the opening goal at Glenavon with a superb chip from 25 yards. Terry Moore had returned to the club after a short spell with Harland and Wolff Welders but there was no sign of either Billy McKeag or Quinton McFall. The excellent displays of defenders Roy Walsh and Rab McCreery earned these two a place in an IFA XI which beat New Zealand 2-0 at the Oval. Reading were rumoured to be after McCreery but no offer materialised.

Our Ulster Cup game with Linfield was the subject of a short documentary on BBC's "Nationwide" in an attempt to show the nation an alternative to popular misconceptions about general life in Belfast. The game itself was a cracker and only a missed penalty by Jamison saved the Blues from defeat. Linfield went on to win the Ulster Cup but we had the consolation of being presented with four sets of a new Adidas playing strip featuring our sponsors Wilson's.

Ronnie McFall showed that was not afraid to wield the axe as Martin and Jamison were dropped after the Ulster Cup. Martin responded with a transfer request, which led to a move to Ards, while Jamison was suspended internally after refusing to act as substitute. Ron Manley made his debut at Coleraine in the Gold Cup and then opened his scoring account with a double against Larne. However our deficiencies were cruelly exposed at Ballymena when the home side contemptuously swept us aside by 4-0. to ensure that they would top the final sectional table.

On the International front two ex-Glenmen were to the fore as Danny Blanchflower resigned as team boss and Billy Bingham appointed as his successor. Bobby McGregor made his 75th "appearance" on the bench for the historic game with the Republic of Ireland.

Fiat dealt a blow to the local game when they announced that they were withdrawing their sponsorship of the Irish League. This season also saw the introduction of a half-time penalty kick competition for local youngsters at home games.

Despite frequently fielding five or six teenagers ourselves we began the league in fine style, remaining unbeaten in the first nine games. The main reason for this was the artistry and craft of Johnny Jamison, a welcome return to form after his previous disagreements. Terry Moore established himself at centre-half with Sammy Cranston relegated to the Seconds and 18 year old Andy Carson came in at right-back. Tom Dickey showed his versatility by going into goals for a spell at Portadown when Matthews was injured. Reserve David Anderson took over for the next match and was equally impressive.

We ended the seventies on a high note as the point gained at home to Cliftonville took us a point ahead of Linfield who lost 0-5 at Ballymena the same day. By the end of the first week of the eighties this lead had been stretched to three points as the Blues went down again, at Portadown.

Further down the club result were pleasing also. The Seconds lifted the George Wilson Cup with a 1-0 win over Linfield Swifts (scorer John Walker) and in the space of a week recorded B Division victories over Glenavon Reserves (9-2) and Larne Olympic (7-0). Eddie Houston was responsible for seven of these 16 goals. The Colts just failed to retain the IFA Youth Cup, going down to Portadown Thirds in the final, but all this caused McFall to surmise, "Things are starting to happen at the Oval again."

He obviously did not foresee the events of the next four months as the fortunes of the Glens totally nose-dived! It all began with a 5-0 defeat by Linfield at Windsor Park in the league. We were totally outplayed in midfield and despite the efforts of Anderson in goals Warren Feeney grabbed a hat-trick. The we lost our next two home games to Crusaders (re-arranged to a misty Tuesday night) and Coleraine (5/1 outsiders), allowing Linfield to take over the league leadership. Roy Walsh blazed a penalty over the bar in the latter when it was 2-0 to Coleraine.

Confidence drained out of the inexperienced team and this was reflected in a mediocre Irish Cup tie with Larne. The game did burst to life in the second half when Larne's Lee Clarke was sent off and Jamison chipped a beautiful goal. Neither side could gain the advantage and the same was true in the Oval replay when 120 minutes football failed to produce a goal.

Robert Strain, a 27 year old left-back who had partnered McFall at Portadown for three seasons, was signed from Crusaders and made his debut at Ballymena. The defence was solid up until the 88th minute when the Braidmen snatched an equaliser. We returned to Ballymena three days later and saw off Larne in the Cup at the third time of asking but this only set up another disaster at Windsor Park in the next round.

From the moment Rafferty put the Blues ahead after only 24 seconds we were swamped in midfield and the eventual margin of defeat was 4-0. Strain had our best chance to score from the penalty spot but shot pitifully at Dunlop. To complete our misery Moore was sent off seven minutes from time.

Results 1979/80

Played 46. Won 20. Drew 13. Lost 13. Goals For 65. Against 57. % 57.6

TC	01/08/79	1	Finn Harps	A	W	3	2	Martin, Rab McCreery, Jamison
TC	07/08/79	2	Dundlak	H	L	1	2	Jamison
UC	18/08/79		Coleraine	H	D	2	2	Martin, Blackledge
UC	22/08/79		Ballymena United	H	L	1	2	Blackledge
UC	25/08/79		Bangor	H	L	1	2	Gracey
UC	28/08/79		Portadown	A	W	2	1	Martin, Blackledge
UC	01/09/79		Larne	A	W	2	1	Jamison (p), Blackledge
UC	08/09/79		Distillery	H	W	3	0	Blackledge, Irvine, Gracey
UC	15/09/79		Cliftonville	A	D	1	1	Martin
UC	22/09/79		Ards	H	W	1	0	Martin
UC	29/09/79		Glenavon	A	W	2	0	Irvine, Porter
UC	06/10/79		Linfield	H	D	1	1	Blackledge
UC	13/10/79		Crusaders	A	L	0	1	-
GC	20/10/79		Coleraine	A	L	0	1	-
GC	27/10/79		Crusaders	A	W	1	0	Blackledge
GC	03/11/79		Larne	H	W	4	1	Ron McCreery, Manley 2, Blackledge
GC	10/11/79		Ballymena United	A	L	0	4	-
GC	17/11/79		Cliftonville	H	D	2	2	Blackledge, Walsh
IL	24/11/79		Coleraine	A	W	3	1	Manley, Blackledge, Jamison
IL	01/12/79		Ballymena United	H	W	2	0	Jamison, Walsh (p)
IL	08/12/79		Bangor	A	D	1	1	Rab McCreery
IL	15/12/79		Portadown	H	W	1	0	Walsh
IL	22/12/79		Larne	H	W	1	0	Gracey
IL	26/12/79		Distillery	A	W	4	0	Walsh 2(1p), Blackledge, Porter
IL	29/12/79		Cliftonville	H	D	1	1	Blackledge
IL	01/01/80		Ards	A	W	3	1	Blackledge, Ron McCreery, Rab McCreery
IL	05/01/80		Glenavon	H	W	3	1	Jamison, Porter, Irvine
IL	12/01/80		Linfield	A	L	0	5	-
IL	22/01/80		Crusaders	H	L	0	2	-
IL	26/01/80		Coleraine	H	L	2	4	Gracey, Blackledge
IL	09/02/80		Ballymena United	A	D	1	1	Houston
IL	16/02/80		Bangor	H	D	1	1	Porter
IL	01/03/80		Portadown	A	D	1	1	Blackledge
IL	08/03/80		Larne	A	W	2	1	Blackledge 2
IL	14/03/80		Distillery	H	W	2	1	Dickey, Irvine
IL	29/03/80		Cliftonville	A	D	2	2	Rab McCreery, Blackledge
IL	05/04/80		Ards	H	W	2	0	Blackledge 2
IL	07/04/80		Glenavon	A	D	1	1	Porter
IL	12/04/80		Linfield	H	L	1	2	Irvine
IL	19/04/80		Crusaders	A	L	0	1	-
IC	02/02/80	1	Larne	A	D	1	1	Jamison
IC	06/02/80	1R	Larne	H	D	0	0	aet
IC	12/02/80	1R2	Larne	BS	W	1	0	Blackledge
IC	22/02/80	2	Linfield	A	L	0	4	-
CAS	22/04/80	1	Cliftonville	A	W	2	1	Strain (p), Dickey
CAS	05/05/80	2	Linfield Swifts	A	L	0	2	-
F	26/07/79		Dundela	H	W	4	1	Jamison 2, Martin, Gracey
F	28/07/79		Cookstown United	A	W	3	1	Gracey, Blackledge, Martin (p) Opening of new Sports Centre
F	14/08/79		Dundela XI	A	L	1	4	Millen Arthur Douglas Testimonial
F	12/03/80		Irish League XI	H	L	1	2	Dickey
F	06/05/80		Linfield	H	W	3	1	Cleary, Unknown 2 Johnny Jamison Testimonial
F	29/05/80		Crewe United	A	W	3	1	Unknown in aid of Cystic Fybrosis

March was a slight improvement as we remained unbeaten during the month in the four league games played but the two points we dropped left us seven behind Linfield with only four matches to go. A section of supporters organised boycotts of the Larne and Distillery games as their patience began to wear thin. Matters weren't really helped by the transfers of Roy Walsh to Swindon Town and Terry Moore to San Diego Sockers. Moore, born in Canada, decided to settle in North America. We lost to an Irish League Select XI in a warm up game for their return fixture with the Scottish League. Gerry Mullan scored both goals for the representative team.

Linfield wrapped up the league title but we gave them a fright at the Oval when Dean Irvine put us 1-0 up after only six minutes. However two second half McKeown penalties gave the Blues a win. Gracey had a great chance to equalise when clean through but was foiled by Dunlop. Our depression was complete a week later when we went down 0-1 at Seaview and missed out on the runners-up spot.

Ballymena were the team to qualify for the UEFA Cup, but they found our Seconds a tough nut to crack in the first round of the County Antrim Shield. Indeed they needed a penalty to triumph 1-0 at the Oval. The Glens 1st XI overcame a difficult hurdle by knocking out holders Cliftonville 2-1 at Solitude (seven players booked) but then crashed to an embarrassing May Day holiday defeat to Linfield Swifts by 2-0!

We restored some pride by beating the Blues 3-1 in a benefit match for Johnny Jamison shortly after. The Glens included Derek Dougan and Portadown's Jim Cleary as guests, with Cleary opening the scoring. In the second half George Dunlop came out to play at centre-forward with Colin McCurdy going into the Linfield net. Dunlop had his problems from the penalty spot, hitting the post after he had previously scored one in a league game versus Portadown. The season was wound up at the end of May with a fixture at Glenavy versus the progressive junior club Crewe United in aid of Cystic Fibrosis research. Pat Jennings guested as an outfield player for the home side but with Peter Rafferty in our ranks we won 3-1. At the end of the season, however, Ronnie McFall was fully aware of the size of the task to put us back to the forefront of local soccer in the 1980's.

There was encouraging news for the two clubs most affected by the Troubles in Ulster at the beginning of the decade. Distillery had finally secured a new ground at Ballyskeagh near Lisburn while up in Londonderry there was bold talk that Derry City would be ready to re-enter the Irish League by 1983.

Appearances and Goals							
	App.	Subs.	Goals		App.	Subs.	Goals
McCreery Rab	43		4	Carson	11		
Gracey	42		4	Anderson	9		
Irvine	42	4	5	Houston	9		1
Blackledge	39		21	Dougan	8		
Porter	38		5	Stewart T.	7		
Jamison	35	2	7	McFall Q.	7	1	
Matthews D.	34			Dickey	6	5	2
Leslie	31	1		Adair	3		
Walsh	27		5	Black	3		
McCreery Ron	27	2	2	O'Neill	3	1	
Carleton	23	1		Cranston	2		
Moore	15	1		McFall A.	2		
Manley	14	1	3	Walker J.		1	
Strain R.	13		1				
Martin	13	1	5	TOTAL	506	21	65

1980/81

New players re-create glory days – Undefeated League campaign – Four kits

Playing matters for the season began on a ludicrously early date of 26th July with the first round of the Tyler All-Ireland Cup games. The Glens had been drawn at home to Sligo Rovers but the tie was switched to Seaview as the Oval pitch was not yet ready. In a drab game on a sun-drenched day two late goals gave Sligo a 3-1 victory. This match marked the only Glentoran appearance for Paul Fielding.

Manager Ronnie McFall was dipping wisely into the transfer market in time for the start of the competitive season proper. He purchased a new centre-half pairing with Alan Harrison (ex-Bangor) and the tall Trevor Erskine (Ex-Finn Harps and Dungannon Swifts) and brought a creative 22 year old midfielder from Portadown, Jim Cleary, to the Oval. The fourth signing was Alan Paterson, then 25, who returned to the Oval after seven years away at Sheffield Wednesday and Sligo Rovers, during which time he played for the League of Ireland against Argentina. The total cost of these signings was approximately £40,000.

Alan Harrison.

This figure coincided with the amount of money our new sponsors, the Clock Shop on the Newtownards Road, were planning to plough into the club over the next six years. Another internal change at the club was the appointment of Gordon Scott as secretary in place of Jack Atkinson who was made a life member.

The Ulster Cup commenced with a difficult encounter at Coleraine but thanks to the brilliance of Paterson we claimed a draw, indeed our new keeper was only beaten by a Robert Strain own goal. Johnny Jamison showed that he had plenty left in him as in the next match against Ballymena he scored both goals, a fine header and a fierce 20 yard drive. By the end of August the team was fitting together nicely as we increasingly looked like a formidable outfit again. Further good news arrived from the other side of the world when New Zealand announced that ex-Glenman John Hill could be leading their side in the 1982 World Cup qualifying campaign.

Our away match with Distillery on 6th September was significant in that it was the first competitive fixture to take place at their new ground at Ballyskeagh. Gary Blackledge had the honour of scoring the first goal there. The second came from our emerging youngster Sammy Troughton, who along with George Neill proved that not all members of the first team panel had been bought in.

Although we sat at the top of the Ulster Cup table it was felt that more players were needed and McFall signed Johnny Charles Jameson from Linfield to supply the ammunition crosses for Blackledge. When Johnny made his debut alongside Johnny Rea Jamison against Cliftonville the inevitable cry of "There's only two Johnny Jami(e)sons!" came from the Oval terraces.

After playing a friendly at Stormont to open Civil Service's new Maynard Sinclair pavilion we travelled to Ards without Paterson and Cleary who had been selected for the Irish League squad to tour Canada. Ricky Adair deputised in goals. We made somewhat heavy weather of winning this match, having to rely on two late Blackledge goals, after Ards had taken the lead in the 78th minute. During the game referee Moffatt had sent off Ron McCreery and Ards' Tom Cullen. Many fans were not immediately aware of what had occurred and there were calls for the re-introduction of yellow and red cards. The Ulster Cup table that night read:

1. Glentoran played 8 points 13, 2. Linfield 8-12, 3. Ballymena United 7-10

For our next game against Glenavon we paraded our new "Clock Shop" sponsored kit and what an eyesore it was! The all-white number with the sponsors name in black, completed by black shorts and red socks was dispensed with after only one game. However our display that day was worse that the strip and, helped by two late Martin Malone goals, Glenavon romped to a 4-0 win.

A week later we ran out at Windsor Park in a white strip with green trim and a red horizontal band with the sponsor's name beneath. Glentoran fans congregated in the Railway Stand had a brilliant view of the opening goal, a superb Cleary free-kick from 35 yards straight into the top corner. Linfield equalised in a stormy second half, when Ron McCreery, Norman Porter and Steve McKee were sent off, but with Ballymena winning their last three games, the drawn result sent the Ulster Cup to the Showgrounds.

We completed our fixtures with a five goal display against the Crues at the Oval, the first time in 103 matches since January 1978 that we had scored more than four goals against a league team. The early sending off of visiting keeper Roy McDonald helped, although the first action of his stand-in Peter Mulhall was to save Strain's subsequent penalty.

In between the Ulster and Gold Cups Glentoran won the Woolco five-a-sides at the Valley Leisure Centre, Newtownabbey. We beat Ballyclare Comrades 6-1 in the final, the goals from Blackledge, Rab McCreery, Cleary, Jameson and Strain(2), having seen off Cliftonville (3-0), Crusaders (4-1) and Glenavon (3-0) on the way. On a sadder note "Stumpy" Jamison's playing days at the Oval were numbered as he was placed on the transfer list and eventually re-joined Crusaders.

Alan Harrison was appointed captain for the Gold Cup as we opened with a home draw against Coleraine. The moment of the match came from Cleary when he magnificently chipped Terry Nicholson from 30 yards. McFall's latest signing, the tigerish Terry Kingon, made his debut in the home 2-0 win over Crusaders. The balding Kingon had seen service with Torquay United, Portadown, Ballymena, Glenavon and latterly Cliftonville and had been bought (with financial assistance from the Amalgamation of Supporters Clubs) to add further bite and experience to the midfield.

We won our next two Gold Cup fixtures to top the section by two points from Cliftonville, but had to play the Reds away in the last game. The Ballymena match was an exciting affair, decided in our favour by a well-struck half-volley from Gary Blackledge. The events were admirably covered by a new local weekly newspaper, the Castlereagh Courier. By now we were sporting our fourth different strip of the season. The latest variation consisted of white with black trim, a red and greed vertical stripe to the left with the "Clock Shop" in a box in the middle. If replica shirts had been available in 1980 you could have spent a fortune!

Over 7,000 attended the deciding Gold Cup game at Solitude. It transpired that if Cliftonville scored a win of any kind they would qualify for the final on goal difference whereas we required only a draw. After 65 minutes of a dramatic encounter the Reds found themselves 2-0 up but Glens substitute Ron Manley came on to score with his first touch to set up a nail-biting finish. Unfortunately for us time ran out and Cliftonville went on to beat Linfield 3-1 in the final.

For the third time in succession Coleraine were our first opponents in a new competition, this time the league itself, and for the third time the game ended all square! The Bannsiders claimed a winner when they thought a Kevin Mahon shot had rebounded back into play from the stanchion but referee Freddie McKnight ruled "no goal". After this match big Trevor Erskine finally conceded that travelling from his Aughnacloy home to play for the

Team Group 1980/1 the undefeated League Champions. Back Row: Ronnie McFall, Davy Roberts, Johnny Jameson, Ron McCreery, Alan Paterson, Trevor Erskine, Norman Porter, Gary Blackledge, Bobby McGregor, Bob Nesbitt Front Row: Terry Kingon, George Neill, Robert Strain, Rab McCreery, Jim Cleary, Tom Dickey, Dean Irvine.

Glens was too much and he returned to Dungannon Swifts. Young Alan McFall came in at centre-back.

The last few weeks of 1980 saw the team in splendid form as we recorded six wins and the goals and breathtaking play flowed from Cleary, Blackledge, Manley and Ron McCreery. Jameson broke his scoring "duck" for the club in the 7-1 thrashing of Portadown and began to win over the die hard fans who resented his previous connection with Linfield. Arguably the best goal of this run was actually scored against us when Ballymena full-back Nigel Worthington drove one past Paterson from around 35 yards.

If the old year had finished with a thrilling revenge win at Solitude (Paterson a vital penalty save) then 1981 certainly opened with a thriller when we beat Ards 4-3 on New Year's Day. Many players surplus to McFall's requirements left the club at this time; Don Leslie and David Anderson went to Chimney Corner, Eddie Houston to Carrick Rangers, Andy Dougan to Bangor and ex-first choice keeper Denis Matthews to Ballymena.

Our first win at Mourneview Park for six seasons kept us one point behind the Blues and set up a keenly awaited Big Two clash at the Oval on 10th January. In front of 12,000 Manley fired us ahead via the crossbar and we held that position until ten minutes into the second half. Then Alan Paterson made a tremendous save from a McKee header, an effort reminiscent of Gordon Banks' effort to deny Pele in the 1970 World Cup finals. However to the amazement of Glenmen Malcolm Moffatt awarded a goal, waving away the inevitable protestors. Somehow we pulled ourselves off the floor and a diving header from Jameson clinched the points and put us on the top of the league.

We obtained hard fought draws in our next two away games while the Blues had a game postponed and lost at home to Cliftonville. Crusaders adopted ultra-negative tactics against us and it was a sad sight to watch Jamison beat two Glens players in the centre-circle and then chip the ball back to his own goalkeeper. The Coleraine game began thirteen minutes late due to bomb scares in Belfast and we had to rely on a late Norman Porter header for our point.

Attention turned to the Irish Cup and we had a more rewarding return visit to Seaview, coming from behind to win 3-1. The next league game contained a goal to sum up the

Glens' form at that time. Cleary won the ball in midfield and spread it wide to Jameson. Johnny sprinted down the right-wing and crossed an inch perfect ball for "Blackie" to thunder into the net past the helpless Matthews. After comfortable wins over Bangor (league) and Ards (cup) we looked to be heading to another victory over Portadown at the Oval, being 2-0 up with twelve minutes remaining. Then in a shock mini-revival Hill and Kirk netted for the Ports and a point had been thrown away.

There were mixed emotions for Gary Blackledge at the beginning of March. On the positive side he was called into the Northern Ireland side for a Birmingham training session but at the same time began a three match suspension for the Glens. Ironically most of his bookings were for retaliation after being kicked around by defenders. The same week the board appointed a Mr. Shahid, a man originally from Bangladesh, as the club surgeon. Down the club the Colts regained the IFA Youth Cup with a 1-0 success over Plunkett Youth Club, Gary Brown the scorer.

Without Blackledge we struggled to a home draw with Larne, Jim Cleary saving our blushes with an 85th minute strike. Linfield only managed to draw 2-2 at Seaview the same afternoon, meaning they still trailed us by a point with six league games left. The team found its shooting boots a week later at Ballyskeagh, coming from behind to wallop the Whites by 7-1. Tom Dickey, standing in for Blackledge, notched two as did Kingon. However Ballymena would be a much more difficult proposition in the Irish Cup semi-final at Windsor Park.

On a sunny afternoon the game was generally a scrappy affair and we were flattered to be 2-0 ahead at the hour mark. However two controversial decisions by referee Alan Snoddy allowed Ballymena to pull it back to level terms. Firstly he awarded a goal when Paterson appeared to be bundled into the net and then gave United a free-kick on the edge of our area when Kingon had blocked a shot with his thigh. Ballymena took full advantage then and in the replay over a demoralised Glentoran side and goals from Paul Malone in the 18th and 89th minutes knocked us out. Blackledge had returned for the replay but was tightly marked by the Braidmen's defence. Ballymena went on to lift the cup by beating Glenavon, surprise winners over Linfield in the other semi, 1-0 in the final.

Just three nights later we faced a difficult league fixture with Cliftonville at the Oval. The game was switched to a Friday night to avoid a clash with a Loyalist demonstration on the Saturday afternoon and proved rewarding as long range goals from Strain and Cleary set up a 2-0 win. Ironically Paul Malone did us a favour the following day when his goal sank Linfield and left us three points clear with only four games to go.

However we stumbled to a draw at Ards in a game where Kingon and Alec Robson, now parading his talents at Castlereagh Park, were given an early bath. After a somewhat anxious win over Glenavon all roads led to Windsor Park on the 18th April for the title showdown. Linfield made the early running and turned round 1-0 up but on 57 minutes Johnny Jameson flashed a volley past Dunlop and the Glentoran fans went crazy. There was a slight scare near the end when the Blues claimed a goal by Peter Dornan but the ball had been clearly over the line, and signalled so, before the cross came in. At the final whistle Ronnie McFall leapt from the bench in the knowledge that the title was almost now secure.

On the Tuesday afternoon Linfield beat Distillery 6-0 meaning we required a point against Crusaders later in the evening to lift the Gibson Cup. On a balmy night before a huge crowd we made no mistake and the 3-1 win meant that we became the first unbeaten Irish League champions since Belfast Celtic in 1929. All this in the "Year of the Cockerel" too! After the trophy presentation Rab McCreery and the rest of the players were mobbed by delirious fans on an attempted lap of honour.

The season wound up with the County Antrim Shield and later the same week the Crues returned to the Oval for a second round tie. It was a completely different setting as hurricane conditions reduced the attendance to around 250 hardy souls. The visitors had the winds in the first half and led 1-0 at the interval and further we had lost Alan Paterson with a broken nose. Norman Porter went into goals and he too became a windswept supporter as we scored four in the second half. After a comfortable semi-final win over Bangor it was Linfield at Windsor again in the final. A jaded Glens went ahead but the Blues, inspired by Willie Gordon, came back to win 4-1 and claim their first trophy of the

Results 1980/81

Played 46. Won 28. Drew 13. Lost 5. Goals For 106. Against 55. % 75.0
Honours: Irish League

TC	26/07/80	1	Sligo Rovers	Sv	L	1	3	Blackledge
UC	16/08/80		Coleraine	A	D	1	1	Blackledge
UC	19/08/80		Ballymena United	H	W	2	0	Jamison 2
UC	23/08/80		Bangor	A	W	4	1	Blackledge 2, Irvine, Jamison
UC	26/08/80		Portadown	H	D	0	0	-
UC	29/08/80		Larne	H	W	2	0	Erskine, Blackledge
UC	06/09/80		Distillery	A	W	2	0	Troughton, Blackledge
UC	13/09/80		Cliftonville	H	D	1	1	Blackledge
UC	20/09/80		Ards	A	W	2	1	Blackledge 2
UC	27/09/80		Glenavon	H	L	0	4	-
UC	04/10/80		Linfield	A	D	1	1	Cleary
UC	11/10/80		Crusaders	H	W	5	1	Strain (p), Blackledge, Dickey, Manley 2
GC	18/10/80		Coleraine	H	D	2	2	Cleary, Blackledge
GC	25/10/80		Crusaders	H	W	2	0	Ron McCreery, Blackledge
GC	01/11/80		Larne	A	W	3	0	Blackledge 2, Ron McCreery
GC	08/11/80		Ballymena United	H	W	2	1	Rab McCreery, Blackledge
GC	15/11/80		Cliftonville	A	L	1	2	Manley
IL	22/11/80		Coleraine	H	D	1	1	Cleary
IL	29/11/80		Ballymena United	A	W	2	1	Manley 2
IL	06/12/80		Bangor	H	W	3	2	Manley 2, Blackledge
IL	13/12/80		Portadown	A	W	7	1	Blackledge 3, Manley 2, Jameson, Ron McCreery
IL	20/12/80		Larne	A	W	3	0	Cleary, Blackledge, Ron McCreery
IL	26/12/80		Distillery	H	W	4	2	Blackledge 2, Jameson, Cleary
IL	27/12/80		Cliftonville	A	W	4	2	Jameson, Harrison, Blackledge, Ron McCreery
IL	01/01/81		Ards	H	W	4	3	Cleary 2(1p), Blackledge, Porter
IL	03/01/81		Glenavon	A	W	2	1	Manley, Blackledge
IL	10/01/81		Linfield	H	W	2	1	Manley, Jameson
IL	17/01/81		Crusaders	A	D	1	1	Cleary (p)
IL	24/01/81		Coleraine	A	D	1	1	Porter
IL	07/02/81		Ballymena United	H	W	2	0	Blackledge 2
IL	14/02/81		Bangor	A	W	3	2	Jameson 2, Cleary (p)
IL	28/02/81		Portadown	H	D	2	2	Blackledge 2
IL	07/03/81		Larne	H	D	1	1	Cleary
IL	14/03/81		Distillery	A	W	7	1	Kingon 2, Strain, Porter, Dickey 2, Manley
IL	27/03/81		Cliftonville	H	W	2	0	Strain, Cleary
IL	04/04/81		Ards	A	D	1	1	Blackledge
IL	11/04/81		Glenavon	H	W	3	1	Cleary (p), Blackledge, Jameson
IL	18/04/81		Linfield	A	D	1	1	Jameson
IL	21/04/81		Crusaders	H	W	3	1	Blackledge 2, Jess og
IC	31/01/81	1	Crusaders	A	W	3	1	Cleary, Blackledge, Manley
IC	21/02/81	2	Ards	A	W	3	1	Blackledge 2, Jameson
IC	21/03/81	SF	Ballymena United	WP	D	2	2	Dickey, Manley
IC	24/03/81	SFR	Ballymena United	WP	L	0	2	-
CAS	24/04/81	2	Crusaders	H	W	4	1	Blackledge 2, Manley, Stewart
CAS	28/04/81	SF	Bangor	H	W	3	0	Cleary, Irvine, Blackledge
CAS	04/05/81	F	Linfield	A	L	1	4	Blackledge
F	07/08/80		Dundela	A	W	2	0	Troughton, Dickey
F	09/08/80		Cookstown United	A	D	1	1	Unknown
F	11/05/81		Land of the Stars	H	W	8	4	Blackledge 2, G.Neill, Paterson 2, Unknown 3

season. Glentoran suffered only five defeats in 1980/1, but crucially each one led directly to the losing of a trophy.

The last match of the season was a charity game against a team of local CB enthusiasts dubbed "the Land of the Stars". For an admission of 10p fans gained an excellent night's entertainment. Glentoran eventually won the game 8-4 with the unusual occurrences of a George Neill goal and two more from Alan Paterson playing as a striker late on. Gary Blackledge claimed a "hat-trick" of sorts, getting two for the Glens in the first half and another after he had changed sides at the interval!

Unsurprisingly for such a successful season there were many individual awards around the club. Blackledge, with 40 goals, was named player of the year by both the NIPFA and the football writers with Ronnie McFall selected as Manager of the Year by the Northern Ireland coaches. Blackledge was joined by Cleary and Paterson in the Irish League panel for the game with the League of Ireland. Groundsman Billy Crawford was again highly praised for his work in getting the pitch into pristine condition. Things were not so bright for Alan McFall, Tom Dickey and Tom Stewart as they were placed on the transfer list at the end of May.

Appearances and Goals

	App.	Subs.	Goals		App.	Subs.	Goals
Strain R.	46		3	Irvine	12	2	2
Blackledge	43		40	Dickey	11	13	4
Cleary	43		14	Troughton	11	1	1
Paterson	43			Jamison	10		3
McCreery Rab	41	1		Stewart T.	7	4	1
Jameson	38		9	Leslie	3	1	
Manley	33	3	15	Adair	2		
McCreery Ron	32	2	5	Carleton	1	1	
Harrison	30		1	Matthews D.	1		
Kingon	27		2	Fielding	1		
Porter	26	13	3	Gracey	1		
Erskine	17		1	Own Goals			1
Neill G.	14	1					
McFall A.	13	6		TOTAL	506	47	106

Gary Blackledge challenges Peter Rafferty during the league game at Windsor Park

1981/82

Club history book marks centenary – Ulster Cup only success –
Sad loss of McGregor

Season 1981/2 marked Glentoran's centenary and we began our 100th season in existence as reigning Irish League champions. During the next fifteen months may events and matches were arranged to commemorate the event and December 1981 a book entitled "The Story of Glentoran" by Malcolm Brodie was published, summarising the history of the club.

The playing staff had been strengthened by the arrival of Barney Bowers and Dermott Keeley from Derby County and Dundalk respectively. Blond midfielder Bowers had previously starred for Cliftonville while the bearded Keeley had a reputation as a tough centre-half who had won most of the available honours in League of Ireland football. One player we missed out on was Roy Walsh who returned to the Irish League with Linfield when most thought that the Glens had first option on him. Young Colts goalkeeper Philip Hughes joined Manchester United and later went on to win three full international caps when with Bury. Other players to leave were Tom Dickey (to Bangor), Ronnie Carleton (Chimney Corner) and Alan McFall (Carrick Rangers). The season was also a benefit year for full-back Rab McCreery.

The directors had lined up an attractive set of pre-season games, the biggest of which was a glamour match with FA Cup holders Tottenham Hotspur. A crowd of over 12,000 saw a crackerjack game on a wet Saturday afternoon. Kingon put us ahead against the London aristocrats but with three minutes remaining Spurs led 3-2 through goals from Glenn Hoddle (a penalty), Mark Falco and the Argentinean World Cup star Osvaldo Ardiles. Then Gary Blackledge sent in a magnificent 25 yard dipping volley to earn a draw.

Our only defeat in the pre-season friendlies had been three days earlier against Norwich City. Joe Royle and Ross Jack scored for the Canaries as we failed to find a way past Chris Woods. Alan Paterson had the satisfaction of saving a late Jack penalty. We rounded off the warm up matches by opening Carrick Rangers' new stand at Taylor's Avenue.

We began the Ulster Cup confidently with wins over Larne, Bangor and Portadown before meeting Linfield at the Oval. We dominated the game but missed an array of chances. With one minute left we held a 1-0 lead through Jameson (on 66 minutes) and had forced a corner. However the ball was crossed straight into Dunlop's hands and the big goalkeeper began a move which ended with John Whitten sliding the ball home past Paterson. The Blues had snatched a draw!

Undeterred we won our next two games to stay top of the table by two points from Cliftonville and Coleraine. The lively game versus Ballymena saw three penalties converted, two by Cleary for us, and two more goals from the ever sharp Blackledge. After a frustrating draw at Seaview we returned to Europe for the first time since 1978.

Hopes were high that we could eliminate our Luxembourg opposition, Progres Neidercorn, but the away first leg ended 1-1. Many felt that the Glens had been robbed of their first away victory in European competition by Belgian referee F. Rion who did not award a goal when a Manley effort appeared to have crossed the line, nor a penalty when the shot was fisted away by a defender! In the return leg we ran out in our new "European" kit of White with separate broad green, red and black vertical stripes. The team's performance was every bit as dazzling and we recorded our biggest European win, 4-0.

Meanwhile the Ulster Cup was heading towards an exciting climax. We defeated Ards, thanks to a first minute own goal by Alec Robson and a second by Cleary, who had been put through by an exquisite Jameson back heel. At Glenavon we found ourselves 0-2 to goals by Mickey McDonald. In a tremendous fightback we went 3-2 up but a lack of concentration allowed winger Alan Wilson to equalise for the home side in the last minute as many were leaving. The table thus read after nine games:

1= Glentoran, Coleraine 15 points, 3= Cliftonville, Linfield 12 points.

We ended the Reds' hopes a week later by defeating them 3-0 at Solitude, all the goals coming in the second half, while the same day Mickey McDonald scored five as Glenavon came from 1-4 down to win 6-4 at Windsor Park. Coleraine kept up the pressure by beating Ards but the following Saturday the Moran's Ulster Cup (and the £1,000 prize) was ours as we comprehensively defeated the Bannsiders 3-0 at a sunny Oval. Coleraine's cause was not helped by having centre-half Jackie Hutton sent off for arguing with referee Gerry Nesbitt.

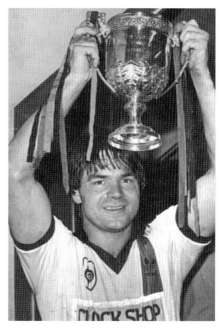

The contribution to the team of Keeley and Bowers was analysed as significant. The former's experience and determination was bringing out the best in the other defenders McCreery, Harrison and Strain while Bowers, although he had yet to find the net, complemented beautifully with Cleary and Kingon in midfield.

The next month or so was to be a melancholy time for Glentoran Football Club. The Gold Cup was a complete disaster as we finished bottom of our section, losing three of the five games. The only bright spot was Bowers' first goal for us, a 20 yard drive during a Friday night game with Larne and the arrival of two new forwards. Sixteen year old John McDaid made his debut in that Larne game while against Cliftonville McFall paraded his latest signing, the ex-Ballymena United striker, Gerry Mullan, signed from Everton for a reported £40,000.

The most embarrassing moment of the Gold Cup came when Jim Cleary put a late penalty right out of Seaview but there were black marks also for Norman Porter and Ron Manley who were sent off in our last two fixtures. Porter appeared to have been harshly dealt with after his clash with Michael Guy, who was only booked, at Ballymena but Manley's dismissal against

Rab McCreery holds aloft the Ulster Cup.

Cliftonville was a major factor in allowing the Reds to beat us at the Oval for the first time in over 16 years.

Our second round European Cup tie with Bulgarians CSKA dealt the club a double blow. After half an hour of the first leg in Sofia Harrison went down injured and as usual Bobby McGregor ran out to treat the player. However within a couple of minutes McGregor himself had collapsed and died to the shock of all. The result (0-2) and the manner of defeat (controversial penalty, Alan Harrison sent off) and our official complaint seemed irrelevant as Glentoran had tragically lost one of their greatest servants and football itself possibly one of its greatest ever healers. It certainly was a sad night in far eastern Europe as grown men, their heads bowed, were reduced to tears.

For the Oval second leg McFall told the players to "go out and do it for Bobby" and they very nearly did. Two spectacular goals from Cleary (fierce right foot shot) and Manley (following a mazy dribble) in the space of three minutes in the middle of the second half sent the game into extra time. Then CSKA cruelly won the tie when a free-kick was deflected into his own net by Kingon, the man of the end of the wall. What a pity that only 4,021 had come through the turnstiles and that BBC Northern Ireland had declined to cover the game. Ronnie McFall had to be congratulated for doing his homework on the Bulgarian champions – this included obtaining a dossier on them from Liverpool manager Bob Paisley. CSKA had lost to Liverpool in Europe in 1980/1 but went on to beat them this season – maybe McFall should have returned the favour!

Although we were knocked out of the Woolco five-a-sides in the first round a team wearing Glentoran shirts did trounce Linfield in a later round. It was Finn Harps, who had borrowed our strip to avoid a colour clash with the Blues!

Results 1981/82

Played 44. Won 27. Drew 6. Lost 11. Goals For 101. Against 46. % 68.2.
Honours: Ulster Cup

UC	15/08/81		Larne	A	W	3	0	Blackledge 2, Cleary
UC	18/08/81		Bangor	H	W	2	1	Cleary (p), Blackledge
UC	22/08/81		Portadown	A	W	2	1	Blackledge, Manley
UC	25/08/81		Linfield	H	D	1	1	Jameson
UC	29/08/81		Distillery	A	W	4	0	Kingon, Cleary, Harrison, Jameson
UC	05/09/81		Ballymena United	H	W	4	2	Cleary 2(2p), Blackledge 2
UC	12/09/81		Crusaders	A	D	1	1	Blackledge
UC	19/09/81		Ards	H	W	2	0	Robson og, Cleary
UC	26/09/81		Glenavon	A	D	3	3	Blackledge 2, Porter
UC	03/10/81		Cliftonville	A	W	3	0	Cleary, Jameson, Kingon
UC	10/10/81		Coleraine	H	W	3	0	Blackledge, Jameson, Manley
EC	16/09/81	1.1	Progres Neidercorn	A	D	1	1	Cleary
EC	30/09/81	1.2	Progres Neidercorn	H	W	4	0	Blackledge 2, Jameson, Manley
EC	21/10/81	2.1	CSKA Sofia	A	L	0	2	-
EC	04/11/81	2.2	CSKA Sofia	H	W	2	1	aet – Cleary, Manley
GC	17/10/81		Coleraine	A	L	1	3	Cleary (p)
GC	24/10/81		Crusaders	A	L	1	3	Blackledge
GC	30/10/81		Larne	H	W	1	0	Bowers
GC	07/11/81		Ballymena United	A	D	1	1	Cleary
GC	14/11/81		Cliftonville	H	L	1	2	Manley
IL	21/11/81		Linfield	A	W	2	1	Strain, Jameson
IL	28/11/81		Crusaders	H	W	6	1	Manley 3, Cleary, Mullan, Jameson
IL	05/12/81		Distillery	A	W	5	0	Cleary, Manley 2, Mullan, Jameson
IL	19/12/81		Bangor	A	L	1	2	Cleary (p)
IL	26/12/81		Portadown	H	W	3	1	Mullan 2, Cleary (p)
IL	01/01/82		Cliftonville	H	L	1	2	McDaid
IL	02/01/82		Larne	A	W	1	0	Strain (p)
IL	16/01/82		Ards	A	W	7	1	Kingon, Blackledge 2, Cleary, Jameson, Manley 2
IL	20/01/82		Coleraine	H	D	2	2	Cleary 2
IL	23/01/82		Glenavon	H	W	3	1	Blackledge 3
IL	06/02/82		Linfield	H	L	1	2	Cleary (p)
IL	13/02/82		Crusaders	A	L	0	3	-
IL	20/02/82		Ballymena United	H	W	3	1	Cleary 2(2p), Blackledge
IL	27/02/82		Distillery	H	W	6	1	Blackledge 3, Cleary, Bowers, Jameson
IL	06/03/82		Coleraine	A	W	2	1	Manley, Blackledge
IL	13/03/82		Bangor	H	W	4	0	Manley, Bowers, Blackledge 2
IL	20/03/82		Glenavon	A	W	3	1	Cleary (p), Jameson, Keeley
IL	27/03/82		Portadown	A	W	4	0	Jameson, Blackledge 2, Mullan
IL	03/04/82		Cliftonville	A	W	1	0	Jameson
IL	10/04/82		Larne	H	W	4	1	Cleary, Rab McCreery, Bowers, Jameson
IL	13/04/82		Ballymena United	A	L	0	1	-
IL	17/04/82		Ards	H	W	2	0	Jameson 2
IC	30/01/82	1	Cliftonville	A	L	0	1	-
CAS	06/04/82	1	Linfield	A	L	0	1	-
F	29/07/81		Newry Town	A	W	3	0	Manley 3 Ambassador Cup
F	01/08/81		Dundalk	H	D	0	0	-

F	05/08/81	Norwich City	H	L	0	2	-
F	08/08/81	Tottenham Hotspur	H	D	3	3	Kingon, Cleary (p), Blackledge
F	11/08/81	Carrick Rangers	A	W	6	2	Jameson 3, Blackledge, Manley, Cleary
F	29/12/81	Arsenal	H	L	0	2	-
F	23/03/82	Leeds United	H	L	2	5	Blackledge 2
F	19/04/82	Liverpool	H	D	1	1	Jameson
F	30/04/82	Linfield	A	W	3	2	D.Neill, Jameson, Manley Len Hiller Testimonial

We began the defence of the league title with a difficult trip to Windsor Park. However within three minutes we had gone ahead thanks to a freakish wind-assisted goal by Robert Strain from nearly 40 yards. Jameson continued his scoring form against his old colleagues in the 25th minute and Linfield's only reply was a McGaughey consolation two minutes from time. Billy Bingham attended the game and was given a standing ovation from both sets of supporters for his achievement of getting Northern Ireland to the World Cup finals in Spain.

The goals flowed in the next two games, Manley scoring five of the eleven, as Jim Cleary ruled the roost in midfield. Then progress was suddenly halted as the Coleraine game was snowed off and we surprisingly lost in gale-force conditions at Bangor. Alan Paterson sustained a leg injury as we lost our first league game for 20 months. With no other goalkeepers of senior experience at the Oval we signed ex-Linfield custodian Ken Barclay on a short term contract, before his imminent emigration to Australia to play for Ringwood City.

Barclay's debut against Portadown was a stormy affair as referee Dessie Campbell booked seven players. Incredibly six of those wore Glentoran shirts, especially as the Ports, geed on by ex-Oval star Johnny Johnston, were the chief aggressors. At least we won 3-1 and the match was a personal triumph for Gerry Mullan, with two clinical strikes. Supporters also had frequent chances to see our new physiotherapist, 23 year-old Tony Wright, in action.

Just three days later over 7,300 fans were back at the Oval to watch a friendly with Arsenal. The match had been arranged at short notice as the Gunners, without a game for three weeks, badly needed some match practice before their FA Cup tie with rivals Tottenham. Paul Davis netted both goals for Arsenal in a tame 2-0 win. The "programme" issued for the game reflected the necessary hastiness – a single yellow sheet. However the Glentoran Gazette, edited by John McCreery, was receiving praise from all quarters. Filled with interesting, informative and topical articles it was expertly laid out and supplemented by top class action photographs from the Castlereagh Courier.

The year of 1982 began badly with another home defeat by Cliftonville and the loss of Keeley to injury in a scrappy 1-0 win at Larne. The Colts brought some joy to the club by defeating Linfield Rangers 3-2 in the IFA Youth Cup final.

We hammered Ards but then dropped a vital point to Coleraine when Des "the Bird" Dickson poached a late equaliser after a masterly Cleary goal on 82 minutes appeared to have set up a victory. All this left the league table as follows in mid-January:
1. Coleraine played 10 points 16, 2. Glentoran 9-13, 3. Linfield 8-11.

Blackledge returned to scoring form with a hat-trick in the space of nine minutes against Glenavon but we then entered a miserable three week period. Firstly bogey team Cliftonville dumped us out of the Irish Cup when Barclay, in his last appearance, "threw in" a Ciaran McCurry effort. We were then left with no goalkeeper for the Linfield match and the programme listed our Number One as "A.N.Other"! Eventually Ricky Adair was persuaded to play in the emergency. Adair had left the Glens earlier in the season to concentrate on Rugby Union with CIYMS. He was powerless to stop goals from McKee and McGaughey in the second half after a Cleary penalty had put us one up. Reggie Hillen was quickly signed from Portadown and made his debut between the sticks at Seaview a week later. Again he could do nothing about the three goals conceded, the first two as a result of mistakes by Rab McCreery and the third an own goal by Bowers in the last minute.

McFall reacted angrily to these defeats and publicly stated that any player not prepared to sweat blood for the club would not be welcome at the Oval. Confidence was restored with comfortable wins over Ballymena and Distillery and then we won the vital game at Coleraine Showgrounds by 2-1. The winner came from Blackledge who, along with McDaid, had just spent a week on trial at Leeds United. Blackie was also on target for the Irish League and two penalties from Cleary helped the local XI draw 3-3 at Windsor Park with OFK Belgrade, who were disguising themselves as the Yugoslavian League.

Around the Oval Dennis Shields succeeded Bimbo Weatherup as Seconds' coach but our latest sponsorship deal with Leisure Automatic Sales Ltd fell through as the company went into the hands of the receiver just two months into the contract.

Leeds United were our next centenary visitors and, with a side managed by Allan Clarke and containing David Seaman, Derek Parlane, Frank Worthington and Kenny Burns, beat us 5-2. We gave the West Yorkshire side a scare though when two goals from Blackledge early in the second half put us 2-1 up. Worthington provided a memorable moment near the end with a beautiful individual goal.

We maintained interest in the league race with five successive victories. The two best goals in this run were scored by Jameson - one a length of the field sprint and finish at Portadown and the other a fine shot to give us a revenge win at Solitude. Linfield and Coleraine though were not dropping points either and our title hopes were finally killed off at Ballymena on Easter Tuesday via a Ronnie Burns goal on 87 minutes. The Irish international full-back Tom Connell, signed from Manchester United for around £30,000, made his Glens debut in that match. We finished second in the table, four points behind Linfield.

We had suffered more disappointment at the hands of the Blues in the County Antrim Shield. Glentoran dominated the match for long spells and only a string of marvellous saves by Dunlop kept the scoresheet blank. Then in the last minute with extra time beckoning, Rab McCreery gave the ball away and Peter Dornan slipped in the winner. The Glenmen, who had been herded below pitch level in front of the closed Railway Stand, just could not believe it. Later that night the unreserved stand at Olympia Drive was destroyed by fire, paving the way for a new grandstand to be built at the national stadium.

In April we had one more "big name" friendly to play versus the newly crowned League Champions Liverpool. They included their full first team squad so the Glens had to line up against the likes of Grobbelaar, Neal, Hansen, Lawrenson, Whelan, Dalglish, Rush and Johnston. Before 15,000 Jameson put us ahead when he outpaced the defence and fired home on the stroke of half-time. Mark Lawrenson equalised on the hour but Cleary almost won the game when he hit the crossbar from 20 yards. David Jeffrey and Kel McDermott guested for us in this match.

After beating Linfield in Len Hiller's testimonial seven of our players took part in the first ever Belfast Marathon in May. Although the domestic season was over for two of our players there was still much to look forward to. Jim Cleary gained a place in the Northern Ireland squad for the Home Internationals, playing against Scotland and Wales. Then both he and Johnny Jameson were named by Bingham in Northern Ireland's World Cup panel. Neither player made an appearance in the memorable finals although Cleary sat on the bench.

Appearances and Goals

	App.	Subs.	Goals		App.	Subs.	Goals
Jameson	44		16	Porter	13	12	1
Bowers	44		4	Hillen	12		
Cleary	43		24	Barclay	7		
McCreery Rab	40		1	McCreery Ron	5	3	
Harrison	39		1	McDaid	4	5	2
Keely	38		1	Connell	2		
Blackledge	37		27	Irvine	1	2	
Manley	35	5	13	Adair	1		
Strain R.	33		2	Stewart T.		1	
Kingon	30		3	Own Goals			1
Paterson	24						
Mullan	18	2	5	TOTAL	484	31	101
Neill G.	14	1					

1982/83

George Best guests – Return to traditional colours - Irish Cup famine ends

Although it would have been impossible to improve on the displays of the previous season, the objectives of all at the Oval would have been to increase the trophy haul – only the Ulster Cup sat in the boardroom after the efforts of 1981/2. Ronnie McFall's message was clear enough, "the side has got to win everything before them this season – second best will just not be good enough!" There were no additional signings to the first team panel but Norman Porter and Ron McCreery were off-loaded to Ards and Portadown respectively while rumours abounded that the out of contract Gary Blackledge would move across town to Windsor Park.

As our centenary year celebrations reached their climax the players again faced a busy and varied pre-season programme. We suffered a shock defeat to Dungannon Swifts and needed penalties to overcome Newry Town and retain the Ambassador Cup. However the warm up concluded in a glamour meeting with Ron Atkinson's Manchester United. In a disappointing game the only player to star was George Best, guesting in the Glentoran number 11 shirt. United's goals in a 2-0 win watched by 12,000 came from Ashley Grimes and Ray Wilkins but other big names such as Buchan, McQueen, Robson, Birtles, Macari and 17 year old Northern Ireland World Cup hero Norman Whiteside failed to impress. Our final pre-season game against Dundalk, a testimonial match for their keeper Ritchie Blackmore, was postponed at short notice. This incensed many supporters' clubs who had already booked buses for the trip south.

George Best in a guest appearance against Manchester United.

A new strip, mainly green with thin red and black vertical stripes replaced the previous "European" one. The design marked a return to traditional colour after a period of 16 years when the team wore a predominantly white jersey.

There was a slight re-organisation too to the season with the Gold Cup played before the Ulster Cup. There were growing complaints from Glenmen regarding the strength of our perennial Gold Cup section as four of the teams had finished in the top five of the last league table. Despite this we coasted through the group with some scintillating football. Cleary dominated the games and set wave after wave of attack in motion. John McDaid enjoyed his run in the first team, scoring in all but one of the matches and, not to be outdone, Ron Manley netted a brilliant hat-trick against Crusaders including a booming 20 yard drive.

A 19 year old midfielder, Raymond Morrison, made his debut in an action packed encounter with Ballymena under the Oval lights. Just before half-time Dermott Keely clashed with Michael Guy and both received their marching orders from Alan Snoddy. The game appeared to be heading for a draw until Manley popped up with the winner in the 81st minute. This assured us of qualification for the final and we completed the group games with a dazzling 5-1 win at Solitude, after trailing early on. We could even afford the luxury of a penalty miss by Sammy Troughton.

Before the Gold Cup final with the Blues we commenced both the Ulster and UEFA Cups. Our European opponents were Banik Ostrava of Czechoslovakia and a disappointingly low crowd watched us go down 1-3 in the home first leg. Barney Bowers had given us hope with an equaliser from a 20 yard free-kick in the 66th minute but defensive lapses led to late goals for Banik through Danek and Antalik. At least we put up a brave display behind the Iron Curtain, holding the fast moving Czechs to a 1-0 scoreline (Valek 48 minutes). McFall had cause to thank local referee Freddie McKnight for his dossier on Banik. Sammy Troughton became the 100th player to represent Glentoran in European competition in the first leg.

After two opening Ulster Cup wins, the highlight of which was a brilliant Morrison volley in the last minute at Bangor, we met Linfield at the Oval in the Gold Cup final on

Dermott Keely and fans with the Ulster Cup .

22nd September. It was to be a night of both triumph and disaster as we dominated from the start. A glancing header from Jameson put us ahead midway through a first half during which Alan Paterson only touched the ball twice! However just before the break young McDaid suffered a fractured leg following a tackle by David Jeffrey. Our sub was Rab McCreery, who was being kept out of the team by George Neill. Cleary and Bowers excelled in midfield throughout but it was left to Jameson to add the coup de gras twelve minutes from time and so the Gold Cup, and Hennessey's £1,500 first prize, was ours.

The Blues had a chance for quick revenge just ten days later when we visited them on Ulster Cup business. After only nine minutes though, we had gone 2-0 ahead with Jameson on target again. However Linfield staged a remarkable second half comeback to win 5-2 with three goals from Billy Murray and a McGaughey brace. For Alan Paterson it was a half to forget as earlier the game had been held up for three minutes while he was being pelted by stones thrown from the Spion Kop.

McFall immediately strengthened the midfield by signing 26 year old Davy Neill from Ballymena. Neill made his Glens' debut against his old team mates the day after the transfer! Three comfortable wins over Crusaders, Ards and Glenavon re-earned the unwanted "team of the season" tag but the Ulster Cup developed into a fight to the finish. We went into the last fixture at Coleraine needing only a draw to lift the Cup whereas the Bannsiders required victory by three clear goals to deny us. An early and rare goal from Keely effectively ended this hypothesis and despite having Manley sent off five minute before half-time we went on to clinch the trophy with a 3-1 victory. It was double celebrations for Jim Cleary as he had just obtained his BA in Business Studies from Ulster Polytechnic.

Two familiar faces left the Oval as Gary Blackledge was loaned to French Third Division side Chaumont (where he linked up with fellow Ulsterman Jim Grattan) and Rab McCreery joined Ballymena. In an open letter to the Gazette McCreery stated that after 13 years with the Glens he did not want to leave the club but felt that he had no option as a first team place could no longer be guaranteed.

We celebrated our 100th anniversary of registering with the IFA by a grand dinner dance at the Park Avenue hotel on 9th November. The event was proclaimed a great success and the board of directors were praised for their efforts in organising the "do". Earlier we had completed our set of centenary friendlies with a visit from Wolves and their Chief Executive

Derek Dougan. The Black Country men won 3-2 with goals from Mel Eves (2) and Wayne Clarke. Other well known personalities in their line up were goalkeeper John Burrows, midfielder Kenny Hibbitt and Scottish centre-forward Andy Gray.

Local marketing executive Mike Wilson put forward his ideas on how Glentoran could woo more fans back through the turnstiles. In a programme article he stated that the club and its matches should be publicised more by experimenting with short bursts on Downtown Radio on Saturday mornings and placing a few posters on appropriate main roads around east Belfast. He advocated the formation of a Glentoran Roadshow complete with a fifteen minute promotional video of great moments from the club's history.

It would have been a shame for any Glenman to have missed our opening Smirnoff Irish League match with Linfield as the balance in Big Two rivalry decisively swung our way. Two goals in two first half minutes from Mullan and the "workaholic" Davy Neill set up a 3-0 victory. You would have thought this to be the perfect launchpad towards league success but amazingly we suffered three defeats in our remaining five games of 1982. Crusaders (two goals from McCurdy), Coleraine and Portadown (an amazing open net miss by Mullan in the 4th minute) were our conquerors. The pundits blamed it on a loss of rhythm caused by the absence of Keely and Manley due to suspension. We even struggled to overcome basement boys Bangor, needing a Mullan goal thirteen minutes from time to earn victory. Young centre-half Jeff Russell made his debut in that match.

In January we got back on course recording five wins on the trot to stay in second place, three points behind Linfield at the half way stage. Highlights of the month were a great first half display at Solitude, Gerry Mullan's hat-trick against Larne and a superb individual goal by Barney Bowers at Ballymena. Barney burst through from midfield and with fans screaming for him to pass it wide he drove home, high and handsome, from 25 yards.

The Colts were also in fine form beating Rooftop 8-1, five of the goals from Gary Hillis and the other three from Paul Millar. On the controversial side, our old adversary Peter Rafferty, now of Ards, was sent off at the Oval by Dessie Campbell for protesting at his decisions. This was despite Glentoran players springing to his defence!

A huge crowd gathered at Windsor Park for the return "big two" league game on 5th February. In the first half the Blues, with the advantage of a gale, went ahead early through Anderson. Then, in a tremendous spell of pressure just before the interval we went ahead thanks to powerful headers from Manley and Bowers. However four minutes into the second half an uncharacteristic attempt at a cheeky backheel from Dermott Keely went straight to Billy Murray who crossed for Dornan to equalise. There was no further scoring and so Linfield remained three points clear.

Meanwhile we progressed to the quarter-finals of the new format 32 team Irish Cup with a comfortable win over Ballymena and a drab victory over juniors Ballymoney. The Glens had been trying to obtain agreement for 3 p.m. kick-offs but the IFA tersely ruled that matches must commence at 2.30 p.m. and floodlights must not be used!

Gerry Mullan.

Two more players left the Oval as Terry Kingon returned to Cliftonville and we loaned Dean Irvine to Distillery to help ease their increasing financial difficulties. Irvine later emigrated to New Zealand before meeting a premature death in a holiday accident. Another person to pass away was 75 year old Johnny Geary, a man who had served the Glens as player, manager and director over many decades.

Results 1982/83

Played 50. Won. 36. Drew 4. Lost 10. Goals For 115. Against 48. % 76.0.
Honours: Irish Cup, Ulster Cup, Gold Cup

GC	21/08/82		Coleraine	H	W	1	0	McDaid
GC	24/08/82		Crusaders	H	W	3	0	Manley 3
GC	27/08/82		Larne	A	W	2	0	McDaid, Manley
GC	31/08/82		Ballymena United	H	W	2	1	McDaid, Manley
GC	04/09/82		Cliftonville	A	W	5	1	Jameson, Connell, Bowers, McDaid, Manley
GC	22/09/82	F	Linfield	H	W	2	0	Jameson 2
UC	11/09/82		Larne	H	W	2	1	Manley 2
UC	18/09/82		Bangor	A	W	5	1	Bowers (p), McDaid 2, Manley, Morrison
UC	25/09/82		Portadown	H	W	1	0	Jameson
UC	02/10/82		Linfield	A	L	2	5	Jameson, Mullan
UC	09/10/82		Distillery	H	W	2	0	Mullan, Cleary
UC	16/10/82		Ballymena United	A	D	1	1	Manley
UC	23/10/82		Crusaders	H	W	4	1	Manley, Cleary (p), Bowers 2
UC	30/10/82		Ards	A	W	5	0	Jameson, Manley 3, D.Neill
UC	06/11/82		Glenavon	H	W	3	1	Cleary, Mullan, Manley
UC	13/11/82		Cliftonville	H	W	3	2	Jameson, Manley, Cleary
UC	20/11/82		Coleraine	A	W	3	1	Keely, O'Kane og, Jameson
UEFA	15/09/82	1.1	Banik Ostrava	H	L	1	3	Bowers
UEFA	29/09/82	1.2	Banik Ostrava	A	L	0	1	-
IL	27/11/82		Linfield	H	W	3	0	Mullan 2, D.Neill
IL	04/12/82		Crusaders	A	L	1	2	Mullan
IL	11/12/82		Distillery	H	W	4	0	Bowers, Cleary, Manley, Morrison
IL	18/12/82		Coleraine	A	L	1	3	Jameson
IL	27/12/82		Bangor	H	W	2	1	Cleary, Mullan
IL	28/12/82		Portadown	A	L	0	1	-
IL	01/01/83		Cliftonville	A	W	3	1	Harrison, Manley, Cleary
IL	03/01/83		Larne	H	W	5	0	Mullan 3, D.Neill, Manley (p)
IL	08/01/83		Ballymena United	A	W	3	1	Jameson, Bowers, Manley
IL	15/01/83		Ards	H	W	4	1	Mullan, Morrison, Jameson, Manley (p)
IL	29/01/83		Glenavon	A	W	3	1	Jameson 2, Mullan
IL	05/02/83		Linfield	A	D	2	2	Manley, Bowers
IL	19/02/83		Crusaders	H	W	3	0	Cleary, Bowers, Morrison
IL	26/02/83		Distillery	A	W	3	1	Morrison, Manley, Bowers
IL	12/03/83		Coleraine	H	L	0	1	-
IL	19/03/83		Bangor	A	W	3	0	Cleary, D.Neill, Mullan
IL	02/04/83		Portadown	H	L	0	1	-
IL	05/04/83		Cliftonville	H	D	1	1	D.Neill
IL	09/04/83		Larne	A	L	0	2	-
IL	15/04/83		Ballymena United	H	W	1	0	Cooke og
IL	19/04/83		Glenavon	H	W	4	1	Manley, D.Neill, Mullan, Stewart
IL	23/04/83		Ards	A	W	3	1	Jameson, Mullan, Manley
IC	22/01/83	1	Ballymena United	H	W	4	0	Jameson, Manley, Mullan, Bowers
IC	12/02/83	2	Ballymoney United	H	W	2	0	Cleary, McDonald og
IC	05/03/83	3	Coleraine	A	W	3	2	Bowers, Mullan, Manley
IC	25/03/83	SF	Ballyclare Comrades	WP	W	3	0	Cleary, Jameson, Manley
IC	30/04/83	F	Linfield	A	D	1	1	Mullan
IC	07/05/83	FR	Linfield	H	W	2	1	Jameson 2
CAS	12/04/83	2	Crusaders	A	W	1	0	Keely

CAS	21/04/83	SF	Ards	CdP	W	2	0	Manley, Cleary
CAS	12/05/83	F	Linfield	A	L	1	4	Manley
F	31/07/82		Dungannon Swifts	A	L	1	2	Mullan
F	03/08/82		Newry Town	A	D	1	1	Bowers (won 9-8 on penalties)
								Ambassador Cup
F	07/08/82		Bohemians	H	L	1	2	Bowers
F	10/08/82		Dundela	A	W	6	3	Troughton, Blackledge,
								Cleary 2, Maxwell og, McDaid
F	14/08/82		Manchester United	H	L	0	2	-
F	19/10/82		Wolverhampton W.	H	L	2	3	Cleary, Mullan
F	24/05/83		Ballyclare Comrades	A	D	1	1	D.Neill

Billy Bingham attended our league match with Crusaders, when we temporarily returned to a white strip, and must have been impressed by the fayre on offer as Cleary, Mullan and Bowers were called into the National squad for a three day training session at Coventry. George Neill was placed on stand-by but only Cleary appeared in the sixteen for the Turkey match. A 23 year-old physiotherapy student, Thorgeir Aalund from Norway, made history when he became the first player from outside the British Isles to represent the club. A friend of club physio Tony Wright, Aalund played centre-forward for the Seconds and scored on his second appearance.

Coleraine provided a double hurdle in March. In a thrilling Irish Cup tie at the Showgrounds we came from behind to win 3-2 but a strike from all of 25 yards from Kevin Mahon the following Saturday all but killed off our league aspirations. This was confirmed three weeks later when we did everything but score against Portadown and then a stray back pass from Strain gave Gary McCullough the chance to bury us. After winning 18 consecutive home games the Glens had lost two in a row! For us the remainder of the Gibson Cup fizzled out and after our defeat at Larne, in a game delayed to 4 p.m. to avoid a clash with the Grand National, Linfield were crowned champions. McFall blooded young midfielder Alan "Alfie"

Stewart in the last few games and he responded with a goal direct from a corner against Glenavon.

For ten long years the Irish Cup had proved elusive but hopes were raised when we drew "B" Division Ballyclare Comrades at the semi-final stage. For some reason the IFA switched the game to a Friday night at Windsor Park, a decision in direct conflict to their earlier policy of disallowing floodlights as this allegedly put sides not

Johnny Jameson scores past George Dunlop in the Irish Cup final replay.

used to them at a disadvantage. In any event we won comfortably, by 3-0, the best goal a lovely chip from Jameson. The Comrades turned out in a blue, white and red strip – no doubt an attempt to win over any neutral support! However, even with ex-Glentoran players Paul Kirk, Andy Dougan and Tom Stewart in their side they never posed a threat. Linfield duly overcame Ards 2-1 the next day to set up a repeat of the 1973 final.

For goalkeeper Alan Paterson, who had obtained the number one jersey back from Reggie Hillen, there was the chance of an unusual cup final hat-trick. He had been a ball-boy when the Glens beat the Blues in the 1966 and was the only playing survivor from ten years before when he had to retire at half-time through injury.

Jameson scores again in the Irish Cup final replay with Lindsay McKeown appearing to be accompanying him on the guitar!

The final at Windsor Park was a poor game and finished all square, a Lindsay McKeown penalty cancelling out Mullan's opener. Many thought we had scored a late winner through Jameson but Hugh Wilson ruled it out for "pushing". The replay took place at the Oval the following Saturday and there was a carnival atmosphere at the Sydenham end of the ground, typified by fans hurling a cockerel onto the pitch. No-one could catch the bird as it strutted around the pitch for the entire game!

A "flyer" of a different kind settled the final between the 30th and 33rd minutes as two strikes from the Blues' bogeyman Johnny Jameson sent us on our way to victory. Even a 74th minute header by McGaughey and the harsh dismissal of Jim Cleary by referee Wilson, who was blowing the whistle for the last time, could not spoil the party as we lifted our third trophy of the season. Rab Strain had performed well in midfield in place of Bowers.

Linfield quickly gained revenge five nights later in the County Antrim Shield final. Indeed the Windsor men went 2-0 up after only eight minutes and, although we had 50% of the subsequent play, there we no complaints at the final 1-4 scoreline. How we had missed the injured Keely and the suspended Cleary. At least Jim had the consolation of being named Ulster Footballer of the Year and making another appearance for Northern Ireland as a substitute against Wales. Gerry Mullan played in all three Home Internationals, adding to his earlier cap versus Albania (as a sub) in the European Championship.

So again the club could look back on a relatively successful season, but once more the league title had eluded us.

The class of 1982/3 with their three trophies.

Appearances and Goals							
	App.	Subs.	Goals		App.	Subs.	Goals
Connell	49		1	Strain R.	19	5	
Neill G.	47			Hillen	16		
Harrison	46		1	Troughton	12	5	
Jameson	46		18	McDaid	7	1	6
Manley	45	1	30	McCreery Rab	6	3	
Cleary	42		12	Stewart A.	5	3	1
Mullan	41		18	Russell	1		
Keely	40		2	Irvine		1	
Bowers	37		12	Kingon		1	
Neill D.	37		6	Own Goals			3
Paterson	34			TOTAL	550	31	115
Morrison	20	11	5				

1983/84

Re-organised competitions – Smithwicks' sponsorship deal -
League title again elusive

The close season of 1983 saw many changes at the Oval. In the boardroom John Crossan became the new chairman replacing Johnston Nelson who took over the role of President. Frank Kerr was appointed as a new director while 32 year-old Mike Wilson was installed as the club's first ever commercial advisor. Wilson was instrumental in setting up the club's open day, organising a new Glentoran newspaper "The Cockerel" to be delivered to 30,000 homes in east Belfast and commencing a new Radio Oval service.

On the playing side our centre-half pairing of the past two seasons moved on. Dermott Keely took up a player manager position in Dublin with UCD, while Alan Harrison was lured to Ballymena by the offer of a better contract. An independent transfer tribunal later set the fee at £18,000. McFall replaced them by signing 23 year-old Paul Dixon from Burnley and the ex-Coleraine pivot John Shannon.

Coaches Dennis Shields and Bob Nesbitt had left the club and so Jim Weatherup returned while Rab Strain was put in charge of the Second XI. Two more old faces returned to east Belfast, Gary Blackledge back from his loan spell in France and also Rab McCreery, who opened the Cock n' Hens bar. Jim Cleary was named as team captain but would first have to serve a six match suspension. Season ticket prices ranged from £10 to £25 with match admission £2 (stand) and £1.30 (terraces).

The pre-season visits to the Oval by Fulham, Bolton and Motherwell certainly lacked the glamour of the previous two years and only the Fulham game provided any real entertainment. The west Londoners, under Malcolm Macdonald, paraded players such as Ray Lewington, Paul Parker, Gordon Davies, Gerry Peyton and Ray Houghton but the goal of the night still came from Cleary, an expertly taken free low kick from 20 yards.

Alan "Alfie" Stewart.

With the elevation to senior status of Newry Town and Carrick Rangers from the "B" Division the number of league clubs increased to fourteen for the first time in 43 years. This created the need for four extra league games plus a total re-organisation of the Gold and Ulster Cups. A degree in advanced logic would have helped you to understand the new format but here goes – the 14 teams were divided up into four groups, two groups having three teams and two having four. Those in the three team groups would play each other team in their group twice and also play each team in the other three team group once! Those in the four team groups would just play each other team in a four team group once. In this way all teams would have seven group games. The winners of each group would then qualify for the semi-final stage. The composition of groups for the Gold Cup, sponsored for the last time by Hennessy, was on a regional basis

Our opening fixture was more special for visitors Newry Town, who were under their guidance of ex-Glenmen Barry Brown and Dennis Shields, as it marked their return to

391

senior circles for the first time since 1939/40 season. However they had a big step up to make, evidenced by our 5-1 victory. We went on to qualify comfortably for the semi-finals overcoming our Section A opponents Ards and Bangor twice by high scoring margins. Indeed we scored 21 goals against the North Down teams with Ron Manley going nap against Bangor at the Oval. Manley's first three goals were solid headers. Defeats at Portadown and Glenavon were meaningless for us but the Lurgan Blues' win ensured they would meet us again at the semi-final stage.

Once more we obtained a favourable European draw, this time French side Paris St. Germain. It was a tall order for the Glens as PSG had players such as Dominique Rocheteau, Gerard Janvion, Patrick Bethanay and the Yugoslav Safet Susic at their disposal. However in the first leg at the Oval Jameson's pace troubled the French and with fifteen minutes remaining the winger fired us ahead with a spectacular volley. PSG fought back however and netted through Zaremba and N'Gom in the 78th and 83rd minutes. This was all the more commendable as the visitors had been reduced to ten men following the dismissal of Luis Fernandez by fussy Belgian referee Alfonse Constantin.

Over 400 supporters made the trip to the Parc des Princes for the return leg and they were rewarded when Gerry Mullan put the Glens ahead on twenty minutes. Goals after the break though from Bathenay and Susic allowed the Parisians to progress to Round Two on a 4-2 aggregate where they would meet Juventus.

Glentoran's Ulster Cup section containing Crusaders (managed by ex-Cougar Tommy Jackson) and Linfield was a more difficult prospect than the Gold Cup. However we began well with an easy win over the Crues and then a brilliant display to beat the Blues at Windsor Park. Long range efforts from Blackledge and Cleary gave us a 2-0 interval lead and when Manley rolled in number three just after the break we were threatening to run up a cricket score. However, in typical fashion, Linfield fought back to reduce the final arrears to 2-3. Our new signing from League of Ireland champions Athlone Town, blond centre-half Harry McCue came into the side as we progressed nicely to top our Ulster Cup section by five clear points.

In the autumn two further obituaries were penned. The first was for Glens' 1st team attendant Davy Roberts, 53, who had been in post for six years. Teddy Horner was named as the new kit-man and a memorial trophy in the name of Roberts was created for the second team player of the month. The legendary Joe Bambrick also passed away. Bambrick, more noted for his scoring exploits for Linfield, Northern Ireland and Chelsea, did have one season with Glentoran in 1926/7 when he appeared in all of our 39 games, scoring 44 of our 93 goals.

By now we had discarded our new green strip with four thin white horizontal bands and returned to the colourful outfit of 1982/3. We were involved in a dramatic Gold Cup semi-final against Glenavon. In a display of all-out attacking football by both teams Glenavon went ahead on 19 minutes but a powerful Manley drive made it 1-1 shortly after. By half-time it was 2-2 but the Lurgan men went ahead again. However their keeper Tasker dropped a cross to leave Blackledge with a simple tap-in to register another equaliser and his 100th goal for the Glens. Extra time produced no further scoring and so the tie went to a penalty shoot out. Each side were successful with their first four kicks before Davy Dennison missed for Glenavon. Gerry Mullan then blasted his kick into the net and so we went through in the cruellest of manners with universal sympathy registered for Dennison.

The Gold Cup final was a "blue" night for us in many ways for not only did we go down 1-3 to Linfield but also lost Davy Neill in the seventh minute to a knee injury which, despite a couple of brave comeback attempts, was to end the Randalstown man's playing career.

By the start of the Irish League McCue had been dropped. Tom Connell moved across to centre-half to partner Dixon with Tommy Leeman coming in at left-back. Leeman's uncle Dick had played for the Glens in the late 1950's before emigrating to South Africa and his grandfather Tommy had also played in the 1930's. We began in style by routing Larne 9-2 and putting another five past Newry. However we were brought down to earth courtesy of another defeat by Linfield at Windsor Park. Dornan, McGaughey and Doherty scored for the Blues after we had been in complete control for the first twenty minutes only to be continually foiled by George Dunlop. To add insult Cleary was sent off for foul language by referee Snoddy and Blackledge had to come off with a thigh injury.

Jameson celebrates Mullan's goal against Paris St Germain in the Parc des Princes.

This defeat was just three days after we had lifted the Ulster Cup in glorious fashion at the same venue. It was a night of personal triumph for Gary Blackledge as he put four past the Bannsiders, including a hat-trick during extra-time, in our 5-2 win.

For Cleary the blow of another suspension was softened by his inclusion in four Northern Ireland squads and a substitute appearance against Turkey in Ankara. His late call up for the West German game necessitated a 100 mile dash from Fermanagh to catch a shuttle from Aldergrove to Heathrow in order to link up with the rest of the party. Being part of the resultant 1-0 win would have made it all worth it. Sammy Troughton was also displaying his skills to a wider audience. Transferred to Wolverhampton Wanderers, he soon broke into the first team making 20 appearances and scoring goals in First Division games versus Norwich and Manchester United.

Meanwhile there were further commercial improvements at the Oval. The Gazette sported a new colour cover with pictures of our celebrating Irish Cup and Ulster Cup teams of 1983 and a second edition of The Cockerel was distributed. More importantly Smithwicks announced that they would be sponsoring the Glens, initially on a three year deal and so another company's name would appear on our jerseys. On the playing side it was revealed that we had made an abortive move to get Dermott Keely back to the club and that twelve months earlier the Glens had made a secret bid to sign Nottingham Forest's unsettled £1 million striker Justin Fashanu on a short term basis!

In December we won three and drew our other three league games to finish the year in second place in the table, just a point behind the Blues. This run began with a 3-3 draw against Ards when we had to come from 0-2 down in the last 29 minutes. There was success down the club too when Glentoran Colts defeated Ballymena United Youth 2-1 in the IFA Youth Cup final at Solitude. Tim Kelly scored the winner in the last minute after Paul Millar had netted the Colts' first equalising goal.

With Davy Neill injured Glentoran employed the services of Tony McCall over the Christmas and New Year period. McCall won many admirers before returning to university in South Carolina. George Neill began 1984 in scoring form with his first competitive goal for the club as did Cleary with a hat-trick against Bangor, the first after only 30 seconds.

The vagaries of the Irish League fixture list decreed that clubs would face each other on consecutive Saturdays as the league passed its half-way stage. We recorded back-to-back victories over Coleraine, a Jameson cross-cum-shot at the Showgrounds and a 25 yard

Results 1983/84

Played 52. Won 34. Drew 9. Lost 9. Goals For 135. Against 49. % 74.0.
Honours: Ulster Cup

GC	20/08/83		Newry Town	H	W	5	1	Manley, Stewart 2, Blackledge, Bowers
GC	23/08/83		Bangor	A	W	7	0	Manley 2, Blackledge, Bowers (p), D.Neill, Jameson, Stewart
GC	27/08/83		Ards	A	W	4	0	Manley 2, Bowers (p), Blackledge
GC	30/08/83		Ards	H	W	5	2	Morrison, Manley, Blackledge 2, D.Neill
GC	03/09/83		Portadown	A	L	0	1	-
GC	06/09/83		Bangor	H	W	5	0	Manley 5(1p)
GC	10/09/83		Glenavon	A	L	1	2	Mullan
GC	04/10/83	SF	Glenavon	WP	D	3	3	aet – Manley, Cleary (p), Blackledge (won 5-4 on penalties)
GC	18/10/83	F	Linfield	A	L	1	3	Blackledge
ECW	14/09/83	1.1	Paris St. Germain	H	L	1	2	Jameson
ECW	28/09/83	1.2	Paris St. Germain	A	L	1	2	Mullan
UC	17/09/83		Crusaders	H	W	5	1	Cleary (p), Mullan, Jameson 3
UC	24/09/83		Linfield	A	W	3	2	Blackledge, Cleary, Manley
UC	01/10/83		Distillery	H	W	2	0	Blackledge, Jameson
UC	08/10/83		Crusaders	A	W	3	1	Cleary (p), Manley 2
UC	15/10/83		Ballymena United	H	W	1	0	Blackledge
UC	22/10/83		Carrick Rangers	A	W	2	0	Blackledge 2
UC	29/10/83		Linfield	H	D	1	1	Stewart
UC	08/11/83	SF	Carrick Rangers	WP	W	4	0	Manley, Cleary 2(1p), Bowers
UC	22/11/83	F	Coleraine	WP	W	5	2	aet – Blackledge 4, McDowell og
IL	05/11/83		Larne	H	W	9	2	Bowers, Manley 3, Cleary 3(2p), Jameson, Sloan og
IL	12/11/83		Crusaders	A	W	3	2	Bowers, Blackledge 2
IL	19/11/83		Newry Town	H	W	5	0	Stewart, Blackledge 2, Mullan 2
IL	26/11/83		Linfield	A	L	0	3	-
IL	03/12/83		Ards	H	D	3	3	Manley, Blackledge, Dixon
IL	10/12/83		Ballymena United	A	W	4	1	Bowers 2, Mullan 2
IL	17/12/83		Carrick Rangers	H	W	6	1	Manley, Mullan, Cleary 2(1p), Bowers, Jameson
IL	24/12/83		Cliftonville	A	W	1	0	Blackledge
IL	26/12/83		Distillery	H	D	1	1	Bowers
IL	31/12/83		Portadown	A	D	0	0	-
IL	02/01/84		Glenavon	A	W	3	1	Cleary, Mullan, G.Neill
IL	07/01/84		Bangor	H	W	6	0	Cleary 3(2p), McCall, Blackledge, Mullan
IL	14/01/84		Coleraine	A	W	1	0	Jameson
IL	21/01/84		Coleraine	H	W	1	0	Cleary
IL	04/02/84		Larne	A	W	2	0	Mullan, Bowers
IL	11/02/84		Crusaders	H	W	1	0	Jameson
IL	25/02/84		Newry Town	A	W	1	0	Manley
IL	03/03/84		Linfield	H	W	4	1	Cleary 2(1p), Mullan, Bowers
IL	17/03/84		Ards	A	D	0	0	-
IL	24/03/84		Ballymena United	H	D	0	0	-
IL	31/03/84		Carrick Rangers	A	W	2	0	Jameson 2
IL	14/04/84		Cliftonville	H	L	1	2	Jameson
IL	18/04/84		Distillery	A	W	4	0	Bowers 2, Blackledge 2

IL	21/04/84		Portadown	H	W	2	0	Blackledge, Morrison
IL	23/04/84		Glenavon	H	D	1	1	Blackledge
IL	28/04/84		Bangor	A	W	4	1	Blackledge, Dixon, Manley, Bradley og
IC	28/01/84	1	H & W Welders	H	W	4	0	Bowers, Cleary, Mullan 2
IC	18/02/84	2	Bangor	A	D	2	2	Bowers, Mullan
IC	27/02/84	2R	Bangor	H	W	3	1	McCue, Mullan, Bowers
IC	10/03/84	3	Glenavon	H	W	1	0	Manley
IC	07/04/84	SF	Carrick Rangers	WP	L	1	2	Bowers
CAS	03/04/84	1	Ballyclare Comrades	H	L	0	2	-
F	02/08/83		Dundela	H	W	2	0	Manley, Jameson
F	05/08/83		Fulham	H	L	1	3	Cleary
F	08/08/83		Bolton Wanderers	H	D	0	0	-
F	11/08/83		Motherwell	H	L	1	2	Bowers
F	13/08/83		Limavady United	A	W	2	1	D.Neill, Bowers
F	20/03/84		Irish League XI	H	D	1	1	Blackledge Johnny Jamison Benefit (Glentoran/Crusaders XI)
F	10/04/84		Bryansburn Rangers	A	W	5	0	Jameson 2, Blackledge, Cleary, Mullan

Cleary drive at the Oval earning us the points. Reserve striker John McDaid was placed on the transfer list and he went to Elland Road on a 10-day trial for a second time. We concluded January with an Irish Cup win over the Harland and Wolff Welders with our former centre-half Sammy Cranston playing against us.

Paul Dixon was in good form as we kept six successive clean sheets in the league. In fact between New Year's Eve and the Saturday before Easter goalkeepers Paterson and Hillen conceded only two goals in 1,000 minutes of football. Tommy Leeman's promise was rewarded with a dream move to Glasgow Rangers in the middle of February as Harry McCue returned to the team after a ten week injury lay-off. McCue set us on the way to victory over Bangor as we qualified for the Cup quarter-finals after needing a late Mullan equaliser to earn a replay.

Linfield visited the Oval on the first Saturday in March for the vital league encounter. What a day it proved to be for the Glens from the moment Cleary put us ahead in the 10th minute from the rebound of a penalty. Dornan equalised for the Blues eight minutes before the break but Linfield were getting little change from our defence which was superbly marshalled by McCue. The Dubliner's performance made a mockery of one banner at the City end proclaiming "Harry Miscue!" Goals in the second half from Mullan, the outstanding Bowers and another Cleary penalty gave the Blues a 4-1 drubbing and only numerous fine Dunlop saves prevented a complete humiliation for our rivals.

So with eight games remaining the Glens held a three point lead but Linfield did have a game in hand. The high spot of the season came the following Saturday as we beat Glenavon 1-0 at home in the Irish Cup but then, quite inexplicably, the team went completely off the boil.

We commenced a run yielding only one win in six games with scoreless draws versus Ards (we hit the bar twice in the closing minutes) and Ballymena when Brian Crockard was outstanding in the Braidmen's nine-man defence. Jameson's two lobs earned a win at Carrick but the next seven days produced two embarrassing defeats. Firstly in the County Antrim Shield when Arthur Stewart's Ballyclare Comrades came to the Oval and won 2-0 to end our twenty match unbeaten run. The goals came from Paul McDowell and Paul Kirk in the 66th and 72nd minutes. Then on the Saturday Carrick Rangers put us to the sword in the Irish Cup semi-final, both of the East Antrim men's goal courtesy of Davy Richardson. Worse was to follow when Cliftonville beat us at home to end our diminished Gibson Cup hopes as much of our commitment and spirit evaporated.

The remainder of the season just fizzled out, but at least Blackie ended his fifteen game scoring drought by netting in all of our concluding four league games and in a friendly against Bryansburn Rangers at Upritchard Park. The Colts entered the Eastercraigs Youth tournament in Scotland and finished fourth, after gaining a 1-1 draw with the eventual winners Doncaster Rovers.

In early 1984 former player Johnny Jamison lost the sight of one eye following a street incident. As "Stumpy" had always been a popular figure at the Oval the club decided to hold a further testimonial match for him with a Glentoran-Crusaders Select XI meeting a Rest of the League XI. However Linfield upset the applecart when they subsequently announced that they had arranged a prestige friendly with Glasgow Rangers at Windsor Park the same evening! After a lot of "to-ing and fro-ing" both games went ahead with the Oval crowd numbering 2,000 compared to 12,000 elsewhere. Glenmen were urged not to attend the Windsor fixture, being told that Rangers would definitely visit the Oval later in the year as part of the Leeman deal. However that match and other proposed fixtures against Glasgow Celtic and Athlone Town fell through. Leeman played the last 25 minutes at Windsor Park as Rangers won 4-0 and over sixteen years later his two clubs finally met, and at Ibrox! The Jamison benefit game finished 1-1, a late Blackledge effort cancelling out Bertie McMinn's opener for the grey-shirted League XI. International winger Ian Stewart came on for the Glens-Crues XI in the second half. Linfield, it must be said, did arrange another benefit match for Jamison when they entertained League of Ireland champions Shamrock Rovers who included Dermott Keely. A crowd of 4,000 saw the Blues win 1-0.

At the end of a very frustrating season collectively, Jim Cleary had one more honour to collect when he was named the N.I.P.F.A. Player of the Year.

Appearances and Goals						
	App.	Subs.	Goals		App.	Subs.	Goals
Bowers	52		18	Leeman	15		
Neill G.	51		1	McCue	15		1
Dixon	48		2	Neill D.	15		2
Manley	46	3	24	Morrison	10	3	2
Connell	45			McCall	6		1
Cleary	42		19	Troughton	5	1	
Jameson	41	4	13	Shannon	5		
Blackledge	38	6	28	Kelly	1	1	
Stewart A.	36		5	McDaid		1	
Paterson	33			Own Goals			3
Mullan	30	10	16	TOTAL	572	29	135
Hillen	19						
Strain R.	19						

Gary Blackledge scores a spectacular late equaliser against Tottenham with Ossie Ardiles helpless.

1984/85

Linfield an early obstacle – Ronnie McFall sacked - A cockerel and a pig

This season marked a much deserved testimonial for 63 year old groundsman Billy Crawford. The Lisburn man had been at the Oval as long as the turf itself as he arrived in August 1949 coinciding with our return from Grosvenor Park. Chairman John Crossan also received an honour when he was appointed to the presidency of the Irish League, the first Glentoran man in this post since Toby Mercer in 1941/2. Billy Stephens came onto the board to replace Dick Bickerstaff.

With no addition to our playing panel we returned an unbeaten record for our six pre-season friendlies. This included a draw with Second Division Brighton and Hove Albion and a narrow win at Moyola Park, Alfie Stewart's old club. A 16 year-old Dundonald schoolboy, Paul Millar, scored two for us at Dundela. Billy McCullough was welcomed back to the club as youth team coach.

The Ulster Cup and TNT Gold Cup were played on the same confusing format as in 1983/4 and once more we qualified comfortably for the semi finals of the Gold Cup, finishing four points ahead of Ards. During the group games there were many notable incidents; Jim Cleary's opening goal of the season and John McDaid's scoring return against Bangor when the saves of Reggie Hillen kept us in the game. In his day job Hillen had been a site engineer on the new North Stand at Windsor Park.

We also had the cool displays of young Tim Kelly to savour, a brilliant Barney Bowers hat-trick in the space of nineteen minutes at Bangor and a great attacking match with Glenavon, even though it finished scoreless! The Lurgan men's glum expressions at the final whistle soon turned to glee when news of Portadown's defeat came through as it meant they qualified to meet us in a repeat of the previous year's

Jim Cleary.

semi. On the negative side Tom Connell broke his ankle in the opening game at Newry and at the age of 26 Johnny Jameson decided to quit football in order to devote more time to youth leadership at his church.

As autumn turned to winter we figured in a mix of Gold Cup play-offs, Ulster Cup fixtures and a European tie. The Glens began the Ulster Cup poorly and a well-organised Linfield side easily beat us 2-0 at the Oval. The first goal was placed into his own net by Harry McCue – this would not have gone down well with the Glenmen displaying the "Prince Harry" banner, a droll double-take a week after the birth of the latest royal!

Billy Caskey returned from the States to the Glens' midfield for the Gold Cup semi-final. What a game this turned out to be as two Blackledge goals had put us ahead before Glenavon pulled one back. Manley soon made it 3-1 but by the 42nd minute the score stood at 3-3! Further goals from Bowers and Blackie swung the tie in our favour after the break.

Barney had also been on target with a curling free-kick just two minutes into our UEFA Cup tie with Standard Liege at the Oval. Overall we gave a brave display against the classy

Belgians but Telen's 59th minute equaliser provided us with an arduous task in Liege. However we battled away in the second leg but after Morrison struck the bar in the 22nd minute things went Standard's way and goals from Dardennes and Jelikic earned them a 3-1 aggregate success.

This match had taken place just four days after a debacle at Ballyskeagh when we went down 2-6 to Distillery. In a complete shambles of a display Davy Neill was all at sea in his comeback match playing out of position at centre-half. The fans hurled verbal abuse at

John McDaid.

manager and directors alike at the finish including many calls for Ronnie McFall's head. The situation went from bad to worse during the remainder of October as Linfield beat us in the Gold Cup final and we plummeted to the bottom of our Ulster Cup section. This culminated with our third defeat of the season to the Blues as arguments raged over the seating and segregation arrangements for supporters at the revamped Windsor Park. The only bright side was in Cleary gaining his fifth international cap in a 3-0 win over Israel at that venue.

McFall attempted to strengthen the defence by signing Portadown's Inter League full-back Jim Smyth for £5,000 and there was Terry Moore's return from America to play at centre-back. Davy Mills was drafted into the midfield and McDaid was taken off the transfer list. The latter responded with a hat-trick for the Seconds against Coleraine Reserves but McCue was made available for transfer after he had refused to play in the same match. Glentoran Colts certainly knew the way to goal as in a run of eight successive victories they saw off

Greenisland Rangers and Queen's Olympic to the tune of 11-1 and 10-0 respectively. Later in the season the Colts took part again in the Eastercraigs festival, eventually losing the third-place play-off 0-2 to Shamrock of Greenock.

Jim Cleary was a class apart as we began the Smirnoff Irish League with a win at Larne but by the beginning of December the team had dropped to ninth place in the table. Defeats to Crusaders, Linfield (who had come back from the dead with two goals in the last thirteen minutes) and Ards (their first win in two months) were the main reasons for the gloom.

Fans gained a glimmer of hope as we won our next two games including against Ballymena, who had Rab McCreery sent off, thanks to an 88th minute winner. Gerry Mullan was playing his heart out for the team but more disappointment came via a pre-Christmas home defeat to Cliftonville. The Reds even built up a 3-0 lead before two late Caskey goals provided a semblance of respectability.

This was the last straw however for the board of directors and Ronnie McFall was sacked after the Distillery fixture on Boxing Day. At least he ended his association with the club on a winning note. There did appear to be a "split" in the board over the decision but they publicly stated that one league title and one Irish Cup success in five and a half seasons was not good enough. McFall countered by pointing out that other trophies had been won, including the Ulster Cup three times in succession, and that he would have been prepared to resign anyway at the end of the season if he failed to bring either league or cup to the Oval.

Coaches Billy McCullough and Jim Weatherup were placed in charge of the team temporarily, commencing with the home meeting with Portadown. It was a game of open football with Sammy Troughton, on a month's loan to the Ports from Wolves, showing some lovely one-touch football. Scottish forward Billy Paton put the visitors into an early lead but McDaid equalised ten minutes into the second half.

The Glens really came to life three days later hammering Glenavon 5-0 on New Year's Day. The visitors' chief tormentor was Johnny Jameson who had returned to the game in vintage form. Terry Moore was forming an effective partnership with our "new" sweeper Bowers as Raymond Morrison was given an extended run in midfield. After an uninspiring win at Bangor the table stood as follows:

1. Coleraine played 12 points 17, 2. Ballymena United 12-16, 3. Linfield 11-15, 4. Glentoran 12-15.

Club sponsors Smithwicks launched a Glentoran "Goal of the Month" competition in January 1985 and Moore was the emphatic inaugural winner with a blistering 35 yard volley past Coleraine's Jim Platt. In a stormy game Manley and Hutton received their marching orders in the 50th minute and Raymond McCoy equalised for the league leaders nine minutes from time. However supersub Gary Blackledge snatched a winner for us five minutes later.

After an easy Irish Cup win over Carrick our return fixture at the Coleraine Showgrounds was postponed just an hour before kick-off. Hundreds of Glenmen fumed at the decision as by then many of them were travelling north.

February was a hectic month for Glentoran. For some time the directors had wanted to play games on Friday nights to see if the attraction of a floodlight match would entice more spectators through the turnstiles. Larne were our meek opponents in the experiment but the idea was deemed unsuccessful as the attendance was 25% lower than the usual and many fans wrote to the club expressing opinion in favour of Saturday afternoon matches. One reason for the lower crowd may have been the TV coverage of the Alex Higgins – Terry Griffiths snooker match after the "Hurricane" had thrilled many by beating Steve Davis in the previous round.

Snow caused the postponement of our league match at Seaview and cup tie at Ballyclare but this was overshadowed by news of the appointment on 13th February of a new manager Billy Johnston. After a successful playing career, cut short by injury, at inside-forward for Glenavon, Oldham Athletic, Coleraine and Northern Ireland (two caps), Johnston had managed Crusaders to a league title and Ballymena to an Irish Cup final. The 43 year old also boasted rugby prowess as he had appeared in the Ulster Schools Cup final for Dungannon in the late 1950's.

Johnston surmounted his immediate hurdle, although we needed a replay to see off the Comrades in the cup. In that match Michael Cullen put Ballyclare ahead with a penalty kick but the night turned sour for him as he suffered a broken leg and Blackledge scored a hat-trick against his team.

Also this month Glentoran fanatic Eric Wright launched a book entitled "Songs of the Glens". It contained over 50 Glentoran songs and poems plus many pictures from earlier days of the club. Eric promoted his work by giving a rendition of one of his favourites on UTV. Many of the poems were penned by Bob Bishop, better known as R.B. Bloomfield.

We loaned Harry McCue to Drogheda and then visited Windsor Park for a vital league game on 3rd March. Once again the Blues highlighted our defensive frailties as Martin McGaughey helped himself to a hat-trick. Linfield had now beaten us five times this season but our cause had not been helped by the dismissal of Blackledge, during his 200th game, in the 21st minute.

However, the remainder of the month saw us progress nicely in the three remaining tournaments. Bangor were beaten in the County Antrim Shield and three league wins kept us four points behind the Blues with two games in hand. It was in the Irish Cup though that we had to rely on luck when meeting Coleraine in the semi-final. Throughout the game we played second fiddle to the Bannsiders and Felix Healey put them ahead on 44 minutes direct from a corner. Then six minutes into the second half we looked dead and buried when McCoy had an open net but somehow Terry Moore got a leg to the ball to knock it clear. As the clock ticked away an equaliser finally came just nine minutes from time when Mullan hit the post and the tireless Raymond Morrison pushed the ball home. Morrison netted again in the 88th minute but there was still time for Roy McCreadie to hit the bar before the final whistle sounded. There was no doubt that these two goals played a big part in earning Raymond the Glentoran player of the season award.

Results 1984/85

Played 55. Won 30. Drew 13. Lost 12. Goals For 108. Against 60. % 66.4.
Honours: Irish Cup, County Antrim Shield

GC	18/08/84		Newry Town	A	W	3	0	Cleary 2(1p), Mallon og
GC	21/08/84		Bangor	H	W	3	0	McDaid, Manley 2
GC	25/08/84		Ards	A	D	0	0	-
GC	28/08/84		Ards	H	D	1	1	Jameson
GC	01/09/84		Portadown	H	W	4	1	Manley 2, Bowers 2
GC	05/09/84		Bangor	A	W	6	0	Mullan, Cleary (p), Bowers 3, Manley
GC	08/09/84		Glenavon	H	D	0	0	-
GC	26/09/84	SF	Glenavon	WP	W	5	3	Blackledge 3, Manley, Bowers
GC	09/10/84	F	Linfield	A	L	0	1	-
UC	15/09/84		Crusaders	A	W	2	1	Mullan, Blackledge
UC	22/09/84		Linfield	H	L	0	2	-
UC	29/09/84		Distillery	A	L	2	6	Manley, Bowers
UC	06/10/84		Crusaders	H	D	2	2	Blackledge, McCue
UC	13/10/84		Ballymena United	A	L	0	3	-
UC	20/10/84		Carrick Rangers	H	W	2	0	Morrison, Cleary
UC	27/10/84		Linfield	A	L	0	2	-
UEFA	18/09/84	1.1	Standard Liege	H	D	1	1	Bowers
UEFA	03/10/84	1.2	Standard Liege	A	L	0	2	-
IL	03/11/84		Larne	A	W	2	1	Cleary, Blackledge
IL	10/11/84		Crusaders	H	L	1	3	Manley
IL	17/11/84		Newry Town	A	W	4	1	Bowers 3(1p), Mullan
IL	24/11/84		Linfield	H	L	2	3	Manley, Mullan
IL	01/12/84		Ards	A	L	1	3	Manley
IL	08/12/84		Ballymena United	H	W	1	0	Mullan
IL	15/12/84		Carrick Rangers	A	W	2	0	McDaid, Bowers
IL	22/12/84		Cliftonville	H	L	2	3	Caskey 2
IL	26/12/84		Distillery	A	W	2	0	Smyth, Manley
IL	29/12/84		Portadown	H	D	1	1	McDaid
IL	01/01/85		Glenavon	H	W	5	0	Cleary, Manley, Morrison 2, Caskey
IL	05/01/85		Bangor	A	W	1	0	Manley
IL	12/01/85		Coleraine	H	W	2	1	Moore, Blackledge
IL	01/02/85		Larne	H	W	6	0	Morrison, Blackledge 2, Manley, Mullan, Cleary
IL	23/02/85		Newry Town	H	W	3	0	Stewart, Bowers (p), Mullan
IL	02/03/85		Linfield	A	L	1	3	Morrison
IL	16/03/85		Ards	H	W	2	0	Blackledge, Bowers (p)
IL	23/03/85		Ballymena United	A	W	3	1	Bowers (p), Mullan, Morrison
IL	06/04/85		Carrick Rangers	H	W	3	0	Mullan, Bowers (p), Jameson
IL	08/04/85		Cliftonville	A	D	1	1	Stewart
IL	11/04/85		Crusaders	A	D	1	1	Bowers
IL	16/04/85		Coleraine	A	D	2	2	Dixon, Mullan
IL	20/04/85		Portadown	A	L	0	1	-
IL	22/04/85		Distillery	H	D	0	0	-
IL	25/04/85		Glenavon	A	W	4	0	Caskey 2, Blackledge 2
IL	27/04/85		Bangor	H	D	1	1	Jameson
IC	19/01/85	1	Carrick Rangers	H	W	3	0	Blackledge 2, Mullan
IC	20/02/85	2	Ballyclare Comrades	A	D	2	2	Blackledge, Cleary
IC	25/02/85	2R	Ballyclare Comrades	H	W	3	1	Blackledge 3
IC	09/03/85	3	Distillery	A	W	3	0	Cleary, Moore, Bowers (p)
IC	30/03/85	SF	Coleraine	WP	W	2	1	Morrison 2
IC	04/05/85	F	Linfield	H	D	1	1	Mullan

IC	11/05/85	FR	Linfield	A	W	1	0	Mooney og
CAS	12/03/85	1	Bangor	H	W	3	1	aet – Jameson, Manley 2
CAS	18/04/85	2	Linfield	A	W	1	0	aet – Jameson
CAS	13/05/85	SF	Ards	A	W	3	2	aet – Blackledge 3
CAS	17/05/85	F	Crusaders	H	W	2	1	Mills, Stewart (p)
F	01/08/84		Brighton & Hove A.	H	D	0	0	-
F	04/08/84		Bohemians	A	D	1	1	Manley
F	07/08/84		Ballymoney United	A	W	2	0	Cleary (p), Stewart
F	09/08/84		Moyola Park	A	W	1	0	Mullan
F	11/08/84		Shelbourne	H	W	4	1	Morrison, McCue, Cleary, Manley
F	14/08/84		Dundela	A	W	5	0	Millar 2, Morrison, Blackledge, McDaid

As the fixture congestion worsened left-back Tommy Leeman returned to Glentoran after an unsuccessful thirteen month stint at Ibrox Park. The league had developed into a three horse race between ourselves, Linfield and Coleraine and we lost vital ground when drawing three tough midweek away fixtures in the space of a week in mid-April. The highlights from these games were a fine angled drive from Alfie Stewart in the 83rd minute at Solitude and a great display of save making from Paterson at Coleraine.

Just two days later we ventured to Windsor Park for a second round Shield tie. Linfield were clear favourites to put one over on us for the sixth time that season but a great display from Paul Dixon kept McGaughey quiet and the game entered extra-time scoreless. With twelve minutes remaining Johnston brought on Jameson and within 120 seconds Johnny had dribbled through the Blues' defence to score the game's only goal. This result ended Linfield's dominance over us and was a great confidence booster for the Irish Cup final in sixteen days time.

Before then the Windsor men secured their fourth consecutive title as we failed to score against either Portadown or Distillery and Coleraine lost at home to Cliftonville. The Bannsiders just pipped us for second place.

Glentoran won the toss for the cup final venue and a large crowd assembled at the Oval on 4th May 1985. Before kick-off Glentoran supporters repeated their act of 1983 by throwing a cockerel onto the pitch. However this time it had a supporting cast in the form of a piglet dubbed in Blue with the letters "L.F.C." A group of fans had obtained the animal from a local farm and fed it on a diet of hamburgers in the days before the final! Note after the game the piglet was returned to the farm unharmed. Needless to say all attempts to catch the two visitors failed with George Dunlop and Teddy Horner most unlucky in their efforts. The game itself was much less interesting and finished in deadlock at 1-1, a deflected George Gibson header two minutes before half-time cancelling out Mullan's opening 24th minute header. Six players were booked in a game which was also hampered by the pitch being covered in hundreds of toilet rolls. To cap it all linesman Jack Poucher was struck by a stone.

The replay at Windsor Park was a much more civilised affair and was decided by a touch of misfortune for Linfield full-back Paul Mooney in the 36th minute. The Glens had a move on the right with George Neill overlapping. The ball came over to Mullan who shot across the goal and Mooney, running in to clear, could only slam the ball into his own net! The Blues brought on Billy Murray at half-time but he was tightly marked by Leeman and at the final whistle the

Ron Manley.

celebrations began as we had maintained our record of not losing to Linfield in an Irish Cup final since 1945.

After securing the "Blue Riband" of Irish football there was still the County Antrim Shield to play for and we visited Ards on the Monday night for the semi-final. Although it was all Glentoran in the early stages the home side forged ahead through Campbell (38 minutes) and Young (72 minutes) before substitute Gary Blackledge took over. Blackie fired in two in the last seven minutes and then grabbled the winner nine minutes into extra-time. Probably the least happy Glenman that night was Billy Caskey who had to jet back to the USA and rejoin Terry Moore, thus missing out on the chance to complete his set of Irish League medals with a Shield one.

The Oval hosted the Shield final against Crusaders on a Friday night and before kick-off a minute's silence was observed in memory of those killed in the Bradford fire disaster. The game itself was hard fought and Paterson had to make many fine saves before Davy Mills opened the scoring after a 30 yard run. McKay levelled a minute into the second half but two minutes later Alfie Stewart netted the eventual winner from the penalty spot after Leeman had been brought down by Albert Holden. For Stewart it was double joy at the end of a hard season as his competent displays had earned him the Young Player of the Year award.

Billy Johnston could rightly look back on his first three months in charge with some satisfaction as he had brought two trophies to the Oval.

Appearances and Goals

	App.	Subs.	Goals		App.	Subs.	Goals
Cleary	53		9	Strain R.	15		
Stewart A.	51		3	McCue	14		1
Bowers	50		18	Smyth J.	12		1
Mullan	48	2	12	Leeman	10	1	
Morrison	44	1	8	Kelly	10	4	
Manley	43	5	16	McDaid	9	4	3
Neill G.	41			Mills	6	5	1
Caskey W.	33		5	Connell	4		
Moore	30	1	2	Neill D.	1	1	
Paterson	29			Russell	1		
Hillen	26			Own Goals			2
Jameson	26	4	5				
Blackledge	25	9	21	TOTAL	605	40	108
Dixon	24	3	1				

1985/86

Disappointing early exits – Dismissals for spitting - Millar's dramatic winner

Glentoran began the season in the North-West of Ireland and finished it ten months later in sun-splashed Florida, covering a lot of miles in between. That pre-season trip to Portstewart produced shock defeats at the hands of junior opposition Roe Valley and Ballymoney, where captain Paul Dixon was sent off for an innocuous challenge, but four days later we had a convincing win at Crothers' Memorial Park, Banbridge. Jim Cowden, an £8,000 buy from Ards, made his debut in that game and set his Oval career off on the right lines with a hat-trick!

Billy Johnston's only other signing was Brian Strain from Amateur League outfit Killyleagh YC, but Terry Moore returned again from his exploits with Tulsa and the Canadian national side. Moving out of the club were Tim Kelly and Stephen Baxter, both to Ards, and John McDaid to Portadown.

We remained unbeaten in the rest of the three warm-up games including an excellent win over Shamrock Rovers, when Ron Manley scored the winner following a jinking run past the entire visitors' defence. It was an unhappy return to the Oval for Dermott Keely who put through his own goal in the 22nd minute. A new strip was on display, a green shirt with a broad horizontal, mainly red with a bit of black, stripe. The Gazette sported a new cover decorated with pictures from the 1985 Irish Cup final.

Thankfully, the complicated Ulster and Gold Cup formats were radically revised. The former was played first and two "B" Division sides were invited to make up four groups of four with the top two in each progressing to the quarter-finals. Missing five regulars, including Jim Cleary, to injury we opened up with a hard fought draw with Chimney Corner, suffering a Dixon own goal and a dismissal for Tom "Leeper" Leeman after only seventeen minutes.

Despite fielding a makeshift team and having Gerry Mullan sent off in injury time at Castlereagh Park for spitting, qualification was ensured with wins over Ards and Glenavon. The home quarter-final clash with Cliftonville was an all out attacking display from both sides with the goal of the game a brilliant Blackledge header from a curling Jameson cross. However the match was still level at 2-2 after extra time and in the resultant penalty shoot-out costly misses by Morrison and Stewart allowed the Reds to go through.

The Gold Cup was played as a mini-league, each team meeting the other once. However the side topping the table would not necessarily win the cup as the top four teams in the table would go through to a play-offs stage! Glentoran began with another poor show against Linfield at Windsor Park in a game brought forward to a 1.30 pm kick-off to avoid clashing with the Black Perceptory parades. Our defence was ripped apart as we won nothing in the air in a 0-4 defeat.

Worse was to follow on the Wednesday evening when Dundela came to the Oval and knocked us out of the County Antrim Shield. The Duns went 2-0 up though Billy Large and Jim Stewart before we pulled back to level terms. Then disaster struck as a harmless cross beyond the far post was first caught then dropped by Reggie Hillen and the ball rolled across the face of the goal for Stephen Milburn to tap into the empty net.

Another poor defensive display prevented us from reaching the second round in Europe. We were favourites against Fram of Reykjavik, indeed the Fram officials had requested the first leg to be switched to their ground. In Iceland things began well and another special free-kick from Barney Bowers gave the Glens a third minute lead. However we were again exposed in the air at the back and Fram struck three times in the second period. So in the return leg we required a 2-0 win to go through but we only managed one, a Mullan effort ten minutes from time. Previously Fram had conceded an average of four goals in every away European tie.

403

Jim Cleary, in his benefit season, had returned to action at Larne the previous Saturday and this coincided with a distinct improvement in both form and results. We returned a 100% record during October to go joint top of the Gold Cup with Coleraine. Cleary scored one of the best goals ever seen at the Oval against Crusaders. He picked the ball up 35 yards out, turned and shot past Dean Smyth to earn rapturous applause from the grandstand and terraces alike. Our run was maintained in a Friday night friendly win over Banbridge in a fixture hastily arranged as our scheduled game at Solitude could not take place.

Two fine professional wins over Coleraine and Cliftonville (re-arranged to the Oval) put us two points clear at the top. Supporters could have celebrated by buying a new replica version of our kit. Despite not winning any of our remaining three games we clinched a top four spot. Two goals from Stephen Baxter gave Ards a 2-0 win over us as Terry Moore and Tim Kelly were ordered off by referee Duffy. Manager Johnston was unable to attend the semi-final with Crusaders due to a stomach ulcer and maybe it was just as well as Kirk Hunter's hat-trick which knocked us out would have done nothing for his health. Ironically the Crues lifted the Gold Cup after needing goal difference to finish fourth in the table!

The Irish League championship commenced in early December and we put previous disappointments behind us in winning our first six games to the turn of the New Year. There was plenty of action at Newry in the second fixture as young Paul Miller had a scoring full debut. Hillen was forced to retire with a head injury and Tom Connell donned the number one jersey. Cowden too left the pitch but under different circumstances as he was dismissed for kicking Marty Magee. Moore was organising the defence well and only Jim Campbell of Ards was able to find our net in the early league fixtures. Later in that game though Campbell, wearing black gloves due to the bitter cold, was sent off as was Ballymena's Colin O'Neill during our New Year's Day noon showdown at the Showgrounds.

Barney Bowers had the misfortune of breaking his leg at Carrick and became another of Tony Wright's long-term injury victims. Davy Neill was bravely attempting to solve his problem with a trip to see Manchester United physio Jimmy McGregor and a subsequent knee operation in Birmingham. Harry McCue left Glentoran for good, signing for Dundalk, and news arrived that Sammy Troughton was now plying his trade for Arcadia in South Africa. A welcome visitor to the Oval over Christmas was centre-forward of the late sixties and early seventies Tommy Morrow, who was enjoying a break back in Ulster from his adopted Australia.

In his role as League President our chairman John Crossen had a battle on his hands as RTE began screening live coverage of an English First Division game every Saturday. Many pubs and clubs installed RTE aerials so creating yet another alternative to standing on the terraces. Matters were not helped by the League insisting on 2.15 or 2.30 pm kick-offs during the winter, thus denying Glentoran and Linfield the use of their floodlights. Irish Cup games, however, were allowed to commence at 3 pm, bringing even more confusion to the average punter.

The rest of January 1986 was not a happy time for us. Firstly our game at Larne was called off an hour before kick-off and the loss in momentum was reflected in an awful display against Glenavon at the Oval a week later. In grim conditions we went down to a Denver goal after 31 minutes, falling four points behind the Blues in the League race. However we had a chance to make amends with a visit to Windsor Park on a Tuesday evening ten days later.

Trevor Anderson gave Linfield a flying start, scoring after only 45 seconds, but Raymond Morrison equalised in the 14th minute. Just before the half-hour Sloan restored the Blues' lead before the controversy of the night after 37 minutes. Johnny Jameson, who had been kicked and elbowed all during the match, won another free-kick and, as he ran away, he spat at the ground. Amazingly Jameson was sent off for this, referee Oliver Donnelly ruling that he had spat at opposition full-back Gary McCartney! During the second half the ten-man Glens swarmed all over the Blues but none of the many chances created were turned into the vital goal. After the match captain Jim Cleary spoke up, voicing an opinion held by Glenmen and supporters of other clubs, by saying that "You get nothing at Windsor Park" inferring that referees are somehow intimidated into giving decisions Linfield's way. Blues manager Roy Coyle thought it was all sour grapes.

We kept our hopes alive by winning the next three league games, including coming from behind at an icy Solitude, while Ards did us a favour by going to Windsor and winning 2-0.

Blackledge made a rare appearance in the first team, deputising for the injured Mullan against Larne, scoring the winner from the penalty spot. With the lanky Paul Millar now a regular up front, Ron Manley was enjoying his new midfield role.

Our results over the next six weeks were extremely inconsistent. Coleraine came to the Oval and, with Felix Healey starring in white gloves, clinically beat us 2-0. However in the return fixture just a fortnight later it was all one-way traffic in the second half as we put five goals past a bemused Jim Platt. We knew we had to beat Linfield at the Oval to stay in the league race and in a tremendous first half spell of nineteen minutes both sides scored twice. It remained 2-2 until the 72nd minute when Terry Moore scored a tragic own goal to give the Blues victory. As a result we trailed by seven points with only one game in hand. Further defeats at Portadown and Crusaders ended our interest in the title. Ex-Glenman McDaid got the winner in the former whilst Pat McCoy tore us apart at Seaview.

On the bright side we had made good progress in the defence of the Irish Cup. Despite a missed penalty by Mullan we overcame Distillery in Round One but then once more we needed a replay to oust the battling Ballyclare. Millar saved our blushes with a late equaliser at Dixon Park and he was on target after five minutes of the replay. Big Paul feat's continued with the only goal in the quarter-final against the Reds when his spectacular strike earned him the Bass "Personality of the Round" award. Gerry Mullan took over the leading role in the semi-final as we comfortably beat "B" Division Brantwood at Windsor in a Friday night. Coleraine beat Ards 2-0 at Ballymena the following day and were immediately installed as cup favourites. Indeed in a poll of the other twelve Irish League manager, ten predicted victory for the Bannsiders.

No doubt they were influenced by our abysmal league form as in a spell of six games we captured only three points, scoring a mere three goals in the process. After pathetic displays against Glenavon and Distillery there were calls for Gary Blackledge to return to the team. Blackie had scored 24 goals in 15 games for the Seconds as they marched towards the "B" Division title. Billy Johnston was warned that although a one-off cup final win would bring short-term joy, it would not paper over the obvious cracks in the team.

It was against this background of despondency that we kicked off the Bass Irish Cup final on 3rd May 1986. On a surprisingly damp day Glentoran Player of the Year Gerry Mullan gave us the lead when he headed home past a flat-footed Platt. But one minute into the second half Coleraine were level when Alan Snoddy awarded them a penalty for "hands" against Moore. Healey converted. With twelve minutes remaining Johnston sent on sub Paul Millar. Millar was disappointed at not making the starting line-up after scoring in all previous matches but he dramatically retained this record in injury time when his speculative volley from the edge of the area flew into the net! There was no time for Coleraine to come back and so we had retained the Cup and won the £5,000 prize money. Millar's memorable day was complete as in the morning he had attended his sister's wedding and become engaged himself.

It was a curio that all of Glentoran's thirteen Irish Cup goals were scored by players whose surname began with M. Terry Moore was also delighted as he left on the Monday to join the Canadian World Cup squad with a winners' medal in his pocket. Moore was unlucky in that despite playing in all but one of the World Cup warm up games he lost his place due to a suspension and failed to appear in the Mexico finals.

The Irish Cup was paraded at the Oval before the Cliftonville game three days later when again Millar was on target in a 1-1 draw. Distillery had just recorded their first Oval victory over us in 25 years and then Bangor obtained their biggest win on our ground since 1932 when they triumphed 4-1! Some normality was restored when we beat Ballymena to finish the league in fourth place. Teenage full-back Philip Major made his debut in this game and set up one of Mullan's goals.

Before setting off on our US trip, which had been organised by Ulsterman Noel Lemon, now a Stateside personality and businessman, we played a couple of testimonials. One was for Linfield's Steve McKee and the other for Dr. Michael Cullen of Ballyclare, the man who had broken his leg against us in the Irish Cup some fifteen months earlier, ending his playing career. The Ballyclare XI included Linfield's Barr and Anderson and Ulster Player of the Year Pat McCoy who we had just signed from Crusaders for the following season.

Results 1985/86

Played 53. Won 30. Drew 9. Lost 14. Goals For 97. Against 58. % 65.1.
Honours: Irish Cup

UC	17/08/85		Chimney Corner	H	D	2	2	Manley 2
UC	20/08/85		Ards	A	W	3	1	Manley, Bowers 2(1p)
UC	24/08/85		Glenavon	H	W	2	0	Morrison, Jameson
UC	28/08/85	QF	Cliftonville	H	D	2	2	aet – Jameson, Blackledge (lost 2-4 on penalties)
GC	31/08/85		Linfield	A	L	0	4	-
GC	07/09/85		Glenavon	H	D	1	1	Stewart
GC	14/09/85		Carrick Rangers	A	W	4	1	Morrison, Jameson 2, Mullan
GC	17/09/85		Bangor	H	W	3	0	Mullan, Bowers (p), Morrison
GC	28/09/85		Larne	A	W	2	1	Mullan, Manley
GC	05/10/85		Ballymena United	H	W	2	1	Mullan, Moore
GC	12/10/85		Distillery	A	W	4	1	Mullan 2, Bowers (p), Jameson
GC	19/10/85		Crusaders	H	W	3	0	Moore, Cleary, Blackledge
GC	02/11/85		Coleraine	A	W	1	0	Mullan
GC	05/11/85		Cliftonville	H	W	5	1	Moore, Stitt og, Blackledge 2, Cleary
GC	09/11/85		Ards	H	L	0	2	-
GC	16/11/85		Newry Town	A	D	0	0	-
GC	30/11/85		Portadown	H	D	2	2	Mullan, Manley
GC	04/12/85	SF	Crusaders	WP	L	2	3	aet – Mullan, Morrison
CAS	04/09/85	2	Dundela	H	L	2	3	Bowers (p), Jameson
ECW	21/09/85	1.1	Fram	A	L	1	3	Bowers
ECW	02/10/85	1.2	Fram	H	W	1	0	Mullan
IL	07/12/85		Portadown	H	W	1	0	Moore
IL	14/12/85		Newry Town	A	W	5	0	Bowers, Mullan, Millar, Jameson, Moore
IL	21/12/85		Crusaders	H	W	1	0	Mullan
IL	26/12/85		Carrick Rangers	A	W	2	0	Millar 2
IL	28/12/85		Ards	H	W	2	1	Mullan, Morrison
IL	01/01/86		Ballymena United	A	W	1	0	Jameson
IL	11/01/86		Glenavon	H	L	0	1	-
IL	18/01/86		Distillery	A	W	1	0	Mullan
IL	21/01/86		Linfield	A	L	1	2	Morrison
IL	25/01/86		Cliftonville	A	W	3	2	Millar, Morrison, Mullan
IL	08/02/86		Bangor	A	W	3	0	Morrison, Millar, Mullan
IL	11/02/86		Larne	H	W	1	0	Blackledge (p)
IL	15/02/86		Coleraine	H	L	0	2	-
IL	01/03/86		Coleraine	A	W	5	1	Cleary (p), Manley 2, Millar 2
IL	08/03/86		Linfield	H	L	2	3	Morrison, Jameson
IL	22/03/86		Portadown	A	L	1	2	Stewart
IL	29/03/86		Newry Town	H	W	4	0	Mullan 2, Morrison 2
IL	31/03/86		Crusaders	A	L	2	4	Jameson, Mullan
IL	08/04/86		Carrick Rangers	H	W	2	0	Jameson, Mullan
IL	12/04/86		Ards	A	D	0	0	-
IL	17/04/86		Larne	A	D	0	0	-
IL	22/04/86		Glenavon	A	L	0	1	-
IL	26/04/86		Distillery	H	L	1	2	Manley
IL	06/05/86		Cliftonville	H	D	1	1	Millar
IL	09/05/86		Bangor	H	L	1	4	Jameson
IL	13/05/86		Ballymena United	H	W	2	0	Mullan 2
IC	01/02/86	1	Distillery	H	W	3	1	Millar 2, Manley
IC	22/02/86	2	Ballyclare Comrades	A	D	1	1	Millar

IC	25/02/86	2R	Ballyclare Comrades	H	W	3	1	Millar, Manley, Morrison
IC	15/03/86	3	Cliftonville	H	W	1	0	Millar
IC	04/04/86	SF	Brantwood	WP	W	3	0	Mullan 2, Millar
IC	03/05/86	F	Coleraine	WP	W	2	1	Mullan, Millar
F	26/07/85		Roe Valley	A	L	2	3	Bowers 2(2p)
F	27/07/85		Ballymoney United	A	L	0	1	-
F	31/07/85		Banbridge Town	A	W	5	2	Cowden 3, Manley, Dixon
F	03/08/85		Shelbourne	H	D	2	2	Dixon, Jameson
F	06/08/85		Dundela	A	W	5	1	Manley 4, Stewart
F	10/08/85		Shamrock Rovers	H	W	3	2	Manley 2, Keely og
F	25/10/85		Banbridge Town	H	W	3	0	Manley, Millar, Bowers
F	20/05/86		Linfield	A	L	0	2	Steve McKee Testimonial
F	22/05/86		Ballyclare Comrades	A	W	3	0	Millar, Morrison, Stewart
								Michael Cullen Benefit
F	30/05/86		Houston Dynamos	A	W	3	1	Millar, Cleary 2
								Spindletop Cup
F	01/06/86		Houston Dynamos	A	D	0	0	(won 8-7 on penalties)
F	03/06/86		Orlando	A	W	3	0	Russell, Mullan, Morrison
F	07/06/86		Tampa Bay Rowdies	A	L	0	1	QPR
F	16/06/86		Meadowbank	A	Unknown			

George Dunlop kept goals for us. For the McKee match a trophy was at stake and the Blues became the first winners of the Windsor Cup.

Our four match American tour began with a game against Houston Dynamos, coached by Keith Weller, in Beaumont, Texas for the Spindletop Cup. Spectators were charged $6 to watch the Glens win 3-1, the first goal coming from Millar, recently named the Ulster Young Footballer of the Year and the NIPFA's most promising newcomer. We defeated Houston on their own ground two days later, albeit in a penalty shoot out. Jeff Russell scored the crucial kick to give us an 8-7 win.

Next it was down to Florida to meet Orlando Lions at the Lake Brantley High School as part of their "world series" matches. On a night of thunder and lightning, which secretary Gordon Scott quipped made the Glens feel at home, we won 3-0, the best goal a bullet header from Mullan. The successful trip concluded with a meeting against Tampa Bay Rowdies, who were really Queen's Park Rangers in disguise. Only Alan McDonald and Terry Fenwick, both a bit further south on World Cup duty were missing from their first choice line-up. It took an 87th minute goal from Gary Chivers to defeat us and QPR's manager Frank Sibley praised the Glens, in particular Cowden, for their efforts. In a remarkable coincidence with the 1967 Detroit Cougars team both Glentoran goalkeepers on tour were actually guests, namely Allen McKnight (Distillery) and Ian Shellard (Banbridge Town).

Appearances and Goals

	App.	Subs.	Goals		App.	Subs.	Goals
Connell	49			Dixon	15	2	
Morrison	49	1	12	Blackledge	13	5	5
Jameson	47	2	12	Mills	12	1	
Stewart A.	40	5	2	Strain B.	5		
Mullan	40	2	25	Smyth J.	3	1	
Moore	39		5	Russell	2	1	
Paterson	34			Keery	2	1	
Neill G.	34			Mathieson	2		
Cleary	34	1	3	Shellard	1		
Manley	33	6	10	Major	1		
Leeman	32	2		Craig	1		
Millar	28	3	15	Own Goals			1
Cowden	27	6					
Bowers	22		7	TOTAL	503	39	97
Hillen	18						

1986/87

*Caskey starts third spell – Jackson replaces Johnston –
Gold and Irish Cup glory*

The earlier start to the season only left enough time for a couple of friendlies prior to competition starting. Billy Johnston had strengthened the playing panel with a couple more shrewd signings to add to that of Pat McCoy. Billy Caskey retuned from the USA for good for his third spell with the Glens and centre-forward Gary Macartney was snapped up from the "B" Division. Macartney, whose uncle Billy had played full-back for Glentoran in 1949/50, was a free scoring striker for many years with the RUC and had eventually been persuaded, in part due to the success at Linfield of his old striking partner Mark Caughey, to try his hand in senior football.

The first of those pre-season games was a scoreless draw at Crewe United when Distillery goalkeeper Allen McKnight played the second half. Johnston failed to sign the big keeper and he later joined Glasgow Celtic and West Ham. Our annual meeting with Dundela doubled as a benefit game for John Walker, a former Colts and Seconds player whose career had been ended prematurely when a "hit and run" driver left him with a serious leg injury. Macartney had a great home debut scoring all four of our goals in a demonstration of what was to come from him. The gate receipts of £852 were made up to £1,000 for Walker by the two clubs.

The Irish League season was given a fixture overhaul. The County Antrim Shield was brought forward to the opening Saturday to be followed by the Ulster Cup. The league championship itself would now commence on the last Saturday in August and finish mid-February and then the regular season would conclude with the Gold Cup, changed to a "two groups of seven" format. The Irish Cup would be played as normal but a new competition would emerge, ironically to fill in the space left by the Shield at the end of the season. It was to be the Irish League Cup, sponsored by Roadferry - the trophy itself was actually the old City Cup last competed for in 1975.

There were further "innovations" of note to the local game. A league win would now be worth three points and two substitutes would be allowed in all games. Belfast's "Big Two" could kick-off at 3 pm during the winter months but the most controversial law introduced was the Professional Form. This stipulated that after a player had appeared in four games for a club he had to sign a "professional" form. The rule was despised by all and was dropped after one season.

George Magill returned to the Oval as physio to replace Tony Wright and inherited the task of looking after long-term casualties Barney Bowers and Davy Neill. Jeff Russell and Reg Hillen moved to seek more regular first team action at Portadown and Carrick respectively while Dean Smyth was signed from Crusaders, initially as cover for Paterson. Right-back George Neill decided to take a break form soccer and, after playing a few game of American Football, settled down to a year of rugby union with Bangor RFC.

The season began well with our midfield of Cleary, Caskey and McCoy supreme. We quickly reached the Shield semi-finals by hammering Bangor but then struggled against the same opponents four days later in the Ulster Cup. The blanket defence of the RUC held us to 0-0 and we had to rely on an 83rd minute McCoy goal at Cliftonville to qualify for the quarter-finals. The Police topped our section on goal difference meaning we faced a difficult away trip to Coleraine on a Tuesday evening.

There we put in a dreadful display as Felix Healey tortured us in the first half hour. Firstly Moore deflected in one of his shots and then Healey cracked in a free-kick from 30 yards. However the moustachioed playmaker was sent off after 27 minutes for persistently fouling Raymond Morrison. We were unable to take advantage however, the nearest to a goal coming when a Macartney lob hit the bar and Raymond McCoy sealed matters with a late third goal. Fans' optimistic hopes of a "clean sweep" were shattered already.

The team showed great character four days later by returning to the scene of the crime and beating Coleraine 2-1 in the opening league encounter. It was a vastly improved display as we threatened to go on the rampage in the second half. During September we recorded easy wins over Bangor (again) and Distillery when Macartney's four goals (including a hat-trick of headers) took him to the top of the league scoring charts. We were involved in a an exciting finish at Solitude. Going into the final ten minutes the Reds led 1-0 but, in a hectic scoring flurry, the game ended 2-2. Away from the league Glentoran beat Ards in the Shield semi-final with Paterson in top form. The only black spot was the nasty injury picked up by Pat McCoy.

We therefore fielded a fairly makeshift XI, with Bowers as a substitute, in our Cup Winners Cup first leg with Lokomotive Leipzig. Despite this Cleary fired us ahead with a 43rd minute volley before a lapse in concentration allowed Lindner in to equalise in the 66th minute. Over 160 supporters travelled for the return leg in East Germany and they were rewarded by witnessing a battling display as we held Lokomotive to 0-2, the second goal coming in the last minute. Alan Paterson certainly earned his corn that night as did the hard-working Macartney and Millar up front. Cleary almost gave us a shock equaliser in the 57th minute when he hit the crossbar. The Germans went on to reach the final but lost 0-1 to Ajax.

Raymond Morrison.

The County Antrim Shield featured clubs from mid-Ulster for the first time ever and our opponents in the final were one such outfit, Glenavon. They agreed to play us at the Oval to cut down on expenses but the decision may have backfired on them as we cantered to a 3-0 victory. Goals from Macartney, Millar and Cleary punished the Lurgan men's defensive lapses.

The remainder of 1986 was given over to the Gibson Cup although a proposed friendly with Tottenham Hotspur on 21st October was cancelled, allegedly due to a disagreement over players' bonuses. Jim Cleary, in his captain's role, wrote to the club programme expressing his regret that the matter had not been kept internal to the club. The Gazette itself now featured the Glentoran shirt on the front cover and was under the enthusiastic editorial control of David McCune.

On 4th October we knocked Larne off the top of the table with a resounding 3-0 win and a week later chinned Ballymena to the tune of 7-2. It was remarked that there was an embarrassing wealth of talent at the Oval. Jim Smyth was solid at the back and even beneficiary Gary Blackledge got in on the act against the Braidmen, netting twice.

Not all things were going our way as we had to scrap for a point at Ards, where keeper McDowell and Damien Byrne shone for the home side, and then suffered our first league defeat at Seaview. Cleary had given us an early lead but the Crues fought back with Gary Hillis outstanding. The most spectacular goal, however, came from Terry Moore, an own goal from all of forty yards! Reggie Hillen gave the customary brilliant display by ex-Glenmen against us but we managed to overcome both Carrick and Newry (with McCoy back in midfield) to leave the league table as follows after eleven games:

1.= Glentoran, Larne 24 points, 3. Linfield 20, 4. Glenavon 19, 5. Newry Town 18.

After a week's rest, caused by the postponement of fixtures due to a mass anniversary demonstration against the Anglo-Irish agreement, we prepared for a "double header" against Linfield. In the first game at the Oval we paralysed the Blues with a superb display. Billy Caskey fired us ahead and just after the interval Morrison nodded us into a 2-0 lead.

Cleary was controlling the midfield and had the chance for number three when a penalty was awarded for a tackle from behind on Caskey. Jim drove the penalty against the bar but after the ball had ballooned high into the air Jameson headed home the rebound. McGaughey's late goal was no more than a consolation for the Blues.

Glentoran thus visited Windsor Park with a seven point advantage over Linfield. The day began badly as Glens' supporters were herded into the Railway end only while the home fans lounged in the North Stand. Worse was to follow when Cleary went off injured in the eighth minute and with Bowers playing his first full game for eleven months we never got going. Martin McGaughey scored the game's only goal on the hour and Larne's 1-0 win over Cliftonville allowed the Inver men to top the table again.

Jim Cowden had a miserable time in early December. First he hit a penalty yards wide as we lost again to Coleraine at the Oval (Ray McCoy with the only goal on 77 minutes) and then suffered a broken shin bone at Bangor.

What was to become a traumatic Christmas and New Year period began with a home game versus Cliftonville. Within 22 minutes we were 2-0 up but the Reds equalised thanks to a freak goal scored from the wing and then from a penalty awarded when Paterson dropped a cross and the ball was driven against the arm of stand-in captain Tom Connell who was covering on the goal-line. The point gained kept our noses just in front of Linfield and Larne.

Dean Smyth made his debut on Boxing Day at Distillery and ex-centre-half Alan Harrison made his first appearance since being signed from Derry City. Caskey and Cleary returned and things looked rosy as "Bamber", playing in his old centre-forward role put us 2-0 up. However we fell away badly and just managed to hold out for a win but the writing was on the wall when we failed to beat Glenavon at the Oval a day later. The game was handled controversially by Jim Duffy and fans staged a furious demonstration at the finish. Five home players were booked and Glenavon's goal came from a penalty, Duncan Lowry netting the rebound after Smyth had saved the first effort. For the after match events the club was fined £75 by the league and ordered to post notices around the ground warning spectators as to their conduct.

Glentoran's "Armageddon" for the season came in East Antrim during the first three days of January 1987. Firstly Larne beat us 4-0 with the help of two late goals and then Ballymena defeated us 2-0 as David Dougherty twice waltzed through our defence. Larne failed to reproduce their form at Windsor Park, where they were hammered 5-0 by Linfield, allowing the Blues to open up a seven point gap over ourselves, Coleraine and Larne with six games to go.

Billy Johnston conceded that the league race was over and a mock "obituary" for our title hopes appeared in the programme for the Ards game. The North Down men inflicted further damage with a 3-2 win and the next day Johnston resigned as manger, jumping before he was pushed. Billy McCullough took over temporarily again but within a fortnight the board had appointed ex-Waterford and Crusaders manager Tommy Jackson to the helm. Forty year old Jackson was, of course, a former player in the late 1960's and had made over 130 Football League appearances for Everton (championship winners in 1970), Nottingham Forest and Manchester United. In addition his tigerish midfield play earned him 35 caps for Northern Ireland.

As so often happens results immediately improved as we won four and drew one of the remaining five league fixtures. Bowers and Brian Strain tightened up the defence and 19 year old winger Robert Craig, son of Tommy, showed lots of promise. There was, however, one more big blow to take before the league curtailed. For the transfer of Harrison from Derry, secretary Gordon Scott had failed to complete the necessary registration form for the movement of a player between leagues of different countries. The IFA imposed fines totalling £900 and also harshly deducted eight points from our league total for this administrative oversight! This resulted in our final league position being adjusted from third to seventh and the loss of Scott who fully accepted responsibility. Alan Crowe was later appointed as his replacement. You cold have been forgiven for thinking that the club was being treated unfairly as the IFA had earlier refused to give any financial assistance towards our floodlights upgrade plan but thousands of pounds was poured into Windsor Park as it was "the National Stadium".

Billy Caskey opens the scoring in the home league game against Linfield as Jameson, Macartney and Moore look on with the visitors McCartney, Doherty, Jeffrey and McGaughey.

The Glens entertained Red Star Belgrade in January and gained a creditable draw against a side containing seven Yugoslav internationals, including Stojanovic and Stojkovic, and were European Cup quarter-finalists.

With spring just around the corner we commenced the Irish Cup, Gold Cup and League Cup almost simultaneously. The Seconds were involved in the latter competition as they had won the George Wilson Cup and they reached the quarter-finals by beating UUC 4-1 and then overcoming Distillery, who fielded ex-Glenman Davy Neill, 4-2 on penalties after a 0-0 draw. Those successful with spot-kicks were Paul Dixon, Alex McDowell, Andy Mathieson and Ian Weatherup (son of Bimbo).

The firsts meanwhile progressed in the Irish Cup with wins over Carrick and Glenavon despite having Blackledge sent off after 55 minutes in the latter. We also went to the top of Section B of the Gold Cup following a "circus" with Ards when Duffy sent off the visitors' Baxter and Kincaid. Two brilliant goals by Cleary against Portadown helped to silence his terrace critics.

The Glens began April with a tough Irish Cup semi-final against Newry Town. Played at Windsor on a Friday night an absorbing battle developed with Mullan's goal on the half-hour cancelling out Marty Magee's early strike. The replay four nights later was just as difficult. The Frontiermen led 1-0 with fourteen minutes to go thanks to an Eamon Hawkins first half penalty, which had been awarded by a linesman for hand-ball against Bowers. Then Cleary equalised and with five minutes to go Gary Macartney poked home the winner.

The wins continued to flow as we qualified for the Gold Cup semi-finals with successes over Distillery and Bangor, Cleary notching his 100th goal for the club in the latter. It was not without a price though as against the Whites Blackledge fell awkwardly and was stretchered to hospital. Happily it proved to be no more serious than a sore back. Glentoran too reached the League Cup quarter-finals to set up an interesting meeting with our Seconds but before that there was the Gold and Irish Cups to settle.

We were down to meet Larne in the Irish Cup final but had a dress rehearsal with them in the Gold Cup semi-final. Goals from Bowers and Jameson helped us to win an excellent match and gain a measure of revenge for that New Year's Day debacle. This set up an intriguing clash with six-time league champions Linfield at the Oval on a sunny Saturday afternoon. In an exciting first half clinical strikes from Macartney and Mullan put us 2-0 up before McGaughey brought the Blues level. Then, with time running out, sub Robert Craig

Results 1986/87

Played 53. Won 33. Drew 11. Lost 9. Goals For 116. Against 53. % 72.6.
Honours: Irish Cup, Gold Cup, County Antrim Shield

CAS	09/08/86	1	Cliftonville	H	W	1	0	Mullan
CAS	12/08/86	2	Bangor	A	W	6	0	Caskey, Jameson 2, Macartney, Cowden, Morrison
CAS	11/09/86	SF	Ards	H	W	4	1	Caskey, Cleary, Macartney 2
CAS	08/10/86	F	Glenavon	H	W	3	0	Macartney, Millar, Cleary
UC	16/08/86		Bangor	H	W	2	1	Jameson, Cleary
UC	20/08/86		R.U.C.	H	D	0	0	-
UC	23/08/86		Cliftonville	A	D	1	1	McCoy
UC	26/08/86	QF	Coleraine	A	L	0	3	-
IL	30/08/86		Coleraine	A	W	2	1	Macartney, Morrison
IL	06/09/86		Bangor	H	W	4	1	Cleary 2(2p), Jameson, Macartney
IL	13/09/86		Cliftonville	A	D	2	2	Morrison, Millar
IL	20/09/86		Distillery	H	W	5	0	Macartney 4, Jameson
IL	27/09/86		Glenavon	A	D	1	1	Macartney
IL	04/10/86		Larne	H	W	3	0	Jameson, Cleary (p), Macartney
IL	11/10/86		Ballymena United	H	W	7	2	Cleary 2(2p), Millar, Macartney, Morrison, Blackledge 2
IL	18/10/86		Ards	A	D	1	1	Millar
IL	25/10/86		Carrick Rangers	H	W	2	0	Jameson, Cleary
IL	01/11/86		Crusaders	A	L	1	3	Cleary
IL	08/11/86		Newry Town	H	W	2	0	Cleary (p), Jameson
IL	22/11/86		Linfield	H	W	3	1	Caskey, Morrison, Jameson
IL	29/11/86		Linfield	A	L	0	1	-
IL	06/12/86		Coleraine	H	L	0	1	-
IL	13/12/86		Bangor	A	W	2	0	Mullan, Millar
IL	20/12/86		Cliftonville	H	D	2	2	Jameson, McCoy
IL	26/12/86		Distillery	A	W	2	1	Caskey 2
IL	27/12/86		Glenavon	H	D	1	1	Caskey
IL	01/01/87		Larne	A	L	0	4	-
IL	03/01/87		Ballymena United	A	L	0	2	-
IL	10/01/87		Ards	H	L	2	3	Macartney, Blackledge
IL	17/01/87		Carrick Rangers	A	W	1	0	Blackledge
IL	24/01/87		Crusaders	H	W	3	0	Macartney, Blackledge, Keery
IL	31/01/87		Portadown	A	W	3	2	Blackledge 2(2p), Macartney
IL	07/02/87		Newry Town	A	D	1	1	Macartney
IL	14/02/87		Portadown	H	W	4	0	Macartney, Davidson og, Blackledge 2(1p)
ECW	17/09/86	1.1	Lokomotiv Leipzig	H	D	1	1	Cleary
ECW	01/10/86	1.2	Lokomotiv Leipzig	A	L	0	2	-
IC	21/02/87	1	Carrick Rangers	H	W	3	1	Bowers, Caskey, Macartney
IC	14/03/87	2	Glenavon	H	W	3	2	Bowers, Burns og, Cleary
IC	03/04/87	SF	Newry Town	WP	D	1	1	Mullan
IC	07/04/87	SFR	Newry Town	WP	W	2	1	Cleary, Macartney
IC	02/05/87	F	Larne	WP	W	1	0	Mullan
GC	28/02/87		Glenavon	A	D	1	1	Jameson
GC	21/03/87		Newry Town	A	W	4	0	Cleary (p), Buchanan og, Caskey 2
GC	25/03/87		Ards	H	W	3	1	Macartney 2, Smyth
GC	28/03/87		Portadown	H	W	4	0	Cleary 2, Bowers, Blackledge
GC	18/04/87		Distillery	H	W	2	0	Morrison, Jameson
GC	20/04/87		Bangor	A	W	5	0	Mullan, Cleary, Macartney, Bowers, Morrison

GC	22/04/87	SF	Larne	WP	W	2	0	Bowers, Jameson
GC	25/04/87	F	Linfield	H	W	3	2	Macartney, Mullan, Craig
ILC	03/03/87	1	R.U.C.	H	W	2	1	Blackledge, Cleary
ILC	13/04/87	2	Carrick Rangers	A	W	2	0	Blackledge 2
ILC	04/05/87	3	Glentoran II	H	W	5	2	Harrison, Macartney 3, Cleary
ILC	06/05/87	SF	Crusaders	WP	L	1	2	Macartney
F	25/07/86		Crewe United	A	D	0	0	-
F	02/08/86		Dundela	H	W	4	1	Macartney 4
								John Walker Benefit
F	26/01/87		Red Star Belgrade	H	D	1	1	Krivolapic og
F	12/05/87		Linfield	H	D	1	1	Blackledge
								(lost 3-5 on penalties)
								Jim Cleary Testimonial for
								the Windsor Cup

scored a dream winner, firing past Dunlop from 20 yards. The result gave Jackson his first trophy as manager and allowed him to "retain" the Gold Cup following Crusaders success under him sixteen months previously.

Now, could the Glens win the Irish Cup for the third time in a row the following Saturday? The answer was yes as Gerry Mullan drove home the only goal of the game in the 33rd minute after being put through by Morrison. For Gerry this maintained the record of scoring in all four of his Irish Cup finals as the Glens completed the first Irish Cup hat-trick by any club since Linfield in 1893 while a large Larne contingent went home disappointed. A newspaper entitled "The Glentoran Supporter" had been on sale before the game.

In the League Cup the following Monday night we beat the Seconds, winners of the "B" Division for the second year in succession, by 5-2 in relaxed style. The Seconds undoubtedly missed their leading scorer, Paul Millar who had been transferred to Ronnie McFall's Portadown. We were denied the prospect of another big two final when Crusaders beat us 2-1 in the semi-final at Windsor after Macartney had opened the scoring after four minutes. This concluded an unbeaten run of twenty matches under Jackson.

The Glens and the Blues did meet once more in a belated testimonial for Jim Cleary. Tommy Wright was Linfield's hero as he saved a Bowers penalty and was instrumental in the Blues taking the Windsor Cup following a penalty shoot-out, during which Lindsay McKeown delighted the crowd with his "Elephant Man" impression.

Billy Caskey was deservedly named the club's player of the year for a season in which he had featured at centre-forward, in midfield and once at centre-half. Gary Macartney finished his first campaign in senior football as the country's leading marksman.

Appearances and Goals

	App.	Subs.	Goals		App.	Subs.	Goals
Cleary	50		20	Harrison	20		1
Macartney	45		28	Millar	15	7	5
Paterson	42			Keery	13	6	1
Smyth J.	42	1	1	Blackledge	13	10	13
Jameson	39	9	13	Smyth D.	11		
Stewart A.	36	5		Craig	11	11	1
Morrison	35	5	7	Strain B.	4		
McCoy	34	1	2	Manley	4	6	
Caskey W.	33	1	9	Major	1	1	
Connell	31			Dixon	1		
Moore	30			Mathieson		1	
Cowden	25		1	Own Goals			3
Bowers	25	3	5				
Mullan	23	5	6	TOTAL	583	72	116

1987/88

The season of 1987/8, Tommy Jackson's first full one in charge, was momentous as the Glens captured the Irish League and Cup double for the first time since 1920/1. We won both trophies in dramatic fashion at the very latest time possible but let us pick up the story in August 1987.

George Neill had returned to the club after his sojourn with the oval ball to link up with new colleagues David Montgomery (a winger from Ballyclare) and Norman McGreevy (ex-Crusaders and Ards), a utility player. On the way out were Brian Strain and Tom Connell (both to Ronnie McFall's Portadown), David Keery to Crusaders and Paul Dixon to Derry City. Off the field ex-BBC commentator Harry Thompson was appointed assistant secretary. Two young English lads, Joe Fitzgerald and Gregoire Murphy, assisted the first team in our successful trio of pre-season friendlies against junior opposition.

Once more the format of the league season was altered. The league was now played after the Gold Cup and in the latter each team would play one fixture against a team from the other group to avoid having an idle Saturday. The League Cup would be slotted in during October and November and there would be two additional tournaments. All Irish League clubs were in the process of installing floodlights and to commemorate this achievement a Floodlit Cup, sponsored by Budweiser, was initiated in November. Finally, to mark their centenary, the County Antrim FA staged a one-off competition at the end of the season for the Cawoods Chalice.

Montgomery and McGreevy both "scored" in our opening County Antrim Shield tie at Inver Park. Larne were 2-0 up before two late goals forced the game into extra time and eventually penalties. Norman put away the decisive kick to earn a second round meeting with Linfield, played the following Thursday because of a waterlogged Oval pitch. After Blackledge had given us an early lead two brilliant efforts from Barney Bowers, fresh from his appearance for the Irish League against Manchester United, secured a satisfying win.

Glentoran sailed through the Ulster Cup section, scoring eleven times in the three games. David Montgomery was a live wire on the wing as Cleary scored in all three games and set up Blackledge's goal at Crusaders, which proved to be Gary's last first team goal for the club. We swept Dundela aside in the quarters, mainly thanks to a superb Gerry Mullan hat-trick, as we raced into a 4-0 lead after only 38 minutes.

The semi-final with Coleraine was played at the Ballymena Showgrounds and without Cleary, due to a family bereavement, we disintegrated in the second half and went down 1-3. Coleraine's goals came from Ricky Wade and McCreadie (two) in front of 4,000, although many thought that the Bannsiders were lucky to be in the semis at all after they had scored "the goal that never was" against Linfield in the previous round. The ball from a header had appeared to go over the bar but the referee had ruled in their favour to give them a 3-2 win!

There was no time for the Glens to lick their wounds as the Gold Cup was in full swing and our European tie just around the corner. We recorded hard fought wins over Glenavon and Ards but were shocked by Newry Town who came to the Oval and beat us 2-0 with late goals from Ralph and Crawley. This was poor preparation for our trip to the tundra to play Rovaneimi SP. Backed by around 80 travelling fans we put in a gutsy display in Finland and earned a scoreless draw. Moreover Gary Macartney appeared to have bundled the ball over the goalline in the 81st minute and despite the linesman awarding a goal the referee thought otherwise. Worse still a defender had pushed the ball away with his hand and no penalty kick was given either!

The return leg at the Oval began a miserable week for Glentoran. Rovaneimi took the lead through Kallio in the 62nd minute while Terry Moore was off having a replacement contact lens inserted. Billy Caskey equalised three minutes later with a bullet header but we failed to find any further way past Martinlussi and so the Finns, managed by ex-Welsh international Graham Williams, progressed on the away goals rule.

Tommy Jackson demanded more effort from the players but on the Saturday we went down 3-4 at Distillery when needing only a point to qualify for the Gold Cup semi-final. Then the following Tuesday Ballymena came to east Belfast and knocked us out of the Shield thanks to a Stevie Conville goal in the 52nd minute. McGreevy, Montgomery and Cleary (for the first time in his career) had been dropped for this game. Jim came on as sub and hit the bar with a late header. The team returned to form with a determined and convincing 4-0 win over Coleraine, qualifying for the Gold Cup semi-final and a mouth watering meeting with the Blues at Windsor Park as a consequence.

Before the championship got underway the League Cup commenced. Glentoran Seconds were again involved and in Round One they beat Limavady 3-1 after extra time. Johnny Jameson had scored the last minute goal which had forced overtime, and two days later he was on target for the first XI in the same competition as we beat the RUC 3-0. Glenavon were humbled 5-0 in Round Two and the team received a standing ovation for their display at the finish. Mullan notched another hat-trick but the goal of the game was provided by Cleary, who slotted home after making a 50 yard run to meet a return ball.

Jim Cleary slots home the penalty to give us the double

The Seconds game at Larne the same evening was postponed and was called off twice more before eventually taking place on 16th November. Despite a gritty display from the reserves Larne won 2-0. By this time the firsts had also been dismissed, going down 1-4 on a Friday night at Portadown after extra time. The Ports fielded five ex-Glenmen and one of them, Paul Millar, scored twice.

The Glens began shakily in the league and twice let a lead slip in our opening fixture with Coleraine. Significantly a diving header from Raymond Morrison gave us victory at Bangor in the next league game. Morrison went on to become our leading scorer in Gibson Cup games, a much happier memory than his experience at Windsor Park in the midweek.

A disappointing Gold Cup semi-final looked to be heading Linfield's way due to a 44th minute goal from Martin McGaughey. However with the referee about to blow for time Cleary blasted in a tremendous volley from 20 yards to send the game into extra-time. There was no further scoring and the Blues went through to the final 5-4 on penalties, the only miss coming when Dunlop saved from Morrison. McGreevy, Cleary, Stewart and Jameson had converted the Glens' other spot-kicks but we still had lost our third semi-final of the season.

Gerry Mullan celebrated his 100th goal for the club in a 3-0 win at Distillery but displays were less than inspiring. Most of the credit to the team was for the defence of Paterson, Neill, the ever-present Stewart, McGreevy and Moore. Following our hiding at Portadown we went seven games without conceding a goal – this run included all Budweiser Cup games as we lifted that trophy with a 1-0 win over Coleraine. The first round tie with Cliftonville, and also our Gold Cup meeting with the Reds, had been switched from Solitude to the Oval due to floodlight work at the North Belfast venue. On 10th December a combined Glentoran/Linfield XI beat the Rest of the League 7-1 at Windsor in aid of the Enniskillen bomb disaster fund.

Our defence was finally pierced by Ballymena after the shutters had been up for 447 minutes. The Braidmen celebrated with a second just two minutes later but we looked to

have earned a draw when efforts from Morrison and Caskey, in 72 and 89 minutes respectively, levelled matters. Then, in dramatic fashion, Young scored their winner in injury time with a thundering shot in fading light from all of 35 yards. Going into the Christmas fixtures it was therefore tight at the top of the league after seven games:
1. Glentoran 14 points, 2. Ards 14, 3. Newry Town 14, 4. Glenavon 13, Portadown 13.

The best goal of our big Boxing Day meeting with Ards was a terrific 30 yard drive by Ron Manley past Paul Kee. For Manley this confirmed his return to the side after he had scored a hat-trick against Larne in only his sixth appearance following a one year lay-off. The remainder of our holiday fixtures were generally dour encounters but we won them all and went back to the top of the table on New Year's Day with a 1-0 win over the Crues. Morrison scored the goal after only 67 seconds.

Paul Millar had an unhappy return to the Oval on 9th January, scoring the decisive goal in the 74th minute when he sliced a John Devine corner into his own net! Devine, just 19, had first appeared on Boxing Day, replacing the injured McGreevy, and immediately made a favourable impression.

Also in January Gary Blackledge was transferred to Glenavon. Blackie had scored successive hat-tricks for the Seconds in two of his last games for the club and showed he was far from done by netting three times on his Glenavon debut within the space of 22 minutes!

Linfield had lurked up to second place in the league by the time we visited them on the 16th of the month. The Blues aerial threat was amply illustrated by headed goals from McLeod and McGaughey from cross-balls in the first half but after 37 minutes Manley pulled one back. The fog around the ground thickened during the half-time interval and on the resumption of the game the referee Alan Snoddy had no alternative but to abandon the affair. Both captains agreed it would have been a farce to attempt to continue. Alan Paterson lost his personal record of not conceding a goal for 941 minutes in this game. The weather again played its hand a week later when our home meeting with Bangor was postponed due to snow.

The replay of the Blues game took place on 2nd February after we had gained a draw on a "mudheap" at Solitude. Again the conditions were atrocious but that was a minor inconvenience to our supporters as Jeff Spiers headed past his own keeper and then Manley wrapped up the points in the 64th minute. The midfielders Cleary and McCoy had been at the centre of everything.

The team was still having to battle in every game as further successes were gained over Distillery, Bangor and Glenavon. Gary Macartney, returning after a three month absence due to glandular fever, scored in all three, while Blackledge scored Glenavon's goal.

The 1987/8 double winning side with their four trophies.

Convincing wins over Larne and Ballymena, which were both featured in the Ulster's new colour photographs, enabled our lead over Linfield to extend to seven points, though they did have a game in hand.

The Irish Cup, again restricted to only sixteen teams, was in full swing and devastating wins over Coleraine and Newry Town, featuring a Mullan hat-trick, got us through to the semi-finals. However the league championship was the prize everyone was after and that moved a touch closer to us when Linfield lost at home to Coleraine on the day when two clinical Cleary penalties saw off Ards. The table read: 1. Glentoran played 20 points 49, 2. Linfield 20-42, 3. Coleraine 19-40.

There was plenty of other activity at the club besides the league race. Michael Cullen was appointed as club doctor and, to the delight of physio George Magill, a new weights and rehabilitation room was constructed at the ground. Goalkeeper Alan Paterson, enjoying his benefit season, received a Civic Reception at the City Hall. The Colts were not to be outdone and they lifted the IFA Youth Cup by defeating Linfield Rangers 4-2. These youngsters also went on to record impressive victories over the Northern Ireland Schools XI, 2-1, and Ards Colts by 10-0 when Erin Montgomery scored five.

Our easiest match on paper in the championship run in was the home meeting with Carrick Rangers. However we stuttered to a draw after Cleary's missed penalty in the sixth minute. Macartney put us ahead midway through the second half when he hooked in an Alfie Stewart cross but in the 73rd minute Carrick were level as Boreland scored after Paterson had turned a Colin Crawford shot onto the post. We then appeared to be losing two more points at Seaview until Morrison popped up with an 84th minute winner. Crusaders had earlier come back from 0-2 down. Extra-time was needed to beat the Police in the Chalice and Morrison was again the hero with the only goal against Newry.

Manager Jackson voiced his views over press reports of Glentoran games. Time and time again, especially away from home, we had gone out to win a game by playing attacking football but received little credit for it.

Portadown presented a double challenge to us in early April. Firstly there was an Easter Tuesday league meeting at a sandy Shamrock Park. In a game of seven bookings Paterson continually thwarted the Ports forwards and goals from Macartney and Morrison earned us the crucial three points. The teams met again at Windsor Park four days later in the Irish Cup semi-final. This time Macartney and Manley put us 2-0 up after 50 minutes but the game really boiled over in the last ten. Greg Davidson netted for the Ports but almost immediately their keeper Mickey Keenan hauled down Jameson and from the resultant penalty Cleary restored our two goal advantage. The drama still had not finished as Kevin McKeever was sent-off for fouling Jameson and then Millar pulled it back to 3-2. The final whistle went soon afterwards to end a clash containing another six bookings but more importantly our dream of the double was still on.

It would have been impossible to have chosen two more difficult fixtures for our last two, Linfield (H) and Coleraine (A). Here is the top of the table after 24 games showing we only required a draw from the Blues game to bring the Gibson Cup back to the Oval:

1. Glentoran 59 points, 2. Linfield 54, 3. Coleraine 52.

Linfield had other ideas and a long range Lee Doherty free-kick flew into our net after only two minutes. That turned out to be the only goal of the game with the outcome that provided the Blues beat Ballymena in their last match (which they duly did 3-1) we had to win at Coleraine to win league. This was because of the Linfield's slightly better goal difference as a draw would send the title to Windsor for the seventh successive season. Amazingly during the week we had to play the Blues again and this time showed our true colours with a comfortable 2-0 success in the Chalice.

Billy Caskey returned in a vital midfield role at Coleraine at a tension-filled and packed Showgrounds. The Glens held the upper hand early on and Devine put us ahead in a goalmouth scramble following a corner before the break. Coleraine equalised early in the second half but just after the hour mark Morrison nodded in the goal that would give us victory and the championship. We had many late chances to add to the lead but 2-1 was sufficient. Seven years of frustration came to an end for the fans as they invaded the pitch at the finish in a state of near delirium.

Results 1987/88

Played 59. Won 43. Drew 9. Lost 7. Goals For 127. Against 44. % 80.5.
Honours: Irish League, Irish Cup, Budweiser Cup, County Antrim Centenary Chalice

CAS	08/08/87	1	Larne	A	D	2	2	Montgomery, Morrison (won 4-3 on penalties)
CAS	13/08/87	2	Linfield	H	W	3	1	Blackledge, Bowers 2
CAS	06/10/87	SF	Ballymena United	H	L	0	1	-
UC	15/08/87		Crusaders	A	W	2	0	Cleary, Blackledge
UC	18/08/87		Ards	H	W	3	1	Cleary, Montgomery, Macartney
UC	22/08/87		R.U.C.	H	W	6	2	Montgomery 2, Mullan 2, Cleary, Macartney
UC	25/08/87	QF	Dundela	H	W	4	0	McGreevy, Mullan 3
UC	01/09/87	SF	Coleraine	BS	L	1	3	Stewart
GC	29/08/87		Glenavon	H	W	3	2	Mullan, Macartney, Moore
GC	05/09/87		Ards	A	W	2	1	Mullan 2
GC	12/09/87		Newry Town	H	L	0	2	-
GC	19/09/87		Cliftonville	H	W	2	0	Macartney, Caskey
GC	26/09/87		Bangor	H	W	5	0	Bowers, Macartney 2, Mullan, Cleary
GC	03/10/87		Distillery	A	L	3	4	Macartney, Cleary, Mullan
GC	10/10/87		Coleraine	H	W	4	0	Macartney 2, Caskey, Mullan
GC	28/10/87	SF	Linfield	A	D	1	1	aet – Cleary (lost 4-5 on penalties)
ECW	16/09/87	1.1	Rovaneimi SP	A	D	0	0	-
ECW	29/09/87	1.2	Rovaneimi SP	H	D	1	1	Caskey
ILC	17/10/87	1	R.U.C.	H	W	3	0	Jameson 2, Caskey
ILC	20/10/87	2	Glenavon	H	W	5	0	Mullan 3, Cleary, McGreevy
ILC	13/11/87	3	Portadown	A	L	1	4	Mullan
IL	24/10/87		Coleraine	H	D	2	2	Mullan, Caskey
IL	31/10/87		Bangor	A	W	1	0	Morrison
IL	07/11/87		Cliftonville	H	D	1	1	Caskey
IL	21/11/87		Distillery	A	W	3	0	Stewart, Manley, Mullan
IL	05/12/87		Glenavon	H	W	1	0	Mullan
IL	12/12/87		Larne	A	W	3	0	Manley 3
IL	19/12/87		Ballymena United	A	L	2	3	Morrison, Caskey
IL	26/12/87		Ards	H	D	2	2	Manley, Cleary
IL	28/12/87		Carrick Rangers	A	W	2	0	Cleary, Morrison
IL	01/01/88		Crusaders	H	W	1	0	Morrison
IL	02/01/88		Newry Town	A	W	2	0	Gray og, Morrison
IL	09/01/88		Portadown	H	W	1	0	Millar og
IL	16/01/88		Linfield	A	A	1	2	Manley. Abandoned after 47 minutes
IL	30/01/88		Cliftonville	A	D	1	1	Mullan
IL	02/02/88		Linfield	A	W	2	0	Spiers og, Manley
IL	06/02/88		Distillery	H	W	1	0	Macartney
IL	10/02/88		Bangor	H	W	3	0	Cleary, Macartney, McCoy
IL	13/02/88		Glenavon	A	W	2	1	Macartney, Stewart
IL	27/02/88		Larne	H	W	4	0	Manley 2, Macartney, Jameson
IL	05/03/88		Ballymena United	H	W	3	0	Caskey, Macartney, Jameson
IL	19/03/88		Ards	A	W	2	0	Cleary 2(2p)
IL	22/03/88		Carrick Rangers	H	D	1	1	Macartney
IL	26/03/88		Crusaders	A	W	3	2	Manley, Morrison 2
IL	02/04/88		Newry Town	H	W	1	0	Morrison
IL	05/04/88		Portadown	A	W	2	0	Macartney, Morrison
IL	16/04/88		Linfield	H	L	0	1	-
IL	23/04/88		Coleraine	A	W	2	1	Devine, Morrison
BC	26/11/87	1	Cliftonville	H	W	2	0	aet – Mathieson, Manley
BC	01/12/87	2	Portadown	H	W	2	0	Morrison, Cleary (p)

BC	08/12/87	SF	Glenavon	WP	W	2	0	Mathieson, Jameson
BC	15/12/87	F	Coleraine	WP	W	1	0	Morrison
IC	20/02/88	1	Coleraine	H	W	3	0	Cleary 2(1p), Moore
IC	12/03/88	2	Newry Town	H	W	5	0	Cleary (p), Mullan 3, Macartney
IC	09/04/88	SF	Portadown	WP	W	3	2	Macartney, Manley, Cleary (p)
IC	30/04/88	F	Glenavon	WP	W	1	0	Cleary (p)
CACC	29/03/88	1	R.U.C.	H	W	2	0	aet Mathieson (p), Mullan
CACC	19/04/88	2	Linfield	A	W	2	0	Jameson, Morrison
CACC	03/05/88	SF	Ards	H	W	1	0	Mathieson
CACC	07/05/88	F	Ballymena United	WP	W	4	2	Mullan 3, Caskey
F	01/08/87		Ballinamallard United	A	W	3	0	Mullan, Macartney, Fitzgerald Opening of New Clubhouse
F	03/08/87		Killyleagh YC	A	W	4	1	Mullan 2, Blackledge (p), Morrison
F	05/08/87		Chimney Corner	A	W	4	1	Blackledge, Caskey, Macartney, Montgomery

The road-show rolled on to a damp Windsor Park the following Saturday. Playing in a new "sponsorless" shirt (green with red sleeves and black trim) because of the Bass-Smithwicks rivalry we had to wait until the 90th minute to defeat Glenavon in a disappointing Irish Cup final. From a corner Billy Caskey headed goalwards but young defender Andy Russell handled it away. Cleary coolly slotted home the resultant penalty, maintaining his record of scoring a spot-kick in every round, to complete the double. This also set a new record for winning the Irish Cup four years in succession. Dean Smyth gained a surprise winners' medal, coming into the team after Paterson had been stricken with chickenpox.

A hat-trick of trophy winning Saturdays was completed by the defeat of Ballymena in the Chalice final. Mullan did the damage with his fourth treble of the season as we coasted to a 4-0 half-time lead. Ballymena fought back to contain the final victory margin to 4-2 but failed to prevent the fourth trophy of the season coming to the Oval.

As is customary for a successful side the individual awards came thick and fast. Tommy Jackson was named Manager of the Year while the evergreen Paterson was voted Ulster Footballer of the Year and also picked up the football writers Player of the Year. Billy Caskey was the choice of the NIPFA for their man of the season. Alfie Stewart was crowned Glentoran Player of the Year. Following his switch from midfield to left-back he had become a model of consistency, only missing one game all season, that at Crusaders on 26th March, when he had fluid on the knee.

Appearances and Goals

	App.	Subs.	Goals		App.	Subs.	Goals
Stewart A.	58		3	Bowers	17		3
Moore	54		2	Smyth D.	15		
Caskey W.	53		9	Harrison	11	2	
Cleary	52	2	18	Montgomery	11	8	4
Jameson	49	1	5	Cowden	9	2	
Paterson	44			Blackledge	6	5	2
Mullan	43	7	27	Mathieson	5	23	4
Neill G.	40	1		Smyth J.	4	2	
McGreevy	37		2	Craig	3	3	
Macartney	34	4	18	Jardine		1	
Morrison	31	5	14	Own Goals			3
Devine	27		1				
Manley	25	5	11	TOTAL	649	78	127
McCoy	21	7	1				

1988/89

Glenmen in Red Square - An unlikely goalscoring hero –
Coly ends our Cup run

The season began on a sour note when club Player of the Year Alfie Stewart was lured to Portadown on contract. Top scorer of 1987/8 Gerry Mullan also left the Oval but in different circumstances as he had decided that the travelling from the North West was too much for him. Mullan joined Coleraine in an exchange deal for Billy Totten. Full-backs Jim Smyth and Philip Major joined Ballyclare and Portadown respectively for first-team football and coming in was ex-Linfield full-back Brian Kennedy and striker Gary Hillis from Crusaders. A tribunal set the Hillis fee at £16,500. We adopted our Cup final kit of 1988 but with black shorts.

The friendlies began in late July with a visit from Limerick City, managed by former Northern Ireland international Billy Hamilton. Indeed Hamilton scored Limerick's equalising goal after Ron Manley had put us ahead after eleven minutes. The remainder of the pre-season games all ended in victory. Hillis put four past an all-star XI but then after netting again at Ballyclare he damaged ankle ligaments and became a long-term injury casualty. George Neill scored twice against Coagh United in a game to officially open their new clubhouse and pitch.

With the County Antrim Shield moved to a more traditional spring slot the competitive season kicked off once more with the Lombard Ulster Cup. We qualified comfortably for the quarter-finals but needed a superior goal difference to top the section ahead of Larne. Cliftonville offered a brave challenge there but once we saw off their early attacks Cleary put us ahead in the 19th minute. Totten, full of confidence, had a sparkling game and he set up Caskey's clinching goal twenty minutes from time.

We continued that good form into the Gold Cup in early September. Raymond Morrison was returning to his old self after a back injury but Manley picked up a broken nose against Ards. With Cleary, Caskey and Morrison dominant in midfield only Glenavon, inspired by Duncan Lowry, could prevent us from winning. Indeed we qualified for the semi-final stage with two games in hand.

The Ulster Cup found its way to the Oval as we beat Coleraine in the semis and then Larne in the final, both at Windsor Park. Manley, back after his nose injury punished Larne with a hat-trick in a comprehensive 5-2 victory.

However the European Cup draw had given us a difficult tie, and a sixteen hour journey, with Spartak Moscow. Over 120 supporters made the trip to the USSR and marked the occasion by posing for photographs in Red Square complete with Polish priests holding up Glens' scarves! In the game itself, played before 40,000, the team battled hard to hold Spartak to a 2-0 scoreline, the goals coming from Ivanov (52 minutes) and Shalimov ten minutes later. We had a great spell just before half-time when Macartney had an effort cleared off the line and Totten sliced wide.

Tommy Jackson stated that Spartak were "world class" but the Glens showed no inferiority complex at the Oval, especially when Terry Moore rose above international goalkeeper Rinat Dasayev to head us into a 46th minute lead. A shock was on the cards as we went all out for that second goal. Maybe the fact that Spartak had lost their playing kit en route and had to wear that of another Irish League club gave us some sort of physchological advantage! However in injury time Cherenkov scored an equaliser which put the issue beyond doubt.

Two nights later we struggled to beat Distillery at the Oval thanks to the brilliance of their goalkeeper Pat Saunders. One reporter surmised, tongue firmly in cheek, that Saunders was a better keeper than Dasayev based on the evidence of their respective performances.

In early October Fred Roberts, scorer of 332 goals in 221 appearances in the late 1920s and early 1930s, passed away. It was in fact a season which marked the death of many ex-Oval stars including Ted Hinton, Arthur Douglas and 84 year-old Tommy McKeague.

The first two rounds of the Roadferry League Cup were played on the middle two Saturdays of October. Despite being without many key players the juniors of Limavady and Omagh never troubled us and we netted eleven times without reply in the two fixtures. David West enjoyed a scoring debut in the former. On a worrying note the Belfast Telegraph carried a story with the headline that Glentoran were heading for bankruptcy. Chairman John Crossan immediately denied such a situation, but did admit that the board were seriously examining additional methods of funding for the club. The first playing disappointment of the season came at Seaview when Portadown knocked us out of the Gold Cup on penalties. Robert Craig had earlier scored the goal of the game with a blistering left foot volley.

Ironically the league championship commenced with a visit to Coleraine Showgrounds, the scene of our memorable title-wining day just six months previously. With a makeshift side, including Neill at centre-half and Jameson wearing the captain's armband, we raced into a 3-1 interval lead, eventually winning 3-2. The side had contained four outside-rights namely the captain, Totten, Craig and Mathieson.

November began badly with defeat at Bangor and the loss of another two points against Cliftonville. The scoreless draw against the Reds was the first such result between the teams for 55 years! George Neill had been sent off at Solitude but the injury crisis was softened by the return to the fold of centre-half Alan Harrison. Although lacking in match fitness the now bearded Harrison added much needed experience to the middle of the defence.

Revenge wins were gained over Bangor and Portadown in the League Cup and we mercilessly hammered Distillery, without Saunders, in the league. The high number of injuries, however, forced the postponement of a friendly with Dundalk.

A large crowd gathered at the Oval for the Glens-Blues League Cup final. During the game Linfield's two African internationals, Tony Coly and Abdeli Khammal, were tastelessly pelted by bananas thrown by Glentoran supporters. This failed to upset the Blues as they went ahead through Mooney and it was not until the 77th minute that Macartney brilliantly equalised after a Cleary corner. Ten minutes later Alan Paterson sent another long punt upfield. Incredibly it bounced over the head of Dunlop and into the Blues' net for the winning goal, ending the Windsor men's 21 match unbeaten run in the process! Everyone was immediately stunned as Paterson became the first goalkeeper to score from open play in a cup final in Ireland. The distance of his "shot" was measured at 94 yards 2 feet 6.5 inches. Dunlop, beaten by Cliftonville's Andy McClean in similar fashion on the opening day of the season, threatened to quit the game. So we gained our sixth trophy in less than a year.

Stephen Douglas is foiled against Larne.

Results 1988/89

Played 57. Won 38. Drew 10. Lost 9. Goals For 131. Against 56. % 75.4.
Honours: Ulster Cup, Irish League Cup

UC	20/08/88		Crusaders	H	W	2	0	Cleary, Macartney
UC	23/08/88		Larne	A	D	1	1	Morrison
UC	27/08/88		Carrick Rangers	H	W	4	0	Cleary, Totten, McCoy 2
UC	30/08/88	QF	Cliftonville	H	W	3	0	Cleary (p), Totten, Caskey
UC	20/09/88	SF	Coleraine	WP	W	2	0	McDowell og, Manley
UC	28/09/88	F	Larne	WP	W	5	2	Manley 3, Bowers, Cleary (p)
GC	03/09/88		Ards	H	W	4	1	Beattie og, Cleary (p), Morrison, Macartney
GC	10/09/88		Glenavon	A	D	1	1	Morrison
GC	17/09/88		Newry Town	A	W	3	0	Manley, Cleary, Craig
GC	24/09/88		Cliftonville	H	W	2	0	Cleary, Morrison
GC	01/10/88		Bangor	A	W	3	0	Macartney 2, Morrison
GC	07/10/88		Distillery	H	W	2	1	Caskey, Macartney
GC	11/10/88		Coleraine	A	D	1	1	Cleary
GC	26/10/88	SF	Portadown	Sv	D	2	2	aet – Caskey, Craig (lost 0-3 on penalties)
EC	07/09/88	1.1	Spartak Moscow	A	L	0	2	-
EC	05/10/88	1.2	Spartak Moscow	H	D	1	1	Moore
ILC	15/10/88	1	Limavady United	H	W	5	0	Jameson, Cleary (p), Macartney 2, West
ILC	22/10/88	2	Omagh Town	H	W	6	0	Manley 4, Craig, Macartney
ILC	08/11/88	3	Bangor	A	W	1	0	Manley
ILC	16/11/88	SF	Portadown	WP	W	3	2	Totten 2, Morrison
ILC	30/11/88	F	Linfield	H	W	2	1	Macartney, Paterson
IL	29/10/88		Coleraine	A	W	3	2	Jameson 2(1p), Macartney
IL	05/11/88		Bangor	A	L	1	2	Macartney
IL	12/11/88		Cliftonville	A	D	0	0	-
IL	19/11/88		Distillery	H	W	8	2	Cleary 2, Macartney 2, Manley 2, Devine, Jameson
IL	26/11/88		Glenavon	A	W	3	2	Morrison, Jameson, Totten
IL	03/12/88		Larne	H	W	3	1	Macartney 2, Morrison
IL	10/12/88		Ballymena United	H	W	3	2	Cleary 2(2p), Jameson
IL	17/12/88		Ards	A	W	5	1	Harrison, Hillis, Morrison, Cleary 2
IL	24/12/88		Carrick Rangers	H	W	4	0	Hillis 2, Macartney, Jameson
IL	27/12/88		Crusaders	A	W	3	0	Bowers, Cleary, Macartney
IL	31/12/88		Newry Town	H	W	2	0	Macartney, Cleary
IL	02/01/89		Portadown	A	L	0	2	-
IL	07/01/89		Linfield	H	L	2	3	Macartney, Hillis
IL	14/01/89		Bangor	H	W	2	1	Cleary (p), Macartney
IL	18/01/89		Distillery	A	W	3	1	Macartney, Manley, Morrison
IL	21/01/89		Cliftonville	H	D	2	2	Cleary 2(1p)
IL	04/02/89		Glenavon	H	L	2	3	Cleary, Caskey
IL	25/02/89		Larne	A	W	1	0	Jameson
IL	04/03/89		Ballymena United	A	W	2	1	Macartney, Manley
IL	18/03/89		Ards	H	W	1	0	Macartney
IL	25/03/89		Carrick Rangers	A	W	3	0	Cleary, Macartney, Hillis
IL	28/03/89		Crusaders	H	W	3	0	Morrison, Macartney, Manley
IL	01/04/89		Newry Town	A	D	1	1	Hillis
IL	15/04/89		Portadown	H	L	0	1	-
IL	22/04/89		Linfield	A	W	2	1	Manley, Jameson
IL	29/04/89		Coleraine	H	D	1	1	Morrison
IC	28/01/89	1	Armoy United	H	W	5	1	Manley, Macartney 2, Cleland, Cleary (p)
IC	18/02/89	2	Omagh Town	A	W	3	2	Jameson, Bowers (p), Macartney

IC	11/03/89	3	Linfield	H	L	0	3	-
BC	31/01/89	1.1	Crusaders	H	W	1	0	Macartney
BC	21/02/89	1.2	Crusaders	A	D	1	1	Mathieson
BC	02/03/89	2	Coleraine	A	L	0	2	aet
CAS	30/03/89	1	Larne	A	W	3	1	aet – Harrison, Cleary, Macartney
CAS	18/04/89	2	Portadown	H	W	2	0	Macartney, Morrison
CAS	10/05/89	SF	Ballymena United	Sv	W	2	0	Macartney 2
CAS	18/05/89	F	Bangor	Sv	L	1	2	aet Cleary (p)
F	30/07/88		Limerick City	H	D	1	1	Manley
F	01/08/88		McCooke Select XI	H	W	8	2	Hillis 4, Craig 2, Cleary, Mathieson. In aid of the McCooke twins
F	05/08/88		Coagh United	A	W	7	2	Neill 2, Cleary (p), Caskey, Hillis, McCoy, og
F	06/08/88		Tobermore	A	W	4	3	Morrison 3, Neill
F	11/08/88		Ballyclare Comrades	H	W	3	1	Hillis, Morrison, Mathieson
F	15/08/88		Dundela	A	W	2	0	Macartney, Morrison
F	06/12/88		St. Patrick's Athletic	H	W	2	0	Macartney, Jameson. Alan Paterson Benefit
F	03/06/89		Abbey Villa	A	W	3	1	Caskey, Morrison, Hillis. Billy Caskey Benefit

Appropriately Paterson staged his testimonial game at the Oval the following Tuesday evening. The opponents were St. Patrick's Athletic, including Damien Byrne, from the League of Ireland and on a freezing night an early goal from Macartney and a late one from Jameson secured a 2-0 win. Events for our next beneficiary Billy Caskey were well under way and, like Paterson, he was to be given a Civic Reception later in the season.

During December the Glens stretched their streak of successive league wins to eight. The most exciting game during this period without doubt was that against Ballymena. With ten minutes to go we trailed 0-2 but fought back to win 3-2 helped by two Cleary penalties, one in the last minute. Gary Hillis had returned from injury and scored two fine individual goals against Carrick on Christmas Eve. Our latest recruit, Tom Cleland signed from Distillery for £14,500, came on as sub for Hillis late in that game.

Seaview was the venue for Glenmen on successive days just after Christmas. On Boxing Day the Seconds, bolstered by many players of first team experience, lost 1-2 to Dundela in the Steel and Sons Cup final. It was a sorry display in our first final appearance in this competition since 1974 with the only bright moment being Jim Cowden's goal. However the following afternoon the 1st XI returned to the scene of the crime and beat Crusaders 3-0, helped by the early sending off of Kirk Hunter for a savage attack on Morrison. Despite a miraculous display from Newry keeper Brian O'Shea we scored two late goals to beat the Bordermen, leaving the last league table of 1988 to read as follows:
1. Glentoran played 11 points 28, 2. Linfield 11-28, 3. Coleraine 11-20.

The New Year began disastrously at Shamrock Park. Portadown beat us 2-0, both goals from Marty Magee, and we also missed two penalties by Cleary (saved by Keenan) and Bowers (hit the crossbar). Linfield rubbed salt into these wounds by coming to the Oval five days later and beating us 3-2. Macartney had opened the scoring in the 46th minute but the Blues, inspired by two goal George O'Boyle, were the better side on the day. Billy Caskey was taken to hospital at half-time with a fractured jawbone.

We stayed in touch by recording hard fought wins over Bangor and Distillery but then slipped eight points behind Linfield when only managing to draw at home to Cliftonville. Our chances slimmed further when we tasted defeat at Glenavon in a stormy game. Referee Magill sent off Duncan Lowry, Mathieson and Kennedy as ex-Glenman Gary Blackledge scored a hat-trick for the home side. Jim Cleary netted for us but had also missed a penalty when we were 0-1 down.

So the thoughts of Glenmen once more drifted to the Irish Cup as our best hope of capturing a major trophy. The Cup had been extended to a 32 team first round again and we took advantage to easily beat Armoy United, who were languishing in the lower reaches of the intermediate league. In Round Two we had to battle to overcome Omagh Town and this set up an exciting third round clash with Linfield at the Oval. A five figure crowd created an electric atmosphere but it proved to be the Blues' day as they won 3-0. The goal of the match was a brilliant 30 yard drive by Coly. Our Cup records were sent tumbling, it was our first defeat in the competition since 1984 and our first Oval loss in thirteen years!

By now we had lost our hold on the Budweiser Floodlit Cup as well. After beating Crusaders 2-1 on aggregate in Round One thanks to a flying header from Andy Mathieson we lost in extra-time at Coleraine in a twice postponed tie. Bowers again hit the woodwork with a spot-kick when it stood 0-0.

Jackson made changes and dropped Caskey and Cleary to the bench for the home game with Ards. Winger Raymond Campbell was signed from Nottingham Forest and Conor McCaffrey, son of our ex-striker Gerry, came into the side at left-back. There was still the prospect of a European place and a sequence of five wins made that seem likelier. However we stumbled by drawing at Newry and then losing at home to Portadown as the players were booed off the pitch. Linfield regained the title that day but it was a sad one for football as over ninety people lost their lives in the Hillsborough disaster in Sheffield.

Once more we quickly gained revenge over the Ports with a County Antrim Shield success three days later when players were fortunate not to be sent off after a second half raucous. Glentoran secured runners-up spot in the league by defeating Linfield 2-1 at Windsor Park. The game will be remembered for Johnny Jameson's 85th minute winner, his 100th goal for the club, and Dean Smyth's last minute penalty save from Lindsay McKeown. Pat McCoy returned to the first team as sub in that match and then donned the number six shirt against Coleraine.

There was still hope of some more silverware in the form of the newly sponsored Cawoods County Antrim Shield. Two exquisite goals from Macartney, named the NIPFA Player of the Year were enough to beat Ballymena in the Seaview semi to take us through to a final with Bangor at the same venue five days later. That game turned into something of a rough-house and Bangor's Eddis was ordered off in the 75th minute. Soon after Jim Campbell put the Seasiders ahead, but a penalty six minutes from time converted by Cleary, which was to be his last goal for the Glens, took the match into extra time. It became end-to-end stuff until George Gibson popped up with the winner after 112 minutes play to end the season.

Glentoran took the field once more in early June at the unlikely setting of Crommelin Park, Donaghadee. The local Glens Supporters' Club had arranged the fixture against Amateur League outfit Abbey Villa in aid of Billy Caskey's benefit. A crowd of about 500 saw the Glens beat the locals, who included Bamber's brother John, by 3-1.

Appearances and Goals

	App.	Subs.	Goals		App.	Subs.	Goals
Macartney	54		33	McGreevy	14		
Caskey W.	52	1	4	Mathieson	10	8	1
Paterson	50		1	Cleland	8	8	1
Cleary	50	1	25	Campbell	8	2	
Morrison	50	1	13	Smyth D.	7		
Totten	41	4	5	McCaffrey	6		
Devine	40	1	1	McCoy	4	2	2
Moore	40		1	Cowden	3	2	
Neill G.	37			Craig	3	9	3
Kennedy	35	2		Montgomery	2		
Bowers	32	3	3	West		1	1
Manley	28	11	17	Own Goals			2
Harrison	20		2				
Jameson	17	21	10	TOTAL	627	82	131
Hillis	16	5	6				

1989/90

The entire Glentoran fraternity was stunned just before the start of the season when Jim Cleary announced his retirement from the game. Cleary, after fifteen years in the Irish League and nine seasons at the Oval, no longer had the motivation for another term and, despite many attempts to get him back in a Glens' shirt, he had made up his mind. Another loss was Alan Harrison who also felt he had no further appetite for the game. Ron Manley left the club to play with Morwell in Australia and Brain Kennedy moved to England where he got fixed up with Colchester United, managed by ex-Rangers boss Jock Wallace. Rumours abounded that Gary Hillis had been placed on the transfer list after he picked up an injury playing in the "frowned upon" summer soccer. Terry Moore was appointed club captain.

The season opened with attractive and well-supported friendlies against WBA and Sheffield Wednesday, managed by Brian Talbot and Ron Atkinson respectively. Although we lost both games narrowly the team, particularly Raymond Campbell, gave a good account of themselves against the likes of Chris Whyte, Colin West, Bernard McNally, Dalian Atkinson, David Hurst, Carlton Palmer, Imre Varadi and Nigel Worthington.

Tommy Jackson dipped into the transfer market and signed Bangor striker Stephen Douglas for around £12,500 and Ron McCreery from Distillery

George Neill's favourite photograph shows him open the scoring in the Irish Cup final against Portadown.

for his second spell at the club. Douglas made his debut against Dundela when Alan Paterson repeated his League Cup final feat by scoring with a long-range punt upfield after coming on as a replacement. Five days previously we had opened the new facilities of Crumlin United, managed by Gerry McCaffrey, in a game where ex-Glens player Alan Jardine suffered a leg-break. Our last friendly was an unpublicised meeting with west Belfast juniors Donegal Celtic. Supporters were angry about not getting the chance to attend the game but given the current circumstances and location of the ground the board of directors thought that they had no option.

Long serving groundsman Billy Crawford was again complemented for the "bowling green" Oval surface and received the BEM for his efforts. Centre-forward of the 1950's Sammy Hughes was made into a life-member of the club.

Glentoran returned a 100% record in the Ulster Cup group games, needing an 85th minute winner in a difficult fixture at Coleraine. This gave us home advantage in the quarter-final tie with Linfield and what a dramatic game that turned out to be! The Blues went ahead through Baxter in the 44th minute and then on 62 minutes Campbell was sent off after an incident with Dehnoun. With just over six minutes remaining Linfield appeared to have sealed victory but a long-range "goal" from Paul Mooney was ruled out for offside. The Glens counter-attacked immediately but McKeown cleared the ball. However referee

Snoddy believed that the ball had struck the defender's arm and awarded a penalty. Now the local game was at last being regularly covered by both television channels and replays confirmed McKeown's opinion. Bowers slotted away the spot-kick but the game was far from over and two late spectacular strikes from Gary Macartney gave us a 3-1 win!

Three days later the Gold Cup commenced in a slightly different format. The clubs were split into two groups of four and one of six. The winners of the two smaller groups qualified for the semi-finals along with the top two from the six-team group. Again we remained unbeaten to qualify the best moment of the campaign being Campbell's 25 yard chip over O'Shea against Newry.

The UEFA Cup draw had paired us with Dundee United and although we lost 1-5 on aggregate it gave fans an excellent chance to promote the name of Glentoran in Scotland.

Barney Bowers.

Over 2,500 made the trip to Dundee to cheer the team on after around 8,000 had attended the Oval leg. Jameson had scored a brilliant equaliser for us in that match but the likes of Maurice Malpas, Kevin Gallagher, John Clark and Jim McInally proved too strong. Dundee United also included Mirodag Krivokapic who had scored an own goal on his last visit to the Oval when playing for Red Star Belgrade.

Back to the Ulster Cup and in one of our best performances for a long time we tore Coleraine to pieces by 4-0 at Ballymena. We carried that form into the first half of the final with Glenavon when two superbly clinical finishes by Macartney helped us to a 3-0 interval lead. The Lurgan men came back after the break and created many chances, but only scored one goal thorough Blackledge on 59 minutes. Hence we retained the Ulster Cup.

The Irish League commenced on 23rd September and only one goal was scored in our opening three games. That came from Robert Craig five minutes from time against Ballymena. Terry Moore and the Ports' Greg Davidson were dismissed at Shamrock Park along with assistant manager Billy McCullough who was ordered from the dugout by referee Magill. The league went into hibernation for three weeks as the opening rounds of the Roadferry League Cup were played.

The Glens regained their scoring form in knocking eight past a helpless Chimney Corner in Round One. Macartney put away four, including a nonchalant reverse flick, and even George Neill got onto the scoresheet. In Round Two we hammered the Blues 4-0 at Windsor, going three up after only 33 minutes! Caskey and Campbell dominated the midfield then but that was not the case in the Gold Cup semi-final when Portadown beat us 5-2. Caskey had opened the scoring but the Ports, helped by a hat-trick of penalties by Roy McCreadie, inflicted our first domestic defeat of the season.

We resumed league business with easy wins over Carrick and Distillery. The latter marked the debut of left-sided player Seamus Heath as substitute. The 27 year-old's nomadic career included service with Cromac Albion, Luton Town, Wrexham, Tranmere, Northwich Victoria and Caernarfon Town in Britain plus six summers in Finland with Tulun Pallaseura, EIS and BK46 of Karis.

The team stuttered badly in mid-November with home defeats by mid-Ulster teams in the space of four days. Firstly Glenavon won an incident-packed league game by 3-2, coming from behind twice with the winning goal a Moore own goal! John Devine now back at centre-half after spells at full-back and in midfield was twice involved in tragic mix-ups with Dean Smyth which both led to Glenavon goals. Next Portadown knocked us out of the League Cup with a Fraser goal on 78 minutes. The game was played in misty conditions and the ill-feeling that had crept into matches between the two clubs spilt over in the 55th minute when a brawl developed. Kevin McKeever and Raymond Morrison were sent off by referee Ritchie.

426

Billy Caskey takes on the Crusaders defence .

The "Fanzine" craze which had hit mainland Britain in the mid to late 1980's spread to Glentoran in November 1989. Three publications emerged, "For Ever and Ever", "A Nightmare on Dee Street" and the one-off "Pride of the East". After a slightly puerile beginning in the case of the former, the two magazines developed into interesting pieces containing both forthright criticism and satirical humour on the Glens and other clubs and events throughout the Irish League scene. They certainly provided an alternative forum for comment to go alongside Paul Vance's much maligned Gazette and "Nightmare" regularly contained excellent interviews with the players.

Still the team found goals hard to come by, just one more in the next three league games into December. However, apart from the Glenavon debacle, Dean Smyth had kept a clean sheet in all the Smirnoff games. Coleraine's McCoy eventually found a way through him in a twice-postponed fixture at the Showgrounds. Earlier in the game this season's beneficiary, Barney Bowers, had put us ahead from the penalty spot.

Gary Macartney netted his 100th goal for the club with a thundering header against Ballyclare Comrades in the Budweiser Cup. Hillis also netted a spectacular goal in our 5-1 win which set us up nicely for the Boxing Day encounter with Linfield – the traditional festive fixture revived after a twelve-year gap.

What an opening 45 minutes Glentoran had as a fierce left foot drive by Tom Cleland, an unmarked Caskey heading home and a brilliant chest-down and dipping volley from Macartney gave us a 3-0 interval lead. "What a load of rubbish", fans chanted as the sorry Linfield XI trooped off. However they came back into it after the break through Grattan (71 minutes) and McGaughey (88 minutes) and almost snatched a draw when we had to clear off the line twice in the last minute!

The Seconds had won the Steel and Sons Cup final the previous day, overcoming a brave East Belfast side 4-1 at Seaview. Man of the match Gary Hillis got two with the other goals coming from McGreevy and the captain Morrison. The Seconds would later lift the "B" Division title too.

Alan Paterson returned in goals for the Cliftonville game when our 1-0 win left the table as follows at the end of the 1980's:

1. Portadown played 13 points 27, 2. Glentoran 12-23, 3. Glenavon 13-23, 4. Cliftonville 13-22, 5. Ballymena 12-21.

January was a bad month for us as we won only two out of seven fixtures, dropping seven league points. We suffered defeat against Ballyclare at Allen Park in the second leg of the Budweiser tie but more crucially lost at home to Portadown in the league race. Conor McCaffrey had to stop playing due to a troublesome chest infection with Heath stepping in as an emergency left-back.

Stephen Douglas scores our second cup final goal against Portadown.

427

Results 1989/90

Played 56. Won 34. Drew 11. Lost 11. Goals For 118. Against 50.% 70.5.
Honours: Irish Cup, Ulster Cup, Budweiser Cup, County Antrim Shield

UC	19/08/89		Larne	H	W	5	0	Douglas, Macartney 2(1p), Campbell, Caskey
UC	22/08/89		Portadown	A	W	2	1	Douglas, Macartney
UC	26/08/89		Distillery	H	W	1	0	Macartney
UC	30/08/89	QF	Linfield	H	W	3	1	Bowers (p), Macartney 2
UC	20/09/89	SF	Coleraine	BS	W	4	0	Jameson, Macartney 2, Caskey
UC	03/10/89	F	Glenavon	WP	W	3	1	Macartney 2, Caskey
GC	02/09/89		Ards	A	W	3	1	Jameson, Douglas, Caskey
GC	09/09/89		Newry Town	H	W	2	1	Jameson, Campbell
GC	16/09/89		Carrick Rangers	A	D	0	0	-
GC	24/10/89	SF	Portadown	WP	L	2	5	Caskey, Macartney
UEFA	13/09/89	1.1	Dundee United	H	L	1	3	Jameson
UEFA	27/09/89	1.2	Dundee United	A	L	0	2	-
IL	23/09/89		Bangor	A	D	0	0	-
IL	30/09/89		Ballymena United	H	W	1	0	Craig
IL	07/10/89		Portadown	A	D	0	0	-
IL	28/10/89		Carrick Rangers	H	W	2	0	Macartney, Totten
IL	04/11/89		Distillery	A	W	3	0	Macartney 2, Morrison
IL	11/11/89		Glenavon	H	L	2	3	Campbell, Scapatticci og
IL	18/11/89		Larne	A	D	0	0	-
IL	25/11/89		Newry Town	H	W	1	0	Macartney
IL	09/12/89		Ards	H	D	0	0	-
IL	12/12/89		Coleraine	A	D	1	1	Bowers (p)
IL	26/12/89		Linfield	H	W	3	2	Cleland, Caskey, Macartney
IL	30/12/89		Cliftonville	H	W	1	0	Douglas
IL	06/01/90		Ballymena United	A	D	1	1	Macartney
IL	09/01/90		Crusaders	A	W	4	0	Douglas 2, Jameson, Hillis
IL	13/01/90		Portadown	H	L	2	3	Macartney, Jameson
IL	27/01/90		Carrick Rangers	A	D	1	1	Macartney
IL	03/02/90		Distillery	H	W	2	0	Hillis, Morrison
IL	10/02/90		Glenavon	A	L	1	2	Macartney
IL	03/03/90		Larne	H	W	2	1	Douglas, Macartney
IL	17/03/90		Newry Town	A	L	0	1	-
IL	24/03/90		Coleraine	H	W	5	3	Jameson 2, Macartney 2, Douglas
IL	31/03/90		Ards	A	L	1	2	Macartney
IL	14/04/90		Crusaders	H	W	6	0	Caskey, Jameson 2, Douglas, Macartney (p), Morrison
IL	17/04/90		Linfield	A	W	3	1	McCaffrey, Macartney 2
IL	21/04/90		Cliftonville	A	D	0	0	-
IL	28/04/90		Bangor	H	L	1	3	Macartney
ILC	14/10/89	1	Chimney Corner	A	W	8	0	Douglas 2, Caskey, Macartney 4, Neill
ILC	21/10/89	2	Linfield	A	W	4	0	Macartney, Bowers (p), Douglas 2
ILC	14/11/89	3	Portadown	H	L	0	1	-
BC	21/12/89	1.1	Ballyclare Comrades	H	W	5	1	Macartney, Caskey, Bowers (p), Hillis, Douglas
BC	01/01/90	1.2	Ballyclare Comrades	A	L	0	1	-
BC	20/02/90	2	Cliftonville	A	W	2	0	Bowers (p), Douglas
BC	28/02/90	SF	Newry Town	NG	W	4	0	Bowers, Devine, Douglas 2
BC	07/03/90	F	Linfield	A	W	4	2	Macartney 2, Campbell, Caskey
IC	20/01/90	5	Cliftonville	H	D	1	1	Jameson
IC	31/01/90	5R	Cliftonville	A	W	1	0	Macartney
IC	17/02/90	6	Barn United	H	W	2	1	Caskey 2

IC	10/03/90	7	Newry Town	A	W	3	2	Douglas 2, Macartney
IC	07/04/90	SF	Linfield	A	W	2	0	Macartney, Campbell
IC	05/05/90	F	Portadown	WP	W	3	0	Neill, Douglas, Morrison
CAS	24/02/90	1	H & W Welders	H	W	3	0	Craig, Douglas 2
CAS	20/03/90	2	East Belfast	H	W	2	0	Bowers (p), Douglas
CAS	28/03/90	SF	Larne	A	W	5	2	Morrison 2, Caskey, Douglas, Jameson
CAS	25/04/90	F	Linfield	H	D	0	0	aet – (won 6-5 on penalties)
F	03/08/89		West Bromwich A.	H	L	2	3	Bowers (p), Talbot og
F	07/08/89		Sheffield Wednesday	H	L	1	2	Totten
F	09/08/89		Crumlin United	A	W	5	1	Caskey 2, Mathieson, Totten, Craig
F	14/08/89		Dundela	H	W	2	1	Paterson, Totten
F	16/08/89		Donegal Celtic	A	W	4	1	Craig 2, Mathieson, Morrison

Senior clubs entered the Irish Cup at the fifth round stage and the draw paired us with Cliftonville at the Oval. We paid the penalty for not putting away our chances and the Reds earned a replay with a 1-1 draw. The Security Forces stipulated that such a Solitude encounter must take place in the afternoon and this caused the Amalgamation of Supporters' Clubs to arrange a boycott of the game and also the Budweiser Cup meeting between the two clubs at the same venue a week later. Ironically the Irish Cup game was postponed after many fans had booked an afternoon off work and the Budweiser tie was played as an evening kick-off following three postponements! In the end Glentoran won both games without conceding a goal. However our championship hopes faltered with a 1-2 defeat in the Mourneview mud.

The rest of February saw us progress on three knockout fronts. Two goals from Caskey saw off Amateur League Barn United in the Irish Cup and then a Craig goal sent us on the way to victory over Harland and Wolff Welders in the County Antrim Shield at a waterlogged Oval. Three days later we reached the final of the Budweiser Cup by beating Newry 4-0 at a snowy Ballyskeagh. Bowers opened the scoring with a free-kick that trickled in from all of 25 yards.

After struggling to beat Larne, Jameson coming off the bench to cross beautifully for Macartney's late winner, we met Linfield again, this time in the Budweiser Cup final at Windsor. The Blues went ahead through McGaughey but we were soon piling on the agony as two Macartney goals wiped this out. Campbell made it 3-1 after a mazy run and by the final whistle we had won 4-2 and in so doing created a club record of five successive wins over Linfield.

We now faced two trips to the Newry Showgrounds where we recorded mixed success. In the Irish Cup quarter-final, or Round Seven, the Glens raced into 3-0 lead after 21 minutes but allowed Newry to pull back to 3-2 and then saw Gray blast a late chance over the bar when faced with an open goal. Newry gained revenge the following Saturday when an Ollie Ralph goal on 50 minutes killed off our fading interest in the Gibson Cup. In between these two games we took part in the inaugural Guinness Sixes at the Dundonald Ice Bowl. After beating Larne 1-0 in Round One we lost to the Blues on penalties following a 1-1 draw. Campbell and Caskey were our scorers.

Jameson stretches to cross ahead of Derek Statham against WBA.

The fixture glut continued as we put five past Coleraine after being 1-3 down at half-time and Larne, to qualify for the final of the Shield, before losing to a managerless Ards. Ex-Glens left-back Tommy Leeman scored with a 25 yard shot. Current left-back Seamus Heath left for a summer season in Finland with BK46.

April commenced with the first of three more meetings with Linfield, this one an Irish Cup semi-final at Windsor Park. It turned out to be another sunny day of happiness for Glenmen as first-half goals from Macartney with a mis-hit shot and Campbell, after another tremendous dribbling run, maintained our domination over our old rivals.

Campbell again created havoc as we hammered the Crues 6-0 and then returned to Windsor Park for a league meeting with the Blues on the evening Easter Tuesday. Sid Burrows put Linfield into an early lead but we equalised with a lovely McCaffrey free-kick after 56 minutes. Then the Blues' executioner-in-chief Gary Macartney took over with goals in the 61st and 83rd minutes to give us a 3-1 victory. Within two days Roy Coyle had resigned as Linfield manager thus ending his fifteen year reign at "The Park".

While we were drawing 0-0 at Solitude, where Bowers missed a penalty, Portadown wrapped up their first league title in beating Ards 1-0 in injury time and the Blues 2-0 in their final game. Glenavon ran them all the way but finished a point behind. Although surprisingly losing to Bangor we finished third just ahead of the Blues on goal difference.

The seventh and last meeting of the season with Linfield came at the Oval in the County Antrim Shield final. The game itself finished scoreless and even extra-time could not produce a goal so it went to a penalty shoot-out. Both sides scored with their first five attempts but then the Blues' young player of the year, Noel Bailie, missed. Conor McCaffrey stepped up to convert his and win us the Shield. It was the first time we had beaten Linfield in the final of this competition since 1968 and it completed our "seven-up" over them that season and was our eighth successive "Big Two" win!

The last match of the season was the Irish Cup final with double-seeking Portadown on a sunny afternoon at Windsor Park on 5th May 1990. In the first half the Glens had been handicapped by the loss of Macartney and Campbell to injury but after 59 minutes we took the lead through, of all people, George Neill. It was only George's third goal of his career but what a time to score it! As the Ports tired substitutes Douglas and Morrison added further goals in the last six minutes to give us an emphatic 3-0 win and our fifth Irish Cup success in six years. Portadown had still never recorded an Irish Cup win over us.

The end of the season brought further joy for John Devine as, after he had gained an under-21 cap against Israel, he was named as a substitute for Northern Ireland against Uruguay in a Windsor Park friendly. Devine came on replacing Colin Hill for the last ten minutes in a 1-0 victory and then completed a "hat-trick" by featuring in an under-23 international against the Republic of Ireland, managing to score in a 2-3 defeat.

On a sadder note the spring had marked the deaths of two former Glentoran stars, namely Tim Williamson and the prince of inside-forwards, Peter Doherty.

Appearances and Goals

	App.	Subs.	Goals		App.	Subs.	Goals
Caskey W.	54		13	Paterson	15		
Macartney	54		39	Totten	13	16	1
Bowers	53	1	7	Craig	13	9	2
Devine	50		1	McCreery Ron	8	1	
Moore	49			Hillis	5	4	3
Douglas	46	5	24	McCoy	2		
Campbell	41	4	5	McGreevy	2		
Smyth D.	41			Mathieson	1	5	
McCaffrey	38		1	Smyth G.	1		
Jameson	36	7	12	West		1	
Neill G.	36	1	2	Own Goals			1
Morrison	22	4	6				
Heath	19	2		TOTAL	616	71	118
Cleland	17	11	1				

1990/91

Two new clubs – Rumanian nightmare – Roadferry success

There were many changes of note at Glentoran and in the wider Irish League scene for the first full season of the 1990's. The number of senior clubs was extended to sixteen with the inclusion of Ballyclare Comrades and Omagh Town. The club launched a telephone-based Glentoran Information Service containing match reports and news stories narrated by Harry Thompson complete with introductory jingle. Dennis Gill replaced Alan Crowe as secretary.

On the playing front Ron Manley returned from Australia and latterly New Zealand while Stephen Fettis and Glen Wilkinson were recruited from Chimney Corner and Carrick Rangers. Players leaving the club included Norman McGreevy and Pat McCoy, both to retirement and the latter to a new life in England, and Ron McCreery and David Montgomery who joined Crusaders and Carrick respectively. One man not on the move was John Devine whose proposed transfer to First Division Southampton never materialised.

We had a limited series of pre-season friendlies, managing a draw with West Bromwich Albion and defeating a combined Dundela / Welders XI in a benefit match to mark Mervyn Bell's 25 years of service. The Glentoran beneficiaries of the previous two seasons, Barney Bowers and Billy Caskey, were finally rewarded with a joint testimonial match against Dundee United. The star of the game was United's Irish international winger Michael O'Neill and the gate receipts from the fixture were kindly donated to the Rumanian Orphans appeal. The team was sporting a new kit, an all green patterned shirt with red collar and cuffs and black shorts. Tommy Jackson was appointed manager to the Irish League XI for their centenary celebration match with Manchester United. Five Glenmen were in the team but United easily won 3-0.

The first two months of the competitive season were extremely disappointing. We comfortably qualified for the Ulster Cup

Gary Macartney.

quarter-finals, despite a missed Bowers penalty at Newry, but then lost our record run against Linfield at that stage. A Stephen Baxter goal three minutes into injury time gave the Blues a 1-0 win. Worse was to follow in the Gold Cup as we failed to qualify for the knockout stage at all. Crusaders beat us for the first time in eleven attempts and we lost at Glenavon despite a goal from Macartney on his return from an ankle injury.

Our European ties with Steaua Bucharest left a nasty taste in the mouth. The Rumanians had been runners up in the 1989 European Cup and despite losing many star players they were still a stiff proposition. The first leg at the Oval was a "night of passion" and the Glens managed a 1-1 draw thanks to a Douglas flick-in, our 50th goal in European competition. Steaua's goal was a penalty by Stan awarded for an alleged foul by Devine.

The return in Bucharest presented an interesting paradox. Away from the match many of the 200 visiting supporters went and made donations to Rumanian orphanages but on the field the Steaua players needlessly put on a display of theatrical acting and spitting. The Albanian referee, Mr. A. Hoxha, totally lost control and ended up sending Billy Caskey off for "spitting"! The Glentoran party boycotted the after match dinner with manager Jackson describing the hospitality as "terrible". The board made a formal complaint to UEFA but the saddest thing of all was that the sometimes brilliant football of Steaua was virtually forgotten. Stan, Ilie Dumitrescu (2), the second a sensational free-kick, and Dan Petrescu (2) scored their five goals.

Caskey was sent off again at Bangor as we crashed out of the Budweiser Cup in the first round after taking the lead. This time his crime for a second booking was kicking the ball away.

The league championship had commenced on 22nd September and we were part of an historic occasion being Ballyclare's first visitors under their new senior status. Bowers ruined the Comrades' day with the only goal after 74 minutes. Apart from the Budweiser loss matters improved during October for both the team and Caskey, who scored his 100th Glens goal with a diving header for the winner at Coleraine. Dean Smyth was dropped after the Bangor defeat and Alan Paterson was recalled at Larne for his 400th appearance. Seamus Heath returned too as the Finnish season concluded.

Action from the away tie with Steaua Bucharest.

Glentoran turned out in white socks for a six match spell and it was during this run that we beat Glenavon 2-0 in an entertaining game. Paterson made many excellent saves but the day was marred by scenes of fighting on the unreserved terraces. As a result a "corridor" was built into the fencing in the middle of the covered portion. Our first league defeat came in a poor display at Newry and left ourselves and Cliftonville tied for second place in the table, five points behind Portadown, who boasted a 100% record after eight games.

After a dispute with the club Robert Craig returned with a goal against Distillery in a re-arranged game but our other absentee Billy Totten was still "AWOL". Another Smyth, defender Gary, appeared on the team sheet as Caskey, Hillis, Bowers and Douglas were dropped for the visit to Bangor. Another Barry McCreadie goal was enough to send us further behind in the league race.

The team responded by producing two breathtaking wins in the next fortnight as twice we came from 0-2 behind to win 3-2 against Cliftonville and Carrick Rangers. Hillis scored a dramatic last minute winner at Taylor's Avenue while the deciding goal against the Reds occurred in the 48th minute when a defender struck the ball against Morrison's back and had to watch it loop into the net!

We had two vital fixtures either side of Christmas versus Portadown and Linfield, both ending in 1-1 draws. The Ports game was a "nail-biter" while the Windsor match was spoiled by the atrocious hurricane-like conditions. The wind did help makeshift right-back Andy Mathieson net our goal though from around 40 yards. The year finished with a dismal and deserved 3-1 defeat by Omagh Town on our first visit to St. Julian's Road.

League form improved in January but the three wins recorded only kept us eight points behind Portadown with a game more played. Gary Macartney continued to haunt teams managed by Roy Coyle when he scored a hat-trick against Ards. We made progress in both the Irish and League Cups against junior opposition but the club was shocked when Dean Smyth resigned. He was frustrated by the lack of first team opportunity due to Paterson's form. Trevor Shaw was subsequently signed from Ards Rangers as goalkeeping cover.

Glentoran Colts captured the "No Smoking" IFA Youth Cup with a 1-0 win over Coleraine Colts at Seaview. Earlier in the competition they had hammered Dungoyne Boys 14-0 and North Fermanagh Youths 9-0. In other news the man who rattled the plastic collection box for spastic children outside the Oval, Billy Young, was named Northern Ireland fundraiser of the year.

Defeat at Crusaders and draws with Glenavon and Newry Town put us entirely out of the running for the title. Indeed we had become embroiled in the battle for the runners-up berth, and a UEFA Cup place, with Bangor. When the Seasiders came to the Oval to win 1-0 it gave Portadown the league. Four days later we sunk to third place when losing at Solitude after Jameson put us ahead in the 85th minute!

Our form was much better in the three knockout tournaments as we featured in some sort of game virtually every mid-week in February and March. In fact Glentoran played sixteen games in those two months alone. Hat-tricks by Macartney and Hillis were the main reason for a 9-1 victory over Tobermore in the Irish Cup when we scored five goals in a ten minute spell during the second half – that after it had stood 1-1 at the interval. This match came in between high scoring League Cup wins over Ballymena and Distillery, indeed fans could have seen seventeen Glentoran goals at the Oval in the space of eight days! In the boardroom long-serving director Tom McNeice resigned to be replaced by Ronnie Rutherford, proprietor of the Strand and Bangor cinema complexes.

Castlereagh Park was the scene for a remarkable League Cup semi-final with Bangor at the end of February. We held a 2-0 lead at one stage but despite them being reduced to ten men for the last 35 minutes, Bangor pulled back to 2-2 and force extra-time. The Glens, however, gained their second wind and scored four more times without replay. A week later we beat the Seasiders at the Oval in the County Antrim Shield. This time we only needed one goal, a beautiful one by Jameson set up by Campbell.

Larne then gave us a hard match in the Irish Cup quarter-final at Inver but a magnificent Morrison volley sent us on the way to an easy 4-1 win in the Oval replay. Raymond's second goal of the night came about as a result of a brilliant run of 60 yards by George Neill.

A large crowd assembled at Windsor Park for the Roadferry League Cup final. Once again Gary Macartney showed a Coyle-led team no mercy and two delightful headers in the 48th and 67th minutes allowed us to pick up our first, and only, trophy of the season and the thirteenth of Tommy Jackson's reign. In between the goals Paterson had made a wonderful and crucial save from Coulter's goal-bound 25 yard drive.

Terry Moore in a race for the ball with Glenavon's Glenn Ferguson.

Glentoran suffered two set-backs in early April. Firstly an understrength side including Trevor Shaw, Stuart Ferguson and Ian McDonald went down in the Shield at Newry. Then Glenavon's Stephen McBride tore us apart in the second half of the Irish Cup semi-final, and scored one of the Lurgan men's three goals with a spectacular long-range shot.

Back to the league and the suffering spectators were given something to shout about when Macartney's glorious header was enough to beat Linfield. It was our first win of the season over the Blues compared to seven in 1989/90. Three days later we battled to beat Carrick but Bangor saw off Distillery to stay two points clear of us with two games left. The Seasiders lost their next game 0-3 at Ballymena while we gained a creditable draw at champions Portadown with Raymond Campbell the man of the match. However our final league win over Omagh was in vain as Bangor clinched the European spot with a 2-1 success against Carrick.

Results 1990/91

Played 52. Won 30. Drew 9. Lost 13. Goals For 99. Against 60. % 66.4.
Honours: Irish League Cup

UC	18/08/90		Coleraine	H	W	1	0	Caskey
UC	21/08/90		Newry Town	A	D	1	1	Douglas
UC	25/08/90		Ballyclare Comrades	H	W	4	0	Hillis, Douglas, West, Morrison
UC	29/08/90	QF	Linfield	H	L	0	1	-
GC	01/09/90		Omagh Town	H	W	2	1	Douglas, McCaffrey (p)
GC	08/09/90		Crusaders	A	L	0	1	-
GC	15/09/90		Glenavon	A	L	1	3	Macartney
ECW	19/09/90	1.1	Steaua Bucharest	H	D	1	1	Douglas
ECW	03/10/90	1.2	Steaua Bucharest	A	L	0	5	-
IL	22/09/90		Ballyclare Comrades	A	W	1	0	Bowers
IL	28/09/90		Ards	H	D	1	1	Macartney
IL	06/10/90		Coleraine	A	W	2	1	Morrison, Caskey
IL	13/10/90		Crusaders	H	W	2	0	Mathieson, Douglas
IL	27/10/90		Larne	A	W	1	0	Jameson
IL	03/11/90		Glenavon	H	W	2	0	Hillis, Macartney
IL	10/11/90		Ballymena United	H	W	2	0	Hillis, Macartney
IL	17/11/90		Newry Town	A	L	0	2	-
IL	01/12/90		Bangor	A	L	0	1	-
IL	04/12/90		Distillery	H	W	3	1	Morrison, Craig, Macartney
IL	08/12/90		Cliftonville	H	W	3	2	Mathieson, Macartney, Morrison
IL	15/12/90		Carrick Rangers	A	W	3	2	Macartney 2, Hillis
IL	22/12/90		Portadown	H	D	1	1	Macartney
IL	26/12/90		Linfield	A	D	1	1	Mathieson
IL	29/12/90		Omagh Town	A	L	1	3	Crilly og
IL	01/01/91		Ballyclare Comrades	H	W	2	1	Douglas, Hillis
IL	12/01/91		Ards	A	W	3	2	Macartney 3
IL	26/01/91		Coleraine	H	W	4	0	Hillis, Jameson, Macartney, Douglas
IL	02/02/91		Crusaders	A	L	0	2	-
IL	09/02/91		Larne	H	W	1	0	Hillis
IL	23/02/91		Glenavon	A	D	1	1	Hillis
IL	02/03/91		Ballymena United	A	W	3	2	Morrison, Manley, Caskey
IL	16/03/91		Newry Town	H	D	2	2	Macartney, Jameson
IL	23/03/91		Distillery	A	W	3	2	Cleland, Macartney, West
IL	26/03/91		Bangor	H	L	0	1	-
IL	30/03/91		Cliftonville	A	L	1	2	Jameson
IL	10/04/91		Linfield	H	W	1	0	Macartney
IL	13/04/91		Carrick Rangers	H	W	2	1	Macartney. Lamont og
IL	20/04/91		Portadown	A	D	0	0	-
IL	27/04/91		Omagh Town	H	W	4	1	Macartney 2, Hillis, Campbell
BC	20/10/90	1	Bangor	A	L	1	2	Mathieson
ILC	05/01/91	1	Banbridge Town	H	W	1	0	Hillis
ILC	12/02/91	2	Ballymena United	H	W	4	2	aet – Morrison, Macartney, Hillis, West
ILC	19/02/91	3	Distillery	H	W	4	0	Caskey, Hillis, Jameson, Macartney
ILC	27/02/91	SF	Bangor	CrP	W	6	2	aet – Dornan og, Hillis 2, Cleland 2(1p), Caskey
ILC	20/03/91	F	Ards	WP	W	2	0	Macartney 2
IC	19/01/91	4	Ballinamallard United	A	W	4	0	Donaldson og, Devine, Moore, Douglas
IC	16/02/91	5	Tobermore United	H	W	9	1	Macartney 3, Hillis 3, Caskey, Bowers, Campbell

IC	09/03/91	6	Larne	A	D	1	1	Caskey
IC	20/03/91	6R	Larne	H	W	4	1	Morrison 2, Bowers, Macartney
IC	06/04/91	SF	Glenavon	WP	L	1	3	Bowers
CAS	05/03/91	1	Bangor	H	W	1	0	Jameson
CAS	01/04/91	2	Newry Town	A	L	1	3	Mathieson
F	04/08/90		West Bromwich A.	H	D	0	0	-
F	07/08/90		Dundela/H&W Weld's	A		W	2	0	Bowers (p), Campbell Mervyn Bell Benefit
F	15/08/90		Dundee United	H	L	0	2	Barney Bowers / Billy Caskey Benefit
F	08/05/91		1980/1 Champions 2 (Cleary 2) 1987/8 Champions 4 (Caskey, Macartney 2, Craig) Robert Strain Testimonial					
F	14/05/91		Linfield	A	W	2	1	Morrison 2 David Jeffrey Testimonial for the Windsor Cup

In the Guinness Sixes we fell in the quarter-finals to Crusaders, 2-4, after topping our group with wins over Cliftonville 3-2, Ballyclare 1-0, and Larne 2-1. Our goals were scored by Hillis (4), Campbell (3) and David West.

We wound up the season with a couple of testimonials. For Second team boss Roberts Strain's benefit a match billed as the "80/1 Champions" versus the "87/8 Champions" took place at the Oval. Although the make up of the sides were not technically correct an enjoyable game was witnessed, resulting in a 4-2 win for the more recent side. Finally we took a team to Windsor to play Linfield in David Jeffrey's testimonial for the "Centenary Cup". Only 1,500 were there to watch Knell put the Blues one up from the penalty spot before two superb shots by Morrison gave us a 2-1 win. One bad moment of the night was the stretchering off of Raymond Campbell.

George Neill was named the Glens player of the year and there was also an award for the Glentoran Gazette. The much-improved programme was named the best in Northern Ireland.

Appearances and Goals

	App.	Subs.	Goals		App.	Subs.	Goals
Campbell	51		2	Mathieson	16	8	5
Moore	49		1	Smyth D.	14		
Morrison	44	1	8	Manley	9	10	1
Bowers	42	1	4	Craig	9	5	1
Neill G.	39			Cleland	6	4	3
Macartney	38	4	27	West	3	7	3
Paterson	37			Fettis	3		
Jameson	34	7	6	Shaw	1		
Caskey W.	30	5	7	Totten		7	
Hillis	29	5	17	Ferguson		1	
Devine	29		1	McDonald		1	
McCaffrey	28	6	1	Own Goals			4
Smyth G.	23	1					
Heath	21	1		TOTAL	572	81	99
Douglas	17	7	8				

1991/92

Heavy friendly defeats – 10,000th goal – League Champions comfortably

During the previous eighteen months there had been much speculation that Glentoran were going to sell the Oval and move to a purpose built all-seater stadium on the waste ground opposite Ashfield school. There were rumours that the directors had been to visit St. Johnstone's new McDiarmid Park for ideas, but as the close season finished the Oval was still our home venue and not for sale. This, among other issues, was a topic for debate for the Glentoran Supporters Action Group, who expressed disappointment with the board. The Action Group urged supporters not to fund club money raising activities such as buying the programme or patronising the club shop.

New signings were Bobby Kincaid, ex-Crusaders and Ards, John McAuley, ex-Cliftonville, Ards and Dunmurry, and Justin McBride from Carrick Rangers. Goalkeeper Dean Smyth decided to return and fight for his place. Ex-Glens players Jim Cowden and

Andy Mathieson.

Norman McGreevy were now trying their hands at rugby union and hockey respectively. Robert Craig did not turn up for pre-season training and eventually joined Ballymena. In the boardroom Derek McKeague was appointed as Secretary / General Manager. Sad news during the season was to be the deaths of three former players of the 1940's and 1950's, namely Peter McKennan, Ben Neill and Walter Kane.

Playing matters began with a match against Everton at the Oval for Tommy Jackson's testimonial. The varied range of contributors to the match programme reflected the man's wide and successful as player and manager, for example, Billy Bingham, Howard Kendall, Dave Mackay, Billy Neill, Tommy Docherty, Pat Jennings, Colin Harvey and Joe Royle. Unfortunately the Glens were outclassed in both this match and four days later against Sheffield Wednesday to the tune of 0-6. Hirst (3), Pearson, Sheridan and McKenzie scored for Wednesday while Newell, McCall, Warzycha, Sheedy, Youds and Beardsley had been on target for the Merseysiders before 5,000. David turned Goliath as we rounded off the pre-season friendlies with an easy 4-1 win over Dundela.

Early displays and results in the Ulster and Gold Cups were good as the team tried to erase the memory of the relatively poor 1990/1 season. In the former we returned a 100% record in the group, the biggest win coming over Ballyclare (5-1) when three goals were scored in a four minute spell to kill the game. George Neill opened the scoring against Cliftonville when his attempted cross-ball eluded 'keeper Paul Rice and finished in the net. Neill then had a taste of goalkeeping himself, standing in for Paterson for twelve minutes in the quarter-final against Newry, when our regular number one was off receiving treatment for damaged ribs. Two powerful headers by Gary Smyth sent us on the way to a 5-0 win in this match.

We opened up our Gold Cup group with a significant 6-3 win at Omagh. McBride scored his first goal for the club and Hillis completed his hat-trick with a late penalty. Andy

Mathieson had the privilege of putting away the club's 10,000th goal in competitive football in the 25th minute of this match, also from the penalty spot.

We met Crusaders in the Ulster Cup semi-final at Castlereagh Park. Glentoran enjoyed lots of pressure and chances but the Crues defence was solid and they gained the only goal of the game when Gary Smyth lobbed over his own goalkeeper, namesake Dean.

The crowd celebrations after we had clinched the league at Carrick.

The Hatchetmen frustrated us again in the Gold Cup as an 87th minute Gary Blackledge effort denied us victory at Seaview. Many supporters thought however that Neill had hooked the ball clear before it had fully crossed the line. In any event the Glens qualified for the quarter-finals thanks to a devastating four-goal first half display against Glenavon.

Now the Budweiser Cup commenced and a brilliant hat-trick by McBride saw off Ballyclare. The games were coming thick and fast as we beat Bangor after extra time in the Gold Cup and then made it fourteen Oval goals in a week by hammering Coleraine 6-1 in the opening Irish League match.

Gary Macartney had been considering retirement but he returned as substitute versus Ards and then four days later he was on the scoresheet against the same opponents in the Budweiser. For that match Glentoran were faced with a goalkeeping crisis as both Paterson and Smyth were injured. Trevor McCullough had offered to come out of retirement but Pat Saunders was signed from Crumlin United. Another player to arrive at the Oval was Ards' Winston "Winkie" Armstrong after he completed his amateur contract with the North Down men.

Down the club the Colts were in scoring mood, recording a 10-1 victory over Lurgan Boys in the IFA Youth Cup and a 13-0 win over Coleraine Colts in the league. Paul Blackledge, brother of Gary, notched five in the latter with Peter Kennedy claiming a hat-trick. They failed to retain the Youth Cup, however, going down 0-5 to Glenavon III in a later round.

We won four league games in a row, including a hard fought 2-0 victory at Glenavon with Macartney scoring twice in the last six minutes, before twice coming a cropper in early November. Returning to Mourneview Park just three nights after the league win we contrived to lose to Omagh Town in Budweiser Cup semi-final. Andy Mathieson blazed a penalty over the bar and missed another glorious chance before scoring in the 25th minute. Harry McCourt netted two for Omagh in their 3-2 success. Then Ballymena ruined our unbeaten league record with a 2-1 win at the Showgrounds.

Glentoran and Cliftonville had not met in a final since the County Antrim Shield of 1930/1, so a novelty factor was attached to our Gold Cup showdown at Windsor Park on 12th November. It proved to be a night of missed chances, none more so when Peter Murray fluffed from only six yards in the 87th minute. Thirty seconds from the end, however, Barney Bowers made no mistake when he slipped the ball home. For Barney, later named man of the tournament, the winning goal capped a run of fine performances.

Bowers was again on target, including one from 30 yards, as we beat Newry and Distillery to stay a point behind Linfield in the title race. In that latter match there was a farcical incident when the Whites' Kennedy passed back to his keeper from all of seventy yards and then watched the ball bounce over the goalie's head and just over the bar!

Raymond Morrison was also finding the net regularly from midfield scoring vital goals in the win over Bangor (league) and Carrick (Shield). That Carrick match developed into something of a rough-house with our McCaffrey and West stretchered off along with their Thompson. Morrison was in his benefit year and to mark the occasion the "Nuts About

Results 1991/92

Played 50. Won 37. Drew 7. Lost 6. Goals For 125. Against 52. % 81.0.
Honours: Irish League, Gold Cup

UC	17/08/91		Distillery	H	W	2	0	Bowers, Hillis
UC	20/08/91		Ballyclare Comrades	H	W	5	1	Hillis 2, Caskey, Craig, Bowers
UC	24/08/91		Cliftonville	A	W	2	1	Neill, Mathieson
UC	27/08/91	QF	Newry Town	H	W	5	0	G.Smyth 2, Hillis 2, Mathieson
UC	04/09/91	SF	Crusaders	CrP	L	0	1	-
GC	31/08/91		Omagh Town	A	W	6	3	Hillis 3(1p), Mathieson (p), Morrison, McBride
GC	07/09/91		Crusaders	A	D	1	1	McBride
GC	14/09/91		Glenavon	H	W	4	2	Hillis, McAuley, Mathieson, Morrison
GC	24/09/91	QF	Bangor	H	W	4	1	aet – Hillis 2, Mathieson, Morrison
GC	30/10/91	SF	Ballymena United	Sv	W	2	1	Macartney, Mathieson
GC	12/11/91	F	Cliftonville	WP	W	1	0	Bowers
BC	21/09/91	1	Ballyclare Comrades	H	W	4	1	McBride 3, Currie og
BC	08/10/91	2	Ards	H	W	4	0	Hillis, Morrison 2, Macartney
BC	05/11/91	SF	Omagh Town	MP	L	2	3	Mathieson, Morrison
IL	28/09/91		Coleraine	H	W	6	1	Mathieson 2, Morrison 2, West, Moore
IL	05/10/91		Ards	A	D	1	1	Morrison
IL	12/10/91		Ballyclare Comrades	H	W	4	2	Morrison, McBride, Mathieson, Bowers
IL	19/10/91		Crusaders	A	W	3	2	McBride 2, Mathieson
IL	26/10/91		Larne	H	W	2	0	Caskey, Mathieson
IL	02/11/91		Glenavon	A	W	2	0	Macartney 2
IL	09/11/91		Ballymena United	A	L	1	2	Morrison
IL	15/11/91		Newry Town	H	W	2	1	Macartney, Bowers
IL	23/11/91		Distillery	A	W	2	0	Bowers, West
IL	30/11/91		Bangor	H	W	3	1	Morrison, Macartney 2
IL	07/12/91		Cliftonville	A	D	0	0	-
IL	14/12/91		Carrick Rangers	H	W	7	0	McBride 3, Hillis 2, Macartney, Campbell
IL	21/12/91		Portadown	A	W	2	1	Mathieson, Campbell
IL	26/12/91		Linfield	H	D	3	3	Morrison, Devine, Campbell
IL	28/12/91		Omagh Town	H	W	4	2	McBride, Jameson, McColgan og, Campbell
IL	01/01/92		Ballyclare Comrades	A	W	2	0	Hillis, Mathieson
IL	04/01/92		Ards	H	D	1	1	McBride
IL	11/01/92		Coleraine	A	W	4	1	Campbell, Macartney 2, Hillis
IL	25/01/92		Crusaders	H	W	1	0	McBride
IL	01/02/92		Larne	A	W	3	2	Morrison, G.Smyth, West
IL	08/02/92		Glenavon	H	W	5	1	Morrison, Macartney, Hillis, McBride 2
IL	22/02/92		Ballymena United	H	W	4	0	Hillis, McBride, Mathieson (p), Campbell
IL	29/02/92		Newry Town	A	W	2	1	Devine, Mathieson
IL	14/03/92		Distillery	H	W	3	0	Morrison, Macartney, McBride
IL	21/03/92		Bangor	A	W	2	1	Douglas, Mathieson
IL	28/03/92		Cliftonville	H	W	1	0	Morrison
IL	11/04/92		Carrick Rangers	A	W	3	0	Macartney, Douglas, McBride
IL	18/04/92		Portadown	H	W	1	0	Macartney
IL	21/04/92		Linfield	A	D	0	0	-
IL	25/04/92		Omagh Town	A	W	4	3	McBride, Hillis 2, Mathieson
CAS	26/11/91	1	Carrick Rangers	A	W	2	1	Morrison, West
CAS	18/12/91	2	Glenavon	A	L	1	4	Bowers

IC	18/01/92	Donegal Celtic	H	W	2	0	Macartney 2
IC	15/02/92	Glenavon	H	D	0	0	-
IC	25/02/92	Glenavon	A	L	0	4	-
ILC	04/02/92	H & W Welders	H	L	0	2	-
F	03/08/91	Everton	H	L	0	6	Tommy Jackson Testimonial
F	07/08/91	Sheffield Wednesday	H	L	0	6	-
F	10/08/91	Dundela	H	W	4	1	Douglas, G.Smyth, Kincaid, Hillis
F	29/01/92	Ards	A	D	4	4	Hillis, Devine, Cleary, Mathieson Tom Kincaid Benefit

Glentoran" video was produced. The tape contained Glens' goal action from the previous ten seasons and numerous interviews with players and staff with a particular emphasis on the contribution of Morrison. A club video was long overdue and, although not professionally produced, this provided supporters with a visual record of or recent achievements.

Glentoran went top of the league on 14th December thanks to a 7-0 thrashing of Carrick Rangers, five of the goals coming in a ten-minute spell. Carrick's over zealous tactics led to five bookings for their players. The following Wednesday we were brought back down to earth with a heavy defeat by Glenavon in the County Antrim Shield. Just before Christmas we visited reigning champions Portadown and came away with a vital 2-1 win. The decisive goal was a brilliant drive by Raymond Campbell, the best answer to his critics who suggested that he did not score enough goals. Glenmen had to celebrate this goal in the rain due to the lack of covered accommodation at Shamrock Park.

A huge crowd, some estimates put it in excess of 18,000, were drawn to the Oval for the Glens-Blues meeting on Boxing Day and they witnessed an exhilarating first 45 minutes. Firstly Terry Moore was stretchered off midway through the first half but on the half-hour we were ahead through Morrison. Moore's replacement John Devine nodded us into a 2-0 lead two minutes later but in a dramatic five minute spell before the break Linfield turned the deficit into a 3-2 advantage with goals from Curry, McGaughey and Beattie. Play was even in the second half and nineteen minutes from time Campbell scored from 25 yards to leave honours even at 3-3. We finished 1991 on a high note with a win over Omagh. Substitute Johnny Jameson brought the game to life in the second half but again the best goal came from Campbell. The last league table of the year read:

1. Glentoran played 15 points 36, 2. Linfield 15-34, 3. Portadown 15-31.

During January and February we showed the consistency required to become league champions. Only two points were dropped at home to Ards when Billy Pyper scored an 86th minute equaliser. Displays were occasionally brilliant though, especially the big home wins over Glenavon and Ballymena. Meanwhile our nearest rivals Portadown and Linfield failed to win many games and by the end of February we had opened up an eleven point gap at the top with only seven fixtures remaining.

All this was being achieved despite a mounting injury list which had become something of a standing "joke" in the media and among supporters. Indeed at one evening training session while six first team members were being put through their paces around a dozen more were in the rehabilitation room under treatment from George Magill and Dr. Michael Cullen.

The players hold aloft the Gibson Cup after Morton McKnight's presentation.

Stephen Douglas returned after a year away to ease the situation slightly but he was obviously not fully match fit. Jackson secured the services of Brendan Kirgan from Ballymoney and Noel McKee from Ards Rangers. Also secured on his return to Ulster from New Zealand's Napier City was ex-Glenavon centre-half Duncan Lowry. Lowry was prevented from making his debut until mid-April as a legal wrangle ensued with the Lurgan men over who had "first refusal" on the player. Lowry himself argued that he had given a verbal agreement to late chairman Wilfie Geddis and ex-manager Terry Nicholson but that it was no longer valid as neither man was still at Mourneview Park.

Our success did not extend to the knock-out competitions. In the League Cup we were humbled at the Oval by Harland and Wolff Welders as latish goals from Robson and Smallwood gave the local juniors a night to remember. We beat Donegal Celtic in the Irish Cup without any rowdy scenes, in a game switched to the Oval. Glenavon gained revenge for their league hammering in Round Six. After an entertaining scoreless draw in east Belfast we were annihilated 4-0 in Lurgan. Our chief executioners were Stephen McBride with a hat-trick and Spurs-bound 17 year old winger Gerard McMahon. The replay had been put back by a week to allow McBride to sit on the bench for Northern Ireland against Scotland at Hampden Park. Ballyclare beat us 3-0 in the opening round of the McEwan's Lager Sixes.

Back to league business and wins over Distillery, when all the goals came in the first half, Bangor and Cliftonville took us to within touching distance of the Gibson Cup. The Oval erupted when Morrison scored a last minute winner against the Reds in what was to be Andy Ritchie's last match as a referee.

So on the 11th April 1992 a large crowd packed into Taylor's Avenue and the Glens did not let them down. Macartney put us ahead on nine minutes and further first half goals from Douglas and McBride wrapped up the title. Glentoran had become champions for the 19th time and victory over Portadown a week later enabled us to set a new Irish League points total record. There were jubilant scenes as the trophy was presented, although we needed some super saves from Paterson, complete with his "Allsport" sponsored gloves to deny the Ports.

After a scoreless draw at Windsor Park we ventured to Omagh for the last game of the season. The match kicked-off at 1 p.m. to allow some players to get back to Belfast for an evening PFA function and by 1.01 p.m. we were a goal down! However we rallied to go 3-1 up and eventually ran out 4-3 winners to maintain our twelve point lead over Portadown in the final league table.

In his first season with us Justin McBride finished joint top scorer and picked up both the PFA's "Most Promising Newcomer" and the Ulster Young Player of the Year awards. Raymond Morrison picked up the senior equivalent and the football writers' Player of the Year while the Northern Ireland coaches plumped for Tommy Jackson as their Manager of the Year. Good times from the past were remembered too as the Detroit Cougars held their Silver Jubilee reunion in the Park Avenue hotel on 16th May.

Appearances and Goals						
	App.	Subs.	Goals		App.	Subs.	Goals
Mathieson	47	1	18	McAuley	7	3	1
Campbell	46		6	West	6	12	4
Morrison	46		18	Douglas	6	4	2
Neill G.	46		1	Craig	5	1	1
Devine	42	8	2	Saunders	4		
Hillis	37	7	20	Lowry	3		
Bowers	37	2	7	Armstrong W.	2	4	
McBride	36	8	20	Manley	1	3	
Macartney	32	3	16	Kincaid	1	2	
Heath	29	1		Jameson		10	1
Smyth G.	29	1	3	Kirgan		2	
Paterson	23			McKee		1	
Smyth D.	23			Own Goals			2
McCaffrey	20	1		TOTAL	550	77	125
Caskey W.	14		2				
Moore	8	3	1				

440

1992/93

Magnificent Marseilles – A worsening injury crisis –
Jackson's reign concludes

The big talking point at the Oval during the summer of 1992 was the European Cup draw against Marseilles of France. With their array of European and African stars they would be an as attractive and skilful side as our previous big name opponents Benfica and Juventus.

The season commenced in early August with the traditional fixture versus Dundela and a testimonial match for Raymond Morrison. That was against League of Ireland winners Shelbourne, the only club on the island with an all-seater stadium. The Glens became unofficial all-Ireland champions, and lifted the Xtra-Vision Cup in the process, by winning 4-2.

There was a new pipe opener to the competitive season with the introduction of the Northern Ireland Charity Shield. We met Irish Cup holders Glenavon and the trophy was shared when a last minute Quigley goal cancelled out Any Mathieson's strike. George Neill captained the side in this match when we paraded our new rig-out of green shirts with red sleeves and a black lace-up collar, entering into the brief retro-shirt trend.

Changes to the playing panel included the arrival of Bangor duo Jim McCloskey and Damian Kelly and Omagh Town midfielder Eamon Kavanagh. The club was fined £2,000 by the Irish League for approaching Kavanagh illegally. Sammy Troughton returned after his South African adventure while on the way out was Conor McCaffrey to Portadown. Winston Armstrong and Seamus

John Devine tries to prevent another Marseilles goal in the Stade Velodrome.

Heath also left to link up with other ex-Glenmen Billy Totten and Tom Cleland at Distillery. Dean Smyth and Stephen Douglas were both "unsettled" and "open to offers". David Chick was appointed as chairman in succession to John Crossan, who was continuing his recovery from illness.

The season saw the introduction of many new laws by FIFA, the most notable being that goalkeepers were no longer able to pick up the ball if it had been passed to them by a colleague's foot. Also the half-time interval was extended to a full fifteen minutes.

We began the Ulster Cup with a hard-earned victory over Carrick Rangers for whom ex-Glenman Gary Blackledge netted. Hillis' winner did not arrive until the 84th minute. However we lost three games in a row to lose interest in the Ulster Cup and in our first Gold Cup fixture as Glenavon ran us ragged at Mourneview Park. Fans vented their frustrations at Omagh and this lead to heated exchanges between a section of them and the chairman at the game's conclusion.

Matters improved and we beat Ards and Ballyclare without conceding a goal to qualify for the Gold Cup quarter-finals. Perhaps the most encouraging news in early September was the inclusion of Raymond Campbell in the Northern Ireland squad for the World Cup qualifier with Albania.

A crowd of around 9,000 came to the Oval for the first leg European Cup match with Marseilles, 2,000 of them sitting in the recently installed "bucket" seats which had replaced the old benches in the grandstand. Marseilles even brought their own chef with them to Belfast and their extrovert millionaire owner, Bernard Tapie, flew in by private jet for the match. The Marseilles team included names such as Rudi Voller, Rafael Martin Vasquez, Basile Boli, Abedi Pele, Marcel Desailly, Allen Boksic, Fabien Barthez, Didier Deschamps and a host of other internationals. "Men from another planet" was one apt description of them as they put in a marvellous display of skills at the Oval, ranging form quick inter-passing and lightning off-the-ball running to long range shooting and sharp finishing.

Glentoran were completely overawed in the first half and turned round 0-4 down to goals from Voller, Martin Vasquez (2) and a magnificent Franck Sauzee free-kick. We

managed to hold them to one more goal in the second half from Ferreri but the prospect of a return trip to their impressive Stade Velodrome was daunting. Although one newspaper described the second leg as a "French lesson for Glentoran" we defended stoutly and were only beaten 3-0 after conceding two early goals. The overall nature of the tie clearly illustrated just how far down the footballing ladder the Irish League was. Barney Bowers could look

Gary Macartney scores against Distillery in the Budweiser Cup.

back with pride on the games as he overtook Billy McCullough's record of 22 European appearances for Glentoran. Marseilles went on to win the European Cup, via the Champions League, beating AC Milan 1-0 in the final. They were later stripped of the title after allegations of bribery against their owner.

We lost at home to another team in white soon after the first leg when Distillery beat us in extra time. Winkie Armstrong scored one and set up the winner for Cleland, taunting the Glens fans in the process.

For the league championship Tommy Jackson signed Ballymena's left back Michael Smyth for £25,000 after rejecting the deal at a higher price. We hammered Newry 6-1 in that opening fixture but a week later went down by the odd goal in three at Seaview despite Crusaders having two men, Gardiner and Lawlor, sent off in the last eleven minutes. Portadown's Peter Murray's goal knocked us out of the Gold Cup as the player gained personal revenge for his miss against us in the previous year's final when he was wearing the red shirt of Cliftonville!

Despite getting back on the rails with an easy win over Larne there were ominous signs as Morrison went off injured in the thirteenth minute to join the growing casualty list. The Glens received national exposure as this match was separately announced on BBC Grandstand as the only late result of the day. Irish League games were making a brief re-appearance on the pools coupons. The Colts too were struggling for form but they recorded their first win of the season with a 10-1 thrashing of Bangor Amateurs III in the Coca-Cola Youth Cup.

Our league form during the rest of October was quite pleasing as we again defeated Ards and Ballyclare comfortably, Macartney netting a hat-trick on both occasions, and also Omagh Town. At the end of the month we stood just a point behind the early pacesetters Crusaders. Then as winter approached we had to reply on last minute headed goals from Macartney to earn a draw at Carrick and defeat Portadown to go top of the table, amidst great joy. A shock awaited us at Coleraine when, on a sodden pitch, we went down 1-2 to a manager-less Bannsiders. Only new boy Kelly impressed.

The ex-RUC, Linfield, Hibernian and Northern Ireland striker Mark Caughey was signed from Bangor and he was on target just before half-time against Cliftonville. Two late goals gave us a 3-0 win over the Reds, who included ex-England winger Peter Barnes. However, apart from a win over Distillery, the team only managed to pick up only one more league point before the New Year. This poor run included a home defeat by 7/1 outsiders Ballymena to the tune of 4-1 and a 0-2 reverse in the Boxing Day encounter with Linfield at Windsor Park. The programme receipts from that Ballymena game were donated to meningitis research. The lack of success was blamed on "the injury crisis" with one match report beginning with "No Macartney, no Campbell, no points!" At one stage during the season as many as seventeen first team players were being treated concurrently for one complaint or another. Also in December Ron Manley was transferred to Cliftonville.

The first two games of 1993 saw us draw with Newry and lose at home to Crusaders as we slipped completely out of the league race. We now lay seventh in the table, eleven points behind the Crues, a far cry from 1991/2. The club then joined the bandwagon for fielding non-Ulster born players by signing Englishmen Tony Henry and Billy Whitehurst on short-term contracts. Henry had seen service with Manchester City, Oldham, Stoke, Bolton, Shrewsbury, Mazola (Japan), Ballyclare and Portadown while bustling centre-forward Whitehurst's previous employers included Hull City, Newcastle United, Sunderland, Sheffield United, Oxford and Doncaster Rovers. Another addition to our panel was big Kevin McKeever, the ex-Finn Harps and Portadown midfielder.

The name of Glentoran was spread further afield on two fronts. The latest teenage craze was fancy computer games and manufacturer Sega launched a European Cup game that included the Glens, Linfield and Bangor as players' choices. Paul Vance, a contributor to and a former editor of the Gazette qualified for the televised stages of Sky's World Cup quiz show "Goal". Eight contestants from 7,000 original entrants reached the finals and Paul easily won his group with three convincing victories. However in the final he unluckily went down 2-3 to Gordon McCubbing, the winning "goal" coming in the last second after Vance had twice been ahead.

The County Antrim Shield appeared to be our only hope of some silverware as we battled through to the semi-final stage. Crusaders were opponents just three days after that league defeat but we triumphed on this occasion, albeit on penalty kicks. Duncan Lowry scored his first goal for the club in the 1-1 draw with a looping header. Troughton, Kelly,

Team Group 1992/3 Back Row: Sammy Troughton, Gary Macartney, Raymond Morrison, Alan Paterson, John Devine, Andy Mathieson Front Row: Johnny Jameson, Eamon Kavanagh, Raymond Campbell, Barney Bowers, Duncan Lowry, Justin McBride, Gary Hillis.

443

Results 1992/93

Played 54. Won 23. Drew 13. Lost 18. Goals For 107. Against 77. % 54.6
Honours: Charity Shield (shared)

CS	08/08/92		Glenavon	WPD		1	1	Mathieson
UC	15/08/92		Carrick Rangers	H	W	3	2	Hillis 2, Mathieson
UC	18/08/92		Bangor	H	L	1	2	Macartney
UC	22/08/92		Omagh Town	A	L	2	3	Macartney, Mathieson
GC	29/08/92		Glenavon	A	L	2	3	Bowers, Kavanagh
GC	05/09/92		Ards	H	W	3	0	Bowers, Mathieson, Campbell
GC	12/09/92		Ballyclare Comrades	A	W	2	0	Mathieson (p), Caskey
GC	07/10/92	QF	Portadown	A	L	0	1	-
EC	16/09/92	1.1	Marseille	H	L	0	5	-
EC	30/09/92	1.2	Marseille	A	L	0	3	-
BC	19/09/92	1	Distillery	H	L	2	3	aet – Neill, Macartney
IL	26/09/92		Newry Town	H	W	6	1	Macartney, Jameson 2, Hillis 2, Devine
IL	03/10/92		Crusaders	A	L	1	2	Devine
IL	10/10/92		Larne	H	W	4	0	Macartney 2, Jameson, Houston og
IL	17/10/92		Ards	A	W	3	0	Macartney 3
IL	24/10/92		Omagh Town	H	W	3	0	Devine, Bowers, Kavanagh
IL	31/10/92		Ballyclare Comrades	A	W	5	2	Devine, Macartney 3, Caskey
IL	07/11/92		Carrick Rangers	A	D	1	1	Macartney
IL	14/11/92		Portadown	H	W	3	2	Davidson og, Macartney 2
IL	21/11/92		Coleraine	A	L	1	2	Devine
IL	28/11/92		Cliftonville	H	W	3	0	Caughey, Campbell, Mathieson
IL	05/12/92		Bangor	A	L	1	2	McGuiness og
IL	12/12/92		Ballymena United	H	L	1	4	West
IL	19/12/92		Distillery	A	W	3	0	Devine 2, Mathieson
IL	26/12/92		Linfield	A	L	0	2	-
IL	28/12/92		Glenavon	H	D	0	0	-
IL	01/01/93		Newry Town	A	D	1	1	Mathieson
IL	02/01/93		Crusaders	H	L	1	2	Douglas
IL	09/01/93		Larne	A	W	4	2	Troughton, Mathieson, Whitehurst, Douglas
IL	16/01/93		Ards	H	D	1	1	Douglas
IL	30/01/93		Omagh Town	A	W	4	0	Devine 2, Kelly, Bowers
IL	06/02/93		Ballyclare Comrades	H	W	5	0	Whitehurst 3, Kelly, Lowry
IL	13/02/93		Carrick Rangers	H	L	1	2	Douglas
IL	27/02/93		Portadown	A	D	1	1	McKeever
IL	06/03/93		Coleraine	H	D	2	2	Hillis, McCloskey
IL	20/03/93		Cliftonville	A	W	3	2	McKeever, Douglas, Macartney
IL	27/03/93		Bangor	H	L	0	2	-
IL	10/04/93		Ballymena United	A	W	8	2	Macartney 3, G.Smyth, Campbell, McCloskey, Devine, Troughton
IL	13/04/93		Distillery	H	D	1	1	McCloskey
IL	17/04/93		Linfield	H	L	1	2	Douglas
IL	24/04/93		Glenavon	A	D	2	2	Morrison 2
CAS	08/12/92	1	Ballyclare Comrades	A	W	4	0	West 2, Caskey, Caughey
CAS	16/12/92	2	Ards	H	W	2	1	Caughey, A.Morrison og
CAS	06/01/93	SF	Crusaders	WPD		1	1	aet – Lowry (won 5-4 on penalties)
CAS	19/01/93	F	Carrick Rangers	WPD		1	1	aet Kelly
CAS	16/02/93	FR	Carrick Rangers	WPL		1	2	Douglas
IC	23/01/93	5	Portadown	H	D	0	0	-

IC	27/01/93	5R	Portadown	A	W	1	0	Macartney
IC	20/02/93	6	Brantwood	A	W	1	0	Douglas
IC	13/03/93	7	Dundela	A	W	2	1	Douglas, Bowers (p)
IC	03/04/93	SF	Bangor	WPL		1	3	Douglas
ILC	02/02/93	1	Dundela	H	W	3	2	Bowers, Douglas, Mathieson (p)
ILC	09/02/93	2	Carrick Rangers	H	W	3	2	aet – McKeever, McCloskey, Martin og
ILC	02/03/93	3	Coleraine	H	D	1	1	aet – Kelly (lost 3-5 on penalties)
F	01/08/92		Shelbourne	H	W	4	2	Morrison, Mathieson, Douglas 2 Raymond Morrison Benefit for the Xtravision Cup
F	03/08/92		Dundela	A	W	2	1	Douglas, McBride
F	05/08/92		Laurelvale	A	W	6	4	Unknown
F	10/08/92		Ballymoney United	A	D	3	3	Macartney, Mathieson, Hillis

Jameson, Mathieson and Douglas converted our spot-kicks while Dean Smyth saved Lynch's penalty to put us into the final.

There we met Carrick Rangers and the game again finished 1-1, Kelly's eleventh minute volley matched by a 30 yard strike from ex-Glenman David Montgomery in the second half. Despite having many more chances we failed to break the deadlock, even when Carrick were without the services of their goalkeeper Moore towards the end of the second period of extra-time.

The Irish Cup commenced on 27th January and Glentoran entertained Portadown in the tie of the round. At an extremely damp Oval the two teams fought out a scoreless draw. Things were equally tight in the Shamrock Park replay until the introduction of Macartney, for his first game in two months, in the 67th minute. Within ten minutes he sent the sizeable travelling support into raptures by heading the only goal of the match in via Major. It was a great way for John Devine to celebrate his 24th birthday as he had curtailed his girlfriend's present of a London holiday to return for the match!

This win inspired our league form and we scored nine times without reply against Omagh and Ballyclare, including a Whitehurst hat-trick. Earlier in the month we had recovered from two down to win 4-2 at Larne but we were still well down the table. Seventeen year-old ex-Lisburn Rangers goalkeeper Neil Armstrong, nephew of Winston, made an unexpected first team debut at Omagh. Dean Smyth had missed the team bus and not only did Armstrong play well, but he became the first Glentoran keeper not to concede three goals in a match at St. Julian's Road! Eamon Kavanagh rejoined Omagh in order to be able to spend more time with his family.

In mid-February we were faced with a "triple-header" against Carrick Rangers. The infamous trilogy began in the Wilkinson Sword League Cup at the Oval which we won 3-2 after extra time thanks to an 119th minute own goal. Despite this result one forthright description of the Glens' performance was "embarrassing". Carrick quickly gained revenge with a league win, again the winning goal coming in the last minute, and then won the Shield for their first time by repeating the 2-1 scoreline, this time at Windsor Park.

Stephen Douglas had scored our late consolation goal in that match and he was on target again in the 87th minute with the only goal of the sixth round Irish Cup versus Brantwood at Skegoniel Avenue. The Glens faced more junior opposition in the quarter-final as we drew a short trip to Wilgar Park to meet Dundela. The match was a 3,000 all-ticket affair and Douglas scored again in a 2-1 win. We had also beaten Dundela in the first round of the League Cup but by this time Coleraine had dismissed us on penalties from that competition. Kelly, our goalscorer in normal time, had his penalty attempt saved by O'Hare on the keeper's 21st birthday. Coleraine returned a 100% spot-kick record, rendering as irrelevant the conversions of Bowers, Troughton and Devine.

Our league form was little better although we won 3-2 at Solitude with Macartney scoring the winner. Bangor were our next opponents in league and cup. The Seasiders gained a psychological advantage for the Irish Cup semi-final with a 2-0 Oval success, their twelfth consecutive win. This was reported on in the new look tabloid size Ireland's Saturday Night, eighteen months before the "Ulster" celebrated its 100th birthday. During the season football editor John Laverty introduced the "Have a Rattle" feedback column and Glentoran supporters were frequent contributors helping to make this popular feature need almost as many square inches as the traditional Soccer Scene!

Bangor repeated their win in the cup semi-final to complete the Glens' miserable season. Although for their first goal the ball appeared to be eighteen inches over the line before it was crossed no-one could deny Bangor their win and a fourth success over us during the season. The Seasiders went on to lift the cup for the first time in their history beating Ards in the final after two replays.

Glentoran responded to this set-back by drubbing Ballymena 8-2 at the Showgrounds with Macartney collecting another hat-trick. The day almost ended disastrously as Justin McBride, back after a seven-month injury layoff, swallowed his tongue. An ambulance had to be driven onto the pitch to whisk him away to hospital and safety.

We still had a big say in the destination of an exciting Gibson Cup finale as we entertained title-seeking Linfield on 17th April. For the first 55 minutes we dominated the match, taking the lead with a beautiful chipped goal by Douglas after he had outpaced the Blues' centre-half Twentyman. Then, after a brilliant save by Wesley Lamont from Campbell, Hunter nodded Linfield level. With only nine minutes remaining Johnston squeezed home their winner and with Crusaders only drawing at home to Ards the Windsor men were 99.9% assured of the championship. On the final Saturday they lost 0-3 to Portadown but the Crues, needing to beat Omagh by nine clear goals to win the league, could only manage a 2-1 success.

The night before we completed our programme of matches with a 2-2 draw at Glenavon. Both goals came from Raymond Morrison, fresh after his visit to the FA rehabilitation centre in Lilleshall. At the conclusion of the season Billy Caskey announced his retirement from the senior game and Stephen Douglas was pondering over a move to New Zealand. Tommy Jackson had a closing message for the fans, "No one knows better than me that you were not satisfied with our performances this season. I can assure you we will not witness a repeat next season."

Appearances and Goals						
	App.	Subs.	Goals		App.	Subs.	Goals
Devine	50		10	Caughey	14	3	3
Neill G.	43	1	1	Whitehurst	14		4
Smyth M.	41			Morrison	13	1	2
Mathieson	40	2	10	McBride	8	3	
Campbell	40	1	3	Smyth G.	8		1
Bowers	40		6	McCloskey	7	15	4
Kelly D.	33	5	4	Caskey W.	7	9	3
Lowry	31	1	2	Jameson	6	6	3
Troughton	30	1	2	Henry	4		
Hillis	29	7	5	West	3	1	3
Paterson	28			Kirgan	1	4	
Smyth D.	25			Armstrong N.	1		
Macartney	24	5	20	McCaffrey	1		
Douglas	23	5	11	Own Goals			5
Kavanagh	15	5	2	TOTAL	594	77	107
McKeever	15	2	3				

1993/94

Derry acquaintances renewed – Strain finds it tough –
Supporters' frustration

It was "all change" at the Oval during the summer of 1993. The club parted company with manager Tommy Jackson and his assistant Billy McCullough and promoted second team manager Robert Strain into the hot seat. Billy Caskey was appointed as his number two, Alan Paterson took over the Seconds' role and Jim Cleary came back to coach on a part-time basis. Strain was busy in the pre-season transfer market, our most notable signing being Scottish forward Neil Candlish from Ballymena for £25,000. He recruited an entire new midfield in the shape of Colin Telford (Raith Rovers), Tommy Mooney (Huddersfield) and a player from Gibraltar, Colin Ramirez (Recreativo Lisnense). Indeed Ramirez was believed to be our first player from outside the British Isles. Leaving the Oval were Stephen Douglas, to Monturia in New Zealand, and Sammy Troughton.

In our pre-season friendlies we suffered heavy defeats against English opposition Sheffield Wednesday and Sunderland but had the consolation of useful wins over League of Ireland sides Derry City and Dundalk. The former match was Terry Moore's testimonial and marked Derry's first visit to the Oval since their Irish League days in 1972. Johnny Jameson netted a spectacular winner.

We managed to scrape through our Ulster Cup group after losing at Bangor to a Marc Kenny free-kick and only managing a scoreless home draw with Cliftonville. All the joy came in an 18 minute spell against Coleraine when Candlish netted twice and set up a third for Kelly to give us a 3-0 interval lead. Mark McWalter led the Bannsiders second half revival but we held out. However the team's obvious deficiencies were exposed in a 0-3 quarter-final defeat at Portadown.

Strain raided the transfer market again bringing in two players from the League of Ireland, goalkeeper John Grace and Scottish midfielder Gerry McCabe. They helped us to successes at Ballymena and Larne in the Gold Cup but we lost again to Portadown despite playing against ten men. In that defeat winger Johnny Jameson suffered a head injury that

Roy Essandoh.

forced him to retire from playing and just miss out by two on 500 career games for the Glens. A combination of qualifying from our Gold Cup group and the reduction in our long injury list brought an optimistic atmosphere to the club but after a long drawn out transfer saga midfielder Raymond Campbell was transferred to Linfield, the final fee set at £33,500.

Our inconsistent form continued as the Irish League commenced in mid-September. We struggled to a scoreless draw against Larne then put Bangor away with consummate ease at Clandeboye, Gary Macartney returning to the scoresheet. A late Keith Percy goal enabled Glenavon to win at the Oval but four days later we gained revenge in a dramatic Gold Cup quarter-final at Mourneview Park. The sides shared six goals before the Glens got through 8-7 on penalties! Distillery though dashed our hopes of glory with an extra-time win in the semi-final and the Whites went on to lift the Gold Cup with a 3-2 win over Bangor.

Tommy Jackson had returned to the local scene as manager of Ballymena and he enjoyed a 3-2 win over us. A curio of this match was our 100th post-war own goal in our favour, the unfortunate man being United's John Heron. Worse was to follow at the end of October when we were hammered 4-1 at home by Cliftonville. The pressure was mounting on Strain

George Neill heads away from Trevor Smith.

as after seven league games the Glens lay in mid-table, already eleven points behind leaders Linfield. Down the club a young coloured striker by the name of Roy Essandoh was making his mark as he found the net regularly for the Seconds and the Colts.

Barney Bowers reached the personal landmark of 100 goals for the club when he netted a hat-trick at Ballyclare in the Budweiser Cup after the first meeting there had to be abandoned less than half an hour in due to floodlight failure. That win set up our first meeting of the season with Linfield but once more we went down in extra-time despite a brave display. More sad news came in the death of Northern Ireland legend Danny Blanchflower, who had begun his career with the Glens in the 1940s.

Raymond Morrison also reached the 100 goals mark when he opened the scoring in our 4-0 win over Newry. More signings were made as Robert Strain tried to find a winning combination. Derek Swan and Stephen Mooney (loan) joined up with emerging youngsters like Darren Parker, Kyle Leckey and Darren Hall but we were very much a mediocre side. Kevin McKeever, Mark Caughey Dean Smyth and Brendan Kirgan were all transferred out in November. Then, after a humiliating County Antrim Shield exit at Ards we managed to record only one league win in December and January.

Off the field Johnny Jameson showed other talents when he released a cassette entitled "Straight Down the Line" as part of his benefit season. No, it wasn't either gospel or Glentoran songs but featured the flying winger singing cover versions of ten of his favourite tracks including "Take it Easy", "Mistletoe and Wine" and "Don't Let the Sun Go Down on Me".

By the turn of 1994 we found ourselves twenty points behind league leaders Portadown. During the 2-2 draw at Larne on New Year's Day the crowd hurled abuse at the board and two weeks later over 150 fans staged a pitch demonstration at half-time in the Ballymena game. The supporters were fed up of the long injury list excuses and wanted to know where the club was heading as rumours about vacating the Oval abounded. They were demanding changes in the boardroom with particular emphasis on chairman David Chick. On the field the Glens stumbled to a draw thanks to a Morrison equaliser in the 79th minute. Recalled 39-year old goalkeeper Alan Paterson had to be on top form with excellent saves from Tully and Speak. Our efforts in the McEwan's Six-a-sides at Dundonald Ice Bowl failed as we lost out on penalties to Ballyclare after beating Coleraine 2-0.

A new Irish Cup had been struck for this season and we travelled to meet Roy Coyle's Ards in the fifth round. Castlereagh Park witnessed an excellent match as Justin

Gary Smyth attempts to block a cross.

Neill shadows Linfield's Raymond Campbell in the Budweiser Cup tie.

McBride put us ahead after only 65 seconds but within half an hour Ards were 2-1 ahead. McBride got his second ten minutes after the break after a brilliant run by George Neill. The replay at the Oval four nights later was also a keen affair and was finally settled in our favour by McCabe.

That joy was short lived however as the following Saturday we crashed at Ballyclare in the league and had Gary Smyth sent off in the process. Assistant manager Billy Caskey was also shown a red card by referee Sammy Meeke for protesting against the decision! The Glens had slumped to ninth in the table and some fans were already getting worried that we may not secure a place in the proposed eight team Premier League due to start in season 1995/6.

We failed to see off Ballymoney United in normal time in the Wilkinson Sword League Cup tie. Three goal in six minutes of extra-time, including one from the returning Stephen Douglas, gave us a flattering 5-2 win. Billy Bingham, just retired as Northern Ireland manager, was made a life member. The rearranged league fixture with Bangor marked Alan Paterson's 500th Glentoran game, just six weeks before his 40th birthday. We drew this game to continue a mini-revival of seven unbeaten games. Barney Bowers also passed the 500 appearances mark later in the season.

We progressed to the quarter-finals of the Irish and League Cups with wins over junior opposition. Gary Macartney notched a hat-trick in the former but the most spectacular goals came from Dundela's Billy McMordie who twice lashed 25 yard shots past Paterson. Results like this would have gladdened the hearts of our most unusual supporters club in Salerno, Italy! Apparently the 30 strong club had been formed by Benevelli Alessandro who had seen the Glens play at Marseille in 1992. The Gazette also went Italian at this time as Paolo Sacchi from Genoa became a regular contributor.

In early March we had a goalscoring bonanza against Coleraine at the Oval. McBride and Kelly put us two up before two-goal Derek Cook inspired Coleraine to go 3-2 ahead. Substitute Candlish then scored twice to put us back in the lead and Justin McBride completed our 5-3 victory in the last minute!

This result lifted confidence before our Irish Cup tie versus Bangor but on the day we were just not up to it as missed chances cost us dear. Two late goals from substitute Paul Gray enabled the Seasiders to repeat their triumph of twelve months previously over us. Before the game the ashes of our ex-chairman Harry McNeely were scattered on the pitch. The rest of March produced three more defeats for us, the most crucial being at Windsor Park to the Blues in the League Cup. Ards equalled their club record of nine successive wins when they beat us 1-0 but such a sequence appeared way beyond us as we lost again at home to league leaders Portadown despite going ahead through Morrison. Once again the Ports did it with ten men after Trevor Smith had been sent off for stamping on our goalscorer

Glentoran's indifferent season drifted to a conclusion in April. From our remaining five league games we picked up

Neil Candlish.

Results 1993/4

Played 49. Won 18. Drew 10. Lost 21. Goals For 82. Against 77. % 46.9

UC	14/08/93		Bangor	A	L	0	1	-
UC	17/08/93		Cliftonville	H	D	0	0	-
UC	21/08/93		Coleraine	H	W	3	2	Candlish 2, Kelly
UC	24/08/93	QF	Portadown	A	L	0	3	-
GC	27/08/93		Ballymena United	A	W	1	0	Bowers
GC	04/09/93		Portadown	H	L	1	2	Jameson
GC	11/09/93		Larne	A	W	4	0	Candlish 2(1p), Hillis 2
GC	06/10/93	QF	Glenavon	A	D	3	3	aet – Candlish, Hillis, Morrison (won 8-7 on penalties)
GC	27/10/93	SF	Distillery	WPL		1	2	aet – Neill
IL	18/09/93		Larne	H	D	0	0	-
IL	25/09/93		Bangor	A	W	3	0	Candlish, Morrison, Macartney
IL	02/10/93		Glenavon	H	L	0	1	-
IL	09/10/93		Ballymena United	A	L	2	3	Morrison, Heron og
IL	16/10/93		Ballyclare Comrades	H	W	3	0	Candlish 2, Bowers
IL	23/10/93		Omagh Town	A	W	3	2	Macartney 2, Morrison
IL	30/10/93		Cliftonville	H	L	1	4	Bowers
IL	06/11/93		Coleraine	A	D	1	1	T.Mooney
IL	13/11/93		Ards	H	W	2	0	G.Smyth, Hall
IL	20/11/93		Portadown	A	L	0	1	-
IL	27/11/93		Newry Town	H	W	4	0	Morrison, McCloskey, S. Mooney, Swan
IL	04/12/93		Carrick Rangers	A	W	2	1	Macartney, McCloskey
IL	11/12/93		Distillery	H	L	0	2	-
IL	18/12/93		Crusaders	A	L	2	3	Morrison 2
IL	27/12/93		Linfield	H	L	0	2	-
IL	01/01/94		Larne	A	D	2	2	Macartney, G.Smyth
IL	08/01/94		Glenavon	A	L	1	2	Morrison
IL	15/01/94		Ballymena United	H	D	1	1	Morrison
IL	29/01/94		Ballyclare Comrades	A	L	1	2	Bowers
IL	08/02/94		Bangor	H	D	2	2	McBride, Bowers (p)
IL	12/02/94		Omagh Town	H	W	3	1	Bowers 2(1p), Macartney
IL	26/02/94		Cliftonville	A	D	1	1	Macartney
IL	05/03/94		Coleraine	H	W	5	3	McBride 2, Kelly, Candlish 2
IL	19/03/94		Ards	A	L	0	1	-
IL	26/03/94		Portadown	H	L	1	3	Morrison
IL	02/04/94		Newry Town	A	D	1	1	McBride
IL	05/04/94		Carrick Rangers	H	W	3	1	G.Smyth, Taylor og, McBride
IL	16/04/94		Distillery	A	W	2	0	Macartney, Kelly
IL	23/04/94		Crusaders	H	L	0	1	-
IL	30/04/94		Linfield	A	L	0	2	-
BC	09/11/93	1	Ballyclare Comrades	A	A	0	0	Abandoned after 29 minutes - floodlight failure
BC	15/11/93	1	Ballyclare Comrades	A	W	3	1	aet – Bowers 3
BC	23/11/93	2	Linfield	A	L	2	3	aet – G.Smyth, McCloskey
CAS	30/11/93	1	Ards	A	L	1	4	Morrison
IC	22/01/94	5	Ards	A	D	2	2	McBride 2
IC	26/01/94	5R	Ards	H	W	3	2	McBride, Candlish, McCabe
IC	19/02/94	6	Dundela	H	W	4	3	Macartney 3, Kelly
IC	12/03/94	QF	Bangor	H	L	0	2	-
ILC	05/02/94	1	Ballymoney United	H	W	5	2	aet – Candlish 2(1p), McBride 2, Douglas
ILC	22/02/94	2	Limavady United	H	W	2	0	McBride, Macartney
ILC	29/03/94	3	Linfield	A	L	1	2	Candlish

F	26/07/93	Sheffield Wednesday	H	L	1	7	Candlish
F	31/07/93	Sunderland	H	L	1	4	Telford
F	04/08/93	Derry City	H	W	2	1	Hillis, Jameson
							Terry Moore Testimonial
F	07/08/93	Dundalk	H	W	1	0	McBride
F	09/08/93	Dundela	H	W	2	1	Telford, Candlish

seven points but there was little to enthuse over. Young Alan Nixon came into the side straight from the third XI and Gary Macartney scored his 192nd and last goal for the club at Distillery to put him joint fourth in our all-time scoring list. Our groundsman Billy Crawford announced he would be retiring in the summer after tending the excellent Oval playing surface for the last 45 years.

We were bit-part players on the final dramatic day of the league season on 30th April. For most of the season the title race appeared to be between Glenavon and Portadown but on the penultimate Saturday Linfield won 2-0 at Shamrock Park to make it a three way race. On the morning of decision day all three clubs were on 67 points and amazingly Glenavon would play Portadown while we visited Windsor Park. We held the Blues to 0-0 at half-time but goals from Fenlon and Gorman earned them a 2-0 win. Meantime down the M1 Glenavon and Portadown fought out a 2-2 draw to slit each other's throats and send the title to Windsor Park! The Ports 84th minute equaliser denied Glenavon a first title in 33 years.

Back to Glentoran and the board's patience with Robert Strain finally ran out and he was demoted to assistant manager. On 2nd June former player Tommy Cassidy was appointed as our new manager and charged with making us a force in the local game once more.

Appearances and Goals

	App.	Subs.	Goals		App.	Subs.	Goals
Smyth G.	46		4	Swan	8		1
Bowers	39	1	10	McCloskey	7	17	3
Candlish	37	2	14	Douglas	6	5	1
McCabe	37	1	1	Devine	6	3	
Smyth M.	36	1		Telford	5	3	
Morrison R.	34	1	11	Mooney S.	4		1
Neill G.	34	1	1	Hall	3	4	1
McBride	24	2	11	Jameson	2	2	1
Paterson	24			Nixon A.	2	2	
Mooney T.	23	6	1	Smyth D.	2		
Grace	23			Dougherty	1	1	
Hillis	22	7	3	Hagan	1	1	
Macartney	22	6	12	Kirgan	1	1	
Ramirez	22	4		McKeever	1		
Parker	22	3		Morrison G.	1		
Kelly D.	17	4	4	West		1	
Lowry	10			Own Goals			2
Mathieson	9						
Leckey	8	2		TOTAL	539	81	82

1994/95

Cassidy's nightmare start – A trophy won on penalties – Relegation averted

New manager Tommy Cassidy was active in the transfer market prior to the start of the new season. Coming into the Oval we had goalkeeper Declan Devine from Omagh, Chris Walker from 1st Liverpool and a clutch of midfield players Eddie Cunnington (Dumbarton), Dave Martindale (Tranmere Rovers), Donal O'Brien (Derry City) and Roddy McDowell (Middlesbrough). Moving on were Billy Caskey (Dundela), Jim McCloskey (Ballymena), Gary Hillis (Larne) and Gary Macartney (back to the R.U.C.) while both Duncan Lowry and Stephen Douglas went further afield to New Zealand and Colin Ramirez to Australia. Douglas also played in Australia before coming home to Bangor. Cassidy also put a number of players, including Raymond Morrison, on the transfer list.

Declan Devine.

The highlights of our busy set of eight pre-season friendlies within 16 days included a win over St. Johnstone and a four-goal salvo from McDowell against Brantwood. Derry City, including ex-Glenman Seamus Heath, provided the opposition for Johnny Jameson's testimonial and the veteran flying winger made a ten-minute farewell appearance towards the end. On the downside Andy Mathieson suffered a fractured cheekbone against East Belfast.

Cassidy's career had seen playing service with Newcastle United, Burnley, Apoel Nicosia and Northern Ireland as well as managerial roles in Cyprus and at Gateshead but even that could not have prepared him for what awaited in his first game in charge of Glentoran. We were annihilated 5-1 at Carrick and worse still had Declan Devine sent-off on his debut. Unsurprisingly we failed to qualify from our Ulster Cup section although if we had taken our numerous chances against Linfield a week later it would have been a different story.

The Glens began to get their act together in the Gold Cup matches. A convincing win at Seaview, with Derek Swann netting twice, was followed up with a revenge win over Carrick and an easy victory against Ards as we topped our section. Retired 71-year old Matt Morrison ran the line in the Carrick game when the best goal came from George Neill. It meant a double celebration for our full-back as he was being sponsored to the tune of £100 a goal by a supporters' club in his benefit season! Cassidy swooped into the transfer market again to obtain Portadown's Scottish forward Trevor Smith with Neil Candlish moving in the opposite direction in time for the start of the league fixtures.

Promotion and relegation in senior football in Northern Ireland had been debated for many years – in 1994/5 it was about to happen but in a complicated fashion! To separate the sixteen teams into two leagues of eight it was decided to take each club's league position from seasons 1993/4 and 1994/5 and add them together. The eight teams with the lowest total would form the new Premier League regardless of how many points they had won. The obvious mathematical flaw in this system would be revealed later but as the

Glens had finished ninth the previous season most observers concluded that we need to finish no lower than around seventh to avoid relegation.

Smith made a scoring debut at Larne in the opening league game but O'Brien was the real star with two goals. We continued this encouraging form to beat Bangor at the Oval but the victory was marred by a horrific facial injury to Barney Bowers when he crashed into a post. We concluded September with a hard fought victory over Cliftonville to reach the Gold Cup semi-final, our winner an own goal by Reds' defender Joe Kerr in extra-time.

Our winning run came to an end at Mourneview Park, where O'Brien missed a penalty but we made satisfactory league progress until losing 0-1 at Solitude. Justin McBride was in goalscoring form, netting a hat-trick at Ballyclare and putting us ahead against Coleraine after only six seconds as we finished October in fourth place in the league just four points behind pacesetters Crusaders.

By then we had the joy of lifting a trophy for the first time in over two years following a nail-biting finale against the Crues. The game itself was something of a dour affair after loan signing from Hamilton Accies Duncan Campbell gave us an early lead. Crusaders equalised through Murray on 32 minutes and even extra time produced no further scoring. So it went down to penalties and a chance for a new Glentoran hero to emerge in the shape of a

Glen Little shows good close control against Ards.

young goalkeeper with the famous name of Neil Armstrong. Crusaders failed to score in the shoot-out as Armstrong saved twice while Darren Parker, Norman Kelly and Alan Nixon converted our penalties. The celebrations were long and loud as it looked like Cassidy, who had just been named Manager of the Month, had the club going forward again. Kelly, from east Belfast, whose career had included spells in the English and Scottish leagues as well as in Brunei, was another short-term loan signing from Raith Rovers.

Distillery brought us back down to earth by knocking us out of the Budweiser Cup but many felt this was a blessing in disguise as it meant we could concentrate on our league form up until the end of the year. We won an incident-packed match at Ards thanks to three goals in an eighteen minute second half spell with the winner coming from the fit-again Bowers. Ards, who included ex-Glenman Raymond Morrison and benefited from a Parker own goal, missed a penalty.

The 19th November 1994 was an historic day in a number of ways. Firstly it marked 100 years of the Ireland's Saturday Night but it was also the day George Neill made his 500th appearance for Glentoran. However it turned into a nightmare as we went down 1-6 at home to Portadown and had keeper Armstrong sent off in the process. Many thought the decision harsh and vented their feelings on referee McDonald. Barney Bowers donned the number one shirt for the resultant penalty and then 17 year old Martin McKenzie came on as sub to be our third goalkeeper in the game. Ex-Glenman Candlish grabbed two of the visitors' goals.

This result knocked us completely out of our stride and we only secured three points from the next five league matches up to Boxing Day and lost interest in the County Antrim Shield courtesy of another 0-1 defeat at Solitude. On the morning of our game at Newry the Glentoran Youth team defeated their Newry counterparts by 15-1 but neither of the senior sides could find the net! We had to battle from 0-2 down to Carrick a week later, one of our goals a 30 yard drive from Cunnington. At least we had some good longer-term news

Results 1994/95

Played 46. Won 21. Drew 11. Lost 14. Goals For 83. Against 66. % 57.6.
Honours: Gold Cup

UC	13/08/94		Carrick Rangers	A	L	1	5	O'Brien
UC	16/08/94		Bangor	A	D	1	1	McBride
UC	20/08/94		Linfield	H	L	0	1	-
GC	27/08/94		Crusaders	A	W	4	2	Swan 2, Cunnington, McBride
GC	03/09/94		Carrick Rangers	H	W	3	0	Cunnington, McBride, Neill
GC	10/09/94		Ards	H	W	3	1	O'Brien (p), McDowell 2
GC	27/09/94	QF	Cliftonville	H	W	2	1	aet – McBride, Kerr og
GC	18/10/94	SF	Coleraine	BS	W	4	2	O'Brien 2, Cunnington, Mathieson
GC	25/10/94	F	Crusaders	WPD		1	1	aet – Campbell (won 3-0 on penalties)
IL	17/09/94		Larne	A	W	4	0	O'Brien 2, T.Smith, McBride
IL	24/09/94		Bangor	H	W	1	0	McBride
IL	01/10/94		Glenavon	A	L	1	3	Parker
IL	08/10/94		Ballymena United	H	W	2	0	McBride 2
IL	15/10/94		Ballyclare Comrades	A	W	4	0	McBride 3, T.Smith
IL	22/10/94		Omagh Town	H	D	0	0	-
IL	29/10/94		Cliftonville	A	L	0	1	-
IL	04/11/94		Coleraine	H	D	1	1	McBride
IL	12/11/94		Ards	A	W	3	2	Bowers, N.Kelly, T.Smith
IL	19/11/94		Portadown	H	L	1	6	N.Kelly
IL	26/11/94		Newry Town	A	D	0	0	-
IL	03/12/94		Carrick Rangers	H	D	2	2	Cunnington, T.Smith
IL	10/12/94		Distillery	A	L	2	3	O'Brien, McBride
IL	17/12/94		Crusaders	H	L	0	2	-
IL	26/12/94		Linfield	A	D	1	1	T.Smith
IL	31/12/94		Larne	H	W	3	1	T.Smith, Cunnington, McBride
IL	02/01/95		Bangor	A	W	3	1	T.Smith, Cunnington, McBride
IL	07/01/95		Glenavon	H	L	1	3	McDowell
IL	14/01/95		Ballymena United	A	D	3	3	McBride, O'Brien, Bowers
IL	28/01/95		Ballyclare Comrades	H	W	3	1	M.Smyth, Little, T.Smith
IL	25/02/95		Cliftonville	H	L	2	3	T.Smith, Tabb og
IL	04/03/95		Coleraine	A	L	0	1	-
IL	10/03/95		Omagh Town	A	D	0	0	-
IL	18/03/95		Ards	H	W	4	1	T.Smith 3, McBride
IL	25/03/95		Portadown	A	W	2	0	Little, T.Smith
IL	01/04/95		Newry Town	H	W	2	1	Cook, M.Smyth
IL	15/04/95		Distillery	H	W	1	0	Walker
IL	17/04/95		Carrick Rangers	A	W	3	2	Little 2, McBride
IL	22/04/95		Crusaders	A	W	2	1	Cook, T.Smith (p)
IL	29/04/95		Linfield	H	D	2	2	T.Smith, Devine
BC	01/11/94	1	Distillery	H	L	2	3	aet – Cunnington, McBride
CAS	29/11/94	1	Brantwood	H	W	3	0	McDowell, T.Smith, McBride
CAS	20/12/94	2	Cliftonville	A	L	0	1	aet
IC	24/01/95	5	Coleraine	H	D	1	1	Bowers (p)
IC	30/01/95	5R	Coleraine	A	L	1	2	T.Smith
ILC	04/02/95	1	Loughall United	H	W	2	1	T.Smith, McBride
ILC	07/03/95	2	Bangor	A	L	2	3	Quigley, T.Smith
F	23/07/94		East Belfast	N*	W	6	0	O'Brien (p), Mathieson (p), Swan 3, McBride
F	26/07/94		St Johnstone	H	W	1	0	Swan
F	28/07/94		Grimsby Town	H	L	0	2	-
F	30/07/94		Brantwood	H	W	8	1	McDowell 4, Telford,

454

							McCloskey, O'Brien, McBride
F	02/08/94	Partick Thistle	H	L	0	2	-
F	04/08/94	Dungannon Swifts	A	W	3	0	O'Brien, McBride, Nixon
F	06/08/94	Derry City	H	D	2	2	Swan, O'Brien
							Johnny Jameson Testimonial
F	08/08/94	Dundela	A	W	4	2	McDowell 2(2p), McBride, D.Kelly

* = at Inverary Avenue

defensively as John Devine returned from injury and Chris Walker made his debut in the Brantwood match.

Nineteen year-old Glen Little did likewise against Crusaders in mid December. The 6'3" Londoner was signed on loan from Crystal Palace following a spell with Derry City. Little missed our battling display at Windsor Park when a long range Trevor Smith goal earned us a point. This result left us in down in ninth place in the league but two good 3-1 wins over the New Year Period against Larne and Bangor raised spirits again. In the latter match all our goals came in a three minute spell.

A hat-trick from Glenn Ferguson, his sixth of the season, helped Glenavon to another Oval success and then we threw away a two goal lead at Ballymena as we plummeted to ninth place again. Our Irish Cup campaign was short-lived too. After rain wiped out the entire fifth round programme we put in a woeful display against Coleraine and were lucky to come away with a draw but the Bannsiders put us out of our misery in the replay. Cassidy publicly apologised for the displays and strengthened the panel by signing James Quigley and Connor McCaffrey. Off the field Jackie Warren was appointed as club secretary.

Around this time there was further speculation and much interest in Glentoran's relocation plans. New sites were considered at Laburnum, the home of Grosvenor Rugby Club, and in the area around the Harbour Estate. However each option brought its own set of problems and issues and the end result was "status quo".

We stumbled to victories over nine-man Ballyclare, Michael Smyth scoring his first-ever Glens' goal in over 100 games, and then juniors Loughall United in the League Cup but a dismal four match run in late February and early March really put us back into the mire. Bangor knocked us out of the League Cup but more importantly we picked up only point in the next three league matches. Barney Bowers' injury problems continued when he damaged a shoulder against Cliftonville in a match that marked the debut of our latest Scottish acquisition Derek Cook, the ex-Kilmarnock and Stranraer striker. Andy Mathieson was sent off in our latest defeat at Coleraine and a dismal scoreless draw on a Friday night at Omagh left us staring relegation in the face.

The equation was simple enough. We had seven league games to go and really had to "get the finger out" or it would be first division football at the Oval the following season. So on the 18th March with rally cries in the press and club programme ringing in their ears the players ran out to take on Ards. Trevor Smith was the hero that day with a hat-trick and he was on target a week later in a impressive 2-0 victory at Shamrock Park. John Devine and Walker comfortably contained any Portadown threats. There was further good news for the future when Glentoran Colts beat Lurgan Town Boys 2-0 in the IFA Youth Cup final, the late goals coming from David Spence and an Andy Kirk penalty. No doubt manager Paul Kirk, Andy's father, was doubly happy!

The supporters too were really getting behind the team and they were rewarded with further victories over Newry and Distillery. They had to be patient in the latter fixture as it was not until the 89th minute before Chris Walker fired in a screamer from all of 30 yards to see off the Whites. Jubilant supporters invaded the pitch at the finish but there was plenty of work to do as we still lay sixth.

After an Easter win at Carrick we finally secured a place in the new Premier League with an excellent victory at runaway champions Crusaders. Maybe we were fortunate with our injury time penalty winner but the team had shown tremendous spirit and pride to rattle off six successive wins when the chips were down. While it was a team effort a lot of the credit could go down to the inspirational form of teenager Glen Little who was clearly enjoying his time in the Irish League. "The Glens fans are brilliant, this club is something special and we were too good to go down", stated Glen.

On the final league Saturday of the season we fought out an entertaining but surprisingly meaningless 2-2 draw with Linfield but there was heartache slightly lower down the table. Bangor lost 2-0 at Ards but in so doing they enabled themselves to stay up! The reason? It meant Ards finished above Coleraine in a congested mid-table and gave Bangor a better two-season placing aggregate over the Bannsiders! If Bangor had managed to win or even draw they would have "earned" relegation. The final table had been so tight that if we had beaten the Blues we would have finished third outright.

So at the end of a topsy-turvy season our immediate future was secure. Manager Tommy Cassidy would be staying on and he was even threatening to bring out an autobiography with surely a chapter headed "the Great Escape" prominent.

Appearances and Goals						
	App.	Subs.	Goals		App.	Subs.	Goals
McBride	45		21	McDowell	9	7	4
Smyth M.	43		2	Kelly N.	8		2
Smith	36	1	19	Lennox	4	1	
Neill G.	33	1	1	Swan	4	1	2
O'Brien	30	5	8	Paterson	3	1	
Cunnington	29		7	Nixon A.	2	9	
Parker	28	6	1	Campbell	2	1	1
Smyth G.	25	1		McCaffrey	1	2	
Mathieson	24	7	1	Beggs	1		
Devine D.	22			Hagan	1		
Armstrong N.	21	1		Moore		7	
Devine J.	21		1	Telford		2	
Bowers	20	1	3	Hall		1	
Martindale	20			Houston		1	
Walker	20		1	McKenzie		1	
Little	18		4	Own Goals			2
Quigley	15		1				
Cook	11		2	TOTAL	506	68	83
Kelly D.	10	11					

1995/96

Winless Windsor streak ends – A transfer saga –
Little lights up the Cup final

Trevor Smith was in fine scoring form in the pre-season friendlies as he netted hat-tricks against his countrymen in games versus Stranraer and Raith Rovers. This, allied to the signings of "B" International Darren Finlay, Ricky McEvoy, Roddy Collins and a permanent deal agreed with Glen Little, would have given supporters hope for the months ahead. Leaving the Oval were Gary Smyth and Donal O'Brien to Glenavon and Crusaders respectively while in September stalwart Barney Bowers departed to Ards after fourteen years service. Cassidy then strengthened the midfield with a third capture from Bangor in the form of Englishman Peter Batey. On the management side Billy Sinclair returned to the club as assistant manager replacing Robert Strain who had returned to Crusaders.

Brantwood were easily shaken aside in the opening League Cup match, a mazy run and deflected in shot from Little putting us on our way, but Linfield were too strong in Round Two. Cassidy remarked that we needed to learn how to win evenly matched games.

We failed to do that at Seaview in our opening Ulster Cup fixture when despite a brilliant two-goal performance by Little we went down by the odd goal in seven. Sinclair was ordered from the dugout by referee Cowie. Derek Cook was on form in our next two games scoring three of our four goals in wins over Omagh and Carrick to get us into the quarter finals. However on the same night the former Dundela captain Michael Goddard died after being struck in the chest during play in a match with Dungannon Swifts. At the

Little torments the Glenavon defence during the Irish Cup final.

end of the season in late May a combined Glentoran / Dundela XI took on a combined Linfield / Dungannon XI in a memorial match. The "home" side lost 2-3 before 3,000 fans, their goals coming from Chris Walker and Finlay.

The Glens also qualified for the Gold Cup quarter-finals but on goal difference in unconvincing fashion. Cook was again on target twice against Larne while in a bruising game with Cliftonville at the Oval the Reds hung on to win despite having Tim McCann sent off just before half-time. We drew at Carrick after falling behind in the second minute.

We had not qualified for European football this season but were offered the chance to play on the continent in a four team tournament in Castlefranco, near Venice, partially organised by a group of ex-pats who were attached to Serie D club Giorgone. Unfortunately the offer had to be turned down as it clashed with the start of the new Smirnoff Premier League we had fought so hard to get into.

Before the league kicked off fans had the chance to pay tribute to stalwart full-back George Neill in his testimonial match. Unfortunately only a very low crowd turned out to see us draw 1-1 with Dundalk, who were managed by ex Glenman Dermott Keely. Cook was again on target. Neill's emerging successor to the number two shirt was Colin Nixon, who showed lots of promise.

We tasted defeat again at Seaview in the opening league fixture and crashed out of the Ulster Cup at Glenavon before drawing three league games in a row in mid October. John Kennedy was signed for £20,000 from Distillery but we needed an injury time header to take a point off Bangor though we had been reduced to ten men with the dismissal of Finlay. Ex-Celtic player Dugald McCarrison made his debut at Solitude in a match where we had Trevor Smith become the latest recipient of a red card. Again we had to come from behind against Portadown, who's minds may have been on the penalties they were incurring over the lack of proof that they had properly registered schoolboy player Gareth Fulton. We eventually gained our first league win at the fifth attempt over Ards, who included ex-Glenmen Morrison and Bowers in their ranks and had keeper Paul Kee sent-off near the end.

A howling gale and heavy rains forced referee Snoddy to abandon our Gold Cup quarter-final at Windsor Park but we were not to be denied in the league on the first Saturday in November.

Little celebrates his Cup final winning goal.

Wearing our all-white new away kit Eddie Cunnington fired us ahead with a magnificent 25 yard strike and in the second-half Little tormented the Linfield left, laying on two goals and slotting home a fourth himself after another mesmerising dribble. What a way to end a sequence of twelve winless games over four years against the Blues! We had moved up to third place in the eight team league but were seven points behind the Ports.

Many people felt that we were still a couple of players short of being a championship chasing team and that theory was borne out by a run of inconsistent results up to Christmas. We unluckily lost to Linfield on penalties in the replayed Gold Cup match after being 2-0 up and went out of the County Antrim Shield at home to Ballymena. Both mid-Ulster teams beat us in the league but there were high spots too including a convincing win over the reigning champions Crusaders, Batey's hat-trick at Newry and a 6-1 victory over his old side at Clandeboye Park when we scored five times in the last twenty minutes. Not satisfied with that Cassidy broke the club's transfer record by purchasing Liam Coyle for £38,000 from Derry City and the striker began to repay that by netting after only sixteen minutes into his debut versus the Reds. However shortly after signing a three year contract Coyle retracted and said that he did not want to play at the Oval – a sequence of events that mystified most.

Meanwhile there was plenty happening off the field. The club installed a new press box in the grandstand while the ground moving plans appeared closer to home as an applications was made for use of the King George V playing fields next door. A renewed sponsorship deal with Smithwicks was announced and a boot deal with New Balance set up. The club even made its first tentative steps onto the world wide web with an Internet site established by supporters John McCreery and Robert Childs.

Boxing Day 1995 was a bad one for the Glens. Not only did we lose at home 0-3 to Linfield but we played for a while with a white ball on a snowy pitch. This was picked up by the BBC Fantasy Football programme and after showing brief action from the game on national television comedians Frank Skinner and David Baddiel sarcastically offered us the loan of an orange one! The top half of the final league table of the year read:

1. Portadown played 13 points 27, 2. Crusaders 14-26, 3. Glenavon 13-23, 4. Glentoran 14-22.

Snow also caused the postponement of our Coca-Cola Floodlit Cup (formerly Budweiser Cup) tie at Newry but when the two legs were played in January we overcame the

Frontiermen 9-2 on aggregate, McBride netting a hat-trick in the home leg. Our league form was also good that month as we recorded wins over Glenavon, after being 0-2 down, the Crues and Bangor to move into third spot. Little scored brilliant goals in the latter two and there was further good news when Liam Coyle announced that he would be returning to the club and Tommy Cassidy was named Guinness "Manager of the Month".

However our inconsistency again set in and we only managed to win one of the next seven league games. This run started with another single goal defeat to Cliftonville and included a thrilling 3-3 home draw with Portadown for whom Gary Halyock was sent off. Two goals from ex-Glenman Paul Millar condemned us to defeat at Windsor Park and a double from Glenavon's Glenn Ferguson at the Oval finally put paid to our league hopes as we dropped down to fifth place, eight points behind leaders Crusaders at the three-quarter way stage.

During that period however we made excellent progress on two cup fronts. Firstly in the Coca-Cola Cup we reached the final after excellent but narrow wins over the Blues, with Coyle scoring the opener, and Portadown. In the Irish Cup we progressed comfortably to the quarter-finals, beating a Distillery side newly managed by Paul Kirk, who a fortnight earlier had been in charge of Glentoran Youth, to meet First Division Ballymena United. That game ended in stalemate with our hero being Batey who played the second half in goal after Declan Devine had to retire at half-time with a broken nose and vertebrae! Glen Little took centre stage in the replay with a stunning hat-trick in our 4-2 success, when again we had to come from two goals down. We had little time to savour that win as six days later we lost to bogey side Cliftonville in the Coca-Cola Cup final. Transfer-listed Derek Cook put us ahead but McCann equalised for the Reds and second half goals from Cross and Stokes finished us off.

In mid March there was bright news for the future when the Glentoran Colts team recorded their 100th league goal for the season. Over half of them came from the prolific Andy Kirk, son of Paul, and Mark Craig backed up by Stuart Elliott. The young Kirk had scored over 120 goals for various junior Glentoran teams in the past two seasons and decided to stay at the Oval despite offers from a couple of Scottish clubs.

We had an Irish Cup semi-final dress rehearsal with leaders Crusaders at the Oval and once more showed a good fighting spirit in twice coming from behind to draw 2-2. Our goalkeeping injury crisis was nearly solved in a novel way when an Austrian named Walter de Vora offered to play for us. Apparently he claimed to be a Glentoran supporter and was at a loose end as he had just lost his first team place at FC Innsbruck but nothing came of the proposed loan move. At the end of March we finally managed to beat Cliftonville, 2-1 at the Oval.

Trevor Smith scoring one of his hat-trick of goals in the pre-season friendly against Stranraer.

Our Irish Cup semi-final was played on a Friday night at Windsor Park. In an exciting game Crusaders went ahead through Baxter early on before John Devine was involved in levelling matters after a fumble by keeper Kevin McKeown. Hunter soon restored the Crues' lead and it stayed that when until the 78th minute when substitute Trevor Smith drove home the equaliser. The replay four days later was a memorable night. The match looked to be heading for extra-time until Liam Coyle, carrying an injury, popped up with the winning goal. It was a bad week for Crusaders as their defeat at Solitude on the Saturday handed the first Premier League title to Portadown.

The Glens warmed up for the cup final with an excellent 3-0 win over Linfield and a win over our final opponents Glenavon on the last day of the league to leap frog above them

Results 1995/96

Played 52. Won 26. Drew 13. Lost 13. Goals For 104. Against 66. % 62.5.
Honours: Irish Cup

ILC	12/08/95	1	Brantwood	H	W	3	0	McGreevey og, McBride, Quigley
ILC	15/08/95	2	Linfield	H	L	0	1	-
UC	19/08/95		Crusaders	A	L	3	4	T.Smith, Little 2
UC	25/08/95		Omagh Town	H	W	2	1	Cook 2
UC	02/09/95		Carrick Rangers	H	W	2	1	Little, Cook
UC	03/10/95	QF	Glenavon	A	L	0	2	-
GC	09/09/95		Larne	A	W	2	0	Cook 2
GC	16/09/95		Cliftonville	H	L	0	1	-
GC	23/09/95		Carrick Rangers	A	D	1	1	T.Smith
GC	24/10/95	QF	Linfield	A	A	1	0	Cunnington (Abandoned after 60 minutes)
GC	28/11/95	QF	Linfield	A	D	2	2	aet – lost 2-4 on penalties – McBride 2
IL	30/09/95		Crusaders	A	L	1	2	Little
IL	07/10/95		Bangor	H	D	1	1	Devine
IL	14/10/95		Cliftonville	A	D	0	0	-
IL	21/10/95		Portadown	H	D	1	1	Batey
IL	28/10/95		Ards	H	W	3	2	T.Smith 2, Cunnington
IL	04/11/95		Linfield	A	W	4	0	Cunnington, McBride, McCarrison, Little
IL	11/11/95		Glenavon	H	L	0	2	-
IL	18/11/95		Crusaders	H	W	3	1	McBride 2, T.Smith
IL	25/11/95		Bangor	A	W	6	1	Kennedy, McBride, Batey, Cunnington, Cook 2
IL	02/12/95		Cliftonville	H	D	1	1	Coyle
IL	09/12/95		Portadown	A	L	1	3	Batey
IL	16/12/95		Ards	A	W	4	1	Finlay, Batey, T.Smith, McBride
IL	26/12/95		Linfield	H	L	0	3	-
IL	01/01/96		Glenavon	A	W	3	2	M.Smyth, Little 2
IL	06/01/96		Crusaders	A	W	3	1	Cook, Mathieson, Little
IL	13/01/96		Bangor	H	W	3	0	Batey, Little, Cook
IL	27/01/96		Cliftonville	A	L	0	1	-
IL	03/02/96		Portadown	H	D	3	3	Nixon, Little, T.Smith
IL	10/02/96		Ards	H	W	3	1	Coyle, Finlay, T.Smith
IL	17/02/96		Linfield	A	L	0	2	-
IL	02/03/96		Glenavon	H	L	1	2	Coyle
IL	16/03/96		Crusaders	H	D	2	2	McBride, Devine (p)
IL	23/03/96		Bangor	A	D	1	1	Parker
IL	30/03/96		Cliftonville	H	W	2	1	Coyle, McBride
IL	06/04/96		Portadown	A	L	2	3	Little, McBride
IL	08/04/96		Ards	A	W	2	0	T.Smith 2
IL	20/04/96		Linfield	H	W	3	0	Little, M.Smyth, Batey
IL	27/04/96		Glenavon	A	W	3	1	Cook 2, Kirk
CAS	21/11/95	1	Newry Town	A	W	4	1	Batey 3, McCarrison
CAS	06/12/95	2	Ballymena United	H	L	1	2	McBride
CCC	17/01/96	1.1	Newry Town	A	D	2	2	T.Smith, McBride
CCC	23/01/96	1.2	Newry Town	H	W	7	0	T.Smith, McBride 3, Little, Batey, M.Smyth
CCC	06/02/96	2	Linfield	H	W	2	1	Coyle, McBride
CCC	06/03/96	SF	Portadown	M	P W	1	0	Batey
CCC	19/03/96	F	Cliftonville	W	P L	1	3	Cook
IC	20/01/96	5	Limavady United	H	W	4	1	Batey, Cook 2, McBride
IC	24/02/96	6	Distillery	H	W	2	0	Cook, Finlay

IC	09/03/96	QF	Ballymena United	H	D	0	0	-
IC	13/03/96	QFR	Ballymena United	A	W	4	2	M.Smyth, Little 3
IC	12/04/96	SF	Crusaders	WPD		2	2	McKeown og, T.Smyth
IC	16/04/96	SFR	Crusaders	WPW		2	1	McBride, Coyle
IC	04/05/96	F	Glenavon	WPW		1	0	Little
F	22/07/95		Stranraer	H	W	4	0	T.Smith 3, McBride
F	26/07/95		Norwich City	H	L	1	2	McEvoy
F	28/07/95		Rangers "A"	H	D	0	0	-
F	29/07/95		Raith Rovers	H	W	3	1	T.Smith 3
F	02/08/95		Greenock Morton	H	L	0	2	-
F	07/08/95		Dundela	H	W	1	0	McBride
F	25/09/95		Dundalk	H	D	1	1	Cook
								George Neill Testimonial

into third place. In the former match all our goals came in a splendid eleven minute first half-spell while in the latter both managers unsurprisingly rested around half a dozen likely cup final starters. Andy Kirk came off the bench to make a scoring debut but the best goal was a 25 yard dipping volley from Derek Cook.

And so to Windsor Park on 4th May where 11,000 fans turned up for the Irish Cup final. It was to be the day Londoner Glen Little earned his name in Glentoran folklore as in the 75th minute he scored a spectacular goal from all of 25 yards as we lifted this trophy for the first time in six years. Darren Finlay was named man of the match for playing out of position at left-back and blotting out the threat of Steven McBride. What a way to end the season with European qualification and a sense of optimism that we were about to become a major force in the local game once more.

Also in May the Glentoran Gazette, under editor Sam Robinson, was named Programme of the Year by both the Northern Ireland and the Wirral collectors' clubs.

Appearances and Goals

	App.	Subs.	Goals		App.	Subs.	Goals
Devine J.	48		2	Neill G.	13		
Smyth M.	47		4	McCarrison	9	5	2
McBride	41	1	19	McEvoy	8	4	
Little	40		17	McCaffrey	7		
Nixon C.	37		2	Hutchinson	2		
Batey	35		12	Kelly D.	1	8	
Armstrong N.	34			McGill	1		
Kennedy	29	3	1	McDowell		5	
Quigley	28	9	1	Houston		3	
Cook	26	10	15	Bowers		2	
Parker	26	9	1	Elliott		2	
Smith	26	7	12	Telford		2	
Walker	25	3		Kirk		1	1
Mathieson	22	6	1	Leeman		1	
Finlay	18	11	3	Moore		1	
Cunnington	17		3	Own Goals			2
Coyle	16	5	6	TOTAL	572	98	104
Devine D.	16						

1996/97

A hot time in Prague – Unwelcome hooliganism – Too many draws

Glentoran's pre-season activities had a distinctly Scottish feel to them as we entertained three visiting clubs and met two more in the Stena Line trophy in Stranraer. That tournament was one to forget for us as after losing to St. Mirren in the semi-final on the Friday we put in a pathetic display to lose 1-6 to the hosts on the Saturday afternoon. Crusaders, who had beaten Stranraer 6-1 in the other semi, restored some Irish League pride by defeating St. Mirren 2-1 in the final. Many of our large travelling support had long since retired to the local bars but not before they had a chance to view our new away strip, a white shirt with a very large green cockerel! The only new player on display was Englishman Steve Baird, who failed to impress. A poor build up was completed when we narrowly lost to Notts County in John Devine's testimonial. A proposed match with Derry City at the Brandywell was aborted due to the Stranraer weekend.

Due to the re-organisation of the European competitions our first competitive match was our Cup Winners Cup tie versus Sparta Prague, a very unsatisfactory situation for Irish League clubs.

Justin McBride in action at Mourneview Park.

The Czechs contained many of their country's squad who had finished runners-up to Germany in Euro '96 in England but we gave them a run for their money at the Oval. Indeed before 4,000 fans we looked to have secured a 1-1 draw until the tall substitute Vratislav Lokvenc headed in the winner in the third minute of injury time. It was a different story in the Golden City of Prague a fortnight later when, helped by a first minute goal, the Czechs hammered us 8-0 in the modern Letna Stadium. Darren Finlay added insult to injury by getting himself sent off for dissent but none of this could dampen the enthusiasm of the large travelling support.

There was better news in domestic football during August as we progressed to the quarter-finals of both the League Cup and Ulster Cup. "B" Division Moyola and Dungannon were defeated in the former and we saw off Bangor 2-1 on aggregate in the latter. Because our European games were played on Thursdays our two following fixtures planned for the Saturday were moved to Monday nights. Two of our players departed for Derry City. Firstly Liam Coyle after a very unsettled "will he or won't he stay" spell and also goalkeeper Declan Devine whose Oval career had been blighted by injury and fitness problems.

Northern Ireland taking part in World Cup qualifiers on Saturdays made our season even more of a stop start nature and after beating Ards in extra time we crashed out of the Ulster Cup to Coleraine at the semi-final stage.

We began our fifth competition of the season (counting the Stranraer trip), the Gold Cup, on 7th September with a 2-2 draw against Cliftonville at Solitude. The game kicked-off in the morning as a ploy to minimise any chance of trouble and thankfully there was none. Although we lost at Omagh in our final section game we qualified in second place on goal difference as Carrick Rangers, after losing by four goals at the Oval, beat Cliftonville 3-2! Glentoran supporters were far from happy however and they subjected the manger to severe verbal abuse at the conclusion of that defeat.

Before the commencement of the Premier League we snapped up defender John Drake and midfielder Philip Mitchell from Distillery whilst Trevor Smith rejoined Portadown. Cassidy also made a trio of loan signings, Rory Hamill from Fulham, Tom McCourt from Ballymena and Andy May from Millwall, to cover for injuries. Another 11 a.m. kick-off and another draw with Cliftonville was followed by three successive defeats in October. Two goal salvos from Glenn Ferguson and Sammy Shiels did the damage for Glenavon and Coleraine with Chris Walker being sent-off at the Showgrounds.

The same month also concluded our interest in two of the knockout tournaments. We battled through to the League Cup final with fine wins over Coleraine and Portadown but went down 0-1 to Crusaders. The Crues were our conquerors in extra-time a week later in the Gold Cup quarter-final.

Around this time there were many unsavoury incidents at local football matches. Cliftonville supporters' buses were stoned on their way into Portadown while Glentoran issued a full page warning in the Gazette stating that spitting on Stewards or throwing coins and bottles at opposing players or match officials was not acceptable behaviour.

After gaining a revenge win over Crusaders we signed one of their ex-players, midfielder Steven Livingstone, in time for the first "big two" clash of the season. It was a game where we had the better play and chances but had to rely on a late Pete Batey goal, when he capitalised on a mistake by Blues keeper David Collins, to equalise Barker's 50th minute strike. When we lost a ding-dong battle at Ards the following week, after three times being ahead, it left us one place of the bottom of the league after the first round of games,

Horst Siegl completes his hat-trick against us in Prague as Parker and Quigley look on.

already a massive 14 points behind early pacesetters Coleraine. Ards' third equaliser was a long-range shot from ex-Glenman Raymond Morrison.

Some of the pressure was eased over the next seven days as we hammered Newry in the Shield and then won at bottom placed Cliftonville. A pleasing aspect was the free flowing scoring of young Andy Kirk, who netted the opener at Solitude and set up Mitchell for the clinching goal. The Reds gained revenge over us shortly after when they knocked us out of the Shield after a penalty shoot out at the Oval.

During the season links between Glentoran and Burnley were re-kindled as we initially met them in a pre-season friendly and then signed one of their young strikers, Ian Duerden, on loan for a couple of games. However there were mixed emotions in East Belfast when Glen Little put pen to paper for the Turf Moor side. No-one begrudged him another crack at full-time English League football but his mazy runs and shooting would be sorely missed. Coming in from England was Rory Hamill who decided to make his loan move to the Oval permanent.

That Solitude victory was the start of a twelve match unbeaten run in the league – however we became the draw specialists in that period as eight of those finished all square, including five in a row over either side of the turn of the year! We began to claw our way up the table, helped by a win over leaders Coleraine in a game where three players were sent off. The Bannsiders' Gaston and McAllister joined Tom McCourt for an early bath.

Results 1996/97

Played 52. Won 23. Drew 14. Lost 15. Goals For 82. Against 61. % 57.7

ECW	08/08/96	1.1	Sparta Prague	H	L	1	2	Little
ECW	22/08/96	1.2	Sparta Prague	A	L	0	8	-
ILC	12/08/96	1	Moyola Park	H	W	3	0	Kirk, Parker, McBride
ILC	14/08/96	2	Dungannon Swifts	H	W	3	1	aet – Elliott, T.Smith (p), McBride
ILC	01/10/96	QF	Coleraine	H	W	4	0	Little 2, Devine (p), Finlay
ILC	08/10/96	SF	Portadown	MP	W	2	1	M.Smyth, Stewart og
ILC	15/10/96	F	Crusaders	WP	L	0	1	-
UC	17/08/96	1.1	Bangor	A	W	1	0	McBride
UC	26/08/96	1.2	Bangor	H	D	1	1	Elliott
UC	28/08/96	QF	Ards	A	W	4	3	aet – Finlay, Kirk 2, McBride
UC	03/09/96	SF	Coleraine	Sv	L	0	1	-
GC	07/09/96		Cliftonville	A	D	2	2	Kirk, McBride
GC	14/09/96		Carrick Rangers	H	W	4	0	McBride, Finlay, Devine, Mathieson
GC	21/09/96		Omagh Town	A	L	0	1	-
GC	22/10/96	QF	Crusaders	H	L	2	3	aet – Mitchell, og
IL	28/09/96		Cliftonville	H	D	1	1	Finlay
IL	12/10/96		Glenavon	A	L	1	2	McCourt
IL	19/10/96		Coleraine	A	L	2	3	Little, Devine
IL	26/10/96		Portadown	H	L	2	3	McCourt, Kirk
IL	02/11/96		Crusaders	A	W	3	2	Little, Mitchell, May
IL	09/11/96		Linfield	H	D	1	1	Batey
IL	16/11/96		Ards	A	L	3	4	Kirk 2, McCourt
IL	23/11/96		Cliftonville	A	W	2	0	Kirk, Mitchell
IL	30/11/96		Glenavon	H	D	2	2	McCourt, Finlay
IL	07/12/96		Coleraine	H	W	1	0	Livingstone
IL	10/12/96		Portadown	A	D	1	1	og
IL	21/12/96		Crusaders	H	D	1	1	Devine
IL	26/12/96		Linfield	A	D	0	0	-
IL	01/01/97		Ards	H	D	0	0	-
IL	04/01/97		Cliftonville	H	D	1	1	Kirk
IL	11/01/97		Glenavon	A	W	2	1	Kirk, Hamill
IL	18/01/97		Coleraine	A	D	0	0	-
IL	01/02/97		Portadown	H	W	2	0	Kirk 2
IL	08/02/97		Crusaders	A	D	1	1	Hamill
IL	15/02/97		Linfield	H	L	0	2	-
IL	01/03/97		Ards	A	L	0	3	-
IL	08/03/97		Cliftonville	A	L	0	1	-
IL	22/03/97		Glenavon	H	W	2	1	Elliott, McBride
IL	25/03/97		Coleraine	H	W	1	0	Quigley
IL	01/04/97		Portadown	A	W	1	0	McCourt
IL	05/04/97		Crusaders	H	W	4	0	Hamill 2, McCourt, McBride
IL	19/04/97		Linfield	A	D	0	0	-
IL	26/04/97		Ards	H	W	2	0	Hamill, McCourt
CAS	26/11/96	1	Newry Town	A	W	5	0	May 2, Livingstone, McCourt 2
CAS	17/12/96	2	Cliftonville	H	D	0	0	aet – (lost 4-5 on penalties)
CCC	28/12/96	1.1	Carrick Rangers	A	W	4	3	Mitchell 2, Kirk, May
CCC	07/01/97	1.2	Carrick Rangers	H	W	1	0	Livingstone
CCC	18/02/97	QF	Ards	H	W	3	0	McCourt, Hamill 2
CCC	04/03/97	SF	Portadown	WP	W	2	1	aet – Kirk 2
CCC	08/04/97	F	Glenavon	WP	L	0	1	-
IC	25/01/97	5	Distillery	H	W	4	0	Mitchell, Kirk, Batey, McCourt
IC	22/02/97	6	Glenavon	A	L	0	2	-
F	20/07/96		Aberdeen	H	L	1	4	Coyle

F	23/07/96	Dundee	H	L	0	1	-
F	24/07/96	Dundela	A	W	3	2	T.Smith 2(1p), Houston
F	26/07/96	St. Mirren	N	L	1	4	Little
							Stena Line Trophy semi-final
F	27/07/96	Stranraer	A	L	1	6	Kirk – Stena Line Trophy
							3rd place play-off
F	30/07/96	Partick Thistle	H	L	0	3	-
F	01/08/96	Burnley	H	L	0	4	-
F	03/08/96	Notts County	H	L	0	1	John Devine Testimonial

The Coca-Cola Cup provided a break form the pressure of the Premier League games and our last match of 1996 at Carrick was certainly an eventful one. Andy May put us ahead in the first minute, Carrick equalised, and then we went on three-goal spree in five minutes just before the interval. However in the last ten minutes the home side scored twice, one an own goal by Livingstone, and our debutant goalkeeper Gavin Cushley was sent off with Paul Leeman going into nets! We secured a more routine second leg victory at the Oval by a single goal.

By early 1997 many were doubting the benefits of an eight team Premier League citing too much pressure and familiarity between the teams. Trevor Anderson resigned as Linfield manger and there were further protests at the Oval after a late Cliftonville equaliser meant yet another draw. Coleraine's big lead at the top had been whittled away by Crusaders and the Blues whilst we now stood fifth, nine points adrift.

Our fine win at Glenavon saw our latest debutant and on-loan signing from Burnley, Tunisian Noureddine Maamria, feature as a substitute. Inevitably nicknamed "Dino" he was an Under-21 international and was trying his hand at British football after a spell with Avenir Sportis Lamarsa in his native land. We got back to drawing ways at the Coleraine Showgrounds a week later, as the Bannsiders broke our record with their sixth draw in a row!

Glentoran began the defence of the Irish Cup with a comfortable 4-0 over First Division Distillery. Maamria impressed with his strong running but the highlight of the game was on overhead kick goal from Kirk. Glenavon put paid to our hopes in Round Six, however, on a day when nothing went right for us from the moment the Lurgan men went ahead in the first minute. Quigley hit the post, Hamill had a goal disallowed after the referee failed to allow an advantage and a second goal from Grant mid-way through the second half sealed our fate.

Around this time we got into a rut in the league losing three games in a row without scoring. Linfield brought our seventeen match unbeaten run to an end at the Oval in a match when we lost Batey to a nasty shoulder injury and saw Kirk miss a penalty. Two Lee Feeney goals helped Ards to a 3-0 win over us, less than two weeks after we had beaten the North Down side by the same score in the Coca-Cola Cup. Indeed that tournament was our last hope of any silverware as we reached the final after a gruelling extra-time win over Portadown at Mourneview Park.

Back to the Premier League and we returned to form with a pleasing run of four victories as the season began to draw to a

Philip Mitchell

465

close. Another non-British player, goalkeeper Guido Van der Kamp from Holland, joined us on-loan from Dunfermline and he proceeded to keep a clean sheet in all of our last five league games. The highlight in April was our 4-0 thrashing of new league leaders Crusaders. Our heroes on the day were two-goal Rory Hamill and the rejuvenated Justin McBride, who netted from all of 35 yards. This win moved us up into third place in the league, which was won by the Crues by three points from Coleraine.

We disappointingly lost the Coca-Cola Cup final to Glenavon, the winning goal coming from Lee Doherty in the 89th minute, and then played out a goalless draw with Linfield before finishing the season with a 2-0 win over bottom club Ards to secure third spot. The unsung Michael Smyth was voted Glentoran Player of the Year, in a season when he passed the 200 appearances mark for the club.

Appearances and Goals

	App.	Subs.	Goals		App.	Subs.	Goals
Devine J.	47		4	Parker	7	2	1
Batey	46	1	2	Van de Kamp	6		
Smyth M.	44		1	Smith	5	3	1
Armstrong N.	38			Cushley	5		
Walker	36	2		Maamria	4	6	
Kirk	35	12	16	Hutchinson	3		
Drake	30	1		Houston	2	3	
McCourt	29	5	11	Cook	2	1	
Quigley	30	4	1	Duerden	2		
Mitchell	24	1	6	Leeman	1	6	
Livingstone	23	5	3	Beggs	1	1	
Finlay	21	7	5	Neill G.	1	1	
May	21		4	Hagan	1		
McBride	21	1	8	Cochrane		3	
Hamill	20	7	7	Hooks		2	
Kennedy	18	5		Newell		2	
Little	17		5	McFadden		1	
Mathieson	13	6	1	Own Goals			3
Nixon	10	1					
Elliott	9	9	3	TOTAL	572	98	82

1997/98

Turbulent times – Coyle in charge – An unlikely hero

There were a few notable changes at the start of the 1997/8 season. The Premier League had been increased in size to ten teams from eight, meaning clubs would play 36 league games in total. To accommodate the extra fixtures the league would start in mid-August and the Ulster Cup would be competed for by First Division sides only. The Gold Cup reverted to a "three groups of six" format played midweek in September and October. George Neill retired from playing, finishing in second place in our all-time appearances chart and took over the managerial reigns of the Seconds.

Our pre-season friendly games including matches against northern England sides Burnley, Blackpool and star-studded Middlesborough. The Glens sported a new kit, a return to a plainer virtually all-green shirt with red collar and cuffs. The Gazette welcomed a new editor in Philip Stevenson and there was an early season message in the programme form club secretary Jackie Warren appealing for better behaviour from supporters and pointing out that the club had to fork out around £7,000 in fines due to the acts of a small minority.

In our opening two rounds of the Wilkinson Sword sponsored League Cup we hammered in fourteen goals, with Andy Kirk netting a personal tally of six and fellow teenager Stuart Elliott scoring a fine individual goal against Tobermore United. We quickly reached the semi-finals of the League Cup with a narrow win over Institute, in a match which marked the debut of our Welsh goalkeeper Wayne Russell.

John Devine was the hero in our opening league fixture with a looping header just before half-time enough to defeat Coleraine. However there was little to celebrate in the rest of August as we lost by a single goal at Glenavon and then put in an inept display to lose at home 0-3 to Linfield. Tommy Cassidy described it as the worst performance since he had taken over as manager over three years previously. Those events were overshadowed somewhat by the death of Diana, Princess of Wales, that night in a car crash and all the following weeks sporting fixtures nationwide were postponed as a mark of respect.

In early September the League Cup was decided. A hard fought win over Glenavon set up a big two final at Windsor Park. Linfield came out on top again in a match where we failed to take our chances and had Chris Walker sent off. Many observers thought that the answer to our problems would be a big, scoring striker who would dovetail with the smaller, nippier Kirk, Elliott and McBride. We got back to winning ways with a comfortable 3-0 win over Ards to send them bottom of the table. This time it was the turn of the visiting manager to bemoan his teams display as Roy Coyle said he was ashamed of his team's performance.

But Glentoran were about to commence a very poor run. After we stumbled to victory at Carrick in the Gold Cup we only won one game out of the next seven. This included embarrassingly heavy defeats at home to Omagh in the league and at Portadown in the Gold Cup when we conceded seven goals for the first time to an Irish League side since New Year's Day 1966! Supporters vented their frustrations after the Omagh debacle with some even threatening to break into the players' entrance and demanded the resignation of club chairman David Chick. Indeed the cries continued before kick-off at Ballymena but some must have turned to cheers when Rory Hamill put us ahead after only eighteen seconds. In the following week Colin Nixon and Andy Kirk had a trial at Leeds but no offers materialised. The Glens were continuing to reap the benefits of Nixon's play as earlier in his career there was a possibility that he would join Glasgow Rangers.

A home loss to Cliftonville and the Portadown defeat brought things to a head and Chick resigned his position the following day. The team battled back on the Saturday and

Results 1997/98

Played 54. Won 27. Drew 12. Lost 15. Goals For 89. Against 60 .% 61.1.
Honours: Irish Cup

ILC	09/08/97	1	Tobermore United	H	W	5	1	Kirk 2, McBride, Elliott, Parker
ILC	12/08/97	2	Dungannon Swifts	H	W	9	2	Kirk 4, Elliott 2, Hamill 2, Livingstone
ILC	26/08/97	QF	Institute	H	W	3	2	Kirk 2, Devine
ILC	03/09/97	SF	Glenavon	A	W	1	0	Hamill
ILC	09/09/97	F	Linfield	A	L	0	1	-
IL	16/08/97		Coleraine	H	W	1	0	Devine
IL	23/08/97		Glenavon	A	L	0	1	-
IL	30/08/97		Linfield	H	L	0	3	-
IL	13/09/97		Ards	H	W	3	0	Hamill, Livingstone, McBride
IL	20/09/97		Portadown	H	D	1	1	Mitchell
IL	27/09/97		Ballymena United	A	W	2	0	McCourt, Hamill
IL	04/10/97		Cliftonville	H	L	0	2	-
IL	11/10/97		Crusaders	A	W	2	0	Parker 2
IL	18/10/97		Coleraine	A	L	1	2	Livingstone
IL	21/10/97		Omagh Town	A	D	1	1	Hamill
IL	25/10/97		Glenavon	H	L	0	1	-
IL	01/11/97		Linfield	A	L	0	2	-
IL	08/11/97		Ards	A	D	1	1	Cash
IL	15/11/97		Portadown	A	L	2	3	Elliott, Hamill
IL	22/11/97		Ballymena United	H	L	1	2	Cash
IL	25/11/97		Omagh Town	H	W	1	0	McBride
IL	29/11/97		Cliftonville	A	W	2	0	Hamill, McBride
IL	06/12/97		Crusaders	H	D	1	1	Leeman
IL	13/12/97		Coleraine	H	W	3	0	Hamill 2, Cash
IL	20/12/97		Glenavon	A	L	0	1	-
IL	26/12/97		Linfield	H	D	1	1	Kirk
IL	01/01/98		Omagh Town	A	W	5	0	McBride 4, Kirk
IL	10/01/98		Portadown	H	W	2	1	Kirk, Elliott
IL	17/01/98		Ballymena United	A	W	2	1	Devine, McBride (p)
IL	31/01/98		Cliftonville	H	W	1	0	McBride
IL	07/02/98		Crusaders	A	W	3	0	McBride 2(2p), Kirk
IL	10/02/98		Ards	H	W	2	0	Elliott, McBride
IL	14/02/98		Coleraine	A	W	5	1	Leeman, Elliott, McBride 2, Kirk
IL	28/02/98		Glenavon	H	W	1	0	Elliott
IL	07/03/98		Linfield	A	L	0	3	-
IL	21/03/98		Omagh Town	H	W	2	0	Kirk 2
IL	28/03/98		Ards	A	W	2	0	McBride, Mitchell
IL	11/04/98		Portadown	A	L	0	2	-
IL	13/04/98		Ballymena United	H	D	2	2	Kirk, Kennedy
IL	18/04/98		Cliftonville	A	D	1	1	Mitchell
IL	24/04/98		Crusaders	H	D	1	1	Kirk
GC	16/09/97		Carrick Rangers	A	W	1	0	McBride
GC	23/09/97		Omagh Town	H	L	1	4	McBride
GC	29/09/97		Cliftonville	H	D	0	0	-
GC	07/10/97		Portadown	A	L	3	7	McBride, Livingstone, Smyth
GC	14/10/97		NewryTown	A	L	1	2	McBride
CAS	18/11/97	1	Distillery	H	D	0	0	aet – (lost 4-5 on penalties)
IC	24/01/98	5	Ballymena United	A	D	1	1	Elliott
IC	27/01/98	5R	Ballymena United	H	W	2	1	Kirk, McBride
IC	21/02/98	6	Coleraine	H	W	3	2	Elliott 2, Kennedy
IC	14/03/98	QF	Armagh City	H	W	3	1	Kirk (p), Mitchell, Leeman
IC	04/04/98	SF	Linfield	A	W	2	1	Kirk 2(1p)

IC	02/05/98	F	Glenavon	WPW	1	0	Kennedy
CCC	03/02/98	1	Newry Town	H D	1	1	aet – Kirk (lost 2-3 on penalties)
F	19/07/97		Dungannon Swifts	A D	1	1	Kirk
F	26/07/97		Burnley	H L	1	4	McBride
F	30/07/97		Blackpool	H D	0	0	-
F	02/08/97		Middlesbrough	H L	0	5	-
F	04/08/97		Dundela	H W	1	0	Kirk

recorded a solid 2-0 win, both goals coming from Darren Parker, who was now sporting a more "slim-line" headband. However that result was something of a false dawn as we failed to register a victory in any of our next nine matches. Indeed seven of those were lost as we failed to qualify for the Gold Cup knock-out stages, fell hopelessly behind in the League race and were knocked out of the County Antrim Shield at the first stage by Distillery on penalties. Cassidy signed Michael Midwood on a loan deal from Huddersfield to play up front but he failed to score in any of his four games.

Early November was a very sad time at the Oval as the club learned of the death of Billy Neill, possibly our greatest ever clubman and one of football's true gentlemen. Then on Saturday we went down 0-2 to Linfield to stay in eighth position in the league. The following day Tommy Cassidy announced his resignation following a meeting with new club Chairman Ted Brownlee. Results were the yardstick of success and despite his unstinting efforts many felt the club needed a change. Billy Sinclair stepped in as caretaker manager.

Michael Cash scored with a curling free-kick at Ards, in his first game for twelve months, to earn us a point but we suffered a week later at Portadown when losing 2-3 after being ahead up until the 84th minute. However fans looked forward to a new era when, on the 18th November 1997, Roy Coyle was appointed as our new manager with Jimmy Brown as his assistant. Coyle had been a Glentoran player over 25 years previously but up to that point was famous for managing Linfield to many trophies over fifteen seasons. Could he repeat the dose with Glentoran? Cassidy soon had taken over Coyle's position as manager of Ards in an un-planned job swap!

After losing at home to Ballymena results improved considerably. In fact of our remaining 28 games this season we were to lose only three outright. We knocked Cliftonville off the top of the table thanks to a fine 2-0 win at Solitude but the performance was tinged with a compound leg fracture for the now veteran Andy Mathieson, an injury that was to effectively end his career. Worse still was the unsavoury antics of the Cliftonville supporters who threw missiles at the player and the stretcher bearers as he was carried off.

Coyle's first signing Paul Dwyer made his debut against his old team mates Crusaders in a 1-1 draw but he was to feature mainly on the bench as the season progressed. An impressive display with Rory Hamill scoring twice saw off Coleraine at the Oval but our mini-revival was halted at Mourneview Park a week later by a Glenn Ferguson header. We finished 1997 by sharing the points with Linfield in an exciting Boxing Day encounter. Inspired by a goal from substitute Kirk we were piling on the pressure before more hooliganism caused the referee to take the teams off the field for six minutes. When play resumed our momentum had been lost and there was no further scoring. Cash suffered two broken ribs in the match and was later released.

January 1998 brought plenty of wins, four in the league and a defeat of Ballymena in the Irish Cup. Helped by the return of many players from injury we moved at last into the top half of the table as confidence was restored. We even managed to overcome the loss of Paul Leeman to a first-half red card to defeat leaders Cliftonville again.

The team continued that form into February where our only "defeat" was to Newry Town on penalties in the Coca-Cola Cup. Penalties helped us to win 3-0 at Seaview as Alan Snoddy awarded us two in two minutes just before half-time, both duly converted by McBride. John Devine made his 400th appearance in that match and McBride too reached a personal landmark of 100 Glentoran goals in an even more impressive 5-1 victory at Coleraine a week later. With eight games to go the table reflected our amazing transformation as follows:

1. Cliftonville 53 points, 2. Glentoran 47, 3=. Linfield, Portadown 46, 5. Crusaders 41.

Team Group 1997/8 Back Row: Paul Leeman, Colin Nixon, Philip Mitchell, Wayne Russell, Andy Kirk, Chris Walker Front Row: John Kennedy, Darren Finlay, John Devine, Rory Hamill, Stevie Livingstone.

We met Coleraine a week later in the Irish Cup sixth round in East Belfast. This time things were much closer and it took a long range free-kick from man of the match Elliott to settle matters in the 84th minute. Also on the scoresheet was John Kennedy who was enjoying a fine run in the side at left-back. The win encouraged talk of a league and cup double, unthinkable only a few months previously but the experienced Coyle reminded supporters with the old cliché that we would take one game at a time.

Out trip to Windsor Park on 7th March brought everyone back to earth on a day many will wish to forget. Under the headlines of "Soccer's Day of Shame" the events unfolded thus. Linfield led 1-0, their new signing Glenn Ferguson continuing his scoring record against us when, just after the half-hour mark, a midfield tussle developed into a melee with all the outfield players and a number of the coaching staff taking part. When the dust had settled referee Frank McDonald singled out Justin McBride and showed him the red card. The Blues went further ahead early in the second half but when Peter Batey was sent off for a second yellow card a riot developed in the North Stand with Glentoran supporters clashing with police. Matters were not helped when Colin Nixon received his marching orders to reduce us to eight men and Ferguson scored again. The fighting continued outside with at least twenty people taken to hospital for treatment as all parties were roundly condemned. Even Roy Coyle was nearly accosted by a Linfield supporter at half-time. The IFA Disciplinary Committee handed us a fine of £2,500 and made a scapegoat out of McBride by giving him a six game ban. Coyle reacted angrily by imposing a blanket ban on all Glentoran media interviews. It was decided that only Chairman Ted Brownlee would communicate with the press.

Now if that was not bad enough both Glentoran and Linfield won their Irish Cup quarter-final ties and were drawn against each other in the semis! The authorities decided to bring forward the kick-off to 11 a.m. and restrict both sides to 3,000 supporters. Back to the league and we stayed in touch with a couple of routine 2-0 victories over Omagh and Ards. The future of the club was further cemented when we announced a nursery side arrangement with Dungoyne Boys and signed David Rainey from Ballyclare.

The cup semi-final was a much happier day for Glentoran as two goals from Andy Kirk, one a penalty, set up our win and both on and off the pitch the game passed off trouble free.

Linfield pulled one back late on but could not recover from conceding their first goal in 661 minutes. As often happens prior to an Irish Cup final our league form dipped off and we only managed to draw three and lose one of our last four games. As a result we ended up in fourth position, nine points behind Cliftonville who were title winners for the first time in 88 years.

Justin McBride had to sit out the Irish Cup final but he would have gained some consolation as being named Glentoran Player of the Year and watching his colleagues regain the Irish Cup as we repeated our 1-0 1996 victory over holders Glenavon. This time the goal came from a less likely source as it was left to full-back John Kennedy to break the deadlock with an angled shot in extra-time. He became the first Northern Ireland born player to score the winning cup goal for six years but that would not have mattered much to the Glentoran supporters who, after a traumatic season, were ready to celebrate. One last piece of good news came as the Seconds lifted the "B" Division title by defeating Portadown Reserves in the last game of the season.

Appearances and Goals

	App.	Subs.	Goals		App.	Subs.	Goals
Nixon C.	50	1		Mathieson	12	4	
Hamill	49	3	10	Armstrong N.	9		
McBride	46		21	Cash	9	1	3
Russell W.	45			Finlay	9	10	
Livingstone	43	3	4	McCourt	5	5	1
Devine J.	41		3	Midwood	4		
Smyth M.	36	2	1	Dwyer	3	7	
Kennedy	35	3	3	McGerrigan	1	7	
Leeman	33	2	3	Quigley	1		
Walker	32	5		Rainey	1	3	
Batey	31	1		Ferguson		2	
Kirk	30	9	22	Maamria		1	
Elliott	26	11	11	TOTAL	594	87	89
Mitchell	26	4	4				
Parker	17	3	3				

1998/99

Israeli adventure – A miraculous comeback – League Champions again

The last full season of the 1990s started early with a mid-July friendly against Queen's Park Rangers. Before kick-off the teams and supporters observed a minute's silence for the popular Glentoran team attendant Teddy Horner, who had passed away after illness. We displayed our new kit, again mainly a silky green but with a red and two black vertical stripes down the left hand side. The returning Justin McBride scored our goal in the 1-2 defeat, a penalty past 6'7" goalkeeper Ademole Bankole.

We used the remainder of the pre-season games, including a well deserved benefit game for Andy Mathieson against Derry City, as warm-ups for our European fixture with Israeli Cup holders Macaabi Haifa. However before that there was the Charity Shield game with Cliftonville to play. The Reds emerged victorious, Tim McCann scoring the only goal, as we failed to find a way past their teenage keeper Michael Ingham.

Glentoran had been relatively quiet on the transfer front during the close season. The only player brought in was David McCallan, who was only to make three appearances, while exiting were Michael Smyth and Darren Parker to Coleraine and Ballymena United respectively.

Many people thought that we showed Haifa too much respect in the Oval leg and we succumbed to a 0-1 defeat, the goal coming from Alon Mizrahi. However those events were overshadowed two days later as we opened our League campaign against Omagh Town. News came through of the bomb blast in the County Tyrone market town and rendered the match virtually meaningless.

We recorded an excellent result at Solitude the following Saturday, Paul Leeman netting a hat-trick including a long range effort from the centre circle, as we gained a quick revenge over Cliftonville before setting off on our longest ever "European" trip. Haifa was located in northern Israel, under the shadow of Mount Carmel and the draw gave over 200 supporters the chance to sample the famous sights of the Holy Land at first hand. In the match itself, in which we turned out in all-black, the Glens fell foul of an early penalty decision but by half-time we had come back into the game and a goal by Pete Batey in the 42nd minute gave plenty of hope for the second-half. However it was not to be and another penalty converted by Mizrahi sent Macaabi through on a 3-1 aggregate.

Glentoran returned to concentrate on domestic matters and we put together an unbeaten run of nine matches as the League and Gold Cup developed. Midfielder Scott Young, signed from Dunfermline, made his debut in a fine 3-1 win at Coleraine as the team won its first six league games. After many years of injury problems a Glentoran manager was now faced with the opposite problem having to leave players out from the first team!

We demolished Glenavon at the Oval at the end of September in a display that aptly illustrated our form of the time. The goals were spread among our forward players of Hamill, Rainey, McBride, Kirk and Elliott in a free-flowing performance prompted by the midfield of Young and Mitchell and would surely have impressed watching Northern Ireland manager Lawrie McMenemy. We now led the table by a point from Linfield but before travelling to meet the Blues we ventured north to play Institute in a game to mark the opening of their new grandstand and floodlights.

The first big two meeting of the season ended all square in front of 8,000 fans when Batey came off the bench to equalise in the 76th minute at Windsor Park. Larmour had earlier put Linfield ahead but a draw was a fair result. Then on the Tuesday we lost at home to champions Cliftonville, who were surprisingly struggling one place off the bottom of the league. There was also a managerial change down the club when George Neill resigned as manager of the Seconds to be replaced by another stalwart in Barney Bowers.

That defeat seemed to re-galvanise the team over the next few weeks as we swiftly returned to winning ways with a string of convincing victories to maintain our league leadership and qualify for the Gold Cup quarter-finals. We reserved the most spectacular of these for the last day of October when Coleraine visited the Oval. The visitors, without a league win on our ground for twelve years, went 2-0 up before David Rainey pulled one back. However by the 70th minute they had scored twice more, Stokes completing a hat-trick, to leave us suddenly dead and buried at 1-4. Then we started one of the greatest comebacks in Glentoran history when Leeman shot through a crowd of players to pull one back with just seventeen minutes remaining. Coleraine's Brendan Aspinall then committed a double crime in the 77th minute. Firstly he flattened Rainey to give us a penalty and found himself sent off for a flare up with the same player. McBride tucked away the penalty and shortly afterwards the Bannsiders found themselves down to nine men when Lynch kicked the ball away and received his second yellow card. Two more defensive errors allowed Elliott and Hamill in to complete the turnaround in the final ten minutes! After all that we led the table by five clear points from thirteen games.

As autumn turned to winter once more we suffered a couple of glitches in the league but progressed well in the knockout tournaments. Both Newry Town and Crusaders came to the Oval in mid-November and left with the points after

The victorious team with the County Antrim Shield.

comfortable wins. There were no comebacks this time but we did twice gain revenge over Newry within the space of seventeen days by beating them in both the Gold Cup quarter-finals and the County Antrim Shield.

Our new signing from Cliftonville, winger Tim McCann, made his debut when the Blues visited the Oval in early December. It was to be Linfield's day as they netted the only goal from a penalty awarded when Batey deliberately pulled the ball down thinking there was a player in a goalscoring position behind him. Our third consecutive home defeat enabled the Blues to go top of the league on goal difference at the half-way stage.

We quickly recovered from this to see off Glenavon in the Gold Cup, now sponsored by Nationwide, semi-final in extra time. Our ex-player Cash had given the Lurgan men the lead but we gradually wore them down, John Devine netting a vital header, to set up a final meeting with Portadown. A crowd of 2,670 were present to witness an excellent display from the Glens as Rory Hamill was on top form, opening the scoring and then crossing for Kirk to make it two. Devine made it three late on before Vinny Arkins netted in injury team for a well-beaten Ports side.

It was Newry Town again for the fourth time in ten matches and they would have been sick of the sight of us as we beat them 5-1 in the league. That set us up nicely for the Boxing Day visit to Windsor Park but there was nothing nice about the weather as a howling gale and driving rain made it virtually impossible to play football. Andy Kirk headed us in front but after Batey had received his marching orders again for attempting to strangle a Linfield player the Blues took advantage to equalise.

Glentoran showed plenty of gritty resolve in the early games of 1999. We needed a John Devine penalty to beat Glenavon on New Year's Day, awarded after Jeff Spiers had handled a corner. By coincidence this was an uncanny repeat of the events in the teams' previous league meeting at Mourneview six weeks earlier. The following afternoon we battled to a

Results 1998/99

Played 57. Won 39. Drew 7. Lost 11. Goals For 125. Against 53. % 74.6.
Honours: Irish League, County Antrim Shield

CS	08/08/98		Cliftonville	H	L	0	1	-
ECW	13/08/98	1.1	Macaabi Haifa	H	L	0	1	-
ECW	27/08/98	1.2	Macaabi Haifa	A	L	1	2	Batey
IL	15/08/98		Omagh Town	H	W	2	0	Mitchell (p), Hamill
IL	22/08/98		Cliftonville	A	W	4	2	Leeman 3, McCallan
IL	01/09/98		Coleraine	A	W	3	1	Nixon, Mitchell, Elliott
IL	05/09/98		Newry Town	A	W	2	1	og, McBride
IL	12/09/98		Ballymena United	H	W	2	1	McBride (p), Elliott
IL	15/09/98		Portadown	H	W	1	0	Rainey
IL	19/09/98		Crusaders	A	D	0	0	-
IL	26/09/98		Glenavon	H	W	5	2	Elliott, Hamill, Rainey, McBride, Kirk
IL	03/10/98		Linfield	A	D	1	1	Batey
IL	06/10/98		Cliftonville	H	L	0	1	-
IL	17/10/98		Omagh Town	A	W	2	0	Mitchell, McBride
IL	24/10/98		Portadown	A	W	3	0	McBride, Hamill, Elliott
IL	31/10/98		Coleraine	H	W	5	4	McBride (p), Rainey, Leeman, Elliott, Hamill
IL	07/11/98		Ballymena United	A	D	1	1	Rainey
IL	14/11/98		Newry Town	H	L	1	3	McBride
IL	21/11/98		Crusaders	H	L	1	4	Rainey
IL	28/11/98		Glenavon	A	W	1	0	Devine (p)
IL	05/12/98		Linfield	H	L	0	1	-
IL	12/12/98		Omagh Town	A	W	4	1	Kirk 3, Leeman
IL	19/12/98		Newry Town	H	W	5	1	Kirk 2, Hamill 3
IL	26/12/98		Linfield	A	D	1	1	Kirk
IL	01/01/99		Glenavon	H	W	1	0	Devine (p)
IL	02/01/99		Coleraine	A	W	1	0	Devine
IL	09/01/99		Cliftonville	H	D	0	0	-
IL	16/01/99		Crusaders	H	W	2	1	Devine, Rainey
IL	30/01/99		Portadown	A	W	3	1	Hamill, McBride, Kirk
IL	06/02/99		Ballymena United	H	W	1	0	McCann
IL	13/02/99		Omagh Town	H	W	2	0	McCann, Elliott
IL	06/03/99		Linfield	H	L	1	2	Finlay
IL	11/03/99		Newry Town	A	L	0	1	-
IL	20/03/99		Glenavon	A	W	1	0	Leeman
IL	23/03/99		Coleraine	H	W	5	0	Devine, Batey, Leeman, Hamill, Rainey
IL	03/04/99		Cliftonville	H	D	1	1	Devine (p)
IL	06/04/99		Crusaders	A	W	3	0	McBride 2, Hamill
IL	17/04/99		Portadown	H	W	3	1	Hamill, Nixon, McCann
IL	24/04/99		Ballymena United	A	W	6	3	Elliott, McCann, Leeman 2, Hamill 2
GC	08/09/98		Ballyclare Comrades	A	W	3	0	Rainey 2, McBride
GC	22/09/98		Larne	H	W	4	1	Hamill, Rainey, Mitchell, Quigley
GC	13/10/98		Ards	A	W	5	0	Leeman, Kirk, McBride 2(1p), Elliott
GC	27/10/98		Portadown	H	D	2	2	Leeman. Elliott
GC	10/11/98		Omagh Town	A	W	3	1	Mitchell (p), Rainey, McBride
GC	24/11/98	QF	Newry Town	A	W	3	1	Kenny og, Leeman 2
GC	08/12/98	SF	Glenavon	WP	W	4	1	aet – Kirk 2, Devine, Young
GC	15/12/98	F	Portadown	WP	W	3	1	Hamill, Devine, Kirk
CAS	01/12/98	1	Newry Town	H	W	2	1	Hamill, Batey

CAS	22/12/98	2	Ballymena United	H	W	1	0	Kirk (p)
CAS	12/01/99	SF	Linfield	A	W	2	1	Kirk, Devine
CAS	02/02/99	F	Cliftonville	WP	W	2	0	Kirk, Elliott
IC	23/01/99	5	Tobermore United	H	W	3	0	McCann, Kirk, McBride
IC	20/02/99	6	Cliftonville	A	L	1	2	Hamill
CCC	16/02/99	1	Dungannon Swifts	H	W	8	0	Elliott 3, Leeman, Kirk 2(1p), Rainey 2
CCC	30/03/99	2	Distillery	H	W	2	1	Elliott, Rainey
CCC	13/04/99	SF	Carrick Rangers	Sv	W	1	0	Leeman
CCC	04/05/99	F	Linfield	A	L	1	2	aet – Young
F	18/07/98		QPR	H	L	1	2	McBride (p)
F	25/07/98		Institute	H	W	2	1	McBride, Kirk
F	29/07/98		Dundela	A	W	4	2	McBride 2, Livingstone, Mitchell
F	01/08/98		Loughall	H	W	2	0	Hamill, Kirk
F	04/08/98		Derry City	H	L	1	2	Rainey
								Andy Mathieson Testimonial
F	29/09/98		Institute	A	D	1	1	Elliott – Opening of new stand and floodlights
F	27/03/99		Stranraer	A	W	1	0	Leeman

single gaol victory at Coleraine, Devine again the match winner with a header fifteen minutes from time to put us five points clear.

After a scoreless draw at home to the Reds we reeled off eight consecutive victories at a vital stage of the season. During this spell we won the County Antrim Shield, defeating Linfield and Cliftonville at Windsor Park in the semis and final. Devine was again the match winner in the former, giving us our only win of the season over the Blues. We also began our defence of the Irish Cup in defeating Tobermore and hammered Dungannon Swifts in the Coca-Cola Cup with Stuart Elliott claiming a hat-trick.

Andy Kirk scored twice in that game and shortly afterwards he was transferred to Hearts. While wishing the young striker with the somersault celebrations well for the future many supporters doubted the timing of the move as the season reached a vital stage.

Rod Lennox was singed on a two game loan deal from Kilmarnock to cover but the worry was emphasised as we stuttered to league defeats versus Linfield and Newry after losing our grip on the Irish Cup via a defeat at Solitude. Rory Hamill was our goalscorer that day and he was in the middle of a period of personal achievement with an appearance for Northern Ireland at B level versus Wales in Wrexham while later in the season he gained a full cap when coming on as a substitute against Canada and was named Glentoran Player of the Year. Elliott got in on the act too by playing for the Under-21 side versus Finland and Scotland while Nixon was called up to the bench for the Moldova game.

However any doubts over our league aspirations were dispelled by a fine win away to Glenavon and a thrashing of Coleraine at the Oval when we scored five again, this time without reply! Thus we maintained our three point lead over

John Devine celebrates with the fans after his vital penalty equaliser against Cliftonville.

Linfield with four games to go. The club then took the chance of a free weekend to pay a visit to Stranraer for a friendly. On this occasion we gave a much better account of ourselves than in 1996 and came away with a solid 1-0 win.

The nerves though appeared against Cliftonville at the Oval on 3rd April. The Reds took the lead with a freak goal as Wayne Russell allowed a free-kick from wide out by Sliney to drift in over his head. Even when the visitors were reduced to ten men with the dismissal of Mulvenna late in the first half we struggled to find a way through. With time ticking away captain Devine once again took centre stage as after being brought down in the area he tucked away the resultant penalty. Linfield could only draw 1-1 with Coleraine so we retained our three point lead.

On the Easter Tuesday we strolled to victory at Seaview while Linfield drew at Glenavon. This set the scene for the Portadown game at the Oval on 17th April. As the Glens led 3-1 towards the end of the game supporters began to congregate around the pitch waiting for the final whistle. When it came there was a joyous pitch invasion as we lifted the Gibson Cup for the first time in seven years. In the last league match we put six past Ballymena to extend our final points margin to eight. Linfield gained a measure of revenge by beating us in the Coca-Cola Final in extra time but once again a team managed by Roy Coyle, with an average age of 22, had landed the biggest prize on offer.

Appearances and Goals

	App.	Subs.	Goals		App.	Subs.	Goals
Hamill	56		17	Mitchell	18	4	5
Walker	56			McCann	17	7	5
Devine J.	54	1	9	Quigley	11	7	1
Leeman	51	3	15	Armstrong N.	7		
Russell W.	50			Finlay	4	8	1
Nixon C.	49		2	Lennox	2		
Young	39	4	2	Livingstone	2	2	
McBride	37	5	15	McCallan	2	1	1
Elliott	33	19	14	Hillis	1		
Rainey	32	12	14	Thornton	1		
Batey	29	9	4	Own Goals			2
Ferguson	29	2					
Kirk	27	13	18	TOTAL	627	103	125
Kennedy	22	4					

Match ticket from our game in Israel, complete with incorrect spelling.
One can only assume the mistake was not repeated in the Hebrew!

1999/2000

Early challenges – A Millennium landmark – The Irish Cup once more

With our European Champions League games scheduled for mid-July the season had almost two start points to it. In fact we took the rare step of playing a game in June against the Irish Universities team who ware warming up for the World Student Games to help with our preparations. We had been drawn against the unknown but very competent Bulgarians Litex Lovech and ended up going down 0-5 on aggregate.

These games were quickly followed by the new Belfast Challenge. The four-team tournament would involve Linfield and Glentoran and two invited top teams, this year Liverpool and Feyenoord. The competition was the brainchild of the Belfast born, Florida based sports promotion businessman Noel Lemon and was certainly an innovative addition with the final game being televised live nationally. We went down 0-2 to Feyenoord on the Friday night before having to settle for a draw with the Blues on the Saturday as they equalised in the last minute.

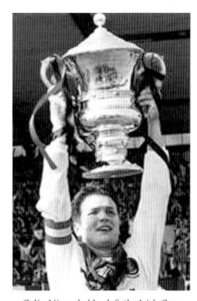

Colin Nixon holds aloft the Irish Cup.

After a couple more friendlies we played the Charity Shield game with Portadown and again lost out by the odd goal before the Smirnoff Irish Premiership kicked off in mid-August. The fixture raised nearly £4,000 for local charities. The main additions to our squad were goalkeeper Alan Gough, signed from Shelbourne from where he had gained a couple of FAI Cup winners medals, Alistair McCombe, a centre-half from Bangor and Brian Russell, a forward from Crusaders. Dubliner Liam Kelly was signed on a loan deal. Leaving the Oval were Wayne Russell to Bohemians and our former skipper John Devine who opted to sign for Coleraine after 11 years and over 450 games for Glentoran. We would also have to do without Justin McBride, in his benefit season, due to a knee injury.

We opened with a victory at Coleraine but were soon pegged back by Glenavon and top flight new boys Distillery whose name was now prefixed by Lisburn in an attempt to drum up support from the town nearest their home stadium. In between these defeats we visited Ards for a testimonial for a former Glentoran servant Raymond Morrison. On the last day of August though we made up for those disappointments when a Stuart Elliott goal gave us an early season victory over Linfield. Once more the match was nearly ruined by hooliganism, this time the referee being struck by a missile, and a subsequent £2,000 fine imposed on the club.

Against Cliftonville we were denied the services of Elliott and full-back Michael Ferguson, but they had a good excuse as they had been selected in the Northern Ireland Under-21 squad for their match in Germany. We gained a point here but generally inconsistent displays meant that by the end of the league's first quarter of fixtures in early October we languished in fifth place, seven points behind joint leaders Linfield and Glenavon. Our most entertaining game was a 5-3 success over Portadown with winger Tim McCann scoring twice on his birthday

The Gold Cup had reverted back to a knockout basis and we progressed to the semi-final with narrow wins over Ards and Glenavon. In the former our latest debutant was young

Results 1999/2000

Played 56. Won 31. Drew 10. Lost 15. Goals For 99. Against 74. % 64.3.
Honours: Irish Cup, Gold Cup, County Antrim Shield

EC	14/07/99	Q.1	Litex Lovech	A	L	0	3	-
EC	21/07/99	Q.2	Litex Lovech	H	L	0	2	-
CS	07/08/99		Portadown	MP	L	1	2	Finlay
IL	14/08/99		Coleraine	A	W	2	1	Elliott, Kelly
IL	21/08/99		Glenavon	H	L	1	2	Elliott
IL	28/08/99		Lisburn Distillery	A	L	0	2	-
IL	31/08/99		Linfield	H	W	1	0	Elliott
IL	07/09/99		Cliftonville	H	D	1	1	Leeman
IL	11/09/99		Crusaders	A	L	0	1	-
IL	18/09/99		Ballymena United	A	D	0	0	-
IL	25/09/99		Portadown	H	W	5	3	McCann 2, Kennedy, Russell, Young
IL	02/10/99		Newry Town	A	L	0	1	-
IL	09/10/99		Coleraine	H	W	3	2	Rainey 2, Elliott
IL	16/10/99		Glenavon	A	D	3	3	McCombe, Elliott, Kennedy
IL	23/10/99		Lisburn Distillery	H	W	3	1	Kennedy, McCann, Elliott
IL	30/10/99		Linfield	A	L	0	2	-
IL	06/11/99		Cliftonville	A	W	2	1	Elliott, Gilzean
IL	13/11/99		Crusaders	H	W	2	0	Elliott, Young
IL	20/11/99		Ballymena United	H	W	3	1	Russell, Young, Gilzean
IL	27/11/99		Portadown	A	L	0	1	-
IL	04/12/99		Newry Town	H	L	0	3	-
IL	11/12/99		Portadown	A	L	0	4	-
IL	18/12/99		Newry Town	H	W	2	1	Young 2(1p)
IL	27/12/99		Linfield	H	D	1	1	McCombe
IL	03/01/00		Glenavon	A	D	3	3	McCann, Gilzean, Kennedy
IL	08/01/00		Lisburn Distillery	H	W	2	0	Gilzean, Elliott
IL	15/01/00		Crusaders	A	D	2	2	Young, Elliott
IL	29/01/00		Coleraine	H	W	2	0	Smyth og, Elliott
IL	05/02/00		Ballymena United	H	W	3	2	Elliott, Young 2(1p)
IL	12/02/00		Cliftonville	A	D	2	2	Gilzean, Russell
IL	26/02/00		Portadown	H	W	1	0	Elliott
IL	03/03/00		Newry Town	A	W	4	3	Russell 2, Hamill, Young
IL	18/03/00		Linfield	A	W	2	1	Rainey, Hamill
IL	25/03/00		Glenavon	H	W	2	1	Rainey, Elliott
IL	01/04/00		Lisburn Distillery	A	L	0	1	-
IL	15/04/00		Crusaders	H	L	1	2	Batey
IL	18/04/00		Ballymena United	A	L	1	2	Elliott
IL	22/04/00		Coleraine	A	W	2	1	Young, Gilzean
IL	29/04/00		Cliftonville	H	W	3	0	Elliott, Hamill, S.Armstrong
GC	05/10/99	1	Ards	A	W	2	1	Rainey 2
GC	23/10/99	2	Glenavon	A	W	2	1	McCombe, Young (p)
GC	06/11/99	SF.1	Cliftonville	H	D	0	0	-
GC	16/11/99	SF.2	Cliftonville	A	D	2	2	aet – McCann, Gilzean (won 4-3 on penalties)
GC	30/11/99	F	Linfield	A	W	4	2	Russell 2, Young, McCombe
CAS	07/12/99	1	Ballyclare Comrades	A	W	2	0	McGreevy og, Young
CAS	31/12/99	2	Linfield	H	W	1	0	Russell
CAS	12/01/00	SF	Ards	Sv	W	4	1	Elliott, McCann, Young, Gilzean
CAS	01/02/00	F	Bangor	CrP	W	2	1	Elliott, Russell
IC	22/01/00	5	Crusaders	H	W	3	0	Gilzean, Young, Elliott
IC	19/02/00	6	Armagh City	A	D	2	2	Hamill, Elliott
IC	22/02/00	6R	Armagh City	H	W	4	0	Young, Gilzean, Elliott, Rainey
IC	11/03/00	QF	Newry Town	A	W	3	1	McCann, Young, og
IC	08/04/00	SF	Linfield	A	W	3	2	Hamill, Elliott, S.Armstrong
IC	06/05/00	F	Portadown	WP	W	1	0	Gilzean

CCC	29/02/00	1	Omagh Town	H	W	3	0	S.Armstrong 2, Rainey
CCC	14/03/00	2	Limavady United	A	L	1	3	Elliott
F	19/06/99		Irish Universities	N*	W	2	0	Elliott, Thornton
F	07/07/99		Dundela	H	W	6	0	Leeman 2, Rainey 2, Hamill, Elliott
F	10/07/99		Armagh City	H	W	6	1	Batey, Rainey, McBride, Leeman, Finlay 2
F	23/07/99		Feyenoord	WP	L	0	2	Belfast Challenge
F	24/07/99		Linfield	A	D	2	2	Finlay, Rainey – Belfast Challenge
F	31/07/99		Carrick Rangers	A	D	0	0	-
F	03/08/99		Loughall	A	L	2	3	Elliott, Rainey
F	24/08/99		Ards	A	W	3	2	Finlay, Leeman, Elliott Raymond Morrison Benefit
F	13/05/00		R.U.C. XI	H	W	9	4	Hamill 2, Livingstone, Halliday, Batey, S. Armstrong, N. Armstrong, Walker, Macartney (p) Gary Macartney Benefit

* = played at Cherryvale

defender Hugh Dickson who gave a sound display. Another famous name to appear on a Glentoran team sheet in October was Gilzean. We signed big forward Ian, son of the famous Alan, from St. Patrick's Athletic for a transfer fee reputed to be £10,000.

We gave a very disappointing display at Windsor Park at the end of October as we went down in a "Big Two" game which unusually contained no bookings for either side! Cliftonville were then frequent opponents in November. Firstly a Gilzean header earned us a league win at Solitude and then after two draws in the two-legged Gold Cup semi-final we kept our nerve to go through on penalties. That game was a triumph for many Glentoran players, Gough for saving a penalty, Scott Young for converting the winning spot-kick but also for the general play of Tim McCann who endured a lot of stick from his former followers.

We showed something of a Jekyll and Hyde character at the end of November as we put in a nondescript display at Portadown in the league. Defeat there left us still in third place but thirteen points behind runaway leaders Linfield. However three days later we ventured to Windsor Park for the Gold Cup final and proceeded to play them off the pitch at times, eventually winning 4-2, two of the goals from Russell who was later named both man of the match and the tournament overall.

This success failed to inspire us much in the league as we suffered heavy defeats to Newry and at Portadown again before we completed the millennium with two more fixtures against our long-standing rivals Linfield at the Oval. The league fixture was drawn but will probably be overshadowed in history by the County Antrim Shield clash four days later as it was the last senior game played anywhere in the United Kingdom before the start of the year 2000. For the record Brian Russell scored the only goal.

We began the new millennium in entertaining style with a 3-3 draw at Glenavon and indeed we did not suffer a defeat until the 14th March, a run of eighteen games unbeaten. The month of January had a "Crusaders" feel to it as we fought out an excellent 2-2 league draw with the North Belfast men before dismissing them from the Irish Cup. Before that we visited Seaview for the Shield semi-final where we dispatched Ards to the tune of 4-1. Once more the cups represented our best chance of success as we had drifted to eighteen points behind Linfield in the League.

Glentoran lifted the first trophy of the 2000's when beating Bangor 2-1 at Castlereagh Park in the County Antrim Shield, gaining a measure of revenge for defeats to the Seasiders in the corresponding games of 1975 and 1989. Elliott scored the first after a deft piece of skill and Brian Russell continued his happy habit of claiming vital goals by coming off the bench to net the winner. There was a change in the boardroom as Chairman Ted Brownlee resigned due to poor health and was replaced by John Parkinson. Around this time the Oval was saddened by news of the death of George Eastham Senior, one of our managers

479

from the early 1970's. Castlereagh Borough Council ensured that one Glentoran legend would never be forgotten when they named the new Soccer Excellent School in Dundonald after Billy Neill.

Armagh City gave us a hard time in the Irish Cup sixth round as they held us to a draw at their pitch before succumbing at the Oval. Stuart Elliott scored in both games meaning he had found the net in all but one of our last eleven fixtures. Towards the end of February the directors indicated that we would be interested in competing in the Inter Toto Cup should we fail to qualify for European football in one of the more traditional ways. Our latest signing Sean Armstrong from Ballyclare made a scoring debut against Omagh in the Coca-Cola Cup.

Just after we had defeated Newry to reach the Irish Cup semi-final our long unbeaten run came to an end in unsatisfactory fashion at Limavady. The team put in a disappointing display, capped by the unfortunate dismissal of Scott Young, as we blew our chances of a clean sweep of all the knockout competitions. However we were soon back on the rails and recorded an excellent away league victory over the Blues. The Gibson Cup was well on its way to Windsor Park but we had made a strong point with the two sides due to meet in the Irish Cup semi-final at the same venue.

That day soon dawned and what a dramatic finale the large crowd were to witness. A superb strike from Hamill and well taken goal from Elliott looked to have earned us a 2-1 win until Murphy equalised for Linfield in injury time. Many of their supporters rushed back to celebrate but before they could find their seats Armstrong sent our supporters delirious with the headed winning goal and gave them another Irish Cup final to look forward to. The club made an important off the field appointment too as John Harvey was installed as Commercial and Fundraising Co-ordinator. John had been a tireless worker on these fronts for a number of years and his role was vital to the future well-being of the club.

Once more our league form dipped slightly leading up to an Irish Cup final and Crusaders and Ballymena took advantage to improve their own causes. However we won the last two games to restore confidence. Stuart Elliott had a double celebration on 29th April as he scored versus Cliftonville and was also named as Glentoran's player of the year.

So to the 6th May and the Irish Cup final against Portadown at Windsor Park. Before the game Roy Coyle decided to stick with the inexperienced 18-year old Hugh Dickson at centre-back and leave Chris Walker out of the team. Walker, who was being married in Sri Lanka at the time of the semi-final, could not force his way back into the team nor even get onto the substitutes bench as three forwards were selected there. The Glens ran out in white shirts and black shorts and Coyle's gamble appeared to have paid off as Dickson and McCombe kept Portadown's Arkins, the county's leading scorer with 34, and Sheridan in check. He gambled again when bringing on Ian Gilzean for Russell but just before the hour mark the substitute cemented his place in Glentoran history. Hamill sent McCann away on the right and his pinpoint cross was met by Gilzean's forehead and the ball flew past Dalton into the net. Neither side really threatened again and all that was left was for Colin Nixon to lift the trophy and for the by now familiar celebrations in the North Stand to begin.

Appearances and Goals

	App.	Subs.	Goals		App.	Subs.	Goals
McCombe	53		4	Ferguson	22	5	
Young	51	3	16	Rainey	18	29	8
Elliott	50	3	23	Armstrong N.	8		
Nixon C.	48	2		Finlay	6	5	1
Gough	48			Dickson	6	1	
Hamill	46	7	5	Livingstone	3	2	
Kennedy	44	2	4	Kelly L.	3	5	1
McCann	42	12	7	Armstrong S.	3	7	4
Batey	39	3	1	Halliday	2	1	
Russell B.	35	8	10	McBride	1	2	
Leeman	34	2	1	Own Goals			3
Walker	30	2		TOTAL	616	114	99
Gilzean	24	13	11				

2000/01

Financial problems – Ibrox at last – A sweet Irish Cup success

Glentoran's first season in the 21st century turned out to be a memorable one in many ways. The highlight of the season undoubtedly was the retaining of the Irish Cup with an extra-time victory over Linfield but we also reached the final of every local knockout tournament entered. We captured the Gold Cup and League Cup, now sponsored by Coca-Cola, and, despite continuing financial problems there were many major developments at the ground. These included the installation of seating on the covered unreserved side of the ground, a makeover for the main grandstand, a revamped souvenir shop and the establishment of a family oriented Milk Bar.

The fiscal situation influenced our transfer market dealings in the summer of 2000. Leaving the club were Ian Gilzean to Shelbourne and Steven Livingstone to Glenavon while Stuart Elliott finally got his big move to the Scottish Premier League with Motherwell for a fee of around £100,000. Within a short space of time Elliott would win his first international caps. Hugh Dickson joined Wigan Athletic and after much legal wrangling we eventually obtained a nominal fee for him. Colin Nixon had the chance to move to Scotland also with Livingston but elected to remain with Glentoran. Coming to the Oval were two Darrens, Lockhart from Crusaders and Fitzgerald from Glasgow Rangers.

Scott Young.

Once more we had a busy pre and early season with a selection of friendlies, the Carlsberg Belfast Challenge, the Charity Shield, a European tie and Justin McBride's testimonial game to fit in before the start of the Smirnoff Irish Premiership in mid-August! Highlights of this were a victory over English Second Division champions Preston and a visit from Liverpool's star studded squad. We wore our latest strip, manufactured by Avec, in this match, a slightly darker green affair with red over the shoulders and a broad white band across the chest.

The game versus Lillestrom was played out in a strange atmosphere as UEFA had decreed that the use of terracing was not allowed. Therefore the crowd of 2,000 crammed into the grandstand while the remaining 80% of the ground was deserted. The Norwegians, helped by the fact that they were already well into their season, proved too strong a team winning easily by 3-0. We put a much more respectable display in the away leg, going down by the only goal.

Our hectic scheduled continued when we were invited to play Glasgow Rangers at Ibrox. The match was partially arranged to give some of Rangers' first team players returning from injury a run out but was also linked to the Tommy Leeman transfer over 16 years previously. Around 2,000 Glentoran supporters made the trip, swelling the crowd to over 16,000, and they sang their hearts out as we took on a full strength Rangers team. Michael Mols put the 'Gers ahead in the tenth minute with a neat turn and finish but we restricted

Fitzgerald makes a run against Lillestrom – note the lack of standing spectators due to a UEFA ruling.

them to just two more from Rod Wallace and Allan Johnston. Glentoran Commercial Department subsequently produced a video entitled "Better Late than Never" covering both this match and the Irish Cup semi-final success over Linfield in April.

Meanwhile in the early league games we failed to get out of the starting blocks and drew four of the first five fixtures. It needed a last minute goal from Lockhart to avoid defeat against Ballymena but then we conceded in a similar time to Linfield when they were awarded a penalty for what appeared to be a very innocuous challenge by Nixon on Ferguson. One of the draws was against Coleraine but when we played them a fortnight later we were roundly hammered 5-2 at the Showgrounds.

Our latest signing Gary Smyth, who had returned to the Oval after a spell with Glenavon, came in to the defence and steadied things at Portadown but we crashed again this time to Smyth's old club at the end of September. The club was rocked by further bad news when UEFA announced that Roy Hamill had failed a drugs test after the European game. To his eternal credit Hamill was very reticent about the affair and bravely faced the media and issued a statement containing, "I have let myself down badly and feel ashamed of my own actions. I have embarrassed my friends and family and have this message for youngsters. Drugs and personal happiness don't mix." However his subsequent suspensions were to haunt him later in the season.

Defeat to Linfield at the end of October left us firmly entrenched in mid-table, already ten points behind the Windsor men. We could take consolation in our Gold Cup progress, however, as two hard earned wins rewarded us with a semi-final tie with Newry. A shock was in store as we lost the home leg 0-1, but after going behind in the return we played some marvellous football to run out 3-2 winners on aggregate with John Kennedy getting the decisive goal.

We played Newry a third time in November and it took a last minute Fitzgerald goal to settle a dour league encounter. That day, or night, will more be remembered for the Legends Dinner at the Park Avenue. Over 30 Glentoran heroes from the past were present at a function to launch the 2001 Legends Calendar. The wonderful reception given to Sammy Hughes, then well into his seventies, in particular will long be recalled.

Current players were making their mark too as Gough, Walker, McBride and Nixon all featured for the Irish League representative team in their 2-0 win over the League of Ireland in Galway. Young would have made it five but for injury. Down the club Glentoran Seconds were also making their mark. Now under George Bowden they lifted the George Wilson Cup with a 2-1 win over Ballymena Reserves and reached the final of the Steel and Sons where they defeated Cliftonville Olympic thanks to a golden goal from Damien McLaughlin. Later in the season the Solitude club gained revenge when their Strollers team beat Glentoran Colts 2-1 in the IFA Youth Cup final.

For the rest of the year our league form continued to be very inconsistent but better news came in the form of a £200,000 grant from the new Northern Ireland assembly towards ground improvements in 2001. Our playing achievement in December was the Gold Cup final victory over Coleraine. In an eventful match Michael Ferguson put us ahead and despite a battling display from the Bannsiders it was left to man of the match Tim McCann to crown our win with the fourth goal. Justin McBride made his 300th Glens appearance in the match while before our next home fixture Roy Coyle was presented with a crystal football boot to mark his 25 years and 40 trophies won as a manger. Another Glentoran servant was celebrating a quarter century achievement as Billy Spence completed 25 years of scouting for the club.

Our playing and results pattern continued in January 2001. We gained only five points from the four league games but were successful in reaching the County Antrim Shield final and seeing off the challenge of Armagh in the Irish Cup. Glenn Ferguson proved to be our downfall and Linfield's match winner once more in the Shield final even though the BBC website falsely lifted the spirits of exiled Glenmen by initially announcing on their website that we had won the match 2-1!

On the 10th February we went down at home to Omagh in a depressing display but this proved to be a spur as the team remained unbeaten in the next fifteen games. That run started with a 4-0 win in the seventh round of the Irish Cup over the first ever winners of that trophy Moyola Park, who were jointly managed by our ex-player Alfie Stewart. We then recorded good league wins over Cliftonville and Ballymena before our progress was halted by events completely outside our control.

A Foot and Mouth crisis had developed all over the British Isles and all sporting events no matter how small, were cancelled in an attempt to contain the spread of the disease. Ironically our scheduled encounter with Linfield on 3rd March was postponed anyway due to ground reconstruction work and the first team squad filled in time with a couple of hastily arranged friendlies against the R.U.C. and the Glentoran Second XI. A couple of players decided their futures would be best served elsewhere as Sean Armstrong joined Coleraine and David Rainey went to Ards. One of our past reserve and colts team players, Roy Essandoh, made a name for himself when he scored Wycombe Wanderers' winning goal against Leicester to earn an FA Cup semi-final appearance against Liverpool. There was some sad news too, though, as the death of Billy Stewart, our centre-half of the mid-1970's, was announced.

The enforced break from action appeared to do us good as we defeated Institute in the Irish Cup and reached the League Cup final, now sponsored by Coca-Cola. We were also hot on the heels of Glenavon as the race for second place in the League heated up.

Paul Leeman had a day of mixed emotions on the 7th April. On the plus side he was part of a Glentoran team that defeated Distillery 2-1 in the Irish Cup semi-final but was also the victim of mistaken identity when the referee sent him off following a mass brawl in which he had taken no part! Thankfully any chance of a suspension receded when the club successfully lodged an appeal against the decision. In the game itself Distillery, against whom in this fixture we maintained our record of meeting in every season since 1883/4, went ahead before McBride equalised from the penalty spot before half-time. A fine run and cross from Hamill was met by Fitzgerald after the break to secure our winner.

After league wins over Crusaders and Portadown we met Glenavon twice towards the end of April. In the Oval league meeting we looked to be on our way to victory until they popped up with a late equaliser which virtually guaranteed them runners-up place in the league. However we made no mistake in the League Cup final the following Tuesday when a Scott Young penalty was enough to bring the second senior trophy of the season to east Belfast. The manger then rested a number of players and our team at Solitude had an experimental feel to it. Damien McLaughlin notched our goal in a 1-1 draw and with others like Martin Hunter, Francis McKeown and Brian Boyd coming through the ranks the future looked very bright.

Results 2000/1

Played 57. Won 31. Drew 12. Lost 14. Goals For 90. Against 54. % 64.9.
Honours: Irish Cup, Gold Cup, Irish League Cup

CS	05/08/00		Linfield	A	L	0	2	-
UEFA	10/08/00	Q.1	Lillestrom	H	L	0	3	-
UEFA	24/08/00	Q.2	Lillestrom	A	L	0	1	-
IL	19/08/00		Ballymena United	H	D	1	1	Lockhart
IL	05/09/00		Coleraine	H	D	1	1	Young (p)
IL	09/09/00		Newry Town	A	W	3	1	McCann, S.Armstrong, Young (p)
IL	12/09/00		Linfield	A	D	1	1	S.Armstrong
IL	16/09/00		Crusaders	H	D	1	1	Rainey
IL	19/09/00		Coleraine	A	L	2	5	McCann, Fitzgerald
IL	23/09/00		Portadown	A	W	3	0	McCann 2, Rainey
IL	30/09/00		Glenavon	A	L	0	3	-
IL	14/10/00		Omagh Town	H	W	2	0	Lockhart, S.Armstrong
IL	21/10/00		Ballymena United	A	W	3	0	McCann, Smyth, McBride
IL	28/10/00		Linfield	H	L	0	1	-
IL	04/11/00		Omagh Town	A	L	1	2	McBride
IL	11/11/00		Newry Town	H	W	1	0	Fitzgerald
IL	18/11/00		Crusaders	A	D	1	1	Fitzgerald
IL	25/11/00		Portadown	H	W	3	1	McCann, Fitzgerald, Lockhart
IL	02/12/00		Glenavon	H	D	1	1	McBride (p)
IL	09/12/00		Cliftonville	A	L	0	1	-
IL	16/12/00		Omagh Town	A	W	3	1	McBride, Nixon, S.Armstrong
IL	23/12/00		Ballymena United	H	W	2	1	McCann, Fitzgerald
IL	26/12/00		Linfield	A	L	0	2	-
IL	01/01/01		Newry Town	A	D	0	0	-
IL	06/01/01		Crusaders	H	W	2	0	McBride 2(1p)
IL	13/01/01		Portadown	A	L	1	4	McCann
IL	27/01/01		Glenavon	A	D	0	0	-
IL	03/02/01		Cliftonville	H	W	1	0	Leeman
IL	10/02/01		Omagh Town	H	L	1	2	Smyth
IL	20/02/01		Cliftonville	H	W	4	0	McBride, Smyth, Fitzgerald 2
IL	24/02/01		Ballymena United	A	W	3	1	Lockhart, McBride (p), Fitzgerald
IL	17/03/01		Coleraine	A	D	1	1	McBride (p)
IL	31/03/01		Newry Town	H	D	0	0	-
IL	14/04/01		Crusaders	A	W	1	0	Batey
IL	17/04/01		Portadown	H	W	4	1	Halliday 2, Hamill, Lockhart
IL	21/04/01		Glenavon	H	D	2	2	Young, Halliday
IL	28/04/01		Cliftonville	A	D	1	1	McLaughlin
IL	08/05/01		Coleraine	H	L	0	1	-
IL	10/05/01		Linfield	H	W	2	0	Fitzgerald, Halliday
GC	03/10/00	1	Cliftonville	A	W	1	0	Young (p)
GC	18/10/00	2	Portadown	H	W	2	1	Lockhart, McBride
GC	08/11/00	SF.1	Newry Town	H	L	0	1	-
GC	22/11/00	SF.2	Newry Town	A	W	3	1	Leeman, Batey, Kennedy
GC	12/12/00	F	Coleraine	WP	W	4	3	Ferguson, Lockhart, Smyth, McCann
CAS	05/12/00	1	Ards	H	W	3	0	Lockhart, Smyth, McBride
CAS	09/01/01	2	Larne	A	W	4	0	Halliday, Nixon, McBride, McLaughlin
CAS	17/01/01	SF	Cliftonville	WP	W	2	0	Batey 2
CAS	30/01/01	F	Linfield	A	L	1	2	Nixon
IC	23/01/01	6	Armagh City	A	W	3	0	McBride 2(1p), Smyth

IC	17/02/01	7	Moyola Park	H	W	4	0	Rainey, McCann, Smyth, Nixon
IC	13/03/01	QF	Institute	H	W	2	1	McCann, Fitzgerald
IC	07/04/01	SF	Lisburn Distillery	WP	W	2	1	McBride, Fitzgerald
IC	05/05/01	F	Linfield	A	W	1	0	Halliday
ILC	06/02/01	1	Limavady United	H	W	2	1	Leeman, Hamill
ILC	19/03/01	2	Armagh City	A	W	1	0	McBride (p)
ILC	28/03/01	SF	Omagh Town	Sv	W	2	0	McCann, Hamill
ILC	24/04/01	F	Glenavon	WP	W	1	0	Young (p)
F	19/07/00		East Belfast	H	W	5	0	S.Armstrong, Lockhart, Hillis, Dickson, Ferguson
F	22/07/00		Shelbourne	H	D	3	3	Young, Armstrong 2 Justin McBride Testimonial
F	26/07/00		Dundela	A	W	1	0	McCann
F	29/07/00		Preston North End	H	W	1	0	Fitzgerald
F	03/08/00		Liverpool	H	L	0	4	Belfast Challenge
F	29/08/00		Glasgow Rangers	A	L	0	3	-
F	Unknown		Supporters XI	H	W	17	1	Unknown
F	03/03/01		Glentoran II	H	W	3	1	Unknown
F	10/03/01		RUC	H	W	5	1	McBride, Nixon, Hamill, Walker, Fitzgerald
F	19/05/01		Sperrin Olympic	A	W	3	2	Fitzgerald 3

The first "Big Two" Irish Cup final in sixteen years came off at Windsor Park on 5th May 2001. Our preparations had been upset by a further suspension, this time from FIFA on the eve of the game, on Hamill until October. A sell-out colourful crowd numbering over 14,000 were present and even the South Stand terracing was opened but the Railway Stand remained closed for alleged safety reasons. The match was also beamed lived by BBC2 Northern Ireland in the province but was made not available to Sky Digital viewers who had to be content with following the game on Radio Ulster or via the internet commentary. The Glens, cheered on by thousands, including the new Roy the Rooster mascot, ran out in another new strip – green shirts with red sides, black shorts and white socks with red tops – anxious to preserve our record of not losing an Irish Cup final to Linfield since 1945.

The early exchanges were equal but as the game progressed it looked like extra time would be required. Alan Gough made a splendid reflex save after a deflection off Leeman and Michael Halliday missed a couple of excellent chances to break the deadlock. However he kept at it and was rewarded by being in the right place at the right time when in the ninth minute of extra-time he side footed in after a McCann header had come off the bar. Linfield posed no further threat and so we had retained the Irish Cup once more. It was to be another night of high celebration in East Belfast and surrounding areas.

There was still a couple of league games to complete the season. Coleraine visited the Oval on the Tuesday and won 1-0 to end their drought of league success at our ground. Then two nights later we had the satisfaction of defeating Linfield again, this time by a 2-0 margin. It was another noteworthy occasion as the new seating on the Sydenham by-pass side of the ground was occupied for the first time. Playing matters for the season were concluded with a visit to Sperrin Olympic in a match to raise funds for Cookstown lad

Darren Fitzgerald.

485

Michael Muldoon who had to have a leg amputated following an accident during a local junior game. Darren Fitzgerald was on form with a first half hat-trick.

More glory came to the club as the youth team won their league and the Gazette was named Programme of the Year again. Rory Hamill decided his future lay elsewhere and signed for Coleraine.

So there you have it. One hundred and nineteen years of Glentoran history, trials and tribulations, successes and failures, devastation and a spirit of rebuilding but a host of memories and achievements. Here's to the future and "Le Jeu Avant Tout."

Appearances and Goals

	App.	Subs.	Goals		App.	Subs.	Goals
McCann	57		12	Hamill	22	14	3
Gough	56			McCombe	19	1	
Nixon	53		4	Armstrong S.	18	12	4
Smyth	44		7	Halliday	16	14	6
McBride	43	5	16	Rainey	10	14	3
Walker	41	4		Hunter	10	4	
Batey	41	2	4	Russell B.	2	5	
Leeman	37	6	3	Armstrong N.	1		
Lockhart	34	6	8	McKeown	1	1	
Fitzgerald	32	20	11	Boyd	1	1	
Kennedy	31	1	1	McLaughlin		2	2
Young	29	4	5	TOTAL	627	120	90
Ferguson	29	4	1				

Appendix

Glentoran Records and Statistics

All details are correct up to the end of season 2000/1.

1. Trophies

Glentoran have lifted 120 major trophies in their history as listed below. In addition the club has also won numerous minor and other awards the detail of which can be found in the text.

Irish League (20 times): 1893/94, 1896/97, 1904/05, 1911/12, 1912/13, 1920/21, 1924/25, 1930/31, 1950/51, 1952/53, 1963/64, 1966/67, 1967/68, 1969/70, 1971/72, 1976/77, 1980/81, 1987/88, 1991/92, 1998/99.

Irish Cup (19 times): 1913/14, 1916/17, 1920/21, 1931/32, 1932/33, 1934/35, 1950/51, 1965/66, 1972/73, 1982/83, 1984/85, 1985/86, 1986/87, 1987/88, 1989/90, 1995/96, 1997/98, 1999/00, 2000/01

Gold Cup (15 times): 1916/17, 1941/42, 1951/52, 1960/61, 1962/63, 1966/67, 1976/77, 1977/78, 1982/83, 1986/87, 1991/92, 1994/95, 1998/99, 1999/00, 2000/01

City Cup (18 times): 1896/97, 1898/99, 1910/11, 1911/12, 1913/14, 1914/15, 1915/16, 1916/17, 1918/19, 1931/32, 1950/51, 1952/53, 1956/57, 1964/65, 1966/67, 1969/70, 1972/73, 1974/75

Ulster Cup (9 times): 1950/51, 1952/53, 1966/67, 1976/77, 1981/82, 1982/83, 1983/84, 1988/89, 1989/90

County Antrim Shield (22 times): 1900/01, 1901/02, 1910/11, 1915/16, 1917/18, 1920/21, 1924/25, 1930/31, 1939/40, 1940/41, 1943/44, 1949/50, 1951/52, 1956/57, 1967/68, 1970/71, 1977/78, 1984/85, 1986/87, 1989/90, 1998/99, 1999/00

Irish League Cup (3 times): 1988/89, 1990/91, 2000/01

Floodlit Cup (twice): 1987/88, 1989/90

Charity Cup (8 times): 1895/96, 1901/2, 1906/07, 1910/11, 1922/23, 1924/25, 1925/26, 1928/29

County Down Cup (twice): 1889/90, 1891/2

Inter City Cup (once): 1943/44

County Antrim Chalice (once): 1987/88

2. Grounds

Glentoran have played their home matches on six different grounds as follows.

1882 to 1886 Ormeau Park

1886 to 1890 King's Field, Westbourne, Ballymacarrett

1890 to 1892 Musgrave Park

1892 to 1903 The Oval, Dee Street

1903 to 2001 The Oval. This was a new ground on the same area as the original Oval, with the pitch rotated to 90 degrees.

1941 to 1949 Following bomb damage to the Oval we used Grosvenor Park as a temporary home.

3. Complete Playing Record

Games Played 4903 Won 2676 Drawn 881 Lost 1346 Goals For 10970 Against 7139 % 63.56

Games decided on penalty shoot-outs are counted as draws. The percentage record is calculated by awarding 100% for a win, 50% for a draw, 0% for a defeat and taking the average over all games. Competitive games only.

4. Playing Record Decade by Decade

Note that the decade is defined as ten seasons starting from the first season commencing within that decade. E.g. The 1930s is defined as seasons 1930/1 to 1939/40.

	Played	Won	Drew	Lost	Goals For	Against	%
1880s	30	17	2	11	96	68	60.0
1890s	201	93	27	81	469	403	53.0
1900s	304	130	70	104	520	421	54.3
1910s	356	211	78	67	711	327	70.2
1920s	444	235	78	131	1002	746	61.7
1930s	486	262	73	151	1303	931	61.4
1940s	441	227	64	150	1097	839	58.7

	Played	Won	Drew	Lost	Goals For	Against	%
1950s	506	291	84	131	1283	772	65.8
1960s	548	311	105	132	1292	771	66.3
1970s	483	260	87	136	958	642	62.8
1980s	525	333	95	97	1154	519	72.5
1990s	522	275	106	141	995	646	62.8
2000s	57	31	12	14	90	54	64.9

5. Leading Goalscorers

		Career Goals	Best Season	Era
1.	Trevor Thompson	375	48	1957-68
2.	Fred Roberts	332	96	1928-33
3.	Sammy Hughes	297	64	1949-59
4=.	Gary Macartney	192	39	1986-94
4=.	Warren Feeney	192	47	1972-78
6=.	Gary Blackledge	159	40	1979-87
6=.	Tommy Morrow	159	41	1966-72
8.	Sammy Lowry	149	34	1949-59
9.	Jimmy Feeney	146	32	1947-54
10.	Jim Cleary	144	25	1980-89
11.	Walter Bruce	140	25	1956-70
12.	Ron Manley	138	30	1979-89
13.	Johnny Jamison	134	24	1970-80
14.	Justin McBride	132	21	1991-01
15.	Jim Lavery	125	32	1937-49
16.	Johnny Jameson	123	18	1980-94
17.	John Boyd	114	25	1913-23
18=.	Gerry Mullan	110	27	1981-88
18=.	Billy Caskey	110	19	1974-93
20.	Sandy McNeill	109	34	1929-37
21.	Barney Bowers	108	18	1981-95
22.	Willie Crooks	106	31	1919-33
23.	Raymond Morrison	105	18	1982-94
24.	Sam Napier	104	23	1909-15

Fred Roberts holds the record for the most goals in one season when scoring 96 times in season 1930/1.

The most number of goals scored by a Glentoran player in one match is six as follows:

Date	Player	Opponents	Venue	Competition
06/11/1886	McManus	Hertford	H	Friendly
25/09/1926	Bambrick	Larne	A	Irish League
14/02/1931	Roberts	Larne	A	City Cup
10/10/1931	Roberts	Larne	H	Irish League
24/09/1932	Roberts	Ards	H	Irish League
09/11/1935	McCrae	Ards	H	Irish League
05/12/1942	Kelly	Cliftonville	GP	Regional League

6. Leading Appearance Makers

Players who have made over 300 appearances. Please note the exact totals may not tally with those given in the seasonal appearances tables. This is because for those games were a full line-up was not available it was possible to identify individual appearances.

		Total	Full+Sub
1.	Billy McCullough	555	549+6
2.	George Neill	531	523+8
3.	Walter Bruce	529	528+1
4.	Barney Bowers	524	510+14
5.	Alan Paterson	517	516+1
6.	Johnny Jameson	498	425+73
7.	Billy Neill	474	474
8.	John Devine	468	455+13
9.	Trevor Thompson	463	460+3
10.	Albert Finlay	456	456
11.	Billy McKeag	449	446+3
12.	Billy Caskey	440	420+20
13.	Raymond Morrison	432	398+34
14.	Noel McCarthy	417	417
15.	Jim Cleary	413	409+4
16.	Johnny Jamison	412	400+12
17.	George Ferritt	404	404
18.	Sammy Hughes	378	378
19.	Ron Manley	376	317+59
20.	Jim Weatherup	363	349+14

			Total		Full+Sub
21.	Jim Murdough		**355**		355
22.	Davy Lyner		**339**		339
23.	Rab McCreery		**335**		324+11
24.	Terry Moore		**333**		328+5
25.	Justin McBride		**330**		302+28
26.	Gary Macartney		**328**		306+22
27.	John Hill		**327**		327
28.	Sammy Lowry		**322**		322
29.	Billy Emerson		**308**		308
30.	Arthur Stewart		**308**		306+2
31.	John Scraggs		**305**		305

7. Managers

The concept of a manager was not really recognised in football terms until the 1930s. Although the actual title may have varied the following is a list of those who have held the post most akin to that of manager. Those who acted as caretaker-managers in the period between appointments are not included.

1932 to 1934	Billy McStay	1966 to 1968	John Colrain
1934 to 1935	David Reid	1968	Alex Young
1936 to 1938	Sam Jennings	1968 to 1971	Peter McParland
1939 to 1940	Louis Page	1971 to 1972	Kieran Dowd
1945 to 1947	Frank Thompson	1972	Alex McCrae
1948 to 1955	Frank Grice	1972 to 1974	George Eastham
1955 to 1957	Jimmy McIntosh	1974 to 1977	Bobby McGregor
1958	Ken Chisholm	1977 to 1979	Arthur Stewart
1958 to 1959	Johnny Neilson	1979 to 1984	Ronnie McFall
1959 to 1960	Tommy Briggs	1985 to 1987	Billy Johnston
1960 to 1961	Len Kane	1987 to 1993	Tommy Jackson
1961 to 1962	Harry Walker	1993 to 1994	Robert Strain
1962 to 1964	Isaac McDowell	1994 to 1997	Tommy Cassidy
1964 to 1965	Gibby McKenzie	1997 to date	Roy Coyle
1965 to 1966	Billy Neill		

8. Best and Worst

Biggest Wins

18-0	v. Montalto (A)	IC	1888
15-1	v. Oldpark (H)	IL	1891
10-0	v. Cliftonville (H)	League	1911
10-0	v. Cliftonville Olympic (H)	CAS	1907
10-1	v. Bangor (H)	League	1968
10-1	v. Coleraine (H)	CC	1939
9-0	v. Milltown (A)	IL	1891
9-0	v. Ligoneil	IL	1891
9-0	v. Derry Celtic (H)	League	1910
9-0	v. Larne (H)	League	1931
9-0	v. Corgy Mills (H)	IC	1951
9-0	v. Coleraine (H)	CC	1952
9-0	v. Cliftonville (H)	League	1972

Biggest Defeats

0-9	v. Ulster (A)	IC	1883
0-9	v. Belfast Celtic (A)	SGC	1946
1-9	v. Ards (H)	CC	1961
0-8	V. Linfield (A)	IL	1892
0-8	v. Ajax Amsterdam (A)	UEFA	1975
0-8	v. Sparta Prague (A)	ECWC	1996
2-9	v. Portadown (H)	League	1938
2-9	v. Belfast Celtic (A)	IC	1944
2-9	v. Linfield (A)	RL	1944
0-7	v. Ulster (A)	IC	1884
0-7	v. Linfield (H)	IL	1890
0-7	v. Linfield (A)	SGC	1944
2-8	v. Glenavon (A)	League	1966
2-8	v. Belfast Celtic (A)	RL	1941

Highest Scoring Draws

6-6	v. Bangor (H)	League	1929
5-5	v. Newry Town (H)	CC	1936
5-5	v Ballymena Utd (H)	CAS	1973 (aet, won on penalties)

Appendix

Miscellaneous Scoring Records

Conceding six and winning
9-6   v. Ards (H)   League   1935

Scoring five and losing
5-6   v. Portadown (A)   League   1941

Most goals scored in a season: 183 in 58 games (average 3.16) during 1952/3
Least goals scored in a season: 32 in 27 games (average 1.19) during 1905/6
Most goals conceded in a season: 121 in 48 games (average 2.52) during 1936/7
Least goals conceded in a season: 18 in 31 games (average 0.58) during 1917/8

9. Record in European Competitions

	Played	Won	Drawn	Lost	GF	GA
European Cup	22	3	6	13	18	42
Cup Winners Cup	22	3	7	12	18	46
UEFA Cup	16	1	3	12	9	43
Fairs Cup	8	1	1	6	7	22
TOTAL	68	8	17	43	52	153

We reached the quarter-finals of the ECWC in 1973/4 before going out to West Germany's Borussia Moenchengladbach.

Our European victories have come against Arsenal (1-0), Chimia Ramnicu Vilcea (2-0), Brann Bergen (3-1), F.C. Basle (3-2), Valur (2-0), Progres Neidercorn (4-0), CSKA Sofia (2-1) and Fram Reykjavik (1-0) all at the Oval.

10. Players Gaining Full International Honours while with the Club

There have been 40 players who have played full international football while registered with Glentoran. They are given below with the number of "caps" won during this time. The list does not include players who made full international appearances before or after they played for the club.

Northern Ireland

6   Billy Emerson

5   Jim Cleary

4   Davy Lyner, Gerry Mullan

3   Jim Lewis, Paddy McCann, George McMaster, Alec Macartney, Hugh Meek, Tommy "Ching" Morrison, Arthur Stewart

2   Walter Bruce, Jack Burnett, James Connor, Johnny Geary, John Lemon, Ralph Lawther, Billy McKeag, John McVicker, Jimmy Maxwell, Johnny Scraggs, R.Crone

1   Billy Andrews, Tom Black, Warren Feeney, Joe Gowdy, Rory Hamill, Johnny Jamison, James Kelly, Jack Lyttle, English McConnell, Sam McGregor, Hugh McKelvey, James McKnight, John Devine, Con Martin, Eddie Mitchell, Cecil Moore, B. Rea, Fred Roberts

Republic of Ireland

3   Con Martin

11. Glentoran Player of the Year Award

1957/8	Billy Neill	1980/1	Gary Blackledge
1958/9	Walter Bruce	1981/2	Johnny Jameson
1959/60	Jimmy Murdough	1982/3	Jim Cleary
1960/1	Jimmy Murdough	1983/4	Tom Connell
1961/2	Matt Crothers	1984/5	Raymond Morrison
1962/3	Eamon Byrne	1985/6	Gerry Mullan
1963/4	Trevor Thompson	1986/7	Billy Caskey
1964/5	Albert Finlay	1987/8	Alfie Stewart
1965/6	Albert Finlay	1988/9	Gary Macartney
1966/7	Arthur Stewart	1989/90	Gary Macartney
1967/8	Billy McCullough	1990/1	George Neill
1968/9	Tommy Morrow	1991/2	Raymond Morrison
1969/70	Tommy Morrow	1992/3	John Devine
1970/1	Roy Coyle	1993/4	Alan Paterson
1971/2	Tony Macken	1994/5	Michael Smyth
1972/3	Roy Stewart	1995/6	Glen Little
1973/4	Warren Feeney	1996/7	Michael Smyth
1974/5	John Hill	1997/8	Justin McBride
1975/6	Warren Feeney	1998/9	Rory Hamill
1976/7	Billy Caskey	1999/00	Stewart Elliott
1977/8	Billy Caskey	2000/1	Tim McCann
1978/9	Roy Walsh		
1979/80	Rab McCreery		

12. Glentoran Cup Final Line-ups

Season	Comp	Team
1885/6	Charity Cup	Lawther, Leslie, Silo, Connor, Baxter, McManus, McVicker, Lemon, Reid, Steele, Sloan
1889/9)	County Down Cup	Sloan, Anderson, Mitchell, Dykes, Taggart, Muir, Gary, Irvine, "McDonnell", Miller, McManus
1891/2	County Down Cup	line-up not traced
1892/3	County Down Cup	Johnston, Purvis, Forbes, Patterson, Sloan, McFall, Sherrard, Stewart, Conway, Clarke, Seddington
1893/4	Charity Cup	Loyal, Patterson, Parks, Freeland, Stewart, Spencer, McLoughlin, Hall, Somerset, King, Millar
1895/6	Irish Cup	E.Johnston, Purvis, McFall, Hattie, Shannon, Burnett, Carmichael, Hall, W.Johnston, Kelly, Somerset
1895/6	Charity Cup	E.Johnston, Purvis, Spencer, Hattie, Shannon, McMaster, Carmichael, Hall, W.Johnston, Kelly, Somerset
1897/8	Charity Cup	Lewis, Purvis, Somerset, Hattie, Shannon, Lyttle, Boyd, Robinson, W.Johnston, Wattie, Duncan
1898/9	Irish Cup	Lewis, Purvis, Kerr, Lyttle, McCann, McMaster, Gill, Smith, W.Johnston, Seaton, Duncan
1900/1	County Antrim Shield	Lewis, "English", Kerr, McCann, Connor, McMaster, Black, W.Johnston, McKinney, Leonard, Wattie
1901/2	County Antrim Shield	Lewis, McAreavey, McMaster, Wattie, Millar, Hattie, Waddell, W.Johnston, McKelvey, Smyth, Gill
1901/2	Charity Cup	Lewis, McAreavey, McMaster, McCann, Millar, Wattie, Blair, Smyth, McKelvey, Booth, Waddell
1902/3	Charity Cup	Lewis, Kerr, McMaster, Blair, Connor, Wattie, Beattie, Booth, McKelvey, Wood, Waddell
1903/4	Charity Cup	Lewis, McClean, McMaster, Rea, Connor, Wattie, McKeown, Smith, Ewing, J.Donoghue, Waddington
1904/5	Charity Cup	Gray, McClelland, McCourt, McConnell, O'Connor, McMaster, McKeown, Leonard, Ward, Kirkwood, Ewing
1906/7	County Antrim Shield	McMillen, King, Dunlop, Stevenson, Rea, Reid, Lyons, Morrison, Andres, Ewing, McDougall
1906/7	Charity Cup	McMillen, King, Finlay, Stevenson, Rea, Reid, Fitzpatrick, Ewing, Andrews, Rooney, McDougall
1909/1)	County Antrim Shield	Kane, Bennett, Cooper, Smyth, Ritchie, Lewis, Lyner, Lawrie, McKnight, Napier, Munro
1910/11	County Antrim Shield	Skene, McCann, Watters, Andrews, Ritchie, Reid, Lyner, Mitchell, Napier, McKnight. Hunter
1910/11	Charity Cup	Gibb, McCann, Watters, Andrews, Ritchie, Reid, Lyner, Mitchell, Napier, McKnight. Hunter
1911/2	"New" Irish Cup	Skene, McCann, Watters, Andrews, Ritchie, Ferritt, Hunter, Mitchell, Napier, Munro, Lyner
1912/3	Irish Cup	Murphy, McAlpine, Watters, Ferritt, Ritchie, Reid, Lyner, J.Lindsay, Napier, McKnight, Munro
1913/4	County Antrim Shield	Murphy, McCann, Annesley, Ferritt, Scraggs, Emerson, Lyner, J.Lindsay, Boyd, Napier, W.Lindsay
1913/4	Irish Cup	Murphy, McCann, Annesley, Ferritt, Scraggs, Emerson, Lyner, J.Lindsay, Napier, Boyd, W.Lindsay
1913/4	Charity Cup	Murphy, McCann, Annesley, Ferritt, Scraggs, Reid, Lyner, J.Lindsay, Smith, Emerson, W.Lindsay
1914/5	County Antrim Shield	Murphy, McCann, Grainger, Ferritt, Scraggs, Emerson, Lyner, Moore, Boyd, Duff, W.Lindsay
1915/6	County Antrim Shield	Steele, Stafford, Grainger, Ferritt, Scraggs, Emerson, Lyner, Duff, Boyd, West, Bookman
1915/6	Irish Cup	Steele, Stafford, Grainger, Ferritt, Scraggs, Emerson, Lyner, Seymour, Boyd, West, Bookman
1915/6	Irish Cup (R)	Steele, Stafford, Grainger, Ferritt, Scraggs, Emerson, Lyner, Seymour, Boyd, West, Snape
1916/7	County Antrim Shield	Steele, G.Moore, Grainger, Ferritt, Scraggs, Emerson, Lyner, Seymour, Clarke, Boyd, W.Moore
1916/7	Irish Cup	Steele, G.Moore, Grainger, Bennett, Scraggs, Ferritt, Lyner, Seymour, Boyd, Emerson, W.Moore
1916/7	Charity Cup	Steele, G.Moore, Grainger, Bennett, Scraggs, Kirkwood, Seymour, Ferritt, Clarke, Boyd, W.Moore
1917/8	County Antrim Shield	Liddell, Brady, Grainger, Ferritt, Scraggs, Emerson, Lyner, Crone, Connor, Boyd, Moore
1917/8	Charity Cup	Liddell, Ferritt, Grainger, Bennett, Scraggs, Emerson, Lyner, Crone, Conor, Boyd, Moore

Season	Competition	Players
1918/9	Irish Cup	Liddell, Spencer, Grainger, Bennett, Scraggs, Emerson, Lyner, Ferritt, Chambers, Mathieson, Moore
1918/9	Irish Cup (R)	Liddell, Spencer, Grainger, Bennett, Scraggs, Emerson, Lyner, Chambers, Boyd, Mathieson, Moore
1918/9	Irish Cup (R2)	Liddell, Spencer, Grainger, Bennett, Scraggs, Emerson, Lyner, Chambers, Boyd, Mathieson, Moore
1918/9	Charity Cup	Liddell, Ferritt, Grainger, Bennett, Scraggs, Emerson, Lyner, Mathieson, Boyd, Croft, Moore
1919/20	Gold Cup	Mehaffey, Kennedy, Ferguson, Ferritt, Scraggs, Emerson, Bingham, Kearney, Gowdy, Grant, Moore
1920/1	County Antrim Shield	Mehaffey, McSeveney, Ferguson, Ferritt, Scraggs, Emerson, McGregor, Crooks, Lyner, Meek, Snape
1920/1	CAS (R)	Mehaffey, McSeveney, Ferguson, Ferritt, Scraggs, Emerson, McGregor, Crooks, Lyner, Meek, Snape
1920/1	CAS (R2)	Mehaffey, McSeveney, Ferguson, Ferritt, Scraggs, Emerson, McGregor, Crooks, Duffy, Meek, Snape
1920/1	CAS (R3)	Mehaffey, McSeveney, Ferguson, Ferritt, Scraggs, Emerson, McGregor, Crooks, Lyner, Meek, Snape
1920/1	Irish Cup	Mehaffey, McSeveney, Ferguson, Ferritt, Scraggs, Emerson, McGregor, Crooks, Davey, Meek, Snape
1920/1	Charity Cup	Mehaffey, McSeveney, Bowman, Ferritt, Scraggs, Emerson, McGregor, Davey, Knocker, Kelly, Snape
1922/3	County Antrim Shield	McCormick, Peden, Tumilson, Reid, Ferritt, Evans, Swindle, McAnally, Keenan, Thompson, Boyd
1922/3	Irish Cup	McCormick, Peden, Ferritt, Reid, Burns, Evans, Swindle, Elwood, Keenan, McAnally, Topping
1922/3	Charity Cup	McCormick, Peden, Ferritt, Reid, Elwood, Evans, McKeague, McAnally, Keenan, Thompson, Harland
1924/5	County Antrim Shield	Bowden, McSeveney, Reid, Inch, Burns, Emerson, McKeague, Rainey, Keenan, Meek, Snape
1924/5	Irish Cup	Bowden, McSeveney, Reid, Inch, Burns, Emerson, McKeague, Rainey, Keenan, Meek, Allen
1924/5	Charity Cup	Bowden, McSeveney, Reid, Inch, Burns, Watson, McKeague, Rainey, Keenan, Meek, Allen
1925/6	County Antrim Shield	Bowden, McSeveney, H.Reid, Rainey, W.Reid, Watson, McKeague, Walker, Armstrong, Geary, Hunter
1925/6	Charity Cup	Bowden, McSeveney, Vance, Kirkwood, W.Reid, Watson, McKeague, Ralph, Armstrong, Hunter, Moore
1926/7	Charity Cup	McDowell, Kirkwood, McCrudden, Gordon, Whitley, Watson, McKeague, McAuley, Bambrick, A.Moore, W.Moore
1928/9	Charity Cup	Ward, Carleton, Allen, Wilson, Stewart, Anderson, McKeown, Crooks, Roberts, Geary, Hutchinson
1929/30	County Antrim Shield	McFarland, McSeveney, Allen, Montgomery, Thoms, McClements, McNeill, Wilson, Roberts, Geary, Hutchinson
1930/1	County Antrim Shield	Fitzroy, McMeekin, Allen, McClements, Mitchell, McClure, Burke, Mathieson, Roberts, Geary, Callaghan
1931/2	Irish Cup	Bennett, Allen, Gibson, Turnbull, Mathieson, McClements, Morgan, Geary, Roberts, Borland, Lucas
1932/3	Irish Cup	Harris, Lyttle, Gibson, Turnbull, Craig, Leathem, McNeill, Crooks, Roberts, Doherty, Hutchinson
1932/3	Irish Cup (R)	Harris, Lyttle, Gibson, Turnbull, Craig, Leathem, McNeill, Crooks, Roberts, Doherty, Hutchinson
1932/3	Irish Cup (R2)	Harris, Lyttle, Gibson, Turnbull, Craig, Arrigan, Doherty, Crooks, Roberts, Leathem, Fitzsimmons
1933/4	Gold Cup	Harris, McClure, Gibson, McCartney, Craig, Leathem, Mitchell, McKnight, Hodder, Duncan, Fitzsimmons
1934/5	Irish Cup	Lewis, Millar, McCaw, Arrigan, Beck, Leathem, Goodwin, Aicken, McNeill, Tyson, Smith
1934/5	Irish Cup (R)	Lewis, Millar, McDiarmid, Arrigan, Leathem, McCaw, Goodwin, Aicken, McNeill, Duncan, Smith
1934/5	Irish Cup (R2)	Lewis, Millar, McDiarmid, Arrigan, Beck, Leathem, Goodwin, Aicken, Duncan, Tyson, Smith
1936/7	County Antrim Shield	Jelly, Stitt, Lee, McNeill, Aiken, Blayney, Williamson, Rigby, Millar, McIndoe, Laverty
1936/7	CAS (R)	Jelly, Stitt, Lee, McNeill, Aiken, Blayney, Williamson, Rigby, Millar, McIndoe, Laverty
1937/8	Charity Cup	Pearson, Stitt, Gray, Patton, Smith, Irvine, Owens, McWilliams, Robinson, Lavery, Fitzsimmons
1938/9	County Antrim Shield	Pearson, Todd, Gray, Wilkins, Murray, Irvine, McCandless, Connor, Taylor, Lavery, Douglas
1939/40	County Antrim Shield	Tizard, O'Neill, Gray, McMillen, Irvine, Stitt, Robinson, Grice, Smith, Lavery, Douglas

1939/40	Charity Cup	Tizard, Thompson, Gray, McMillen, Bryson, Wilkins, Douglas, Sloan, Smith, Grice, Lavery
1940/-	County Antrim Shield	Hinton, Young, Gray, McMillen, Irvine, McDermott, Douglas, Grice, Robinson, Weir, Lavery
1941/2	Irish Cup	Hinton, Gager, Aston, McDermott, Bray, Kirkham, Wright, Keddie, Robinson, Matthias, Douglas
1942/3	Irish Cup	Beale, Hickman, Henderson, McDermott, Dykes, Stevenson, Wright, Beattie, Kelly, Grant, Douglas
1943/4	County Antrim Shield	Vernon, Tyrie, Lavery, Nimmick, Dykes, Wright, Mackin, Ramscar, Neary, Gregg, Deakin
1943/4	Inter-City Cup (1)	Vernon, Tyrie, Lavery, Nimmick, Dykes, Wright, Mackin, Ramscar, Neary, Gregg, Deakin
1943/4	Inter-City Cup (2)	Vernon, Tyrie, Lavery, Nimmick, Dykes, Wright, Todd, McIlroy, Bradford, Gregg, Douglas
1944/5	Irish Cup	Vernon, McIlroy, Gilmore, McDermott, Dykes, Wright, McIlvenny, Hill, Nimmick, Deakin, Langton
1946/7	Irish Cup	McKee, Kane, B.Neill, Blanchflower, Watters, T.Hughes, Wright, Kelly, McCormack, Lawlor, Lavery
1948/9	Irish Cup	Moore, B.Neill, McCarthy, Blanchflower, T.Hughes, Ferran, Nimmick, Peacock, McFarlane, Kerr, Feeney
1949/50	County Antrim Shield	Beare, Lewis, McCarthy, B.Neill, T.Hughes, Ferran, Bingham, Ewing, S.Hughes, S.Lowry, Feeney
1950/1	Gold Cup	Moore, King, McCarthy, Mulholland, T.Hughes, Ferran, Bingham, Ewing, S.Hughes, McFarlane, Feeney
1950/1	Ulster Cup	Moore, Dunlop, McCarthy, Mulholland, Lewis, McDermott, Cunningham, Ewing, S.Hughes, McFarlane, Feeney
1950/1	Irish Cup	Moore, Dunlop, McCarthy, Mulholland, T.Hughes, Ferran, Cunningham, Ewing, S.Hughes, Williamson, Feeney
1951/2	Gold Cup	Clark, Lucas, McCarthy, W.Neill, T.Hughes, McFarlane, S.Lowry, Ewing, S.Hughes, Williamson, Feeney
1951/2	Irish Cup	Clark, Lucas, King, W.Neill, T.Hughes, McFarlane, S.Lowry, Ewing, S.Hughes, Williamson, Feeney
1951/2	County Antrim Shield	Clark, McCarthy, King, W.Neill, T.Hughes, McFarlane, S.Lowry, Ewing, S.Hughes, Williamson, Feeney
1952/3	Ulster Cup	Clark, McCarthy, King, W.Neill, Corbett, McFarlane, S.Lowry, Ewing, S.Hughes, Williamson, Deakin
1953/4	Irish Cup	Bond, McCarthy, King, W.Neill, Murdough, Lewis, S.Lowry, Clugston, S.Hughes, Cunningham, Feeney
1953/4	Irish Cup (R)	Bond, McCarthy, King, W.Neill, Murdough, Lewis, S.Lowry, Clugston, S.Hughes, Cunningham, Feeney
1953/4	Irish Cup (R2)	Bond, McCarthy, King, W.Neill, Murdough, Lewis, S.Lowry, Clugston, S.Hughes, Cunningham, Feeney
1955/6	Irish Cup	McMahon, McCarthy, Cush, W.Neill, Murdough, T.Lowry, S.Lowry, Fogarty, S.Hughes, Mulvey, Nolan
1955/6	Irish Cup (R)	McMahon, McCarthy, Cush, W.Neill, Murdough, T.Lowry, S.Lowry, Fogarty, S.Hughes, Mulvey, Nolan
1955/6	Irish Cup (R2)	McMahon, McCarthy, Lucas, W.Neill, Murdough, Dubois, S.Lowry, Fogarty, Mulvey, Bruce, Nolan
1956/7	County Antrim Shield	McMahon, Lucas, McCarthy, W.Neill, Murdough, Truesdale, S.Lowry, Fogarty, Thompson, S.Hughes, Mulvey
1956/7	CAS (R)	McMahon, Lucas, McCarthy, Truesdale, Murdough, Dubois, S.Lowry, Fogarty, Thompson, S.Hughes, Mulvey
1957/8	Ulster Cup	Fullerton, Lucas, Dubois, W.Neill, Murdough, Truesdale, S.Lowry, Bruce, S.Hughes, Fogarty, Lindsay
1957/8	Ulster Cup (R)	Dunlop, Lucas, Dubois, W.Neill, Murdough, Truesdale, S.Lowry, Fogarty, S.Hughes, Mulvey, Lindsay
1958/9	Gold Cup	McMahon, Lucas, Elder, W.Neill, White, Dubois, Ashe, Bruce, Thompson, Spiers, Calderwood
1960/1	Gold Cup	McGonigal, Borne, Crothers, W.Neill, Murdough, Drennan, Reynolds, Bruce, Thompson, O'Neill, Mitchell
1960/1	County Antrim Shield	McGonigal, O'Neill, Crothers, W.Neill, Murdough, Drennan, Smyth, Bruce, Thompson, M.Doherty, Harvey
1960/1*	North South Cup (1)	McGonigal, Kennedy, Crothers, W.Neill, McCullough, Stewart, M.Doherty, Hume, Thompson, Bruce, T.Doherty
1960/1*	North South Cup (2)	McGonigal, Kennedy, Crothers, W.Neill, McCullough, Stewart, M.Doherty, Hume, Thompson, Bruce, T.Doherty
1961/2	Ulster Cup	McGonigal, Borne, Crothers, McCullough, Geoghegan, Forde, Callender, Stewart, Thompson, Bruce, Shields
1961/2	Gold Cup	Bradley, Borne, Crothers, Stewart, Murdough, McCullough, Reynolds, Bruce, Thompson, Forde, Smyth
1961/2	County Antrim Shield	Savage, Kennedy, Crothers, W.Neill, Murdough, McCullough, M.Doherty, Stewart, Thompson, Bruce, Todd

1962/3	Gold Cup	Rea, Borne, Wilson, McCullough, Byrne, Stewart, Pavis, Hume, Thompson, McDowell, Mitchell
1963/4	Gold Cup	Finlay, Creighton, Wilson, Byrne, McCullough, Bruce, Warburton, Curley, Thompson, Ross, Pavis
1963/4	Gold Cup (R)	Finlay, Creighton, Wilson, Brannigan, Byrne, Bruce, Warburton, Curley, Thompson, Stewart, Pavis
1963/4	Irish Cup	Finlay, Creighton, Borne, Byrne, McCullough, Bruce, Pavis, Curley, Thompson, Brannigan, Green
1963/4	County Antrim Shield	Finlay, Creighton, Borne, Byrne, McCullough, Bruce, Warburton, Stewart, Thompson, Brannigan, Pavis
1964/5	Ulster Cup	Finlay, Creighton, Borne, Stewart, McCullough, Bruce, Warburton, Turner, Thompson, Brannigan, Gillespie
1965/6	Irish Cup	Finlay, Creighton, Borne, McCullough, Byrne, Bruce, Conroy, Stewart, Thompson, McDonnell, McAlinden
1966/7	Gold Cup	Finlay, Creighton, McKeag, Sinclair, McCullough, Bruce, Colrain, T.Conroy, Thompson, Ross, Weatherup
1966/7	Irish Cup	Finlay, Creighton, McKeag, Jackson, McCullough, Stewart, Weatherup, Bruce, Thompson, Ross, Morrow
1967/8	County Antrim Shield	J.Cassidy, Creighton, Wright, Hill, McCullough, Bell, Johnston, Welsh, Thompson, M.Conroy, Weatherup
1967/8	CAS (R)	J.Cassidy, Creighton, Wright, Hill, McCullough, Bell, Welsh, Johnston, Thompson, Morrow, Weatherup
1968/9	Gold Cup	Finlay, Creighton, McKeag, Hill, McCullough, Bell, Hutton, Weatherup, Heron, D.Johnston (sub A..Welsh), Morrow
1968/9	Gold Cup (R)	Finlay, Creighton, McKeag, Hill, McCullough, Bell, Hutton, Morrow, Heron, Macken, Weatherup
1969/70	City Cup	Finlay, Hill, McKeag, Coyle, McCullough, Bruce, Weatherup, T.Cassidy, Patterson, Morrow (sub Hutton), Lavery
1969/70	Gold Cup	Finlay, Hill, McKeag, Coyle, McCullough, Macken, Weatherup, Hutton, Henderson (sub Patterson), Morrow, Lavery
1970/1	Gold Cup	Finlay, Hill, McKeag, Coyle, R.Stewart, Macken, McCaffrey, Bruce (sub Weatherup), Magill, Kirk, Morrow
1970/1	County Antrim Shield	Finlay, Hill, McKeag, Coyle, McCullough, Macken, Magill, McCaffrey, Hall, Morrow, Jamison
1972/3	City Cup	Paterson, Hill, McKeag, R.Stewart (sub Murray), McCullough, Weatherup, Jamison, McCreery, Morrow, Dickson, Feeney
1972/3	Irish Cup	Paterson (sub Walker), Hill, McKeag, R.Stewart, Murray, Anderson, Weatherup, McCreery, Hall, Jamison, Feeney
1974/5	Gold Cup	McCullough, Hill, Craig, Walsh, W.Stewart, Dougan, W.Caskey, Moreland, Robson, Jamison (sub McIlwaine), Feeney
1974/5	County Antrim Shield	McCullough, McKeag, Craig, Walsh, W.Stewart, Dougan, W.Caskey, Jamison, Robson, Clarke (sub Campbell), Feeney
1974/5*	City Cup	McCullough, McCreery, Craig, Walsh, Robson, Dougan, W.Caskey, Moreland, Dickinson, Jamison (sub Kennedy), Feeney
1976/7	Gold Cup	Matthews, McCreery, R.McFall, Moreland, Robson, Dougan, Jamison, McVeigh, W.Caskey, Dickinson, Feeney, sub Walsh
1976/7	County Antrim Shield	Matthews, McCreery, R.McFall, Walsh, Robson, O'Neill, Moreland, McVeigh, W.Caskey, Jamison, Feney, sub Dougan
1977/8	Gold Cup	Matthews, Dougan (sub O'Neill), R.McFall, Walsh, Cranston, Dougan, Dickinson, Jamison, W.Caskey, Q.McFall, Feeney
1977/8	County Antrim Shield	Matthews, McCreery, R.McFall, Walsh, Cranston, Dougan, Dickinson, Beattie, Jamison, Q.McFall, Feeney
1980/1	Gold Cup	Paterson, Rab McCreery, Strain, Harrison, Porter, Cleary, Jameson, Ron McCreery, Blackledge, Manley, Kingon, sub Irvine
1982/3	Gold Cup	Paterson, G.Neill, Connell, Keely, Harrison, Cleary, Jameson, Bowers, Manley, McDaid (sub Rab McCreery), Morrison
1982/3	Irish Cup	Paterson, G.Neill, Connell, Keely, Harrison, Cleary, Jameson, Bowers (sub Morrison), Manley, Mullan, D.Neill
1982/3	Irish Cup (R)	Paterson, G.Neill, Connell, Keely (sub Morrison), Harrison, Cleary, Jameson, Strain, Manley, Mullan, D.Neill
1982/3	County Antrim Shield	Paterson, G.Neill, Connell, Troughton, Harrison, Morrison, Jameson (sub Stewart), Strain, Manley, Mullan, D.Neill
1983/4	Ulster Cup	Paterson, G.Neill, Connell, Dixon, McCue, Cleary, Jameson, Bowers, Blackledge, Manley, D.Neill (sub Mullan)
1983/4	Gold Cup	Paterson, G.Neill, Connell, Dixon, Strain, Cleary, Jameson (sub Mullan), Bowers, Blackledge, Manley, Stewart
1984/5	Gold Cup	Hillen, Kelly, Stewart, Moore, McCue, Cleary, Morrison, Bowers (sub D.Neill), Blackledge, Manley, Mullan
1984/5	Irish Cup	Paterson, G.Neill, Leeman, Morrison, Dixon, Cleary, Stewart, Bowers, Blackledge, Mullan, Caskey
1984/5	Irish Cup (R)	Paterson, G.Neill, Leeman, Morrison, Dixon, Cleary, Stewart, Bowers, Blackledge (sub Jameson), Mullan, Caskey

1984/5	County Antrim Shield	Paterson, G.Neill, Leeman, Connell, Dixon, Mills (sub Moore), Jameson, Morrison, Blackledge, Manley, Stewart
1985/6	Irish Cup	Paterson, G.Neill, Leeman, Connell, Moore, Cleary, Jameson (sub Millar), Morrison, Manley, Mullan, Stewart
1986/7	County Antrim Shield	Paterson, J.Smyth, Cowden, Connell, Moore, Cleary, Jameson, Morrison, Macartney, Millar, Stewart
1986/7	Gold Cup	Paterson, J.Smyth, Stewart, Bowers, Harrison, Cleary. Jameson (sub Craig), Caskey (sub Manley), Mullan, Macartney, Morrison
1986/7	Irish Cup	Paterson, J.Smyth, Stewart, Bowers, Harrison, Cleary. Jameson (sub Craig), Caskey, Mullan, Macartney, Morrison
1987/8	Budweiser Cup	Paterson, G.Neill, Stewart, McGreevy, Moore, Cleary, Morrison, Caskey, Mullan, Manley, Jameson (sub Mathieson)
1987/8	Irish Cup	D.Smyth, G.Neill, Stewart, Devine, Moore (sub Mathieson), Cleary, Morrison, Caskey, Macartney, Mullan (sub Manley), Jameson
1987/8	County Antrim Chalice	D.Smyth, G.Neill, Stewart, Devine, McGreevy, Cleary, Morrison, Caskey, Macartney, Mullan (sub Manley), Jameson (sub Mathieson)
1988/9	Ulster Cup	Paterson, G.Neill, Kennedy, Bowers, Moore, Cleary. Totten, Caskey, Macartney, Manley, Morrison
1988/9	Irish League Cup	Paterson, G.Neill (sub Kennedy) , McGreevy, Harrison, Devine, Cleary, Totten, Caskey, Macartney, Hillis (sub Jameson), Morrison
1988/9	County Antrim Shield	D.Smyth, G.Neill, Devine, Bowers, Moore, Cleary, R.Campbell, Totten (sub Mathieson), Caskey, Hillis (sub Jameson), Morrison
1989/90	Ulster Cup	D.Smyth, McGreevy, McCaffrey, R.Campbell, Moore, Devine, Totten, Caskey, Macartney, Craig (sub Cleland), Douglas (sub Mathieson)
1989/90	Budweiser Cup	D.Smyth, Morrison, Heath, Devine, Moore, Bowers, R.Campbell, Caskey, Macartney, Douglas, Craig (sub Jameson)
1989/90	County Antrim Shield	D.Smyth, G.Neill (sub Totten), McCaffrey, Devine, Morrison, Bowers, R.Campbell, Caskey, Macartney, Douglas (sub Cleland), Jameson
1989/90	Irish Cup	D.Smyth, G.Neill, McCaffrey, Devine, Moore, Bowers, R.Campbell (sub Morrison), Caskey, Macartney (sub Totten), Douglas, Jameson
1990/1	Irish League Cup	Paterson, G.Neill, McCaffrey, Morrison, Moore, Bowers, R.Campbell, Caskey, Macartney, Hillis (sub G.Smyth), Jameson (sub Mathieson)
1991/2	Gold Cup	D.Smyth, G.Smyth, McCaffrey, Morrison, Devine, Bowers, R.Campbell, Moore, Macartney, Mathieson, Hillis (sub West)
1992/3	County Antrim Shield	D.Smyth, G.Neill, M.Smyth, Henry (sub McCloskey), Lowry, Devine, Caughey (sub Jameson), Mathieson, Douglas, Whitehurst, D.Kelly
1992/3	CAS (R)	D.Smyth, G.Neill, M.Smyth, Bowers, Lowry, Devine, R.Campbell, Mathieson, Douglas, Whitehurst, D.Kelly
1994/5	Gold Cup	Armstrong, G.Neill, M.Smyth, Parker, G.Smyth, Mathieson (sub D.Kelly), N.Kelly, Martindale (sub A.Nixon), D.Campbell, Cunnington, McBride
1995/6	Coca-Cola Cup	Armstrong, C.Nixon, M.Smyth, Kennedy, Devine, Walker (sub Coyle), Quigley (sub Parker), Little, Cook, Batey, McBride
1995/6	Irish Cup	D.Devine, C.Nixon, Finlay, Walker, Devine, Parker, T.Smith, Little, Coyle, Batey, McBride
1996/7	Irish League Cup	Armstrong, Drake, M.Smyth (sub Parker), Walker, Devine, May, Finlay, Little, McCourt, Batey, Hamill
1996/7	Coca-Cola Cup	Van de Kamp, C.Nixon, M.Smyth, Kennedy, Devine, Quigley, McBride, McCourt, Hamill (sub Kirk), Batey, Elliott
1997/8	Irish League Cup	Russell, C.Nixon, M.Smyth, Walker, Devine, Parker, Mathieson, Mitchell (sub Elliott), Hamill (sub Kirk), Livingstone, McBride
1997/8	Irish Cup	Russell, C.Nixon, Kennedy, Walker, Devine, Leeman (sub Livingstone), Mitchell, Finlay, Kirk, Batey, Hamill
1998/9	Gold Cup	Russell, Leeman, Ferguson, Walker, Devine, Quigley, Elliott, Hamill, Kirk, Batey, Young
1998/9	County Antrim Shield	Russell, C.Nixon, Ferguson, Walker, Devine, Leeman, Elliott, Hamill, Kirk (sub Kennedy), Young, McBride (sub Rainey)
1998/9	Irish League Cup	Russell, C.Nixon, Kennedy, Walker, Devine, Leeman, Elliott, Hamill, Elliott, Batey (sub Young), McBride (sub Rainey)
1999/00	Gold Cup	Gough, C.Nixon, Ferguson, Walker, McCombe, Young, McCann, Hamill, Russell, Batey, Rainey (sub Leeman)
1999/00	County Antrim Shield	Gough, Leeman, Kennedy, Walker, McCombe, Young, McCann (sub Russell), Hamill, Gilzean, Batey, Elliott
1999/00	Irish Cup	Gough, C.Nixon, Kennedy, Dickson, McCombe, McCombe, Young, McCann, Hamill, Russell (sub Gilzean), Batey, Elliott
2000/1	Gold Cup	Gough, C.Nixon, Ferguson, Leeman, McCombe, McCombe, G.Smyth, McCann, Lockhart, Fitzgerald, Batey (sub Halliday), McBride
2000/1	County Antrim Shield	Gough, C.Nixon, Kennedy, Walker, McCombe (sub Rainey), G.Smyth, McCann, Lockhart (sub Halliday), Hamill, Leeman, McBride
2000/1	Irish League Cup	Gough, Nixon, Ferguson, Young, Leeman, G.Smyth, McCann, Hamill (sub Fitzgerald), Halliday (sub McBride), Batey, Lockhart
2000/1	Irish Cup	Gough, Nixon, Ferguson, Young, Leeman, G.Smyth, McCann, Halliday, Fitzgerald, Batey, Lockhart (sub McBride)

* Game played during the following season

Subscribers

1. Girvan Wiltshire
2. Peter Lee
3. Roy France Snr.
4. Darren Gowdy
5. Chris Irvine
6. Philip Stevenson
7. Jim Welsh
8. Alan Carr
9. Graeme Kinkead
10. Graham Watt
11. Graham King
12. Stafford Reynolds
13. Richard McVeigh
14. David Kennedy
15. Louise France
16. Steven Nairn
17. Noel Irwin
18. William Noel Irwin
19. Norman Reid
20. Aubry Ralph
21. Michael Ralph
22. Christopher Ralph
23. Marshall Gillespie
24. Sarah Jane Reynolds
25. Alan Busby
26. George Dorrian
27. Marty Lowry
28. David Busby
29. Davy Brownlee
30. Gary Dunlop
31. Robert Morrow
32. David Wylie
33. John McCreery
34. Gavin Campbell
35. Noel Nicholl
36. Bill Lennon
37. David McAlister
38. Pete Brett
39. S.Stockton
40. Maurice Kinkead
41. Stephen Gorman
42. Jim Kelly
43. George Ruddell
44. Brian McClelland
45. John Stewart
46. Tom McStraw

47. Mark Anderson
48. Charles McCullough
49. Michael Loughnan
50. John Spence
51. David McKay
52. Gary Smyth
53. Norman Downey
54. Christopher Downey
55. John Moore
56. David Dean
57. Eddie Kelly
58. Lorraine France
59. Colin Davidson
60. Michael Fee
61. Dean Hogg
62. Chris Holt
63. Gary Eaton
64. Rodney Thomas
65. Martin Harris
66. Ian Lemon
67. Laura Spence
68. Louise Spence
69. Mark Wilson
70. Hugh Rodgers
71. Philip Rodgers
72. Bertie Reynolds
73. Denis Adams
74. Russell Moore
75. George Radcliffe
76. Robert Craig
77. Stevie Lee
78. Rodney Thom
79. Scott Mathieson
80. Pamela Abernethy
81. Davy Hawkes
82. Jim Hawkes
83. Brendan McDonnell
84. Johnny McIlwaine
85. Roy Halliday
86. Stephen Reid
87. Maurice Campbell
88. Colin Wotherspoon
89. Brian Robinson
90. Ian Sloan
91. John Duffy
92. David McMordie

93. Gary McMordie
94. Simon Boyd
95. Stephen Gardiner
96. Andy Harrison
97. Nichola Henry
98. Brian Payne
99 Trevor Roberts
100. Jim Welsh (2)
101. Sandy Burrows
102. Bryan Milne
103. David Stewart
104. David Allen Stewart
105. Philip Briggs
106. Stephen Henderson
107. Bryan Henderson
108. Paul Ritchie
109. Robbie Burns
110. Robbie Burns (2)
111. Michael Cockcroft
112. George Glass
113. Paolo Sacchi
114. Ken Holt
115. Judith France
116. Audrey France
117. William Moore
118. Claire Palmer
119. Ian Milligan